INNOVATION

In recent years, a great deal of attention has been focussed on the undertaking of managing innovation. Without the right focus, resourcing and capabilities, firms struggle to create value through innovation. However, the task of managing innovation is one of continuous paradoxes where an overly structured mind-set can impede entrepreneurship, creativity, culture and the right conditions for disruption. The question remains of how we can have the right lens to properly understand and appreciate innovation, and how we can have a flexible set of tools, techniques and perspectives to support innovation.

This concise text introduces readers to one of the fundamental ideas in the business world.

Insights into the key ingredients of innovation, including business models, services, entrepreneurship and creativity are analysed alongside core contexts, such as disruptive technology. Students of business and management will appreciate additional coverage of the future of the field, including open innovation and the dark side of digital disruption.

This accessible book provides a thought-provoking, stimulating perspective that will make it a valuable resource for a range of academic and student audiences across business and management disciplines.

Renu Agarwal is Professor in Management at the UTS Business School, Sydney. Her research interests are quite diverse including the disciplinary fields of service innovation, service value networks, supply chain management, dynamic capability building, management practices, innovation and productivity. Her research study and teaching include strategic supply chain management, innovation and entrepreneurship, fostering and measuring dynamic management capabilities that enhance organisational and managerial capabilities.

Eric Patterson is a Director for a multinational consulting firm advising major government organisations on business planning and strategy execution. He works across multiple levels of Australian government on programmes and priorities delivering new infrastructure and services, and improvements in the workings of government. His expertise spans government portfolio management, investment planning and programme assurance in transport, education, justice/defence, civil government, and energy and utilities.

Sancheeta Pugalia is a final-year Doctorate student in the School of Information, Systems, and Modelling at University Technology Sydney, Australia. Her area of expertise is entrepreneurship and innovation. Building on her expertise, her doctorate research focusses on looking at women entrepreneurs in the technology sector where she closely monitors the root causes of lower participation rate of women entrepreneurs in this industry. Prior to pursuing her PhD, she did her Master by Research programme from the Indian Institute of Technology Madras, India, and focussed her research in the area of student entrepreneurship.

Roy Green is Emeritus Professor and Special Innovation Advisor at the University of Technology Sydney. Roy graduated with first-class honours from the University of Adelaide and gained a PhD in Economics from the University of Cambridge, where he was also a Research Fellow. He has worked in universities, business and government in Australia and overseas, including as Dean of the UTS Business School, Dean of the Macquarie Graduate School of Management and Dean and Vice-President for Research at the National University of Ireland, Galway. He is also a Conjoint Professor at the University of Newcastle and a Fellow of the Irish Academy of Management.

INNOVATION

Edited by
Renu Agarwal, Eric Patterson,
Sancheeta Pugalia and Roy Green

Routledge
Taylor & Francis Group

LONDON AND NEW YORK

Cover image: Getty/Eoneren

First published 2023
by Routledge
4 Park Square, Milton Park, Abingdon, Oxon OX14 4RN

and by Routledge
605 Third Avenue, New York, NY 10158

Routledge is an imprint of the Taylor & Francis Group, an informa business

British Library Cataloguing-in-Publication Data
A catalogue record for this book is available from the British Library

Library of Congress Cataloging-in-Publication Data
A catalog record has been requested for this book

ISBN: 978-0-367-36442-7 (hbk)
ISBN: 978-0-367-34302-6 (pbk)
ISBN: 978-0-429-34603-3 (ebk)

DOI: 10.4324/9780429346033

Typeset in Bembo
by codeMantra

CONTENTS

FIGURES

TABLES

EDITORS

Renu Agarwal is Professor in Management at the UTS Business School, Sydney. Her research interests are quite diverse including the disciplinary fields of service innovation, service value networks, supply chain management, dynamic capability building, management practices, innovation and productivity. Her research study and teaching include strategic supply chain management, innovation and entrepreneurship, fostering and measuring dynamic management capabilities that enhance organisational and managerial capabilities.

Renu is the Director of management practices projects and has been instrumental in managing several Australian federal and state government research project grants including the 2009 landmark study – *Management Matters in Australia – Just how productive are we?* – which has had an impact on government policy-making and contributed to the broader world management survey study. Over the past 12 years, Renu is passionate about bringing insights from different disciplines to explore complex issues and phenomena and lately is pioneering research at the nexus of ordinary and dynamic management capability building spanning across multidisciplinary fields of management and economics, influencing productivity, innovation and policy-making. Renu has worked on a number of research projects with industry, Australian state and federal government, as well as with other governments internationally, e.g. New Zealand, the US and India.

Renu has extensive industry and academic experience as an innovative educator and facilitator in the fields of business strategy, capability building innovation and productivity and has published widely in top-tiered academic journals and books, and her work has been presented and recognised at a number of international conferences.

Eric Patterson is a Director for a multinational consulting firm advising major government organisations on business planning and strategy execution. He works across multiple levels of Australian government on programmes and priorities delivering new infrastructure and services, and improvements in the workings of government. His expertise spans government portfolio management, investment planning and programme assurance in transport, education, justice/defence, civil government, and energy and utilities.

Eric is a researcher focussed on innovation management with a specialisation in innovation portfolio management and public sector innovation. He has published on innovation management with papers and conference presentations on topics including business model innovation and innovation process management. Eric is currently completing his doctorate research on Innovation Portfolio Management across the Australian Government. This looks at the prevalence and success rate of government investments in innovation. He is currently examining the innovation outcomes in over $500bn of investments across the Australian Commonwealth Government. He is examining the mechanisms to improve innovation success and encourage more diversified innovation portfolios in government.

Prior to his advisory and research career, Eric was a member of the Australian Public Service working in innovation policy and business support programmes. He holds Masters Degrees in Innovation Management, Public Administration and Management.

Sancheeta Pugalia is a final-year Doctorate student in the School of Information, Systems, and Modelling at University Technology Sydney, Australia. Her area of expertise is entrepreneurship and innovation. Building on her expertise, her doctorate research focusses on looking at women entrepreneurs in the technology sector where she closely monitors the root causes of lower participation rate of women entrepreneurs in this industry. Prior to pursuing her PhD, she did her Master by Research programme from the Indian Institute of Technology Madras, India, and focussed her research in the area of student entrepreneurship.

Sancheeta has also received world renowned scholarships, including DAAD and JASSO scholarship for Germany and Japan, respectively. She has worked on multiple projects including the entrepreneurial ecosystem, management capabilities, business advisory services and escalated her research skills. These projects were conducted with Georges River Council, Engineers Australia, Australian Supply Chain Institute, Department of Industry, Innovation and Science and National Heart Foundation. Her work has been published in journals, conferences and books.

Apart from her research career, she is actively involved in promoting women in STEM and is an ambassador of Women in Engineering & IT.

Emeritus Professor Roy Green is Special Innovation Advisor at the University of Technology Sydney. Roy graduated with first-class honours from the University of Adelaide and gained a PhD in Economics from the University of Cambridge, where he was also a Research Fellow. He has worked in universities, business and government in Australia and overseas, including as Dean of the UTS Business

School, Dean of the Macquarie Graduate School of Management and Dean and Vice-President for Research at the National University of Ireland, Galway. He is also a Conjoint Professor at the University of Newcastle and a Fellow of the Irish Academy of Management.

Roy has advised and published widely in the areas of innovation policy and management as well as trends in business education. He has undertaken research projects with the OECD, European Commission and other international bodies. Roy chaired the Australian Government's Innovative Regions Centre, CSIRO Manufacturing Sector Advisory Council, NSW Manufacturing Council and Queensland Competition Authority. He also participated in bodies such as the Prime Minister's Manufacturing Taskforce.

Roy conducted the Australian Government's Review of the Textile, Clothing and Footwear Industries, led Australian participation in a global study of management practice and productivity, coordinated an Australian Business Deans Council project on the future of management education, and prepared the report on Australia's Innovation System for the Australian Senate.

More recently, Roy joined the Research Advisory Committee of the Centre for Policy Development, the Board of the Innovative Manufacturing CRC and the newly established Australian Design Council. He is also currently Chair of the Advanced Robotics for Manufacturing Hub and the Port of Newcastle.

CONTRIBUTORS

Renu Agarwal is an Associate Professor, Operations and Supply Chain Management and the Director of Strategic Supply Chain Management programmes at UTS Business School. She provides leadership in the disciplinary fields of service innovation, service value networks, supply chain management, dynamic capability building, management practices, innovation and productivity. Renu is also the Director of management practices projects and has been instrumental in managing several Australian federal and state government research project grants including the 2009 landmark study – *Management Matters in Australia – Just how productive are we?* – which has had an impact on government policy-making and contributed to the broader world management survey study. Over the past 12 years, Renu has been the project lead for many research projects totalling AUD$4M funded by government, industry and universities, has published in many top tier international journals and has edited several books.

Ali Ahmadi holds a MBA in strategy from the Industrial Management Institute of Tehran, Iran, and is a PhD student in strategy at the Smith School of Business – Queen's University, Canada. Ali is interested in competitive dynamics, dynamic capabilities and innovation in high-velocity contexts.

Emil Åkesson is a PhD student at Faculty of Engineering LTH, Lund University. His research focusses on the cognitive/conceptual challenges of business model innovation at established firms, as well as how these challenges may be better supported through the application of appropriate tools. Emil has a background in engineering physics and has previously worked as a software development engineer and consultant in a variety of industries.

Ekaterina Albats is a postdoctoral researcher at LUT University, School of Business and Management, Finland. Ekaterina works in the fields of innovation and technology management, open innovation and university-industry collaboration. Ekaterina has been running multiple research and consulting projects on open innovation and business model development, knowledge transfer, published her research results in multiple academic journals and books. Among the past projects most relevant to this piece, Ekaterina has been managing The Open Innovation Academic Network (www.oi-net.eu), led the working group in the INSPIRE project on open innovation in small and medium-size enterprises (SMEs) (www.inspire-smes.com), managed the work on Business Model Development in the platform development project C3PO (www.itea4.org/project/c3po.html) on smart city co-design. Of the latest projects, during a two-year postdoctoral appointment at Stanford University, The Scandinavian Consortium for Organizational Research, Ekaterina has been researching knowledge and technology transfer at Stanford and Silicon Valley, as well as explored the role of digital platforms in facilitating academia-business collaboration. Ekaterina has published her work in such highly ranked academic journals as *Technological Forecasting and Social Change, Journal of Business Research* and *Journal of Technology Transfer*. Ekaterina has also been serving as a guest Editor at the *Triple Helix* journal.

Felix Arndt is the John F Wood Chair in Entrepreneurship at the Gordon S Lang School of Business and Economics at the University of Guelph. He has published widely on the topics of entrepreneurial, organisational and technological change.

Lars Bengtsson is a full Professor in Industrial Engineering and Management at Lund University, Faculty of Engineering LTH and holds a PhD from the School of Economics and Management, at the same university. He has published some 100 books, book chapters and journal articles in strategic management, entrepreneurship and innovation, university-industry collaboration and research method issues. Currently, he focusses his research on open innovation and technology-based business models, especially with connection to digitalisation and sustainability.

Ann Dadich is a registered psychologist, a full member of the Australian Psychological Society, and a Justice of the Peace in New South Wales. She has accumulated considerable expertise in health service management, notably knowledge translation. This encompasses scholarship on the processes through which different knowledges coalesce to promote quality care. This is demonstrated by her publishing record, the grants she has secured and the awards she has received. A/Prof. Dadich holds editorial appointments with several academic journals, including the *Australian Health Review*. She is also the Deputy Director of the Sydney Partnership for Health, Education, Research and Enterprise (SPHERE) Knowledge Translation Strategic Platform; she chairs the Australian and New Zealand Academy of Management (ANZAM) Health Management and Organisation (HMO) Conference Stream; and she convenes the ANZAM HMO Special Interest Group. Additionally, A/Prof. Dadich supervises doctoral candidates and teaches undergraduate units on change management, innovation, creativity and organisational behaviour.

Ilse Svensson de Jong (M.Sc) holds a PhD in Industrial Engineering and Management with a focus on innovation measurement and control systems at the Faculty of Engineering LTH, Lund University. She obtained her Master's in International Business, specialised in Accounting and Accountancy, at Tilburg University, the Netherlands. Simultaneously she worked on her Master Study in Management of Technology at Lund University and CBS Copenhagen. The preferred research method is thereof mixed, combining both quantitative and qualitative methods. As a practitioner, she has been working as a management accountant at large organisations as well as entrepreneurial organisations. Her research and teaching interest lie in intersectional fields of innovation, management control and emerging subjects such as social sustainability and digitalisation.

Mark Dodgson has studied innovation management for nearly 40 years, and has written or edited 19 books and over a hundred articles and book chapters on the subject. He has been on the board of two multi-billion dollar companies and five start-ups. He has advised numerous companies and governments throughout Europe, Asia and North and South America and has researched and taught innovation in over 60 countries. He writes a regular blog on innovation and entrepreneurship for the World Economic Forum. Mark's current research encompasses innovation in China, the development of fusion energy, innovation in philanthropy and innovation in the 18th-century English pottery and textile industries. Illustrating the ubiquity of the study of innovation, he has published on innovation in academic journals in management, organisation studies, geography, history, economics, engineering, science, information systems, research policy, transportation, projects, international business, social relationships, work and higher education. In 2019, he was appointed an Officer in the Order of Australia (AO) for distinguished service in the field of innovation. His website can be found at www.markdodgson.org.

Mathew Donald has worked in large organisations for over 35 years, experiencing and leading change throughout his career. His qualifications include a Bachelor of Economics (Maj Acctg) from Macquarie University, being a Fellow of CPA Australia (FCPA) and a Member of Australian Institute of Project Management (MAIPM). Dr Mat also holds a Master of Project Management Degree from The Adelaide University and a PhD (Business) from Western Sydney University, where his research featured organisational change, leadership and management topics. In recent times this author has become an opinion writer for several institutions, an author, also lecturing and tutoring at Charles Sturt

University and Macquarie University in a range of business subjects. This author has regularly presented at conferences, webinars and podcasts on business-related topics where organisational change, disruption and leadership, a number of those can be sourced at www.drmat.online.

Samrat Gupta is currently an Assistant Professor in the Information Systems area at the Indian Institute of Management (IIM), Ahmedabad. He did his doctorate in IT & Systems from the Indian Institute of Management (IIM), Lucknow. His current research interests include complex networks, online platforms and soft computing. His research has been published in journals such as *Information Sciences, Decision Support Systems, Data & Knowledge Engineering, Information Technology and People, Journal of Decision Systems* and *Journal of Prediction Markets*. His research has been funded and awarded by reputed organisations such as SPARC, MHRD, Indian Institute of Management (IIM) Bangalore, Institute for Development and Research in Banking Technology (IDRBT), Hyderabad, India, Complex Engineering Systems Institute (ISCI), University of Chile, Santiago and International Academy, Research, and Industry Association (IARIA).

Athanasios Hadjimanolis has received his first degree (in Chemistry) from the University of Athens and the MBA and PhD from Brunel University in London (UK). The topic of his PhD thesis was: 'Management of technological innovation in small manufacturing firms'. He has published many papers in international journals like *Research Policy, Technovation,* etc., and has contributed a chapter to the *International Handbook on Innovation* (2003) and to several other international handbooks. A. Hadjimanolis has worked for many years in industry and universities and is currently Emeritus Professor at the Business School of the European University Cyprus (Nicosia, Cyprus). He has served as the Chairman of the Management and Marketing Department for five years.

Pia Hurmelinna-Laukkanen is a Professor of Marketing, especially International Business at the Oulu Business School, University of Oulu, and an Adjunct Professor (Knowledge Management) at the LUT University. She has published about 75 refereed articles in journals such as *Journal of Product Innovation Management, Industrial and Corporate Change, Industrial Marketing Management, International Business Review, R&D Management* and *Technovation*. Most of her research has involved innovation management and appropriability issues, including examination of different knowledge protection and value capturing mechanisms. The research covers varying contexts like internationalisation and inter-organisational collaboration in ICT and healthcare sectors.

Jayshree Jaiswal is currently working as a research associate at the Indian Institute of Management, Ahmedabad (IIMA). She is a PhD scholar at the Institute of Management, Nirma University. She has earned management degree specialising in marketing and bachelors of engineering in electrical. Her research interests are green marketing, consumer behaviour, innovation adoption and sustainable development. She has more than years of experience with leading organisations like IIMA, Gujarat Chamber of Commerce & Industry and MICA.

Carol Jarvis is a Professor in Knowledge Exchange and Innovation in the Bristol Business School at the University of the West of England, where she plays an active role in the design and delivery of leadership development interventions. Working from a complexity perspective and focussing on lived experience, her current research interests encompass leadership learning and practices, leadership for innovation. She has a strong commitment to building and delivering sustainable organisational improvements, achieved through collaboration and individual, team and organisational learning and development, leadership of innovation and practice-led learning. She has published in *Management Learning* and *Entrepreneurship Education and Pedagogy*.

Rajul G. Joshi is an interdisciplinary professional with proven excellence in Higher Education teaching, training, research and supervision. Dr Joshi holds extensive industry and academia experience in India and Australia. She is equipped with teaching learning scholarship, networking, communication, project management, mentoring and consulting skills. Dr Joshi had been part of two ARC research project teams in Australia and armed with grant-based research project undertaking and research training skills. She has co-edited two books and has few articles in peer-reviewed journals. Dr Joshi is active in India-Australia engagement and she has been invited for key note speech, to conduct workshops and initiates community engagement and research projects between India and Australia. She completed her PhD in Management and MBA in Business Information Technology from the University of Technology Sydney. Her research interests are in Management Science, Organisation Studies, Strategic Management, Entrepreneurship, Innovation, Development Studies, Philosophy and Management Education.

Selen Kars-Unluoglu is a Senior Lecturer in Organisation Studies in the Bristol Business School at the University of the West of England. Her research focusses on understanding the ways organisations develop and deploy their intangible resources, such as knowledge, capabilities and networks. Informed by interpretative phenomenology and practice-based approaches, she has a commitment to understanding the everyday experience of innovation and capability development in organisations. Her work on innovation and capability development has appeared in *Innovation: Management, Theory and Practice, International Small Business Journal* and *Journal of Management and Organization*.

Tony Katsigiannis is an Australian-based consultant. He co-authored *Business Model Approach to Public Service Innovation* with Dr Renu Agarwal and Kai Jin PhD (published in *The Handbook of Service Innovation*, Springer 2015). Tony's interest in innovation began in 2013 when, as a member of the National Standing Committee on Policy Submissions of the Institute of Public Administration of Australia, he helped instigate a report on public sector innovation entitled *Actively Shaping the Future Through Co-Creation*. Tony has extensive industry experience in the public, not-for-profit and commercial sectors, including 13 years in the NSW Public Sector. He has worked as both a Probity Manager and Human Resources Manager in the Transport and Arts portfolios respectively. He has an MBA from Macquarie University and a Bachelor of Mathematics from the University of Newcastle.

Catherine Killen is the Director of the Postgraduate Project Management Program in the School of Built Environment, Faculty of Design Architecture and Building at the University of Technology Sydney (UTS), Australia. Catherine's teaching and research builds upon her engineering background and her experience with new product development and innovation projects. Her research in the areas of innovation and project portfolio management has been published in more than 90 journal articles, book chapters and conference papers. Catherine is regularly invited to speak to industry audiences about her practice-based research and its implications for modern project management. Her current research themes include organisational capabilities for survival in dynamic environments, strategy and project portfolio management decision making in a variety of contexts, effectuation as a decision logic in project environments, the use of data visualisations to support project and portfolio decision making.

Andrew Levi serves as senior manager for global strategy and operations manager at Emerging Public Leaders, a pan-Africa-focussed Public Leadership Development organisation. He has spent several years working on governance, policy, crisis and organisational change research and capacity building; working alongside senior executives in the Academy, Business, Government and Non-Profit sectors. He formerly worked in PwC's global crisis advisory practice in the UK and East Africa; McKinsey & Company's Center for Government in Washington, D.C.; at Strathmore University and the premier government-run public policy think-tank and financial services regulator in Kenya. He is an alumnus of the Blavatnik School of Government at Oxford University and Cambridge University's Faculty of Law; and a recipient of scholarships to Harvard and Yale Universities. He considers himself a corporate and public governance reformist, drawing on his knowledge of Africa, Asia, Europe, North America and the Middle East.

Hussan Munir is an Assistant Professor at Malmö University and holds a PhD in Software Engineering from Lund University. He has collaborated with Sony Mobile, Axis Communications, Scania and Volvo cars during his research work. His research interest encompasses open innovation, open-source programme office and digitalisation, business models and ecosystem. Furthermore, he worked as a software developer at Ericsson and a former developer advocate at Axis communication. He was involved in setting up the Unimatrix community under the Linux Foundation and a maintainer of Axis Camera application platform on GitHub.

Anna Nikina-Ruohonen is a Researcher, Entrepreneurship and Business Renewal, Haaga-Helia University of Applied Sciences, Helsinki, Finland. Anna specialises in work life transformation from various perspectives, including innovation ecosystems and areas of innovation, the impact of AI and new technologies, innovation management, entrepreneurship and evolution of psychological contract. Anna has about 20 years of professional, industry, entrepreneurial, start-up and academic experience in Finland, across Europe and globally. An internationally published scholar and a Recipient of 'Academic Paper Most Relevant to Entrepreneurs Award' presented by United States Association for Small Business and Entrepreneurship. Author and editor of *Areas of Innovation in a Global World: Concept and Practice.* Her ongoing RDI projects address the role of artificial intelligence, robotics and new technologies on work life, including individual, team and organisational levels. See, e.g. AI-TIE – AI Technology Innovation Ecosystems for Competitiveness of SMEs and AI is here – support, skills and cooperation are the way forward.

Vincent Ogutu is the Vice Chancellor Designate of Strathmore University in Nairobi, Kenya. A career educationist, Vincent sees teaching as an opportunity to dedicate oneself to the gathering and sharing of powerful insights. He has held senior positions in the university's management board and in Strathmore Business School. His undergraduate and master's degrees were in Economics from the University of Nairobi and the University of London respectively. He undertook his doctorate in Organisational Behaviour at Rutgers University in the US on a Fulbright Scholarship and studied social entrepreneurs from the viewpoint of the Psychology of Meaningful Work. In his interaction with entrepreneurs in New York and New Jersey, he was selected to present a tech innovation of his at Google in New York, an adventure that led to his next discovery – *The Innovation Algorithm.* He has taught this innovation technique in Kenya, Uganda, Germany, Uruguay and the US.

Eric Patterson is a Director for a multinational consulting firm advising major government organisations on business planning and strategy execution. He works across multiple levels of Australian government on programmes and priorities delivering new infrastructure and services, and improvements of workings of government. Eric is a published author on innovation management with papers and conference presentations on topics including business model innovation and innovation process management. Eric is currently completing his doctorate research on Innovation Portfolio Management across the Australian Government. This looks at the prevalence and success rate of government investments in innovation. Prior to his advisory and research career, Eric was a member of the Australian Public Service working in innovation policy and business support programmes.

Daria Podmetina is an associate professor and an academic director of Innovation and Logistics (INLOG) Master programme at LUT University, School of Engineering Science, Finland. Daria work in the fields of innovation management, international business, open and collaborative innovation, and sustainability. Daria has been developing and managing several research and consulting projects on innovation management and new educational practices and published her research results in academic journals and books. Currently Daria is a coordinator of international educational project ArtIST (www.artistandinnovation. eu) developing 21st-century skills for students and new European curriculum on STEAM – integrating arts into innovation management and entrepreneurship education. In the recent years Daria has been promoting open innovation research and teaching in large international projects such as the Open Innovation Academic Network (www.oi-net.eu), the INSPIRE project on open innovation in SMEs (www.inspire-smes.com) and European project for entrepreneurship, sustainability and social innovation for school education (DOIT project www. doit-europe.net). Daria is also project director of Innovation Capacity building for Enhancing Sustainable growth and Employability (INCREASE) (increase. erasmus.site/) developing innovative solutions for Sustainability in Education and Policy & Challenge University Business Collaboration Platform (PoliUni-Bus). Daria is also an active member of the Academy of Management, scientific board member of ISPIM and WOIC conferences and serves as a reviewer in several top academic journals. Daria has published her work in such highly ranked academic journals as *Technological Forecasting and Social Change, Management Decisions* and *Journal of Small Business Management.*

Sancheeta Pugalia is a PhD student in the School of Information, Systems, and Modelling at University Technology Sydney, Australia. Prior to pursuing her PhD, she did her Master by Research programme from the Indian Institute of Technology Madras and focussed her research in the area of entrepreneurship. She has also received world renowned scholarships, including DAAD and JASSO scholarship for Germany and Japan, respectively. She has worked on multiple projects including the entrepreneurial ecosystem, management capabilities, business advisory services and escalated her research skills. Along with publishing her work in journals, conferences and books, she is an ambassador of Women in Engineering & IT.

Minna Saunila (D.Sc. Tech.) is an Associate Professor at LUT University, School of Engineering Science, Department of Industrial Engineering and Management. Her research covers topics related to performance management, innovation, service operations, as well as sustainable value creation. Recently, her research projects have been related to digitisation of services and production. She has previously published in *Technovation, Computers in Industry, Journal of Engineering and Technology Management* and *Technology Analysis and Strategic Management* among others. Since 2018, she has also been a docent of the University of Jyväskylä School of Business and Economics.

Rob Sheffield is the Director of Bluegreen Learning and Visiting Fellow at the University of the West of England. His passion is in helping leaders enable innovation in their teams and organisations. He has tutored thousands of leaders from healthcare, professional services, energy, tech and education, nationally and internationally, to help them build climates that support innovation while aligning their innovation efforts with organisational strategy. He is co-founder of the Bristol Innovators' Group, a city-wide cross-sectoral network to help people apply innovation practices; and the Co-Leader of Global Practice for the Innovation Leadership special interest group at ISPIM innovation network. His first book *How Leaders Learn to Enable Innovation in Teams: Innovation Catalysts* was published in January 2019.

Pavan Soni is an Innovation Evangelist by profession and a teacher by passion. He is the founder of Inflexion Point, offering programmes on Design Thinking, Strategic Acumen and Consulting Skills. He is the author of the book, *Design Your Thinking,* published by Penguin Random House in 2020. Apart from being an Adjunct Faculty at ISB Hyderabad and IIM Bangalore, Pavan is a columnist at *Mint, YourStory, Inc42, Entrepreneur* and *People Matters.* Dr Soni was the only Indian to be shortlisted for the prestigious 'FT & McKinsey Bracken Bower Award for the Best Business Book of the Year 2016'. He has been invited five times to speak at the TEDx, and is featured as one of the '100 Digital Influencers of 2020' by YourStory. He is Gold Medalist from MBM Engineering College Jodhpur, did his PGDIE from NITIE Mumbai and Doctoral Studies from IIM Bangalore in the domain of innovation management.

Onnida Thongpravati, PhD, has earned Degrees in BBus eCom(SUT), Grad-CertEd (LTHE-SUT), MBus and InfTech(Melb), PhD (RMIT). She is Senior lecturer and Director of the Master Program in Entrepreneurship and Innovation, Tasmanian School of Business and Economics. She has publications on new product development, entrepreneurship and innovation management and related education and training aspects including future curriculum design, multi-stakeholder supervisory and mentorship, industry-oriented and cross-disciplinary STEM. She has extensive experience developing, teaching and revising education programmes and units in management and marketing across higher education levels. She previously held academic appointments at Swinburne University of Technology, RMIT, RMIT Online and Deakin University, and was a Postdoctoral Researcher (Entrepreneurship and Innovation) at the Australian Research Council Training Centre in Biodevices. She has been appointed as a project manager/consultant for various industries in Thailand and worked full-time as a procurement and logistics planner at an Australian division of the world's second largest IT distributor.

Amit Anand Tiwari is an Assistant Professor at IIM Rohtak. He received his doctoral degree from the Indian Institute of Management Lucknow. His research focusses on contemporary issues in creative industries and cultural products. His research interests span over various areas like service dominant logic, products coolness and complex networks brand implications. His work has been published in *Journal of Retailing and Consumer Services, Marketing Intelligence & Planning, Measuring Business Excellence* and *Journal of Decision Systems*. His projects on cultural products and echo chambers have received funding from MHRD (Ministry of Human Resource Development, India) under prestigious granting initiatives such as SPARC. His paper on technology convergence has received award from IIM Ahmedabad.

Jialei Yang is a doctoral researcher at the University of Oulu, supervised by Professor Pia Hurmelinna. She will be a Scancor scholar at Stanford University and she was a visiting scholar at UC Berkeley sponsored by Professor Henry Chesbrough. Her research focusses on innovation management (especially innovation appropriability and open innovation), and she has 10+ publications including journal, conference and white papers. She serves as a scientific panel member and coordinator at ISPIM, editorial board member of WOIC, and reviewer for *AOM, EURAM* and *Journal of Innovation Management*.

PREFACE

Managing innovation will increasingly become a challenge to management, and especially to top management, and a touchstone of its competence.

Peter Drucker (2013). People and Performance, p.149, Routledge

Peter Drucker's comment is as relevant now as it was then, possibly more so in these volatile, uncertain and complex times. It is increasingly recognised that innovation is vital to the success of organisations and entire economies. However, as a commonly used 'buzzword' it is often misapplied and misunderstood. Originating from the Latin *innovare*, meaning to bring in something new, innovation is essentially about the creation of value, in other words less about the generation of ideas than their translation into commercial or social outcomes. What makes innovation interesting and important is its role not just in shaping historical or contemporary narratives but also in preparing us for a more prosperous, healthy and sustainable future. As Theodore Levitt put it, 'Creativity is thinking up new things. Innovation is doing new things'. In this context, innovation is the indispensable driver of modernity, underpinning human progress and now critically the health and prosperity of entire populations as well as the survival of the natural world around us, through changing technologies, business models and modes of social organisation. The existential nature and impact of innovation has earned the topic close attention among both researchers and practitioners, and in doing so it has also given rise to the famous aphorism 'innovate or die'.

In recent years, such attention has shifted to the management of innovation as well as its content in firms and organisations, together with supportive public policy which recognises its inherent complexity and paradoxes. We realise that to innovate we cannot rely purely on luck, which is why the focus of this Handbook is on the 'how' of innovation – how to lead technological change and innovation, how to set strategic innovation goals, how to direct resources to these goals and how to establish effective processes to facilitate implementation.

With the proliferation of approaches to innovation management, it is important not to confine ourselves to a narrow perspective on innovation or to a closed and excessively rigid approach, such as those we might find in linear 'lab to market' commercialisation solutions. This would fail to accommodate the multi-layered and interdisciplinary nature of the topic, let alone to recognise the risks and opportunities involved with its practical application. It cannot be emphasised enough that the study of innovation resists categorisation as a single overarching framework.

Approaches to innovation encompass economic and management perspectives, an all-important science and technology dimension and inevitably cultural and human-centred approaches. Acknowledging these diverse approaches, we seek to explore the nature and impact of innovation holistically across multiple dimensions and in a broad range of contexts and settings. To this end, we have brought together a distinguished collection of global authors from a mix of industry, public policy and academic backgrounds. Some are seasoned executives and academics, others are emerging researchers or those working in niche industries or start-ups. The nearly 40 authors who have contributed to the Handbook subscribe to the premise that for innovation to happen, and to succeed, it must be proactively managed at the organisational level. Only with the right focus, resourcing and capabilities, as well as a systematic national policy framework, can firms and organisations consistently innovate at high quality with positive outcomes. Not all innovation meets with success, of course, but the point is to maximise the chances of it doing so.

It would be no exaggeration to say that innovation is the 'hidden engine' that powers today's advanced economies, as it generates new forms of value to challenge traditional industries and occupations and to create new ones, requiring new skills, technologies and infrastructure. While past economic orthodoxy abstracted from the dynamic role of innovation in its static equilibrium modelling, more recent developments in economic theory have begun to recognise and account for its significance in capital accumulation and growth. In addition, both research and experience have now begun to demonstrate some generalisable features of successful innovation, albeit in different regional, industrial and societal contexts. This Handbook will bring to life the contemporary innovation debate in multiple contexts ranging across large and small organisations, developed and developing countries, and across industry sectors from high tech manufacturing to healthcare. It will demonstrate the value of having a flexible set of tools, techniques and perspectives to support innovation management in these contexts and will unpack what the evidence would suggest constitutes success, in five Parts.

Part 1 'A call to action for innovation management' outlines the contemporary challenges and key considerations in preparing to manage and promote innovation at the organisational level. This Part comprises two chapters, the first of which by Dodgson in 'The changing nature of innovation management: A reflective essay' provides an overview of the state of play in the academic literature and practice on innovation management. This is followed by Donald's chapter on 'Setting up for innovation management' which discusses the rapid pace of technological change and innovation in the context of uncertainty and risk.

Part 2 'Key ingredients for successful innovation management' introduces the role of innovation leadership, management control and problem-solving. Sheffield, Kars-Unluoglu and Jarvis in 'Climate for innovation: A critical lever in the leadership of innovation' assess how leadership influences the climate that may, in turn, support or hinder innovation. Saunila's chapter 'Mobilising management controls in innovation projects' investigates the characteristics and potential of management controls in innovation projects. Lastly, Ogutu and Levi in 'Unveiling "The Innovation Algorithm": The New Approach to Raising Your Capacity to Innovate' examine a mechanism that enables problem-based bottom-up innovation.

Part 3 'What innovation leaders are doing' emphasises the importance of bringing an organisational mindset to the innovation challenge and investigates the role of specific management approaches, tools and market engagement strategies in embedding the process of innovation. Dadich in 'Brilliant positive deviance: Innovation beyond disconnected and disciplined domains' shows how innovation may be sourced internally to support improvements in healthcare. Joshi and Soni in 'How managers shape innovation culture: Role of talent, routines and incentives' identifies the routines, incentives and talent that are required for middle managers in transforming the organisational culture. Munir, Bengtsson and Åkesson in 'Management tools for business model innovation – A review' scan the literature on mechanisms to target and facilitate business model innovation. Thongpravati in 'Origins of innovation: Market-driving innovation vs market-driven innovation' considers the balance between demand- and supply-driven innovation with a focus on market dynamics. Finally, Nikina-Ruohonen in 'Innovation ecosystems as a source of renewal for innovative enterprises' explores ways of navigating complex stakeholder environments to secure innovation goals. This Part highlights the need for an innovative mindset internally at all levels within organisations and in relation to the external environment, with a focus on the active inclusion of stakeholders, especially through 'co-creation' with employees and customers.

Then Part 4 'The trend toward boundaryless innovation' indicates the importance of capitalising on innovation opportunities outside and across organisational boundaries, sometimes depicted as 'open innovation'. This approach has changed the world of business and indeed the public sector by consciously blurring traditional boundaries and expanding the scope and prospects of innovation, particularly for small and medium-size enterprises (SMEs) in innovation networks and ecosystems. Albats and Podmetina in 'Houston, we have a problem: Ambiguity in perceiving "open innovation" by academia, business and policy-makers' introduces the concept of open innovation as a domain of productive ambiguity. Hadjimanolis in 'Innovation management in small and medium size enterprises (SMEs): New perspectives and directions' extends the concept to the role of SMEs, often perceived as innovation laggards, and their current and prospective contribution to broader industrial transformation, Of course, innovation is not confined to the private sector, and Katsigiannis closes this Part with a chapter on 'Leading Public Sector Innovation Management', which reviews and challenges the compartmentalisation of the public sector in the innovation literature and practice.

Lastly, Part 5 'The new normal for managing innovation effectively ' returns to the role of leadership in the design and delivery of innovation outcomes. Clearly, leaders are critical to contemporary innovation success in a volatile, complex and fast-changing environment. Killen in 'Effectuation: A decision logic for innovation in dynamic environments' begins this Part with a fresh look at innovation management, and Yang, in 'Benefiting from innovation – Playing the appropriability cards' shows how innovation can be targeted in different contextual circumstances to optimise execution and impact. Jaiswal, Tiwari, Gupta and Agarwal in 'Frugal innovation: A structured literature review of antecedents, enablers, implications and directions for future research' consider the new opportunities and options available for driving innovation in the context of 'new geographies'. Ahmadi and Arndt in 'Dynamic capabilities and innovation' take this further as a strategy for building dynamic capabilities for innovation at the organisational level. Finally, Patterson, Pugalia and Agarwal in 'Innovation management as a dynamic capability for a volatile, uncertain, complex and ambiguous world' summarise the prospects for innovation in conditions of constant and unrelenting disruption, exacerbated most recently by the COVID-19 pandemic. This concluding Part emphasises the need for practical approaches suited not only to prevailing circumstances but also to those we have hardly begun to anticipate, again reinforcing the importance of positioning innovation as a dynamic capability that can shape as well as adapt to the external environment.

Our hope is that the great value of this Handbook will be seen in the unique perspectives that individual contributors have brought to the study of innovation and its management in firms, organisations and the wider community. These have important implications not just for the robustness of post-COVID economic recovery but also for the *quality* of this recovery, particularly with the new and growing longer term challenges we face in public health, social inequality and climate change. We would like to sincerely thank all the authors for persisting with their contributions in the face of a global pandemic, and the publishers for their patience. It has not been an easy time for anyone. More than ever, the world will need resilient and innovative organisations to chart a way forward, together with governments that can provide well-targeted, system-wide policy support. We are confident that this Handbook, drawing on relevant lessons of the past, will convey a broad and comprehensive understanding of what is required for success in the future.

Renu Agarwal, Eric Patterson, Sancheeta Pugalia and Roy Green

PART 1

A call to action for innovation management

The Handbook starts with the theme of introducing innovation management, and looking into how to understand the field and set for success innovation management. Through this part...

Dodgson reflects upon the present understanding about innovation management in "The changing nature of innovation management: a reflective essay". Building on the three concepts of innovation management, the essay will put forward the values from an era of planning to plasticity, and answer to digital and data-rich technologies, thereby contemplating on how innovation management might contribute to a new form of capitalism.

In "Setting up for innovation management" Donald puts forward the technology change that is taking place as a result of fast-paced environments filled with uncertainty and risk. By building on the past research, Donald presents a theoretical framework that can help lead to organization success.

DOI: 10.4324/9780429346033-1

1

THE CHANGING NATURE OF INNOVATION MANAGEMENT

A reflective essay[1]

Mark Dodgson

Introduction

The theory and practice of innovation management is currently experiencing a period of rapid and profound change. A subject that addresses issues such as 'disruption' and 'transformation' is itself going through a disruptive and transformative change. Innovation management is changing dramatically because the context in which it performs is altering so markedly. Since the turn of the century, the changes in the circumstances in which organizations function have accelerated spectacularly; in technologies, markets, organizational structures, and skills requirements. Even the ostensible primary driver of capitalism since the 1970s, increasing shareholder value, is increasingly under question. The primacy of financial capitalism is eroding in the face of the growing importance of human, social, and natural capital. Innovation management is changing accordingly and, indeed, has an added obligation to contribute to these changes in responsible and ethical ways.

There is an extensive academic literature on innovation management,[2] and this chapter will base its argument around three robust and enduring insights of value that are binary in nature, and will be used as lenses to explore broader issues. The first is the distinction between *mechanistic* and *organic* forms of organization and management (Burns and Stalker, 1961). The second is James March's (1991) distinction between *exploitation* and *exploration* in organizational learning. The third, associated particularly with David Teece and colleagues (e.g. Teece et al., 1997; Teece, 2007), is the distinction between *operational routines* and *dynamic capabilities*. Each binary concept co-exists in complementary ways, and is connected over time. As well as acceleration in the connections between them, the centre of gravity in their distinctions, the balance of attention in innovation management, has moved distinctively from mechanistic *to* organic, exploitation *to* exploration, and

DOI: 10.4324/9780429346033-2

operational routines *to* dynamic capabilities. By selecting these binary analyses it is intended to simply illustrate the dynamic changes that have occurred, and their consequences. The aim of the chapter is also to highlight in the field of innovation management, which is notoriously prone to elevating the latest tool/practice/solution as being the definitive answer to its problems, there is virtue in stepping back and celebrating insights that demonstrate sustained value.

The chapter will analyse why these changes have occurred. It will argue innovation management has altered and continues to change as a result of the movement from an era of planning to plasticity, massive changes in digital technologies, and the necessary reformation of capitalism to address the connected challenges of global health, environmental sustainability, and social equity. It will contend the changes required have been, and remain, extremely challenging for many organizations. The chapter will conclude by arguing the need for innovation managers and researchers to respond to this historic shift.

Three frameworks[3]

Tom Burns and G.M. Stalker's (1961) *The Management of Innovation* was one of the first books on the subject, and it made the seemingly obvious, but actually profound, observation that different forms of management and organization are needed for different business conditions. *Mechanistic* systems are needed when conditions are stable and predictable, and organizations display high degrees of centralization and job specialization, and rigid structures. *Organic* systems are appropriate for changing conditions and unpredictable circumstances, and possess low degrees of centralization and job specialization, and fluid structures. Difficulties arise when mechanistic systems are applied to unpredictable and unstable business conditions, and organic systems to predictable and stable conditions. Challenges occur as organizations increasingly need to utilize organic systems that often conflict with well-established, highly planned, hierarchical, command-and-control management systems.

James March, in a classic 1991 article on organizational learning, distinguished between *exploitation*, characterized by words such as production, efficiency, implementation and execution, and *exploration*, characterized by words such as flexibility, risk-taking, experimentation, and innovation. He argued that maintaining an appropriate balance between the two is a primary factor in an organization's survival and prosperity. He also argues that a focus on exploitation often restricts exploration. Focussing on what is already known, he contends, produces returns that are positive, proximate, and predictable; focussing on the novel produces returns that are uncertain, distant, and often negative. March suggests an antidote to this tendency is the possibility of making 'small experiments with wild ideas', while retaining the possibility of diffusing those that proved to be good ones (March, 2006:210). The notion of 'ambidexterity' offered another solution, with organizations challenged to simultaneously function in explore and exploit mode (Duncan, 1976), although it is widely accepted that this poses significant challenges for managers. Organizations increasingly need to overcome any such difficulties and encourage exploration. The challenges of encouraging experimentation include overcoming tendencies to focus on the 'already known', accepting greater levels of risk and greater preponderance of failure, and introducing incentive and reward systems that are harder to assess and quantify (Muller, 2018).

The concept of *dynamic capabilities* was designed to theorize the emerging and evolving elements of strategy as firms seek to survive in turbulent and uncertain environments. They are identifiable strategic processes by which firms purposefully adapt, integrate, and reconfigure their competences, resources, and routines to address a changing technological, market, and regulatory environment (Teece et al., 1997; Teece, 2007, 2010). Dynamic capabilities are commonly rooted in creative managerial and entrepreneurial acts, and "reflect the speed and degree to which the firm's idiosyncratic resources/competences can be aligned and realigned to match the opportunities and requirements of the business environment" (Teece, 2010:692).

Dynamic capabilities are used to create or change 'lower-order' *operational routines* (Zollo and Winter, 2002; Helfat and Winter, 2011). Operating routines refer to the repetitive tasks that a firm performs by producing and selling existing products or services. They provide stability and direction for recurring tasks.

The nature and distinction between dynamic capabilities and operational routines has preoccupied much of the strategic management literature, often, it must be said, without much enlightenment for management practice. However, there are insights if it is asserted that operating routines are the activities that deliver day-to-day value, such as production, logistics, information systems and human resource management, and dynamic capabilities are those activities that reconfigure the construction of value, such as R&D, new product development processes, collaborative research partnerships, and business model innovation. Organizations need increasingly to nurture dynamic capabilities in order to address the challenge of the *lack* of stability in existing markets and technologies. Their products and services are continually changing and therefore the strategic capabilities that redirect and reconfigure them, and the speed of their influence, are increasingly important.

The three concepts selected here are binary but not mutually exclusive, they co-exist and can be complementary. They are linked over time – as innovations develop they commonly move from organic to mechanistic structures, from exploration to exploitation – and as dynamic capabilities shape operating routines. Success, it is argued, lies with organizations that manage to balance their forms of organization, their focus on utilizing existing capabilities and developing new ones, and their operational and dynamic efforts. The balance between them all, however, has changed. Organic forms of management have become more important relative to mechanistic ones, exploration is more essential vis-à-vis exploitation, and strategic capabilities are more imperative for the sustainable creation of value in organizations as they regularly have to redefine operational routines. Furthermore, the pace of their connections has accelerated:

the transitions from organic to mechanistic, exploring to exploiting, dynamic capabilities to operating routines, has accelerated.

That is not to deny the essential importance of operational and routine tasks, and the search for efficiencies in exploiting these areas is a continuing management of innovation concern. It is simply to assert that, for the reasons to be discussed below, these tasks are likely to be more transient and changeable. It is also the case that over time there has been extensive learning through experience of managing such issues, and there are ever-increasing opportunities for technologies, such as AI and robotics, to automate any routine activities.

From planning to plasticity

These shifts, and associated changes in innovation management, are the result of changing context and circumstances, one element of which can be characterized as a move in organizations from an era of *planning* to one of *plasticity*. In the planning era, the assumptions were that there was an element of stability in markets, technologies, and business conditions, and the future was more or less predictable. Risk could be measured and probabilities assessed in an actuarial manner. Innovative efforts could be designed and directed with a degree of certainty. Operations, new product developments, and R&D projects could be planned with a sequence of activities leading to predetermined goals. In the era of plasticity, there is endemic instability in markets, technologies, and business conditions, and the future is unknowable. Unlike risk, uncertainties cannot be allocated probabilities and measured, and the need is for flexibility and responsiveness. Plasticity lies in the capacity for continuous change and rapid adaptation to the environment (Table 1.1).

TABLE 1.1 From the era of planning to the era of plasticity

From: Planning	To: Plasticity
Environment predictable, stable	Environment unpredictable, unstable
Innovation is linear	Innovation is emergent and iterative
Hierarchical organizations searching for control	Networked organizations searching for influence, and use of empowerment
Strategy as plans	Strategy as craft
Lean thinking	Need for slack
Outputs clearly measured by metrics	Contingent assessment of outcomes
Search for optimization	Search for learning
Risk managed by assessing probabilities	Uncertainties mitigated by experiments, assessed by real options
Search for best practice	Search for good practice
Focus on capital investments, R&D, and highly structured processes	Focus on human and intellectual capital, and fluid and iterative processes
Innovation primarily occurs in autarkic firms	Innovation occurs in range of evolving ecosystems

The US military loves an acronym, and its use of VUCA (volatility, uncertainty, complexity, and ambiguity) has been embraced in the world of management (See McChrystal et al., 2015 and special edition of California Management Review, 2018). It is widely recognized that contemporary organizations are surrounded by volatility, uncertainty, complexity, and ambiguity. Even before the shocks of the 2020/21 global pandemic, the scale, pace, and unpredictability of change are breathtaking. It is not hard to find examples of how quickly and extensively circumstances can transform. In the ten years following its emergence in a Harvard University dormitory, Facebook grew bigger than the Bank of America. Founded in 1984 to sell books, Amazon achieved sales of $100 billion within 30 years. In 2020 it is estimated there will be 3.8 billion mobile internet subscriptions. India launched its Aadhar biometric digital identity in 2009, and there are now 1.2 billion enrolled. And the lifespan of a Fortune 500 company has declined from 40 to 15 years. The speed and extent of change diminish the potential of planning and require plasticity in response.

It has long been recognized that innovation is not a linear process. In connecting and realizing technology, market, and organizational opportunities, there are feedbacks, iterations, and fluidity which commonly produces unexpected outcomes, and often rely on serendipity and luck. Planning proves difficult in such circumstances. Organizationally, responding to the unpredictability and velocity of change requires replacing old hierarchies and control structures with empowered people utilizing diverse networks for creating and diffusing innovations. The days have passed when a strategic plan descended annually from head offices explaining what needs to be done to achieve well-defined objectives. It is impossible to determine what needs to be done to get from A to B if B is unknowable. Instead, innovation strategy becomes a craft, melding capabilities and opportunities, experiments and learning (Dodgson et al., 2013; Schrage, 2014; Dodgson and Gann, 2018; Schilling, 2019).

Much past attention in innovation management has focussed on the notion of 'lean': removing excess and waste from systems on the grounds of efficiency. This is fine as far as it goes, but efficiency that diminishes effectiveness is counterproductive. Lean is appropriate for repetitive, routine tasks – exploitation in mechanistic organization – but inappropriate for creative, dynamic tasks – exploration in organic organization – where slack is needed. Slack gives degrees of freedom for people to get excited about new ideas, often unaccounted for in traditional ways, and incentivized to reward long-term outcomes rather than short-term outputs. New metrics for performance involve moving from "how many more have you made/sold" and "how have you improved the ratio of price to cost", to "what new opportunities have you created", and "what have you done to add value to what we do". The search for optimization continues, but as its objectives and performance boundaries are constantly changing, the aim is to maximize learning. Risk becomes uncertainty and the actuarial application of probabilities diminishes in utility, replaced by experiments, rapid learning, and fast scaling of successful developments. In these circumstances, the use of real options provides the best indicators of performance (Trigeorgis and Reuer, 2017). There is no 'best' practice in these environments, given so many contingencies, and the idiosyncratic circumstances of every organization, only 'good' practices.

One of the major changes to have affected the binary distinctions is the shift that has occurred in the constitution of value-creating activities. These have moved from capital-intensive to human-intensive investments. Much of the focus of innovation managers has moved from large capital plant and equipment, and substantial internal R&D projects, to the construction and management of entrepreneurial and highly incentivized individuals and teams, and effectively leveraging innovation networks and ecosystems. As attention has shifted from producing standardized goods to producing bespoke services and experiences, and this requires much closer attention to human factors and connection with increasingly discerning consumers, concerned not only with price and performance but also environmental and social costs.

It has long been recognized that firms do not innovate in isolation, and collaboration is essential (Dodgson, 1993/2018). Nevertheless, many firms approach innovation as something that could be planned as an autarkic process, failing to recognize the wide range of actors – research institutions, users, suppliers, start-ups, partners – that affect the nature and direction of innovation. Analyses of this trend, such as open and democratic innovation (Chesbrough, 2003; von Hippel, 2005), which captured well-established practices, are now being supplemented by more interesting analyses of emerging phenomena, including innovation ecosystems and platforms (Autio and Thomas, 2014; Gawer and Cusamano, 2014).

Digital and data-rich technologies

New technologies have encouraged and facilitated the shifts and speeds of transitions in the binary concepts. Strategy and organization, and innovation management, have been profoundly affected by, among others: digital technologies and big data, biosciences and bioengineering, Artificial Intelligence/machine learning, robotics, additive manufacturing, and the cloud. Innovation has not only created these technologies, which are transforming the world, but the ways it is managed have been changed by their use. Technologies for design and prototyping – what Dodgson et al. (2005) identified as 'innovation technologies' – are intensifying the innovation process in a wide range of sectors. The process of drug discovery, for example, is being transformed by CRISPR gene editing and high throughput chemistry. The design and construction of buildings and infrastructure is changing through the use of Building Information Modelling. The use of AI is enhancing innovation in the health sector, from improving medical diagnoses to better allocation of resources. Communications across all sectors are enhanced by the internet, shared databases, high-fidelity video conferencing, etc. Virtual and augmented reality and simulation technologies are offering new insights and opportunities for innovation. Production and operations, and supply chains, are controlled by robots and algorithms to assure maximum efficiency. These technologies are automating routine and adding firepower to creative tasks.

The 'data deluge' of daily production of massive amounts of data is changing the nature of innovation management. Data that can be stored on the cloud, and rapid growth of smart connected devices to collect, analyse, and share data, for example, are providing innovators with enhanced consumer insights and opportunities. It is hard to imagine trends in innovation management, such as 'open' (Chesbrough, 2003) and 'democratic' (von Hippel, 2005) innovation, without the digital technological infrastructure and tools that assist them. The ability to rapidly and cheaply prototype, test, and play with new ideas as they transform into practice has fundamentally changed how innovation occurs.

Despite these advances we need to be wary. Schumpeter's great dictum that innovation involves a process of creative destruction continues to be as opposite as ever. For all the benefits that technological innovation has provided, for example, in extended life spans and greater opportunities for communication and education, it has also given us weapons of mass destruction. It has given us chernobyl, thalidomide, oxycontin, and the mortgage-backed securities and collateralized debt obligations that contributed so importantly to the global financial crisis in 2008. The gift of greater connectivity comes alongside the dangers of cyber security and misuse of personal information.

The Schumpeterian notion of creative destruction applies just as much to the activities of innovative individuals, and is personified by Thomas Midgely (1889–1944). Midgely was instrumental in developing refrigeration, and when he was approached to confront the challenge of knocking on car engines (where there are problems with the mixture of fuel and air), he helped solve the problem. In this regard he changed the world, massively altering retailing and distribution and patterns of domestic consumption, and in helping create the auto industry, build transportation networks, and democratize travel. Unfortunately, he developed refrigeration by using chlorofluorocarbons, and solved engine knock by adding lead into petrol, both with devastating consequences for environmental pollution. An inventor to the end, confined to bed suffering from polio, Midgely developed a system of ropes and pulleys to move him around. The system malfunctioned one night and strangled him to death.

This anecdote reveals how at the societal and individual level, advances in technology can have unforeseen, and occasionally catastrophic, consequences. Writing about AI, Stephen Hawking, said that we are at the most dangerous moment in the development of humanity. His concerns lay with how AI will accelerate the already widening inequality around the world, and is socially destructive. The management challenge remains to accentuate the creative side of innovation and try and foresee and mitigate the destructive part. It is to encourage advances such as Midgely's while avoiding the unforeseen, or lack of concern for, their negative consequences.

Mitigating the adverse consequences of technological change, and indeed increasing its creative potential, will require much greater concern on the part of innovation managers for the social consequences of what they do. It will also depend upon a broader franchise among its leaders and developers. The dangers of excluding women in innovation, resulting in development of male-dominated, sub-optimal technologies, are revealed in Caroline Criado Perez's *Invisible Women* (2019). Engaging diversity in all its forms in innovation is likely to produce technologies more relevant and useful for diverse societies. As the cost of innovation-supporting technologies comes down, there are opportunities to place these creative tools in the hands of more and more diverse people: truly democratic innovation.

A different kind of capitalism

The different kinds of capitalism in the world have shaped the context in which innovation is managed. Bank-based capitalism, such as in Germany and Japan, has encouraged longer-term investments in incremental innovation. Stock market-based capitalism, such as in the USA and the UK, has supported riskier investments, but with shorter time horizons. State-based capitalism, such as in China and some other Asian countries, has seen governments involved in encouraging different models of industrial development, with profound implications for innovation management (see, e.g. Zhang et al., 2021). Thus Korea has enabled the growth of large industrial conglomerates, Taiwan small high-tech firms based around research centres, Singapore has leveraged off foreign direct investment, and China, pragmatically, has encouraged all of these models.

Although all these kinds of capitalism differ in many regards, they all offer incentives for innovation. With an evolutionary economics perspective, capitalism is a very effective stimulus to the creation of variety, and markets and governments provide selection mechanisms for promulgating innovations that fund next generations of variety. It is this evolutionary model of capitalism that has since the Industrial Revolution lifted life expectancy globally from 30 to 71, and raised world GDP per capita, at adjusted prices, from $666 to over $10,000.

Despite its successes, the problem with capitalism in its most current forms is that it has proven incapable of dealing with the challenges of the age: environmental and climate change, and growing social inequalities. The Covid-19 crisis in 2020 can in part be explained by the degradation of humankind's relationships with nature and its consequences exacerbated by social inequalities in the guise of unequal access to medical care, the differential abilities in poorer households to socially isolate, and higher levels of co-morbidity among the socially disadvantaged.

These challenges emerge as a direct result of the belief, articulated by economists such as Milton Friedman, that the main responsibility of the capitalist corporation is the maximization of shareholder value. While there have been notable exceptions to this, for example, in those organizations led by religious beliefs, such as Quaker-owned companies or the Tata group in India, the search for shareholder value has generally superseded concerns for its consequences for society or the environment.

In 2019 the Business Roundtable, the group representing the CEOs of the USA's 200 largest businesses, officially recognized that the maximizing shareholder value model of capitalism was past its sell-by date, and that companies have to address a broader community of stakeholders, including employees, suppliers and customers. Respected commentators in publications such as the *Financial Times* and *Economist* are speculating about the challenges to capitalism and its need to reform. Economists warn of the damage done to national economies by the populism that leads to anti-internationalization, manifested, for example, by US/China trade wars and Brexit. A key driver of that populism is a form of capitalism that accentuates inequalities, makes employment precarious, and removes hope that the next generation will have better life opportunities. The massive destruction wreaked by bushfires in Australia in 2020 makes it all too apparent what appalling devastation occurs when capitalism fails to consider its environmental consequences.

There are, of course, alternatives to capitalism, seen in social enterprises and cooperatives, and capitalism takes different forms, perhaps most starkly in China. Assuming that the Western-style, Anglo-Saxon capitalism, as practised in the USA, the UK, Australia, and elsewhere, will remain the primary form of industrial and business organization in large parts of the world, it will in future need broader inclusivity and a wider purpose in order to survive. The construction of economic value is based upon and embedded in social cohesion and progress. The first principle of any organization's social and legal licence to operate has to become 'do no harm'. This applies environmentally, from sustainable energy production to waste management and the circular economy. And it applies socially, where the consequences of new products and services need to be fully appreciated and accounted for, from the sale of opioids and automated vehicles, to promotion of financial services, to the hitherto ignored responsibilities of social media platforms. It also applies to consideration of the quality and quality of employment, where primary concern should lie with supporting jobs that complement technology advances and offering opportunities for retraining those disadvantaged by them.

The demand of citizens, consumers, and contemporary workforces dominated by millennials, is for an economic system that offers hope and optimism, based on a confidence that change will improve rather than damage. It is the obligation of those studying and practising innovation management to contribute fully to the shift in capitalism towards greater social equity and environmental responsibility.

A form of economic relations is needed that creates value not only for financial capital, but also for human, social and natural capital. The Covid-19 pandemic raises the distinct possibility of a reconsideration and re-set of a capitalism that neglects the social basis of all value creation. The World Economic Forum calls this transformation the 'Great Reset'.

This will not occur if organizations and their leaders continue to do things as they did in the past. The management strategies, organizational routines, structures, and processes of the past have contributed to environmental degradation and social disruption, and to contribute to address these problems, there is the need for new, transformative leadership and management of innovation. To contribute to a new form of capitalism, businesses need to be fundamentally disrupted: business purpose needs to be expanded, attitudes to growth amended, strategies changed, governance restructured, incentive systems adjusted, and organizational structures and cultures realigned.

The future of innovation management

Innovation will play a crucial role in the transformation of capitalism: it produces the new products, processes, organizations, and business models that create the future. Innovation, simply, has the potential to make the lives of each generation better. Ever since the Industrial Revolution, the continuous application of technique to translate ideas into actions has led to improvements in people's standard of living and quality of life. The author hopes to live a longer and healthier life than his parents, and has enjoyed a massive difference in the opportunities open to him in his life compared to his grandparents. Given the extent of the changes needed in our economic system, whether this trajectory of generational improvements will continue is, disturbingly, open to question. It is by no means certain that the author's grandchildren will have better standards of living and quality of life than his children's. Existential threats confront us, including the environmental and health crises associated with climate change and growing social inequalities and associated political turbulence. Innovation has contributed to these threats, and will be part of their mitigation. All the learning that has occurred in innovation management to deal with technological and market disruption now needs to be additionally applied to the turbulence caused by the multiple and existential threats that confront us all. Innovation is not something that occurs unattended: it needs to be managed. How it is managed will be a crucial determinant in whether the next generation will have longer, healthier, more rewarding, and enjoyable lives than this one.

Some of the future challenges of innovation management are encapsulated by the dynamic changes occurring in the three selected fundamental insights in the field that are binary in nature. Given the dramatically changing market, technological, competitive, and political environment, the significance of organic organizational structures, and strategies that accentuate experimentation and dynamic capabilities are substantially enhanced. The tempo and quality of connections between creativity, exploration, and flexibility, and routine, discipline, and accountability has intensified. These changes provide lenses into the broader dynamics in the environment in which innovation is managed and the difficulties it faces.

Managing innovation was much easier in the planning era. Forecasts could be accurate, and plans could work out as envisaged. Innovation management operated in a more stable world, where the trajectories of markets and technologies were predictable, and organizations operated in long-standing hierarchies and authority structures. The challenges were mainly around efficiency and optimization. This was appropriate for industrial production and operations, but even in R&D, where it might be assumed organic structures and new explorations would be more fitting, there were assumptions that activities could readily be mapped, planned, optimized, and measured.

The advent of digital and data-rich technologies is, on the one hand, creating new insights and business models, and facilitating more, faster, and cheaper experimentation and adaptation. On the other hand, they are contributing to what D'Aveni (1994) and McGrath and Kim (2014) call 'hyper-competition'. In this highly unstable and rapidly changing environment, the management of innovation becomes ever more challenging as barriers to entry are lowered, including from entrants in different industries, and the resources firms need to compete for exist often reside in external networks and innovation ecosystems, rather than internally.

The idea that the ultimate purpose of the firm was to create shareholder value was simple, clear, and unifying, even though its consequences could be environmentally and socially destructive. This abrogation of responsibility is now not only rejected by environmental and social pressure groups, but by consumers, employees, and increasingly the leaders of major organizations. Managing for a triple bottom line – financial, environmental, and social – adds significantly to the complex challenges of capitalism.

Innovation management has to respond to turbulence and disruption of the era of plasticity, digital and data-rich technologies, and the need for a new form of capitalism. New forms of capitalism will not emerge fully formed: existing practices have deep roots, and conflict and contestation is inevitable. Paraphrasing Gramsci, the old is dying and the new will struggle to be born. In such circumstances the value of experimentation, of organic and emergent practices, and of continual dynamism in the capabilities of organizations, will be key to successful change.

Innovation management cannot dispassionately sit by: it has responsibilities. It is beholden on those that create the future to hold to account those who claim they want that future to meet environmental and social needs. Innovation managers need to *accentuate* Schumpeter's and Midgely's creative, and *mitigate* their destructive, elements of innovation. The dangers of approaches such as

Facebook's "move fast and break things" are evident in its casual response to its promotion of violent and anti-democratic forces. Innovation management has to be responsible and ethical management.

The broader inclusivity of capitalism includes greater global integration. At a time of rising nationalism, with the prospect of destructive competition between nations over technology and technical standards, innovation managers need to circumvent the rhetoric of divisive politicians, and contribute to the only way of overcoming environmental degradation, poverty, and social exclusion, and health pandemics, which is to develop global solutions. Innovation managers in the public and private sector have to carefully weigh the rewards of temporary national advantage in constructed trade wars, compared to the universal benefits when there is uninterrupted flow of knowledge between nations.

What are leaders of innovation to do in these circumstances, and how are they to manage innovation? First and foremost they need to appreciate the VUCA circumstances in which their organizations operate, and develop appropriate responses. As Napoleon said, the job of the leader is to describe reality and provide hope. These responses will involve more organic organization, greater experimentation, and enhanced dynamic capabilities, and speedier transitions between them and their binary partners. As well as creating incentives for innovation, they will involve far greater concern for overcoming its obstacles. These include the innovation antibodies of organizational policies and procedures that stifle initiative, and the organizational permafrost of usually middle-level managers wary of change. Innovation leaders will articulate the concern for environmental sustainability, need for social equity, and benefits of globalization, and pursue them relentlessly.

One opportunity lies in the way innovation management is becoming more relevant to a broader range of institutions and organizations. As more is learnt about innovation in public services, NGOs, philanthropy, and in social and humanitarian innovation, there are opportunities to transfer management lessons on innovation for social good to innovation for profit, and vice versa (Dodgson and Gann, 2020). There are also opportunities for greater input from sociology and behavioural economics and psychology, providing their insights into how individuals and populations alter behaviours (e.g. Ozaki et al., 2013; Halpern, 2015).

Other prospects lie with the increasing use of innovation technologies. The tools of virtual and augmented reality, simulation and modelling, and massive availability of data alongside tools for its integration and interrogation, provide huge opportunities for the democratization and inclusiveness of innovation. These technologies help bring multiple perspectives to bear in the creation and diffusion of innovation. They connect different professions and skills, producers and users, the private and public sectors and citizens. The ability to cheaply and quickly play in the digital world with potential future configurations of products and services, before creating them in the real world, will improve the range of options, reduce the chances of mistakes, and produce better outcomes.

As a result of the broad move from capital-intensive investments to investments in people, innovation management increasingly has to focus on human factors. As organizations have moved from hierarchies to networks, from controlling to empowering, from plans to experiments, new skills, and capabilities are becoming ubiquitous. The abilities of leaders to craft new solutions to problems in the face of uncertainty and imperfect information become crucial. There is a need for substantially greater diversity in the field, especially with more women contributing to the design and features of innovation. Encouraging greater diversity in the workforce, especially bringing the creative and collaborative skills of women more to the fore, and providing the tools for innovation to previously excluded workers in developing economies, offers the greatest opportunities for realizing the potential for innovation management to make a better world.

Acknowledgement

The author wishes to acknowledge the helpful comments from Sam MacAulay on a draft of this chapter.

Notes

1 As well as being reflective, the essay is selective, not offering a review of the field, but more of a personal interpretation of some of its key issues.
2 See, for example, from this author, Dodgson et al. (2014), the four volumes of Dodgson (2016, 2018, 2021).
3 The concepts outlined here for illustrative purposes are much richer than these short summaries suggest. Only a few headline features of the concepts are described, with little of the nuance they deserve.

References

Autio, E., and Thomas, L. (2014), "Innovation ecosystems: implication for innovation management," in Dodgson, M. Gann, D., and Phillips, N. (eds), *The Oxford Handbook of Innovation Management*, Oxford: Oxford University Press.

Burns, T., and Stalker, G. (1961), *The Management of Innovation*, London: Tavistock.

California Management Review. (2018), Special Section on VUCA, Vol 61:1.

Chesbrough, H. (2003), *Open Innovation*, Boston, MA: Harvard Business School Press.

D'Aveni, R. (1994), *Hypercompetition: Managing the Dynamics of Strategic Maneuvering*, New York: Free Press.

Dodgson, M. (1993/2018), *Technological Collaboration in Industry: Strategy Policy and Internationalization in Innovation*, London: Routledge. Republished 2018.

Dodgson, M. (ed), (2016), *Innovation Management: Critical Perspectives on Business and Management*. Volume 1: *Foundations*; Volume 2: *Concepts and Frameworks*; Volume 3: *Important Empirical Studies*; Volume 4: *Current and Emerging Themes*, London: Routledge.

Dodgson, M. (2018), *Innovation Management: A Research Overview*, London: Routledge.

Dodgson, M. (2021), "The strategic management of technology and innovation," in *Oxford Research Encyclopedia of Business and Management*. Oxford: Oxford University Press. https://doi.org/10.1093/acrefore/9780190224851.013.145

Dodgson, M., Gann, D., and Salter, A. (2005), *Think, Play, Do: Technology, Innovation and Organization*, Oxford: Oxford University Press.

Dodgson, M., Gann, D., and Phillips, N. (2013), "Organizational learning and the technology of foolishness: the case of virtual worlds in IBM," *Organization Science*, 24, 5: 1358–1376.

Dodgson, M., Gann, D., and Phillips, N. (eds), (2014), *The Oxford Handbook of Innovation Management*, Oxford: Oxford University Press.

Dodgson, M., and Gann, D. (2018). *The Playful Entrepreneur: How to Survive and Thrive in an Uncertain World*, London: Yale University Press.

Dodgson, M., and Gann, D. (2020). *Philanthropy, Innovation and Entrepreneurship: An Introduction*, London: Palgrave Macmillan.

Duncan, R. (1976), "The ambidextrous organization: designing dual structures for innovation," in Kilmann R., Pondy L., and Slevin D. (eds), *The Management of Organization Design*, New York: Elsevier, pp. 167–188.

Gawer, A., and Cusumano, M. (2014), "Platforms and innovation," in Dodgson, M., Gann, D., and Phillips, N. (eds), *The Oxford Handbook of Innovation Management*, Oxford: Oxford University Press.

Halpern, D. (2015). *Inside the Nudge Unit*, London: Penguin.

Helfat, C., and Winter, S. (2011). "Untangling dynamic and operational capabilities: strategy for a (n)ever-changing world," *Strategic Management Journal*, 32: 1243–1250.

March, J. (1991), "Exploration and exploitation in organizational learning," *Organization Science*, 2, 1: 71–87.

March, J. (2006), "Rationality, foolishness, and adaptive Intelligence," *Strategic Management Journal*, 27: 201–214.

McChrystal, S., Collins, T., Silverman, D., and Fussell, C. (2015), *Team of Teams: New Rules of Engagement for a Complex World*, Penguin.

McGrath, R., and Kim, J. (2014), "Innovation, strategy, and hypercompetition," in Dodgson, M., Gann, D., and Phillips, N. (eds), *The Oxford Handbook of Innovation Management*, Oxford: Oxford University Press.

Muller, J. (2018), *The Tyranny of Metrics*, Princeton, NJ: Princeton University Press.

Ozaki, R., Shaw, I., and Dodgson, M. (2013), "The co-production of 'sustainability': negotiated practices and the prius," *Science, Technology and Human Values*, 38, 4: 518–541.

Perez, C. (2019), *Invisible Women: Exposing Data Bias in a World Designed for Men*, London: Chatto and Windus.

Schilling, M. (2019), *The Strategic Management of Technological Innovation*, New York: McGraw Hill.

Schrage, M. (2014), *The Innovator's Hypothesis*, Cambridge, MA: MIT Press.

Teece, D., Pisano, G., and Shuen, A. (1997), "The dynamic capabilities and strategic management," *Strategic Management Journal*, 18, 7: 509–533.

Teece, D. (2007), "Explicating dynamic capabilities: that nature and microfoundations of (sustainable) enterprise performance," *Strategic Management Journal*, 28, 13: 1319–1350.

Teece, D. (2010), "Dynamic capabilities," in Hall, B., and Rosenberg, N. (eds), *Handbook of the Economics of Innovation*, Oxford: Elsevier.

Trigeorgis, L., and Reuer, J. (2017), "Real options theory in strategic management," *Strategic Management Journal*, 38, 1: 42–63.

von Hippel, E. (2005), *Democratising Innovation*, MIT Press.

Zhang, M., Dodgson, M., and Gann, D. (2021), *Demystifying China's Innovation Machine: Chaotic Order*, Oxford: Oxford University Press.

Zollo, M., and Winter, S.G. (2002), "Deliberate learning and the evolution of dynamic capabilities," *Organization Science*, 13, 3: 339–351.

2

SETTING UP FOR INNOVATION MANAGEMENT

Mathew Donald

Introduction

Globalisation has emerged to form great interconnectedness in trade and business that has accelerated the speed of change, otherwise named disruption, whilst also increasing the unpredictability and risk of future change (Donald, 2019). Whilst there is little evidence of research indicating that current organisational models are ineffective or failing, there is research arguing that the models may be too inflexible, slow and controlled to be effective in a new age of fast-paced ongoing change. Organisational change and any associated resistance may be multidimensional (Dent & Goldberg, 1999; Taylor & Cooper, 1988), where recent research indicates links between change and a range of leadership and management factors (Donald, 2014, 2016, 2017, 2019). A multifaceted approach to change may also include a range of new innovation concepts with beneficial influence (West & Farr, 1989; West, Hirst, Richter, & Shipton, 2004).

This chapter reviews the background of organisational design in respect to structure and process against traditional management centric model that has for so long been based on status, power and control. In an age where change is almost constant, new data and information will all too often present with little or no predictability or certainty. The decision models of old were based on reasonable predictability and certainty, based on a premise that management could control or even optimise. This chapter provides evidence from past research as an assessment of management, process and structures and discusses their applicability for a new disruption environment.

Proposed in this chapter is a new organisational model that is less prescriptive, being more of a free framework that allows organisations to adapt dynamically to ongoing change. This chapter as a result envisages that all stakeholders will be elevated to the decision-making role in the new age, where all their skills,

DOI: 10.4324/9780429346033-3

concerns and opinions are taken into account in almost real time. The newly proposed model will not be without criticism and assessment as it is a theoretical starter, one based on the literature, yet to be tested and researched. For the practitioner the environment has changed, where new ideas and models are required to avoid potential misalignment with stakeholders and loss of corporate value.

Literature Review

In response to the changes in global trade and business it has been proposed that organisational structures, processes and even governance may need to adapt in response to the pace, uncertainty and risk involved in this new form of change (Donald, 2019). The following literature review is the result of investigating organisational structures and processes so as to understand past research and their applicability to the modern age with its faster pace, uncertainty and risk. The nature of this literature review is important as a changing business environment has the potential to significantly disrupt the traditional business decision models based on inadequacies of management skills, tools and processes (Basile & Faraci, 2015; Donald, 2019). The review commenced with an investigation of past research into business systems, organisational environments, processes and structures, so as to understand the potential for that understanding to contribute towards the future of organisational models in the faster, more disruptive new age.

Organisational Structure

Organisations in a disruptive environment may need to be faster and more nimble (Denning, 2018; Donald, 2019), where the traditional control mechanisms may limit those attributes in larger more established businesses. Organisational change may now be considered a continuous process (Burnes, 2004; Král & Králová, 2016), where change and adaptation may be important for organisational survival (Donald, 2019). The staged change process described in early resistance research (Lewin, 1945) may no longer be possible when change is almost continuous. In today's environment, the various changes in organisational structures may be a measure of change (Král & Králová, 2016). Empirical studies for change and structure is uncommon, where the studies may, over time, assess the models used or proposed, yet communication is considered one element that may be important to change (Král & Králová, 2016). In more recent research communication was also linked with at least seven other change factors (Donald, 2017, 2019).

Corporate structure supports the control systems, so various corporate controls may need to be reviewed and adjusted when organisations change (Maciejczyk, 2016). Structure, on the other hand, is an enabler of successful strategy and operations, where the matrix structure was supposed to improve the functional and operational divide (Peters, 1993). Organisational structure may be a result of factors including strategy, environment, technology and organisational size (Daft,

2012; Král & Králová, 2016) and may influence technological innovation (Hu, 2014). Often large corporate organisations may seek centralisation of strategy, yet they may allow decentralisation of operational matters (Romelaer & Beddi, 2015). A wide range of organisational models exist ranging from country of origin through to globally orientated (Heenan & Perlmutter, 1979; Perlmutter, 1969; Romelaer & Beddi, 2015), product diversity including the more popular models like the matrix structure, divisional structure, product structure and area structures (Romelaer & Beddi, 2015; Stopford & Wells, 1972; Williams, McWilliams, & Lawrence, 2016).

Organisational structures can be classified along the lines of functions, departments, regions, product or matrix (Williams et al., 2016), or that of functions, divisions and matrix (Maciejczyk, 2016). Large global organisations are often designated into regions, countries or products, where diversity may be allowed based on culture, religion or historical context (Stverkova & Pohludka, 2018). Structural design is not necessarily fixed, rather it may vary based on management and market environment at a point in time (Maciejczyk, 2016; Williams et al., 2016). The management control system is often also dependent upon job descriptions, reporting relationships and compensation guidelines (Guadalupe, Li, & Wulf, 2013).

Globalisation

Globalisation, otherwise characterised as interconnected trade, has potential to become unstable or chaotic (Roome, 1998, 2011), or unpredictable, uncertain and risky (Donald, 2019). The new landscape has resulted in mergers that once may have been unthinkable, including water and power sectors (Roome, 2011). Many organisations have focussed their core activities since globalisation emerged, yet non-core activities have been often offshored, all in the pursuit of increased efficiency and profits (Sarmiza, 2010). Whilst benefits were expected in globalisation, the benefits have not been uniformly distributed, leading to increases in world migration and the number of people identifying as refugees (Roome, 2011).

Larger, more powerful brands have thrived in the new opportunity presented by globalisation (Roome, 2011), where corporations are now described as owning systems rather than merely products or assets (Roome, 1998, 2011). In globalisation work has changed, with divergence in worker arrangements that were split between those in full time secure work against casual workers that have emerged with less protection over their rights (Ekberg et al., 2016; Virtanen et al., 2005). To compete on a global basis, employers have sought more flexible arrangements through the use of casual labour (Blanck, 2014; Schur, Kruse, & Blanck, 2013; Virtanen et al., 2005). Flexible working arrangements may be under-researched in respect to their ability to reduce workplace harm, where the lack of guidance may have led to ambiguity and lack of worker protection (Ekberg et al., 2016).

The multinational corporation is complex, with increasing interconnectedness and a range of interdependencies (Ghoshal & Westney, 1993; Romelaer & Beddi, 2015). It is acknowledged that using elements of power, control, strategy and knowledge are insufficient to create a comprehensive model of the multinational, where more elements are likely to be required for complete understanding (Romelaer & Beddi, 2015). The matrix structure as a popular structure for technical environments (Anderson, 1994; El-Najdawi & Liberatore, 1997; Kuprenas, 2003) allows functional specialists to be deployed quickly throughout the operations, yet the resulting diverse agendas may emerge to slow the organisation down (Anderson, 1994). IKEA, on the other hand, has developed a business model of global replication, where the modifications are allowed as it replicates through a process of learning whilst allowing for local variations based on regional differences (Jonsson & Foss, 2011). A replication strategy is thought to be explicitly expansive in its nature, so in the IKEA model there is significant codification of processes, with instructions and a lot of detail (Jonsson & Foss, 2011).

Some argue that the emerging corporate social responsibility (CSR) and ethics may be contrary to the whole notion of capitalism (Friedman, 1970), or may even harm business models (Albach, 2005, 2007). Others argue that CSR and ethics may be an essential requirement to globalisation and the emerging landscape (Pies, Beckmann, & Hielscher, 2010). When change is almost constant and written rules are not able to be maintained regularly enough, ethics may be the staff guidance to replace written rules (Donald, 2019). CSR is not a clear concept, where the topics have at least 25 acknowledged definitions (Carroll, 1999; Dahlsrud, 2008; Guthey & Morsing, 2014), although it has been characterised with elements of adaptability and resilience (Guthey & Morsing, 2014). Some argue that there is a natural tension between social performance and economic objectives, where they may cause organisations to confront dilemmas and trade-offs, whilst acknowledging that divergent goals may be useful to understanding and society (Guthey & Morsing, 2014; Margolis & Walsh, 2003).

In an online interconnected environment, business leaders that connect with others may be more successful than others (Nann et al., 2010), so mere structural and process changes may be insufficient for this new age. The changing business environment, with its chaotic nature, increasingly challenges business to develop relationships to include both flexibility and credibility (Juras, Brockmeier, Niedergesaess, & Brandt, 2014). Creativity and innovation may be ways to create flexibility and credibility for this new age (Donald, 2019), this is not to say that control systems will not be of benefit. There is a relationship between budget adoption and organisational performance, even if start-ups do not use these in their initial phases (Foster, 2005). Informal systems may be too difficult to maintain during growth as there is a positive association between start-up growth and the adoption of management control systems (Davila & Foster, 2007). Many Chief Executive Officers (CEOs) leave start-ups as the formality of management systems is introduced, perhaps recognising that the controls may be too restrictive for entrepreneurs (Davila & Foster, 2007). The traditional gating system used to control and improve project success may also be too restrictive in almost constant change, leading to a re-thinking of the model, as a way to increase pace and adaptability (Cooper, 2017). Any new stage gating may need to be adaptive and responsive to customer changes, potentially emerging as an iterative rather than a fixed model, or with unison multiple cycles that are not merely sequential (Cooper, 2017). Should multiple cycles emerge it is important to remember that over constrained resources in multiple cycles are possible, so additional dedicated resources may be required (Cooper, 2017).

Beyond the control systems and structures there are other factors at play in organisations where some argue that authority and accountability should be aligned (Arya, Glover, & Radhakrishnan, 2007; Bedford, Malmi, & Sandelin, 2016; Giraud, Langevin, & Mendoza, 2008; Jevtić, Jovanović, & Krivokapić, 2018; Merchant & Otley, 2006) to yield improved organisational results (Daft, Jonathan, & Willmott, 2010; Jevtić et al., 2018; Khandwalla, 1973; Mintzberg, 1979; Simons, 2005, 2013). Leadership has been found to be a factor that influences change (Donald, 2016, 2017, 2019) amongst at least seven other change factors being leadership, workload, management, monitor, planning, power and culture. Cross functional team research also indicates that leadership can have positive effects, where management skills can improve competition whilst improving co-operation (Lado, Boyd, & Hanlon, 1997; Strese, Meuer, Flatten, & Brettel, 2016). Past organisational design may have been based on control, research now indicates that formalisation can yield positive effects, centralisation negative effects, whilst co-operation and competition can yield improved financial results (Luo, Slotegraaf, & Pan, 2006; Strese et al., 2016). Further manager pays and responsibilities appear to vary with centralisation of decision making and organisational synergies may diminish as organisations diversify (Guadalupe et al., 2013).

This literature review calls out that management controls organisations through a variety of means that include design and structure. The controls and structures of past organisational design may require redesign to provide a platform that is more able to cope with a faster, more unpredictable and uncertain environment that has emerged out of globalisation, the internet, technology and social media (Donald, 2019). The following section discusses the gaps identified from this literature review.

Gaps in the Literature

After consideration and review of the literature review above it is apparent that many of the past models are based on management control or power, aimed at delivering consistency, quality or growth. The paradigm of management control was evident in the original change research by Lewin (1945), yet modern research still may support some of Lewin's original research findings (Donald, 2017, 2019). Contrary to the linear change assumption in Lewin's work, it has been argued as being too simple for this more complex environment (Dent & Goldberg, 1999; Donald, 2019).

Control may have been essential to the structures of the past, yet research now suggests that centralisation may have negative effects, whilst cooperation and competition may improve results (Luo et al., 2006; Strese et al., 2016). Multiple structural types may have existed for many years, be that of the matrix, the divisional, functional, the regional or product (Maciejczyk, 2016; Williams et al., 2016), yet the models have rarely been tested on factors outside of control or power. Whilst some existing structures may allow some flexibility for regional and cultural differences (Maciejczyk, 2016; Williams et al., 2016), structure has also been used for control, power or for expansion in the case of IKEA (Jonsson & Foss, 2011). Whilst existing structures may have been researched on the basis of control or flexibility for local or cultural reasons (Stverkova & Pohludka, 2018), there appears to be little research on a wider range of criteria.

Performance measures are widely used in business, future research may be able to use those metrics to see if they are also applicable and relevant to alternate structures (Kuprenas, 2003). If the new age is faster and more unpredictable, it may be useful for research in the future to compare structures and even industries with alternate criteria such as adaptability, creativity and speed (Donald, 2017, 2019). Whilst formalisation may yield benefits to an organisation, centralisation does not (Luo et al., 2006), so more research into the differences and effects of formalisation versus centralisation may assist.

The traditional gating system used to control and improve project success may be also too restrictive in almost constant change so some are re-thinking the model as a way to increase pace and adaptability (Cooper, 2017). The new stage gating may need to be adaptive and responsive to customer changes so it may emerge as an iterative rather than a fixed model, or may develop with unison multiple cycles rather than merely sequential (Cooper, 2017). There appears to be little modern research around how organisations may already be emerging to respond to the new age environment. The literature has a lot of research into the traditional business models, yet there is little research into modern organisations against alternate criteria that may be more appropriate for a constantly changing environment. The following discusses how this research was approached.

Research Approach

Organisational design has been researched for a long time, where the common research paradigm has assumed management control over design, structure and processes by using the power, control and position. The new age business environment that is faster, more uncertain, less predictable and consequentially more risky than previous times (Donald, 2019), so the various organisational structures may no longer be as relevant as in previous times when change was less frequent and more predictable.

This research offers a theoretical solution based on past research knowledge that may be useful for practitioners and academics to review and consider in the future. The traditional management models, may have limited creativity, critical thinking and flexibility as it was so rule based, written and offering consistency. This research has not conducted assessments of existing or new structures and processes and their applicability to the new disruptive age, rather it has removed the manager as centric to the design and has sought to table a new model from the literature based on key themes and concepts identified. The new age that may be faster, more unpredictable and uncertain, otherwise referred to as Volatility, Uncertainty, Complexity and Ambiguitys (VUCA), where the concept of management control and power may need to be replaced (Ramakrishnan, 2021) with leadership that is more adaptive and agile (Kaivo-oja & Lauraeus, 2018). Extending this concept it is clear that many corporates replaced slow and conservative processes with new flexible and speedy processes, yielding new innovated solutions that may not have been possible previously (Osland et al., 2020).

The literature review above determined that control, accountability and leadership are key concepts used in traditional organisational design. This research has used those key concepts as a means to propose an alternate and new organisational model, where the concepts have been compared against a new age that requires organisations to operate faster with less certainty. It is appreciated that in this faster new age practitioners will want to trial new models and concepts now rather than waiting for trials and research findings that may take years to develop and understand. Organisational design is rarely standard, rather they are often defined based on the circumstance, market position or by specific management criteria, varying over time. No two organisations are likely to be the same at any point in time, even if they compete and exist in the same market, so this research has sought factors that may be useful in the new age with its fast pace with great uncertainty. The following findings and related model are based on the literature review above, where it is a framework with principles that may be tested and trialled by academics and practitioners alike.

Findings and Proposed Frameworks

As discussed above, this research is based on the contention that the past array of organisational structures and processes, with their management power and control, may no longer be appropriate for a globalised, disruptive environment (Donald, 2019). Whilst some organisations already allow local cultural and customer differences in regions (Jonsson & Foss, 2011), the great number of policies, processes and structures are designed to remove variation, or to control (Maciejczyk, 2016) through common standards. There are efficiencies that result from control and standardisation, be that in management knowledge, reduced variation and errors, or in governance, yet the mechanisms of control have the potential to restrict creativity and critical thinking. The new age environment with its faster, less uncertain and unpredictable nature may require deeper thought, broader ideas and multiple opinions if it is to find and assess options as multiple unpredictable changes emerge. The fast identification and assessment of a range of solutions may be required to adapt when change is unpredictable and uncertain.

It has been proposed that organisational structures be assessed on their openness, including elements of vision and innovation, where organisations often seek to experiment with structures during times of change (Nisar, Palacios, & Grijalvo, 2016). Even large successful organisations can diminish in size and value in disruption, even the once dominant market position of Kodak diminished substantially as it failed to identify, monitor and respond to the digitisation of photography (Donald, 2019). The cause of the demise of Kodak is unclear yet it led to loss of value and market share, where the structure, process or management strategy may have been contributors.

Overall structures are a choice of management, split against global control and local responsiveness (Romelaer & Beddi, 2015). Despite the control of strategy, a global diverse organisation may allow individualised strategies based on local sales, structures, finance and marketing influences (Alford & Greve, 2017; Porter, 1996; Stverkova & Pohludka, 2018). Organisational structures may vary based on adaptability, innovation and scale across countries and across organisational age (Kim & Utterback, 1983). The organisational structure has more importance than merely providing control, as structures and product architecture have also been linked to quality issues (Gokpinar, Hopp, & Iravani, 2010). Whilst there are discussions of new organisational models to respond to the disruptive environment, new sources of data analysis may be required as the old tools may be too restrictive when executives have changing needs (Cheung & Babin, 2006).

The future of organisational control systems and structures research may be insufficient, so authority and accountability alignment may be required, where further understanding of the benefits may be useful (Arya et al., 2007; Bedford et al., 2016; Giraud et al., 2008; Jevtić et al., 2018; Merchant & Otley, 2006) in improving organisational results (Daft et al., 2010; Jevtić et al., 2018; Khandwalla, 1973; Mintzberg, 1979; Simons, 2005, 2013). Whilst organisations may experience issues in change, a cohesive overriding force may enable adaptive and fluid organisations to perform with reliability (Grabowski & Roberts, 2011), indicating that metrics or objectives may be useful in supplying such force. Whilst some may question the classical product and geographic models (Gebauer & Kowalkowski, 2012), other structures may change in response to customer requirements (Homburg, Hoyer, & Fassnacht, 2002). Whilst structure may be important to stability and control, too many changes in structure may lead to instability and reduced organisational effectiveness (Rapoport, 1989).

Some may argue that a corporation has a simply primary goal to return financial outcomes to its shareholders (Beets, 2011), yet it may also have a variety of secondary goals (Beets, 2011; Friedman, 1970; Grubbs, 1998; James & Rassekh, 2000; Kamani, 2010; Manne, 2008; Silver, 2005). As organisations grew larger towards the end of the 20th century a tension has grown around the responsibilities of functional and operational management (Quail, 2008), where such tension may need resolution in new models of the future. It is acknowledged that using elements of power, control, strategy and knowledge is insufficient to create a comprehensive model of the multinational, where more elements are likely to be required for complete understanding (Romelaer & Beddi, 2015).

The various traditional structures may have served business well over the past 50 or more years, yet they are not without criticism or issues. The matrix structure has emerged as a common structure of many large organisations, is characterised as one where functional specialists provide independent professional advice without having to consider the trade-offs or general management responsibility. Tensions can emerge between the operational general management and the specialist when the general manager decides to operate alternately to the advice based on risk, trade-offs, profit or people considerations.

Despite the perceived benefits many in matrix organisational structures experience confusion over their roles and responsibilities (Johns, 1999; Kuehn, Khandekar, & Scott, 1996), slower results and conflict (Kuprenas, 2003), as well as being ambiguous and lacking efficiency (Goold & Campbell, 2003). Any appointments of a functional and an operational leader with similar power and titles led to conflict and delays, both contrary to the benefits perceived in the matrix structure (Anderson, 1994). So apart from the current disruptive nature of the modern business environment, issues remain in the past structures, processes and governance that need resolution in any new models that are proposed.

Turbulence, or otherwise described as disruption (Donald, 2019), is causing something akin to a revolution, where adaptation and the reorganising of corporate structures may be required to survive and adapt (Stverkova & Pohludka, 2018). The past structures may be inadequate to resolve the emerging issues over economic distribution, power and the environment (Roome, 2011). Whilst structure may be important to stability and control, too many changes in structure may lead to instability and reduced organisational effectiveness (Rapoport, 1989).

The matrix organisation appears to suffer less issues than the alternate structures despite its relatively high complexity, potentially due to the way processes are varied (Rapoport, 1989). So a key challenge for management is to design a structure that meets the organisational strategy and returns whilst seeking to reduce the negative effects from any change (Rapoport, 1989). It has been argued that goal orientated functional organisations may be more able to adjust structures with relative stability (Rapoport, 1989).

The structural design and outcome may not be the only consideration for design of organisations in the future as knowledge and technology sharing can assist in developing innovative business models (Guan & Huang, 2014), where innovation can be achieved through efficiency and novelty models if training is included (Hu, 2014). It has been discussed that future organisations may need to consider ethics, society and community given the power that many current organisations hold (Beets, 2011). Matrix structures have also been found to have improved if leaders provide tools to implement it combined with training (Kuprenas, 2003). In a changing environment some have argued that new governance is required (Donald, 2019; Roome, 2011) as the structure is not the only organisational factor that may need to adjust to disruption and its faster environment.

As discussed in the gaps section of this research, some organisations like IKEA adopt expansive strategies that pursue replication through processes, yet allow local variations (Jonsson & Foss, 2011). Whilst the IKEA model reduces management control through regional decision making, it relies on processes to assist in alignment without prescribing decisions and outcomes as other multinationals may. In traditional structures it is possible that management control and rules may become overly prescriptive, thereby inhibiting agility and responsiveness. This does not suggest that some form of alignment or control is unwarranted, rather that growth is possible with a less rigid structure when strong processes are defined and trained.

The organisational structure may not be the only element, as flexible working arrangements also assist in the pursuit of efficiency that has translated to numerous workplace changes like additional flexibility and cross- skilling (Ekberg et al., 2016). The choices of structure and design closely align with the operational and process activities of a business (Basile & Faraci, 2015). With a faster less certain environment the organisation may be incapable of keeping up the old control processes like documentation and training, where instead a higher level advice system, like ethics, may be more useful (Donald, 2019). CSR, being a connection between organisation and society values, has been characterised with elements of adaptability and resilience (Guthey & Morsing, 2014) that may be useful in an environment of fast and uncertain change.

Business management innovations have been defined as new ways of working (Basile & Faraci, 2015; Hamel, 2006) or as a new process or structure (Basile & Faraci, 2015; Vaccaro, Volberda, & Van Den Bosch, 2012). Innovation in the organisational context is certainly more than the traditional product-based models, so now includes innovation in terms of administration (Damanpour, 1987; Pisano, 1996), management (Basile & Faraci, 2015; Birkinshaw & Mol, 2006; Hamel, 2006; Markides, 1997) and even organisation (Basile & Faraci, 2015; Damanpour, 1987; Damanpour & Aravind, 2011; Damanpour & Evan, 1984).

One might consider that apart from power and control, organisational structures and processes are often designed in an attempt to gain advantage or implement strategy, or simply as a means to meet new real or perceived issues in past structures. Based on the literature review above and the discussion around the limits of current organisational structures and processes, a new model for the organisation of the future is proposed in the following discussion. The new model is based on the faster, more unpredictable and uncertain risk of the emerging globalised interconnected environment.

Risk registers have often been used by organisations to identify and prepare for risk before they occur, yet in this more connected new age the risks are increasingly harder to predict, as they can now transcend markets and industries, where the possible rather than the probable can occur in fast time (Donald, 2019). The proliferation of the internet, email and social media occurred with little notice based on their perceived benefits and functionality, each now allows information and understanding to be transmitted almost instantly, without filtering or analysis in many cases. The old risk register does not appear to be appropriate for this new age, where disruption preparation and registers are proposed as extensions for the future (Donald, 2019).

New Model Inputs

The new model proposed for the future of organisations is one that prepares the organisation for ongoing change, a change embracing culture and innovative thinking where change is sought to be understood prior to it occurring. It is proposed here that business models should be measured for appropriateness and success against new criteria rather than the power and control models of the past Power and control have been used as ways for management as a means to ensure success or to ensure that their strategy and outcomes are met, in an ever-changing environment the power and controls of the past may be too rigid and slow to adapt so regularly. More than one factor has been interlinked with change and one another (Donald, 2017, 2019) so the key to organisations adapting in a faster moving environment may not be simple nor singular, rather a multiple of adaptation techniques may be required through new thinking and innovation.

It will be beneficial to see inputs as being more than physical business requirements, rather it will improve speed and agility if the inputs of the new model include a culture of openness, vision and inclusion. Speed will be improved if these new inputs are shared and trained in the organisation, as that will reduce any staff resistance or time required to explain and gather support or appreciation to the constantly changing environment.

New Model

If the above new inputs are embraced and achieved, they will likely enable the organisation to adapt and react to changes as they are identified or occur. Staff that are trained and cognisant of constant change will be more likely to accept change when it occurs, thereby improving their ability to move towards resolutions and options than if they had not been aware of the potential for change. To react and adjust to change that is sudden and constant routine decision making may be too slow, so enablers that allow and encourage solutions to be creative and flexible may be important to commercial success. Balancing the flexibility with the potential to harm society or cross societal values is important to limit the power and risk to an organisation with these new enablers (Donald, 2019). Hence it is considered prudent to include ethics and society in staff training to limit the potential for creativity and flexibility to harm or impede organisational value.

Staff attitudes and requirements are likely to change in a less certain, faster changing environment (Donald, 2019), where the IT industry is one that confronted this issue earlier than others. The IT industry has already examples of issues surrounding the attraction of talent and maintaining skills talent in a fast moving uncertain environment, where new ways of managing and developing their staff are required (Chaudhuri, Hirudayaraj, & Ardichvili, 2018). In an environment of high competition and rapid change the IT industry has emerged with a number of flexible designs that were aimed to promote continuous innovation (Bahrami, 1992) and may be of use in the future of organisations.

The new organisational model that is proposed is not based on power, control or even efficacy as the unpredictable nature of the new age may require inefficient adjustments in order to survive and thrive. The proposition of a new model is to not prescript structures and processes or even roles, rather the new model seeks to add financial value to the organisation, whilst achieving societal requirements through innovation, speed and adaptability. The new model proposed expands the notion of CSR whilst acknowledging its place in a faster more uncertain new age. Rather than measuring management on financial success alone the new model seeks to measure their ability to adapt, where budget and even strategic goals can quickly and easily be overridden by change in a globalised, technological environment. Even the product or service being offered may quickly be fundamentally changed when new tariffs arise, drones and artificial intelligence develop, so it may be unfair or inappropriate to measure and reward merely on financial or strategic grounds.

New Organisational Model Measures

From the literature review there appear to be a range of factors that may assist in the achievement of the new model measures, as outlined above in this section. The key requirements of a modern new age organisation for the new age may be measures against an uncertain, unpredictable and risky environment, where control is not considered as the sole requirement, where the traditional financial measures may be insufficient. Whilst financial measures may continue to be a focus for investors, the broader stakeholders may prefer to have a longer-term view, or see value to society and other stakeholders as also being important.

Innovation, speed and organisational adaptability are proposed as two additional measures for organisations in the new model. In any new model, the traditional manager and leader roles will take on new balancing skills. The new measures will measure organisational success through the combination of innovation, speed and adaptability, rather than merely financial or society. These two additional measures for the organisation are required with financial and societal measures so as to recognise that at times the new age will result in the suboptimal, due in part to the unforeseen, speed and the lack of control over global events. Investors in this new age may be accommodating if new robots, tariffs or other disruptions emerge so long as the organisation is able to adapt and innovate solutions that allow it to survive and thrive in the longer term. Essentially investors exist to achieve returns, where the fixed measure of budget or market forecast may no longer be an appropriate measure when changes are interconnected beyond the control of the management.

Furthermore, a new model is proposed below that is based on outcome assessments rather than being prescriptive in its nature. So, innovation is required, achieved through the use of creativity with flexibility that react and assess to ongoing change where the adaptability is not pre-defined, rather the solutions are a range of possibilities that are assessed by their potential outcomes. Whilst management should be responsible for identifying new, sudden and unpredictable change, any notion of fixed and unvarying results is unlikely in this new age. Innovative management skills are likely to entail early change identification, option evaluation and critical thinking. The new organisational model proposed is shown in Figure 2.1.

This new model in Figure 2.1 does not prescribe processes, structures or governance, leaving the exact form to the processes of design using the inputs listed above. Recent research indicates that some organisations are experiencing almost constant change, some larger organisations with more than 50 significant changes in just a three-year period (Donald, 2017). Remaining with the traditional strategy, hierarchical structures, written processes and financial targets may simply be too few in number and too rigid when the environment is uncertain, unpredictable and risky.

As discussed previously, an iterative rather than a fixed model, with multiple cycles (Cooper, 2017) may allow organisations to move away from sequential project control processes, hence increasing speed. An iterative model, with delegated decision making and cells that are allowed to operate flexibility and creatively, may improve speed and responsiveness. Rather than management losing control of change it may be beneficial to consider this iterative model with

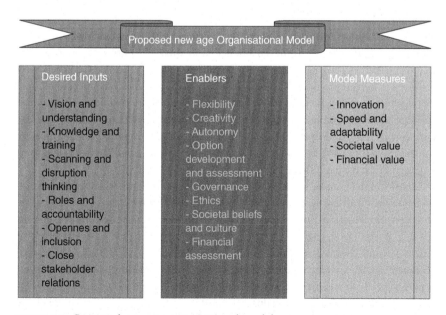

FIGURE 2.1 Proposed new age organisational model.

gates, timeframes and targets, so allowing the cell to solution goals and optimise in between gates that have to be passed through.

For flexibility it is argued that roles and responsibilities should not be overly prescriptive, as large documents may often not be used (Goold & Campbell, 2003), where the more important than the role description may be the purpose of a role (Goold & Campbell, 2003; Merton, 1968), or an understanding of disruption (Donald, 2019). The new model proposed in this research sets the measures for organisational success, yet allows for flexibility within the model to achieve those goals, as in disruption structures, processes and stakeholder involvement may be under constant change. Rather than defining roles and responsibilities, accountabilities are deemed more important, allowing more creative solutions. The following is a discussion of the practical applications for this research and proposed model as well as a discussion for practitioners and future research directions.

Practical Applications, Future Study and Practitioners

The new model being proposed has implications for the enterprise and management innovation. The se implications affect organisation structure, processes and governance. The model proposed above was designed from the literature, yet there are likely to be practical applications of this model for those wanting to adapt and adjust to the faster new age disruption environment, so it is discussed in this section.

Enterprise Implications

With a less certain, more unpredictable and riskier environment the traditional models of setting strategy, annual budgets and financial measures appear to be inappropriate, lacking flexibility and acknowledgement of creativity that may be required when unpredictable changes occur. Past structures and processes may have been effective when measured against power and control, it is perceived that they are too rigid and slow to be appropriate for an environment that is in almost constant change. Entrepreneurs may have the requisite creativity to design new solutions, so long as they can engage stakeholders with close relations as trust and engagement have been linked to change success (Donald, 2019).

Traditional organisational models rely upon governance through reporting of deviations and inefficiencies, yet governance is often retrospective and slow in larger organisations, occurring well after any decision-making process. This is not too push governance into the irrelevant, rather it may hold higher relevance counter the creativity and risk profiles of the creative and entrepreneurial (Donald, 2019). Governance may need to be closer to decision-making timing, where it is involved in the development of options and their critical assessment before decisions are made (Donald, 2019). Of course, if governance is to be closer to decision makers their independence can be compromised. Although there are benefits of real time independent advice that may outweigh independence issues as closer governance, in real time may be beneficial in avoiding the illegal or unethical actions. The measures for organisational success are no longer purely financial in this proposed model, rather ethics and society value needs to also balance with the creative and innovation. Governance should not be limited to pure financial audits, rather it should provide independent advice against all four of the measures proposed in this new model in Figure 2.1.

Manager Implications

For managers and leaders trained in past times it may be confronting or quite difficult to contemplate a model without management centricity, power and control. The traditional model was based on expectations that the business environment was reasonably predictable and controllable, where the manager was in control with great knowledge to solve and propose solutions. In the new age with its faster, less uncertain and riskier environment, management is unlikely to be all knowledgeable, nor be the source of all the creativity and best options. Management will need the support and skills of staff and the broader stakeholders if they are to quickly identify issues and best fit solutions, management may now be the facilitator of the flexible and the adaptive rather than merely being the controller of the financial outcomes.

Furthermore, the new model removes the notion that management make decisions independently, where they merely seek to consult or communicate after decisions are made. The old process is considered to be too slow and may inhibit trust, so it may be advantageous to share the environment and broader business issues before decisions are made in this new age. Inclusion and consultation occurring as decisions are made may be more engaging, as staff, customers and suppliers are allowed to have more information and understanding of the issues. Of course, these new relations need to be genuine, where staff and others are allowed to give negative feedback, or make suggestions and assessments without fear of retribution or criticism. Trust and engagement have both been closely linked to a number of other change factors (Donald, 2017, 2019), so in constant change a broad set of factors should be included in the new processes.

It is important to consider how divergent this proposed model will be for those trained in leadership and management in past times. Existing managers and leaders may not fully appreciate the new age, its fast pace, uncertainty and risk so may continue to work in the old power and control modes of the past. Organisations that do not seek to inform, train and increase knowledge on disruption and the associated changes required in a new organisational model may find their management disillusioned, or even subversive, towards the goals and operations of a new model. Knowledge and training have been associated with innovative business models (Guan & Huang, 2014), where innovation can also be achieved with efficiency and novelty models if training is included (Hu, 2014). It is therefore important for organisations seeking to modernise for this new age, or to adopt this proposed new model, to be conscious of the size of the change required and to not leave their managers behind in the transition.

As the new age will not only be full of constant change (Donald, 2019), it is likely to yield new transactions, new tools and opportunities with its new technology, artificial intelligence and interconnectedness brought upon by globalisation. New management techniques are required as a result of this new age, irrespective of the organisational model adopted as the old models often are too slow for this new age and potentially stifle creativity and innovation. Merely changing a model, he organisational processes and structures may be insufficient for a complete transition in this new age, rather a broad and multiple dimension change approach is more likely required to cover all the issues that may arise. Alternately, ignoring the new age, not changing away from the management centric models may leave the organisation unable to adapt or transition to the new creative and innovative approaches that competitors may achieve.

Contribution to Innovation

Innovation may have at least five dimensions including strategy, structural, staff motivation and its ability for cohesion (Kraśnicka, Głód, & Wronka-Pośpiech, 2016). The new age is faster, more unpredictable and more uncertain than in the past, where new situations, new transactions and new possibilities may emerge (Donald, 2019). Organisations wanting to survive and thrive in this new age will likely need to be early identifiers of change, good at analysis with critical thinking of the options, where each of those elements will not be automatic nor easily available. Management and leadership of the future will be challenged like never before as technology moves from the change itself to the enabler of faster and more uncertain change.

Change in this new age will likely accelerate in speed, so limiting the management centric models of power and control, simply the manager of the future is unlikely to be knowledgeable on all aspects of the organisation, nor the global interconnected changes occurring all around the world. Rather management will be more dependent on their staff, customers and suppliers to identify risks and opportunities, more dependent upon others to analyse and to provide reasonable alternatives and assessments. The manager and leader of the future will likely require skills of creativity, inclusion, openness and ethics that may not have been so important in a more stable environment.

This research has contributed to the innovation topic by firstly reviewing organisational models and associated research including their assessment and evolution. In that process several factors linking innovation to organisational success were identified, be that through creativity, knowledge and training. This research has reviewed the differences of this new age and their potential effects on organisational structures, processes and stakeholder relations. The new age is likely to be constantly changing, yet holding great uncertainty, unpredictability and risk due to globalisation and the way technology is now an enabler of information sharing and transmission.

Summary of Model Changes

Table 2.1 presents a summary of model changes. The case for less management centric organisational models has been made in this chapter as a means to allow faster adaptation to risks and opportunities as they present. The model proposed in this research has added new measures of organisational success beyond the mere financial outcome, arguing for flexible adjusting targets rather than the traditional fixed budget requirements. Without the manager making all decisions in the new model, it is recommended that all stakeholders be included in decision making as a way to gather more ideas, reducing trust issues and as a way to build understanding and engagement. The model proposed has innovation as a measure, yet its design is also innovative and potentially thought provoking for those trained in management of past times.

There are many examples of flexible models emerging in the IT industry, where the industry is adapting to fast emerging new technology and innovations. The future of the organisational model is already in development and so it will be useful and important to compare these emerging models to those proposed above as well as to the existing models. Future research may be able to monitor and assess these emerging models in terms of their success or benefits, so being useful to those in control of business models of the future.

TABLE 2.1 Summary of model changes

Organisational element	Old model	New model
Management	Control and rule	Iteration and targets with gates
Leadership	Top down communication of plans	Collaboration, close relationships and two way involvement
Structures	Rigid and defined	Flexible and adaptive
Ethics and society	Backward looking, reporting focus	Actively considered at time of decision making
Change	Reactive once change occurs or is reasonably likely	Forward looking and preparing for change that may only be possible
Planning and budgets	Rigid and defined, tracked and measured	Flexible options under constant review. Prepared to alter previous targets regularly
Creativity and innovation	Controlled through formal proposals and review	Flexible cells allowed to work autonomously within iterative goal setting and gates

References

Albach, H. (2005). Betriebswirtschaftslehre ohne Unternehmensethik *ZfB – Zeitschrift für Betriebswirtschaftslehre, 75*(9), 809–831.

Albach, H. (2007). Betriebswirtschaftslehre ohne Unternehmensethik – Eine Erwiderung. *ZfB – Zeitschrift für Betriebswirtschaftslehre, 77*(2), 195–206.

Alford, J., & Greve, C. (2017). Strategy in the public and private sectors: Similarities, differences and changes. *Administrative Sciences, 7*(4), 35.

Anderson, R. E. (1994). Matrix redux. *Business Horizons, 37*(6), 6–10. doi:10.1016/S0007-6813(05)80238-1

Arya, A., Glover, J., & Radhakrishnan, S. (2007). The controllability principle in responsibility accounting: Another look. In F. G. R. Antle, & P.J. Liang (Ed.), *Essays in accounting theory in honour of Joel S. Demski* (pp. 183–198). New York: Springer Nature.

Bahrami, H. (1992). The emerging flexible organization: Perspectives from Silicon Valley. *California Management Review, 34*(4), 33–52. doi:10.2307/41166702

Basile, A., & Faraci, R. (2015). Aligning management model and business model in the management innovation perspective. *Journal of Organizational Change Management, 28*(1), 43–58. doi:10.1108/JOCM-10-2013-0199

Bedford, D. S., Malmi, T., & Sandelin, M. (2016). Management control effectiveness and strategy: An empirical analysis of packages and systems. *Accounting, Organizations and Society, 51*, 12–28. doi:10.1016/j.aos.2016.04.002

Beets, S. D. (2011). Critical events in the ethics of U.S. corporation history. *Journal of Business Ethics, 102*(2), 193–219. doi:10.1007/s10551-011-0805-1

Birkinshaw, J., & Mol, M. (2006). How management innovation happens. *MIT Sloan Management Review, 47*(4), 81–88.

Blanck, P. (2014). The struggle for web eQuality by persons with cognitive disabilities. *Behavioral Sciences and the Law, 32*, 4–32. doi:10.1002/bsl.2101

Burnes, B. (2004). Kurt Lewin and the planned approach to change: A re-appraisal. *Journal of Management Studies, 41*(6), 977–1002. doi:10.1111/j.1467-6486.2004.00463.x

Carroll, A. B. (1999). Corporate social responsibility: Evolution of a definitional construct. *Business and Society, 38*(3), 268–295.

Chaudhuri, S., Hirudayaraj, M., & Ardichvili, A. (2018). Borrow or grow: An overview of talent development/management practices in Indian IT organizations. *Advances in Developing Human Resources, 20*(4), 460–478. doi:10.1177/1523422318803345

Cheung, W., & Babin, G. (2006). A metadatabase-enabled executive information system (Part A): A flexible and adaptable architecture. *Decision Support Systems, 42*(3), 1589–1598. doi:10.1016/j.dss.2006.01.005

Cooper, R. G. (2017). Idea-to-launch gating systems: Better, faster, and more Agile: Leading firms are rethinking and reinventing their idea-to-launch gating systems, adding elements of Agile to traditional Stage-Gate structures to add flexibility and speed while retaining structure. *Research-Technology Management, 60*(1), 48–52. doi:10.1080/08956308.2017.1255057

Daft, R. L. (2012). *Organization theory and design* (11th ed.). Mason, OH: Cengage Learning.

Daft, R. L., Jonathan, M., & Willmott, H. (2010). *Organization theory and design*. USA: Cengage Learning.

Dahlsrud, A. (2008). How corporate social responsibility is defined: An analysis of 37 definitions. *Corporate Social Responsibility and Environmental Management, 15*(1), 1–13.

Damanpour, F. (1987). The adoption of technological, administrative, and ancillary innovations: Impact of organizational factors. *Journal of Management, 13*(1), 675–688.

Damanpour, F., & Aravind, D. (2011). Managerial innovation: Conceptions, processes, and antecedents. *Management and Organization Review, 8*(2), 423–454.

Damanpour, F., & Evan, W. M. (1984). Organizational innovation and performance: The problem of 'organizational lag'. *Administrative Science Quarterly, 29*(3), 392–409.

Davila, A., & Foster, G. (2007). Management control systems in early-stage startup companies. *The Accounting Review, 82*(4), 907–937. doi:10.2308/accr.2007.82.4.907

Denning, S. (2018). Succeeding in an increasingly Agile world. *Strategy & Leadership, 46*(3), 3–9. doi:10.1108/SL-03-2018-0021

Dent, E., & Goldberg, S. (1999). Challenging "resistance to change". *The Journal of Applied Behavioral Science, 35*(1), 25–41. doi:10.1177/0021886399351003

Donald, M. (2014). *Project Managers beware: The resistance to change you experience may be due to Senior Leadership rather than just your methods or employees.* Paper presented at the AIPM National 2014 Conference Proceedings, Brisbane, Australia. http://www.aipm2014.com.au/images/files/papers/Donald-M.pdf; http://www.aipm2014.com.au/images/files/papers/AIPM_2014_Conference_Proceedings.pdf

Donald, M. (2016). *Organisational change factors: More than disgruntled employees or poor process.* Paper presented at the AIPM 2016 Inaugral Regional Conference (Peer Reviewed Paper), Sydney, Australia. https://www.aipm.com.au/documents/aipm-key-documents/aipm_2016_national_conference_papers.aspx

Donald, M. (2017). *Resistance to change forms and effects in Greater Western Sydney: A multidimensional approach* (Doctor of Philosphy- Business). Western Sydney University, Sydney, Australia.

Donald, M. (2019). *Leading and managing change in the age of disruption and artificial intelligence* (1st ed.). United Kingdom: Emerald.

Ekberg, K., Pransky, G., Besen, E., Fassier, J.-B., Feuerstein, M., Munir, F., & Blanck, P. (2016). New business structures creating organizational opportunities and challenges for work disability prevention. *Journal of Occupational Rehabilitation, 26*(4), 480–489. doi:10.1007/s10926-016-9671-0

El Najdawi, M. K., & Liberatore, M. J. (1997). Matrix management effectiveness: An update for research and engineering organizations. *Project Management Journal, 28*(1), 25–31.

Foster, G. (2005). Management accounting systems adoption decisions: Evidence and performance implications from early-stage/startup companies. *The Accounting Review, 80*(4), 1039–1068. doi:10.2308/accr.2005.80.4.1039

Friedman, M. (1970). The social responsibility of business is to increase its profits. *New York Times Magazine, 122–126*(September), 32–33.

Gebauer, H., & Kowalkowski, C. (2012). Customer-focused and service-focused orientation in organizational structures. *Journal of Business & Industrial Marketing, 27*(7), 527–537. doi:10.1108/08858621211257293

Ghoshal, S., & Westney, D. E. (1993). Introduction and overview. In S. Ghoshal, & D. E. Westney (Eds.), *Organization theory and the multinational corporation.* New York: Saint Martin's Press.

Giraud, F., Langevin, P., & Mendoza, C. (2008). Justice as a rationale for the controllability principle: A study of managers' opinions. *Management Accounting Research, 19*(1), 32–44. doi:10.1016/j.mar.2007.09.002

Gokpinar, B., Hopp, W. J., & Iravani, S. M. R. (2010). The impact of misalignment of organizational structure and product architecture on quality in complex product development. *Management Science, 56*(3), 468–484. doi:10.1287/mnsc.1090.1117

Goold, M., & Campbell, A. (2003). Making matrix structures work: Creating clarity on unit roles and responsibility. *European Management Journal, 21*(3), 351–363. doi:10.1016/S0263-2373(03)00048-3

Grabowski, M., & Roberts, K. (2011). High reliability virtual organizations: Co-adaptive technology and organizational structures in tsunami warning systems. *ACM Transactions on Computer-Human Interaction (TOCHI), 18*(4), 1–23. doi:10.1145/2063231.2063233

Grubbs, K. E. (1998). Profits and prophets. *World Trade, 11*(3), 96.

Guadalupe, M., Li, H., & Wulf, J. (2013). Who lives in the C-suite? Organizational structure and the division of labor in top management. *Management Science, 60*(4), 824–844. doi:10.1287/mnsc.2013.1795

Guan, Y., & Huang, G. (2014). Empirical study on the influencing factors of business model innovation. *Applied Mechanics and Materials, 687–691*(Manufacturing Technology, Electronics, Computer and Information Technology Applications), 4746–4749. doi:10.4028/www.scientific.net/AMM.687-691.4746

Guthey, E., & Morsing, M. (2014). CSR and the mediated emergence of strategic ambiguity. *Journal of Business Ethics, 120*(4), 555–569. doi:10.1007/s10551-013-2005-7

Hamel, G. (2006). The why, what and how of management innovation. *Harvard Business Review, 84*(2), 72–84.

Heenan, D., & Perlmutter, H. V. (1979). *Multinational organization development.* Reading, MA: Addison-Wesley.

Homburg, C., Hoyer, W. D., & Fassnacht, M. (2002). Service orientation of a retailer's business strategy: Dimensions, antecedents, and performance outcomes. *Journal of Marketing, 66*(4), 86–101.

Hu, B. (2014). Linking business models with technological innovation performance through organizational learning. *European Management Journal, 32*(4), 587–595. doi:10.1016/j.emj.2013.10.009

James, H. S., & Rassekh, F. (2000). Smith, Friedman, and self-interest in ethical society. *Business Ethics Quarterly, 10*(3), 659–674.

Jevtić, M., Jovanović, M., & Krivokapić, J. (2018). A new method for measuring organizational authority and accountability: Quantitative approach. *Industrija, 46*(3), 47–69. doi:10.5937/industrija46-18041

Johns, T. G. (1999). On creating organizational support for the project management method. *International Journal of Project Management, 17*(1), 47–53.

Jonsson, A., & Foss, N. (2011). International expansion through flexible replication: Learning from the internationalization experience of IKEA. *Journal of International Business Studies, 42*(9), 1079–1102. doi:10.1057/jibs.2011.32

Juras, A., Brockmeier, J., Niedergesaess, V., & Brandt, D. (2014). Trust and team development to fight chaos: Three student reports. *AI & Society, 29*(2), 267–275. doi:10.1007/s00146-013-0484-9

Kaivo-oja, J. R. L., & Lauraeus, I. T. (2018). The VUCA approach as a solution concept to corporate foresight challenges and global technological disruption. *Foresight, 20*(1), 27–49. doi:10.1108/FS-06-2017-0022

Kamani, A. (2010). The case against corporate social responsibility. *Wall Street Journal, August* (23), R1.

Khandwalla, P. N. (1973). Viable and effective organizational designs of firms. *Academy of Management Journal, 16*(3), 481–495. doi:10.2307/255008

Kim, L., & Utterback, J. (1983). The evolution of organizational structure and technology in a developing country. *Management Science, 29*(10), 1185–1197. doi:10.1287/mnsc.29.10.1185

Král, P., & Králová, V. (2016). Approaches to changing organizational structure: The effect of drivers and communication. *Journal of Business Research, 69*(11), 5169–5174. doi:10.1016/j.jbusres.2016.04.099

Kraśnicka, T., Głód, W., & Wronka-Pośpiech, M. (2016). Management innovation and its measurement. *Journal of Entrepreneurship, Management and Innovation, 12*(2), 95–122.

Kuehn, R. R., Khandekar, R. P., & Scott, C. R. (1996). The effects of marginality ad reward on matrix conflict. *Project Management Journal, 27*(3), 17–26.

Kuprenas, J. A. (2003). Implementation and performance of a matrix organization structure. *International Journal of Project Management, 21*(1), 51–62. doi:10.1016/S0263-7863(01)00065-5

Lado, A. A., Boyd, N. G., & Hanlon, S. C. (1997). Competition, cooperation, and the search for economic rents: A syncretic model. *Academy of Management Review, 22*(1), 110–141.

Lewin, K. (1945). The research center for group dynamics at Massachusetts Institute of Technology. *Sociometry, 8*(2), 126–136.

Luo, X., Slotegraaf, R. J., & Pan, X. (2006). Cross-functional "coopetition": The simultaneous role of cooperation and competition within firms. *Journal of Marketing, 70*(2), 67–80. doi:10.1509/jmkg.70.2.67

Maciejczyk, A. (2016). Challenges of control in functional organization structures: Example of outsourcing sector. *Journal of Economics & Management, 25*(25), 48–62. doi:10.22367/jem.2016.25.04

Manne, H. G. (2008). Milton Friedman was right. *Wall Street Journal, November* (24), A12.

Margolis, J. D., & Walsh, J. P. (2003). Misery loves companies: Rethinking social initiatives by business. *Administrative Science Quarterly, 48*(2), 268.

Markides, C. (1997). Strategic innovation. *Sloan Management Review, 38*(3), 9–23.

Merchant, K. A., & Otley, D. T. (2006). A review of the literature on control and accountability. *Handbooks of Management Accounting Research, 2*, 785–802. doi:10.1016/s1751-3243(06)02013-x

Merton, R. (1968). *Social theory and social structure.* New York: Free Press.

Mintzberg, H. (1979). *The structuring of organisations: A synthesis of the research.* New Jersey: University of Illinois.

Nann, S., Krauss, J., Schober, M., Gloor, P. A., Fischbach, K., & Führes, H. (2010). Comparing the structure of virtual entrepreneur networks with business effectiveness. *Procedia – Social and Behavioral Sciences, 2*(4), 6483–6496. doi:10.1016/j.sbspro.2010.04.050

Nisar, A., Palacios, M., & Grijalvo, M. (2016). Open organizational structures: A new framework for the energy industry. *Journal of Business Research, 69*(11), 5175. doi:10.1016/j.jbusres.2016.04.100

Osland, J. S., Mendenhall, M. E., Reiche, B. S., Szkudlarek, B., Bolden, R., Courtice, P., … Maznevski, M. (2020). Perspectives on global leadership and the COVID-19 crisis. In J. S. Osland, B. Szkudlarek, M. E. Mendenhall, & B. S. Reiche (Eds.), *Advances in global leadership* (Vol. 13, pp. 3–56). UK, Emerald Publishing Limited.

Perlmutter, H. V. (1969). The tortuous evolution of the multinational corporation. *Columbia Journal of World Business, 4*(1), 9–18.

Peters, J. (1993). On structures. *Management Decision, 31*(6), 60.

Pies, I., Beckmann, M., & Hielscher, S. (2010). Value creation, management competencies, and global corporate citizenship: An ordonomic approach to business ethics in the age of globalization. *Journal of Business Ethics, 94*(2), 265–278. doi:10.1007/s10551-009-0263-1

Pisano, G. P. (1996). Organizing for innovation. *Harvard Business Review, 74*, 162.

Porter, M. E. (1996). What is strategy? *Harvard Business Review, 74*(61), 61–78.

Quail, J. (2008). Becoming fully functional: The conceptual struggle for a new structure for the giant corporation in the US and UK in the first half of the twentieth century. *Business History, 50*(2), 127–146. doi:10.1080/00076790701853363

Ramakrishnan, R. (2021). Leading in a VUCA World. *Ushus Journal of Business Management, 20*(1), 89. doi:10.12725/ujbm.54.5

Rapoport, V. (1989). Constancy and change: Flexible organization structures. *Systems Practice, 2*(4), 433–450. doi:10.1007/BF01062327

Romelaer, P., & Beddi, H. (2015). Strategy and structure in international multi-business groups: Looking beyond global integration-local responsiveness. *International Studies of Management & Organization, 45*(4), 359–378. doi:10.1080/00208825.2015.1006040

Roome, N. (1998). *Sustainability strategies for industry: The future of corporate practice.* Washington, DC: Island Press.

Roome, N. (2011). A retrospective on globalization and sustainable development: The business challenge of systems organization and systems integration. *Business & Professional Ethics Journal, 30*(3/4), 195–230. doi:10.5840/bpej2011303/410

Sarmiza, P. (2010). New faces of globalization: Market integration, production disintegration, genesis of new global organizational structures for production and trade. *Revista de Economie Mondială, 2*(3), 11–28.

Schur, L., Kruse, D., & Blanck, P. (2013). *People with disabilities: Sidelined or mainstreamed?* Cambridge: Cambridge University Press.

Silver, D. (2005). Corporate codes of conduct and the value of autonomy. *Journal of Business Ethics, 59*, 3–8.

Simons, R. (2005). *Levers of organization design: How managers use accountability systems for greater performance and commitment.* USA: Harvard Business Press.

Simons, R. (2013). The entrepreneurial gap: How managers adjust span of accountability and span of control to implement business strategy. *Harvard Business School Accounting & Management Unit Working Paper No. 13–100.* Retrieved from doi:10.2139/ssrn.2280355

Stopford, J. M., & Wells, L. T. (1972). *Managing the multinational enterprise.* New York: Basic Books.

Strese, S., Meuer, M. W., Flatten, T. C., & Brettel, M. (2016). Organizational antecedents of cross-functional coopetition: The impact of leadership and organizational structure on cross-functional coopetition. *Industrial Marketing Management, 53*, 42. doi:10.1016/j.indmarman.2015.11.006

Stverkova, H., & Pohludka, M. (2018). Business organisational structures of global companies: Use of the territorial model to ensure long-term growth. *Social Sciences, 7*(6). doi:10.3390/socsci7060098

Taylor, H., & Cooper, C. (1988). Organisational change-threat of challenge? The role of individual differences in the management of stress. *Journal of Organizational Change Management, 1*(1), 68–80.

Vaccaro, I. G., Volberda, H. W., & Van Den Bosch, F. A. J. (2012). Management innovation in action: the case of selfmanaging teams. In T. S. Pitsis, A. Simpson, & E. Dehlin (Eds.), *Handbook of organizational and managerial innovation* (pp. 138–162). Cheltenham: Edwar Elgar.

Virtanen, M., Kivima¨ki, M., Joensuu, M., Virtanen, P., Elovainio, M., & Vahtera, J. (2005). Temporary employment and health: A review. *International Journal of Epidemiology, 34*, 610–622.

West, M. A., & Farr, J. L. (1989). Innovation at work: Psychological perspectives. *Social Behaviour, 4*(1), 15–30.

West, M. A., Hirst, G., Richter, A., & Shipton, H. (2004). Twelve steps to heaven: Successfully managing change through developing innovative teams. *European Journal of Work and Organizational Psychology, 13*(2), 269–299. doi:10.1080/13594320444000092

Williams, C., McWilliams, A., & Lawrence, R. (2016). *MGMT3* (3rd ed.). Australia: Cengage Learning Australia.

PART 2

Key ingredients for successful innovation management

In the second part of the publication, "Key ingredients for successful innovation management", we include three chapters that introduce contemporary and successful innovation approaches. Through this part...

In "Climate for innovation: A critical lever in the leadership of innovation" Sheffield et al. outline organisational climate through the context of healthcare teams. Using longitudinal case study approach, this chapter draws insights into how leadership can influence climate to support or hinder innovation. Through their analysis, it can be observed that for leadership interventions and practices to flourish, climate for innovation is required.

Saunila covers the topic of management control in "Mobilizing management controls in innovation projects". Given the rise of innovation projects it is important to understand on what management controls are mobilised in managing innovation. The findings suggest the need for multiple controls during innovation projects, both interactive and diagnostic. Additionally, through the empirical study it is found that the use of control is not linear.

Ogutu and Levi reflect upon different innovation algorithm in "Innovation management tools – The Innovation Algorithm". The author looks on holistic and specific challenges to innovation managers. While introducing the algorithm, there is a good balance of how innovation works and how the approach works.

DOI: 10.4324/9780429346033-4

3

CLIMATE FOR INNOVATION

A critical lever in the leadership of innovation

Rob Sheffield, Selen Kars-Unluoglu and Carol Jarvis

Introduction

Innovation involves an uncertain journey and, although leadership cannot ensure innovation success, it can influence its odds (Van de Ven, 2017). In this chapter, we explore leadership of innovation through the lens of organisational climate, an arena where leadership can have a significant influence (Isaksen, 2007). Our research was conducted with a range of teams in the National Health Service (NHS) in England, from different disciplines but with a shared interest in innovations to improve patient care.

While the context of the healthcare sector in England is specific, it has wider resonance. The sector is facing, and struggling to meet, a tsunami of challenges including: rising demand from an aging population with increasingly complex health needs coupled with static or shrinking budgets (NHS England, 2014, 2017); and an existing problem with staff shortages (Nuffield Trust, 2017) compounded by the uncertainty around the implications of Brexit for EU nationals. As with many organisations, across numerous sectors and geographies, this creates a pressing need to improve their capacity for innovation (Carruthers, 2011; Rose, 2015).

These challenges have encouraged a climate characterised by time pressures, with every minute routinised, where a focus on providing evidence-based management and audit trails (Ham, 2014) preferences predictability and control over risk, playfulness and idea-time associated with innovation (Isaksen et al., 2011). Thus, at a time when innovation has increasing importance, the climate poses barriers to innovation that are hard to surmount. Challenges may vary from sector to sector, but the experience of closer monitoring and competing demands for scarce resources is ubiquitous. It is in this context that we explore leadership practices and their influence on climate for innovation.

DOI: 10.4324/9780429346033-5

We next outline some key thinking on climate for innovation. We then summarise our research approach and drawing on insights from six case studies explore ways in which leadership can influence climate to support or hinder innovation. We conclude by posing questions leaders can consider for improving the climate for innovation in their teams and organisations.

Understanding the role of climate for innovation

The growing pressure for developing and delivering creative products and services has generated increased interest in innovation leadership among scholars and practitioners (Byrne et al., 2009). Despite its central importance to any organisation, because different disciplines have studied it from different perspectives, "the term 'innovation' is notoriously ambiguous and lacks either a single definition or measure" (Adams et al., 2006: 22). Other scholars (e.g. Baregheh et al., 2009) have aimed for a synthesis of these definitions, a task beyond the scope of this chapter. We define innovation as a "multi-stage process whereby organizations transform ideas into new/improved products, service or processes, in order to advance, compete and differentiate themselves successfully in their marketplace" (Baregheh et al., 2009: 1334). We focus on the impact these changes make directly on an organisation, like the magnitude of novelty and of progress the organisation experiences (Mulgan & Albury, 2003). Doing so allows us to distinguish between incremental (with minor magnitude and impact), radical (major breakthroughs) and transformational (fundamental, organisation-wide impacts) innovation (Mulgan & Albury, 2003).

Much remains to be understood about how best to facilitate innovation. While it is widely accepted that innovation involves an uncertain journey and its success cannot be ensured (Van de Ven, 2017), leaders can influence the odds. By encapsulating and communicating their organisation's true priorities, leaders can have a significant influence on organisational climate and advance the organisational innovation outcomes (Isaksen, 2007; Hunter & Cushenbery, 2011).

Climate is described as the general psychological atmosphere in an organisation (Isaksen et al., 1995) as discerned through observable attitudes and recurring behaviour patterns. Daily exposure to a particular climate, defined as employee interpretations of their everyday experience of working in a given organisational environment, generates a lasting effect on employee behaviour (Ekvall, 1987), influencing their mental and physical efforts (Pace, 2003). This suggests a link between climate and organisational success. Climate differs from culture which reflects the deeper ideological foundations of the organisation at the level of values, beliefs, traditions (Isaksen et al., 2011). Climate is more amenable to deliberate change efforts than culture (Ehrhart et al., 2013; Isaksen, 2017) as it operates at the level of visible and audible behaviour patterns and processes which can be locally created by what leaders do (Schein, 2000).

Over time, improving climate can shift culture, changing how the organisation views innovation. For example, research suggests leaders of innovative organisations implement a developmental culture, and attach importance to generating ideas, tracking technological frontiers, flexibility and adaptability (Büschgens et al., 2013). Their employees' behaviour patterns, which may, for example, exhibit greater willingness to take risks, then differ from those working in a hierarchical culture that emphasises stability and following rules and procedures.

Growing evidence suggests that shifting climate enhances innovation (Patterson et al., 2005); hence shaping climate is a leadership priority (Amabile et al., 2004). Leaders then can play the role of 'tempered radicals' (Meyerson, 2008) to affect innovation through relatively small changes, shaping climate through their everyday leadership behaviour and using it as a lever to affect more radical responses. Understanding how to foster innovation through climate interventions can help leaders identify and build upon structures, processes and practices that are working well in supporting innovation and modify those that are not.

Clarifying constructs to study climate for innovation

Above we demonstrate the importance of climate in leading innovation in organisations, but how do we define it? Ekvall (1987, 1996) offers one of the main attempts to conceptualise climate for innovation, which developed into The Situational Outlook Questionnaire® (SOQ®) (Isaksen et al., 1995).

The SOQ® assesses climate on nine dimensions, outlined in Table 3.1, which are found to predict higher levels of organisational support for creativity and innovation and effectively discern climates that either encourage or discourage innovation (Isaksen et al., 2001).

The SOQ® comprises 53 quantitative rating items, related to the nine dimensions and includes three open-ended questions. These qualitative questions

TABLE 3.1 SOQ dimensions (from: https://www.soqonline.net/)

Dimension	Description
Challenge/ involvement	The degree to which people are involved in daily operations, long-term goals, and visions
Freedom	The independence in behaviour exerted by the people in the organisation
Trust/openness	The emotional safety in relationships
Idea-time	The amount of time people can (and do) use for elaborating new ideas
Playfulness/ humour	The spontaneity and ease displayed within the workplace
Conflict	The presence of personal and emotional tensions in the organisation
Idea-support	The ways in which new ideas are treated
Debate	The occurrence of encounters and disagreements between viewpoints, ideas, differing experiences and knowledge
Risk-taking	The tolerance of uncertainty and ambiguity exposed in the workplace

surface information about positive and negative tensions in the organisational climate, and encourage respondents' ownership by asking them to come up with actions to improve the climate.

Climates conducive to innovation have been investigated at the organisational level (Abbey & Dickson, 1983; Amabile & Gryskiewicz, 1987). However, team climate has received less attention, and this forms our focus. In an era in which 'everyone will have a part to play as the creator and implementer of new ideas' (West & Rickards, 1999: 55), the need to source novel ideas has spread to all areas of the workforce. This democratisation of innovation calls for a shift in focus to and to understand how leaders can improve their team climates since teams are increasingly becoming hotbeds for innovation (Lipman-Blumen & Leavitt, 1999).

However, the reality of producing innovations in teams is not straightforward. Teamwork involves social and psychological processes that can influence innovation processes. For example, team members are unlikely to generate and communicate novel ideas if they expect these to be dismissed or criticised (West & Anderson, 1996). They require a psychological atmosphere that allows novel ideas to be openly communicated, fairly evaluated and properly implemented (Amabile & Gryskiewicz, 1987).

The value of team-based organising is particularly visible in healthcare organisations. Teams have long been used to maximise effectiveness and efficiency in healthcare (Poole & Real, 2003) and are advocated as the optimal work design for delivery of high-quality patient care (Baker et al., 2006), resulting, for example, in lower error rates and lower mortality rates (Hughes et al., 2016) and higher patient satisfaction (West et al., 2001). The imperative for effective teamwork is also consistently emphasised by policymakers (Department of Health, 2012).

The demand for improved effectiveness and system efficiencies fuelled by increasing demand on health services, increasing cost of medical technology and medication, more informed, sophisticated and demanding patients, and shrinking or static budgets, creates a pressing need for healthcare organisations to improve their teams' capacity for innovation in the UK (Carruthers, 2011) and the USA (Weberg, 2012). These can be in the form of product innovation or structural innovation to the way organisations' business model operates in healthcare delivery (Varkey et al., 2008). However, the uncertainty inherent in innovation can increase anxiety and stress, discouraging risk-taking and creativity and encouraging habitual behaviours (Goleman & Boyatis, 2008). This can increase further under pressure of time (Amabile et al., 2002), further increasing the significance of instilling a high perceived level of support for creativity and innovation. Beyond the healthcare context, this will have resonance in any high-stakes, high-pressure environment, where the imperative for an innovation to demonstrate maturity before supplanting existing processes or products can discourage innovative behaviour (Varkey et al., 2008). This is amplified in healthcare organisations where decisions and actions resulting from risk-taking, playfulness or freedom – important dimensions of an innovative climate – can be, quite literally, a matter of life and death, making the study of, and interventions in, climate for innovation crucial.

This literature on team climate for innovation provides a theoretical foundation for our analysis, as we address the following research question: how can leaders influence innovation outcomes of their teams and organisations through their deliberate efforts to foster a climate for innovation? In addressing this question, we go beyond mainstream studies, typically quantitative 'snapshots' in time explaining the relationship between team/ organisational climate and team/ organisational innovation performance (e.g. Bain et al., 2001; Isaksen, 2007). Instead we take a qualitative and longitudinal approach measuring team climate pre-study; looking into what leaders did with these new insights on their teams' climate; and re-measuring the same teams' climate post-study to establish the impact of leaders' interventions. Joining Isaksen (2017), we believe that the field would benefit from an improved understanding of leadership behaviours that help and hinder innovation in their teams. Our research approach has allowed us to identify specific and durable ways in which leaders can change their team climates, and to encourage more reflective leadership practices for innovation. It is the details of this research we turn our attention to next.

Our research approach

Our exploration of the climate for innovation focusses on the everyday practices of healthcare leaders in England, as they try to make innovation happen. The research was undertaken with participants on two cohorts of a leadership development programme, tailored for the healthcare sector and run between November 2011–September 2012 and February 2013–January 2014. All programme participants were leading on an innovation project of regional or national significance designed to improve patient care, a criterion for selection onto the programme. However, none of the participants were dedicated innovation managers; their leadership of innovation was taking place alongside their busy day jobs. A competitive, over-subscribed application and selection process may also suggest participants were deemed 'successful' in their leadership of innovation.

Longitudinal data were collected from participants through a mixed-methods approach. This included administering the SOQ® with participants and up to five team members from a team they were leading (conducted both pre- and post-programme by 18 teams) and 21 in-depth interviews with participants 6–8 months after programme completion.

In this chapter we focus on stories from six participants, all of whom completed the SOQ® pre-and post-programme and were interviewed. Three of these participants saw significant improvement to their team climate on at least one SOQ® dimension,[1] and three experienced climate deterioration as revealed by the analysis of the quantitative SOQ® data by paired t-test to compare changes in dimension means over time. For each story, significant changes, at 95% confidence levels, are shown in bold. In Table 3.2, highlighted changes show significant climate improvement, while in Table 3.3, they show significant climate deterioration. The tables also include team climate benchmarks generated from earlier research from Isaksen and Lauer (2002).

As their innovations evolved to extend their reach and influence, follow-up interviews were completed with the team leaders in Stories 1 and 2 in January 2020 and in Story 3 in April 2017. We did not undertake follow-up interviews with participants in Stories 4, 5 and 6 because their ideas had not evolved.

We selected these stories because they illustrate how team climate can change, for better or worse, and in a short time. They are drawn from different parts of

TABLE 3.2 Pre- and post-programme scores on SOQ® climate dimensions (Stories 1–3)

SOQ dimensions	Most creative team benchmark (n=154)	Least creative team benchmark (n=154)	Case 1 Time 1	Case 1 Time 2	Case 2 Time 1	Case 2 Time 2	Case 3 Time 1	Case 3 Time 2
Challenge	260	100	224	227	214	248	210	264
Freedom	202	110	152	202	177	192	169	200
Trust and openness	253	88	183	177	168	187	193	233
Idea time	227	65	145	140	153	164	108	156
Playfulness	235	77	124	143	160	194	200	256
Conflict	27	123	88	105	30	50	44	25
Idea-support	218	70	197	231	208	233	203	260
Debate	231	83	195	217	193	217	192	197
Risk-taking	210	65	177	234	164	197	150	200

TABLE 3.3 Pre- and post-programme scores on SOQ® climate dimensions (Stories 4–6)

SOQ dimensions	Most creative team benchmark (n=170)	Least creative team benchmark (n=170)	Case 4 Time 1	Case 4 Time 2	Case 5 Time 1	Case 5 Time 2	Case 6 Time 1	Case 6 Time 2
Challenge	260	100	253	236	179	223	232	237
Freedom	202	110	142	158	192	142	204	183
Trust and openness	253	88	196	160	123	165	180	164
Idea time	227	65	150	142	83	90	113	97
Playfulness	235	77	165	158	100	160	142	133
Conflict	27	123	80	104	152	106	108	117
Idea-support	218	70	215	180	123	173	150	156
Debate	231	83	205	167	154	183	163	143
Risk-taking	210	65	189	170	115	140	120	152

the health sector, including primary and acute care, and from different – rural and urban – environments, illustrating a range of organisational contexts. Also, some leaders have clinical professional backgrounds, while others are non-clinical leaders. For ease of introduction, we provide a short summary of each story in Table 3.4. Throughout this chapter we use pseudonyms to protect participants' confidentiality.

TABLE 3.4 Overview of selected stories

Story	Setting and innovation description	Type of innovation Service: an innovation focus on healthcare services to patients. Organisational: an innovation focus on infrastructure that delivers services. For example, changes in roles, structures, human capabilities, buildings.	Degree of innovation (incremental/ radical/ transformational)
1	The creation of a community support hub to improve community care across multiple organisations in a geographical region.	Service	Transformational
2	The creation of an external partnership to supply pharmacy services, affecting services both within the trust and for some external organisations.	Service and organisational	Radical
3	Introduction of a series of organisational and service improvements across multiple healthcare organisations to improve diabetes long-term care.	Service and organisational	Incremental
4	Radical healthcare service innovation across a city, requiring consensus from senior healthcare institution leaders in a major regional city.	Service	Transformational
5	Service redesign for healthcare commissioners, aimed at their own unit.	Service	Incremental
6	A series of interventions aimed at culture change that would 'ripple out' to other organisational units.	Organisational	Incremental

Findings

Below for each story, we describe the nature of the innovation, its main challenges and achievements. We then review how our participants sought to influence team climate through their leadership practices, and how the presence, or lack, of wider leadership support also affected climate. We also unpack how these leadership practices and changes in team climate influenced innovation outcomes.

Story 1 – General practices as a community hub

In 2013, Hilary, a general practitioner (GP), was also federation chair across her region, supported by the local Clinical Commissioning Group (CCG).

From April 2013 onwards, in her role as federation chair, Hilary collaborated with a group of other practices to create a community support hub, which evolved over time to provide holistic, human–centred care to more than 43,000 people. This story is an example of collaborative and transformational clinical service redesign across multiple organisations in a geographical region. Its uniqueness comes from the integration of personal, GP and community services into a single hub model.

In 2013 the hub received £110,000 of funding from the CCG to initiate the innovation. They employed a community development worker, who catalogued the support schemes existing in the area, and created a website to share them. Later, they created a team of 'health connectors', to help people manage multiple and complex medical conditions and trained 'community-connectors' (now numbering some 1,400), to spread awareness of the approach.

Positive results from the pilot, led to the CCG awarding a further £300,000, to develop and extend the hub model across a region of 115,000 people. Despite positive results emerging, there remained uncertainty around the sustainability of the innovation, since funding was short-term, and as the scale was extended, more resources were needed.

However, in 2018 a national newspaper published an article on the innovation, bringing worldwide interest and raising its profile. Coupled with close alignment to the policy agenda and the growing importance of Health Integration Teams, the project's prospects received a boost.

As the hub model developed, fewer people reported themselves to hospitals. Unplanned admissions dropped in the area by 14%, from April 2013 to December 2017, while the adjacent regions experienced an increase of 29%. This led to cost savings of nearly £1.2 million – a reduction of 21%.

Considering how the innovation developed, Hilary reports a personal motivation for wanting to improve care:

> My career has been in smaller practices. Then here, with 30,000 patients and a whole team, you can run the risk of de-personalising what's going on...I'm

used to knowing the person… you could see that life and medicine are not distinct. I felt it more keenly, moving from a smaller to bigger practice.

(Hilary, January 2020)

Hilary's GP team members completed the SOQ® in April 2013 and again in January 2014 with statistically significant improvements in risk-taking and freedom. In January 2014 team members described how freedom to move forwards with and test out new ideas had improved:

> I believe that the current leadership has fostered a more open culture that enables freer discussion, addresses issues in the group at an early stage and therefore allows people to bring forward ideas that can be discussed openly.

Through interview, Hilary reported a shift in their attitude towards risk:

> The fact that you can trial something, and move lightly, and implement something if it seems to be working, with it not being a black mark if it's not quite so good…Not everything you test has to work…The effort involved in being absolutely sure things are going to work, before you test them, saps your energy to test anything else.
>
> *(Hilary, May 2014)*

Hilary also made it a priority to gain idea support and agreement. Aware that *"if you don't have that engagement it bites you back later"* (Hilary, January 2020), she purposefully set time aside to plan how to engage people and gain a platform of support for her innovation:

> There is progress, but it's a lot of softer progress…– it's that chipping away and moving people's opinions forward so that you can start something and show that it works…If it's embedded in the whole [the region], it's there for ever and safe. If you do your own little bit of change…the danger is someone else does something completely different, and you find you're undermined and the direction's changed.
>
> *(Hilary, May 2014)*

As a result of her emerging thinking about relations and networks, she focussed on telling her story in a way different audiences could hear and appreciate it and she worked hard to get appropriate opportunities and venues to tell it.

A supportive wider context played an important role too. Key figures in the CCG were interested in distributed leadership and encouraged initiatives from ground level. And the town itself has a reputation for 'independence' and encouraging local action, rather than waiting for top-down permission.

Hilary's story shows a clear sense of purpose: providing holistic, human-centred care across a region. It also foregrounds a highly relational approach, working closely with others and agreeing means and ends to embed and sustain innovation. Her team benefitted from her commitment to making the uncertainty of doing something radical 'safe enough'; accepting that there would be setbacks and communicating this to her team, giving them permission to experiment and take risks without expecting perfection.

Story 2 – Revisiting delivery of pharmacy services

In May 2015, a leading retailer opened a pharmacy at this UK trust, the outcome of a procurement dialogue with potential suppliers which started in June 2013. While not new to the sector, for this organisation it is a radical service redesign through partnership, affecting an outpatient population of more than 450,000 and many services within the Trust and some external organisations.

The innovation resulted from a series of structural and cultural changes initiated by the Trust to promote local, autonomous decision-making and clarify accountability for local performance. This context influenced the thinking of Chief Pharmacist David seeking to ensure the performance and longer-term sustainability of the Pharmacy service. Outsourcing promised benefits as David reported in 2014:

> This is about us consolidating our resources in doing what we do best: clinical service provision and frontline patient care. And bringing in people who are much better at dispensing outpatient prescriptions all day...I want to release my staff to be patient facing,

The results are impressive: 90% of patients are now waiting less than 20 minutes for their prescription, when previously on a bad day, wait times were 90 minutes, which has increased patient satisfaction and reduced complaints.

While the Trust achieved cost savings of almost £47,000 per month, no jobs were lost, and time was saved to train and develop staff.

The same retailer has won contracts with three other Trusts in the region, with David diffusing the innovation and encouraging its adoption through the network of Chief Pharmacists across the region that meets regularly to share experiences and practices.

Reviewing the origin of the innovation, David describes a process of reflection with the team and of personal learning. When the first climate results were shared in April 2013, he asked the team what they needed from him as a leader. They replied:

> You're not telling us enough...you need to share more with us...rather than trying to be involved in every meeting we might have...commission that from us, and we'll deliver to you in a set timescale.
>
> *(David, May 2014)*

Recognising the limit of his control over change and wanting to build real accountability with his staff, David and his team initiated a sustained process of reflection on their ways of working:

> We thought about what things could change...I got the pharmacy team to think about...where we are now and we need to be in 5 years' time...they had to tell me things they'd start doing and stop doing.
>
> *(David, May 2014)*

This reflective process had an effect. The second climate results in January 2014 showed statistically significant improvements in playfulness/humour, idea support and risk-taking, with team member comments describing what aids innovation:

> Having time away from the day job. Listening and encouraging team to voice their ideas even if unusual. Discussing in non-judgmental way.
>
> Our team leader leads by example. He is innovative and supportive of changes suggested by the team.

In analysing David's story, we are struck by the change in his approach as a leader. Realising his efforts alone would be insufficient to drive and sustain innovation, David delegated and devolved more power to the team, instead of trying to be operationally involved in everything. This reflection drove him to tap into the energy and ideas of the team and instil long-term, purposeful, patient-centred innovation. Combined with a commitment to providing support and encouragement to the team as they took risks, this change in leadership practices was crucial in nurturing ideas that later evolved into genuine innovation.

Story 3 – Improving diabetes long-term care

In 2013, Ben assumed leadership of a Musculo-Skeletal Services team, which managed a wide range of services, including diabetes. Later, Anne took on responsibility for managing the team to implement their diabetic improvement plans. In their large, regional city, diabetes was a growing problem with higher lower-limb amputation rates compared to most of the country.

Between 2013 and 2018, the team introduced a series of city-wide clinical service innovations, coordinated across multiple healthcare organisations, and including local doctors. In 2014 they secured £330,000 funding to develop a prioritised service for most-at-risk diabetes patients. A risk-line was introduced that allowed patients to ring a clinician for signposting to appropriate care. Local doctors were encouraged to refer diabetic patients for assessment, and community wound clinics with dedicated specialist resource combined to ensure a more standardised approach. Internally, staff were trained in clinical competencies, with risk cards introduced to stratify and prioritise cases. Taken together, this series of incremental service innovations made a substantive difference, cutting waiting times for most-at risk-patients from around 18 to 4 weeks allowing more and better treatment options for patients.

However, the popularity of the services produced capacity challenges – referrals increased and waiting times started to rise. In 2017, the team won a further £220,000 funding, to refine and extend their services. They reviewed their criteria for 'high-risk' and agreed an integrated approach with GPs and hospitals, supported by an electronic referral process, with a single point of access for acute treatment. These innovations secured regular, timelier, quicker diabetic foot checks for 4,500 patients with positive impact on earlier diagnosis.

These innovations emerged from structure and role refinements Ben initiated in 2013 to create a highly engaged team involved in developing ideas to support strategic aims. He ensured the senior team made time for idea development, and that these ideas were shared more widely. This emphasised the importance of creativity, sending out clear messages about involvement, time for creativity and follow-through to implementation. For example, in one exercise the wider team generated more than 300 ideas and developed these into ten broad challenges. By mid-2014, seven of these were already being implemented and contributed to the rise in the reputation of the team in the organisation.

The second climate results in January 2014, revealed statistically significant improvements in challenge/involvement, playfulness/humour and risk-taking. Team members' comments from the second SOQ® suggest the inclusive approach to innovation, led by the senior leadership team and guided by Ben, contributed to trust and relationship building:

> I think the idea support in this team is great. [Our]team is excellent at working together in creating innovative solutions to solving problems.
>
> The level of trust in the team is very high. Creative problem-solving techniques are used early to predict future opportunities and solve existing issues.
>
> The members all support one another and are never critical of new ideas/suggestions.

Team members also commented on the improvement in challenge/involvement by highlighting the importance of team leadership to focus the team's ideas and prioritise areas that needed attention.

Inevitably there were many challenges through this time, as Ben reports:

> The hardest thing was risk-taking. The level of bureaucracy in a clini-cal organisation is difficult to overcome. So, we took risks in a measured way. We developed small wins with the team, and this has been of critical importance in demonstrating a measured approach to risk taking.
>
> *(Ben, August 2017)*

As Anne took on project implementation, she framed her role as maintaining a now-healthy team climate, in particular, providing idea-time and idea support:

> I was thinking: 'we don't have the luxury of time, so how can we manage it effectively?' We made sure we were protected from the hustle and bustle of everyday work. We'd use clinical rooms, so people didn't know where we were. We engaged the team constantly, and used ideas from them, to get their buy in, from the ground-up. I did a lot of coaching through 1:1s with my team.
>
> *(Anne, August 2017)*

Ben and Anne's achievement highlights the importance of approaching innovation in a way that fits with the broader organisational culture. This requires an awareness of the wider context – not only of the overarching agenda and strategic priorities but of preferred approach to addressing these. With this awareness, Anne and Ben emphasise taking 'measured risks' and securing small, incremental innovations. They exercise leadership in more localised, diffused and modest ways than traditional forms of innovation leadership. However, they still effect significant changes with a substantial impact. As in David's story they show commitment to developing their team, providing opportunities for team members to grow their awareness of the wider context and to exercise their agency in crafting innovative responses.

Stories 4, 5 and 6 – What can we learn from stories of partial change?

We now explore three stories of interrupted change, where some progress was reported, often at a slower pace than the leaders would have liked. The leaders were focussing on different types of innovation: a radical service innovation across a city, involving multiple organisations (Story 4); an incremental service redesign for healthcare commissioners, affecting their own unit (Story 5); and an executive team with the intent to model incremental cultural change that would affect other organisational units (Story 6). On the second measurement of team climate, each of them saw statistically significant deterioration in a dimension: risk-taking in Story 4, freedom in Story 5 and idea-time in Story 6.

Because these teams introduced less innovation, we focus on the climate conditions that frustrated the leaders and hindered innovation. There were notable common themes across the stories.[2]

Lack of, or inconsistent, senior support or the undermining of efforts by more senior people appears to be a major factor, highlighting once more the importance of awareness of the wider context and of securing a 'champion':

> It does feel quite risky. The risk is above me in the organisation...We pretend to make decisions in an inclusive manner, in reality the decisions are

made by two or three senior people…It feels an arms-length organisation…
[senior leaders] feel they must be 'in charge' and make the decisions…

(Story 5, Interview with leader, May 2014)

…could we have done more in managing the organisational stakeholders who
were putting constraints in the way? That includes very much dealing with
senior players…we probably could have done more to get them on board.

(Story 4, Interview with leader, February 2013)

As illustrated in the more successful stories above, leaders soon work out who
they need to talk to and whose support is essential to drive forward their innovation. Where this support is lacking or insufficient, they may seek to introduce
change 'below the radar':

From a personal perspective, it's about getting a grip and doing it. But the
culture is when you do that, you either get chopped off at the knees, or it's
too late for it. If you can get to the point where you can share how great
it's been, before anyone gets to stop if, it's fine. So, it's about trying to be
canny…and getting past those original hurdles.

(Story 6, interview with leader, February 2014)

Being unable to escape a short-term focus, and constrained by limited, or changing, resources, priorities and audiences was another theme:

Doesn't feel like there is room to be innovative…due to lack of funds
Longer term we'll need to be innovative for that exact reason, but short
term it still feels that we are being stifled.

(Story 5)

We spend more time on minutiae and crisis management. Priorities change
daily.

(Story 6)

It's been a very new team coming together, and the team itself has evolved
so much during the year…The impact has been less evident, than it would
have been with a more stable team…stakeholders have changed and evolved.

(Story 4, interview with leader, February 2013)

Finally, poor intra-group relations sometimes hindered work and innovation
outcomes:

Competitiveness between members. People look to criticise other team
members. Power struggles. Lack of support towards others.

(Story 5)

In stories 4, 5 and 6, lack of senior support, was compounded by a focus on the short-term. In this context, and with scarce, changing resources, the perception of risk from introducing innovation was sometimes deemed too high. This is not a case of outright opposition to change, more one of insufficient, meaningful support. As a consequence, leaders and teams made slow progress. Reflecting on the whole experience, one leader summed up succinctly how 'success' in innovation can sometimes prove elusive:

> Our interventions have helped avoid things completely failing, but we would be hard pressed to identify real benefits.

While it is not part of this study, we had ongoing contact with these leaders from stories 4, 5 and 6 who noted they applied their leadership learning in other contexts and teams, over the same time period, with greater success. Our analysis suggests when wider contexts are adverse, even effective and motivated leaders will likely struggle to improve climate for innovation, and to deliver innovation. In the next section we look at the practical implications of these findings for leadership in introducing sustainable innovation.

Practical implications

Our analysis shows how innovation outcomes can be improved when an agenda for purposeful (in this case patient-centred) innovation is established, and team members are involved in meaningful work challenges. We illustrate different ways in which leaders and team members acted in ways that mitigated risk, bounded their experimentation, used available resources, evidenced change, reported to more senior influencers and protected ideas in early, fragile stages.

A number of key themes emerge. First, in Stories 1, 2 and 3, while the impetus for innovation was crafted at local level, their broader contexts were change-receptive, with leaders and their teams receiving explicit support from more senior people and being able to access them when hurdles were encountered. In Stories 4, 5 and 6, there was variable agreement on the innovation agenda, and insufficient senior support.

The more radical the innovation and the broader its scope, the greater the unpredictability and the higher the perceived risk. As risk and unpredictability increase, so does the importance of senior leadership support for the innovation to be seen as credible, valuable and feasible (Côté-Boileau et al., 2019).

The more leaders build wider goodwill and networks of relationships, from senior leaders and peers across and between organisations, the more likely they can call upon it at moments of challenge and crisis. And the more likely the innovation will survive. This resonates with Ballard's (2005) work on the importance of Agency (the power to take action), Association (the need to build networks and connections to amplify voices) and Awareness (of the strategic agenda and limits of human agency). Ballard (2005) stresses a need for all three to be present.

In this case, for example, without Association, the result is the isolated activist who is ignored, and possibly stressed.

Second, the three 'success' stories show an awareness of the local context (Ballard, 2005) which shapes their approach. Stories 1 and 2 brought highly novel change within a receptive and supportive context. Without this supportive context, radical innovations are likely to meet stiffer resistance, especially when their scope is pervasive and their consequences disruptive (Totterdell et al., 2002). Aware of this, in Story 3, Ben and Anne took the approach of the 'tempered radical' (Meyerson, 2001) implementing far-reaching change through a series of incremental innovations appropriate to their local clinical context that was more amenable to a more linear approach. They emphasised taking measured risks and securing small wins yet their moderate, quiet and 'tempered ways' achieved revolutionary impact.

Third, in Stories 1, 2 and 3, leaders focussed on Agency (Ballard, 2005), devolving power to act to team members. This required them to improve the climate for risk-taking to ensure team members felt they would be supported if their actions did not achieve the desired results. They built confidence, providing team members with development opportunities and distributed leadership responsibilities.

Fourth, innovations had varying adoption rates beyond their unit/ service/ organisation. Story 1 has been the most widely spread; Story 2 has led to some wider adoption and Story 3 introduced the least. Why was this?

- The leader in Story 1 saw spread as key to sustainability from the outset. She deliberately slowed the pace of task activity, concentrating on relationship building and joint working. The quality of these relationships benefitted the innovation eventually, bringing publicity, agreement on how to proceed, and energy in sharing the story with wider populations.
- In Story 2, the leader was part of a network of Chief Pharmacists that met regularly to share experiences. This acted as a mechanism for spreading the innovation, as well as learning and support, and for mitigating any risks associated with adoption in other areas.
- In Story 3, the leaders targeted energy at the local stakeholders, rather than wider stakeholders. What seems to be missing is a deliberate attempt, throughout the process, to consider and plan for wider spread that would secure the longer-term sustainability.

In summary, there is evidence that longer-term sustainability and spread should be part of the early-stage innovation process. Leaders should envision sustainable innovation in their contexts, build stakeholder relationships and think about communication and sharing of good practice from the outset.

Finally, cultivating stakeholder relationships helped the leaders in our stories avoid change fatigue (McMillan & Perron, 2013) in a context where change fatigue is often endemic (Lubitsh et al., 2005). In our stories, where innovation was congruent with wider strategies, and was agreed and sought by a powerful group of senior stakeholders, the energy and enthusiasm generated provided a powerful antidote to change fatigue, helping team members avoid losing trust (Reineck, 2007) or from feeling disorientated or dysfunctional as a result of too much stimulation (Stensaker et al., 2002). Where this was lacking as in Story 4, where the innovation team met with active resistance and struggled to gain a common agreement from powerful interest groups, the chances of successful implementation are greatly reduced.

As this discussion suggests, in a supportive context, improvements in team climate are amplified, and emerging ideas are more likely to be encouraged. Purposeful innovations, aligned to strategy, aided by senior support, with freedom devolved to local teams have proved a powerful combination.

Conclusion

This chapter provided insights into the hurdles leaders faced in managing innovation in their teams and their interventions to climate for overcoming these. Table 3.5 summarises some of the practical steps leaders across our broader study took to shift their climate for innovation.

While our research has taken place in the NHS in England, our findings have relevance for innovation leaders in other sectors. We highlight the importance of understanding the wider context and demonstrate climate for innovation is amenable to leadership interventions and practices. These practices can be adapted and adopted in many organisational contexts and will have particular resonance for innovation leaders in high-stakes and/ or highly regulated environments.

There are, however, limitations of using team climate to understand support for innovation. The scope of the innovation may outgrow its source team, requiring leaders to switch their efforts to stakeholders beyond their team to influence innovation success. Hence, over time, the impact of initial team climate improvement can get diluted. This makes attribution of cause and effect more difficult and highlights the need to consider the impact of climate on innovation within the wider context of time and space, encompassing a multitude of conversations and actions taking place within and beyond the team and the organisation, only a proportion of which leaders could ever attend to and influence (Aasen, 2009). More fundamentally, as the latter three stories point out, no one, leaders included, can control the responses of the wider context to their interventions in the never-ending swirl of activity surrounding the innovation agenda. As such, the climate and the resulting innovation outcomes do not capture everything about the learning of leaders and their teams regarding supporting and managing innovation.

Despite these limitations, the chapter shows climate can provide fertile soil for ideas to flourish. It can also be the barren land where lie the withered and forgotten ideas. In the fuzzy front end of innovation, it is instructive to look at team climate as long as we pay attention to the leadership practices within a broader organisational context, over a period of time.

TABLE 3.5 Leadership practices to promote climate health

Dimension	Leadership practices that encouraged ...
Challenge and involvement	• Increased collaboration/earlier involvement of others • Seeking perspectives beyond own team/organisation • Greater, earlier patient involvement • Use of peer networks to test and challenge new ideas
Freedom	• Increased delegation of power and authority • Active discouragement of permission-seeking culture • Avoiding 'over-planning' • Expecting the unexpected
Trust/openness	• Appreciative enquiry – taking energy from what we do well • Seeking and providing opportunities for constructive feedback • Promoting coaching and active listening
Idea-time	• Allocating and protecting time in team meetings, away days/off-sites • Making time and space to reflect on and in action
Playfulness/humour	• Taking time out as team for informal conversation • Use of creative methods; e.g. drawing, storytelling, Lego Serious Play™
Conflict (reduction)	• Valuing diversity and difference • Surfacing and dealing with issues in timely and transparent fashion
Idea-support	• Storytelling targeted to audience • Delegation – increases time to promote projects and seek support • Fostering "innovation champions"
Debate	• Valuing diversity of views and all the different expertise available to you • Allowing time to get beneath surface issues
Risk-taking	• Accepting failure as inevitable side effect of innovation – and learning from it • Awareness (of self, impact, organisational priorities, costs, etc.) mitigates risk

The questions to guide further research and debate are: how can leaders aid innovation efforts with an increased awareness of the wider context (and the systemic opportunities and barriers it poses)? And how can leaders gain an enlightened acceptance of their agency (and its limits) to empower action in association with others?

Notes

1 The SOQ® provides a score between 0 and 300 on each of nine dimensions and shows the team's mean scores and range against benchmarks for innovative and 'stagnant' organisations. In addition, each respondent receives a report showing their scores in relation to the range for their team.
2 Note that the quotes below are all from team members, from their second experience of the SOQ® survey, unless indicated otherwise.

References

Aasen, T. M. B. (2009). A complexity perspective on innovation processes for subsea technology development. *International Journal of Learning and Change, 3*(3), 294–307. https://doi.org/10.1504/IJLC.2009.024694

Abbey, A., & Dickson, J. W. (1983). R&D work climate and innovation in semiconductors. *Academy of Management Journal, 26*(2), 362–368. https://doi.org/10.5465/255984

Adams, R., Bessant, J., & Phelps, R. (2006). Innovation management measurement: A review. *International Journal of Management Reviews, 8*(1), 21–47. https://doi.org/10.1111/j.1468-2370.2006.00119.x

Amabile, T., & Gryskiewicz, S. S. (1987). *Creativity in the R&D laboratory – Report.* Center for Creative Leadership.

Amabile, T. M., Hadley, C. N., & Kramer, S. J. (2002). Creativity under the gun. *Harvard Business Review, 80,* 52–63.

Amabile, T. M., Schatzel, E. A., Moneta, G. B., & Kramer, S. J. (2004). Leader behaviors and the work environment for creativity: Perceived leader support. *The Leadership Quarterly, 15*(1), 5–32. https://doi.org/10.1016/j.leaqua.2003.12.003

Bain, P. G., Mann, L., & Pirola-Merlo, A. (2001). The innovation imperative: The relationships between team climate, innovation, and performance in research and development teams. *Small Group Research, 32*(1), 55–73. https://doi.org/10.1177/104649640103200103

Baker, D.P., Day, R., & Salas, E. (2006). Teamwork as an essential component of high-reliability organizations. *Health Services Research, 41*(4 Pt 2), 1576–1598. https://doi.org/10.1111/j.1475-6773.2006.00566.x

Ballard, D. (2005). Using learning processes to promote change for sustainable development. *Action Research, 3*(2), 135–156. https://doi.org/10.1177/1476750305052138

Baregheh, A., Rowley, J., & Sambrook, S. (2009). Towards a multidisciplinary definition of innovation. *Management Decision, 47*(8), 1323–1339. https://doi.org/10.1108/00251740910984578

Büschgens, T., Bausch, A., & Balkin, D. B. (2013). Organizational culture and innovation: A meta-analytic review. *Journal of Product Innovation Management, 30*(4), 763–781. https://doi.org/10.1111/jpim.12021

Byrne, C. L., Mumford, M. D., Barrett, J. D., & Vessey, W. B. (2009). Examining the leaders of creative efforts: What do they do, and what do they think about? *Creativity and Innovation Management, 18*(4), 256–268. https://doi.org/10.1111/j.1467-8691.2009.00532.x

Carruthers, I. (2011). *Innovation Health and Wealth, Accelerating Adoption and Diffusion in the NHS.* Department of Health, NHS Improvement & Efficiency Directorate, Innovation and Service Improvement. https://webarchive.nationalarchives.gov.uk/20130107013731/http://www.dh.gov.uk/en/Publicationsandstatistics/Publications/PublicationsPolicyAndGuidance/DH_131299

Côté-Boileau, É., Denis, J. L., Callery, B., & Sabean, M. (2019). The unpredictable journeys of spreading, sustaining and scaling healthcare innovations: A scoping review. *Health Research Policy and Systems, 17*(1), 84–110.

Department of Health and Social Care. (2012). *The NHS constitution.* www.nhs.uk/choiceintheNHS/Rightsandpledges/NHSConstitution/Pages/Overview.aspx

Ehrhart, M. G., Schneider, B., & Macey, W. H. (2013). *Organizational climate and culture: An introduction to theory, research, and practice.* Routledge.

Ekvall, G. (1987). The climate metaphor in organization theory. In B. Bass & P. Drenth (Eds.), *Advances in organizational psychology* (pp. 177–179). Sage.

Ekvall, G. (1996). Organizational climate for creativity and innovation. *Journal of Work and Organizational Psychology, 5*(1), 105–123. https://doi.org/10.1080/13594329608414845

Goleman, D., & Boyatzis, R. (2008). Social intelligence and the biology of leadership. *Harvard Business Review, 86*(9), 74–81.

Ham, C. (2014). *Reforming the NHS from within: Beyond hierarchy, inspection and markets.* King's Fund. https://www.kingsfund.org.uk/publications/reforming-nhs-within

Hughes, A. M., Gregory, M. E., Joseph, D. L., Sonesh, S. C., Marlow, S. L., Lacerenza, C. N., Benishek, L. E., King, H. B., & Salas, E. (2016). Saving lives: A meta-analysis of team training in healthcare. *Journal of Applied Psychology, 101*(9), 1266. https://doi.org/ 10.1037/apl0000120

Hunter, S. T., & Cushenbery, L. (2011). Leading for innovation: Direct and indirect influences. *Advances in Developing Human Resources, 13*(3), 248–265. https://doi.org/10.1177/1523422311424263

Isaksen, S. G., & Lauer, K. J. (2002). The climate for creativity and change in teams. *Creativity and Innovation Management Journal, 11*, 74–86. https://doi.org/10.1111/1467-8691.00238

Isaksen, S. G., Lauer, K. J., Murdock, M. C., Dorval, K. B., & Puccio, G. J. (1995). *Situational outlook questionnaire: Understanding the climate for creativity and change (SOQ™)—A technical manual.* Creative Problem Solving Group.

Isaksen, S. G. (2007). The climate for transformation: Lessons for leaders. *Creativity and Innovation Management, 16*(1), 3–15. https://doi.org/10.1111/j.1467-8691.2007.00415.x

Isaksen, S. G. (2017). Leadership's role in creative climate creation. In M. Mumford & S. Hemlin (Eds.), *Handbook of research on leadership and creativity* (pp. 131–158). Edward Elgar Publishing. https://doi.org/10.4337/9781784715465.00014

Isaksen, S. G., Lauer, K. J., Ekvall, G., & Britz, A. (2001). Perceptions of the best and worst climates for creativity: Preliminary validation evidence for the situational outlook questionnaire. *Creativity Research Journal, 13*(2), 171–184. https://doi.org/10.1207/ S15326934CRJ1302_5

Isaksen, S. G., Dorval, B. D., & Treffinger, D. J. (2011). *Creative approaches to problemsolving: A framework for innovation and change* (3rd ed.). Sage.

Lipman-Blumen, J., & Leavitt, H. J. (1999). *Hot groups: Seeding them, feeding them, and using them to ignite your organization.* Oxford University Press.

Lubitsh, G., Doyle, C., & Valentine, J. (2005). The impact of theory of constraints (TOC) in an NHS trust. *Journal of Management Development, 24*(2), 116–131. https:// doi.org/10.1108/02621710510579482

McMillan, K., & Perron, A. (2013). Nurses amidst change: The concept of change fatigue offers an alternative perspective on organisational change. *Policy, Politics, and Nursing Practice, 14*(1), 26–32. https://doi.org/10.1177/1527154413481811

Meyerson, D. E. (2001). Radical change, the quiet way. *Harvard Business Review, 79*(9), 92–100.

Meyerson, D. E. (2008). Rocking the boat: How tempered radicals effect change without making trouble. MA: Harvard Business Review Press.

Mulgan, G., & Albury, D. (2003). *Innovation in the public sector.* Cabinet Office Strategy Unit, United Kingdom Cabinet Office. https://www.alnap.org/system/files/content/ resource/files/main/innovation-in-the-public-sector.pdf

NHS England. (2014). *Five year forward view.* https://www.england.nhs.uk/wp-content/ uploads/2014/10/5yfv-web.pdf

NHS England. (2017). *Next steps on the five year forward view.* https://www.england.nhs. uk/wp-content/uploads/2017/03/NEXT-STEPS-ON-THE-NHS-FIVE-YEAR-FORWARD-VIEW.pdf

Nuffield Trust. (2017). *Facts on staffing and staff shortages in England.* https://www. nuffieldtrust.org.uk/resource/the-nhs-workforce-in-numbers#references

Pace, R. W. (2003). *Organizational dynamism: Unleashing power in the workforce.* Quorum.

Patterson, M. G., West, M. A., Shackleton, V. J., Dawson, J. F., Lawthom, R., Maitlis, S., & Wallace, A. M. (2005). Validating the organizational climate measure: Links to managerial practices, productivity and innovation. *Journal of Organizational Behavior, 26*(4), 379–408. https://doi.org/10.1002/job.312

Poole, M. S., & Real, K. (2003). Groups and teams in health care: Communication and effectiveness. In T.L. Thompson, A. Dorsey, R. Parrott & K. Miller (Eds.), *Handbook of health communication* (pp. 369–402). Routledge.

Reineck, C. (2007). Models of change. *The Journal of Nursing Administration, 37*(9), 388–391. https://doi.org/10.1097/01.NNA.0000285137.26624.f9

Rose. (2015). *Better leadership for tomorrow: NHS leadership review.* Department of Health and Social Care. https://www.gov.uk/government/publications/better-leadership-for-tomorrow-nhs-leadership-review

Schein, E. H. (2000). Process Consulting for the Organization of the Future: Building a Helping Relationship. Germany, EHP-Verlag Andreas Kohlhage.

Sommers, L. S., Marton, K. I., Barbaccia, J. C., & Randolph, J. (2000). Physician, nurse, and social worker collaboration in primary care for chronically ill seniors. *Archives of Internal Medicine, 160*(12), 1825–1833. https://doi.org/10.1001/archinte.160.12.1825

Stensaker, I., Falkenberg, J., Meyer, C. B., & Haueng, A. C. (2002). Excessive change: Coping mechanisms and consequences. *Organizational Dynamics, 31*(3), 296–296. https://doi.org/10.5465/apbpp.2001.6133700

Totterdell, P., Leach, D., Birdi, K., Clegg, C., & Wall, T. (2002). An investigation of the contents and consequences of major organizational innovations. *International Journal of Innovation Management, 6*(04), 343–368.

Varkey, P., Horne, A., & Bennet, K. E. (2008). Innovation in health care: A primer. *American Journal of Medical Quality, 23*(5), 382–388. https://doi.org/10.1177/1062860608317695

Van de Ven, A. H. (2017). The innovation journey: You can't control it, but you can learn to maneuver it. *Innovation: Organization & Management, 19*(1), 39–42. https://doi.org/10.1080/14479338.2016.1256780

Weberg, D. (2012). Complexity leadership: A healthcare imperative. *Nursing Forum, 47*(4), 268–277. https://doi.org/10.1111/j.1744-6198.2012.00276.x

West, M., & Rickards, T. (1999). Innovation. In S. Pritzker & M. Runco (eds.), *Encyclopaedia of creativity* (Vol. 2, pp. 45–55). Academic Press.

West, M. A., & Anderson, N. R. (1996). Innovation in top management teams. *Journal of Applied Psychology, 81*(6), 680–693. https://doi.org/10.1037/0021-9010.81.6.680

West, M. A., Borrill, C. S., Dawson, J. F., Scully, J., Carter, M., Anelay, S., Patterson, M., et al. (2001). The link between the management of employees and patient mortality in acute hospitals. *The International Journal of Human Resource Management, 13*(8), 1299–1310. https://doi.org/10.1080/09585190210156521

4

MOBILIZING MANAGEMENT CONTROLS IN INNOVATION PROJECTS

Minna Saunila and Ilse Svensson de Jong

Introduction

Successful companies are found to be characterized by being able to ensure both operational excellence and to take a more systematic approach in managing innovation. Comprehension about how innovation projects deliver outcomes is pivotal in the management of innovation projects, which makes management control a critical effort for managers in many contemporary companies (Ylinen & Gullkvist, 2014; Lopez-Valeiras et al., 2016). Management control has been defined as "systems, rules, practices, values and other activities management put in place in order to direct employee behavior" (Malmi & Brown, 2008, p. 290). Prior research has concluded that innovation and control practices are connected (cf. Cardinal, 2001; Labitzke et al., 2014; Bisbe & Malagueño, 2015; Janka et al., 2019; Henri & Wouters, 2020).

Still, the connection between management control and innovation at the project level remains challenging (Ylinen & Gullkvist, 2014; Lopez-Valeiras et al., 2016), Research on innovation and management control has primarily been survey- or conceptual-based studies that lack an in-depth understanding of how the approaches of management control function in real innovation projects contexts (Ylinen & Gullkvist, 2014; Lopez-Valeiras et al., 2016). This research gap has brought in a new stream of research that studies the relation between innovation and management control by taking into account both the complexity of innovation and the ways by which inputs are transformed into outcomes (Hashi & Stojcic, 2013). Given these points, there is a need for qualitative approaches to provide fine-grained evidence on the use of management control for fostering innovation (Barros & da Costa, 2019). Thus, this chapter focuses on management control in innovation projects. More specifically the purpose of this chapter is

DOI: 10.4324/9780429346033-6

to examine how multiple management controls are mobilized by managers in innovation projects.

Management control for innovation

Origins of management control in innovation studies

Accounting and management journals have paid a lot of attention to the role that management controls can play in innovation in recent years, with a significant increase in published publications (Speklé et al., 2017; Aaltola, 2018; Barros & da Costa, 2019). Innovation research is reaching strongly toward an enhanced comprehension about innovation as a managed and controlled effort (Davila et al., 2009; Janssen et al., 2011; Saunila et al., 2014). Innovation, and innovation projects, is referred to in this chapter as the chain from idea generation to execution and value capture (Davila et al., 2012).

While management control has been thought to be harmful to innovation in the past, recent research suggests that innovation can benefit from it (Barros & da Costa, 2019; Fagerlin & Lövstål, 2020; Henri & Wouters, 2020). Nowadays, management control is considered more widely as a means to manage uncertain conditions, for example, innovation (Bisbe & Malagueño, 2009; Revellino & Mouritsen, 2009; Chenhall & Moers, 2015). Management control has transformed to be more open in taking into account the internal and external factors that drive innovation (Chenhall & Moers, 2015). This emerging paradigm, where management control supports innovation, however, does not imply that traditional management control practices will be abandoned. These management controls are coexisting alongside newer ones, contributing to the development, articulatement, legitimization, and visibility of the role of innovation within organizations (Chenhall & Moers, 2015; Barros & da Costa, 2019).

Previous research seems to indicate that managing innovation projects necessitates the use of multiple controls that evolve over time, which are used at specific moments and should vary depending on the type of innovation that is involved (Barros & da Costa, 2019). This may require the parallel usage of several controls transforming over time (Bedford, 2015; Barros & da Costa, 2019; Müller-Stewens et al., 2020), consideration of the type of control used in specific moments (Chiesa et al., 2009; Revellino & Mouritsen, 2009; Barros & da Costa, 2019), and the type of control varying according to the type of innovation (Labitzke et al., 2014; Barros & da Costa, 2019; Guo et al., 2019).

Management control literature gives numerous conceptualizations that assist us to comprehend the use of controls in a broader sense (Barros & da Costa, 2019). These include, for example, Simons' levers of control (LOC) framework in which the use of interactive, and diagnostic control is explored (Bisbe & Otley, 2004; Bisbe & Malagueño, 2009, 2015; Chiesa et al., 2009; Revellino & Mouritsen, 2009; Müller-Stewens et al., 2020), and input or clan, behavior, and output control (Cardinal, 2001; Li et al., 2011; Guo et al., 2019).

Simon's levers of control

The most used typology is Simons' levers of control (LOC) framework, which is one of the taxonomies that recognizes the use of multiple controls and styles in their use (Chenhall & Moers, 2015; Curtis & Sweeney, 2017). Most prominently in this work is the interactive and diagnostic use of management control. This diagnostic formal management control was based on cybernetic controls that assist in setting goals, comparing inputs and outputs with the goals, and taking appropriate corrective actions as well as revising the goals accordingly (Chenhall & Moers, 2015). Müller-Stewens et al. (2020) consider that management control can happen either diagnostically to track the progress toward intended goals; but also, interactively to share information within an organization and to communicate top management's concerns. Interactive use has been widely suggested to be supportive of innovation (Bisbe & Otley, 2004; Bisbe & Malagueño, 2009, 2015; Chiesa et al., 2009; Revellino & Mouritsen, 2009; Müller-Stewens et al., 2020).

According to these studies, interactive use of management control promotes innovation by offering direction for seeking, legitimacy for autonomous initiatives, and stimulus for initiatives in low-innovation organizations (Bisbe & Otley, 2004; Barros & da Costa, 2019). Bedford (2015) stated that the efficiency of interactive flexible control is dependent on the type of innovation that the company targets: they improve performance in companies that develop exploratory innovation but not exploitative innovation. Lopez-Valeiras et al. (2016) revealed a positive relationship between interactive control and organizational innovation. Further, interactive management control has been found to possess a positive connection with creativity in both conservative and entrepreneurial companies (Bisbe & Malagueño, 2015). Müller-Stewens et al. (2020) found that interactive controls drive product innovation regarding product newness and innovation rate. However, in uncertain environments, interactive controls facilitate innovation rates directly, but in stable environments, the influence is vicarious via coordination routines.

Diagnostic use of management control has achieved some dubious findings (Barros & da Costa, 2019). While studies are reporting their constraining effect (Bisbe & Malagueño, 2015), others have reported a positive contribution to the deployment of innovation (Bedford, 2015; Müller-Stewens et al., 2020). Müller-Stewens et al. (2020) found that the diagnostic controls are positively driven product innovation in terms of product newness and innovation rate both directly and via coordination routines. Bedford (2015) found to support that also passive and conventional uses of accounting controls positively contribute to innovation. The results achieved by Bisbe and Malagueño (2015) suggest that diagnostic management control plays a minor role in each of the various phases of the innovation development.

Input or clan, behavior, and output control

The second typology looks into the object of control and makes a distinction between input, behavior, and output controls (Merchant & Van der Stede,

2007). Guo et al. (2019) state that input controls deal with the management of innovation-related resources. Behavior control includes the mechanisms that monitor the tasks associated with the introduction of innovation and determine how information is coordinated and spread across the company. Finally, output control assists in regulating outcomes of innovation. Poskela and Martinsuo (2009) revealed that input control is required in attaining strategic renewal at the early phases of innovation. The study of Cardinal (2001) revealed that input, behavior, and output controls all contribute to radical innovation, whereas only input and output controls contribute to incremental innovation. Li et al. (2011) studied the role of controls in terms of clan, behavior, and output control, in the relation between knowledge exploitation and endogenous innovation. They refer to clan controls as socialization mechanisms that determine employee stances based on organizational norms, shared values, and beliefs. They found that all types of controls play moderating roles in the knowledge exploitation-endogenous innovation relationship. Guo et al. (2019) found a positive connection between management control and product and process innovation. However, the role of behavior and input controls was even more highlighted in process innovation.

In summary, the main takeaways from the previous research are that the use of management controls in innovation comprehends a set of controls used in different ways, with different results being expected (Revellino & Mouritsen, 2015; Barros & da Costa, 2019). Depending on the way they are used, controls produce different results and can provide different routines that impact innovation either by supporting or constraining it (Barros & da Costa, 2019). In this chapter, the mobilization of multiple management controls in innovation projects will be documented. When analyzing and interpreting the empirical material, it became clear that innovation projects indeed require a set of controls used in different ways.

Research approach

Empirical research setting

The empirical evidence builds on a single case on the mobilization of managerial controls in innovation projects. The prior purposes of the innovation projects are to translate the strategy into action and to ensure the continuation and renewal of future business. Case studies are utilized to understand phenomena with complex and multiple facets and processes (Yin, 2003). A medium-sized media company forms the empirical case environment of the study. The company consists of multiple business units that execute distinct roles and tasks in a company with both independent and shared functions. The business includes three printed newspapers; web services; radio; printing service; distribution service; and traditional supportive facilities, for example, administration and ICT. The company employs about 270 persons in total. Like the company's competitors, the company under investigation suffers from the changes in the industry digitalization and continuously intensifying competition and uncertain business environment. The company possesses both exploitative and exploratory innovation as it has realized that innovation and tomorrow's business prosperity require both; reducing costs is not a sufficient means to assure competitiveness.

In the company, innovation is understood in several different ways depending on the job description. In content production, the daily making of a paper is seen as a process of innovation. In sales, innovation can be a repackaged product or a flyer tailored to a customer event. New ways of working and forms of services are innovations in the online service context. Thus, the classification of innovations is considered important: the development work within the unit and the strategic renewal covering the entire company should be separated. Innovation projects are mostly incremental in nature. They target developing existing operations and aim to build renewal by networking. Thus, the company is actively searching for possibilities to support innovation through the utilization of outside parties as well. The company can recognize areas where, for example, digitalization could be used to support innovation at the company. However, these recognized advantages seem to rely on boosting existing business elements and optimizing processes. Due to the operating logic, it is hard to separate innovation from daily activities because the company does not make a clear distinction between product and service development and innovation. While incremental innovations are the main focus, radical innovations also have their own path. Utilizing innovation projects to develop and ideate something completely new is still rare, even though their supporting elements as a part of innovation are understood.

Data and analysis

The empirical data is composed of semi-structured one-on-one interviews involving 14 individuals with distinct roles and responsibilities in the company under investigation. Interviewees were chosen based on the criteria that they had innovation-related tasks at the group or department level. Thus, they were, for example, having project manager roles in innovation projects or they were managers of the functions that conducted the innovation projects. Table 4.1 provides information on the interviews. The questions of the interviews were carefully constructed beforehand. Still, the topics were debated informally with the interviewees and complemented by fine downing questions and comments from the interviewer. Interviewers took notes and made observations during interviews. These notes and observations were then compared and compounded to the interview recordings and transcriptions. These allowed for in-depth analysis. The interviews were chosen as a data collection method because it is probable to attain a deep and detailed picture of the research theme. The validity of the data was verified by substantiating the questions on a robust scientific basis. Interviewed persons were carefully chosen based on pre-determined characteristics explained above. The interviews were targeted on the persons' experiences about the innovation project design and implementation, the creation of ideas, and the measurement and

TABLE 4.1 Information about the interviews

Unit	No. of interviews	Interviewees' roles in the company	Interview duration
Paper 1	3	Employee/innovation project manager, two managers	58.36–74.14 min
Paper 2	2	Employee/innovationprojectmanager,manager	39.59–52.27 min
Paper 3	2	Employee/innovation project manager, manager	46.45–49.18 min
Radio	2	Employee/innovation project manager	47.03 min
Web services	2	Employee/innovation project manager, manager	57.24–69.34 min
Sales	4	Two employees/innovation project managers, two managers	42.53–77.08 min

management of these phases in the company. Without any guidance in terms of the forms of control consequential to innovation projects, interviewees utilized prior understanding to qualify both negative and positive effects that emerge.

Data analysis was performed utilizing a content analysis method based on the guidance of the prior literature. The data analysis aimed to recognize the key managerial means used for innovation project control and the moments in which they are being used. Since the aim of the research wasn't to obtain scientific generalizability, theory concepts and conclusions from the existing studies were used for analysis themes (Yin, 2003). Although an initial understanding of the nature of management control practices in innovation was formed based on prior literature, themes of analysis were also allowed to emerge exploratorily. The final results were formed using a cyclic analytical process, including the preceding steps: (1) reading the transcripts and deciphering the content; (2) categorizing the material into themes; and (3) piecing the themes together. After these, a comprehensive understanding of the topic was developed.

Findings

The differences in the approaches of management control that are utilized to guide innovation as well as in what moments they are being used can be seen in the combination of control mechanisms used by the company. Managerial controls were mobilized at different levels of the company. However, the focus of this chapter is management control at the innovation project level and the analysis concentrates on project level control although authority was used by persons with higher hierarchical levels than project management. Table 4.2 summarizes the findings with illustrations of management control mechanisms revealed by the case and an overview of the types of management control highlighted in a different situation related to innovation projects. The following sections discuss and elaborate upon these findings.

TABLE 4.2 Management control in innovation projects

Type of activity	Innovation project characteristic	Type of control (LOC)	Type of control (input/ output/ behavior)
Designing the project	Providing collaboration possibilities for cross–border information acquisition and sharing Incorporating all functions in idea development Forming cross-functional teams linked to organizational strategy. Fostering learning in the company via accountable persons	Interactive/ diagnostic control	Behavior/output control
Taking responsibility for the project	Guiding the initiative from idea to a project.	Diagnostic control	Input control
Directing the project	Defining the roles and responsibilities at different levels (individual, project, unit, company). Building common "project spirit" and goal orientation. Focusing the innovation sufficiently. For example, forming the link to strategy, annual plans, or interests of the management. Matching unit-level and company-level goals. Matching short-term and long-term goals.	Interactive/ diagnostic control	Behavior/input control
Managing ownership	Assigning the "ownership" of an idea to a person with real changes of taking it forward. For example, sufficient knowledge, capabilities, resources, and authority.	Diagnostic control	Input/output control
Targeting resources for the project	Forming a unified view of how resources are allocated. Prescribing available resources between units and functions. Incorporating the right knowledge and expertise.	Diagnostic control	Input/output control
Launching	Prioritizing projects and informing the staff about them. Communicating innovation internally before external actions.	Interactive control	Behavior control
Coordination and execution	Aligning project design and project management with company goals. Resourcing, project coordination, systematization and monitoring of processes, and involvement of people. Gathering user/customer feedback for all levels. Constructing metrics that comprise the innovation project.	Diagnostic control	Output control

Designing the project

The rise of innovation projects was generally guided by general company-level goals to pursue innovation and to make innovation a part of everyone's work. When designing innovation projects, actions taken must lead to more targeted, yet proactive, and multi-faceted idea refinement processes. Supporting and encouraging active individuals was considered to enable learning throughout the company. Measures to be taken by the active individuals included mapping the current situation and commissioning-related customer research, interpreting the results and assessing future trends, and defining innovation generation processes. They also improved the flow of information between units. Managerial means are required to motivate employees to take a more active approach in revealing their ideas. This highlights the managers' ability to create collaboration possibilities for cross-border information acquisition and sharing. In a fast-changing environment, deeper collaboration between different units is considered essential. Crossing unit boundaries is perceived as a difficult but necessary condition especially in developing radical innovation. All units needed to be involved in idea refinement. Also, external experts, such as suppliers or customers, were considered as crucial sources of innovation project inputs.

> Innovation has been commonplace in a small unit all along. Many issues and discussions and meetings have been related to these same issues. The fact that this activity [innovation] is organized, is related to the improvement of cooperation between units of the company.

The link between innovation and strategy and the strategy process needed to be strong. The role of management control is about involving different units working together upon shared goals, involving and supporting people, and arranging opportunities, time, and freedom for those involved in innovation. These means assist in forming a common concept and language for innovation between different units and functions and to make innovation more commonplace. They also assist in forming cross-functional teams linked to organizational strategy.

> A good strategy is needed for the organization to guide that work [innovation] clearly. The management should be clear about it and of course, everyone should be able to mirror it against themselves.

To sum up, in this type of activity, management control was characterized by general company-level goals to pursue innovation and to make innovation a part of everyone's work. Thus, management control included a combination of different types of control.

Taking responsibility for the project

The control was characterized by allocating time for innovation and investing in idea collection systems supporting innovation. In this sense, management controls were targeted defining the roles and responsibilities at different organizational levels (individual, project, unit, company). Responsibility for the innovation project's daily operation is divided into three levels. The strategic level is the responsibility of the management team. The head of development is responsible for the coordination of innovation and the innovation manager, together with his / her supervisor, is responsible for the third, operational level activity. Reporting takes place in the company from the bottom up.

> It's such a big organization that coordination is definitely in place, but the fact that someone would be in charge of leading the whole company's innovation makes it feel somewhat difficult.

Managers are expected to tend to come up with ideas and a good horizontal view of the company's operations: content production, the impact of digitalization, a sales perspective, and financial boundaries. Management should look at the company operations as a whole and, if necessary, also question working practices. This requires time and freedom. The role is seen to involve more process coordination than actual implementation tasks. Thus, it was seen important that managers guide the initiative from an idea to a project.

To sum up, in this type of activity, management control was characterized by allowing time for innovation and providing idea-collection systems supporting innovation. Thus, management control included mainly diagnostic, input type of control.

Directing the project

Management control was used to communicate the importance of innovation along with the importance of company goals. Thus, one of the important roles of control is to focus innovation sufficiently. This means, for example, forming the link to strategy, annual plans, or interests of the management. The innovation projects to be conducted support daily business and strategy, emphasizing customer needs. Although the management team defines the priorities for innovation, the project-level management takes care of directing operations to the prioritized areas. However, more radical innovations can also challenge and question a company's strategy.

Decision-making in the company is decentralized. In smaller units, decision-making is perceived to work. But when dealing with higher levels of the company, managers are expected to be more and more aware of the necessities in matching unit-level and company-level goals. The company's industry is currently undergoing major changes, and management struggles with its position concerning the operating environment. This highlights the importance of directing the innovation projects: the focus of the action needs to be clear; it cannot provide a little bit of everything for everyone. Smaller units are agile to implement product innovations, but larger units are slow and cumbersome to implement. The company has a long history and has several business units; as a result, the response to change is slow. Strong traditions and high market share can further complicate adaptation to innovation. Short-term goals are traditionally emphasized but management is more and more aware of the necessity to change the course toward long-term goals. Thus, managerial means emphasized the importance of matching the short-term and long-term goals of the company.

To sum up, in this type of activity, management control was characterized by communicating innovation as important along with the importance of company goals. Thus, management control included a combination of different types of control.

Managing ownership

In the company, decision-making authority has traditionally been at the top management. However, top management is not always familiar enough with the daily process of innovation to make the right decisions, which may result in a mismatch between decision-making authority and the information needed in decisions. It was considered important that an idea must always be assigned a "sponsor" who is responsible for refining the idea until a decision is made to start the project. The role of innovation manager and other formal innovation roles were used to tackle the issue.

> The task of an innovation manager is not to innovate or come up with ideas, not to do those things in practice, to be responsible for what needs to be done. But to make sure that innovation happens. That those ideas get the attention and treatment they deserve and they then go effectively through the process towards practical implementation.

The responsibility then passes to the designated project manager, who must also be allocated the resources needed to carry out the project. Important is to assign the "ownership" of an idea to a person with real changes of taking it forward. This requires, for example, sufficient knowledge, capabilities, resources, and authority. The original developer of the idea is kept aware of the course of the process.

Further, the roles, goals, operating methods, and division of responsibilities between innovation managers and other forms of innovation roles needed to be kept clear. Otherwise, it causes pressure and uncertainty and reduces the motivation of the people in those roles. The development of the company is a completely new area for some people with formal innovation roles, while some see the role as a natural fit for the current job description. Building trust in the group is essential that the fear of stealing ideas does not hinder innovation. People with formal innovation roles hope that the role will create opportunities for networking and bringing insights into strategy work, as well as support and positive encouragement from related parties.

To sum up, in this type of activity, management control was characterized by utilizing innovation managers and other formal innovation roles. Thus, management control included mainly diagnostic, input and output types of control.

Targeting resources for the project

The allocation of resources was perceived as the most challenging issue in unified innovation. Management was responsible for forming a unified view of how resources are allocated and prescribing available resources between units and functions. The resources of the units are budgeted for innovation projects. This means time, money as well as people and their skills. If necessary, external resources will be allocated to the activities. Targeting of resources is dependent on the type of innovation pursued, either incremental or radical.

> Any kind of ideas, ideas that develop company operations would be desirable. However, it would be needed to classify those ideas. This is such a small thing, and this is quick to do, it can be done right away. That would bring results quickly and people would feel that my idea was implemented.
>
> Many good ideas are slated into the same thing that we don't have the resources. I think it's a shame that then if we really want to change things and do things in a new way, then we should also think about our resources in a new way. Leave something else out that we get that done.

Typical first steps in both types are problem definition, ideation, idea evaluation, further processing, and conceptualization of ideas. These require supportive managerial means discussed earlier. After that, the process can be roughly divided into two different categories that require different procedures and managerial means. In the occurrence of incremental innovation, the process is characterized by small improvements to the existing ways of action guided by the constraints of the prevailing situation. Its implementation is determined by socialization mechanisms among company employees. In the case of radical innovation, it is about implementing selected ideas; innovation is built from the concept created as a result of the idea refinement process. This is typically a traditional project-like approach with clearly defined stages.

The project's management draws up a project plan, to make a schedule for the project and to document the progress of the project. The manager is accountable for the project, which means allocating tasks within the company and defining and monitoring the use of the necessary external resources, as well as reporting. This requires vision in relation to incorporating the right knowledge and expertise. When starting an innovation project, sufficient resources are allocated to it and a project schedule is planned. The schedule can be drawn up backward from the required completion date, if required, or according to the time taken by the tasks and resources. A connection to the resources available is essential. The schedule should include certain common checkpoints. The timetable must also take into account the time required for internal marketing and training. A common buffer time is reserved for the end of the schedule in case of possible delays.

> We need to define how that idea starts to refine. A clear path to what happens first, what happens next. In the same way, for those different projects, whatever there is in practice, such a clear responsibility that who takes care of it, who has any responsibilities in that project. And tracking it around how that project is progressing there in the background.

To sum up, in this type of activity, management control was characterized by following stage-gate type of process for radical innovation, and informal processes for incremental innovation. Thus, management control varied based on innovation type but included mainly diagnostic, input and output types of control.

Launching

The launch of a project follows the company's general guidelines and the operating models of the business units and areas of responsibility. The overall communication about the importance of innovation was highlighted at the starting of the project as well. The wealth of ideas resulted from the need of prioritizing projects and informing the staff about them.

> …this type of prioritization and project management skills. And it requires and demands systematicity in the activities, that is documentation, that is project reviews and that kind of thing.

The schedule of communicating about the project depends on whether it is a unit-level or a company-level effort. The unit's projects are decided by the unit's management team, and at the company level, the decision is made by the top management team. The reasons shall state the reasons why the project is placed in either level. Similarly, justification must be given for not starting to implement the idea and the decisions and reasons are to be documented. Also, communicating innovation internally before external actions were crucial. The project manager together with the Innovation manager and people with formal innovation roles are responsible for internal communication and information on the progress of the project.

> Internal communication and everything else needs to work so that it is known what will be coming. Knowing who it influences, how it influences, what it requires, how it is sold, how it is marketed, that all that pipe is pre-thought out.

To sum up, in this type of activity, management control was characterized by communication about the importance of innovation. Thus, management control included mainly interactive, behavioral types of control.

Coordination and execution

It was felt that there was still plenty of room for improvement in design and project management. Initiatives were made to aligning project design and project management with company goals. This means resourcing, project coordination, systematization, and monitoring of processes, and involvement of people. The innovation project follows a pre-planned procedure that analyzes the project's progress and external changes related to the project. Managers will guide the refinement and drawing up the specifications for the innovation, as well as define the measures to track the process. A crucial part of the control was constructing metrics that comprise the innovation project. The schedule and project implementation are monitored during the project, if necessary, additional resources will be allocated to the project or the schedule will be adjusted according to the available resources. It is essential to take into account the synchronization of different projects (even between different units) and the connections to other projects, as well as the use of common resources (e.g. information and financial management). During the project, a prototype is tested by users/customers to gain practical insight. Management was responsible for gathering user/customer feedback for all levels.

> When those goals are clear enough and understandable at all levels, then better ideas may emerge that genuinely deliver innovations that benefit that business. Also, get started with those ideas. There may be less innovation that doesn't support that core business.

One part of the project is the implementation. The resources and processes required for deployment and maintenance of the innovation must be defined in advance throughout the innovation life cycle. The project manager transfers ownership of the product to the product manager or unit manager. The project manager makes sure that the parties understand their respective roles.

To sum up, in this type of activity, management control was characterized by meeting specific goals for operations, budgets, and sales targets. Thus, management control included mainly diagnostic, output type of control.

Conclusions

This chapter contributes to the growing research on the interplay between innovation and management control (e.g. Bisbe & Otley, 2004; Bisbe &

Malagueño, 2009, 2015; Revellino & Mouritsen, 2009; Chenhall & Moers, 2015; Guo et al., 2019; Müller-Stewens et al., 2020) and builds on the need of more in-depth insights gained by qualitative approaches (Barros & da Costa, 2019). The chapter focused on managerial controls in innovation projects building on a qualitative analysis that focuses on innovation projects carried out in a company operating in the media sector. Thus, this chapter complements and extends the current understanding of management controls in innovative projects (Ylinen & Gullkvist, 2014; Lopez-Valeiras et al., 2016). By examining multiple types of control this study reveals whether and how the approaches of managerial controls are mobilized by managers. To do so, we empirically demonstrated how the approaches of management control are utilized to guide innovation, and in what moments they are being used. Thus, the results support prior research suggesting that innovation at the project level requires simultaneous usage of several controls (Bedford, 2015; Barros & da Costa, 2019; Müller-Stewens et al., 2020), as well as consideration of innovation type in management control (Labitzke et al., 2014; Barros & da Costa, 2019; Guo et al., 2019).

The main conclusions are as follows. *First*, the results highlight the necessity of multiple controls during innovation projects, both interactive and diagnostic, input, behavior, and output types of control. The findings reveal that managers should be very open in observing the need for different types of management controls in innovation projects. Although interactive and behavioral forms of control are highlighted in study findings, diagnostic and output types of control are needed in certain situations to guide the project. This is in line with the findings of the vast majority of studies showing that interactive control is supportive for innovation (Bisbe & Otley, 2004; Bisbe & Malagueño, 2009, 2015; Chiesa et al., 2009; Revellino & Mouritsen, 2009; Müller-Stewens et al., 2020). Diagnostic control assists in clarifying the path from accelerating ideas into innovation; it should support interactive forms of control by representing effective and seamless paths that fit the company's operation type and strategic goals.

Second, the empirical evidence shows that the use of control is not linear, i.e., innovation and management controls interact to influence innovation, and thus control practices need to transform according to specific situations in innovation projects. The study supports prior studies showing that distinct management controls are required in distinct phases of the innovation project (cf. Chiesa et al., 2009; Revellino & Mouritsen, 2009). However, the empirical evidence reveals that there are no linear relationships between the innovation project phase and the type of control. Thus, the study challenges the predominant view that early phases require interactive control, whereas later phases are more structured, interactive control. Based on the empirical evidence, the reality is more nuanced, and managers are required to find the right combination of multiple controls in each type of activity in an innovation project.

Third, a single manager cannot control all activities and situations of an innovation project. It requires "frames" and strategies with the art of information sharing and collaboration. This means that diagnostic control forms the backbone of innovation project control. However, it is complemented with interactive, behavior type of control that enables the transformation from strategy into daily action.

This research, however, is limited to a certain group of people and a specific set of innovative projects. It also considers only a few forms of management controls. With slight modifications, the proposed approach can be evaluated with other innovation projects and different management controls. Table 4.2 can be used as a framework in future studies to assess the types of management control in innovation projects. Further research could also assess whether and how specific types of management controls contribute to innovation project results. The results of this chapter can be used as a reference to focus on a specific type of activity in the innovation project of the project as a whole.

References

Aaltola, P. (2018). Investing in strategic development: Management control of business model and managerial innovations. Qualitative Research in Accounting and Management, 15(2), 1–40.

Barros, R. S., & da Costa, A. M. D. S. (2019). Bridging management control systems and innovation. Qualitative Research in Accounting & Management, 16(3), 342–372.

Bedford, D. S. (2015). Management control systems across different modes of innovation: Implications for firm performance. Management Accounting Research, 28, 12–30.

Bisbe, J., & Malagueño, R. (2009). The choice of interactive control systems under different innovation management modes. European Accounting Review, 18(2), 371–405.

Bisbe, J., & Malagueño, R. (2015). How control systems influence product innovation processes: Examining the role of entrepreneurial orientation. Accounting and Business Research, 45(3), 356–386.

Bisbe, J., & Otley, D. (2004). The effects of the interactive use of management control systems on product innovation. Accounting, Organizations and Society, 29(8), 709–737.

Cardinal, L. B. (2001). Technological innovation in the pharmaceutical industry: The use of organizational control in managing research and development. Organization Science, 12(1), 19–36.

Chenhall, R. H., & Moers, F. (2015). The role of innovation in the evolution of management accounting and its integration into management control. Accounting, Organizations and Society, 47, 1–13.

Chiesa, V., Frattini, F., Lamberti, L., & Noci, G. (2009). Exploring management control in radical innovation projects. European Journal of Innovation Management, 12(4), 416–443.

Curtis, E., & Sweeney, B. (2017). Managing different types of innovation: Mutually reinforcing management control systems and the generation of dynamic tension. Accounting and Business Research, 47(3), 313–343.

Davila, T., Epstein, M., & Shelton, R. (2012). *Making innovation work: How to manage it, measure it, and profit from it*. Upper Saddle River, NJ: FT press.

Davila, A., Foster, G., & Oyon, D. (2009). Accounting and control, entrepreneurship and innovation: Venturing into new research opportunities. European Accounting Review, 18(2), 281–311.

Fagerlin, W. P., & Lövstål, E. (2020). Top managers' formal and informal control practices in product innovation processes. *Qualitative Research in Accounting & Management*, 17(4), 497–524.

Guo, B., Paraskevopoulou, E., & Santamaria Sanchez, L. (2019). Disentangling the role of management control systems for product and process innovation in different contexts. European Accounting Review, 28(4), 681–712.

Hashi, I., & Stojčić, N. (2013). The impact of innovation activities on firm performance using a multi-stage model: Evidence from the Community Innovation Survey 4. Research Policy, 42(2), 353–366.

Henri, J. F., & Wouters, M. (2020). Interdependence of management control practices for product innovation: The influence of environmental unpredictability. Accounting, Organizations and Society, 86, 101073.

Janka, M., Heinicke, X., & Guenther, T. W. (2020). Beyond the "good" and "evil" of stability values in organizational culture for managerial innovation: The crucial role of management controls. Review of Managerial Science, 14(6), 1363–1404.

Janssen, S., Moeller, K., & Schlaefke, M. (2011). Using performance measures conceptually in innovation control. Journal of Management Control, 22(1), 107.

Labitzke, G., Svoboda, S., & Schultz, C. (2014). The role of dedicated innovation functions for innovation process control and performance—An empirical study among hospitals. Creativity and Innovation Management, 23(3), 235–251.

Li, Y., Li, X., Liu, Y., & Barnes, B. R. (2011). Knowledge communication, exploitation and endogenous innovation: The moderating effects of internal controls in SMEs. R&D Management, 41(2), 156–172.

Lopez-Valeiras, E., Gonzalez-Sanchez, M. B., & Gomez-Conde, J. (2016). The effects of the interactive use of management control systems on process and organizational innovation. Review of Managerial Science, 10(3), 487–510.

Malmi, T., & Brown, D. A. (2008). Management control systems as a package—Opportunities, challenges and research directions. Management Accounting Research, 19(4), 287–300.

Merchant, K. A., & Van der Stede, W. A. (2007). Management control systems: Performance measurement, evaluation and incentives. Pearson Education.

Müller-Stewens, B., Widener, S. K., Möller, K., & Steinmann, J. C. (2020). The role of diagnostic and interactive control uses in innovation. Accounting, Organizations and Society, 80, 101078.

Poskela, J., & Martinsuo, M. (2009). Management control and strategic renewal in the front end of innovation. Journal of Product Innovation Management, 26(6), 671–684.

Revellino, S., & Mouritsen, J. (2009). The multiplicity of controls and the making of innovation. European Accounting Review, 18(2), 341–369.

Revellino, S., & Mouritsen, J. (2015). Accounting as an engine: The performativity of calculative practices and the dynamics of innovation. Management Accounting Research, 28, 31–49.

Saunila, M., Pekkola, S., & Ukko, J. (2014). The relationship between innovation capability and performance: The moderating effect of measurement. International Journal of Productivity and Performance Management, 63(2), 234–249.

Speklé, R. F., van Elten, H. J., & Widener, S. K. (2017). Creativity and control: A paradox—Evidence from the levers of control framework. Behavioral Research in Accounting, 29(2), 73–96.

Yin, R. K. (2003). Case study research. Design and methods. Sage Publications: US.

Ylinen, M., & Gullkvist, B. (2014). The effects of organic and mechanistic control in exploratory and exploitative innovations. Management Accounting Research, 25(1), 93–112.

5

UNVEILING "THE INNOVATION ALGORITHM"

The New Approach to Raising Your Capacity to Innovate

Vincent Ogutu and Andrew Levi

Covid-19 and the New Innovation Imperative

It would not be a stretch of the imagination to assume that since the emergence of Covid-19 in late 2019, virtually every leader of a mission-oriented team, organization or country has found herself or himself grappling with a variant of the question: *"How should my organization outthink and act its way out of the current Covid-19 economic crisis and its ripple effects?"*

It is a fact that Covid-19 has been enormously disruptive for many organizations – upending operating models, revenue streams and value chains (El Baz & Ruel, 2021). Since its onset, businesses, governments and non-profits have found themselves pressed to quickly reimagine and reinvent their product and service delivery models, internal systems and processes and the markets and networks within which they interact. Simply put, a major outcome of the ensuing global health and economic crisis is an undeniably fierce urgency for innovation.

Increasingly, innovation is perceived as a powerful predictor of organizational survival post this Covid-19 crisis (Caballero-Morales, 2021); in much the same way that innovations in vaccine production and global public health supply chains seemingly hold the key to human survival through this pandemic (Ndwandwe & Wiysonge, 2021). Thus, with no clear immediate end to this pandemic or its ripple effects in sight, Covid-19 focusses attention on the importance for leaders of today's organizations to affirm and build the innovative capacity of their organizations and staff. This book chapter specifically unveils *The Innovation Algorithm* – an innovation 'short-code' developed in 2016 by Dr. Vincent Ogutu, to offer leaders, followers and their organizations, a new dependable pathway to innovate at will. The Innovation Algorithm by-passes conventional psychological and perceived resource barriers to innovation, and breaks down the innovation process into simple steps that will make innovation accessible to most people.

DOI: 10.4324/9780429346033-7

In order to help you appreciate the potential value of *The Innovation Algorithm*, we will now proceed in the next section to give you a short review of early calls to innovation, and a review of the barriers that have typically stood in the way of innovation. We will outline how such barriers could be lowered and then explain how far methods like *Design Thinking* have gone in overcoming these barriers. We shall conclude by suggesting how we think *The Innovation Algorithm* responds to these barriers and how it compares to *Design Thinking* as a tool for innovation.

The Persistent Call to Innovate

Whereas the current innovation imperative is closely linked to the ongoing Covid-19 pandemic, the globalization of innovation neither finds its genesis nor its basis in the current global health crisis. On the contrary, David de Pury (1994) forewarned in a prescient article published three decades earlier on the globalization of trade, that future organizations would increasingly face a persisting ultimatum to – innovate or die – in the context of a globalizing world economy.

Recent waves of global innovation have also been associated with global catalytic conditions, as captured in the US military acronym – VUCA – used in reference to a global operating context characterized by *Volatility, Uncertainty, Complexity and Ambiguity*. This is affirmed by McChrystal et al. (2015), who point out that leaders of organizations and teams increasingly find themselves continuously navigating through a global operating environment whose rules of engagement seem ever more unstable, undefined, convoluted, confusing and demanding of new problem-solving approaches.

To these four catalytic factors, we would add two additional catalysts for increasing levels of global innovation. The first of these factors, *Co-opetition*, concerns the undeniable observation that there is increased competition nowadays, coupled with the growing need to simultaneously collaborate with other industry players thus giving rise to prospects of innovation fuelled by inspiration, collaboration, rivalry or any combination thereof (Brandenberger & Nalebuff, 1996). The second factor is the need to satisfy an *Upswing-in-Demand*, referring to intensification of consumer expectations, choice, appetite and reach. The importance of this factor is supported by Christensen and Eyring (2011), who posit that rising levels of innovation are driven, in part, by the prospect of reaching new or disenfranchised consumer markets and leveraging greater economies of scale.

We sum up these combined incentives for innovation, in the acronym – CUVUCA – in reference to the prevailing global market conditions of *Co-opetition, Upswing-in-Demand, Volatility, Uncertainty, Complexity and Ambiguity*. Admittedly, this is inspired by the military term VUCA and the Kiswahili word *kuvuka* (to cross over to the other side). These six conditions, have in our estimation, intensified the push and pull to innovate globally. In our view, it follows that for any organization or leader, their capacity to fabricate innovative solutions at will, will be the single most defining differentiator between those organizations and leaders who will and won't navigate beyond this global crisis safely and successfully.

Barriers to Organizational and Individual Innovation

Despite the fact that today, most leaders recognize the imperative for innovation, not all organizations and leaders are actively engaged in innovation. We consider this to be due to several intrinsic and extrinsic impediments to innovation, as described below.

Intrinsic Obstacles to Innovation

In many cases, organizations and leaders need to overcome rigid intrinsic cultures and attitudes in their organizations which stifle and incapacitate innovation (Bessant & Tidd, 2007; Christensen, 1997).

Status Quo Bias

A common impediment to innovation within organizations is resistance to change – a bias towards the status quo. There is often a belief that past success rules out the need to innovate and, much less, do so continuously. Thus, rather than pursuing continuous and iterative learning-led innovation, previously successful organizations will opt to engage in one-off or arbitrary innovation. This hubristic posture gives rise to a climate of inertia that correlates past success with future prosperity.

Over time, collective lethargy, conformity and confirmation bias justify and further entrench the way things already get done. Eventually, self-congratulation and the prestige of temporary incumbency obfuscate any clear line of sight towards shifting operational and strategic dynamics (Cabinet Office, 2010; Christensen & Eyring, 2011); rendering such organizations and leaders oblivious to shifts within their internal and external environments that warrant innovation. It is at this perceived peak of accomplishment and celebration, when such organizations, societies and leaders stand to miss disruptive market innovations and new entrants with the potential to threaten the continued success of their organizations or societies (Christensen, 1997).

Regrettably, among such organizations and leaders, the pursuit of innovation is relegated as being the preserve of start-up and less successful organizations and societies; or simply a nice-to-have among more currently successful organizations and leaders (Christensen & Raynor, 2003).

Fear of Failure

For other organizations, societies and leaders, the perceived challenges, risks and repercussions of innovating pose a major barrier to innovation. Some organizations and leaders consider the prospect of failure and public shame in the pursuit of innovation as being too high a price to risk the endeavour. In response, scholars such as Christensen (1997, p. 159) have hastened to draw the distinction between the 'failure of an idea and the failure of a firm', in an attempt to diminish the shame of past or possible failure. On the contrary, they point out a positive correlation between successful innovation and perseverance in the face of failure, as it is likely those '...who leave room to try, fail, learn quickly, and try again, [who] can succeed at developing the understanding of customers, markets, and technology needed to commercialize disruptive innovations' (Christensen, 1997, pp. 209, 210).

Insecurity and Apathy

As we see it, perhaps the most significant threat to innovation in the 21st century, lies not in the factors mentioned thus far, but from an unwarranted sense of ineptness in the pursuit of innovation – a poverty of self-confidence in one's own ability to bring forth into the world that which is simultaneously new and relevant. Owing in large part to pervasive top-down, expertise-driven cultures in many organizations, sectors and societies, most have incorrectly come to believe that the responsibility of and capacity for innovation lies not with the ordinary employee or citizen, but rather with special cadres of subject-matter experts.

As a result, we witness in many organizations today, that the work of innovation is delegated away to designated R&D functions, strategy groups or design teams, if not out-sourced to supposedly more capable strategy consulting firms. This has the inevitable effect of conveying a resounding message to the rest of our organizations or societies, to leave innovating up to expert groups. De-responsibilized in matters of innovation, the majority of us in our organizations, societies or industries, hence find a convenient scape-goat for our lack of innovation.

As a result, the majority of us as non-experts view ourselves as lacking in either sufficient legitimacy, creativity, intelligence, know-how, training, resources, justifiable self-esteem or youthful dynamism to be effective innovators, compared to so-called subject-matter or innovation experts (Christensen, 1997). By virtue of their professional qualifications and/or experience, we often assume that this latter group has both higher prospects of and legitimacy to generate innovative solutions to address challenges or opportunities that arise. This paradigm suggests that innovation ought to emerge exclusively from those individuals, teams, organizations or societies possessing pre-deterministic traits of genius (as evidenced by a track-record of maverick achievements), expertise, high competence or a reliable propensity for good fortune. This entrenched bias regarding sources of innovation, is best captured today in our inordinate faith in the innovation quotients of individuals such as Elon Musk and Jeff Bezos and in organizations like Tesla, Amazon and Apple – our belief that innovation ought to descend from on high down to more modestly endowed organizations and societies.

As a result of such biases, indigenous creative potential in the Global South (countries seen as operating on the periphery, non-Western countries) is often internally overlooked, in favour of foreign experts or organizations who supposedly hold the keys to innovatively solving developmental challenges they have little personal exposure to. In the end, this results in a dichotomy between

Innovation's Global North (also known as the West) from whence innovations originate, and Innovation's Global South, comprising not of innovators, but innovation end-users and innovation 'emulators' (Christensen & Eyring, 2011).

Extrinsic Obstacles to Innovation

Aside from the intrinsic obstacles, organizations, societies and leaders also face external inhibitors to innovation. We shall not dwell much on these since this chapter is mostly about overcoming the intrinsic obstacles. Extrinsic obstacles include extraneous conditions such as over-regulation, resulting in *regulatory drag*. Also, stark asymmetries between organizations and societies in information and factors of production, result in differential levels of know-how and wherewithal for, particularly for high-end or costly innovation.

For instance, limited access to essential technologies like the Internet in certain societies, presents an external impediment to the pursuit of innovation among small or remotely situated enterprises (Christensen & Eyring, 2011).

What Bessant and Tidd (2007, p. 111) term as 'responsible innovation', the need to balance human technological advancement with environmental concerns has also placed a necessary inhibition on the development and use of innovations that might yield long-term adverse impacts on our environment.

Lowering the Barriers to Innovation

General Approaches to Spurring Innovation

Contemporary scholars have sought to respond to this rising interest in and appetite for innovation by amplifying research on ways of spurring and stimulating innovation. Progressively, this quest to demystify the innovation process has led scholars such as Christensen and Raynor (2003) to conclude that, on the basis of the resultant academic research, the black box of innovation has, by and large, been unlocked and its mechanisms made apparent to organizations and individuals.

Summarizing key approaches to spurring innovation, a first among these approaches would be the innovation as a result of brainstorming. Based on a publication by the Harvard Business School (2009, pp. 41–46), brainstorming is a key component of the innovation process, more so when involving open informal engagement, crowd-sourced ideation, Socratic dialogue, group anonymization, systematic identification and elimination of technical contradictions, or snowballing off of existing solutions. Also cited as key ingredients of the innovation process and specifically, idea-generation, is the exploitation of new or under-exploited knowledge, customer ideas, learnings from lead users, ethnographic insights, research and development lab findings and open innovation (Harvard Business School, 2009).

Innovation scholars like Bessant and Tidd (2007), posit that organizations and individuals stand to improve their capacity to think and act creatively by, among other things, striving to: think differently; strengthen their analytical skills; enhance their internal expertise; foster collaboration and interdisciplinarity; and integrate opposing ideas through cross-pollinating concepts across different domains of knowledge and practice.

Consequently, scholars are increasingly converged around the idea of innovative and creative aptitudes as being 'less about one's personal or organizational "wiring" than about one's willingness and ability to execute a goal-oriented systematic process for the development and expression of novel ideas aimed at solving problems or satisfying needs' (Harvard Business School, 2009, p. 167).

Among other documented approaches to spurring innovation, particularly within organizational teams, are intensifying reward-based incentives; permitting greater staff autonomy; promoting lofty goal-setting; enabling informal communication structures; and leveraging senior executive support. Echoing this stance, Christensen and Eyring (2011) present a related notion of the innovation process, as being a methodical approach combining aspects of incentivization, specialization, hybridization, collaboration and the modification of metrics and indicators, towards the development of a desired outcome-driving solution.

Better but Still Limited: Spurring Innovation Through Design Thinking

Design Thinking offers a general theory of the innovation process; one that represents a more integrated and systematic approach to creative problem-solving than many previous conceptions. Methodologically, it is also one that seeks to make both replicable and predictable, the process of generating novel solutions in response to challenges, needs and/or opportunities. Innovation from a Design Thinking approach fundamentally involves an iterative process consisting of 5 key steps (Figure 5.1):

According to Dam and Siang (2018), innovation through Design Thinking requires that the prospective innovator first *gain a deep understanding of the seriousness and scale* of the problem or innovation opportunity at hand through *empathic data collection.* This can involve consulting in depth with targeted beneficiaries of the desired innovation, as well as technical experts on the identified challenge or opportunity. This enables the potential innovator to move to the second rung of the Design Thinking process, of stepping into the shoes of the target population and generating a *clearer, more structured definition of the problem to be solved, need to be met or opportunity to be seized.* This second step would culminate in the development of a *human-centred problem statement,* framed in respect of the interests of target beneficiaries and not prospective innovators, as the latter often tend to be personally detached from the lived experiences and realities of the situation for which the innovation is sought.

Design Thinking's third stage involves *ideation,* defined as an *attempt to contrive novel, out-of-the-box ideas in relation to the problem, need or opportunity*; and based on a robust understanding of the circumstances prompting innovation, distilled, as we indicated, into a human-centred problem statement. At this stage, the budding

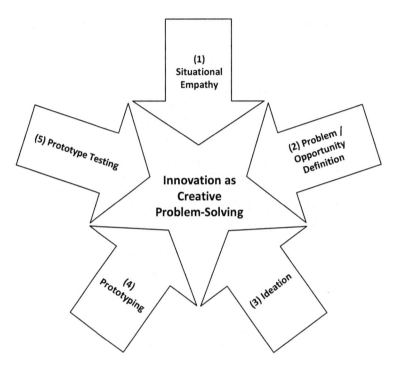

FIGURE 5.1 Graphical representation of Design Thinking methodology.

innovator attempts to view the problem or opportunity from multiple perspectives and deploys a variety of conventional ideation techniques such as structured and informal brainstorming; systematic identification and elimination of technical contradictions; idea crowd-sourcing; Socratic dialogue; and snow-balling, in pursuit of an innovative solution. The purpose of this phase is to generate as wide an array of solutions as possible, before gradually narrowing down to the best possible solutions to address the identified problem, opportunity or situation.

The fourth and penultimate step of this process involves *solution prototyping*. Having conceptualized and narrowed one's solution-set to few potentially viable innovations, the prospective innovator fabricates his or her conceptualized solution into an early-stage product or service aimed at addressing the problem or opportunity. Finally, the prototype solution is *tested for efficacy, efficiency, precision, safety, utility and user-friendliness*, among other things. As an iterative innovation process, test outcomes would dictate the need to further attempt to refine the proposed innovative solution at any of the stages set our earlier in the Design Thinking process.

Design Thinking has its limitations. First and foremost is its insistence that Design Thinkers be led in their innovation efforts by empathy for target beneficiaries. This pre-requisite for altruism ignores that people also have self-interested leanings. This precondition also limits the innovative capacity of those less inclined to engage empathetically with a situation. On the contrary, by not better leveraging innate self-interest, Design Thinking misses a huge opportunity to further incentivize innovation as being an avenue of personal accomplishment or fulfilment, as much as one of altruism.

Relatedly, in underscoring the need for empathy towards target beneficiaries, Design Thinking tacitly assumes that prospective innovators are usually outsiders to the situation in need of intervention – and that the innovator is a foreigner and not indigenous to the challenges or opportunities – and hence needs to collect data from persons more local to the situation, in order to adequately comprehend the problem or opportunity at an intellectual and emotional level. This implicit bias towards 'foreign' innovation, overlooks home-grown and indigenous problem-solving potential. Worse still, it threatens to perpetuate the perception and existence of asymmetries in innovative quotient between populations, for instance, between the Global North who may represent beneficent innovators and the Global South, perceived as non-agentic beneficiaries of innovation; or between the poor inner city communities and elite benefactors in those countries.

Third and most evidently, Design Thinking does not adequately guide its users on how to generate novel ideas. It gives useful tips like re-examining assumptions, but doesn't go deep enough or clearly enough to help the average user understand how to think outside the box.

Finally, baked into Design Thinking's testing requirement is a limiting condition to immediately appreciate and adequately demonstrate the utility of one's nascent innovation. We think this ignores the fact that numerous innovations including the Internet and medical products like Sildenafil, have tended to be developed often decades before grasping the full potential or optimal application of such innovations. Rather, through this utility precondition, we run a new inherent risk of restricting innovation. A more beneficial approach might be to distinguish innovation design efforts from utility optimization efforts.

In view of the above, we seek to introduce an alternative schema for innovation, which we consider to have most of the benefits of Design Thinking, while largely overcoming its afore-stated limitations.

Limitless Innovation: An Introduction to The Innovation Algorithm

We would now like to give you a brief history of *The Innovation Algorithm* before we walk you through its five-step approach. Developed in 2015 by Dr. Vincent Ogutu, then a management doctoral candidate at Rutgers University, *The Innovation Algorithm* offers a new approach to creative problem-solving; one which facilitates both creativity and problem-solving in equal measure; embraces simple, effective steps for novel ideation; and fosters a climate of limitless innovation in removing prerequisites of the prospective innovator, whether of empathy, prior knowledge or expertise.

We consider *The Innovation Algorithm* to be a stepwise innovation formula designed to unlock and boost the innovative capabilities of individuals and organizations alike, irrespective of subject-matter expertise. The Innovation Algorithm draws on *cognitive* techniques to simplify the innovator's path towards developing new solutions, while *affectively*, maximizing his or her motivation towards innovating, by assuaging negative affects which so often stifle one's capacity or confidence to innovate.

At a cognitive level, *The Innovation Algorithm* enables the prospective innovator to identify the cognitive limitations that give rise to *problem-solving path dependence*, while offering practical ways to literally think outside-of-the-box – *generate new paths or streams of ideation and action.* Centrally, The Innovation Algorithm empowers innovation by *unbundling the simplicity of the innovation process*; rendering it accessible to people who are not subject-matter experts.

A Brief History of The Innovation Algorithm

While studying entrepreneurs, a key type of innovator, on his doctoral research programme in New York, Dr. Ogutu accepted an invitation to participate in a 'Solve for X' competition organized by Google Development Group North Jersey, which was soliciting radical solutions to complex problems. Selected as one of seven finalists to present his moon-shot idea at the Google offices in New York, his innovative idea on simulating teleportation was well received. As a non-engineer and lacking formal training in technology, Dr. Vincent Ogutu was as surprised as anyone else that virtually overnight, he had suddenly become a tech-innovator, as assessed by some of the leading technologists in the world.

What followed next was a case of further discovery through action research. Seeking to understand how he had come to innovate, Dr. Ogutu began a process of reflexively examining the individual mental steps he had followed and the emotions he had experienced leading up to the moment on that day, when he got his moonshot idea. When he had submitted the broad concept, he was told it was impossible – unless he could resolve two major constraints that were pointed out to him. He was also told on the same day that Google were excited about his idea and were wondering how he would overcome the constraints. It was this latter piece of news that enthused him enough to find the answer in five minutes – something he would have considered himself incapable of doing. Realizing that two major acts of innovation on the same day were unlikely to be randomly occur, Dr. Ogutu set out to understand the thought and affective processes that must had led to his innovations, and this led to his discovery of *The Innovation Algorithm.*

The next step Dr. Ogutu followed was to test whether the algorithm was just a case of him fitting his own data onto his explanation, or whether it was actually generalizable. He then proceeded to test it in different settings and fields to see if it would work if other people applied it. He began with an inner-city school in New York and was pleased when both classes he taught came up with patentable innovations. He has since tested it with audiences in three continents. It has been applied and appreciated by students and leading-edge professionals alike, by mental health clinicians as much as by musicians and realtors, in different continents. In 2016, Dr. Ogutu presented *The Innovation Algorithm* before a Professional Development Workshop on Creativity at the Academy of Management in Anaheim, California. Later, following a presentation of The Innovation Algorithm to a group of Ugandan executives, an economist, Japheth Kawanguzi was inspired by the algorithm to establish Uganda's Innovation Village. Subsequently, students from Strathmore University in Kenya, successfully drew on their understanding of *The Innovation Algorithm* to develop a clean energy solution, the *Kijiji Project;* winning first prize in the 2019 *Initiate! Impact Challenge*, a clean energy access for Africa competition in Cape Town, South Africa. They then went on to win Bronze in a global competition held in the UK, the *Efficiency for Access Design Challenge, 2020*. Dr. Ogutu has since taught *The Innovation Algorithm* to MBAs in Germany and Uruguay and to other audiences in Kenya, Uganda and the US.

Understanding The Innovation Algorithm

The Innovation Algorithm offers us a simple articulation of the mechanics of innovating. It is an explanation of the sequence of thoughts and feelings that enable an individual or organization to think and act innovatively. It can be broken down into five steps:

Step 1: Innovators Must Forge Deep Emotional Connections with the Problems/Opportunities

The Innovation Algorithm requires as its first step, that a prospective innovator build a *deeply personal emotional connection* with the problem or opportunity at hand. Distinctively, this catalytic affective component of The Innovation Algorithm extends far beyond the notion of empathy found in Design Thinking. Empathy within the context of The Innovation Algorithm applies in a more intimate way by asking not only how resolving the situation would make our target beneficiaries feel, but instead redirecting the question as to how the innovator himself/herself would feel if he/she succeeded in delivering the solution to the target beneficiaries.

The salience of this deeper personal emotional connection to the context cannot be overstated. Copious evidence points to felt emotions as being sources of arousal, capable of stimulating sensemaking, possibly leading to the reframing of issues and circumstances in ways that result in new conceptions of one's agency in his or her environment (Maitlis & Sonenshein, 2010; Sonenshein, 2009). Maitlis and Sonenshein (2010) postulate that 'negative emotions may trigger a sense that change is necessary' (pp. 567, 570), as can positive emotions which act as sense-giving resources, broadening the attention and repertoire of responsive actions among persons within an organization. Similarly, Fredrickson and Joiner (2002, p. 172) point to the tendency of positive emotions to enable 'flexible and creative thinking', expanding the range of action alternatives one perceives and is likely to take; further citing the role of joy in generating an impulse for exploration.

Under the schema of The Innovation Algorithm, it is not simply the need to merely establish an emotional connection to an intervention situation which is crucial, but the need to ensure a *profound* emotional connection to the situation. Studies point to the crucial role of emotional intensity in guiding one's choice-perception and behavioural decision-making in problem-solving and opportunity-seeking situations (Wikström et al., 2012). It is assumed that a strong emotional connection to a desired end state increases one's eagerness, attentiveness, ingenuity and forbearance towards working through challenges or opportunities standing in the way of the desired state; as is the general conception of passion projects and personal vocations. It is this kind of innovator who is best poised to deploy his or her best energies to find new solutions to challenges or opportunities that might otherwise appear insoluble. The saying "necessity is the mother of invention" speaks to this very concept – that one is more likely to innovate if one deeply feels the need to do so.

Step 2: Innovators Must Deconstruct and Express Their Problems/ Opportunities in the Simplest Yet Most Accurate Terms Possible

A major impediment to the generation of solutions to situations is the extent to which the innovator in question truly understands the challenge or opportunity. Innovators will often find themselves limited by their knowledge of the problem or opportunity at hand; and it can often be intimidating to wade through the seas of jargon that surround certain opportunities and challenges. Successful innovators overcome this complexity hurdle by intentionally attempting to arrive at the true essence of the problem or opportunity that they seek to address.

Take cancer treatment for example. The World Health Organization describes it as caused when abnormal cells grow uncontrollably in a multi-stage process, going beyond their usual boundaries to invade adjoining parts of the body and/ or spread to other organs, progressing from a pre-cancerous lesion to a malignant tumour. Users of *The Innovation Algorithm* would necessarily look past this jargon and convolution towards a more basic expression of cancer – *that even a 7-year-old could accurately grasp and formulate new ideas about*. This however stands as paradoxical for most adults, who naturally try to formulate accurate logical and grammatically correct definitions when asked to define concepts.

Children on the other hand, typically respond with simple descriptions, at the end of which their listeners often have a clear sense of the situation they face. Box 5.1 shows you Step 1 in action by providing a typical description the authors of this article have used in the past to give a simple explanation of what cancer is.

Box 5.1 *Bradley (a 7-year old): Uncle Vince, What's Cancer?*

Uncle Vince: It's a very bad illness. Here, I'll explain how it works. You know your body is so clever, it knows how to repair itself whenever it gets broken (see how you grew a brand new skin after you fell and cut yourself last week?). It also knows exactly how it should grow. You were shorter last year, but this year you've grown taller. And guess what, your little finger is still shorter than your middle finger. It's because your body knows which part needs to grow slower and which part should grow quicker. However, once in a while, a part of your body may get confused and start growing much faster than it should, and that's what we call cancer. If that happens in the wrong part of your body, like next to your heart or in your head, you could die. Normally if an insect bites you or if you eat something poisonous, your body will usually know an enemy has entered it, and it will fight it. But if a part of you gets confused and starts growing too fast, your body will not fight it because it thinks that is part of it growing. It won't see it as an enemy the way it did with the insect bite and the poison. That's why cancer is so dangerous, because your body thinks the part that is growing too fast is part of it, and so it doesn't fight it.

Most adults we presented with this explanation complained that it was too long-winded compared to a concise more adult-type definition. They agreed, however, that it would be simple enough to help a child get a good grasp of what cancer is – good enough in fact to allow them to distinguish it from other ailments they might already know. They also agreed that it was not a case of an adult using fairy-tale language and analogies to try and 'dumb down' a complex concept to a child's level – and that it was instead an honest attempt to actually describe a complex concept in simple, accessible terms, without sacrificing any of the accuracy needed to give the listener a competent grasp of the concept.

By making its users go through an extended exercise of expressing problems or opportunities in the simplest yet most accurate terms possible, *The Innovation Algorithm* accomplishes several useful gains. At a cognitive level, it helps the prospective innovator identify the smallest unit of analysis and/or lowest common factor to be considered in addressing the situation, thus reducing the intellectual hurdles an innovator might face when analyzing a multifaceted situation. Effectively, this step alleviates the sense of intimidation with which an innovator might otherwise approach a problem they already consider to be 'wicked'. As a consequence, the innovator's sense of self-confidence is intensified as they begin to see the problem/opportunity at hand as a situation simple enough for them to grasp and possibly even address. Thus, *The Innovation Algorithm* seeks to build in the innovator not just a desire but an *expectation* to intervene capably in a situation, thereby fostering what we are calling, *innovation confidence* – being a minimum threshold of confidence required to deliberately apply new thinking to address a problem or opportunity.

Step 3: Innovators Must Identify Pathways of Innovation by First Categorizing and Expressing All Existing Efforts at Addressing the Situation, in the Simplest Yet Most Accurate Terms Possible

The next step towards deploying *The Innovation Algorithm* consists of creating a clear visual map of solutions that are already in existence. Here, the innovator should seek to research and comprehensively identify the efforts to resolve the situation that have already been attempted and to understand them in their simplest expression.

Having achieved a simplified understanding of these efforts, the innovator would cluster similar ones (solution efforts that follow a similar approach) into a common pathway. By the conclusion of this step, the innovator should be able to visualize the universe of distinct clusters or pathways deployed in attempts to address the challenge or opportunity. As a result of this step, the innovator develops a clear and robust yet simplified cognitive map of what general approaches have been applied without success to the resolution of the situation; and more importantly, a sense of what general approaches have never been attempted. This is precisely the level of clarity that we think is needed as a prelude to the radical creative thinking that follows in subsequent steps of innovating.

Box 5.2 What follows (see Box 5.2) is an illustration of this process of identifying, deconstructing and clustering the existing solution-set.

Reverting to the cancer example, one might list some of the existing solutions (interventions) as including open surgery, chemotherapy, laparoscopy, amputation, radiotherapy and use of laser treatment. However, upon simplifying and clustering these approaches, one might categorize them – using 7-year-old terms – into two pathways, aimed at either 'removing' or 'killing' the cancer. Those that seek to remove cancerous tumours include (aggressive amputation, or open surgery in the targeted area, or the less invasive laparoscopy technique). Those that attempt to kill the cancer cells do so by using different types of "weapons", by poisoning the cancer cells (chemotherapy), pounding on them (radiotherapy) or burning them (laser treatment). It is essential to suppress the understandable adult urge to reject this "simplistic or childish attempt to express in simple terms what are really very complex concepts" and to complete the exercise. Only then will the efficacy of this way of thinking be fully experienced. Just remember, there must be a reason kids are the most creative people around.

Step 4: Innovators Should Focus on Generating New Solution Pathways

In this step of executing The Innovation Algorithm, the innovator seeks to generate new ideas – solution pathways – based on their cognitive map of the solution universe broken down and expressed as simply as possible. While this is an ideation exercise, it is distinct from most brainstorming exercises in which the innovator's goal is to develop final or ultimate solutions. In contrast, in this penultimate stage of deploying *The Innovation Algorithm*, the innovator focusses on identifying a new *generic pathway, not a final solution*, to address the challenge or opportunity. Cognitively, this presents a much smaller hurdle for the innovator than envisioning an actual final solution, which may be considerably technical in nature.

Turning back to the example of cancer treatment (see Box 5.3), this would be akin to moving beyond *removal* or *killing* the condition, to something equally simple and generic that any non-expert and child could conceive, such as *surrounding or ring-fencing* cancer cells; *high-jacking or reprogramming* the cancer cells to disrupt their multiplication; or *slowing down* the growth of the cancer cells or indeed *starving* them of nourishment.

Crucially, *The Innovation Algorithm* embraces a new locus of innovation in changing the focus of innovation from generating new end-solutions to identifying novel paths and mechanisms towards desired goals. The true novelty in

---

Box 5.3 *Example of cancer treatment*

In some training simulations Dr. Oqutu had with non-medics, including young middle-schoolers, on solving the cancer problem, participants were able to generate approaches or pathways that had only recently been discovered in Oncology. For instance, some participants suggested finding a way to "tell the cells what to do so that they're no longer confused". At this point, we invariably congratulated them for essentially, in just a few minutes of applying The Innovation Algorithm to solving cancer, having conceived a pathway that was first attempted barely a handful of years ago by seasoned medical researchers.

While the technology to attempt to programme cells already existed when the human genome was decoded more than two decades ago, this re-programming approach had not been considered then. Instead, scientists had been focussed on getting better and better solutions along the existing pathways, such as chemotherapy, for instance. A crucial insight and question here is, what might have been the outcome had those earlier scientists taken a step back and focussed on creating novel pathways for cancer treatment? It is likely that their journey along the pathway of cell-hijacking would have reached a much more advanced stage sooner rather than later, with possible implications on lives saved, prolonged or improved.

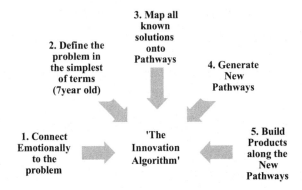

FIGURE 5.2 The Innovation Algorithm, graphically represented.

The Innovation Algorithm lies in prioritizing this path-centric focus over a solution-centric focus to innovation – the belief that novelty exists at the level of the pathway not just the product. By pointing out where path dependence is likely to occur (mapping of existing pathways), *The Innovation Algorithm* enables out-of-the-box thinking to occur by precisely identifying and labelling the "boxes" (the existing pathways) and providing instructions to extend beyond those particular boxes to create and explore new ones. Further, it is noteworthy that whereas focussing on the development of solutions is often enticing, the development of end-products will tend to automatically exclude less technical contributors or non-subject-matter experts, from making deliberate and meaningful contributions to innovation. The evaluation and creation of simple conceptual pathways of innovation is, however, a more reasonable threshold enabling participation of experts and non-experts alike (Figure 5.2).

Step 5: Innovators Should Build End-Products or Services Along the Newly Identified or Expanded Solution Pathways

The final stage in applying *The Innovation Algorithm* involves drawing on the newly identified pathways to design trial solutions to address the challenge or opportunity in focus. By this stage, the lion's share of the innovation process has been completed and the innovator may either elect to personally develop the end-solution based on the newly identified pathway(s) if they have sufficient expertise, or opt to hire domain-specific experts to build end-solutions to operationalize the new or expanded pathway.

This final step of deploying *The Innovation Algorithm* could therefore be as simple as approaching experts, presenting to them the new pathways generated in stage 4 and then hiring them to operationalize the ones for which adequate technology already exists to build those solutions. It follows that a significant benefit of *The Innovation Algorithm* is that it acts as a great equalizer in the arena of innovation – equipping laypersons and subject-matter experts alike with the capacity to make meaningful contributions towards advances in addressing the challenges and opportunities we face as individuals or organizations. Indeed, for experts, The Innovation Algorithm overcomes what has often prevented experts from arriving at radically new pathways – their *path-dependence* – resulting from biases towards professional risk aversion and gradualism. These five steps to using *The Innovation Algorithm* hold the key to unlocking and fundamentally raising the capacity to innovate among organizations and decision-makers today.

People often ask us if we have any success stories yet. Even though the algorithm is still relatively new and we have not gone to any great lengths to popularize it, we are encouraged by the results we have seen so far. On the very first attempt by the first author to teach it in an inner-city school in New York, a high school class set out to solve the social problem occurring at the time whereby people of colour who were later proved innocent and unarmed were shot by the police in regrettable incidents. They came up with the concept of a "smart gun" that would shoot not bullets but tranquilizer darts, and which would use its camera to determine the best exposed body part to target and then accurately guide the dart to its target. The user needed no longer be a marksman and just had to point and shoot (to disable, never to kill). A more recent example was the innovation that a team of Strathmore University engineers came up with to win an affordable energy competition in South Africa. They then went on to win an award in a global competition as well. They simplified the energy or power problem to one of literally "bringing power to people". Inspired by Uber's model of summoning or hailing a cab through an app, they came up with the concept of "uberization of power". A person in a remote village in Africa would just "summon" a battery pack through an app or a phone call, and it would be delivered by a cyclist from a central location where all batteries would be charged using solar panels on the roof and walls of a discarded transport container. The cyclist would then pick up the used battery and take it back to the container to be recharged. Their solution was favoured by the judges because of its great simplicity, utility, practicability and affordability.

Conclusion: Democratizing Innovation

Faced with existential comorbidities, diminishing resources, heightening competition, globalized demand and increasingly frequent black swan events, companies, societies and entire nations need to innovate or risk collapsing into oblivion. This truth rings truer today than when de Pury (1994) sounded this caution nearly three decades ago. Ever more apparent is the fact that we live now in an age of co-opetition, upswing-of-demand, volatility, uncertainty, complexity and ambiguity – CUVUCA. The emergence and persistence of an unprecedented global health pandemic in Covid-19, has only intensified the challenges and opportunities in the global theatre of action. Innovation has replaced physical fitness as the rule for survival. Innovation has usurped our corporate strategies, become our institutional culture, embedded itself in our daily operations. And those who are thriving are those who have accepted that it is innovation, differentiation and disruption and no longer standardization, benchmarking and homogeneity which are the touchstones of this 21st century. Whether by choice or compulsion, all of us now sit at the table of innovation.

Yet many organizations and individuals have yet to embrace this paradigm shift in its fullness. Regarding this sweeping tide of global innovation, many have resigned themselves to change resistance, apathy, insecurity and the fear of failure or experimentation (Heidenreich & Speith, 2013). Others simply lack the know-how, confidence or opportunity to initiate change through innovation (Koellinger, 2008). Still others we surmise, disinclined to the idea of innovation, delegate away any personal obligations to drive towards or attempt innovation. Yet it is in these times that we posit that no organization, team or individual can afford to overlook their capacity to innovate, or safely exist as mere end-users of imported innovations.

In the wake of mounting demand for innovation globally, we firmly submit that the enterprise of innovation must be decentralized across diverse fields and geographies. It is unsustainable to continue to expect innovations from Silicon Valley and San Francisco but not Siberia or Sierra Leone; from software engineers but not from sculptors. No single geography or professional domain should exercise full or partial hegemony over addressing the world's challenges and opportunities.

Through *The Innovation Algorithm*, we have unveiled in this book chapter a means of democratizing innovation. Levelling the playing field of innovation, we seek to equip those right at the coalface of opportunity or challenge with the know-how and confidence to innovate. We have done so recognizing that, only two things are guaranteed going into the foreseeable future: the fact that the world will likely continue in similar flux; and the fact that the value of any single organization or individual is likely to rise in tandem with their capacity to innovate. From a future research perspective, we will continue teaching the algorithm and then documenting actual cases of its application in order to both provide evidence that it works, and also in order to get a deeper understanding of what makes it work. We hope to collaborate with innovators from different sectors like healthcare, engineering and music to see if it works in the same way across domains. We hope that by providing more evidence of its success in terms of numbers and across multiple domains, we will convince more people of its utility. Most of all, having equipped young and old, non-experts and experts alike through *The Innovation Algorithm*, we hope we will have settled the debate on whether innovative leaders are born or made in favour of the latter, of course.

Acknowledgement

We would like to thank Todd Nakamura, Founder of the Google Development Group North Jersey for insisting on the fact that anyone can innovate if they have a huge problem that they care about, and for challenging the principal author to create his first moonshot and present it at Google in New York. This is what unlocked the subsequent discovery of *The Innovation Algorithm*. We also acknowledge the help we got from all the people who tried out our new approach in three continents and confirmed us in our belief that it really works.

References

Bessant, J., & Tidd, J. (2007). *Innovation and entrepreneurship*. New Jersey: John Wiley & Sons.

Brandenburger, A. M., & Nalebuff, B. J. (1996). *Co-opetition*. New York: Bantam Doubleday Dell Publishing Group.

Caballero-Morales, S. O. (2021). Innovation as recovery strategy for SMEs in emerging economies during the COVID-19 pandemic. *Research in International Business and Finance, 57*, 101396.

Cabinet Office. (2010). *Mindspace: Influencing behaviour through public policy*. London: Institute for Government.

Christensen, C. M. (1997). *The innovator's dilemma: When new technologies cause great firms to fail*. Boston, MA: Harvard Business School Press. 179 p. *Technology Assessment*.

Christensen, C. M., & Eyring, H. J. (2011). *The innovative university: Changing the DNA of higher education from the inside out*. New Jersey: John Wiley & Sons.

Christensen, C. M., & Raynor, M. E. (2003). *The innovator's solution: Creating and sustaining successful growth*. Boston, MA: Harvard Business School.

Dam, R., & Siang, T. (2018). What is design thinking and why is it so popular? *Interaction Design Foundation, 1*, 1–6.

de Pury, D. (1994). 'Innovate or die' is the first rule of international industrial competition. *Research Technology Management, 37*(5), 9–11.

El Baz, J., & Ruel, S. (2021). Can supply chain risk management practices mitigate the disruption impacts on supply chains' resilience and robustness? Evidence from an empirical survey in a COVID-19 outbreak era. *International Journal of Production Economics, 233*, 107972.

Fredrickson, B. L., & Joiner, T. (2002). Positive emotions trigger upward spirals towards emotional wellbeing. *Psychological Science, 13*(2), 172–175.

Harvard Business School. (2009). *The innovator's Toolkit: 10 practical strategies to help you develop and implement innovation*. Harvard: Harvard Business Press.

Heidenreich, S., & Spieth, P. (2013). Why innovations fail—The case of passive and active innovation resistance. *International Journal of Innovation Management, 17*(05), 1350021.

Koellinger, P. (2008). Why are some entrepreneurs more innovative than others? *Small Business Economics, 31*(1), 21.

Maitlis, S., & Sonenshein, S. (2010). Sensemaking in crisis and change: inspiration and insights from Weick (1988). *Journal of Management Studies, 47*(3), 551–580.

McChrystal, G. S., Collins, T., Silverman, D., & Fussell, C. (2015). *Team of teams: New rules of engagement for a complex world*. London: Penguin.

Ndwandwe, D., & Wiysonge, C. S. (2021). COVID-19 vaccines. *Current Opinion in Immunology, 71*, 111–116.

Sonenshein, S. (2009). Emergence of ethical issues during strategic change implementation. *Organization Science, 20*(1), 223–239.

Strathmore News. https://www.strathmore.edu/news/strathmore-team-wins-bronze-at-efficiency-for-access-design-challenge/

WHO. Definition of cancer. https://www.who.int/health-topics/cancer#tab=tab_1

Wikström, P. -O. H., Oberwittler, D., Trieber, K., & Hardie, B. (2012). *Breaking rules: The social and situational dynamics of young people's urban crime*. Oxford: Oxford University Press.

PART 3

What innovation leaders are doing

The third part, 'What innovation leaders are doing', observes specific management approaches, tools, and market engagement approaches to embed innovation. Through this part…

Healthcare topic is of utmost importance given the changing scenario worldwide. Thus, Dadich in 'Brilliant positive deviance: Innovation beyond disconnected and disciplined domains' argues on the importance of innovation sourced from internal instances of positive deviance. By looking from a healthcare case, this chapter investigates internally conceived, undisciplined innovation – specifically, positive deviance. Future research can examine the relationship between positive deviance and innovation – conceptually, theoretically, methodologically, and empirically.

Joshi looks at this innovation management from manager's perspective in 'How managers shape innovation culture: Role of talent, routines, and incentives'. The chapter explores the drivers of organisational change and identifies three key levers: routines, incentives, and talent. It identifies how middle management enables the right routines and incentive structures to hire and motivate the talent to bring about organisational transformation.

In 'Management tools for business model innovation – a review' Munir et al. presents a literature review to identify and classify proposed business model innovation tools. Managers can apply Business Model Innovation (BMI) tools to change their business model in three types of situations; changes due to digitalisation, to develop and sharpen the company's competitive advantages, and when developing new businesses.

Thongpravati in 'Origins of innovation: Market-driving innovation vs market-driven innovation' investigates different innovation. By looking into multiple studies from associated to new product development (NPD),

DOI: 10.4324/9780429346033-8

product innovativeness and management in relation to the 'market-driving' and 'market-driven' paradigm, this study unfolds the origins of innovation.

As a concluding chapter for this part, 'Leading and managing areas of innovation: The multi-stakeholder perspective', Nikina-Ruohonen looks at innovation challenges from multi-stakeholder perspective. This chapter looks at areas of innovation from both practice-oriented and management-centred approach and to assist in productive management practices.

6

BRILLIANT POSITIVE DEVIANCE

Innovation beyond disconnected and disciplined domains

Ann Dadich

Introduction

Innovation is often understood to be a product, process, position, or paradigm that is externally conceived – directly or indirectly – and tweaked for a prevailing organisational context (Kickbusch, Krech, Franz, & Wells, 2018). Direct examples include the introduction of lean thinking and balanced scorecards from firms that manufacture vehicles or electronics into health and mental health services (Robinson et al., 2014). Indirect examples include research and development (R&D) activities within an organisation to pursue innovation (Bauer & Schimpf, 2018). Yet R&D activities embed plans, protocols, and processes into a prevailing configuration, 'privileg[ing] existing businesses over new products' (Dougherty & Hardy, 1996, p. 1196). This can 'put... discipline into a process that [might otherwise be]... ad hoc' (Cooper, 1990, p. 53).

These direct and indirect examples suggest there is little to learn from what serendipitously occurs within an organisation, in a perhaps unmanaged or undisciplined way. Instead, the organisation requires innovation that is sourced from disconnected and disciplined domains – be it a different sector, another organisation (potentially within the same sector), or specialised R&D activities within the organisation. Consider, for instance, research about high-tech industries that suggests the value of R&D intensity, particularly during recession periods – conversely, low-tech industries are said to benefit from opening their innovation processes (Zouaghi, Sánchez, & Martínez, 2018). Similarly, in their research involving innovation managers, Jones, Cope, and Kintz (2016, p. 50) concluded:

> [They] find themselves needing not only to more effectively manage improved processes and efficiencies in internally focused R&D efforts

DOI: 10.4324/9780429346033-9

but also to learn effective approaches to monitor, tap into, and integrate innovative technologies from an increasingly diverse set of external sources.

Although fresh ways of working, sourced from these (and potentially other) disconnected and disciplined domains might seem exotic, appealing, and well-informed, they suggest there is little to learn from serendipitous or undisciplined internal moments. It can convey to those within and beyond an organisation that innovation needs to be sourced from elsewhere, even if from within the organisation, and in an organised, if not a controlled way.

The aforesaid message can be problematic for (at least) three key reasons. First, it can denigrate the nous and creativity of those who are intimately familiar with how an organisation operates and functions. Second, it can stymie the likelihood that personnel will recognise and share their different ways of working. And third, primary (if not sole) reliance on innovation from disconnected and disciplined domains can be costly (Godin & Vinck, 2017). Consider: the cost of purchasing intellectual property; the cost of adapting it; and the cost of securing and sustaining colleague buy-in. Beyond these are the costs identified by Biggi and Giuliani (2020), which include: 'the negative consequences of open innovation as a powerful search strategy, encompassing the generation, capture and employment of new knowledge at firm-level' (pp. 8–10). This dark side is relevant to this chapter. The authors reported, 'a high level of openness to external knowledge could harm the production of new knowledge and, subsequently, firms' performance' (p. 11) – this was partly because such openness can risk imitation.

This is not to suggest that reliance on internal knowledge is necessarily better. Privileging institutional logics can hamper innovation (Kooijman, Hekkert, van Meer, Moors, & Schellekens, 2017). This was indicated by Dougherty and Hardy (1996) who found: 'large, mature organizations could not achieve sustained innovation because innovators within them could not solve innovation-to-organization problems' (p. 1146). This finding underscores the limits of a myopic understanding of innovation, whereby attempts are made to fit a square peg into a round hole (Wilf, 2019). It also intimates that 'there is no one true path to innovation' (Satell, 2017, p. 41).

To redress this seeming preoccupation with disconnected and disciplined domains, this chapter considers the potential of internally conceived, undisciplined innovation – specifically, positive deviance (DeGraff & Roberts, 2012). Furthermore, given that the future of work is human (Deloitte, 2019), this chapter is situated in healthcare.

The value of this chapter is threefold. First, it recognises that innovation can come from those serendipitous or undisciplined experiences within an organisation – those moments that brought joy, generated delight, and exceeded expectation; that is, moments that were brilliant, as deemed by those who were involved, directly or indirectly. Second, the chapter recognises that all that glitters might not be gold, as innovation often requires adaptation and refinement (Mattsson, Helmersson, & Stetler, 2016; Rehn, 2019). And sometimes this adaptation and refinement represent a sunk cost. Third, harnessing the internal expertise and prowess that manifests during unbridled, joyful moments can serve to build capability (Barker Caza & Milton, 2012). Recognising, supporting, and promoting what people are doing well, if not brilliantly, can ignite an upward spiral within organisations (Fredrickson, 2003). Just as negativity begets negativity, positivity begets positivity.

This last contribution is important given that many have largely espoused discipline – a principled approach that is purposeful and focussed (Drucker, 2002; Keeley, Walters, Pikkel, & Quinn, 2013; Waitzkin, 2007). This is not to diminish the value of discipline; but rather, to argue the complementary value of indiscipline to afford a collective opportunity to learn from positive deviants – those who enact 'strategies to solve a problem from within the same community experiencing the problem' (O'Hara et al., 2018, p. 276), offering 'alternatives that are "invisible in plain sight"' (Martínez, 2019, p. 54). And by doing so, '[these] strategies are, arguably, more likely to be adopted and sustained by the wider community' (O'Hara et al., 2018, p. 276).

The three aforesaid contributions are purposely situated in healthcare. Healthcare is something we all need, either for ourselves or a loved one. Furthermore, our need for quality healthcare has never been greater, given our ageing populations and the rise of multi-morbidities (WHO, 2011, 2014, 2018).

Managing the demand for healthcare can be difficult. This is partly because healthcare is challenged by multiple agendas, some of which conflict (Spyridonidis & Currie, 2016). This is not to suggest that other sectors (or the settings, therein) are devoid of the multiplicities of the healthcare sector. Rather, unlike healthcare, other organisations are seldom in the business of saving lives or moderating the sequelae among patients and carers, while simultaneously managing the bottom line.

Given the complexity of the healthcare sector, the lessons presented in this chapter are relevant to other sectors. If we can understand how to promote and sustain innovation in this complex sector, we are likely to understand how it might be achieved further afield.

This chapter commences with an overview of positive deviance. Drawing on healthcare exemplars, it then demonstrates that much can be learnt from brilliant moments of positive deviance. The chapter concludes by explicating key implications.

Positive Deviance

Since its introduction to address public health issues (Wishik & Vynckt, 1976), positive deviance has gained traction within management studies. As part of a positive approach to organisational scholarship – which focusses on 'that which is positive, flourishing, and lifegiving in organizations' (Cameron & Caza, 2004, p. 731) – positive deviance is a 'collection of behaviours that depart from the norms of a referent group, in honourable ways' (Spreitzer & Sonenshein, 2003,

p. 209). These behaviours are honourable because of the associated effects, enabling organisations to flourish. As such, positive deviants depart from expected practices to invigorate, strengthen, or galvanise a group of individuals who pursue a common goal (Mertens, Recker, Kohlborn, & Kummer, 2016). Although Gary (2013) described positive deviance as intentional, the value of the behaviour might only become apparent when positive outcomes and/or experiences emerge. For this reason, positive deviance might encompass both intentional and unintentional behaviour.

Conceptually, positive deviance is asset (rather than deficit)-based; it recognises the value of local (rather than external) expertise to address intractable issues (Luft, 2010); and it is socially driven and sustainable, whereby positivity begets positivity (Marsh, Schroeder, Dearden, Sternin, & Sternin, 2004). For two key reasons, these represent points of difference from quality improvement exercises and (participatory) action research (Bradley et al., 2009). First, the preferred or best practices are assumed to already exist – they are not introduced via an innovation sourced from a different sector, another organisation within the same sector, or specialised R&D activities within the organisation; nor are they introduced via an intervention, even if co-developed by personnel. Second, variation is expected – rather than examine phenomena through experimentation and/or feedback mechanisms, positive deviance prizes learning from exceptional exemplars. As Tarantino (2005) explained, 'The statement becomes, "This is how we can do what we want to do," rather than the question "How can we get them to do what we want them to do?"' (p. 63).

Positive deviance has been used to examine myriad constructive deviations from organisational norms (Spreitzer & Sonenshein, 2003). For instance, in an examination of 'diamonds in the rough', Clancy (2010) found that clinicians with managerial responsibilities did not necessarily value nurses who blindly complied with organisational standards and policies – but rather, they valued the nurse who, '"always finds a way to get the job done," "is the glue that holds us all together," and "is extremely resourceful, knowledgeable, and adaptable"' (p. 54). These individuals used effective workarounds to realise an organisational aim. The promise of positive deviance was also reported with reference to: green management practices to promote environmental sustainability (Jaaffar & Amran, 2017); ways to address federal recidivism on the border between the United Stated and Mexico (Durá, Perez, & Chaparro, 2019); frontline personnel in the retail and services sector who 'break the rules' to benefit customers and their organisation (Fazel-e-Hasan, Mortimer, Lings, & Drennan, 2019, p. 836); as well as effective organisational communication (Bisel, Kavya, & Tracy, 2020). Furthermore, positive deviance is deemed to be one of the 'key ingredients for success' (Melnyk & Davidson, 2009, p. 294) when creating a culture of innovation or an entrepreneurial orientation (Zbierowski, 2019).

Should leaders wish to 'go above and beyond normal expectations in positive ways' (Williamson, Buchard, Winner, & Winston, 2017, p. 30), research suggests four values are pertinent – namely: connections with others, both within and beyond the organisation; learning and development; courageous action; as well as shared (rather than top down) leadership. Although many leaders might appear to prize (or pay lip service) to these values, it is important to 'walk the talk' (Meyer & Hühn, 2020, p. 14) by embodying and enacting these values.

This is not to suggest that positive deviance is the panacea for all organisational or administrative woes by discounting or, worse still, ignoring organisational challenges. But rather, it can help to redress the attraction to problems and gaps among scholars, policymakers, and managers, among others (Gkeredakis et al., 2011; Healy & Walton, 2016). Redressing this preoccupation can foster: the psychological safety required for frank and honest conversations, where colleagues feel less compelled to be cautious or defensive (Nembhard & Edmondson, 2012); knowledge sharing; and innovation. To demonstrate the potential value of positive deviance in innovation, the following section presents exemplars of brilliant healthcare, which afforded personnel with managerial and/or clinical responsibilities, opportunities to learn – not from disconnected and disciplined domains, but from each other.

Exemplars

Having serendipitously learnt – via their personal networks – of health services that delivered superior (health)care in disparate domains, relative to their counterparts, a few research teams (whose members represented disparate organisations) have used unconventional methodologies and methods to learn from these instances of positive deviance that typically exceeded the expectations of those involved. The studies spanned paediatric care (Hopwood, Dadich, Elliot, & Moraby, 2021), renal care (Kippist, Fulop, Dadich, & Smyth, 2020), and palliative care (Dadich, Collier, & Hodgins, 2019; Dadich, Collier, Hodgins, & Crawford, 2018). However, given the rise of multi-morbidities and the social determinants of wellbeing (Fleming & Baldwin, 2020), personnel at the different sites often addressed myriad matters, including (but not limited to) mental health issues, accommodation issues, family discord, spiritual wellbeing, and limited social support. As such, while the personnel had expertise in a particular speciality, their knowledge and skill-base were far more expansive.

Given the aim of this chapter, this section does not present empirical findings – some of these are reported elsewhere (Dadich et al., 2018, 2019; Hopwood, Elliot, Moraby, & Dadich, 2020; Kippist et al., 2020). Rather, the purpose is to demonstrate how a deliberate and considered focus on internal moments of brilliance can serve to distinguish and learn from innovation that is not sourced from disconnected and disciplined domains. As such, this section describes how the studies were conducted and some of the findings from one study.

To examine, understand, and learn from these 'pockets of brilliance' within the health system (Dadich et al., 2015, p. 752), unconventional approaches were used. This followed four reasons. First, much of the guidance on how to examine positive deviance suggests a linear approach, comprised of seemingly discrete and predetermined activities (Klaiman, 2011). Furthermore, the identification of positive deviants often entails a statistical approach or a normative approach. The former assumes behaviours and outcomes are normally distributed, and it involves the determination of confidence intervals by which deviance is identified (Spreitzer & Sonenshein, 2004). The normative approach focusses on the phenomenon of positive deviance, the contexts in which it emerges, and the factors that shape it (Warren, 2003). Although this guidance can be helpful, how might positive deviance be studied in contexts that shun it, explicitly or implicitly? This includes 'today's highly regulated health system environment' (Clancy, 2010, p. 55), where directives and decrees dominate – be they in the form of government policies, organisational protocols, clinical guidelines, or the mandates of professional bodies. A culture that prizes conformity and compliance can mask deviance in all its forms – including that which is positive. For instance, following their study on disciplinary processes and the management of poor performance among nurses, Traynor, Stone, Cook, Gould, and Maben (2014) revealed a 'lack of systematic recording and reporting... and... examples of deliberate concealment' (p. 57) – and according to the authors, this demonstrated 'increased managerial power'. These observations are noteworthy because, as Gary (2013) noted, 'when nurses don't report the exact care provided, the outcomes of positive deviance are lost' (p. 31). Given that positive deviance research requires the identification of positive deviants and promulgating their practices (Lawton, Taylor, Clay-Williams, & Braithwaite, 2014), it is important to consider unconventional methodologies and research methods that are conducive to the examination of this concept in complex contexts (Lindberg & Clancy, 2010), like health services.

The second reason for the unconventional approaches was because, given the serendipitous and mercurial nature of brilliance, it might not be readily recognised within an organisation. This is particularly the case when there is limited opportunity for regular reflection, as in some busy, if not chaotic health services (Stander, Grimmer, & Brink, 2020). It was therefore important to consider how *in situ* practices might be captured and examined.

Third, given the connection between positive deviance and humility, participants might not readily recognise their practices, or their role(s) therein, as brilliant (Pina e Cunh, Rego, Simpson, & Clegg, 2020). As such, conventional methods like a survey, an interview, or a focus group, with directed questions were unlikely to be fit-for-purpose.

Fourth, to learn from these brilliant moments, the expertise and skills of the researchers alone were likely to be insufficient, for the researchers stood behind an 'understandascope' (Tonson, 2012). Their view of these complex contexts was incomplete – not wrong, inaccurate, or misguided; but imperfect. As such, it was important to respectfully involve individuals who are typically relegated to the role of 'subject' or 'participant' as co-researchers to make sense of these moments in context, paying heed to a polyphony of experiences, shaped by the pasts, the presents, and the futures (Bakhtin, 1984; Dawson, 2019).

For the aforesaid reasons, the research teams used: POSH-VRE, which coalesces positive organisational scholarship in healthcare (POSH) and video reflexive ethnography (VRE); discovery interviews (Dawood & Gallini, 2010) and world cafés (Anderson, 2011). Although different, they all encourage reflective and reflexive practices – specifically:

> Reflection refers to the common practice of thinking back to an event and assessing it and our conduct in relation to it… [It] is personal, focused and purposive… Reflexivity, in contrast, refers to our capacity to monitor and affect events, conducts and contexts in situ… [It] is collaborative in nature, diffuse in focus, open-ended in purpose and immediate in effect… reflexivity is a fully internalised and socially distributed monitoring and adjusting of the safety gradient of practice.
>
> *(Iedema, 2011, pp. i83–i84)*

Further detail on these three approaches can be sourced elsewhere (Dadich et al., 2018, 2019; Hammill et al., 2018; Kippist et al., 2020; Moraby, Dadich, Elliot, Diamantes, & Hodge, 2018).

One of these studies involved the use of POSH-VRE with clinicians who delivered community-based palliative care. Ostensibly, community-based palliative care is that which is delivered by clinicians to individuals with a life-limiting illness who remain at home, as well as their family members, to ultimately improve their quality of life. For (at least) three key reasons, this model has attracted increasing interest, particularly from Western governments. First, although many individuals are living longer (UN, 2020), they are likely to experience chronic illness (Etkind et al., 2017). Second, the cost of hospital-based care can be exorbitant, particularly during times of financial austerity, like COVID-19 (Rosenthal & Frenkel, 2018) – although it is unclear whether community-ty-based palliative care represents an economical alternative to hospital-based care (Gomes, Calanzani, & Higginson, 2014), it can prevent unnecessary admissions (Spilsbury, Rosenwax, Arendts, & Semmens, 2017). Third, many individuals would prefer to die at home, or at least claim this to be their wish (Hoare, Morris, Kelly, Kuhn, & Barclay, 2015).

Although operationalised in different ways (Stevens & Milligan, 2018), community-based palliative care in the study reported, largely involved nursing and medical palliative care specialists who lent their expertise to community-based generalist nurses, allied health professionals, as well as clinicians within residential aged care facilities. These specialists visited patients and family members at home; they participated in multidisciplinary team meetings; they orchestrated services and equipment that would enable individuals to die at home; and they regularly reviewed patient clinical records. Sometimes the specialist clinicians and their generalist counterparts consulted patients and family members together, and sometimes they did this independently, pending workload, as well as the needs and preferences of patients and family members. As such, these clinicians were sometimes 'sole traders' and were not always privy to what each other did, how they did it, or why.

To capture (potentially) brilliant moments, members of the research team as well as members of the clinical team (or co-researchers) captured video-recordings of palliative care *in situ*. Video-recordings were captured within the health service, while on commute to patient homes and meetings, during team discussions and telephone conversations, as well as during home visits – before, during, and/ or after a patient death (see Figure 6.1). The video-recordings were then amateurishly (rather than masterfully) edited into brief clips for analysis by the wider clinical team during reflexive sessions. During these sessions, the clinicians were invited to watch, critique, and interpret each clip, highlighting: what (if anything) epitomised brilliant palliative care; why; what (might have) enabled it, regardless of whether this was within or beyond the lens of the video-camera; the associated effects, be they evident or tacit; and how such brilliance can be promoted.

Although the clinicians were all skilled in palliative care and familiar with evidence-based practices (Australian Commission on Safety and Quality in Health Care, 2015), this deliberate and considered focus on daily, otherwise mundane practices served to visualize those which were brilliant (Iedema et al., 2018). For instance, the clinicians recognised that brilliant palliative care involved a bespoke blend of several ingredients, pending what the circumstances required. For instance, it involved: 'knowing what you don't know'; and 'an ability to shed your skin', so as not to contaminate interaction with pessimism:

> to me, a brilliant person asks questions and never assumes… to me, brilliance is about… knowing what to ask, in what context and not pretending you're… the expert.
>
> There's always organisational issues and it's about how you adapt, how to adjust to them… You might walk in because you've had a fight with your old man, and you kick… and punch [your colleague]. But you walk out and go out to a patient and that changes… It's like taking off your skin… It's like… 'I'm really frickin' pissed off today – but, it's okay'.

FIGURE 6.1 Home visits.

According to the clinicians, brilliant palliative care also involved extemporised engagement, devoid of the pomposity that can sometimes accompany the health-care hierarchy (Dadich & Olson, 2017). Furthermore, it involved relational investment – despite the organisational protocols that specified the minutes and consultations afforded to each patient, time was purposely invested into rapport building to ultimately improve the patients' and family members' quality of life:

> I love how the… [clinician] look[s] like it's their house. They know the kitchen… It kind of looks like your family and you know it so well… I guess it's that bond that you've created.
>
> It's an investment to spend that time because, in the end, you're going to get compliant patients, you're going to have less problems, less likely to go into hospital. So really, when you look at cost and time, you're saving a lot… Acknowledging the lady… That lady walks away saying, 'That's a good doctor'. The same with any of us when we go to a GP… if they listen to us and we felt heard, we walk away saying, 'That's my GP. I'm going to go back'. That ends up being a GP for ten, 15 more years… And that's the difference… 'If that doctor tells me I need to this, I'm going to be compli-ant because that's my doctor. He listens to me, he cares'. So… your clinical outcomes… are reflected and it pays offs.

Relational investment afforded these clinicians the opportunity to use their limited resources – including time – effectively and efficiently. For instance, the clinical consultations were not dictated by organisational protocols or clinical measures, but by the patient and/or family member. The clinicians explicitly directed their atten-tion to and validated the concerns and preferences of patients and family members – this bolstered the rapport. And by being perceptive and effecting a 'discipline of noticing' (Mason, 2002), the clinicians assessed a patient's clinical and psychosocial situation without assessing – as such, they asked questions, without asking:

> It's the patient and the concerns of the carers that is our number one pri-ority, regardless of the disease process. We say to them, 'What is your most concerning issue today?' If these spots on the feet are the first thing that they want to list, then that has to become my first area of concern… regardless of whether I think it's important or not… I need to address it, explain it for them so they've got an understanding of what it might be, why it might be there, why they shouldn't need to worry too much about it… because you can't address any of the other things you might think are important if you don't address what their primary concern is first. I mean, they're a human, a whole human, not a disease.
>
> As soon as you walk into the patient's house, there goes your assessment. Your assessment's already started – by the way you look at the patient, how they walk, how they stand from the chair, how they walk from the chair, from the lounge room to the kitchen. That's already part of your assessment.

it's… that interaction… you're sort of asking questions as you went along… but it flowed really well. And even though you're asking questions… You're doing it in a way that nobody really realises or can see exactly why you're asking. It's just a like a normal conversation between two people, but you're getting all the information that you need.

According to the clinicians, these and other ingredients were associated with brilliant palliative care. Their individual and collective practices sometimes exceeded their own expectations and/or those of the patients and family members they supported. This was aptly demonstrated by: the unsolicited notes of appreciation and gifts they received (see Figure 6.2); the luncheon that one grieving family hosted for the clinical team, following a patient's death; as well the clinicians' MacGyver-esque quality, able to imaginatively use limited resources to improve patients' and family members' quality of life. As 'sole traders' who largely worked beyond the reach of a health service storeroom of equipment and supplies, this skill was particularly important:

It's the, 'Well, I don't have this that I really should have but, you know, if I actually tweak this a little bit and turn it around and put it… back to front, it still be the same thing', because they do this all the time… It can come down to some days that you know, 'Where am I going to put the stuff?' as you walk in the house… and I only have this much room and I need this much or you know, the bed's here or there's no light and I can't see anything. All that stuff… you don't think about until you actually come out in the community to do.

FIGURE 6.2 Unsolicited appreciation from bereaved family members.

Collectively, these exemplars demonstrate how turning the collective cognitive gaze to moments of brilliance within an organisation can serve to recognise and learn from innovation beyond disconnected and disciplined domains. Furthermore, it can duly affirm the qualities of personnel, whose virtues might otherwise remain un(der)valued.

Implications

The thesis of this chapter has key implications for scholars, managers, and their personnel, as well as consumers. For scholars, there is considerable opportunity to clarify the relationship between positive deviance and innovation – conceptually, theoretically, methodologically, and empirically. To avert the oft-cited, if not obligatory call for 'more research', particular lines of enquiry include (but are not limited to): the conditions that help or hinder positive deviance, particularly in highly regulated contexts, given the rise of neo-liberalism and the associated effects (Penz & Sauer, 2019); how adversity and crises – including COVID-19 – influence positive deviance, particularly as it relates to innovation; the methodologies and research methods that are particularly appropriate and conversely, inappropriate, for this area; how diversity can be embraced with reference to, for instance, epistemologies, disciplines, traditions, values, identities, and cultures (among others), to ultimately avert a 'monocultural tint' (Spreitzer & Cameron, 2012, p. 1042); 'Can there be too much positivity?' (Spreitzer & Cameron, 2012, p. 1042); the dark sides of positive deviance; as well as whether (and how) positive deviance can be institutionalised, without binding it to a disconnected or disciplined domain, lest it be compromised.

Further to this last line of enquiry, research is especially required to determine whether innovation that is *not* sourced from disconnected and disciplined domains, like positive deviance, represents a dynamic capability for innovation management (Teece, Peteraf, & Leih, 2016). If so, research is then needed to determine the dark sides of clarifying – with measurable specificity – an organisation's 'ability to integrate, build, and reconfigure internal and external competences to address rapidly changing environments' (Teece, Pisano, & Shuen, 1997, p. 516). Although there might be value in monitoring, measuring, and engineering conditions that are (likely to be) conducive to positive deviance, its serendipitous nature will be compromised, if not lost. Arguing this point, Zbierowski (2019) advised, 'organisations should be careful with using some other high performance indicators grouped in factors "workforce quality" and "long-term orientation" [as]... those factors introduce high level of stability that can be harmful to positively deviant behaviours' (p. 229). Although he sagaciously suggested a need to reconcile the 'contradiction between stability and flexibility', how one might walk this tightrope, why, the associated effects, and how one might readily recognise a reconciliation, are yet to be clarified.

For managers and their personnel, this chapter provokes potentially challenging questions about how to involve colleagues and consumers in positive deviance and relatedly, innovation. This is likely to require them to encourage an authorising environment (Moore, 1995), where individuals and collectives can exercise agency, unshackled from a fear of being reprimanded when an experience is less than brilliant (Janssen & Huang, 2008). Of particular value are efforts to: explicitly and implicitly value (rather than shun) individual and collective differentiation; enable conditions that promote positive deviance, like individual differentiation; and remove those conditions that (might) thwart it, like group identification (Kim & Choi, 2018).

However, by loosening the managerial reins and affording greater control to colleagues, positive deviance – as a form of innovation that is beyond disconnected and disciplined domains – might challenge one's professional identity. This is because it can encroach on lines of authority, roles, functions, and areas of expertise, perceived or otherwise (Hannen et al., 2019; Lifshitz-Assaf, 2018). Perhaps a more progressive approach to promote positive deviance – and potentially reconcile the aforesaid contradictions (Zbierowski, 2019) – is through the concept of leaderfulness (Raelin, 2003, 2004).

Not to be confused with distributed or shared leadership, leaderfulness is relational, communal, and dynamic. It is, 'The practice of involving everyone in leadership, that leadership can be a collective property' (Raelin, 2004, p. 65). Leaderful practices can be energising – this is because, 'Everyone's talent is allowed to shine through and contribute to team goals. People can bring their whole selves to work and feel at home contributing to the greater good' (p. 66). Leaderfulness is comprised of four critical tenets – namely: collective; concurrent; collaborative; and compassionate. As Raelin explained:

> **Collective** leadership means that everyone in the group can serve as a leader; the team isn't dependent one individual to take over.
> **Concurrent** leadership means that not only can many members serve as leaders, but also they can do it at the same time. No one, not even a supervisor, has to stand down when any team member is making his or her contribution as a leader.
> **Collaborative** leadership means that everyone is in control of and can speak for the entire team. All members pitch in to accomplish the work of the team. Together, they engage in a mutual dialogue to determine what needs to be done and how to do it.
> **Compassionate** leadership means that team members commit to preserving the dignity of every individual on the team, considering each when a decision is made or action taken (original emphasis).

According to Raelin (2003), leaderfulness is important for (at least) two key reasons. First, it can contribute to the 'Bottom Line Impact' of an organisation. This is because leaderfulness can enhance: quality, innovation, change management, flexibility, learning, supervision, resilience, proactivity, output, and commitment. Second, leaderfulness can encourage individuals to 'Bring... [the] Whole

Person to Work'. Leaderful practices do not reinforce a false dichotomy that separate the professional from the personal, but they acknowledge and celebrate the symbiotic relationship between the two.

Developing leaderfulness requires mindfulness – that is, a 'discipline of noticing' (Mason, 2002), akin to that demonstrated by the clinicians in the exemplars. It is a capability that can be nurtured by becoming mindful or self-aware. However, contrary to its label, self-awareness is not solely an introspective endeavour; it is also extrospective, for it encompasses the self in relation to others. As Goleman (2015) explained:

> People with strong self-awareness are neither overly critical nor unrealistically hopeful. Rather, they are honest – with themselves and with **others**. People who have a high degree of self-awareness recognize how their feelings affect them, **other people**, and their job performance.
>
> *(p. 231, emphasis added)*

Self-awareness is both internal and external. The former denotes, 'how clearly we see our own values, passions, aspirations, fit with our environment, reactions (including thoughts, feelings, behaviors, strengths, and weaknesses), and impact on others' – this category 'is associated with higher job and relationship satisfaction, personal and social control, and happiness; [while] it is negatively related to anxiety, stress, and depression' (Eurich, 2018, para. 7). The latter represents an 'understanding [of] how other people view us... For leaders who see themselves as their employees do, their employees tend to have a better relationship with them, feel more satisfied with them, and see them as more effective in general' (para. 8). These interrelated categories recognise self-awareness as a relational construct, whereby self-understanding comes from understanding the self in relation to, and with others. As Merton (2005) eloquently conveyed:

> We are warmed by fire, not by the smoke of the fire. We are carried over the sea by ship, not by the wake of a ship. So too, what we are is sought in the depths of our own Being, not in our outward reflection of our own acts. We must find our real selves not in the froth stirred up by the impact of our Being upon the beings or things around us, but in our own Being, which is the principle of all our acts.
>
> *(p. 123)*

Through self-awareness comes a better understanding of limitations – or, knowing what you do not know – once again, akin to that demonstrated by the clinicians in the exemplars. This requires humility (Caldwell, Ichiho, & Anderson, 2017) or servant leadership that is 'other-oriented' (Eva, Robin, Sendjaya, van Dierendonck, & Liden, 2019, p. 114), whereby the authority of a single individual is relinquished to be shared and strengthened with others. This too was demonstrated by the clinicians whose style was unpretentious and unobtrusive. Like energy, leaderfulness – as form of leadership – is not created or destroyed, but is transformed. Furthermore, that which is 'exceptional, virtuous, life-giving, and flourishing phenomena' (Barker Caza, 2017, p. 4) can 'spread via social contagion to followers' (Owens & Hekman, 2016, p. 1088).

Although leaderfulness is a worthwhile pursuit of its own accord, its inclusion in this chapter and the accompanying explication follow its role in positive deviance and relatedly, innovation. Specifically, leaderfulness can encourage a 'team to take the time necessary for tacit knowledge to surface... [and for] collaborative learning' (Vuojärvi & Korva, 2020, pp. 12–13). As such, a key message for managers and their personnel is to be leaderful. Although definitive instructions are unlikely to be helpful – lest they compromise the authenticity of four aforesaid tenets – it can be helpful, in the first instance, to be mindful or to consciously notice the seeming mundanity of organisational life – what individuals and collectives do; how they do it; who or what they do it with; why; and the associated effects. This might help to recognise and enact communication styles that respectfully navigate and weave social interactions that may or may not be simultaneous or congruent in form, content, or regularity. Akin to 'professional artistry' (Rycroft-Malone et al., 2004, p. 88), leaderfulness welcomes, if not encourages ambiguity to respect and pay heed to different forms of knowing, thereby widening otherwise narrow interpretations of situations and experiences, to foster cultures of productivity (Morley & Hosking, 2003) and collective progress. Leaderful communication is demonstrated through 'skilful relating' (Fulop & Mark, 2013, p. 256). Communication that promotes leaderfulness involves crafting 'intelligible formulations' from perhaps a 'chaotic welter of impressions' (Fairhurst, 2007, p. 57). Communication is much more than what one says and does – it also encompasses what is unsaid, what is purposely not said, when, and how.

Through mindfulness, managers and their personnel might also become more personally and socially tuned and therefore better able to manage the self and the collective (Suriyankietkaew, 2013). This follows three key reasons. First, just as 'energy begets energy' (Pratsei, 2018; Taylor, 2008), leaderfulness fosters personal and social agency – that is, 'agentic collaboration in which one harnesses the agentic capabilities of others to serve goals that lie beyond any one individual' (Raelin, 2011, p. 199). Thus, managing the self serves to manage social interactions, which serve to manage the self. Second, to manage priorities and optimise wellbeing, particularly during difficult circumstances, leaderful practices foster enriching experiences to help otherwise weary individuals to: persevere; weather otherwise precarious periods; and buoy each other. Third, leaderfulness requires one to be comfortable with ambiguity to recognise relational nuances – that is, to exercise the 'discipline of noticing' (Mason, 2002).

Finally, for consumers, given the (seeming) importance of innovation across the public, private, and third (or not-for-profit) sectors (De Vries, Bekkers, & Tummers, 2016; Drucker, 2015; Godin & Vinck, 2017), and the limited opportunities for consumer engagement in related processes, this chapter invites consumers to ask how they too can demonstrate their leaderful and positively deviant capacities. This is not synonymous with crowdsourcing and related efforts – these largely represent engineered efforts to solicit novel ideas (Afuah & Tucci, 2012; Wexler, 2011), rather than practices that have actually been enacted and experienced; nor is it tantamount to citizen (social) science (Dadich, 2014; Heiss & Matthes, 2017; Leach, Parkinson, Lichten, & Marjanovic, 2020; Tauginienė et al., 2020), whereby volunteers contribute to research and/or development that might otherwise be conducted by those who are paid. Instead, consumers are encouraged to connect with organisations, problematise the oft-cited calls for 'consumer engagement' and 'consumer participation' (Hall et al., 2018; Sarrami-Foroushani, Travaglia, Debono, & Braithwaite, 2014; Solomon & Martin-Hobbs, 2018), and raise the profile of the moments they deem to be brilliant.

Conclusion

This chapter has argued a need to redress the preoccupation with innovation sourced from disconnected and disciplined domains. Equally important is innovation sourced from internal instances of positive deviance – particularly those serendipitous moments of brilliance, be they intentional or unintentional. Mindful recognition and a respectful examination of these moments can offer opportunities for vicarious learning, whereby managers and their personnel can learn without learning. For instance, rather than an expressed focus on, 'How can we improve?', as is the focus of appreciative enquiry (Bright & Miller, 2013; Head, 2013), the focus is, 'What makes us brilliant and why?' Whether and how lessons are garnered, are directed by the self and the collective, lest change fatigue be exacerbated. It is important to explicitly recognise the confluence of energy that enables 'agentic collaboration' (Raelin, 2011, p. 199). This can respectfully rekindle hope within and among those who have grown weary by innovation sourced from elsewhere, even if from an internal specialised unit. Furthermore, demonstrations of legitimate compassion for individuals and collectives reflect the four tenets leaderfulness.

Innovation sourced from internal instances of positive deviance might also benefit disconnected and disciplined domains. For instance, others might be inspired by stories of experiences that exceeded expectation and adapt lessons to foster joy and delight in their own organisation, regardless of sector, organisation-type, or specialisation. Consider the stories that some have shared about their own positive experiences within organisations, not to necessarily change others, but to promote positivity. These can potentially inspire a different way of working and/or a different approach to scholarship to understand these experiences, without necessarily imposing change. For example, drawing on his experiences as a hospital manager and Disney employee, Lee (2004) shared lessons from the field and uncommon wisdom to 'bring out the best behaviors in workers and provide the best emotional for patients'. Similarly, colleagues and I have drawn inspiration from international stories about 'What's right in health care'

(Studer Group, 2007) to reimagine research and pursue methods that democratise scholarship – like discovery interviews and world cafés – to ultimately widen our understandascope. These external instances of brilliance can helpfully complement internal instances.

Acknowledgements

The author extends sincere appreciation to the researchers involved in the studies described within this chapter, whose respective contributions helped to advance the arguments presented. They include: Dr Aileen Collier (University of Auckland); Mr Michael Hodgins, Dr Louise Kippist, and Dr Katie Hammill (Western Sydney University); Ms Janeane Harlum and Ms Therese Smeal (South Western Sydney Local Health District), Prof. Meera Agar and A/Prof. Nick Hopwood (University of Technology Sydney); Em. Prof. Liz Fulop (Griffith University); Ms Anne Smyth (Organisational Consulting); Dr Christopher Elliot (South Eastern Sydney Local Health District); and Ms Khadeejah Moraby (SA Health). These studies were collectively supported by: the NSW Agency for Clinical Innovation; the Western Sydney University; and the Maridulu Budyari Gumal Sydney Partnership for Health, Education, Research and Enterprise (SPHERE) Early Life Determinants of Health (ELDoH) Clinical Academic Group (CAG).

References

Afuah, A., & Tucci, C. L. (2012). Crowdsourcing as a solution to distant search. *Academy of Management Review, 37*(3), 355–375.

Anderson, L. (2011). Use the world café concept to create an interactive learning environment. *Education for Primary Care, 22*(5), 337–338.

Australian Commission on Safety and Quality in Health Care. (2015). *National consensus statement: Essential elements for safe and high-quality end-of-life care.* Sydney, NSW: Australian Commission on Safety and Quality in Health Care.

Bakhtin, M. (1984). *Problems of Dostoevsky's poetics* (C. Emerson, Trans.). Minneapolis: University of Minnesota Press.

Barker Caza, B. (2017). An introduction to positive organizational scholarship. In A. J. G. Sison, G. R. Beabout, & I. Ferrero (Eds.), *Handbook of virtue ethics in business and management* (Vol. 1, pp. 533–546). Dordrecht: Springer.

Barker Caza, B., & Milton, L. P. (2012). Resilience at work: Building capability in the face of adversity. In K. S. Cameron & G. M. Spreitzer (Eds.), *Oxford handbook of positive organizational scholarship* (pp. 895–908). New York, NY: Oxford University Press.

Bauer, W., & Schimpf, S. (2018). *Understanding the history of industrial innovation: Developments and milestones in key action fields of R&D management.* Milan: R&D Management Conference.

Biggi, G., & Giuliani, E. (2020). The noxious consequences of innovation: What do we know? *Industry and Innovation, Epub-ahead-of-print, 28*(1), 1–23.

Bisel, R. S., Kavya, P., & Tracy, S. J. (2020). Positive deviance case selection as a method for organizational communication: A rationale, how-to, and illustration. *Management Communication Quarterly, 34*(2), 276–296.

Bradley, E. H., Curry, L. A., Ramanadhan, S., Rowe, L., Nembhard, I. M., & Krumholz, H. M. (2009). Research in action: Using positive deviance to improve quality of health care. *Implementation Science, 4*(25), 1–11.

Bright, D. S., & Miller, M. T. (2013). Appreciative inquiry and positive organizational scholarship: A philosophy of practice for turbulent times. In J. Vogelsang, M. Townsend, M. Minahan, D. Jamieson, J. Vogel, A. Viets, C. Royal, & C. Valek (Eds.), *Handbook for strategic HR: Best practices in organization development from the OD network* (pp. 399–410). New York, NY: American Management Association.

Caldwell, C., Ichiho, R., & Anderson, V. (2017). Understanding level 5 leaders: The ethical perspectives of leadership humility. *Journal of Management Development, 36*(5), 724–732.

Cameron, K. S., & Caza, A. (2004). Contributions to the discipline of positive organizational scholarship. *American Behavioral Scientist, 47*(6), 731–739.

Clancy, T. R. (2010). Diamonds in the rough: Positive deviance and complexity. *Journal of Nursing Administration, 40*(2), 53–56.

Cooper, R. G. (1990). Stage-gate systems: A new tool for managing new products. *Business Horizons, 33*, 44–54.

Dadich, A. (2014). Citizen social science: A methodology to facilitate and examine workplace learning in continuing interprofessional education. *Journal of Interprofessional Care, 28*(3), 194–199.

Dadich, A., Collier, A., & Hodgins, M. (2019). Navigating and understanding organisational complexity in health services: The value of POSH-VRE. *Journal of Management & Organization, 26*(3), 375–390.

Dadich, A., Collier, A., Hodgins, M., & Crawford, G. (2018). Using POSH VRE to examine positive deviance to new public management in healthcare. *Qualitative Health Research, 28*(8), 1203–1216.

Dadich, A., Fulop, L., Ditton, M., Campbell, S., Curry, J., Eljiz, K., Fitzgerald, A., Hayes, K. J., Herington, C., Isouard, G., Karimi, L., & Smyth, A. (2015). Finding brilliance using positive organizational scholarship in healthcare. *Journal of Health Organization and Management, 29*(6), 750–777.

Dadich, A., & Olson, R. (2017). How and why emotions matter in interprofessional healthcare. *International Journal of Work Organisation and Emotion, 8*(1), 59–79.

Dawood, M., & Gallini, A. (2010). Using discovery interviews to understand the patient experience. *Nursing Management, 17*(1), 26–31.

Dawson, P. (2019). *Reshaping change: A processual perspective* (Second ed.). Routledge.

De Vries, H., Bekkers, V., & Tummers, L. (2016). Innovation in the public sector: A systematic review and future research agenda. *Public Administration, 94*(1), 146–166.

DeGraff, J., & Roberts, D. N. (2012). Innovativeness as positive deviance: Identifying and operationalizing the attributes, functions and dynamics that create growth. In K. S. Cameron & G. M. Spreitzer (Eds.), *Oxford handbook of positive organizational scholarship* (pp. 703–714). New York, NY: Oxford University Press.

Deloitte. (2019). *The path to prosperity: Why the future of work is human.* New York, NY: Deloitte Touche Tohmatsu Limited.

Dougherty, D., & Hardy, C. (1996). Sustained product innovation in large, mature organizations: Overcoming innovation-to-organization problems. *Academy of Management Journal, 39*(5), 1120–1153.

Drucker, P. (2002). The discipline of innovation. *Harvard Business Review, 80*(8), 95–102.

Drucker, P. F. (2015). *Innovation and entrepreneurship: Practice and principles.* Oxon: Routledge.

Durá, L., Perez, L., & Chaparro, M. (2019). Positive deviance as design thinking: Challenging notions of stasis in technical and professional communication. *Journal of Business and Technical Communication, 33*(4), 376–399.

Etkind, S. N., Bone, A. E., Gomes, B., Lovell, N., Evans, C. J., Higginson, I. J., & Murtagh, F. E. M. (2017). How many people will need palliative care in 2040? Past trends, future projections and implications for services. *BMC Medicine, 15*(102), 1–10.

Eurich, T. (2018, January 4). *What self-awareness really is (and how to cultivate it)* [Website].

Eva, N., Robin, M., Sendjaya, S., van Dierendonck, D., & Liden, R. C. (2019). Servant leadership: A systematic review and call for future research. *Leadership Quarterly, 30*(1), 111–132.

Fairhurst, G. T. (2007). *Discursive leadership: In conversation with leadership pyschology.* London: Sage Publications.

Fazel-e-Hasan, S. M., Mortimer, G., Lings, I., & Drennan, J. (2019). Examining customer-oriented positive deviance intentions of retail employees. *International Journal of Retail & Distribution Management, 47*(8), 836–854.

Fleming, M. -L., & Baldwin, L. (Eds.). (2020). *Health promotion in the 21st century: New approaches to achieving health for all.* Oxon: Routledge.

Fredrickson, B. L. (2003). Positive emotions and upward spirals in organizations. In K. S. Cameron, J. E. Dutton, & R. E. Quinn (Eds.), *Positive organizational scholarship: Foundations of a new discipline* (pp. 163–175). San Francisco, CA: Berrett Koehler.

Fulop, L., & Mark, A. L. (2013). Relational leadership, decision making and the messiness of context in healthcare. *Leadership, 9*(2), 254–277.

Gary, J. C. (2013). Exploring the concept and use of positive deviance in nursing: 'Responsible subversion' and why accurate documentation matters. *American Journal of Nursing, 113*(8), 26–34.

Gkeredakis, E., Swan, J., Powell, J., Nicolini, D., Scarbrough, H., Roginski, C., Taylor-Phillips, S., & Clarke, A. (2011). Mind the gap: Understanding utilisation of evidence and policy in health care management practice. *Journal of Health Organization and Management, 25*(3), 298–314.

Godin, B., & Vinck, D. (Eds.). (2017). *Critical studies of innovation: Alternative approaches to the pro-innovation bias.* Cheltenham: Edward Elgar Publishing.

Goleman, D. (2015). What makes a leader? In L. W. Porter, H. L. Angle, & R. W. Allen (Eds.), *Organizational influence processes* (Second ed., pp. 229–241). Oxon: Routledge.

Gomes, B., Calanzani, N., & Higginson, I. J. (2014). Benefits and costs of home palliative care compared with usual care for patients with advanced illness and their family caregivers. *Journal of the American Medical Association, 311*(10), 1060–1061.

Hall, A. E., Bryant, J., Sanson-Fisher, R. W., Fradgley, E. A., Proietto, A. M., & Roos, I. (2018). Consumer input into health care: Time for a new active and comprehensive model of consumer involvement. *Health Expectations, 21*(4), 707–713.

Hammill, K., Dadich, A., Aggarwal, R., Peronchik, J., Vasquez, D., & Bejjani, C. (2018). *A family-video to die for: Bringing the family back to family-centred palliative care with VRE.* In Conference Proceedings: ACSPRI Social Science Methodology Conference, University of Sydney, 12–14 December, 2018, 69–78.

Hannen, J., Antons, D., Piller, F., Salge, T. O., Coltman, T., & Devinney, T. M. (2019). Containing the not-invented-here syndrome in external knowledge absorption and open innovation: The role of indirect countermeasures. *Research Policy, 48*(9), 1–17.

Head, T. C. (2013). Appreciative inquiry: Debunking the mythology behind resistance to change. In J. Vogelsang, M. Townsend, M. Minahan, D. Jamieson, J. Vogel, A. Viets, C. Royal, & C. Valek (Eds.), *Handbook for strategic HR: Best practices in organization development from the OD network* (pp. 576–583). New York, NY: American Management Association.

Healy, J., & Walton, M. (2016). Health ombudsmen in polycentric regulatory fields: England, New Zealand, and Australia. *Australian Journal of Public Administration, 75*(4), 492–505.

Heiss, R., & Matthes, J. (2017). Citizen science in the social sciences: A call for more evidence. *GAIA, 26*(1), 22–26.

Hoare, S., Morris, Z. S., Kelly, M. P., Kuhn, I., & Barclay, S. (2015). Do patients want to die at home? A systematic review of the UK literature, focused on missing preferences for place of death. *PLoS One, 10*(11), e0142723.

Hopwood, N., Dadich, A., Elliot, C., & Moraby, K. (2021). How is brilliance enacted in professional practices? Insights from the theory of practice architectures. *Professions & Professionalism, 11*(2), 1–22.

Hopwood, N., Elliot, C., Moraby, K., & Dadich, A. (2020). Parenting enterally fed children: How families go from surviving to thriving. *Child: Care, Health and Development, 46*(6), 741–748.

Iedema, R. (2011). Creating safety by strengthening clinicians' capacity for reflexivity. *BMJ Quality & Safety, 20*(Suppl. 1), i83–i86.

Iedema, R., Carroll, K., Collier, A., Hor, S., Mesman, J., & Wyer, M. (2018). *Video reflexive ethnography in health research and healthcare improvement.* Milton Park: Taylor & Francis.

Jaaffar, A. H., & Amran, A. A. (2017). The influence of leaders' past environmental-related experiences and positive deviance behaviour in green management practices. *Jurnal Pengurusan, 51*, 1–18.

Janssen, O., & Huang, X. (2008). Us and me: Team identification and individual differentiation as complementary drivers of citizenship and creative behaviors of members of middle management teams. *Journal of Management, 34*(1), 69–88.

Jones, J. N., Cope, J., & Kintz, A. (2016). Peering into the future of innovation management. *Research-Technology Management, 59*(4), 49–58.

Keeley, L., Walters, H., Pikkel, R., & Quinn, B. (2013). *Ten types of innovation: The discipline of building breakthroughs.* Hoboken, NJ: John Wiley & Sons.

Kickbusch, I., Krech, R., Franz, C., & Wells, N. (2018). Banking for health: Opportunities in cooperation between banking and health applying innovation from other sectors. *BMJ Global Health, 3*(Suppl. 1), 299–323.

Kim, M. J., & Choi, J. N. (2018). Group identity and positive deviance in work groups. *Journal of Social Psychology, 158*(6), 730–743.

Kippist, L., Fulop, L., Dadich, A., & Smyth, A. (2020). Brilliant renal care: A really positive study of patient, carer, and staff experiences within an Australian health service. *Journal of Management & Organization, 26*(3), 355–374.

Klaiman, T. (2011). Learning from top performers using a positive deviance approach. *American Journal of Medical Quality, 26*(5), 422.

Kooijman, M., Hekkert, M. P., van Meer, P. J. K., Moors, E. H. M., & Schellekens, H. (2017). How institutional logics hamper innovation: The case of animal testing. *Technological Forecasting & Social Change, 118*, 70–79.

Lawton, R., Taylor, N., Clay-Williams, R., & Braithwaite, J. (2014). Positive deviance: A different approach to achieving patient safety. *BMJ Quality & Safety, 23*, 880–883.

Leach, B., Parkinson, S., Lichten, C., & Marjanovic, S. (2020). *Emerging developments in citizen science: Reflecting on areas of innovation.* Santa Monica, CA: RAND Corporation.

Lee, F. (2004). *If Disney ran your hospital: 9 1/2 things you would do differently.* Bozeman, MT: Second River Healthcare.

Lifshitz-Assaf, H. (2018). Dismantling knowledge boundaries at NASA: The critical role of professional identity in open innovation. *Administrative Science Quarterly, 63*(4), 746–782.

Lindberg, C., & Clancy, T. R. (2010). Positive deviance: An elegant solution to a complex problem. *Journal of Nursing Administration, 40*(4), 150–153.

Luft, H. S. (2010). Data and methods to facilitate delivery system reform: Harnessing collective intelligence to learn from positive deviance. *Health Services Research, 45*(5 Pt 2), 1570–1580.

Marsh, D. R., Schroeder, D. G., Dearden, K. A., Sternin, J., & Sternin, M. (2004). The power of positive deviance. *British Medical Journal, 329*, 1177–1179.

Martínez, E. (2019). Invisible in plain sight: A reflection on the potential and perils of an action research study of "positive deviants". *Action Research, 15*(1), 53–56.

Mason, J. (2002). *Researching your own practice: The discipline of noticing.* London: Routledge.

Mattsson, J., Helmersson, H., & Stetler, K. (2016). Motivation fatigue as a threat to innovation: Bypassing the productivity dilemma in R&D by cyclic production. *International Journal of Innovation Management, 20*(2), 1–23.

Melnyk, B. M., & Davidson, S. (2009). Creating a culture of innovation in nursing education through shared vision, leadership, interdisciplinary partnerships, and positive deviance. *Nursing Administration Quarterly, 33*(4), 288–295.

Mertens, W., Recker, J., Kohlborn, T., & Kummer, T. -F. (2016). A framework for the study of positive deviance in organizations. *Deviant Behavior, 37*(11), 1288–1307.

Merton, T. (2005). *No man is an island.* Boston, MA: Shambhala Publications.

Meyer, M., & Hühn, M. P. (2020). Positive language and virtuous leadership: Walking the talk. *Management Research, 18*(3), 263–284.

Moore, M. (1995). *Creating public value: Strategic management in government.* Cambridge, MA: Harvard University Press.

Moraby, K., Dadich, A., Elliot, C., Diamantes, M., & Hodge, K. (2018). *How to reveal and encourage brilliant feeding care.* In Conference Proceedings: ACSPRI Social Science Methodology Conference, University of Sydney, 12–14 December, 2018, 108–118.

Morley, I., & Hosking, D. M. (2003). Leadership, learning and negotiation in a social psychology of organizing. In N. Bennett & L. Anderson (Eds.), *Rethinking educational leadership: Challenging the conventions* (pp. 43–60). London: Sage Publications.

Nembhard, I. M., & Edmondson, A. C. (2012). Psychological safety: A foundation for speaking up, collaboration, and experimentation in organizations. In K. S. Cameron & G. M. Spreitzer (Eds.), *Oxford handbook of positive organizational scholarship* (pp. 490–503). New York, NY: Oxford University Press.

O'Hara, J. K., Grasic, K., Gutacker, N., Street, A., Foy, R., Thompson, C., Wright, J., & Lawton, R. (2018). Identifying positive deviants in healthcare quality and safety: A mixed methods study. *Journal of the Royal Society of Medicine, 111*(8), 276–291.

Owens, B. P., & Hekman, D. R. (2016). How does leader humility influence team performance? Exploring the mechanisms of contagion and collective promotion focus. *Academy of Management Review, 59*(3), 1088–1111.

Penz, O., & Sauer, B. (2019). *Governing affects: Neoliberalism, neo-bureaucracies, and service work.* London: Routledge.

Pina e Cunh, M., Rego, A., Simpson, A. V., & Clegg, S. (2020). *Positive organizational behaviour: A reflective approach.* Oxon: Routledge.

Pratsei, A. (2018). *Doing care, doing citizenship: Towards a micro-situated and emotion-based model of social inclusion.* Cham: Palgrave Macmillan.

Raelin, J. (2004). Preparing for leaderful practice: Learn to let go. *T+D, 58*(3), 65–70.

Raelin, J. (2011). From leadership-as-practice to leaderful practice. *Leadership, 7*(2), 195–211.

Raelin, J. A. (2003). *Creating leaderful organizations: How to bring out leadership in everyone.* San Francisco, CA: Berrett-Koehler Publishers.

Rehn, A. (2019). *Innovation for the fatigued: How to build a culture of deep creativity.* London: Kogan Page.

Robinson, S., Radnor, Z., Fitzgerald, A., Hayes, K. J., Sohal, A., & Sloan, T. (2014). Lean in healthcare - History and recent developments. *Journal of Health Organization and Management, 28*(2), 99–108.

Rosenthal, M. M., & Frenkel, M. (Eds.). (2018). *Health care systems and their patients: An international perspective.* New York, NY: Routledge.

Rycroft-Malone, J., Seers, K., Titchen, A., Harvey, G., Kitson, A., & McCormack, B. (2004). What counts as evidence in evidence-based practice? *Journal of Advanced Nursing, 47*(1), 81–90.

Sarrami-Foroushani, P., Travaglia, J., Debono, D., & Braithwaite, J. (2014). Implementing strategies in consumer and community engagement in health care: Results of a large-scale, scoping meta-review. *BMC Health Services Research, 14*(402), 1–16.

Satell, G. (2017). *Mapping innovation: A playbook for navigating a disruptive age.* New York, NY: McGraw-Hill Education.

Solomon, L., & Martin-Hobbs, B. (2018). *Five preconditions of effective consumer engagement - A conceptual framework.* Melbourne, VIC: Consumer Policy Research Centre.

Spilsbury, K., Rosenwax, L., Arendts, G., & Semmens, J. B. (2017). The impact of community-based palliative care on acute hospital use in the last year of life is modified by time to death, age and underlying cause of death. A population-based retrospective cohort study. *PLoS One, 12*(9), 1–15.

Spreitzer, G. M., & Cameron, K. S. (2012). A path forward: Assessing progress and exploring core questions for the future of positive organizational scholarship. In K. S. Cameron & G. M. Spreitzer (Eds.), *Oxford handbook of positive organizational scholarship* (pp. 1034–1048). New York, NY: Oxford University Press.

Spreitzer, G. M., & Sonenshein, S. (2003). Positive deviance and extraordinary organizing. In K. Cameron, J. Dutton, & R. Quinn (Eds.), *Positive organizational scholarship: Foundations of a new discipline* (pp. 207–224). San Francisco, CA: Berrett-Koehler.

Spreitzer, G. M., & Sonenshein, S. (2004). Toward the construct definition of positive deviance. *American Behavioral Scientist, 47*(6), 828–847.

Spyridonidis, D., & Currie, G. (2016). The translational role of hybrid nurse middle managers in implementing clinical guidelines: Effect of, and upon, professional and managerial hierarchies. *British Journal of Management, 27*(4), 760–777.

Stander, J., Grimmer, K., & Brink, Y. (2020). Time as a barrier to evidence uptake – A qualitative exploration of the concept of time for clinical practice guideline uptake by physiotherapists. *Journal of Evaluation in Clinical Practice, 27*(2), 280–290.

Stevens, E., & Milligan, S. (2018). Home palliative care in the United Kingdom and Europe. In Holtslander L., Peacock S., & Bally J. (Eds.), *Hospice palliative home care and bereavement support* (pp. 45–62). Cham: Springer. doi:https://doi.org/10.1007/978-3-030-19535-9_4

Studer Group. (2007). *What's right in health care: 365 stories of purpose, worthwhile work, and making a difference.* Gulf Breeze, FL: Fire Starter Publishing.

Suriyankietkaew, S. (2013). Emergent leadership paradigms for corporate sustainability: A proposed model. *Journal of Applied Business Research, 29*(1), 173–182.

Tarantino, D. P. (2005). Positive deviance as a tool for organizational change. *Physician Executive, 31*(5), 62–63.

Tauginienė, L., Butkevičienė, E., Vohland, K., Heinisch, B., Daskolia, M., Suškevičs, M., Portela, M., Balázs, B., & Prūse, B. (2020). Citizen science in the social sciences and humanities: The power of interdisciplinarity. *Palgrave Communications, 6*(89), 1–11.

Taylor, R. B. (2008). *White coat tales: Medicine's heroes, heritage and misadventures*. New York, NY: Springer.

Teece, D., Peteraf, M., & Leih, S. (2016). Dynamic capabilities and organizational agility: Risk, uncertainty, and strategy in the innovation economy. *California Management Review, 58*(4), 13–35.

Teece, D. J., Pisano, G., & Shuen, A. (1997). Dynamic capabilities and strategic management. *Strategic Management Journal, 18*(7), 509–533.

Tonson, J. (2012). Understandascope. *Eingana, 35*(3), 10–11.

Traynor, M., Stone, K., Cook, H., Gould, D., & Maben, J. (2014). Disciplinary processes and the management of poor performance among UK nurses: Bad apple or systemic failure? A scoping study. *Nursing Inquiry, 21*(1), 51–58.

UN (United Nations). (2020). *World population ageing 2019*. New York, NY: UN (United Nations), Department of Economic and Social Affairs, Population Division.

Vuojärvi, H., & Korva, S. (2020). An ethnographic study on leadership-as-practice in trauma simulation training. *Leadership in Health Services, 33*(2), 185–200.

Waitzkin, J. (2007). *The art of learning: A journey in the pursuit of excellence*. New York, NY: Free Press.

Warren, D. (2003). Constructive and destructive deviance in organizations. *Academy of Management Review, 28*, 622–632.

Wexler, M. N. (2011). Reconfiguring the sociology of the crowd: Exploring crowdsourcing. *International Journal of Sociology and Social Policy, 31*(1), 6–20.

WHO (World Health Organization). (2011). *Global health and ageing*. Geneva: WHO.

WHO (World Health Organization). (2014). *Global status report on noncommunicable diseases*. Geneva: WHO.

WHO (World Health Organization). (2018, November). *Health statistics and information systems: Disease burden and mortality estimates* [Website]. Retrieved from http://www.who.int/healthinfo/global_burden_disease/estimates/en/index2.html

Wilf, E. Y. (2019). *Creativity on demand: The dilemmas of innovation in an accelerated age*. Chicago, IL: University of Chicago Press.

Williamson, B., Buchard, M. J., Winner, W. D., & Winston, B. E. (2017). Internal factors that enable positive deviance to occur in leaders: A phenomenological description. *International Leadership Journal, 9*(1), 30–56.

Wishik, S. M., & Vynckt, S. (1976). The use of nutritional 'positive deviants' to identify approaches for modification of dietary practices. *American Journal of Public Health, 66*(1), 38–42.

Zbierowski, P. (2019). Positive deviance as a mediator in the relationship between high performance indicators and entrepreneurial orientation. *Entrepreneurial Business & Economics Review, 7*(2), 217–233.

Zouaghi, F., Sánchez, M., & Martínez, M. G. (2018). Did the global financial crisis impact firms' innovation performance? The role of internal and external knowledge capabilities in high and low tech industries. *Technological Forecasting and Social Change, 132*, 92–104.

7

HOW MANAGERS SHAPE INNOVATION CULTURE

Role of talent, routines, and incentives

Rajul G. Joshi and Pavan Soni

Introduction

The last decade witnessed the demise of house-hold brands such as Nokia, Eastman Kodak, Blockbuster, Readers Digest, and Lehman Brothers, among others. Although the survival, revival, and relevance of mature growth-phase large organisations are not guaranteed, a few companies have managed to negotiate turbulent times to emerge more relevant to their customers, employees, and investors. While the presence of new-age companies, such as Tesla, Facebook, Alibaba, and Netflix, should be of no surprise to anybody, the more impressive ones are the large organisations, such as Siemens, Philips, Unilever, and DuPont, among others. Such large companies from traditional industries have demonstrated strategic renewal through organisational transformation and fostering of an innovation culture.

Large firms are complex adaptive systems of business organisations built on structural and managerial principles, where structural principles deal with the design of the system and the managerial principle reflect the application of the intelligence and intentionality provided by humans (Reeves et al., 2016). Being closer to internal and external operations, behaviours, and the organisation routines, middle management recognises both the need for change or continuity more than most others and they can initiate change appropriately. Middle management, an integral layer, is channel of communication for initiating and implementing innovation. This middle layer translates vision into actions and influences behaviours through the orchestration of tactical objectives at the operational level. Thus, making it imperative for firms to focus on the 'dynamic managerial capabilities' (Adner & Helfat, 2003) to focus on the incentives for the actors enacting the micro-level routines. Managers influence the orchestration of routines and policies through nudging the choice architecture (Felin, 2014) and

DOI: 10.4324/9780429346033-10

the social contract of employees to achieve both the organisational and personal goals in an organisational setting. Talent acquisition is one of the most essential capabilities of an organisation (Felin & Hesterly, 2007) striving for innovation culture because the right talent insinuates organisation performance. This puts forward a significant question about how the middle managers shape a culture of innovation in an organisation while making it more resilient in the face of rapid external change.

Borrowing from the literature on routines, behavioural economics, and organisational design, this chapter offers a model of how middle managers shape a culture of innovation while making it more resilient in the face of rapid external change. The three-pronged lever available with the middle manager comprises routines, talent, and incentives; which roughly translate into the How, Who, and Why dimensions of innovation culture, respectively. The question underpinning this chapter is how middle managers of large organisations enable culture transformation through innovation. Since so much is being spoken about the leaders as enablers of change and innovation culture, by focussing on the middle layer of the organisation, the chapter brings to fore one of the overlooked dimensions of change – the agency at the middle of the organisation. Further, by anchoring the study on an organisation that is large and has managed to reinvent itself, the chapter offers practical insights for managers.

Literature review

Large organisations such as 3M, Corning, Google, Microsoft, Nike, SAP, Cisco, and Tata Group, to name a few, are enlivening the innovation culture thereby embracing strategic renewal and change effectively. Innovation culture is a significant factor of growth for such large organisations. Innovation culture is a multidimensional perspective entailing the intention, the infrastructure, and operational level behaviours necessary to influence a market and value orientation and the environment to implement innovation (Dobni, 2008). According to Birdi (2020), innovation culture entails norms with a focus on continuous improvement through the generation and implementation of ideas across the organisation. Likewise, it is an expression of people, their past, and their current ideas, beliefs, and behaviours which create innovation consistently over time (Morris, 2007). Overall, innovation culture challenges the entrenched mode of thinking and paves way for fresh ideas, attracts new talent, and retains quality personnel, redefines risk, enables growth, and disrupts competition. Due to the multitude of variables of culture, the concept of culture for innovation is still fragmented, and the inclusion of this concept in management theory is still missing (Büschgens et al., 2013).

Tushman and O'Reilly (1996) delineates that culture influences innovation through socialisation processes and the value proposition communicated through structures, routines, policies, and day-to-day artefacts and practices and procedures. This is especially difficult for large organisations that are confronted with rapidly changing task environments. The fundamental pressure for the large organisations is the long-run survival and handling the paradoxical tensions of exploration and exploitation to configure and reconfigure resources to capture existing and new opportunities (March, 1991). Shaping innovation culture through managerial cognition, incentives, and motivational influence can ease such paradoxical tensions of innovation and change. Managers not only influence the innovation process and outcome but also determine the organisation's innovativeness. The most probable actors to promote the espoused value of the organisation are managers (Argyris & Schon, 1974). While managers nurture shared values, they also identify routines, talents, and practices that reinforce those values to propel innovation. This necessitates the coherent understanding of social order through routine dynamics in organisations and organising for innovation (Dougherty, 2008).

Organisational routines are an important source of change, innovation, and flexibility (Nelson & Winter, 1982; Feldman, 2000; Feldman & Pentland, 2003; Pentland et al., 2012). Routines are essential for the understanding of innovation and organisational change (Becker et al., 2005). Nevertheless, over a while routines lead to the development of cultural inertia and institutional isomorphism. To impede such issues, scholars such as Tushman and O'Reilly (1996) argue that routine work should be separated from innovation. Moreover, as routine enables to capture changes it is integral for innovation and organisational transformation. Both the corresponding normative considerations and cultural influence becomes vital aspects of the cognitive representation in a formal organisation (Koumakhov & Daoud, 2017). For prospering innovation culture, firms should further view routine from a dynamic perspective embodied through managerial cognition.

In this chapter, routines are taken as internal dynamics and will be discussed from the ostensive-performative (OP) framework of practice theory which focusses on operationalisation and enactment of routines, actors' influence on their co-constitution, and how they emerge and change (Parmigiani & Howard-Grenville, 2011). Central to this framework is the OP element of routine; where ostensive relate to the abstract idea of the routine (structure) and performative relate to the actual performances of the routine by specific people in a spatial and temporal context. As this framework focusses on subjectivity, improvisation, people, agency, and reflexive behaviour, it enhances the understanding of the impact of routines on performance, culture, and change. Routines, here, is a generative system producing repetitive, recognisable patterns of interdependent actions, carried out by multiple actors (Feldman & Pentland, 2003; Pentland et al., 2012). Furthermore, the proponents of the practice perspective of routines propose that routines are rule-based behaviour driven by reflexivity, agency, contextuality, and individual discretion in an organisation (Feldman, 2000; Feldman & Pentland, 2003).

Managerial practice requires an underlying structure to decide what culture should be implemented to foster innovation and to assess if a specific culture is an effective and efficient coordination instrument (Büschgens et al., 2013). Moreover, to alter the behaviour of the people in a predictable manner, managerial decision-making should focus on motivation, incentives, and influence through a set of repeatable patterns of behaviour. Here, culture building is relatively relevant, requiring managers to promote culture by shaping and modelling norms and value to support creativity with rigorous selection and socialisation process of the right people for innovative culture (Dougherty, 2008) and monitoring action through the system of reward (Ghosal & Moran, 1996; Dougherty, 2008).

Westley (1990) purports that middle managers on getting access to the framing rules of top management can effectively negotiate and potentially alter those rules; implicating a web of meanings and redefinition of interpretive schema through ideology and policies. Concurrently, Feldman and Pentland posit that some forms are more flexible allowing for managerial discretion in their execution (2003). Within the managerial hierarchy, the role of top management and middle management is distinct (Floyd & Lane, 2002); while the focus of the former is on decision-making the latter focusses on the execution of strategy, communication of information, and development of tactical objectives (Huy, 2002). According to Nonaka, middle management plays a significant role in initiating strategic change and the socialisation process (1988). Besides, the middle management layer can influence the choice architecture for managing innovation, strategic renewal, and change. For managers and organisations, nudge-related experimental insights help in shaping the welfare of employees thereby influencing the performance of organisations for innovation and growth (Felin, 2014).

The notion of nudging the choice architecture and nudge management is built on the basic tenets of nudge theory and provides a cognitive and psychology perspective to organisational learning and development. According to Thaler and Sunstein, nudge theory provides a choice architecture that alters people's behaviour predictably without removing any options or significantly changing their economic incentives (2008). Choice architecture is the interface of routines, work settings, culture, and policies; and employees are consumers and users of the same (Felin, 2014). Besides, choice architectures have implications for how employees behave, interact, and perform in organisations (Felin, 2014). Moreover, the conceptualisation of nudge is rooted in dual-process theories of information processing and cognition focussing on heuristics and biases (Kahneman & Tversky, 1979).

The basic intuition behind nudging is that how choices are presented, ordered, and structured – essentially, the interface provided to employees – can powerfully impact outcomes (Felin, 2014). Moreover, as motivation and influence is a core element of behaviour and change, the nudge theory can be used to further influence the social, environmental, and economic decisions, managing change and making decisions under uncertainty (Kahneman & Tversky, 1979; Kahneman, 2011). This will further complement the routines construct, which is silent about the mobilisation of motivation and intelligent adaptive efforts (Foss et al., 2012). Tidd and Bessant (2009) posit that there are no guaranteed recipes for innovation success, some organisations have developed pragmatic ways of acting and putting innovation in practice, experiments, or patterns linked to an innovation-friendly culture.

Gaps in the literature and opportunities for studies

Economic approach dominates majority of the innovation studies, allowing little room for the analysis of innovation and creative change within the organisation; thereby creating a need for approaching organisation as a learning system and to direct our attention to the role of actor cognition, internal organisational dynamics, and behaviour in shaping the external environment and outcomes of organisation change (Lam, 2005). Furthermore, the discourse on innovation and management of innovation is inundated with tech-start-ups, entrepreneurship, business model, and dynamic capabilities perspective; creating a scope of generating a narrative on the managerial cognition and innovation management in the incumbent large and old firms. Empirical research is also required to investigate how firms organise themselves to enhance the learning and motivation of organisation members (Foss et al., 2012). Additionally, there is also a need to extend the work of strategy and innovation context into how human capital might be nudged in appropriate ways to ensure the best individual and organisational outcomes (Felin, 2014). Moreover, the phenomenon of organisational innovation, especially on change and adaption, does not have a single coherent conceptual framework; because it is rooted in varied theoretical paradigms that use different research methods (Lam, 2005). Furthermore, for an innovative organisation, there is a continual need for not only motivating and enabling people to undertake complex work (Amabile & Conti, 1999) but also for shaping an integrative mind-set where people see problems as being correlated with broader wholes (Kanter, 1983).

Research approach

In management research, the field of strategic management must delve into the world of practice, and that explains the emergence of the sub-field of 'strategy as a practice'. The chapter builds on the consultative experience of the authors, insights from practical observations, and anecdotal evidence seeing how organisational transformation takes place and the way middle managers bring about the same. The intent here is to distil the practices, identify broad patterns and draw practical inferences that can inform managers attempting a similar cultural transformation.

For the empirical part of the research, an anchor organisation is studied, and the inferences are substantiated with the help of observations from relevant organisations wherever applicable. The anchor organisation is Anand Group (AG), one of India's largest auto-ancillary makers, and the organisational transformation is that from a focus on process improvement to a culture of breakthrough innovations. The level of observation is the middle managers and the unit of observation are the talent, routines, and incentives that have enabled such a transformation.

The data source primary consists of company reports, annual reports, internal memos, personal interviews, and factory visits. The interview transcripts and data sources are carefully coded on the dimensions of talent (both middle and senior), routines (explicit and implicit), and incentives (monetary and non-monetary). On the basis of identified pattern of the transition, a series of propositions are offered on how middle managers enable organisation transformation by orchestrating the levers of talent, routines, and incentives. Extant literature related to routines and capabilities, managerial choices and actions, nudge theory, and behavioural economics has helped to analyse, evaluate of case organisation, and propose our model.

A model of shaping organisational culture

A simplified model of innovation culture transformation comprising of three levers of change: talent, routines, and incentives is proposed in here. Talent refers to the people resources, across the length and breadth of the organisation. Routines are the ostensive and performative activities performed by the talent to achieve the desired outcome. Incentives are monetary and non-monetary causes that set talent to adopt a certain routine.

The internal dynamics of routines have the potential to promote continuous change and innovation (Feldman, 2000). Such underpinning influence of routines, especially ostensive aspects – shared understanding or shared schemata (Feldman, 2000; Feldman & Pentland, 2003; Becker, 2004) on the behaviour of the actors (Feldman, 2000; Feldman & Pentland, 2003), in an organisation is quintessential for innovation culture. Further, Tucker (2019) posits that informal managerial controls are associated with culture controls; thereby managers energising employees through the adequate and comprehensive system of rewards, and rigorous selection and socialisation process to bring in the right talent that nourishes and nurture innovation culture (Dougherty, 2008). Furthermore, routines can steer employees in a particular direction and nudge their behaviour; however routine construct, according to Foss et al. (2012) is silent about motivation. Hence, it is important to focus on talent (who) and incentives (why) to establish a well-rounded culture model.

As Thaler and Sustein (2008) assert different nudges can be used to change thinking. An appropriate incentive system with talent management routines facilitated a culture of innovation for large firms. Managers can use talent and incentives as nudges to build an innovation culture. A manager must identify the contexts where motivational dynamics are really at the core of the action (Foss et al., 2012).

Figure 7.1 presents a parsimonious model of change, anchored on routines, incentives, and talent that the middle management influences to bring about the desired change. The specific talent, routine, and incentive levels interventions at the organisation rolled out to bring about the desired transformation are outlined in the subsequent sections. Through interviews and field observations various

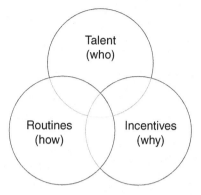

FIGURE 7.1   Three levers of cultural transformation: Talent, Routines, and Incentives.

practices are identified under each of the three levers, and then inferences are drawn with an implication for research and practice.

About Anand Group

Anand Group (AG) is one of India's largest auto-ancillary manufactures. Founded in 1961, the company has stitched together a series of strategic joint ventures (JV) and technology partnerships to introduce a wide range of technologies and world-class products to the Indian automobile market. As of 2020, the company supplies, at least, one component to most of the major Original Equipment Manufacturers (OEMs) in India. The customers include all major two-wheelers, three-wheelers, four-wheel passenger vehicles, commercial vehicles, tractors, earth moving equipment, and railways.

Headquartered in New Delhi, the group has 19 companies and manufacturing plants at 57 locations across 11 states in India. It has 23 partnerships with global technology leaders, of which 16 are in the form of JV, and seven are in technology licencing agreements. The company closed the FY 2019–2020 with a consolidated revenue of INR 100 billion and 14,000 employees.[1] In 2014, AG was awarded the Golden Peacock Award for enrolling and enabling innovators across the company's functions and levels.[2]

Notes Deep Anand, the Founder and Chief Mentor of AG:

> We encourage 'out of the box thinking' and being open to making mistakes and learning from them. I keep telling my management that let's take some chances and some risk. Life is all about daring. If you make some mistakes, so be it. But if you don't take any risk, you will stay still.[3]

The following section presents the specific interventions, along with timelines over the years, that have helped transform the firm's culture from a process-centric to an innovation-centric.

Enablers of the innovation culture at Anand Group

Specific organisational practices and initiatives around innovation management introduced at AG between the 1960s and 2020 which highlight the role of talent, routines, and incentives are discussed in here.

Talent

Four key initiatives relating to talent management have been identified and deliberated upon with managerial practices that have enabled organisational transformation by managing talents.

A belief that 'business is 90 percent people' (1961 onwards)

Deep Anand, founder of AG, is often heard saying – 'business is 90% people', and there is no better way of demonstrating this ethos than to look at some of the group's remarkable people practices. Two of the unique programmes having a direct impact on innovation culture are the 'Return to India' programme and 'Deputation with JV partners' programme.

Return to India (R2I) is a recruitment initiative to attract experts from some of the leading manufacturing companies in the US and Europe. Initiated in 1974, the programme aims at sourcing, at least, two managers every year to create a group-wide resource to manage assignments in various functions and companies of AG.

As a part of deputation with JV partners, AG sends about seven employees each year to its various JV partners for long durations for building expertise on various technical domains. On their return to India, these employees share and deploy the best global practices within AG companies. Between 1998 and 2012, more than 40 Anand managers were sent on long-term deputation to several of the JV partners in the US, Germany, France, Sweden, Korea, and Japan for periods ranging from one year to five years.[4]

Operating Engineers Model (1994 onwards)

One of the distinctive features of people development at AG is the Operating Engineer (OE) Model, the backbone of continuous improvement and innovation at the group companies. OE model is a unique approach to creating 'knowledge workers' on the shop floor. This programme was started on an experimental basis in 1994, and today has become an industry benchmark. Instead of hiring the unionised workforce, which is a practice in the manufacturing sector, the OE model works on employing diploma graduates and train them for four years for them to take up important roles and responsibilities at the company. This young and dynamic workforce, in the age group of 22–24 years, forms the backbone of a typical AG factory.

Operating Engineers (OEs) are put through a minimum of 40-hour training per year and are encouraged to complete their graduation/further education alongside their jobs. Typically, an OE at the end of their tenure turns out to be a seasoned operator who is fully capable of taking up more complex responsibilities and leading teams. The model has built-in planned attrition of 25%, which means that these OEs must ideally move into higher roles, such as supervisory or functional, or leave the company to give room to yet younger OEs. This ensures continuous refreshing of talent and ideas and doesn't let the OEs or managers fall for the complacency trap.

The company hires around 1,500 diploma graduates every year for the OE programme. To ensure diversity, the firm has a rule to not hire more than 20% of people from any single state. This makes the employees highly adaptive and mobile. At the end of the four years, knowledge-wise most of these OEs, who are still in their early 20s, are equivalent to the supervisor on a shop floor, except for the rigid attitude. Some of the most enduring benefits of the OE model include autonomy at the workplace, continuous training, multi-skilling and job-rotation, leadership qualities, and rapid knowledge enhancement of the Operating Engineers and fellow employees.

Sourcing innovation expertise from external consultants (2010–2015)

To source innovation capabilities, especially new routines and incentive mechanisms, AG engaged with a Bangalore-based innovation consultant, Erehwon Innovation Consulting. For the engagement, Erehwon's Orbit-Shifting Innovation™ methodology was adopted. The core framework, called Erehwon's Three Gear Thinking,[5] comprises three broad planks. Firstly, to develop multi-directional thinking, while staying away from root cause analysis; secondly, to seek hidden or invisible insights, both on problems and solutions; and finally, to challenge fundamentals while closely observing principles of the outside industry.

An important factor of the innovation programme is the evolution of the scope. When the programme started in 2010, the primary focus was on quality, cost, and delivery. By 2011, the focus shifted to manufacturing and operations; then by 2012, it got broadened to incorporate growth, business, and processes. By 2014, the scope encompassed innovations in products and businesses. Going forward, the team envisages applying the approach to address problems at the levels of society and the ecosystem.

As Rajendra Abhange, Senior Director and CTO of Gabriel India, observes:

> The greatest contribution of Erehwon was to bring the outside-in view of how the method has worked for several other companies and to help get the initial buy-in at the group level. The engagement with Erehwon has helped us develop the skills on challenging the assumptions and the given rules of the game. They taught us to think in compartments and to multiply ideas, while not dumping anything which sounds innocuous.[6]

The association with Erehwon started to ramp down towards 2016, and by then many of the innovation champions at the group were capable of replicating the best practices of innovation in a very systematic manner.

Routines

Following discussion entails key routines and processes that got developed and implemented at the AG companies enabling the proliferation of an innovation culture.

Nurturing long-term partnerships with global innovators (1961)

In 1961, Deep Anand established his first business venture called Gabriel India in collaboration with Maremont Corporation (now Gabriel Ride Control Products of Arvin Meritor Inc., USA) for the manufacture of shock absorbers at Mulund in Mumbai. Since then the group has forged over 15 partnerships with international manufacturers, from across the US, Japan, Korea, the UK, and several European countries.

Partners of AG are global leaders in their respective segments, and the same reflects in their JV positions in the Indian market. These partners come from various advanced countries and, together, span almost the entire automotive value chain.

On the synergies between AG and the JV partner, Arul Kumar, the MD of Spicer India (a JV with Dana Corporation of USA), says:

> Both Anand and Dana Corporation are batting on each other's strengths. The technology, design, and program management processes are all from Dana while the people processes and customer relationship management practices are from AG. We have shown enormous respect for the other's competence over the last 20 years, and that is what keeps the JV going. Because of the good faith of Dana, today we have the Chairman and the Managing Director of Spicer India from Anand.[7]

There were several good practices that Anand has borrowed from Dana Corporation, such as the Anand U, which are adapted from Dana U, and the people processes, which were adopted from Dana Operating System. Such partnerships allow for constant enhancement of talent and transfer of robust routines from the world's best-run manufacturing innovators.

Co-creation with leading Indian OEMs (2000 onwards)

One way of sourcing new routines and making the existing routines better is to engage with the demanding customers directly. The Indian market offers some of the most stringent requirements for automobile companies. One remarkable example of an India-driven innovation is the HVAC unit that MAHLE Behr designed for Tata Nano in 2007. The climate control system was entirely designed at the Indian R&D unit in Pune, when, in the first place, the German partner – Behr – almost ridiculed the price of the product. But in the process, the company developed several new competencies in design and manufacturing, which had later served well in other projects.[8]

On the Tata Nano project, Sunil Kaul reflects:

> Immediately after we developed HVAC for Nano, I received a senior delegation from Mercedes Benz, Germany and they asked us – "How do you design an AC?". I quipped – "You should be talking to Germans, I learned AC designing from them," To my rebuttal, they said – "You guys are good at making the basics in air conditioners. So, if I need something more, I will add on to that. Whereas a German would only think of the most luxurious AC and then de-feature, and that will not reduce the cost." That is the kind of capability we can build in India.[9]

Such challenging conditions and customers enable experimentation and new routine formation, which would have otherwise taken AG years to develop in isolation. The duration of partnership that AG has managed to sustain is remarkable and sort of an exception in the highly dynamic automotive industry.

Participation in VSME programme (2010)

Another important source of competence for AG is the domestic manufacturing ecosystem. AG is a part of the unique VLFM (Visionary Leaders For Manufacturing) programme, where CII teamed with the National Manufacturing Competitiveness Council (NMCC), Japan International Cooperation Agency (JICA), IIT-Madras, IIT-Kanpur, and IIM-Calcutta. The objective of VLFM is to create Visionary Leaders skilled to transform Indian manufacturing by conveying the management concept of Japanese manufacturing to senior and middle managers. Under the programme, the managers and workers from carefully identified SMEs are mentored by these larger companies over a year to transfer the best practices in manufacturing and management.

AG has taken a lead in driving the VSME programme in its supplier community. During the facilitation of transformation, Anand participants and suppliers undergo specially designed training to learn and apply various tools, such as workplace transformation, value stream maps, Heijunka planning, machine transformation, quality stabilisation, and control by pull.

Notes MS Shankar:

> The VSME program has made the procurement, production, and delivery cycles less fluctuating. It has offered us an opportunity to think beyond the production issues and help us focus on creating breakthroughs while

challenging the limits. This has helped us free our people's time and attention from managing low-complexity tasks to now focusing on innovation.[10]

Thanks to programmes like VSME, once the routines become deeply entrenched and almost automatic, the management and employees could start developing higher-order routines and that's how the layers of competencies get created.

Creating the innovation architecture (2013 onwards)

So far the various innovation initiatives, as a part of external engagements with Erehwon, SMEs, OEMs, and JV partners, were shaping up as islands of excellence, and it was time for the Technology Office at the company to bring all of these under one umbrella.

Starting April 2013, the innovation team at Anand started to work on a reference document for the innovation that would offer guidelines on various techniques, practices, examples, and insights drawn from the past four years of the innovation programme. Dubbed as the 'Architecture for Innovation', the manual provides a set of guidelines, which can be deployed by the innovation champions at the various group companies, to foster, sustain, and fission a culture of innovation.

The five elements of the Architecture are Strategy, Processes of Pursuit of Challenges, People Capability, Practices, and Platforms. Architecture has helped set the culture of innovation by helping build capabilities of employees in adopting a systematic innovation methodology, and yielding results that are quantum in nature. Table 7.1 details the Innovation Architect.

Incentives

Getting the appropriate talent and setting the suitable routines are only as useful as the talent's ability and willingness to follow those routines well and change those along the way. While the Innovation Architecture lays out ostensive aspects of the routines, the incentives would ensure that routines are indeed performed as intended and that they also improve basis the changing organisational requirements and external realities. Critical incentives that AG laid down for employees to embrace change and for enduring transformation are outlined in here.

TABLE 7.1 Innovation architecture at Anand Group

Innovation architecture at Anand Group   **Key objectives:**   − To create a quantum impact in areas of influence   − Develop Innovation Champions   − Creative breakthrough results

Strategy	Processes	People capacity	Practices	Platforms
– Portfolio of challenges and aspirations – People ecosystem for innovation – Trackers to map the evolution of journey, challenges, and people	– Identification of challenges – Pursuing challenges – Recognising the closure of challenges	– Evolving clarity of roles – Embedding breakthrough thinking and engagements – Evolving twin-track KRA systems	– Innovation principles – Interpersonal alignment for enrolment – Rewards – Live Concourse – Innovation review – Publishing Lighthouse	– Creating banks for challenges, ideas, frames, and insights – Implementation platform

Five key elements of driving innovation

Formation of Innovation@Anand Group (2010)

To give a formal shape to various innovation initiatives, in 2010 AG launched Innovation@Anand. The objective was to graduate from seeking continuous improvement to creating breakthroughs by adopting a systematic and repetitive process for developing innovation champions across levels and functions.

The initiative, led by MS Shankar and Sunil Kaul, resulted in wide-spread participation of the people for two primary reasons. First, through the several *Live Concourse* sessions, the innovation champions could demonstrate that 'it works', and how ordinary people could achieve extraordinary feats by applying methods. Second, the employees could see the leadership being supportive and encouraging to take risks and even fail at times.

On building the culture of innovation, Sunil Kaul reflects:

> To instill the belief in our people, we first worked with the non-R&D employees and let them chose projects which are closer to their heart and where they can bring about improvements at their levels. Trained on the Erehwon methodology, the people did pick up projects around quality improvement, waste reduction, power savings, and other functions. Seeing the success, we then took up the engineers and looked at product innovations.
>
> Culture is built when you touch 40% of your people and not just 5–10%. The key was a mindset change and not innovation as a project. The start from non-R&D people was the key to instill a sense of 'can do' attitude in our people.
>
> Today when you challenge a shop floor person to look at a 100% improve-ment, the response is 'let me try'. We have been able to start a 'movement', and not just train people on techniques. That to me is the greatest source of satisfaction.

There are a couple of interesting insights one could draw from the statement. First, the Innovation Group didn't limit innovation or radical improvement to the most obvious areas of product development or R&D, but instead broad-based it. Second, a tipping point is identified in terms of the number of people who must be influenced to bring about a lasting change. Thirdly, there's a testimony to how incentives lead to confidence building. Such an approach helped scale innovation across the group companies.

Innovation champions at group companies (2011 onwards)

To ensure the proliferation of the learning of the innovation programme, the group formed an Innovation Task Force, called *i5*, in each group company. This was apart from the *i7* team that would operate at the group level. The i5 would have the COO and a few functional heads to reinforce the insights from the innovation programme and have one full-time leader anchoring the journey. These Innovation Leaders would identify challenges, and enable competence building across functions. By recognising the enthusiasts and evangelists of innovation at the company and group level, an additional external incentive is provided for one to continue on the innovation journey.

Between 2011 and 2013, the Innovation@Anand programme successfully launched the initiatives called Firestarters@Anand, FirestarterLeaders@Anand, and InnovationStarters@Anand. These are titles given to people who have contributed significantly to the innovation process and achieved remarkable results. Table 7.3 depicts the various innovation champions formed at AG as a part of the innovation programme.

TABLE 7.2 Some of the innovation champion programmes identified at Anand Group

Mechanisms	Purpose	Participants
Innovation @Anand	Embedding a culture of innovation at Anand Group companies. Creation of Innovation Champions	All employees
i7@Anand	Conceptualising, creating, and steering the journey.	Sponsors from Anand Executive Committee, Leaders at Anand Corporate, and Leaders from group companies
i5@Individual Company	Creating, enabling, and steering innovation challenges at each company.	Company COO, Innovation Leaders, Innovation Anchor, Leader at Anand Corporate
FireStarter@Anand/ InnovationStarter@ Anand	Identifying individuals who have either taken series of challenges or the first challenge at any company	Employees

At the Innovation Concourse held at Gabriel India in December 2015, Late Dr. APJ Abdul Kalam, former President of India, advised the leadership team at the company on furthering innovation. He said:

> It is a great achievement that from a centralized drive, a culture of innovation has started taking root at Gabriel. To take it to every employee, one has to follow the method of 'nuclear fission', that is, to set up innovation centers at each production center to nurture innovative ideas and shape those into products needed for the customers. Auto-component manufacturers need to innovate and create better and global leadership products.[11]

Further, the innovators are given time and space to work on these projects, outside of their work schedule. What was needed next is avenues for employees to display their talent and creations, and this happened through the Live Concourse sessions. Table 7.2 depicts the various titles given to innovation champions at AG.

Live Concourse for demonstrating innovation success stories (2010 onwards)

Nothing gives more confidence to ideators and innovators than a public acknowledgment of their efforts and results, both successful and not so much. To demonstrate some of the concepts and the outcomes of the innovation programme, AG conducted the first Live Concourse in Pune in December 2010. The Live Concourse served as a mechanism to inspire stakeholders of the company, especially the OEs.

Deep Anand reviewed the projects and the progress. His presence was vital to further the innovation drive at the group. There were individual contributors identified at various companies to further facilitate the proliferation of these concepts and practices. These were later called 'Fire Starters'. The idea was to infuse fission across teams, such that these were self-sustaining. By the time the second Concourse was held in March 2011, the programme had become pan-Anand and experienced very high visibility. The participation levels became so huge that each of the group companies then started organising their separate Live Concourses to showcase their innovations.

Rewards and recognition programmes (2014)

In August 2014, Innovation@Anand formally rolled out the Rewards and Recognition initiative for the innovation programme. On the impact of rewards and recognition programme Manoj Kolhatkar notes:

> Right from the senior level, we have impressed upon setting a mechanism of rewarding people for their contribution. We not only reward people for what they have achieved but, more importantly, for what they have undertaken.

> The results are not as important as the participation, and the efforts. That has helped encourage the 'freedom to fail' at the organisation.[12]

Once again, the focus is not on results as much as on the process, and that, in many ways, is the reason for the success of the innovation programme at AG. Since 2014, Innovation@Anand has become a part of the Annual Strategy making process at the group, and there are specific targets and challenges identified to be achieved by the innovation programme.

These rewards are threshold-based and are not ranked. The two criteria are – capabilities demonstrated and results achieved. The fixed portion of the rewards is aimed at recognising capabilities during ideation and prototyping, while the variable category is focussed on sustaining the result. The rewards are through a point system. Further, as of 2015, the practice had been rolled out across the group companies, which participated in the journey – Innovation@Anand.

Together, the formation of Innovation@Anand, identification of various roles and titles around innovation, demonstration through Live Concourse, and formal rewards and recognition programmes have helped embed routines into the consciousness and practices of talent and enabled organisational transformation.

Inferences from the case study

The case elucidates specific factors and approaches the middle management adopted in shaping talent base, organisational routines, and incentive mechanisms to bring about a cultural transformation. Table 7.3 depicts a sequential

TABLE 7.3 Plotting the various talent, routines, and incentive level interventions across the timeline

Timelines/ levers	1960–1990	1991–2000	2001–2010	2011–2020
Talent	A belief that 'business is 90 percent people'			
Routines	Nurturing long terms partnerships with global innovators			
Talent		Operating Engineers Model		
Routines			Co-creating with leading Indian OEMs	
Routines			Participation in VSME programme	
Talent			Sourcing innovation expertise from external consultants	
Incentives			Formation of Innovation@Anand Group	
Incentives			Live Concourse for demonstrating innovation success stories	
Routines				Creating the Architecture of Innovation
Incentives				Innovation champions at group companies
Incentives				Rewards and recognition programmes

model transformation at AG, where specific practices are routines, incentives and talent are identified chronologically.

The founder Deep C Anand believed that 'business is 90 percent people' that helped set the stage for transformation, for has it not being for a focus on talent, any changes in routines or even incentives are not sustainable. The seeding of world-class innovation routines and competencies, first around process innovations and later around product innovation, is a direct consequence of selective and enduring partnerships with world-class manufacturing companies, and almost all joint ventures formed over the years remain to date.

The OE Model, launched in the mid-1990s, further introduced a steady stream of talent into the organisation that would embrace the new processes and routines more readily than the unionised workers and the built-in attrition ensures that complacency doesn't set in either for the managers or the employees.

The co-creation of products with leading Indian OEMs helped Anand benchmark its product development and process creation capabilities with the best in the industry and often to exacting standards set by Indian companies and MNCs working in India. This also helped the transfer of higher-order routines between the customers, JV partners, and suppliers. The VSME programme further helped the company formalise some of its routines of problem-solving, process improvement, and product development while engaging with and teaching small and medium-sized suppliers and vendors.

With these interventions and building up of absorptive capacity, AG was at the right juncture to engage with external experts on innovation framework, and Erehwon taught a group of Anand managers routines of structured problem solving and seeded enabled projects to demonstrate a transformation from process innovations to product innovations.

Such practices later got scaled with the introduction of Innovation@Anand and conducting of Live Concourses which helped formalise the processes and practices of innovation. The creation of Innovation Architecture and incentives in terms of identification and celebration of innovation champions and formal rewards and recognition programme ensured that there is an explicit reason for employees to continue showing interest in the initiative and also improve the routines along the way.

As seen in the case, if any of the three elements are missing, the transformation won't take place. A change in talent, both fresh talent from outside and renewed talent from within is the starting point, and this needs to be following a new set of routines, which come from both top-down (ostensive), and bottom-up (performative), and are held together with incentives. If the incentives, both monetary and non-monetary, are missing the talent would not have reason to move from one set of practices to another, and they would recoil to their previous selves. Similarly, the routines cannot be static either, else they would not keep pace with external changes.

Conclusion

Building new capabilities sustainably and predictably is the holy grail of organisations. In this chapter, we have identified three levers of innovation culture:

routines, talent, and incentives. Together, the talent, routines, and incentives denote the 'who', 'how', and 'why' dimensions of organisational transformation, respectively. Taking the case of India's Anand Group, a total of 11 organisational practices, initiated over 60 years, from 1961 till 2020, are identified around the dimensions of talent, routines, and incentives.

The chapter offers three key practical applications. First, it brings to the attention the importance of the middle manager, which is often overlooked in the discourse on cultural transformation because most of the previous work has focussed on the leaders or the senior management team. Second, the case study-based work synthesises the literature on routines, talent, and incentives, bringing in three otherwise disparate literature into the stream of organisational capability creation. By borrowing relevant concepts from disparate domains and contextualising them to the capability creation realm, the work offers a coherent, more practical view. Finally, the paper offers in detail how such a cultural transformation has taken place in an organisation from the emerging economy, India, and shares, with anecdotal evidence and first-hand research, how middle management plays a significant role in ushering innovation culture.

From a theoretical vantage point, the research furthers the investigation of micro-foundations of strategy, in terms of the sources of sustainable competitive advantages and how new capabilities come into being. By adopting a case study based research, a much more granular treatment is dealt with for the trajectory of capability creation and the role of the agency, which offer the much-needed ammunition to the 'strategy as a practice' stream of research.

In terms of furthering the research, the conceptual model of three levers can be tested out with a large sample size, to validate the correctness and completeness of the model. Given the nature of the investigation, qualitative research, based on longitudinal data would be more suitable for such an attempt. It would be useful to nuance with a specific set of routines, talent, and incentive mechanisms amicable for capability creation and organisational transformation. Though the model starts with the middle management, in a mid-sized organisation, there is no reason to believe that the findings would be limited to just about that size or organisational composition.

Notes

1 Auto component maker Anand announces senior management appointments. September 22, 2020. https://auto.economictimes.indiatimes.com/news/auto-components/auto-component-maker-anand-announces-senior-management-appointments/78237327#:~:text=Anand%20Executive%20Board%20New%20Delhi,Jubilee%20year%20of%20the%20company.
2 ANAND – winner of prestigious Golden Peacock Award Innovation Management (2014). Anand Group India Stories. November 1, 2014. Available at: http://www.anandgroupindia.com/stories/434-anand--winner-of-prestigious-golden-peacock-award--innovation-management-2014-nov-01-2014.aspx
3 From an address by Deep Anand to his employees made in May 2006 at New Delhi.
4 ANAND Interaction. Volume LVI, May 2012 (pp. 1).
5 Erehwon presentation adapted by Anand Group.

6 Based on interview with Rajendra Abhange on November 6, 2015 at Gabriel Hosur.
7 Based on interview with Arul Kumar on October 19, 2015 at Spicer India Pune campus.
8 Nano suppliers think smart. The Auto Car Professional. April 1, 2009. Available at: http://www.autocarpro.in/features/nano-suppliers-smart-3643
9 Based on an interview with Sunil Kaul on February 18, 2016 at MAHLE Behr Pune campus.
10 Based on a conversation with Shankar on February 18, 2016 at Spicer India plant in Pune.
11 As recollected by Shankar during an interview on February 18, 2016 at Spicer India plant in Pune.
12 Based on interview with Manoj Kolhatkar on October 21, 2015 at Gabriel Pune campus.

References

Adner, R., & Helfat, C. E. (2003). Corporate effects and dynamic managerial capabilities. *Strategic Management Journal*, 24(10), 1011–1025.

Amabile, T. M., & Conti, R. (1999). Changes in the work environment for creativity during downsizing. *Academy of Management Journal*, 42(6), 630–640.

Argyris, C., & Schon. (1974). *Theory in Practice: Increasing Professional Effectiveness*. Jossey-Bass.

Becker, M. C. (2004). Organisational routines: A review of the literature. *Industrial and Corporate Change*, 13(4), 643–678.

Becker, M. C., Lazaric, N., Nelson, R. R., & Winter, S. G. (2005). Applying organisational routines in understanding organisational change. *Industrial and Corporate Change*, 14(5), 775–791.

Birdi, K. (2020). Insights on impact from the development, delivery, and evaluation of the CLEAR IDEAS innovation training model. *European Journal of Work and Organizational Psychology*, doi: 10.1080/1359432X.2020.1770854

Büschgens, T., Bausch, A., & Balkin, D. B. (2013). Organisational culture and innovation: A meta-analytic review. *Journal of Product Innovation Management*, 30(4), 763–781.

Dobni, C. B. (2008). Measuring innovation culture in organisations: The development of a generalized innovation culture construct using exploratory factor analysis. *European Journal of Innovation Management*, 11(4), 539–559.

Dougherty, D. (2008). Bridging social constraint and social action to design organisations for innovation. *Organisation Studies*, 29(3), 415–434.

Feldman, M. S. (2000). Organisational routines as a source of continuous change. *Organisation Science*, 11(6), 611–629.

Feldman, M. S., & Pentland, B. T. (2003). Reconceptualizing organisational routines as a source of flexibility and change. *Administrative Science Quarterly*, 48(1), 94–118.

Felin, T. (2014). *Nudge: Manager as Choice Architect*. Oxford University working paper, SSRN. 10.2139/ssrn.2523922.

Felin, T., & Hesterly, W. S. (2007). The knowledge-based view, nested heterogeneity, and new value creation: Philosophical considerations on the locus of knowledge. *Academy of Management Review*, 32(1), 195–218.

Floyd, S. W., & Lane, P. J. (2000). Strategizing throughout the organisation: Managing role conflict in strategic renewal. *Academy of Management Review*, 25(1), 154–177.

Foss, N. J., Heimeriks, K. H., Winter, S. G., & Zollo, M. (2012). A Hegelian dialogue on the micro-foundations of organizational routines and capabilities. *European Management Review*, 9(4), 173–197.

Ghoshal, S., & Moran, P. (1996). Bad for practice: A critique of the transaction cost theory. *Academy of Management Review*, 21(1), 13–47.

Huy, Q. N. (2002). Emotional balancing of organisational continuity and radical change: The contribution of middle managers. *Administrative Science Quarterly*, 47(1), 31–69.

Kahneman, D. (2011). *Thinking, fast and slow*. Macmillan.

Kahneman, D., & Tversky, A. (1979). On the interpretation of intuitive probability: A reply to Jonathan Cohen. *Cognition*, 7, 409–411.

Kanter, R. M. (1983). *The change masters: Innovation for productivity in the American corporation*. Simon and schuster.

Koumakhov, R., & Daoud, A. (2017). Routine and reflexivity: Simonian cognitivism vs practice approach. *Industrial and Corporate Change*, 26(4), 727–743.

Lam, W. (2005). Successful knowledge management requires a knowledge culture: A case study. *Knowledge Management Research & Practice*, 3(4), 206–217.

March, J. G. (1991). Exploration and exploitation in organisational learning. *Organisation Science*, 2(1), 71–87.

Morris, L. (2007). *Creating the Innovation Culture: Geniuses, Champions, and Leaders*. Innovation Lab White Papers, Innovation Labs. http://www.innovationlabs.com/publications/creating-the-innovationculture/

Nelson, R. R., & Winter, S. G. (1982). *An Evolutionary Theory of Economic Change*. Harvard University Press.

Nonaka, I. (1988). Toward middle-up-down management: Accelerating information creation. *MIT Sloan Management Review*, 29(3), 9.

Parmigiani, A., & Howard-Grenville, J. (2011). Routines revisited: Exploring the capabilities and practice perspectives. *Academy of Management Annals*, 5(1), 413–453.

Pentland, B. T., Feldman, M. S., Becker, M. C., & Liu, P. (2012). Dynamics of organisational routines: A generative model. *Journal of Management Studies*, 49(8), 1484–1508.

Reeves, M., Levin, S., & Ueda, D. (2016). The biology of corporate survival. *Harvard Business Review*, 94(1), 2.

Thaler, R., & Sunstein, C. (2008). *Nudge: Improving Decisions about Health, Wealth and Happiness*. Yale University Press.

Tidd, J., & Bessant, J. (2009). *Managing Innovation: Integrating Technological, Market, and Organisational Change*. John Wiley & Sons.

Tucker, B. P. (2019). Heard it through the grapevine: Conceptualizing informal control through the lens of social network theory. *Journal of Management Accounting Research*, 31(1), 219–245.

Tushman, M. L., & O'Reilly, C. A. (1996). Ambidextrous organizations: Managing evolutionary and revolutionary change. *California Management Review*, 38(4), 8–29. doi:10.2307/41165852

Westley, F. R. (1990). Middle managers and strategy: Microdynamics of inclusion. *Strategic Management Journal*, 11(5), 337–351.

8

MANAGEMENT TOOLS FOR BUSINESS MODEL INNOVATION – A REVIEW

Hussan Munir Lars Bengtsson and Emil Åkesson

Introduction

The concept of business model innovation (BMI) has attracted researchers for almost 20 years and developed rapidly as a research concept (Foss and Saebi, 2017). BMI is often portrayed in the academic literature as a new type of innovation that "complements the traditional subjects of process, product, and organizational innovation" (Zott et al., 2011). Despite many years of research on BMI, it is still relatively unclear how companies and their managers innovate their business models and what management tools they use to manage the BMI process (e.g., Heikkilä et al., 2018a). Overall, it is assumed in the academic literature that managers try to maintain consistency between the company's strategic activities and core components of the business model by monitoring external and internal risks that may harm the current business model, anticipate potential consequences and implement actions to modify the business model to preserve or increase performance (Demil and Lecocq, 2010). However, practitioners seem to struggle to identify appropriate tools to manage BMI (Chesbrough, 2010) as well as a unifying conceptualization of the BMI tools (e.g., Remane et al., 2017b).

The empirical knowledge on how managers manage BMI mainly concerns stages in the BMI process (Frankenberger et al., 2013) as well as the complex, emergent and experimental (Berends et al., 2016; Laudien and Daxböck, 2017) character of the process, contrasting to the more rationally assumed process in the conceptual research literature (e.g., (Demil and Lecocq, 2010). However, in none of these empirical studies on the BMI process, management tools are focused. Thus, there is a lack of knowledge of what management tools managers use to manage the BMI process. While this naturally calls for empirical research on BMI tools, we first need to know what management tools that could be in use and for what purpose. Similar to strategic management and innovation

DOI: 10.4324/9780429346033-11

management, researchers on BMI have developed and proposed management tools to use when managing this process (Heikkilä et al., 2018a).

The purpose of this chapter is to identify and classify proposed BMI tools, through a literature review of academic publications, intending to provide answers to the research question:

Which are the different types of BMI tools proposed by academic research?

What types of strategic objectives and innovation contexts are intended using BMI tools?

Our main findings are that the overall number of BMI tools described in the research literature is limited mostly to facilitate design processes rather than for test or implementation purposes. Moreover, the identified tools are based on conceptual reasoning and not on empirical studies of tools used by managers. The findings imply a need to do empirical investigations of the diffusion of BMI tools to managers and include strategy tools in such a study, as well as investigating the effectiveness of such tools.

The chapter proceeds as follows. First, we introduce a definition of BMI tools. Second, we describe the literature review we have done resulting in identifying 35 peer-reviewed journal articles containing proposals for BMI tools. Third, we review and classify all the tools and analyze our findings, i.e., evaluate the collection of tools in terms of the number of tools, distribution of purpose and evidence of use and effectiveness. Fourth, we conclude with a summary of our findings and avenues for further research.

Definition of Business Model Innovation Tool

Defining the concept BMI is not an easy exercise. Indeed, as demonstrated in recent reviews of the business model (Massa et al., 2017) and BMI literature (Foss and Saebi, 2017), researchers have so far failed to unite around a single definition of both concepts. Depending on how one interprets the business model, BMI concepts one may lean in different directions for what should constitute a BMI tool. There is, however, among researchers a definitional convergence that a business model concerns value creation, value delivery and value capture mechanism in a firm (Foss and Saebi, 2017; Massa et al., 2017). The most often used definition of a business model is the one proposed by Teece (2010:172) "the design or architecture of the value creation, delivery, and capture mechanisms of a firm", which we will adopt in this chapter. In line with this BMI will here be defined as "designed, novel, and non-trivial changes to key elements of a firm's business model and/or the architecture linking these elements" (Foss and Saebi, 2017:216).

One solution is to lean on proposed tools in the academic literature to identify BMI tools. In defining a BMI tool, we pragmatically fall back on the proposed tools in the literature. We define a BMI tool to be any tool that is intentionally and explicitly (by a researcher) proposed to be used to facilitate a change of the way a firm creates value, delivers and captures value from it, both in terms of changes in key elements and/or links in the architecture of elements. A BMI

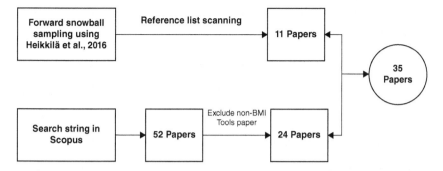

FIGURE 8.1 Research method.

tool, for the purpose of our analysis, then, is generally any tool that is provided with the intention to facilitate business model change or innovation.

Research Method

We performed a literature review using a search string in Scopus and forward snowball sampling method by using the paper based on empirical studies of BMI tools (Heikkilä et al., 2016a). As far as we know this is the only paper, so far, that explicitly studies how managers manage BMI paths and relate appropriate BMI tools to these paths. The search query was composed of the following keywords "business model innovation★" AND "tool★" in Scopus. The search string only included peer-reviewed articles in the English language and the keywords were searched in fields title, keywords and abstract. The search query yielded 52 articles on BMI tools. We excluded all papers that do not present BMI tools and filtered 24 papers addressing sustainable BMI tools. Moreover, we performed a forward snowball sampling and found 11 more relevant papers in scanning the reference list, giving a total of 35 selected academic papers. Figure 8.1 shows the literature review method.

Classification of Business Model Innovation Tools

As defined above BMI can be seen as changes in both key elements of the firm's business model, such as non-trivial changes in the pricing structure, and in the whole architecture of the business model which may involve a whole ecosystem of firms. An example of BMI could be changing from products to services to attract new customer groups, moving the company's processes to the cloud (e.g., data analytics), outsourcing/insourcing of key resources (e.g., value network), changes in pricing strategies (e.g., pay per use) or monetization and revenue, e.g., ads (Heikkilä et al., 2016a). There are several methods, frameworks, and templates, referred to as tools (Bouwman et al., 2012), which have been developed to facilitate BMI but overall BMI literature lacks classification (Bouwman et al., 2012). Following the innovation management literature we may differentiate between BMI phases or stages in the innovation process as proposed by (Bouwman et al., 2012; Heikkilä et al., 2016a), i.e., exploration, design, test and implementation. In line with strategic management literature, we may differentiate between different objectives with the BMI changes: for the start of a new business, profit or growth (Heikkilä et al., 2018a). Finally, we can use entrepreneurship literature to differentiate between start-ups, small and medium size enterprises (SMEs), and large firms. BMI tools can be then classified into three possible categories which are as follows.

• Innovation process stages
• Strategic objectives
• New firm or size of a firm

The classification of all the tools found in the literature review can be found in Appendix 8.1.

Process-based tools classification

This classification is based on exploring BMI stages (Bouwman et al., 2012; Heikkilä et al., 2016a). The exploration phase refers to tools to scan the environment analyzing the conditions for BMI and/or identifying opportunities for BMI. Our review has not found any specific BMI tool for exploration. Instead, the use of well-known strategic management tools, such as PESTEL, SWOT and Porter's 5-forces tool (Porter, 2008), which may indicate both opportunities and threats to BMI, are mentioned as exploration tools by Heikkilä et al. (2016a).

The design phase refers to tools that facilitate the design of a new or changed business model either in a holistic way, such as the CANVAS (Osterwalder and Pigneur, 2002), or focus on different aspects of BMs, e.g., the BM Cube (Lindgren and Horn Rasmussen, 2013) that can address value sharing between network partners. The test phase refers to the use of tools analyzing the viability of the company's business model or intended changes in it. For instance, the use of success factors as proposed in STOF approach (Bouwman et al., 2008) and six-step stress testing for the BM (Haaker et al., 2017). The implementation phase concerns the implementation of a new or a planned change in the BMI, e.g., tools that deal with scalability and agility. Moreover, the tools related to roadmaps and the order in which certain steps have to be followed are also relevant in this stage.

Objective-based tools classification

This classification is based on the strategic objectives of the firm concerning BM innovation (Heikkilä et al., 2016a). The objectives are as follows.

• O1: Start a new business
• O2: Make the business profitable
• O3: Make the business grow

O1 refers to the start of a new business that requires more exploratory scanning of the target market, target customers, develop the value proposition, identify potential competitors, a viable revenue model, etc. O2 deals with the improved use of internal resources, explores new revenue models, customer analysis, use-value networks, stakeholder analysis, new ideas, etc. Finally, O3 may entail attracting more customers, market analysis, improve the firm's branding, improve offerings and value proposition based on market analysis, and build a supplier and partner network to find new channels to expand indigenous or foreign markets.

Organizational size-based tools classification

This classification is based on the size of the firms and includes start-ups and established firms. To start a new business is obviously the main objective for start-ups rather than established firms with an existing business model. However, also established firms may start new businesses, i.e., corporate entrepreneurship, and start-ups may after some time aim to grow their business. Overall, this classification implies that different organizational sizes may require using different BMI tools.

Reviewing the BMI Tools – Findings

Table 8.1 lists the BMI tools in chronological order, in terms of names or acronyms and literature reference, i.e., when they have been first published. The first tools to appear on the list are established strategic management tools, such as the SWOT and five-forces that have been used for decades in strategic decision-making, but later have been described as useful also in management processes related to business model innovation. An example is the five-forces framework first introduced by Michael Porter in a HBR-article (Porter, 1979) and then described as a BMI tool by Osterwalder and Pigneur (2010) and Heikkilä et al. (2016a). The first genuine BMI tool to appear is the CANVAS model (Osterwalder and Pigneur, 2002, 2010) which has greatly influenced the subsequent development of the field, in terms of both research and development of new tools.

In terms of the tools main intended stage, intended objectives and main intended size or context we get the following distribution (Table 8.2):

Most tools are based on conceptual reasoning and in many of them case studies are used to illustrate the applicability and value of the tool. In three papers the tools are based on a systematic literature review, such as the review of software tools that may facilitate various tasks related to business model innovation (Szopinski et al., 2020). Only in five papers the tools are based on a more substantial empirical base.

BMI tools – innovation process stages

In terms of the main stage most proposed tools are intended to be used in the design phase, facilitating managers to design changes or new business models. Among the design tools we find the most well-known tool: the business model

TABLE 8.1 Classification of tools

No	References (in chronological order)	Method (Conceptual, empirical, lit review)	Main intended stage				Main intended objective			Main intend size
			Expl	De-sign	Test	Impl	New bus	Profit	Growth	Startup/Establ/Both
1	PEST-analysis (Aguilar, 1979; Gupta, 2013)	Conc	X					X	X	Est
2	Five forces framework (Porter, 1979, 2008)	Conc and case studies	X					X	X	Est
3	SWOT (Piercy and Giles, 1989)	Conc	X					X	X	Est
4	E-business model/ Business Model CANVAS (Osterwalder and Pigneur, 2002, 2010)	Conc		X			X	X	X	Both
5	The elements of a successful business model (Johnson et al., 2008)	Conc and illustr cases				X			X	Est
6	STOF (Bouwman et al., 2008)	Conc				X		X		Est
7	An activity system design framework (Zott and Amit, 2010)	Conc		X			X	X		Both
8	The white space (Johnson and Lafley, 2010; Leavy, 2010)	Conc and illustrat cases	X				X	X	X	Est
9	Designing for performance-a technique for business model estimation (Heikkilä et al., 2010)	Conc				X		X		Est
10	ANCHOR (Deshler and Smith, 2011)	Conc		X				X		Est
11	Differentiators (Deshler and Smith, 2011)	Conc		X				X		Est
12	Functional Alignment Matrix (Deshler and Smith, 2011)	Conc				X		X		Est
13	Lean venturing (Breuer, 2013)	Conc+illustrative cases				X	X			Est

#	Tool	Type						Class
14	Business model roadmapping (De Reuver et al., 2013)	Conc		X		X		Est
15	VISOR (El Sawy and Pereira, 2013)	Conc	X				X	Both
16	Innovation readiness levels for BMI (Evans and Johnson, 2013)	Conc		X			X	Est
17	The 4I-framework of BMI (Frankenberger et al., 2013)	Emp: 14 case studies		X	X			Est
18	BM Cube (Lindgren and Horn Rasmussen, 2013)	Conc + illustr cases	X				X	Est
19	Business Model Navigator (Gassmann et al., 2014a, 2014b)	Emp 250 business models	X				X	Est
20	The innovation pivot framework for startups (García-Gutiérrez and Martínez-Borreguero, 2016)	Conc		X	X			St
21	BM analysis using computational modeling (Groesser and Jovy, 2016)	Conc + illustrat case			X		X	Est
22	Metrics for BMs (Heikkilä et al., 2016b)	Conc + 4 illustr cases	X		X		X	Est
23	360° business model innovation (Rayna and Striukova, 2016)	Conc + illustr cases	X				X	Est
24	A five-V framework to map out potential innovation routes (Taran et al., 2016)	Systematic lit review	X		X		X	Est
25	Performance assessment and experimentation tool for BMI (Batocchio et al., 2017)	Conc + illustr case			X	X		St
26	Business model stress testing (Haaker et al., 2017)	Conc + illustr case	X				X	Est
27	Digital business models in traditional industries (Remane et al., 2017a)	Conc	X				X	Est
28	The BM Pattern Database-A Tool (Remane et al., 2017b)	Systematic li review		X			X	Est

(Continued)

No	References (in chronological order)	Method (Conceptual, empirical, lit review)	Main intended stage				Main intended objective			Main intend size
			Expl	De-sign	Test	Impl	New bus	Profit	Growth	Startup/Establ/Both
29	Visual tools for BMI (Täuscher and Abdelkafi, 2017)	Systematic lit review		X						Est
30	From strategic goals to business model innovation paths (Heikkilä et al., 2018b)	Emp: 11 case studies				X	X	X	X	Est
31	A BMI Tool for Established Firms (Trapp et al., 2018)	Conc + 4 case studies		X			X	X		Est
32	Business model schema (Kim et al., 2020)	Conc		X				X		Est
33	Digital business using a freemium BM (Panda, 2019)	Conc		X					X	St
34	Software tools for business model innovation (Szopinski et al., 2020)	Emp: review of software tools		X				X		Est

TABLE 8.2 Distribution of BMI tools in the review

Method	Main intended stage				Main intended objective			Main intended size	
	Expl	Design	Test	Impl	New business	Profit	Growth	Startup	Est
Conceptual incl cases -27									
Empirical -5 Syst lit review -3	4	17	3	11	8	23	10	6	31

Canvas (Osterwalder and Pigneur, 2002, 2010) which have inspired other BMI tools too in this review. In 15 of the reviewed papers the business model Canvas has been used in different ways to develop new BMI tools. The design tools can be divided into two types of tools – the modeling tools and the pattern matching tools. Zott and Amit (2010) provide a theoretical grounding for both types of tools, as tools to design elements (content, structure, governance) and tools for design themes. The modeling tools allow managers to experiment with different designs, in terms of both components and architecture. Among the modeling tools we find the Canvas (Osterwalder and Pigneur, 2002, 2010), the Visor for digital business models (El Sawy and Pereria, 2013), the Business Model Cube (Lindgren and Horn Rasmussen, 2013), 360 degree business model innovation (Rayna and Striukov, 2016) and software tools for BMI (Szopinski et al., 2020). The second type of design tool is the templates or patterns of business models, such as the Business Model Navigator (Gassman et al., 2014a, 2014b), Remane et al.'s (2017b) 182 different business model patterns and the Five-V framework (Taran et al., 2016). The pattern matching tools allow the manager to match the pattern with their current business model, or mix and match patterns in new or certain configurations, to redesign the business models. Many design tools draw on strong visual representation as a way to support collaborative cognitive processes in the design phase of a new business model.

The exploration tools are all well-known strategy tools to analyze the external environment, such as the PEST (Gupta, 2013) and five-forces framework (Porter, 2008), and the alignment with the firm internal environment, i.e., the SWOT-framework (Piercy and Giles, 1989) and identification of white spaces (Leavy, 2010). Thus, the exploration of external and internal conditions for BMI may be managed by existing tools in strategic management.

Researchers have put somewhat less effort in developing or proposing test and implementation tools. We have identified three test tools; they all provide stress test tools. Groesser and Jovy (2016) and Haaker et al. (2017) have designed stress test tools based on the Canvas. Groesser and Jovy (2016) provide a computational modeling tool and Haaker et al. (2017) a scenario planning tool to evaluate different BMI options including the risks and stress related to implementation.

Evans and Johnson (2013) present a stress test tool analyzing investment readiness levels to implement a specific business model to evaluate the amount of stress the organization is likely to experience in the implementation process.

Among the implementation tools, we have identified three types of management tools. The first type of tool provides checklists that managers should follow when organizing the BMI-initiative, such as organizing the new business model in a separate organizational unit or integrate it in a current unit (Johnson et al., 2008), possible redesign of a culture, leadership and reward systems (Deshler and Smith, 2011), and operational issues such as customer services (Heikkilä et al., 2010). The second type of group of implementation tools is process maps for managers to guide them through the whole BMI-process (Bouwman et al., 2008; Breuer, 2013; De Reuver et al., 2013; Frankenberger et al., 2013; Garcia-Gutierrez and Martinez-Borreguero, 2016; Heikkilä et al., 2018b). The third type of tools is performance management tools providing metrics for managers to monitor the implementation of a new business model (Heikkilä et al., 2016b; Batocchio et al., 2017).

BMI tools – strategic objectives and size

Heikkilä et al. (2018b) point out that it is important to clarify the strategic objective of BMI, i.e., profit, growth or new businesses. Most BMI tools are designed to support the strategic objective of profit making. Some tools are intended to develop new businesses (Breuer, 2013; El Sawy and Pereira, 2013; Frankenberger et al., 2013), this is of course natural in the case of start-ups (Garcia-Gutierrez and Martinez-Borreguero, 2016; Batacchio et al., 2017). Other tools focus on growth (Johnson et al., 2008; Rayna and Striukova, 2016), which could be especially important for platform-based digital business models (El Sawy and Periera, 2013; Panda, 2019; Li, 2020). Finally, we found that most tools assume an established company context and not a start-up context, i.e., assuming there already is an existing business model in need of change, rather than searching for and designing a completely new business model.

Implications for Practitioners

Our findings from this review of BMI tools have a number of implications for practitioners. First, when performing different kinds of explorations or analyses of trends in the wider society, or industry, or competitors, specific BMI tools do not seem to have any significance. These kinds of exploration and analysis are still handled best by established strategic management tools such as the SWOT and five-forces framework.

Second, most BMI tools are intended for, and have their strength in, experimenting with the design or redesign of a business model, placing it in a value chain and value network ecosystem. As most of these BMI tools have a visual representation, such as the business model canvas, they facilitate creativity and analysis work in management groups with different functions, e.g., in workshops with visual boards. Thus, BMI tools have their strength in collective problem-solving rather than individual problem-solving. Thus, BMI tools may be especially well suited to use the collective intelligence of a management group representing different company functions, possibly including representatives from partners in customer, supplier, or development companies. BMI tools may then be instrumental in building and maintaining company internal networks across functions or other intra-organizational boundaries. In a work life with increasing levels of distant work this may prove to be even more important.

Third, in terms of implementation BMI tools provide mainly variants of standard management tools such as checklists and key performance indicators. This may imply that managers need to look elsewhere for more advanced management tools to manage BMI implementation.

Fourth, while most BMI tools assume the profit objective it is important for managers to make the objective of the BMI process explicit as many of the tools may be used also for growth or creating new businesses. Making the objective explicit might be especially important for managers in government or non-profit organizations as these organizations often have other objectives than profit and growth. Moreover, managers in government and non-profit organizations often face complex situations with multiple and non-aligned objectives, making it important to know which objective(s) the BMI tool is (are) addressing.

Fifth and finally, BMI tools are mainly developed to support managers when established companies need to change their business model in three types of situations; changes due to digitalization, to develop and sharpen the company's competitive advantages, and when developing new businesses i.e. corporate venturing.

Concluding Remarks

To our knowledge, this is one of the first studies to systematically review BMI tools proposed in the academic literature. Overall we found a limited number of tools and most of them are related to the design phase of the BMI process. This finding indicates that managers overall have a limited toolbox to draw from and particularly so when it comes to testing and implementing phases of the BMI process. One tool has a special standing, the business model canvas (Osterwalder and Pigneur, 2002, 2010), as it seems to be the most common tool to refer to in the academic literature and has inspired many other researchers to design new and modified tools based on the canvas. One solution to this lack of specific available management tools for BMI, especially for exploration purposes, seems to be to complement standard management tools from strategic and innovation management such as the SWOT and five-forces industry analysis, this is particularly evident in the exploration phase. Thus, the diffuse relations between strategy and business models often noted in the academic literature (DaSilva and Trkman, 2014) are mirrored also into the academic discourse of BMI tools.

Moreover, we found that the proposed tools are based mainly on conceptual reasoning, with very few cases of empirical grounding of the tools. Hence, we do not know to what extent these tools are used, adapted to specific industries and companies, nor how effective they are in regards to specific strategic objectives. For instance, Heikkilä et al. (2018b) found that SMEs used different BMI paths depending on the strategic objective of the company, i.e., profitability, growth or starting a new business. The tools we have identified in the literature mostly assume a profit objective, if that corresponds with managers' needs we do not know.

We found that most tools are intended for an established company context and not a start-up context, i.e., an existing business model in need of change, rather than designing a completely new business model. While this seems to be an unsurprising finding, given that we found the tools in management journals, the lack of tools for start-ups, e.g., in entrepreneurship journals, still is a bit puzzling. Perhaps the term BMI and tool are not as frequently used in the entrepreneurship field. The widespread use and focus on the lean start-up method (e.g., Blank, 2013) might be one reason for this. Finally, this study paves the way for future research on the identified BMI tools by empirically evaluating the viability of these tools in the context of different companies.

References

Aguilar, F. J. (1979). *Scanning the business environment*. MacMillan Co.

Batocchio, A., Ferraz Minatogawa, V. L., & Anholon, R. (2017). Proposal for a method for business model performance assessment: Toward an experimentation tool for business model innovation. *Journal of Technology Management Innovation*, 12, 61–70.

Berends, H., Smits, A., Reymen, I., & Podoynitsyna, K. (2016). Learning while (re) configuring: Business model innovation processes in established firms. *Strategic Organization*, 14, 181–219.

Blank, S. (2013). Why the lean start-up changes everything. *Harvard Business Review*, 91(5), 63–72.

Bouwman, H., De Reuver, M., Solaimani, S., Daas, D., Haaker, T., Janssen, W., Iske, P., & Walenkamp, B. (2012). Business models tooling and a research agenda. *BLED 2012 – Special Issue*. 7.

Bouwman H., Faber E., Haaker T., Kijl B., & De Reuver M. (2008). Conceptualizing the STOF model. In: Bouwman, H., De Vos, H., & Haaker, T. (eds) *Mobile service innovation and business models*. Springer.

Breuer, H. (2013). Lean venturing: Learning to create new business through exploration, elaboration, evaluation, experimentation, and evolution. *International Journal of Innovation Management*, 17(3), 1340013.

Chesbrough, H. (2010). Business model innovation: Opportunities and barriers. *Long Range Planning*, 43(2–3), 354–363.

DaSilva, C. M., & Trkman, P. (2014). Business model: What it is and what it is not. *Long Range Planning*, 47(6), 379–389.

Demil, B., & Lecocq, X. (2010). Business model evolution: In search of dynamic consistency. *Long Range Planning*, 43(2–3), 227–246.

De Reuver, M., Bouwman, H., & Haaker, T. (2013). Business model roadmapping: A practical approach to come from an existing to a desired business model. *International Journal of Innovation Management*, 17(1), 1340006.

Deshler, R., & Smith, K. (2011). Making business model innovation stick. *People and Strategy*, 34(4), 18.

El Sawy, O. A., & Pereira F. (2013). *Business modelling in the dynamic digital space*. Springer Briefs in Digital Spaces. Springer.

Evans, J. D., & Johnson, R. O. (2013). Tools for managing early-stage business model innovation. *Research-Technology Management*, 56(5), 52–56.

Foss, N. J., & Saebi, T. (2017). Fifteen years of research on business model innovation: How far have we come, and where should we go? *Journal of Management*, 43(1), 200–227.

Frankenberger, K., Weiblen, T., Csik, M., & Gassmann, O. (2013). The 4I-framework of business model innovation: A structured view on process phases and challenges. *International Journal of Product Development*, 18(3–4), 249–273.

García-Gutiérrez, I., & Martínez-Borreguero, F. J. (2016). The innovation pivot framework: Fostering business model innovation in startups: A new tool helps entrepreneurs design business models by identifying the sources of competitive advantage embedded in an innovation. *Research-Technology Management*, 59(5), 48–56.

Gassmann, O., Frankenberger, K., & Csik, M. (2014a). Revolutionizing the business model. In: Gassmann O., & Schweitzer F. (eds) *Management of the fuzzy front end of innovation*. Springer, pp. 89–97.

Gassmann, O., Frankenberger, K., & Csik, M. (2014b). *The business model navigator: 55 models that will revolutionise your business*. Pearson.

Groesser, S. N., & Jovy, N. (2016). Business model analysis using computational modeling: A strategy tool for exploration and decision-making. *Journal of Management Control*, 27(1), 61–88.

Gupta, A. (2013). Environment & PEST analysis: An approach to the external business environment. *International Journal of Modern Social Sciences*, 2(1), 34–43.

Haaker, T., Bouwman, H., Janssen, W., & de Reuver, M. (2017). Business model stress testing: A practical approach to test the robustness of a business model. *Futures*, 89, 14–25.

Heikkilä, M., Bouwman, H., Heikkilä, J., Haaker, T., Lopez-Nicolas, C., & Riedl, A. (2016a). Business model innovation paths and tools. *Bled 2016 Proceedings 6*.

Heikkilä, M., Bouwman, H., Heikkilä, J., Solaimani, S., & Janssen, W. (2016b). Business model metrics: An open repository. *Information Systems and e-Business Management*, 14(2), 337–366.

Heikkilä, M., Bouwman, H., & Heikkilä, J. (2018a). From strategic goals to business model innovation paths: An exploratory study. *Journal of Small Business and Enterprise Development*, 25(1), 107–128.

Heikkilä, J., Heikkilä, M., Niemimaa, M., & Järveläinen, J. (2018b). Means to survive disruption: Business model innovation and strategic continuity management? *Bled 2018 Proceedings 3*.

Heikkilä, J., Tyrväinen, P., & Heikkilä, M. (2010). Designing for performance-a technique for business model estimation. *Proceedings of EBRF; 1797-190X*.

Johnson, M. W., Christensen, C. M., & Kagermann, H. (2008). Reinventing your business model. *Harvard Business Review*, 86(12), 57–68.

Johnson, M. W., & Lafley, A. G. (2010). *Seizing the white space: Business model innovation for growth and renewal*. Harvard Business Press.

Kim, I. H. S., Ku, T. Y. D., & Lee, B. Y. M. (2020). Business model schema: Business model innovation tool based on direct causal mechanisms of profit. *Technology Analysis & Strategic Management*, 32(4), 379–396.

Laudien, S. M., & Daxböck, B. (2017). Business model innovation processes of average market players: A qualitative-empirical analysis. *R&D Management*, 47(3), 420–430.

Leavy, B. (2010). A system for innovating business models for breakaway growth. *Strategy & Leadership*, 38(6), 5–15.

Li, F. (2020). The digital transformation of business models in the creative industries: A holistic framework and emerging trends. *Technovation*, 92–93(3), 102012.

Lindgren, P., & Horn Rasmussen, O. (2013). The business model cube journal of multi business model innovation. *Journal of Multi Business Model Innovation and Technology*, 1(3), 135–182.

Massa, L., Tucci, C. L. & Afuah, A. (2017). A critical assessment of business model research. *Academy of Management Annals*, 11(1), 73–104.

Osterwalder, A., & Pigneur, Y. (2002). An eBusiness model ontology for modeling eBusiness. *BLED 2002 Proceedings 2*.

Osterwalder, A., & Pigneur, Y. (2010). Business model generation: a handbook for visionaries, game changers, and challengers (Vol. 1). UK: John Wiley & Sons.

Panda, B. K. (2019). Application of business model innovation for new enterprises. *Journal of Management Development*, 39(4), 517–524.

Piercy, N., & Giles, W. (1989). Making SWOT analysis work. *Marketing Intelligence & Planning*, 7(5/6), 5–7.

Porter, M. E. (1979). The structure within industries and companies' performance. *The Review of Economics and Statistics*, 61(2), 214–227.

Porter, M. E. (2008). The five competitive forces that shape strategy. *Harvard Business Review*, 86(1), 25–40.

Rayna, T., & Striukova, L. (2016). 360° Business Model Innovation: Toward an Integrated View of Business Model Innovation: An integrated, value-based view of a business model can provide insight into potential areas for business model innovation. *Research-Technology Management*, 59(3), 21–28.

Remane, G., Hanelt, A., Nickerson, R. C., & Kolbe, L. M. (2017a). Discovering digital business models in traditional industries. *Journal of Business Strategy*, 38(2), 41–51.

Remane, G., Hanelt, A., Tesch, J. F., & Kolbe, L. M. (2017b). The business model pattern database—A tool for systematic business model innovation. *International Journal of Innovation Management*, 21(01), 1750004.

Szopinski, D., Schoormann, T., John, T., Knackstedt, R., & Kundisch, D. (2020). Software tools for business model innovation: Current state and future challenges. *Electronic Markets*, 30(3), 469–494.

Taran, Y., Nielsen, C., Montemari, M., Thomsen, P., & Paolone, F. (2016). Business model configurations: A five-V framework to map out potential innovation routes. *European Journal of Innovation Management*, 19(4), 492–527.

Täuscher, K., & Abdelkafi, N. (2017). Visual tools for business model innovation: Recommendations from a cognitive perspective. *Creativity and Innovation Management*, 26(2), 160–174.

Trapp, M., Voigt, K. I., & Brem, A. (2018). Business models for corporate innovation management: Introduction of a business model innovation tool for established firms. *International Journal of Innovation Management*, 22(01), 1850007.

Zott, C., & Amit, R. (2010). Business model design: An activity system perspective. *Long Range Planning*, 43(2–3), 216–226.

Zott, C., Amit, R., & Massa, L. (2011). The business model: Recent developments and future research. *Journal of Management*, 37(4), 1019–1042.

APPENDIX 8.1

SHORT DESCRIPTIONS OF PAPERS IN REVIEW

No	References (in chronological order)	Description
1	PEST-analysis (Aguilar, 1979; Gupta, 2013)	PEST analysis refers to a framework of macro-environmental factors used in the environmental scanning component of strategic management. These factors include political, economic, socio-cultural, and technological aspects.
2	Five forces framework (Porter, 1979, 2008)	This framework is used for analyzing the competition of a business. The five forces included in the framework are a threat of new entrants, threat of substitutes, bargaining power of customers, bargaining power of suppliers, competitive rivalry.
3	SWOT (Piercy and Giles, 1989)	SWOT analysis represents the strengths, weaknesses, opportunities, and threats of a company.
4	E-business model/ Business Model CANVAS (Osterwalder and Pigneur, 2002, 2010)	Business Model Canvas is a business tool used to visualize the important building blocks of the business, such as value customer segments, value propositions, channels, customer relationships, revenue streams, key resources, key activities, key partnerships, and cost structure.
5	The elements of a successful business model (Johnson et al., 2008)	This study defines the elements of a successful business model, which includes customer value proposition, profit formula, key resources, and key processes.
6	STOF (Bouwman et al., 2008)	This business model tool describes the business from four connected perspectives, namely service, technology, organization, and finance.

(Continued)

No	References (in chronological order)	Description
7	An activity system design framework (Zott and Amit, 2010)	The framework provides insights by giving BM design a language, concepts, and tools. The design elements include content, structure, and governance, and the design themes include novelty, lock-in, complementarities, and efficiency.
8	The white space (Johnson and Lafley, 2010; Leavy, 2010)	The study explains how to develop an innovative BM. It starts with finding an important unfilled job-to-be-done and look at the world of the customer in a new way from the outside in rather than through the lens of current products or approaches to segmentation.
9	Designing for performance-a technique for business model estimation (Heikkilä et al., 2010)	The model helps in estimating the feasibility of the business ideas. It explicitly defines the metrics for measuring the success of the business model in terms of the strategic goals of the organization.
10	ANCHOR (Deshler and Smith, 2011)	The ANCHOR tool helps in clarifying what is most important to the customer and how your organization fits in your customer's world. ANCHOR consists of five components, namely audience, need, channel, omit, and revenue.
11	Differentiators (Deshler and Smith, 2011)	This tool assists organizations to identify and define the capabilities of the organization, so those capabilities drive distinctiveness (e.g., develop key activities, develop resource implications, prioritization, etc.).
12	Functional Alignment Matrix (Deshler and Smith, 2011)	This tool provides an organized and systematic way for helping each function in the organization break the inertia of past choices and realigns in support of the new business model (e.g., element of BM and functional choices for new BM).
13	Lean venturing (Breuer, 2013)	It allows organizations to actively experiment with BMs through trial-and-error learning, continuous testing, and support qualifying central BM elements.
14	Business model roadmapping (De Reuver et al. 2013).	It shows the practical approach make from the transition from an existing BM to the desired business model.
15	VISOR (El Sawy and Pereira, 2013)	The VISOR framework aimed to understand ecosystem dynamics in digital platforms. The framework consists of key components that specify for digital business, such as value proposition, interface, service platforms, organizing model, and revenue/cost structure.

16	Innovation readiness levels for BMI (Evans and Johnson, 2013)	The tool allows a quantitative assessment of the organization's state of readiness to implement a specific business model and a measure of the amount of stress an idea is likely to create for the organization.
17	The 4I-framework of BMI (Frankenberger et al., 2013)	This framework refers to four iterative business model innovation phases of initiation, ideation, integration, and implementation.
18	BM Cube (Lindgren and Horn Rasmussen, 2013)	The BM Cube is proposed as a generic framework for working with any business model.
19	Business Model Navigator (Gassmann et al., 2014a, 2014b)	It is a business model tool aimed to facilitate the key aspects of a business model success, such as business offerings, revenue stream, value proposition, value chain, and customers.
20	The innovation pivot framework for startups (García-Gutiérrez and Martínez-Borreguero, 2016)	This framework aims to foster the creative process of generating promising applications for an invention. It has four key aspects, which include innovation object, impact, uncertainty, and sustainable competitive advantage.
21	BM analysis using computational modeling (Groesser and Jovy, 2016)	The analysis is organized into five sections which include where models are used, why model, making and using models, types of model and analysis, and future directions.
22	Metrics for BMs (Heikkilä et al., 2016b)	The study presents an open repository of metrics related to core BM concepts.
23	360° business model innovation (Rayna and Striukova, 2016)	This study introduces a comprehensive framework that provides an integrated view of all of the critical components of the business model.
24	A five-V framework to map out potential innovation routes (Taran et al., 2016)	The five V framework addresses five BM aspects: value proposition, value segment, value configuration, value network, and value capture.
25	Performance assessment and experimentation tool for BMI (Batocchio et al., 2017)	This study presents a method that combines the practices of the Balanced Scorecard with the BM Canvas to access the performance measurement of a BM.
26	Business model stress testing (Haaker et al., 2017)	The tool visualizes challenges and suggests ways to increase the robustness of BM. The stress testing approach is particularly useful in a stage of business model experimentation.
27	Digital business models in traditional industries (Remane et al., 2017a)	This study allows managers to systematically analyze, discover digital business models, and better cope with the digital transformation of their industrial businesses.

(Continued)

No	References (in chronological order)	Description
28	The BM Pattern Database-A Tool (Remane et al., 2017b)	The database helps to systematically innovate the business model.
29	Visual tools for BMI (Täuscher and Abdelkafi, 2017)	This study contributes to the broader understanding of how visual tools can support business model innovation at a cognitive level.
30	From strategic goals to business model innovation paths (Heikkilä et al., 2018b)	The study helps to analyze how different strategic goals of (micro, small and medium-sized firms) relate to the business model innovation (BMI) paths when improving their business.
31	A BMI Tool for Established Firms (Trapp et al., 2018)	This tool operationalizes BMI and offers criteria and indicators to accelerate BMI in established firms.
32	Business model schema (Kim et al., 2020)	The schema provide cognitive structures that consist of concepts and relations among them that organize managerial understandings about the design of activities and exchanges that reflect the critical interdependencies and value-creation in their organization's exchange networks.
33	Digital business using a freemium BM (Panda, 2019)	Digital business model refers to a BM where some services or content are provided free of charge while other content or more advanced features must be paid for.
34	Software tools for business model innovation (Szopinski et al., 2020)	The study provides a classification of existing software tools for the taxonomy.
35	The digital transformation of business models (Li, 2020)	The study contributes to the understanding of business models and how digital technologies facilitate business model innovations in the creative industries.

9

ORIGINS OF INNOVATION

Market-driving innovation vs market-driven innovation

Onnida Thongpravati

Introduction

In today's turbulent business environment and digitalisation, innovation has become a buzz word in the 21st century. 'Innovate or die' – the mantra that has been recognised and reused repeatedly by governments, businesses, academics and consultants. This is exceptionally the case in the time of crisis and pandemic. The Second World War, for instance, has fostered new ideas and inventions such as the first digital computer for code breaking 'Colossus', the first jet engine for mass air travel, the first rocket, and nuclear as a weapon and a source of energy generation. A pandemic like the COVID-19 has also stimulated the development of innovation for necessity or what so called 'crisis-driven innovation' – a next wave of innovation that has often emerged from crisis situations or extreme conditions driving radically new thinking and different perspective. Notably they instigate an entrepreneurial and innovative mindset and a sense of urgency for firms to address pressing needs by developing new solutions particularly market-driving or breakthrough trajectories (Bessant, Rush, & Trifilova, 2015). There is thus a recent call for more research highlighting the importance of market-driving or 'market shaping' to solve real-world issues and wicked problems (Nenonen, Fehrer, & Brodie, 2021).

While many terms have been used by researchers and firms to identify different types of innovations, there is an inconsistency regarding the definition of 'innovation' specifically for breakthrough types. Breakthrough innovations can sometimes be referred to as "market-driving innovations" as they drive the market in their character (Thongpravati, Reid, & Dobele, 2020). They are also being referred to as 'discontinuous', 'radical', 'disruptive', 'exploratory', 'revolutionary' innovation and/or other terms (Garcia & Calantone, 2002; Harmancioglu, Dröge, & Calantone, 2009; O'Connor, 2008; Song & Montoya-Weiss,

DOI: 10.4324/9780429346033-12

1998; Story, Hart, & O'Malley, 2009). This creates different expressions and a lack of clear distinction between the terms and difficulties in their interpretations (Danneels & Kleinschmidt, 2001; de Brentani, 2001).

Market-driving or breakthrough innovations are argued to be a source of sustainable competitive advantage that can importantly contribute to a firm's growth and profitability in dynamic settings (e.g. Chandy & Tellis, 1998; Cho & Pucik, 2005; Hauser, Tellis, & Griffin, 2006; Sorescu, Chandy, & Prabhu, 2003; Thongpravati et al., 2020). This type of innovation has been designated as a significant research topic by the Marketing Science Institute (MSI) (Story et al., 2009). Market-driving innovations can revolutionise an industry and fundamentally redefine the market structure, preferences and even behaviour of all players in the market (customers, competitors and other stakeholders) (Jaworski, Kohli, & Sahay, 2000). Firms that focus on developing market-driving innovations are considered to be 'market-driving' as opposed to being 'market-driven' (Kumar, Scheer, & Kotler, 2000; Schindehutte, Morris, & Kocak, 2008). Market-driving firms can therefore change the rules of the competitive game, enabling them to transcend 'the zero-sum game' that specifies various industry battlegrounds (Bessant, Birkinshaw, & Delbridge, 2004).

Notwithstanding the significance of market-driving innovation to firm's survival, only a minority of firms develop a large majority of this type of innovation (O'Connor, Ravichandran, & Robeson, 2008; Sorescu et al., 2003). Jaworski, Kohli, and Sarin (2020) stated "while the concept of shaping or driving markets has received limited research attention, the *implementation* of the concept – e.g. a structured set of steps firms may take – has received even less attention" (p. 142). Incremental innovations is dominated in most companies' new product development (NPD) portfolio, accounting up to 90% of new product introductions (Spanjol, Tam, Qualls, & Bohlmann, 2011). In other words, only 10% of new product introductions are real breakthroughs (Griffin, 1997; Reid & de Brentani, 2004). Those real breakthroughs, nevertheless, generate 24% of profits (Martin, 1995). It is evident that successful breakthrough innovation can positively create better performance outcomes compared to incremental innovations and would pay off more than proportionally (Kleinschmidt & Cooper, 1991; Rubera & Kirca, 2012). A strong financial performance is thus found in firms which develop breakthrough innovations, especially those with high pre-product levels of marketing and technology support.

The aim of the chapter is threefold: first, it reviews the literature to present an operationalisation of product innovativeness and the resource-based perspective (RBV) of new product development; second it addresses the gaps in the literature by defining and classifying the types of product innovation, in particular, the varying degree of breakthroughness using the notion of 'market-driving' and 'market-driven' paradigm through the lens of the RBV as proposed in the dynamic capabilities literature (Eisenhardt & Martin, 2000; Jaworski et al., 2000; Teece, Pisano, & Shuen, 1997), and proposes a new 'Market-Driving Innovation and Market-Driven Innovation Model' (MDIM) for different types of innovation development, along with an illustration of a conceptual focus of changing market orientation; third, it offers both practical and political implications as well as theoretical contributions to the study of innovation management including future study area.

Literature review

New product development and product innovativeness

In general, the new product development (NPD) process or product innovation process is about bringing new products to market. A new feasible product idea can be called an invention. An invention that has progressed through the stages of production, marketing and diffusion into the marketplace, and has been adopted by customers can be called a product innovation (Garcia & Calantone, 2002). According to Garcia and Calantone (2002, p.112), "the innovation process comprises the technological development of an invention combined with the market introduction of that invention to end-users through adoption and diffusion".

The NPD process is iterative, which involves the first introduction of a product innovation followed by subsequent reintroduction of an improved version. The degree of newness of a product innovation is often measured by its innovativeness. Product innovativeness has been measured according to both the product's newness to the marketplace (macro-level) and the product's newness to the firm (micro-level) (Garcia & Calantone, 2002; Harmancioglu et al., 2009; Song & Montoya-Weiss, 1998). The term 'newness' alone is related to 'change' (Baregheh, Rowley, & Sambrook, 2009). More specifically, Johnson and Jones (1957) suggested that the term 'newness' can be measured in *technological* and *market* dimensions. On one hand, the technological dimension verifies a paradigm shift in the science and technology of a new product. On the other hand, the market dimension verifies the extent to which the new product generates a paradigm shift in the market structure in an industry (Chandy & Tellis, 1998; Garcia & Calantone, 2002). The technological and market dimensions have become widely recognised in studies of new product success factors and related NPD strategies, development processes and performance (Harmancioglu et al., 2009).

Accordingly, the degree of newness of a product at both macro- and micro-levels can be measured by its discontinuity in technological and/or marketing dimensions (Garcia & Calantone, 2002). The discontinuity of a new product at the macro-level causes "a paradigm shift in the science and technology and/or market structure in an industry" (Garcia & Calantone, 2002, p.113). The discontinuity of a new product at the micro-level influences "the firm's existing marketing resources, technological resources, skills, knowledge, capabilities, or strategy" (Garcia & Calantone, 2002, p.113).

Figure 9.1 unpacks how product innovativeness can be operationalised through macro-level and micro-level discontinuities and their corresponding marketing and technology dimensions.

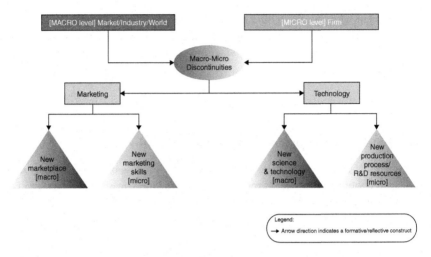

FIGURE 9.1 Operationalisation of product innovativeness.
Source: Adapted from Garcia and Calantone (2002).

As shown in Figure 9.1, the operationalisation of product innovativeness demonstrates the possible varying degree of newness that can be used to explain different types of product innovations.

The higher order view of macro- and micro-level product innovativeness 'form' or 'build' a formative construct, i.e. 'macro–micro discontinuities'. The macro–micro discontinuities 'reflect' or 'depict' a reflective construct, i.e. the two dimensions of marketing and technology. The marketing dimension is measured with a set of respective indicators, i.e. new marketplace (macro-level) and new marketing skills (micro-level). The technology dimension is measured with another set of respective indicators, i.e. new science and technology (macro-level) and new production process/research and development (R&D) resources (micro-level).

The different level of macro–micro discontinuities and the marketing-technology dimensions primarily lead to three types of product innovations. This could be from more radical ones that illustrate all macro–micro discontinuities of market-technology dimensions, really new innovations that illustrate discontinuities in either marketing or technology dimension at macro-level and any combinations at micro-level, and less innovative ones that illustrate only micro discontinuities of marketing and/or technology dimensions. Examples of these innovations are the World Wide Web that causes discontinuity to the world (all macro–micro levels of marketing and technology dimensions), the Sony Walkman which causes discontinuities to electric industry and creates a new mobile entertainment market (all macro-micro-levels of marketing dimensions and a micro-level of technology dimension) and a digital automotive control system which only causes a technology discontinuity at micro-level, respectively (Garcia & Calantone, 2002).

It is also important to emphasise that there is often a tension between the marketing and technology dimensions. This is aligned with the models of 'market pull' or 'customer insight' and 'technology push' or 'executive foresight'. While the market pull model focusses on marketing as a source of ideas for R&D direction, the technology push model focusses on R&D for the market to receive the R&D outcomes (Hobday, 2005; Wind & Mahajan, 1997). These different focusses of the models could influence the level of product newness.

Many other terms have been used by researchers to identify different types of product innovations according to their level of innovativeness. In the marketing literature, a new-product breakthrough is the principal meaning of the term 'innovation' (Han, Kim, & Srivastava, 1998). In essence, product innovation primarily ranges from 'continuous' to 'discontinuous' innovation. Continuous innovation can be referred to terms such as 'evolutionary', 'sustaining', 'incremental' and 'minor' innovation. Discontinuous innovation can be referred to terms such as 'revolutionary', 'disruptive', 'breakthrough', 'radical', 'really new' and 'major' innovation (Garcia & Calantone, 2002; Harmancioglu et al., 2009; O'Connor, 2008; Song & Montoya-Weiss, 1998; Story et al., 2009). Some highly innovative firms such as 3M and Corning have categorised the degree of product innovativeness as 'horizon 1, 2, 3' and 'today, tomorrow and beyond' (O'Connor, 2010, p.2). Researchers and firms are thus far from a consensus in framing the types of innovation (McDermott & O'Connor, 2002).

According to March (1991), radical innovation can be differentiated from incremental innovation by its *exploration* competencies. Leifer et al. (2000) described exploration as involving "something fundamentally new, including *new products, processes*, or combinations of the two" (p.5). In contrast, incremental innovation is based on *exploitation* competencies, and has to do with refining and improving the cost or features of existing products. This terminology has been used by the majority of the researchers to make the distinction between radical and incremental innovation (Leifer et al., 2000).

Verganti (2008) refers to radical innovation as 'design-driven innovation' by means of recognising possible radical changes and redesigning or redefining product meanings for a customer. In a similar vein, Atuahene-Gima (2005) refers to 'radical innovation' as new products that "involve fundamental changes in technology for the firm, typically address the needs of emerging customers, new to the firm and/ or industry, and offer substantial new benefits to customers" (p.65). In contrast to radical innovation, 'incremental innovation' refers to "product improvements and line extensions that are usually aimed at satisfying the needs of existing customers. They involve small changes in technology and little deviation from the current product-market experience of the firm" (Atuahene-Gima, 2005, p.65).

Product innovation is also related to being market focussed or market leading. Jaworski et al. (2000) suggested that firms can be *market driving* (driving markets) or *market driven*. Being market driving means that firms challenge the *status quo* to discover latent or unarticulated needs of customers to develop breakthrough innovations in a new (unpredictable) market (Deszca, Munro, & Noori, 1999; Kumar et al., 2000; O'Connor, 1998; Varadarajan, 2009). The market structure and the behaviour of market players are manipulated, which increases the competitiveness of the industry. The market structure can be changed in three ways: "(1) eliminating players in a market (deconstruction approach), (2) building a new or modified set of players in a market (construction approach) and (3) changing the functions performed by players (functional modification approach)" (Jaworski et al., 2000, p.45). Moreover, changing the mindset of customers, competitors and other stakeholders may directly influence market behaviour. As opposed to being market driving, market driven means that a firm reactively responds to customer's preferences and follows other players' behaviour to develop incremental innovations within a given market structure (Jaworski et al., 2000; Kumar et al., 2000).

According to Zortea-Johnston, Darroch, and Matear (2012), "innovations that create new customers, lead existing customers, meet latent needs, and reshape product/market spaces" are referred to as "driving markets innovations" (p.146). Zortea-Johnston et al. (2012) advocate that driving markets innovations are considered to be *radical* or *breakthrough* in nature (i.e. new to the world innovations or those innovations that either change consumer behaviour or market structures). These types of innovations enable firms to "renew their competitive position and delay eventual firm decline" (Zortea-Johnston et al., 2012, p.146). Other researchers have also described driving markets innovation as "market-driving innovation" (e.g. Kumar et al., 2000; Schindehutte et al., 2008). Schindehutte et al. (2008) state "market-driving firms must search for their next market-driving innovation, or lose its competitive advantage to a new incumbent" (p.17). In contrast to market-driving innovation, "market-driven innovation" is considered to be incremental in nature. This type of product innovation is developed within the confinement of the existing market structure and does not, or at most very little, alter consumers' usage pattern or behaviour (Zortea-Johnston et al., 2012).

Recent research by Jaworski et al. (2020) explained a seven-step approach on driving markets and further identified the typology of 'market-driving' processes, which entail four distinct characteristics: (1) *Pied Piper* "an individual firm influencing preferences of customers and market actors in favor of functional benefits offered by a technological innovation", (2) *Guild* "a collaborating set of firms influencing preferences of customers and market actors in favor of functional benefits offered by a technological innovation", (3) *Evangelist* "an individual firm influencing cultural tastes, values, and symbols in a direction beneficial to the firm" and (4) *Apostles* "a collaborating set of firms influencing cultural tastes, values and symbols in a direction beneficial to the firms" (p.143). Examples of these four typologies include ResMed – medical devices and cloud-based software solutions provider for sleep-disordered breathing, FM Radio, McDonald phasing out its foam packaging, and the rise of US Craft Breweries Industry, respectively.

Resource-based perspective and new product development

Over the past decade, resource-based theory (RBT) (Penrose, 1959) has been an important although somewhat controversial perspective used in strategic management literature to explain a firm's success. RBT postulates that a firm's resources are the primary determinants of sustainable competitive advantage and superior performance (Conner, 1991; Penrose, 1959). The resources in themselves, nonetheless, appear to be less valuable without the organisational capabilities to manage them. Porter (1991, 1996) stated that the processes and activities for creating advantage are more important to focus on and analyse than the firm's resources. 'Organisational capabilities' are the embedded processes, routines and current practices of learning, organising and getting specific activities done in a firm (Eisenhardt & Martin, 2000; Teece et al., 1997). A unique combination of both strategic and complementary key resources, particularly those with the potential to generate rents, may allow a firm to develop inputs to organisational capability, critical competences and embedded routines (Tallman, 2005).

This broader capability view of RBT reflects the resource-based view (RBV) of the firm as proposed in the dynamic capability literature (Barney, 1986; Montgomery, 1995; Rumelt, 1984; Wernerfelt, 1984). The RBV of the firm has emerged as one of the most fruitful trends within the RBT (Acedo, Barroso, & Galan, 2006). This is because the traditional RBT does not provide an adequate explanation of how and why firms achieve superior long-term performance in rapidly changing and unpredictable situations.

In this vein, the importance of the RBV perspective in explaining the sources of a firm's performance is recognised by many authors (e.g. Amit & Schoemaker, 1993; Barney, 1991; Mahoney & Pandian, 1992; Peteraf, 1993; Peteraf & Barney, 2003). A central premise of RBV is that a certain set of resources and capabilities enables firms to survive in highly challenging settings. Numerous RBV researchers have focussed on "look within the enterprise and down to the factor market conditions that the enterprise must contend with, to search for some possible causes of sustainable competitive advantages", holding constant all other factors outside the firm (Peteraf & Barney, 2003, p.312). This inward-looking perspective has proved to be useful for analysing various strategic issues and diversification (Foss & Knudsen, 2003). In addition, recent research on RBV has emphasised intangible assets, which include dynamic capabilities (Teece et al., 1997).

Dynamic capability theory extends RBV to incorporate the process dimension of gaining and sustaining advantage over time (Teece, 2007; Teece et al., 1997). Winter (2000) strategically defined dynamic capabilities as effecting organisational change by changing the path of evolution and development to match the requirements of the changing environment. The term 'dynamic' refers to:

> the capacity to renew competences so as to achieve congruence with the changing business environment; certain innovative responses are required when time-to-market and timing are critical, the rate of technological change is rapid, and the nature of future competition and markets difficult to determine.
>
> *(Teece et al., 1997, p.515)*

'Dynamic capabilities', likewise, can be referred to "a learned and stable pattern of collective activity through which the organization systematically generates and modifies its operating routines in pursuit of improved effectiveness" (Zollo & Winter, 2002, p.340). The dynamic capabilities of firms are heterogeneous in respect to resources, capabilities and endowments that are difficult to modify (Amit & Schoemaker, 1993; Barney, 1991; Mahoney & Pandian, 1992; Penrose, 1959; Wernerfelt, 1984).

For this reason, the RBV of a firm and its dynamic capabilities reflect the firm's ability to develop new capabilities through constant reconfiguration, recombination and the accumulation of different types of resources (i.e. skill acquisition, learning and other intangible assets). The firm can therefore develop new applications and attain new and innovative forms of competitive advantage to meet changing market demands (Eisenhardt & Martin, 2000; O'Regan & Ghobadian, 2004; Teece et al., 1997).

In relation to product development and management, the RBV of the firm provides a perspective that explains how the resources of the functional and integrative capabilities of the firm influence its process efficiency and product effectiveness (Verona, 1999). As resources are the inputs into the production process (Grant, 1991), the firms that realise a uniqueness and superiority of resources and capabilities can engage in NPD and innovations that "produce more economically and/or better satisfy customer wants by creating greater value or net benefits" (Peteraf & Barney, 2003, p.311). This can lead a firm to achieve a competitive advantage over its competitors by means of attaining aggressive pricing and high sales volume (cost leadership) and/or differentiated products that facilitate premium pricing, positive brand image and customer loyalty (Porter, 1980, 1985).

In addition, it is also important to differentiate the terms 'capability', 'competence' and 'capacity' when analysing a firm's ability to innovate. Generally, 'capability' refers a collaborative process that can be deployed or improved and through which an individual's know-how – i.e. competence – can be exploited. 'Competence' is about getting the right people with certain skills (sufficient knowledge, strength and abilities) to successfully perform and process critical work functions, through capability, in a defined work setting (Vincent, 2008). The relevant questions for firms to ask themselves in relation to 'capability' are: "How can we get done what we need to get done?" and "How easy is it to access, deploy or apply the competencies we need?" (Vincent, 2008, para. 4–5), and importantly "What can the firm do more effectively than its rivals?" (Grant, 1991, p.115). The questions related to "competence" are: "Who knows how?" and "How well do they know?" (Vincent, 2008, para. 4–5). The questions "Do we have enough?" and "How much is needed?" refer to the "capacity" to hold, receive or accommodate amount/volume (Vincent, 2008, para. 6).

Gaps in the literature and opportunities for studies

The terminology and theoretical work of other researchers has provided value in terms of distinguishing the types of innovations. Although there are varied definitions and frameworks for defining innovations, a practical definition is required based on the resource-based view (RBV) of the firm as proposed in the dynamic capabilities literature to gain insights into the emerging 'market-driving' concept and innovation developments.

In the environment of dynamic marketplace and market-driving innovation, firms require different approaches, a paradigm beyond the traditional RBV (Eisenhardt & Martin, 2000; O'Connor, 2008; Teece et al., 1997). Previous research on RBV has often viewed resources as a stable concept that can be identified at a point in time and will endure over time (Dunford, Snell, & Wright, 2003). The RBV perspective thus applies to known markets where the industry/market structure, boundaries and value chain are relatively stable and clear.

Recent studies have used the RBV to investigate the role of a firm's resources in addressing the dynamic business environment (de Brentani, Kleinschmidt, & Salomo, 2010; Paladino, 2007). The RBV of the firm, as proposed in the dynamic capabilities literature, provides an overall theoretical perspective (Eisenhardt & Martin, 2000). The RBV focusses on a firm's internal resources that are valuable, rare, inimitable and nonsubstitutable (Barney, 1991). Importantly, these resources need to be modified, integrated and reconfigured to adapt to the changing environment. This is the dynamic nature of the capability of a firm to alter its internal resources in advantageous ways to improve firm performance (Teece et al., 1997). Internal resources, particularly the intangible resources (skills and knowledge) and an entrepreneurial orientation (proactiveness and innovativeness), are essential for creating sustainable advantage (Bakar & Ahmad, 2010).

Cast in RBV, product innovation has been regarded as an engine of corporate renewal and is a dynamic capability of the firm (Danneels, 2002; Knight & Cavusgil, 2004; McNally & Schmidt, 2011; Zahra, Sapienza, & Davidson, 2006). The abilities of a firm to exploit its existing resources and skills and to change the routines for product development can enhance new product performance and firm performance, and are therefore important for scholarly examination (Cooper & de Brentani, 1991; Cooper & Kleinschmidt, 1993; De Clercq, Thongpapanl, & Dimov, 2011; Kleinschmidt & Cooper, 1991; Song & Parry, 1997a, 1997b; Zirger & Maidique, 1990).

Past empirical research has leant towards an internal firm perspective rather than an external customer perspective to measure innovativeness (Harmancioglu et al., 2009; Song & Montoya-Weiss, 1998). The firm perspective is consistent with the RBV of the firm or inward-looking view. Innovation has been extensively identified in both the technological and the market dimensions and the perspectives on changes made in an organisation (Damanpour, 1991; Garcia & Calantone, 2002). Despite the fact that the degree of newness of a product innovation can be measured by the level of innovativeness, the dimensions and classifications to measure the innovativeness are often limited to the exploration of new technologies or products stemming from technology. Henderson and Clark (1990), for instance, identified a framework of architectural innovation that captures two dimensions of the types of technological change: (1) an innovation's impact on core design concepts of a technology embodied in components and (2) the impact on the linkages between the core concepts and components.

Many of the limitations and gaps relate to the dominant literature on disruptive technology and innovation deriving from science and technological advances. There is an overemphasis on technological innovation, which leads to our underdeveloped conceptualisation of market-driving paradigm, i.e. the RBV market-driving lens. Over time, it fosters a major misconception of mindset that undermines the true nature of breakthrough innovations and their development. Breakthrough innovations are indeed not limited to high-tech products but are across all industries including low-tech ones. Innovative products that are new to both dimensions necessitate more learning/unlearning and organisational changes.

In this regard, radical innovations require a greater variety of resources, new skills, learning/unlearning, flexibility and capabilities quite apart from existing technology and practices (McDermott & O'Connor, 2002). Radical innovations involve more uncertainty and a higher proportion of experimentation than incremental innovations that involve only extensions, refinements or adaptations of established product designs (Kessler & Chakrabarti, 1999; Ottum & Moore, 1997; Sethi, 2000; Sivadas & Dwyer, 2000). Mohr, Sengupta, and Slater (2005, p.18–19) considered that "breakthrough (radical) innovations are so different that they cannot be compared to any existing practices or perceptions. They employ new technologies and create new markets. Breakthroughs are conceptual shifts that make history".

Research approach

This chapter reviews numerous studies associated with the NPD process and definitions of innovation from a firm perspective as reflected in the RBV literature and dynamic capability theory grounded in this study. A clear definition and set of criteria are important to provide structure to the body of the research and the intended meaning of the innovation construct and its domains, including the operationalisation implications (Varadarajan, 1996). Cast in RBV, the 'market-driving' and 'market-driven' paradigm provides a lens for further analysing the origins of innovation and classifying related terms and definitions. The analysis of the studies leads to a construction of a framework that captures the exploration of new ideas in addition to new technologies. The scope of the framework is broadened to reflect the varying degree of breakthroughness and describes each dimension and associated considerations with each one.

The later sections present the findings of the research by further exploring and analysing the operationalisation of product innovativeness and surfacing a guidance for defining the types of product innovation and their implications. A 'Market-Driving Innovation and Market-Driven Innovation Model' (MDIM) is proposed to close the knowledge gap in the conceptualisation of breakthrough innovations.

It must also be noted that the traditional market orientation and the concept of 'market-driven' have been dominant in the strategic marketing literature (Jaworski et al., 2000; Stathakopoulos, Kottikas, Theodorakis, & Kottika, 2019). However, research on market-driven orientation has appeared to offer little explanation on the behaviour of market-driving firms and their development of breakthrough innovations. The need to shift the emphasis of innovation research from the traditional market orientation is essential to market-driving innovation (Hills & Sarin, 2003; Kumar et al., 2000; Thongpravati et al., 2020); hence, a conceptual focus of changing market orientation is subsequently formed to illustrate the required movement.

Findings of research

This research merges views from previous studies and defines "market-driving [product] innovation" as "breakthrough product innovation, which *explores* new ideas or technologies that significantly transform existing markets or create new ones", and therefore require "*market-driving* competencies" (Thongpravati et al., 2020, p.123). Market-driving competencies are about getting "outside the immediate voice of the customer" and proactively reshaping customers' product preferences (Jaworski et al., 2000, p.45).

As the majority of definitions of product newness describe the two common dimensions of (1) technology and (2) markets, this research has adopted criteria and extended these dimensions to measure the newness of product innovation. For the purpose of this study, the merged definition of 'market-driving innovation' refers to a product identifiable by one or both of the following criteria:

(1) builds on a very new idea or very new technology that has never been used in the industry or market before, and/or;
(2) is one of the first of its kind introduced into the market and/or has an impact or causes significant changes in the industry or product category (either offers 5–10 times improved benefits or 30% cost reduction compared with the previous generation) (Leifer et al., 2000; O'Connor, 1998; O'Connor & Rice, 2001; Song & Montoya-Weiss, 1998).

These criteria identify what makes a product new to a firm. The first criterion verifies the extent to which the idea or technology embedded in a new product is different from existing ideas or technologies. Firms must have technological competence or very new ideas to develop advanced technology or products that are able to drive the market. The second criterion verifies the extent to which the new product is new to the market and/or impacts on the current markets or industries or creates new ones. Firms must have market competence to offer products better than existing products by discovering additional or unarticulated needs of customers (Chandy & Tellis, 1998; Damanpour, 1991; Danneels & Kleinschmidt, 2001; Veryzer, 1998).

NEWNESS/ IMPACT TO MARKET/ INDUSTRY		NEWNESS OF IDEAS/ TECHNOLOGY	
		Low	*High*
	Low	**(4) Incremental innovation** *(Market-driven innovation)*	**(2) Technological breakthrough/ Really new innovation** *(Market-driving innovation)*
	High	**(3) Market breakthrough/ Really new innovation** *(Market-driving innovation)*	**(1) Radical [breakthrough] innovation** *(Market-driving innovation)*

FIGURE 9.2 Defining types of product innovation.
Source: Adapted from Chandy and Tellis (1998, 2000), Garcia and Calantone (2002), and Zortea-Johnston et al. (2012).

Correspondingly, the two levels (low and high) for each criterion conceptually lead to four types of product innovations (see Figure 9.2): (1) radical [breakthrough] innovation, (2) technological breakthrough, (3) market breakthrough and (4) incremental innovation. This study adopts one of the most prevalent typologies in innovation research (Harmancioglu et al., 2009), primarily based on the work by Chandy and Tellis (1998), Garcia and Calantone (2002), Song and Montoya-Weiss (1998) and Zortea-Johnston et al. (2012).

Figure 9.2 presents the types of product innovation.

As shown in Figure 9.2, technological breakthroughs and market breakthroughs are referred to as really new innovations (Garcia & Calantone, 2002). Both *technological* breakthroughs and *market* breakthroughs, along with *radical* [breakthrough] innovation can be classified as market-driving innovations. The remaining incremental innovation is classified as a 'market-driven' innovation (Chandy & Tellis, 1998, 2000; Zortea-Johnston et al., 2012).

The following section explains the types of product innovations in more detail.

Market-driving innovation

Radical [breakthrough] innovation

In radical innovation, discontinuities happen at both macro- and micro-levels and along sublevels in both marketing and technological dimensions by requiring: (1) a new state of idea/science and technology embedded in a product ("never used in the industry before"), (2) a new marketplace ("the first of its kind and totally new to the market"), (3) a new production process and/or new R&D resources and (4) new marketing skills (Song & Montoya-Weiss, 1998, p.126).

As reflected in Figure 9.2, a radical [breakthrough] innovation meets all the described criteria, requiring changes in both existing ideas/technology and market/industry infrastructure. In other words, 'radical innovations' are breakthrough new products that create significant discontinuities and are new for both the firm and the marketplace – a new line of business or new product line. Radical innovation provides an entirely new level of functionality to customers and substantially transforms the way the current markets/industries operate or forms new ones (Leifer et al., 2000). An example of a radical innovation is the first consumer refrigerator; the many subsequent improvements were not radical innovations. Another example of radical innovation using a very new idea that has become the first of its kind introduced into the market and has a significant impact on the fashion industry is the famous Coco Chanel's little black dress. With its radical design, the dress has become a uniform for women and has represented 'fashion' since the 20th century through to the 21st century, making Coco Chanel one of the world's most prestigious fashion houses.

Technological breakthrough and market breakthrough as really new innovation

For really new innovation, discontinuity happens at the macro-level, either in the technological dimension through a new state of idea/science and technology embedded in a product ("never used in the industry before") or in the marketing dimension through a new marketplace ("the first of its kind and totally new to the market"); whereas at the micro-level discontinuities can happen in any combination by requiring new a production process/R&D resources and/or new marketing skills (Song & Montoya-Weiss, 1998, p.126).

As reflected in Figure 9.2, a really new innovation can be either a technological breakthrough or a market breakthrough but will not incorporate both. In this study, '*technological breakthroughs*' refer to products that build on a new or novel idea/technology that has never been used in the industry before. The product may not be new to the market but the technology application is. An example of a technological breakthrough is the first true mobile computer (Laptop), which used new technology to extent the existing product line of the desktop computer [the existing computer market]. '*Market breakthroughs*' refer to products that build on an existing idea or technology and create a new market, being the first of their kind and totally new to the market, and/or causing significant changes in the industry or product category (Song & Swink, 2009). An example of a market breakthrough is the iPod, which used existing technology (MP3) within a new platform to create a new market.

Market-driven innovation

Incremental innovation

For incremental innovation, discontinuity happens only at the micro-level, from a technological dimension which requires new production process/R&D resources and/or from a marketing dimension, which requires new marketing skills (Garcia & Calantone, 2002; Song & Montoya-Weiss, 1998). In other words, an incremental product is new either to the firm or to the customer. This type of product innovation can also be referred to as 'market-driven innovation' (Jaworski et al., 2000; Zortea-Johnston et al., 2012) because it is an adaptation of an existing product which only provides "new features, benefits, or improvements to the existing technology in the existing market" (Garcia & Calantone, 2002, p.113).

As reflected in Figure 9.2, this study refers to incremental ('market-driven') innovation as an improvement of an existing product, which *exploits* existing ideas/technologies in the existing market, and therefore requires market-driven competencies (Garcia & Calantone, 2002; Jaworski et al., 2000; Leifer et al., 2000). Market-driven competencies are about listening to the voice of the customer and being reactive to articulated product preferences in existing (predictable) markets (Jaworski et al., 2000; Varadarajan, 2009). An example of an incremental innovation is the Apple iPhone11 Pro, where incremental improvements to the iPhone11 introduced new benefits based on the existing platform.

Classifying market-driving innovation (radical and really new innovation)

By defining the types of product innovation, radical innovations and really new innovations are discontinuous and can be distinguished from the others. Most discontinuous innovations are often classified as really new innovations – specifically, technological breakthroughs or market breakthroughs. This is because new product development seldom results in both new marketing and technical infrastructures at the macro-level, as occurs in radical innovation. A really new innovation is not as innovative as a radical innovation and is less able to influence the market and/or reshape the nature of competition in the industry. According to Garcia and Calantone (2002), really new innovations are considered as moderately innovative products, as defined by Kleinschmidt and Cooper (1991, p.243) as "consisting of lines to the firm, but where the products were not as innovative (that is not new to the market) and new items in existing product lines for the firm". There may also be fewer risks and uncertainties associated with the development of a really new innovation than with the development of a radical innovation (Garcia & Calantone, 2002; Kleinschmidt & Cooper, 1991).

For generalisation and simplification of terms, it is proposed that 'breakthrough' or 'market-driving' innovation is composed of both radical and really new innovations (i.e. *radical* breakthroughs, *technological* breakthroughs and *market* breakthroughs new products) (Chandy & Tellis, 1998, 2000; Garcia & Calantone, 2002; Zortea-Johnston et al., 2012). The classification of market-driving innovation is consistent with that of O'Connor (2008), who treated and labelled radical and really new innovations collectively as 'major innovation'. Although radical innovation and really new innovation involve different degrees of product newness, the strategic challenges of these two types of innovation are of like kind. A firm engaged in developing radical or really new innovation is required to shift outside its realms of knowledge and experience (O'Connor, 1998). This means that the firm cannot rely completely on its current technology and customers, as in the NPD scenario of incremental innovation (O'Connor, 2008).

Figure 9.3 ultimately introduces the 'Market-Driving Innovation and Market-Driven Innovation Model' (MDIM) by capturing the operationalisation of macro-level and micro-level discontinuities and the marketing and idea/technology dimensions leading to different types of innovation development.

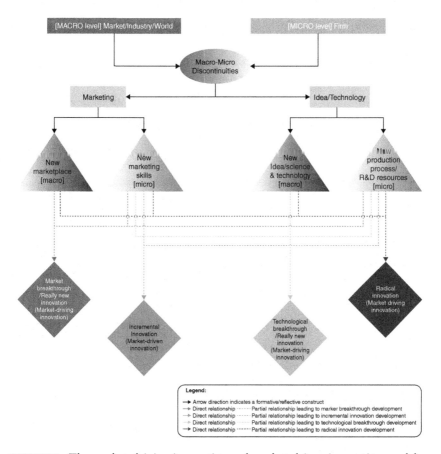

FIGURE 9.3   The market-driving innovation and market-driven innovation model.

In principle, the innovation practices, capabilities and competencies required to develop 'market-driven' innovation often do not work well for market-driving innovation (Leifer et al., 2000; Rice, Leifer, & O'Connor, 2002). Firms, managers and employees require different structure, process, skills and mindsets to navigate their development of 'market-driven' innovation and market-driving innovation (Barczak & Kahn, 2012; O'Connor, 2008).

For instance, one of the key competencies for market learning and the development of successful market-driving innovations is 'market visioning' as opposed to 'market listening'. Under the notion of 'market-driving', 'market visioning competence' can be defined as "the ability of individuals or NPD teams in an organisation to link new ideas or technologies to future market opportunities" to result in a market vision – "a clear and specific early-stage mental model or image of a product-market" that enables the NPD teams to maintain the level of innovativeness or 'breakthrough integrity' of new product concepts from the front end of innovation through to launch (Thongpravati et al., 2020, p.124).

With respect to the front end of market-driving innovation, the strategic focus and research reflect a firm's continuing endeavours of engaging in market-driving behaviour and a *forward-sensing, proactive* strategy to discover latent consumer

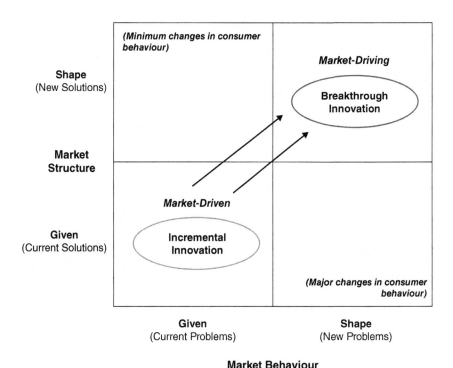

FIGURE 9.4 The changing focus of market orientation from "market-driven" to "market-driving".

Source: Adapted from Jaworski et al. (2000, p.46), Wind and Mahajan (1997, p.3).

needs and/or new technologies and to link them to new forms of markets. Market-driving firms develop highly innovative products based on their foresight by acquiring new technical/market knowledge and information that underlie their innovative capacity (absorptive capacity) (Cohen & Levinthal, 1990).

In the circumstance of pandemic like the COVID-19, it has also profoundly influenced the way people live their life. This raises major changes in consumer behaviour patterns and new opportunities to unlearn and relearn what becomes a 'new normal' that fosters more developments of breakthrough innovations. Market-driving firms develop 'new solutions' to 'new problems' that have not been solved previously; this enables them to shape the market structure (Jaworski et al., 2000). Thus, there is a need to shift the focus from market-driven orientation to market-driving orientation (Hills & Sarin, 2003; Kumar et al., 2000).

Figure 9.4 illustrates the changing focus of market orientation.

The changing focus of market orientation from market driven to market driving is shedding light on the development process of breakthrough innovation that has remained elusive to date. While market-driven firms are excellent at developing incremental innovations, market-driving firms are excellent at developing breakthrough innovations (Hills & Sarin, 2003; Leifer, O'Connor, & Rice, 2001; Stolper, Blut, & Holzmueller, 2009).

Practical implications

This chapter has significant implications for managers, entrepreneurs and NPD team members related to how they can best facilitate the development of product innovations. The better understanding of the Market-Driving Innovation and Market-Driven Innovation Model (MDIM) and its operationalisation, the better they can develop their mental models and visualisations for breakthrough thinking in terms of the level of innovativeness and the types of innovation development.

Although the focus of the chapter is specifically on the types of 'tangible' market-driving new products, the implications also extend to 'intangible' services or process innovations. It is crucial to understand that 'process innovation' and 'innovation process' is not the same notion and needs to be distinguished. An innovation process or "a production process [innovation] is the system of process equipment, work force, task specification, material inputs, work and information flows, and so forth that are employed to produce a product or service" (Utterback & Abernathy, 1975, p.641). When the innovation process is operationalised, the development of process innovations can thus improve both efficiency and effectiveness of new product or service innovations (e.g. increase the value and volume the product or service innovations in terms their cost advantage, quality, speed-to-market and output productivity).

The Pilkington's float glass process, for instance, can be considered as a 'technological breakthrough' where the market-driving process innovation emerged from the existing plate glass industry using new float glass technology for its manufacturing to reduce glass production time and cost as well as improving quality of plate glass. By further adopting such existing technology to sheet glass industry, it also creates a 'market breakthrough' in process innovation that reshapes the sheet glass product market.

Other new services can also be viewed through the lens of MDIM to explore their level of discontinuities and innovativeness dimensions in service concepts. Even the emerging business model innovation concept needs to measure its market-driving and/or market-driven competencies. This is significant because business model innovation occurs at the strategic or organisational level, as opposed to the project/programme or functional level as product or service innovation.

In an accelerated and rapidly changing world, firms should face the challenges and be engaged in market-driving innovative activities (be it new products, services, or processes) rather than being market-driven to survive. Managers should resist the temptation to fall back on "me-too" or market-driven innovations even though undertaking market-driving innovation tends to increase the levels of uncertainty and complexity in the development process. This is a competitive necessity for firms to achieve sustainable competitive advantage. To be involved in a project associated with high risk and uncertainty does not necessarily result in poor performance. A competitive advantage can often be gained by undertaking more difficult and complex tasks than the competitors do. Top performing firms are thereby fostering a higher proportion of highly innovative, risky and long-term NPD projects (as reflected in market-driving innovations) (Cooper & Kleinschmidt, 2010). Hence, it requires the right mix and balance between market-driven and market-driving breakthrough projects within a firm's NPD portfolio.

Political implications

All in all, the focus on developing market-driving innovations can foster a country's innovation performance and international competitiveness and participation in global value chains. Several countries are predominantly developing more market-driven innovations than market-driving innovations. Analysis over number of studies suggest that innovation capabilities issues remain, for instance in Australia, in terms of innovation efficiency ratio of output over input and the level of innovativeness embedded in innovation developments.

According to the 2012 INSEAD Global Innovation Index, Australia was ranked 13th on the calibre of its innovation input and 31st on innovation output, while the innovation efficiency ratio of output over input placed the country at 107 out of 141 countries assessed.

(Thongpravati, 2017, p.62)

Additionally, Australia has dropped its ranking of innovation capabilities from 20th in 2018 to 23rd in 2020 among the 131 economies being featured (University, INSEAD, & WIPO, 2020). In terms of innovativeness, the Australian Innovation System Report by the Office of the Chief Economist reveals that new-to-market innovation is accounted for only 5.7% of Australian businesses in

2012–2013 (Thongpravati, 2017). One of the reviews of Innovation and Science Australia (ISA) in 2016 indicates that the development of business innovations was incremental as opposed to major new-to-world innovation. As a consequence, the recent Government amended the statutory board of ISA to *Industry, Innovation and Science Australia* (IISA) to ensure that its innovation policy benefits Australian industry and encourages market-driving 'true to type' developments (Brennan, 2021).

The ongoing innovation capabilities issues can undermine the nation's return on investment in research and product development and the ability to attract private and foreign investment (Thongpravati, 2017). As highlighted in the MDIM, the development of a market-driving innovation such as a radical innovation requires a high level of newness in terms of ideas/technology and a high level of newness in the way in which it impacts the market/industry. While it could be more difficult for countries that may play a role of technological catching-up to develop a radical innovation, it is important for policy makers to articulate that a new idea can be exercised and incorporated into innovation and entrepreneurship based on an 'existing technology'. This type of development still has a potential to be 'market-driving', i.e. a market breakthrough type, which can simply lead to an increased development of breakthroughs at the national level.

Theoretical implications

This chapter contributes to the study of innovation management mainly in threefold.

First, it bridges the gap in the traditional market orientation to NPD through the resource-based view (RBV) and dynamic capability theory and the notion of 'market driving'. The paradigm of the traditional RBV alone, as asserted by most researchers, does not sufficiently capture today's highly competitive and dynamic marketplace (due to either pace or ambiguity). This is especially true for an investigation of market-driving innovation in the context of dynamic capability (Eisenhardt & Martin, 2000; O'Connor, 2008; Teece et al., 1997). Hence, the present study adds to the theoretical argument of RBV and dynamic capability literature as a robust approach to the analysis of sustainable competitive advantage, particularly for market-driving innovation.

Second, it advances our knowledge about breakthrough innovation through the lens of market orientation. The study unfolds the definitions of the types of product innovation especially the varying degree of breakthroughness. It broadens the view of the exploration competencies in terms of the newness in ideas using the notion of "market-driving". Although the 'market-driving' is an alternate paradigm for marketing in high-tech industries (Hills & Sarin, 2003), it can also be applied to low-tech industries. It deep-dives to simplify our understanding by operationalising the level of innovativeness under an umbrella of 'market-driving' and 'market-driven' behaviours, i.e. market-driving innovation vs market-driven innovation.

Third, the operationalisation of product innovativeness and the proposed 'Market-Driving Innovation and Market-Driven Innovation Model' can be extended to other types of innovation such as new services, process and/or business model innovations. Future studies should further explore this venue of study to increase our understanding of the concept of 'market-driving' and the development of 'intangible' innovations. Empirical research could also be done on the market-driving behaviour of firms and their antecedents (Ghauri, Wang, Elg, & Rosendo-Ríos, 2016) and/or number of contingencies influencing the market-driving process (Jaworski et al., 2020), among other gap of studies.

References

Acedo, F. J., Barroso, C., & Galan, J. L. (2006). The Resource-based Theory: Dissemination and Main Trends. *Strategic Management Journal, 27*(7), 621–636. https://doi.org/10.1002/smj.532

Amit, R., & Schoemaker, P. J. H. (1993). Strategic Assets and Organizational Rent. *Strategic Management Journal, 14*(1), 33–46. https://doi.org/10.1002/smj.4250140105

Atuahene-Gima, K. (2005). Resolving the Capability-Rigidity Paradox in New Product Innovation. *Journal of Marketing, 69*(4), 61–83. https://doi.org/10.1509/jmkg.2005.69.4.61

Bakar, L. J. A., & Ahmad, H. (2010). Assessing the Relationship between Firm Resources and Product Innovation Performance: A Resource-Based View. *Business Process Management Journal, 16*(3), 420–435. https://dx.doi.org/10.1108/14637151011049430

Barczak, G., & Kahn, K. B. (2012). Identifying New Product Development Best Practice. *Business Horizons, 55*(3), 293–305. https://10.1016/J.BUSHOR.2012.01.006

Baregheh, A., Rowley, J., & Sambrook, S. (2009). Towards a Multidisciplinary Definition of Innovation. *Management Decision, 47*(8), 1323–1339. https://doi.org/10.1108/00251740910984578

Barney, J. B. (1986). Strategic Factor Markets: Expectations, Luck, and Business Strategy. *Management Science, 32*(10), 1231–1241. https://dx.doi.org/10.1287/mnsc.32.10.1231

Barney, J. B. (1991). Firm Resources and Sustained Competitive Advantage. *Journal of Management, 17*(1), 99–120. https://doi.org/10.1177/014920639101700108

Bessant, J., Birkinshaw, J., & Delbridge, R. (2004). Innovation as Unusual. *Business Strategy Review, 15*(3), 32–35. https://doi.org/10.1111/j.0955-6419.2004.00324.x

Bessant, J., Rush, H., & Trifilova, A. (2015). Crisis-driven Innovation: The Case of Humanitarian Innovation. *International Journal of Innovation Management, 19*(6), 1–17. https://doi.org/10.1142/S1363919615400149

Brennan, T. (2021, April 12). Industry, Innovation and Science Australia, Parliament of Australia. Retrieved from https://www.aph.gov.au/About_Parliament/Parliamentary_Departments/Parliamentary_Library/FlagPost/2021/April/Industry_Innovation_and_Science_Australia

Chandy, R. K., & Tellis, G. J. (1998). Organizing for Radical Product Innovation: The Overlooked Role of Willingness to Cannibalize. *Journal of Marketing Research, 35*(4), 474–487. https://doi.org/10.2307/3152166

Chandy, R. K., & Tellis, G. J. (2000). The Incumbent's Curse? Incumbency, Size, and Radical Product innovation. *Journal of Marketing, 64*(3), 1–17. https://doi.org/10.1509/jmkg.64.3.1.18033

Cho, H. -J., & Pucik, V. (2005). Relationship between Innovativeness, Quality, Growth, Profitability, and Market Value. *Strategic Management Journal, 26*(6), 555–575. https://doi.org/10.1002/smj.461

Cohen, W. M., & Levinthal, D. A. (1990). Absorptive Capacity: A New Perspective on Learning and Innvoation. *Administrative Science Quarterly, 35*(1), 128–152. https://doi.org/10.2307/2393553

Conner, K. (1991). A Historical Comparison of Resource-Based Theory and Five Schools of Thought Within Industrial Organization Economics: Do We Have a New Theory of the Firm? *Journal of Management, 17*(1), 121–154. https://doi.org/10.1177/014920639101700109

Cooper, R. G., & de Brentani, U. (1991). New Industrial Financial Services: What Distinguishes the Winners. *Journal of Product Innovation Management, 8*(2), 75–90. https://doi.org/10.1016/0737-6782(91)90002-G

Cooper, R. G., & Kleinschmidt, E. J. (1993). Major New Products: What Distinguishes the Winners in the Chemical Industry? *Journal of Product Innovation Management, 10*(2), 90–111. https://doi.org/10.1016/0737-6782(93)90002-8

Cooper, R. G., & Kleinschmidt, E. J. (2010). Success Factors for New Product Development. In *Wiley International Encyclopedia of Marketing*. John Wiley & Sons, Ltd. https://doi.org/10.1002/9781444316568.wiem05021

Damanpour, F. (1991). Organizational Innovation: A Meta-Analysis of Effects of Determinants and Moderators. *The Academy of Management Journal, 34*(3), 555–591. https://doi.org/10.5465/256406

Danneels, E. (2002). The Dynamics of Product Innovation and Firm Competences. *Strategic Management Journal, 23*(12), 1095–1121. https://doi.org/10.1002/smj.275

Danneels, E., & Kleinschmidt, E. J. (2001). Product Innovativeness from the Firm's Perspective: Its Dimensions and Their Relation with Project Selection and Performance. *Journal of Product Innovation Management, 18*(6), 357–373. https://doi.org/10.1111/1540-5885.1860357

de Brentani, U. (2001). Innovative versus Incremental New Business Services: Different Keys for Achieving Success. *Journal of Product Innovation Management, 18*(3), 169–187. https://doi.org/10.1111/1540-5885.1830169

de Brentani, U., Kleinschmidt, E. J., & Salomo, S. (2010). Success in Global New Product Development: Impact of Strategy and the Behavioral Environment of the Firm. *Journal of Product Innovation Management, 27*(2), 143–160. https://doi.org/10.1111/j.1540-5885.2010.00707.x

De Clercq, D., Thongpapanl, N., & Dimov, D. (2011). A Closer Look at Cross-Functional Collaboration and Product Innovativeness: Contingency Effects of Structural and Relational Context. *Journal of Product Innovation Management, 28*(5), 680–697. https://doi.org/10.1111/j.1540-5885.2011.00830.x

Deszca, G., Munro, H., & Noori, H. (1999). Developing Breakthrough Products: Challenges and Options for Market Assessment. *Journal of Operations Management, 17*(6), 613–630. https://doi.org/10.1016/S0272-6963(99)00017-0

Dunford, B. B., Snell, S. A., & Wright, P. M. (2003). Human Resources and the Resource Based View of the Firm, School of Industrial and Labour Relations. *Center for Advanced of Human Resource Studies* (pp. 1–35). Ithaca, NY: Cornell University. https://hdl.handle.net/1813/77397

Eisenhardt, K. M., & Martin, J. A. (2000). Dynamic Capabilities: What Are They? *Strategic Management Journal, 21*, 1105–1121. https://doi.org/10.1002/1097-0266(200010/11)21:10/11<1105::AID-SMJ133>3.0.CO;2-E

Foss, N. J., & Knudsen, T. (2003). The Resource-Based Tangle: Towards a Sustainable Explanation of Competitive Advantage. *Managerial and Decision Economics, 24*(4), 291–307. https://doi.org/10.1002/mde.1122

Garcia, R., & Calantone, R. J. (2002). A Critical Look at Technological Innovation Typology and Innovativeness Terminology: A Literature Review. *Journal of Product Innovation Management, 19*(2), 110–132. https://doi.org/10.1111/1540-5885.1920110

Ghauri, P., Wang, F., Elg, U., & Rosendo-Ríos, V. (2016). Market Driving Strategies: Beyond localization. *Journal of Business Research, 69*(12), 5682–5693. https://doi.org/10.1016/j.jbusres.2016.04.107

Grant, R. M. (1991). The Resource-Based Theory of Competitive Advantage: Implications for Strategy Formulation. *California Management Review, 33*(3), 114–135. https://doi.org/10.2307/41166664

Griffin, A. (1997). PDMA Research on New Product Development Practices: Updating Trends and Benchmarking Best Practices. *Journal of Product Innovation Management, 14*, 429–458. https://doi.org/10.1111/1540-5885.1460429

Han, J. K., Kim, N., & Srivastava, R. K. (1998). Market Orientation and Organizational Performance: Is Innovation a Missing Link? *Journal of Marketing, 62*, 30–45. https://doi.org/10.2307/1252285

Harmancioglu, N., Dröge, C., & Calantone, R. J. (2009). Theoretical Lenses and Domain Definitions in Innovation Research. *European Journal of Marketing, 43*(1/2), 229–263. https://doi.org/10.1108/03090560910923319

Hauser, J. R., Tellis, G. J., & Griffin, A. (2006). Research on Innovation: A Review and Agenda for Marketing Science. *Marketing Science, 25*(6), 687–717. https://doi.org/10.1287/mksc.1050.0144

Henderson, R. M., & Clark, K. B. (1990). Architectural Innovation: The Reconfiguration of Existing Product Technologies and the Failure of Established Firms. *Administrative Science Quarterly, 35*, 9–30. https://doi.org/10.2307/2393549

Hills, S. B., & Sarin, S. (2003). From Market Driven to Market Driving: An Alternate Paradigm for Marketing in High Technology Industries. *Journal of Marketing Theory and Practice, 11*(3), 13–24. https://doi.org/10.1080/10696679.2003.11658498

Hobday, M. (2005). Firm-Level Innovation Models: Perspectives on Research in Developed and Developing Countries. *Technology Analysis & Strategic Management, 17*(2), 121–146. https://doi.org/10.1080/09537320500088666

Jaworski, B. J., Kohli, A. K., & Sahay, A. (2000). Market-Driven Versus Driving Markets. *Journal of the Academy Marketing Science, 28*(1), 45–54. doi:10.1177/0092070300281005

Jaworski, B. J., Kohli, A. K., & Sarin, S. (2020). Driving Markets: A Typology and a Seven-Step Approach. *Industrial Marketing Management, 91*, 142–151. https://doi.org/10.1016/j.indmarman.2020.08.018

Johnson, S. C., & Jones, C. (1957). How to Organize for New Products. *Harvard Business Review, 35*(3), 49–62.

Kessler, E. H., & Chakrabarti, A. K. (1999). Speeding Up the Pace of New Product Development. *Journal of Product Innovation Management, 16*(3), 231–247. https://doi.org/10.1111/1540-5885.1630231

Kleinschmidt, E. J., & Cooper, R. G. (1991). The Impact of Product Innovativeness on Performance. *Journal of Product Innovation Management, 8*(4), 240–251. https://doi.org/10.1016/0737-6782(91)90046-2

Knight, G. A., & Cavusgil, S. T. (2004). Innovation, Organizational Capabilities, and the Born-Global Firm. *Journal of International Business Studies, 35*(2), 124–141. https://doi.org/10.1057/palgrave.jibs.8400071

Kumar, N., Scheer, L., & Kotler, P. (2000). From Market Driven to Market Driving. *European Management Journal, 18*(2), 129–142. https://doi.org/10.1016/S0263-2373(99)00084-5

Leifer, R., McDermott, C. M., O'Connor, G. C., Peters, L. S., Rice, M. P., & Veryzer, R. W. (2000). *Radical Innovation: How Mature Companies Can Outsmart Upstarts.* Boston, MA: Harvard Business School Press.

Leifer, R., O'Connor, G. C., & Rice, M. P. (2001). Implementing Radical Innovation in Mature Firms: The Role of Hubs. *Academy of Management Perspectives, 15*(3), 102–113. https://doi.org/10.5465/ame.2001.5229646

Mahoney, J. T., & Pandian, J. R. (1992). The Resource-based View within the Conversation of Strategic Management. *Strategic Management Journal, 13*(5), 363–380. https://doi.org/10.1002/smj.4250130505

March, J. G. (1991). Exploration and Exploitation in Organizational Learning. *Organization Science, 2*(1), 71–87. https://doi.org/10.1287/orsc.2.1.71

Martin, J. (1995). Ignore Your Customer. *Fortune, 131*(8), 123–126.

McDermott, C. M., & O'Connor, G. C. (2002). Managing Radical Innovation: An Overview of Emergent Strategy Issues. *Journal of Product Innovation Management, 19*(6), 424–438. https://doi.org/10.1111/1540-5885.1960424

McNally, R. C., & Schmidt, J. B. (2011). From the Special Issue Editors: An Introduction to the Special Issue on Decision Making in New Product Development and Innovation. *Journal of Product Innovation Management, 28*(5), 619–622. https://doi.org/10.1111/j.1540-5885.2011.00843.x

Mohr, J. J., Sengupta, S., & Slater, S. F. (2005). *Marketing High Technology Products and Innovations.* Englewood Cliffs, NJ: Prentice-Hall.

Montgomery, C. A. (1995). *Resource-Based and Evolutionary Theories of the Firm: Towards a Shynthesis.* Boston, MA: Kluwer Academic Publishers.

Nenonen, S., Fehrer, J., & Brodie, R. J. (2021). Editorial: JBR Special Issue on Market Shaping and Innovation. *Journal of Business Research, 124*, 236–239. https://doi.org/10.1016/j.jbusres.2020.11.062

O'Connor, G. C. (1998). Market Learning and Radical Innovation: A Cross Case Comparison of Eight Radical Innovation Projects. *Journal of Product Innovation Management, 15*(2), 151–166. https://doi.org/10.1111/1540-5885.1520151

O'Connor, G. C. (2008). Major Innovation as a Dynamic Capability: A Systems Approach. *Journal of Product Innovation Management, 25*, 313–330. https://doi.org/10.1111/j.1540-5885.2008.00304.x

O'Connor, G. C. (2010). Radical Innovation. In *Wiley International Encyclopedia of Marketing.* New Jersey: John Wiley & Sons, Ltd.

O'Connor, G. C., Ravichandran, T., & Robeson, D. (2008). Risk Management through Learning: Management Practices for Radical Innovation Success. *Journal of High Technology Management Research, 19*(1), 70–82. https://doi.org/10.1016/j.hitech.2008.06.003

O'Connor, G. C., & Rice, M. P. (2001). Opportunity Recognition and Breakthrough Innovation in Large Established Firms. *California Management Review, 43*(2), 95–116. https://doi.org/10.2307/41166077

O'Regan, N., & Ghobadian, A. (2004). The Importance of Capabilities for Strategic Direction and Performance. *Management Decision, 42*(2), 292–313. https://doi.org/10.1108/00251740410518525

Ottum, B. D., & Moore, W. L. (1997). The Role of Market Information in New Product Success/Failure. *Journal of Product Innovation Management, 14*(4), 258–273. https://doi.org/10.1111/1540-5885.1440258

Paladino, A. (2007). Investigating the Drivers of Innovation and New Product Success: A Comparison of Strategic Orientations. *Journal of Product Innovation Management, 24*(6), 534–553. https://doi.org/10.1111/j.1540-5885.2007.00270.x

Penrose, E. (1959). *The Theory of the Growth of the Firm.* New York: Wiley.

Peteraf, M. A. (1993). The Cornerstones of Competitive Advantage: A Resource-Based View. *Strategic Management Journal, 14*(3), 179–191. https://doi.org/10.1002/smj.4250140303

Peteraf, M. A., & Barney, J. B. (2003). Unraveling the Resource-Based Tangle. *Managerial and Decision Economics, 24*(4), 309–323. https://doi.org/10.1002/mde.1126

Porter, M. E. (1980). *Competitive Strategies.* New York: The Free Press.

Porter, M. E. (1985). *Competitive Advantage.* New York: The Free Press.

Porter, M. E. (1991). Towards a Dynamic Theory of Strategy. *Strategic Management Journal, 12,* 95–117. https://doi.org/10.1002/smj.4250121008

Porter, M. E. (1996). What Is Strategy? *Harvard Business Review, 74*(6), 61–78.

Reid, S. E., & de Brentani, U. (2004). The Fuzzy Front End of New Product Development for Discontinuous Innovations: A Theoretical Model. *Journal of Product Innovation Management, 21*(3), 170–184. https://doi.org/10.1111/j.0737-6782.2004.00068.x

Rice, M. P., Leifer, R., & O'Connor, G. C. (2002). Commercializing Discontinuous Innovations: Bridging the Gap from Discontinuous Innovation Project to Operations. *IEEE Transactions on Engineering Management, 49*(4), 330–340. https://doi.org/10.1109/TEM.2002.806721

Rubera, G., & Kirca, A. H. (2012). Firm Innovativeness and Its Performance Outcomes: A Meta-Analytic Review and Theoretical Integration. *Journal of Marketing, 76*(2), 130–147. https://doi.org/10.1509/jm.10.0494

Rumelt, R. P. (1984). Towards a strategic theory of the firm. *Competitive Strategic Management, 26*(3), 556–570.

Schindehutte, M., Morris, M. H., & Kocak, A. (2008). Understanding Market-Driving Behavior: The Role of Entrepreneurship. *Journal of Small Business Management, 46*(1), 4–26. https://doi.org/10.1111/j.1540-627X.2007.00228.x

Sethi, R. (2000). New Product Quality and Product Development Teams. *Journal of Marketing, 64*(2), 1–15. https://doi.org/10.1509/jmkg.64.2.1.17999

Sivadas, E., & Dwyer, F. R. (2000). An Examination of Organizational Factors Influencing New Product Success in Internal and Alliance-Based Processes. *Journal of Marketing, 64*(1), 31–49. https://doi.org/10.1509/jmkg.64.1.31.17985

Song, X. M., & Montoya-Weiss, M. M. (1998). Critical Development Activities for Really New Versus Incremental Products. *Journal of Product Innovation Management, 15,* 124–135. https://doi.org/10.1016/S0737-6782(97)00077-5

Song, X. M., & Parry, M. E. (1997a). The Determinants of Japanese New Product Successes. *Journal of Marketing Research, 34*(1), 64–76. https://doi.org/10.1177/002224379703400106

Song, X. M., & Parry, M. E. (1997b). A Cross-National Comparative Study of New Product Development Processes: Japan and the United States. *Journal of Marketing, 61*(2), 1–18. https://doi.org/10.1177/002224299706100201

Song, X. M., & Swink, M. (2009). Marketing-Manufacturing Integration Across Stages of New Product Development: Effects on the Success of High- and Low-Innovativeness Products. *IEEE Transactions on Engineering Management, 56*(1), 31–44. https://doi.org/10.1109/TEM.2008.2009790

Sorescu, A. B., Chandy, R. K., & Prabhu, J. C. (2003). Sources and Financial Consequences of Radical Innovation: Insights from Pharmaceuticals. *The Journal of Marketing, 67*(4), 82–102. https://doi.org/10.1509/jmkg.67.4.82.18687

Spanjol, J., Tam, L., Qualls, W. J., & Bohlmann, J. D. (2011). New Product Team Decision Making: Regulatory Focus Effects on Number, Type, and Timing Decisions. *Journal of Product Innovation Management, 28*(5), 623–640. https://doi.org/10.1111/j.1540-5885.2011.00833.x

Stathakopoulos, V., Kottikas, K. G., Theodorakis, I. G., & Kottika, E. (2019). Market-Driving Strategy and Personnel Attributes: Top Management Versus Middle Management. *Journal of Business Research, 104*, 529–540. https://doi.org/10.1016/j.jbusres.2018.09.020

Stolper, M., Blut, M., & Holzmueller, H. H. (2009). *Market Driving and Firm Performance.* Paris: International Marketing Trends Congress.

Story, V., Hart, S., & O'Malley, L. (2009). Relational Resources and Competences for Radical Product Innovation. *Journal of Marketing Management, 25*(5–6), 461–481. https://doi.org/10.1362/026725709X461803

Tallman, S. (2005). Forming and Managing Shared Organization Ventures: Resources and Transaction Costs. In D. Faulkner & M. De Rond (Eds.), *Cooperative Strategy: Economic, Business, and Organizational Issues.* Oxford: Oxford University Press.

Teece, D. J. (2007). Explicating Dynamic Capabilities: The Nature and Microfoundations of (Sustainable) Enterprise Performance. *Strategic Management Journal, 28*(13), 1319–1350. https://doi.org/10.1002/smj.640

Teece, D. J., Pisano, G., & Shuen, A. (1997). Dynamic Capabilities and Strategic Management. *Strategic Management Journal, 18*(7), 509–533. https://doi.org/10.1002/(SICI)1097-0266(199708)18:7<509::AID-SMJ882>3.0.CO;2-Z

Thongpravati, O. (2017). The Student of the Future. In R. Gutierrez (Ed.), *The University of the Future: Evolutions, Revolutions and Transformations* (pp. 59–83). Sydney: LeeHechtHarrison.

Thongpravati, O., Reid, M., & Dobele, A. R. (2020). Unfolding Market Vision Quality: Understanding its Dimensions, Drivers, and Before-Launch Performance. *Journal of Strategic Marketing, 28*(2), 123–135. https://doi.org/10.1080/0965254X.2018.1488701

University, C., INSEAD, & WIPO. (2020). *The Global Innovation Index 2020: Who Will Finance Innovation?* Retrieved from Ithaca, Fontainbleau, and Geneva: https://www.wipo.int/edocs/pubdocs/en/wipo_pub_gii_2020/au.pdf

Utterback, J. M., & Abernathy, W. J. (1975). A Dynamic Model of Process, and Product Innovation. *Omega, 33*, 639–656. http://dx.doi.org/10.1016/0305-0483(75)90068-7

Varadarajan, P. R. (1996). From the Editor: Reflections on Research and Publishing. *Journal of Marketing, 60*, 3–6. https://doi.org/10.1177/002224299606000402

Varadarajan, P. R. (2009). Fortune at the Bottom of the Innovation Pyramid: The Strategic Logic of Incremental Innovations. *Business Horizon, 52*, 21–29. https://doi.org/10.1016/j.bushor.2008.03.011

Verganti, R. (2008). Design, Meanings, and Radical Innovation: A Metamodel and a Research Agenda. *Journal of Product Innovation Management, 25*, 436–456. https://doi.org/10.1111/j.1540-5885.2008.00313.x

Verona, G. (1999). A Resource-Based View of Product Development. *The Academy of Management Review, 24*(1), 132–142. https://doi.org/10.5465/AMR.1999.1580445

Veryzer, R. W. (1998). Discontinuous Innovation and the New Product Development Process. *Journal of Product Innovation Management, 15*(4), 304–321. https://doi.org/10.1111/1540-5885.1540304

Vincent, L. (2008). Differentiating Competence, Capability and Capacity. *Innovating Perspectives, 16*(3), 1–2.

Wernerfelt, B. (1984). A Resource-Based View of the Firm. *Strategic Management Journal, 5*(2), 171–180. https://doi.org/10.1002/smj.4250050207

Wind, J., & Mahajan, V. (1997). Issues and Opportunities in New Product Development: An Introduction to the Special Issue. *Journal of Marketing Research, 34*(1), 1–12. https://doi.org/10.2307/3152060

Winter, S. G. (2000). The Satisficing Principle in Capability Learning. *Strategic Management Journal, 21*(10), 981–996. https://doi.org/10.1002/1097-0266(200010/11)21:10/11<981::AID-SMJ125>3.0.CO;2-4

Zahra, S. A., Sapienza, H. J., & Davidson, P. (2006). Entrepreneurship and Dynamic Capabilities: A Review, Model and Research Agenda. *Journal of Management Studies, 43*(4), 917–955. https://doi.org/10.1111/j.1467-6486.2006.00616.x

Zirger, B. J., & Maidique, M. A. (1990). A Model of New Product Development: An Empirical Test. *Management Science, 36*(7), 867–883. http://dx.doi.org/10.1287/mnsc.36.7.867

Zollo, M., & Winter, S. G. (2002). Deliberate Learning and the Evolution of Dynamic Capabilities. *Organization Science, 13*(3), 339–351. https://doi.org/10.1287/orsc.13.3.339.2780

Zortea-Johnston, E., Darroch, J., & Matear, S. (2012). Business Orientations and Innovation in Small and Medium Sized Enterprises. *International Entrepreneurship and Management Journal, 8*(2), 145–164. https://doi.org/10.1007/s11365-011-0170-7

10

INNOVATION ECOSYSTEMS AS A SOURCE OF RENEWAL FOR INNOVATIVE ENTERPRISES

Anna Nikina-Ruohonen

Introduction

Innovation ecosystems have persistently dominated business dialogue and research. This trend has amplified following the COVID-19 crisis that has pushed the corporate world to regroup, harness the abilities of networks and establish collaborations that enable business renewal.

At the same time, when addressing innovation ecosystems from an enterprise perspective, the existing body of research has mainly focussed on the firm as the unit of analysis. Studies addressing the enterprise perspective with the ecosystem level being the unit of analysis are scarce (Yaghmaie & Vanhaverbeke 2020). However, a functioning innovation ecosystem is based on the principles of reciprocity, and adopting purely the biased perspective of an individual firm on their interests may result in the misalignment of those with other ecosystem participants (Vanhaverbeke et al. 2014).

The present chapter focusses on the multi-stakeholder perspective, where an enterprise collaborates within an innovation ecosystem with the consideration of partners' interests and aims. However, it is not the enterprise innovation ecosystem that is the focus here, as it implies an ecosystem established and governed by specific enterprise. Rather an individual enterprise – as understood by an established corporation or firm – is one of the innovation ecosystem members. For over a decade the innovation ecosystem as a concept has attracted varied interest of scholars and practitioners, and knowledge in the area has remained fragmented (Gu et al. 2021), leading to a plethora of mixed definitions and conceptualization efforts of innovation ecosystems (see, e.g. Jacobides et al. 2018). For the purposes of the current discussion, innovation ecosystems are viewed as a constellation of members, such as corporations, startups, investors, universities, regions and community at large. This is supported by the view of innovation ecosystems

DOI: 10.4324/9780429346033-13

as a combination of heterogeneous actors and their complex value-creating interrelationships that follow the principles of co-evolution (see, e.g. Adner 2016; Iansiti & Levien 2004; Zahra & Nambisan 2011).

The chapter is structured in the following way. First, innovation ecosystems are placed within the current context of business renewal from the perspective of enterprises. Second, the multi-stakeholder perspective of innovation ecosystems is addressed with the respective implications for enterprises. Third, managerial outcomes and considerations are offered for key interrelationships.

The chapter builds up to the conclusion that contemporary innovation management practices within the context enterprises as members of innovation ecosystems are no longer focussed merely on separate needs, wants and interests of the key innovation process stakeholders, but rather on the proactive search for sustainable and effective networks and partnerships.

Business renewal as the new norm

COVID-19 transformed the world of business, pushing for the reinvention and development of business practices, and offered a unique opportunity for learning. Business leaders are faced with an amalgam of demands, ranging from navigating through uncertain landscapes, supporting employees and stakeholders through unpredictability, coping with the major impacts occurring at a high speed. At this critical moment, relying on existing partnerships, efficiently developing the new ones, adopting the bird's-eye view of an ecosystem and its members is imperative in looking for, creating and bringing to life new and redefined business models, products and services.

A recent study of firm founders and CEOs in Finland (Harmaala & Nikina-Ruohonen 2021), showed that the first moments of COVID-19 crisis in the spring 2020 were paralysing for enterprises, as everything stopped and the business activities were at the zero-mark, the business leaders felt that the situation was out of their hands and nothing could be done. Following the initial shock and after having considered to whether give in to the situation or act upon it, the majority of the leaders took the matters into their hands, decided to act and pushed back. As one of the CEOs commented, "Corona made us take a huge jump in how the whole business is run. We had development and new business ideas prior to it, but COVID forced action". As crisis put many business operations on hold, this created the space for reflection of the company and business model fundamentals that had previously been overshadowed by the rush of everyday business activity. As a result, crisis has invigorated the innovation management practices within enterprises, calling for reinforced employment of and engagement in innovation ecosystems.

Recognizing the crisis, envisioning the path forward and acting on it, helps business leaders to overcome the "normalcy bias", preventing them from underestimating the possibility of a crisis and the difference that it could make (Alon & Omer 1994). In all researched cases (Harmaala & Nikina-Ruohonen

2021), the response of business leaders to the crisis was in line with the classic path of change management, which evolves from the initial stagnation and resistance to committing to change, seeking and pursuing fresh opportunities. It is proposed here that in this critical turning point, the effective employment of innovation ecosystems supports enterprises as they set out to create new business models, test and launch new or improved products and services, and to develop their business, adapting to the new environment. The companies that are a part of a stronger network have stronger chances at successful and timely business renewal.

Engagement in an innovation ecosystem supports enterprise leaders as they actively and curiously explore the business environment that emerged from the new situation, and learning became more strategic. In the aftermath of COVID-19, the business renewal it to become and permanently claim its place as the new norm. Innovation ecosystems have the capacity to foster organizational learning, when it is necessary for enterprises to place business operations under scrutiny, examine scenarios and develop new business opportunities or adjust the old business models.

Innovation ecosystems are effective platforms for business renewal, as they serve as dynamic integrators for its members and with the consideration of the surrounding environment, making them visible and impactful to the community at large. This is supported by multiple examples internationally. The Silicon Valley in the USA is regarded by many as an exemplar innovation ecosystem, not least for its capacity for continuous reinvention and renewal (Koh et al. 2005). Other innovation ecosystems connect innovation process and the city (e.g. Ann Arbor SPARK in the USA or Porto Digital in Recife, Brazil), create innovation cities from scratch (e.g. Sophia Antipolis in France). Furthermore, innovation ecosystems do not need to be characterized by physical borders – the place can be a virtual one, supported by the digitalization. One example are the innovation centres created by Cisco in a virtual community format around the world, where companies and experts can share ideas or collaborate on new products.

The value of the abilities of enterprises to function within innovation ecosystems is highlighted by the current business environment, as shaped by world of pandemic. More classical views of crisis management imply the necessity and availability of a predefined response plan. For example, Fink (1986, 15) suggests that planning for a crisis "…is the art of removing much of the risk and uncertainty to allow you to achieve more control over your own destiny". Instead, the nature, the scope, the speed of COVID-19 crisis has pointed towards the need for an expedited learning curve in enterprises, where their leaders develop behaviours and mindsets that "prevent them from overreacting to yesterday's developments and help them to look ahead" (D'Auria & De Smet 2020, 2). The networks, resources and interrelationships between ecosystem members are an invaluable source for achieving and sustaining the business renewal practices within innovative enterprises.

Innovation ecosystems connect enterprises to new trends, technologies and startups

With business renewal as an inevitable prerequisite for an enterprise competitiveness and competitive advantage, the integrative role of innovation ecosystems is essential helps to bring research and industry closer. In the industry helix, the special emphasis is placed on research and development activities that produce marketable outputs and knowledge, and this requires multi-member network configurations involving a diversity of academic bodies and firms.

From an enterprise perspective, it is a balancing act, where in addition to a major internal R&D unit, the open innovation activities play a role including partnerships and cooperation with new business ventures, establishing or being a part of startup accelerators, making strategic acquisitions of the prominent ventures and startups. Innovation ecosystems are designed to enable the open innovation principles in practice and with a reasonable investment an enterprise is able to select and accelerate relevant startups, provide them access to resources, mentorship and network.

Interestingly, corporations tend to navigate towards startup groups rather than individual startups (Nikina-Ruohonen 2021), and, therefore, innovation ecosystems offer greater opportunities as they consolidate and attract larger numbers of startups. One example of this, is a recently established innovation centre by Cisco in Barcelona, Spain. The centre is open to any startups, entrepreneurs, experts that may contribute to the development of new solutions within Internet of Things (IoT) as applied to city environment especially. Barcelona was a natural choice for this as it already had a ready innovation ecosystem in place for smart city and related innovations (Satyam 2016). The example illustrates how an existing ecosystem is valuable for the development of new and innovative topics, with the potential to attract local and global talent to concentrate expertise on key technology areas valuable for the enterprise.

Being a part of an innovation ecosystem enables an enterprise to spot new trends, technologies and solutions early. Enterprises then have the opportunity to involve experts and business leaders early on to help to develop the initial business models, with the focus towards practical outcomes, such as new products and services. Ideally, enterprises are able to rely on innovation ecosystems to help them establish connections to some of the best startups, as the ecosystems are uniquely positioned in their ability to do so.

Enterprises and their multi-stakeholder perspective of innovation ecosystems

Innovation ecosystems imply value creation, making it necessary to understand and embrace the various stakeholders as the key element for enterprises in effective innovation ecosystem engagement. Within the definition of value creation collaborative processes and the interrelational dimension is emphasized, and the value capture is enabled by enterprise's ability to actualize the related profit achieving competitive advantage (Ritala et al. 2013). Essentially, this is achievable by an enterprise when value capture is reached by the means of value creation (Adner & Kapoor 2010), and the multi-stakeholder perspective being an enabling mechanism for it.

Innovation ecosystems bring together a vast scope of heterogeneous stakeholders, some of which would otherwise be in direct competition, such as enterprises from the same industry or investors that search for the most prominent early-stage business ventures. Gomes et al. (2016) addressed the stakeholder perspective of innovation ecosystems and demonstrated the view of how they are "composed of interconnected and interdependent networked actors, which includes the focal firm, customers, suppliers, complementary innovators and other agents as regulators", indicating a co-evolution process of cooperation and competition. Innovation ecosystems enable synergies, effective networks and coopetition – all of the elements that enterprises may benefit from.

There are main components to any working innovation ecosystem: entrepreneurs, investors, universities, regional impact, the surrounding community in terms of press and public, and of course – enterprises (Harthorne & Nikina 2016). These perspectives are addressed next in relation to enterprises as ecosystem members.

Enterprises and high-tech startups

Cooperation with startups is central to enterprise's capacity to reinvent itself, and may take several different forms, such as forming a strategic partnership, creating spin-offs, investing in prominent startups, engaging startups within corporate accelerators or acquiring them. In this manner, startups are the key motivator for enterprises and the main attraction of innovation ecosystems. This is manifested in ecosystem's drive to attract, engage and promote the best-value startups. For the purposes of the present discussion, the term startup refers to a business venture in its first stages of operations that is founded with the purpose to develop a product or service with the potential market demand.

The startup aspirations within innovation ecosystem engagement are to establish a strong network of fellow-entrepreneurs, experts, skills, investors, customers, etc. Enterprises are a resource that may offer insight and knowledge, better access to top R&D and infrastructure, customer and investor roles.

As a result, by far the most significant variable of an effective ecosystem are the startups that it is able to attract. Prominent high-growth startups have the potential to make a notable impact, to create new jobs and support economic outputs. From the perspective of an enterprise, a single startup is unlikely to reshape its direction. However, groups of startups that work on interconnected topics are more likely to make a meaningful contribution. In this respect, the groups of startups rather than individual ventures or entrepreneurs are of the most significance, making innovation ecosystems especially valuable.

Search for investment is one of the key drivers for many startups, with enterprises in the position to meet the need. Enterprises have a wider view of the market and the trends, they work on the abilities to see complementarities and put the main elements together for the most effective outcomes. Enterprises bring together and match finances, ideas, business ideology, talents, customers and partners. In order for an enterprise in the role of an investor to achieve this there is a requirement of focussed expertise and experience, market and trend understanding, capability of noting emerging talents and community interests. For enterprises, innovation ecosystems are a key asset in supporting these processes.

Accessing skills and talents within innovation ecosystems

Startups are one of the key talent pools for enterprises within innovation ecosystems, but not the only one. Noting talents early on, having an all-encompassing view of skill needs and knowing where to find the right expertise is what makes enterprises desirable partners and investors.

Innovation ecosystems are based on or created in close proximity to university environments. There are multiple mechanisms for university-enterprise engagements, ranging from event organization, integration of cooperation modules into teaching, launching joint startup platforms and many others. The universities and higher education institutions are consolidations of skills and talents, both in terms of experts, who have a solid background and pedagogical expertise, which translates into corporate services and cooperation, and in respect to graduates and their recruitment.

Both technological and business-oriented universities and higher education institutions are valuable members of innovation ecosystems. Research equipment, access to researchers with a proven track record, having a solid base for company operations are some of the elements that make universities valuable to startups. Technology universities growing new scientific talent, conduct scientific research, have the infrastructure that might be in demand by startups and corporations alike. Business universities share knowledge about current management trends, inspire entrepreneurship and business renewal, form entrepreneurship and management skills, move forward innovation management education and help create entrepreneurial atmosphere. In combination, these provide a powerful human resource base for innovation.

The entrepreneurial spirit of universities as organizations and their readiness to engage in corporations-startups-universities partnership vary. Some universities will be oriented towards theoretical knowledge and do not advance the skills needed to cooperate with the private sector, in which case their value for the industry is, for example, more in the recruitment opportunities of graduates. In other institutions, university professors make an effort to be more in touch with the market and many of them have former business experience. This reflects in the dedication and the mindset that the professors display; and the essential soft skills may prevail over the in-depth knowledge of technologies. Both approaches and attitudes might be required, depending on the needs of the company at a given moment.

Regional and community considerations for enterprises within innovation ecosystems

Regions often have their focus strategies, allowing them to raise profile, attract funds, create firms and develop expertise within specific industries. This makes it easier for investors, enterprises and other key actors to direct their resources and capital accordingly.

For example, Singapore has an established reputation within fintech landscape, which has provided grounds to attracting and building companies that will become notable industry makers with international outreach. Furthermore, this is an opportunity for innovation ecosystem and its members to advance a multi-dimensional ecosystem, and extend the core fintech expertise to, for example, big data, analytics and digital media. The connections to the educational sector and universities also become apparent within this example, it is noted to be one of the best in the world for maths and science. By employing the focussing strategy, Singapore is able to grow and strengthen its innovation ecosystem, while offering lucrative opportunities for enterprises specialized in the same fields. In contrast, in other sectors Singapore would not be able to compete for global talents equally effectively, because there is no industry core strength for it or a natural focus.

Every region has its own unique, multifaceted scenery (Etzkowitz & Leydesdorff 2000), where a range of enterprises, startups, policy makers and academic institutions interact and shape their own work, outcomes and knowledge capacities (Doloreux 2002). The community, the public and the press offer an effective check to the realities of how convincing an innovation is for the market, and serve as an important source for validation in creating and launching new products and services (Harthorne & Nikina 2016).

Managing the interrelations within innovation ecosystems

Relations in an innovation ecosystem have their own specific patters and attributes and might be more unstable and evolving – for example, moving from cooperation to competition and in reverse (Adner & Kapoor 2010). Hence, the underlying processes of relationships among ecosystem members are not always explicit, apparent or predictable.

In order for an innovation ecosystem to be a valuable platform for enterprise business renewal, there has to be value, mutuality and impact within the interrelations of members within it. The effort of this chapter has been to identify and discuss some of the key stakeholders within innovation ecosystems from the perspective of enterprises, and to offer a practical view of establishing reciprocal exchanges.

Table 10.1 offers a summary of examples of sources of business renewal via enterprise interrelations with ecosystem members. Innovation ecosystem acts as an enabler for stakeholders' interrelations that attracts a body of heterogeneous members to the ecosystem from within various stakeholder groups, and supports stakeholders' co-evolution and complex value-creating interrelationships.

TABLE 10.1 Sources of business renewal via enterprise interrelations with innovation ecosystem members

Stakeholder groups in innovation ecosystems	Examples of sources of business renewal via enterprise interrelations with ecosystem members	Innovation ecosystem as enabler for stakeholders' interrelations
Other enterprises	• Joint pursuit of new trends, co-opetition, synergies, partnerships	Attracting a body of heterogeneous members to the ecosystem from within various stakeholder groups, supporting stakeholders' co-evolution and complex value-creating interrelationships
Startup groups	• Spotting the prominent startup groups and new talent, help in focussing the efforts of startups, acceleration of selected startups, providing them with access to resources, mentorship and network; exploring various mechanisms for cooperation, such as startups accelerators, acquisitions, venture investments	
Universities	• Access to skills pool and talent acquisition; establishing startup-enterprise-university cooperation to enable R&D infrastructure access, support to startup learning orientation, knowledge, training, technological and entrepreneurial skills, acceleration support	
VCs and investors	• Co-opetition for the most prominent startups, synergies in investing in new trends, partnerships for startup financing, mentorship, startup selection and support of investment-ready startups	
Region	• Strategy and priority areas of a region focus resources and capital of enterprises, while making them more accessible to other ecosystem members	
Community	• Positioning of company and its brand within community, testing and validating new products or services in the market	

As portrayed by the summary in Table 10.1, in respect to other enterprises within an ecosystem, the relations are defined by the possibility of joint pursuit of new trends, identifying the potential for co-opetition, synergies and partnerships. Startup groups (rather than individual startups) form the key interest for enterprises. Engaging in innovation ecosystems allows to spot the prominent startup groups and new talent. Following the mutuality principle, enterprises may help in focussing the efforts of startups, accelerate selected startups, provide them with access to resources, mentorship and network. Multiple mechanisms for enterprise-startup cooperation are possible, such as startups accelerators, acquisitions, venture investments and other.

Innovation ecosystems offer vast opportunities for skills and talent access for enterprises and other ecosystem members. Universities and higher education institutes (technological and business-oriented) are in the central role in offering access to skills pool and talent acquisition. Furthermore, from the perspective of an enterprise and the startups in which an enterprise is invested in, universities may enable R&D infrastructure access, offer support to startup learning orientation, knowledge, training, technological and entrepreneurial skills, and provide acceleration support in cooperation with the industry.

Interrelations of an enterprise with VCs and investors may involve the co-opetition for the most prominent startups, looking for synergies in investing in new trends, establishing partnerships for startup financing, mentorship, startup selection and support of investment-ready startups.

The community engagement principle from the perspective of an enterprise advances the positioning of a company and its brand within community, enables testing and validation of new products or services in the market.

Understanding the regional focus of an innovation ecosystem helps to shape enterprise's own strategy and priority areas along with the decisions on resource and capital allocation. Simultaneously, the alignment between the regional focus and the business of an enterprise makes it more accessible to other relevant ecosystem members and desired partners with similar interests.

Certainly, the innovation ecosystem in itself is a renewing and evolving concept. As one of the key related concepts, the Triple Helix model of the university-industry-government relations (Etzkowitz 1993, 1996; Etzkowitz & Leydesdorff 1995) supports the interactive principles of innovation, stepping aside from linear knowledge flow interpretations towards non-linear transitions The step further from this is the Quadruple Helix that takes into account the viewpoints of civil society and media, and the environmentally oriented Quintuple Helix completes the original framework with the natural environment (Carayannis & Campbell 2009, 2011; Carayannis et al. 2012). This presents a dynamic, varied and evolving landscape of innovation ecosystems. There is a great and growing scope of perspectives and stakeholders impacting the formation and functioning of innovation ecosystems, and this continues to offer new opportunities to enterprises.

Conclusion

Business renewal is increasingly important for enterprises, and the key to coping with the turbulences of the external environment. Innovation ecosystems are uniquely positioned to enable the business renewal of enterprises with the consideration of the exchanges of members within innovation ecosystems that are based on understanding, appreciating and responding to each other's needs.

Provided that the interrelations between an enterprise and other members of an innovation ecosystem are established constructively, the mutuality is bound to support not only the enterprise's own business renewal, but also that of the interacting parties. Table 10.1 offers vivid examples of such principle. For instance, IoT is a prominent and still largely unknown area. GE, SAP, Cisco and other enterprises share the understanding that this is one of the notable sources of potential business renewal, but innovating alone would not offer the necessary speed or impact. Therefore, following the principles of co-opetition a 150 million USD investment was made into a joint innovation centre on IoT (Satyam 2016), offering the basis for business renewal not only to each individual enterprise as a participant, but to them all – and further to those startups, universities and other ecosystem members that will become engaged.

In addition to interrelational reciprocity and the mutual business renewal of well-orchestrated relationships, it is essential to consider the interrelations between ecosystem members beyond the two-dimensional axis, where enterprise is one of the two involved parties. The multilayered connections between different members of an ecosystem offer an interesting perspective and potentially lead to greater implications for gaining competitive edge. In this manner, for example, instead of addressing separately the university-startups, startups-enterprises, enterprises-universities connections, new insight may be gained by establishing the interrelations within enterprise-universities-startup configurations. This way enterprises would see universities not only as access points to skills and talents, but, for instance, as a support network to startups within their investment pool. It is the exploration of the multitude of dependencies and interests within ecosystem members that offers the greatest potential for business renewal for enterprises and connected stakeholders.

Further discussion of the enterprise perspective may benefit from the consideration of the innovation ecosystem life-cycle stages. Innovation ecosystems may be viewed as evolving structures in their movement through life-cycle phases and evolution (launch, growth, maturity) – requiring for an equally dynamic approach and role adaptiveness from involved enterprises.

The chapter adopted a practice-oriented and management-centred approach to addressing innovation ecosystems from the perspective of enterprises and in relation to other ecosystem members or stakeholders. While the higher lever management view is valuable and necessary, it is to be noted that the relational patterns and the stakeholder interactions may and often do take place and different organizational levels. This notion offers great potential for future investigations into human-to-human interactions and organizational roles as a source of business renewal within innovation ecosystem context.

To conclude, the chapter stresses the value of innovation ecosystems for business renewal of innovative enterprises. The need to observe the ecosystem engagement via the ecosystem and the stakeholder levels of analysis rather than the biased single-firm view is highlighted. The contributions of such approach indicate that provided that the interrelations between an enterprise and other members of an innovation ecosystem are established constructively, the mutuality is bound to support not only the enterprise's own business renewal, but also that of the interacting parties – creating exponential value.

References

Adner, R. 2016. Ecosystem as structure, *Journal of Management*, 43(1), 39–58.

Adner, R., & Kapoor, R. 2010. Value creation in innovation ecosystems: How the structure of technological interdependence affects firm performance in new technology generations, *Strategic Management Journal*, 31(3), 306–333.

Alon, N., & Omer, H. 1994. The continuity principle: A unified approach to disaster and trauma, *American Journal of Community Psychology*, 22(2), 273–287.

Carayannis, E., & Campbell, D. 2009. Mode 3" and "Quadruple Helix": Toward a 21st century fractal innovation system, *International Journal of Technology Management*, 46 (3–4), 201–234.

Carayannis, E., & Campbell, D. 2011. Open innovation diplomacy and a 21st century fractal research, education and innovation ecosystem: Building on the Quadruple and Quintuple Helix innovation concepts and the "Mode 3" knowledge production system, *Journal of the Knowledge Economy*, 2, 327–372.

Carayannis, E., Barth, T., & Campbell, D. 2012. The Quintuple Helix innovation model: Global warming as a challenge and driver for innovation, *Journal of Innovation and Entrepreneurship*, 1(2), 1–12.

D'Auria, G., & De Smet, A. 2020. Leadership in a crisis: Responding to the coronavirus outbreak and future challenges. *Organization Practice*, March 2020, McKinzey Company.

Doloreux, D. 2002. What we should know about regional systems of innovation, *Technology in Society*, 24(3), 243–263.

Etzkowitz, H. 1993. Technology transfer: The second academic revolution, *Technology Access Report*, 6, 7–9.

Etzkowitz, H. 1996. From knowledge flows to the triple helix: The transformation of academic industry relations in the USA, *Industry & Higher Education*, 337–342.

Etzkowitz, H., & Leydesdorff, L. 1995. The Triple Helix: University-industry-government relations, a laboratory for knowledge based economic development, *EASTT Review*, 14(1), 14–19.

Etzkowitz, H., & Leydesdorff, L. 2000. The dynamics of innovation: From National Systems and 'Mode 2' to a Triple Helix of university-industry-government relations, *Research Policy*, 29(2), 109–123.

Fink, S. 1986. *Crisis Management: Planning for the Inevitable*, American Management Association, New York, NY.

Gomes, L.A.V., Facin, A.L.F., Salerno, M.S., & Ikenami, R.K. 2016. Unpacking the innovation ecosystem construct: Evolution, gaps and trends, *Technological Forecasting and Social Change*, http://dx.doi.org/10.1016/j.techfore.2016.11.009.

Gu, Y., Hu, L., Zhang, H., & Hou, C. 2021. Innovation ecosystem research: emerging trends and future research, *Sustainability*, 13, 11458.

Harmaala, M.-M., & Nikina-Ruohonen, A. 2021. Crisis as a leadership learning experience. *Work 2021 Conference*, Finland, online, August 18–19, 2021.

Harthorne, J., & Nikina, A. 2016. High-tech companies – The heart of areas of innovation. In *Areas of Innovation in a Global World: Concept and Practice*. IASP.

Iansiti, M., & Levien, R. 2004. Strategy as ecology, *Harvard Business Review*, 82(3), 68–78.

Jacobides, M.G., Cennamo, C., & Gawer, A. 2018. Towards a theory of ecosystems, *Strategic Management Journal*, 39(8), 2255–2276.

Koh, F., Koh, W., & Feichin, T. 2005. An analytical framework for science parks and technology districts with an application to Singapore, *Journal of Business Venturing*, 20(2), 217–239.

Nikina-Ruohonen, A. 2021. Leading and Managing Areas of Innovation: The Multi-Stakeholder and Startup Perspectives. *eSignals Research, HHBIC 2020,* 17–18.11.2020, Online.

Ritala, P., Agouridas, V., Assimakopoulos, D., & Gies, O. 2013. Value creation and capture mechanisms in innovation ecosystems: A comparative case study, *International Journal of Technology Management,* 63(3/4), 244–267.

Satyam, A. 2016. Industry: Changing reality, updated needs. In Marcus, A., & Nikina, A (Eds.), *Areas of Innovation in a Global World: Concept and Practice.* IASP.

Vanhaverbeke, W., Chesbrough, H., & West, J. (2014). Surfing the new wave of open innovation research. *New Frontiers in Open Innovation,* 281, 287–288.

Yaghmaie, P., & Vanhaverbeke, W. 2020. Identifying and describing constituents of innovation ecosystems: A systematic review of the literature, *EuroMed Journal of Business,* 15(3), 283–314.

Zahra, S., & Nambisan, S. 2011. Entrepreneurship in global innovation ecosystems, *AMS Review,* 1(1), 4–17.

PART 4

The trend toward boundaryless innovation

Part IV builds on the key learning that we must capitalize on innovation from outside of one's organizational boundaries. These authors help us learn to embrace an innovative culture and innovation that transcend organizational boundaries and extend across industries and regions. Through this part...

As an opening chapter for Part 4, we look closely at open innovation in "Houston, we have a problem: Ambiguity in perceiving 'open innovation' by academia, business and policy-makers" written by Albats and Podmetina. In this chapter, they are trying to answer the crucial question of how the open innovation concept manages its multi-lingual job of speaking to diverse stakeholder and organizational groups? Using past studies on open innovation, they present a comprehensive understanding of the phenomenon.

In "Innovation management in small and medium size enterprises (SMEs): New perspectives and directions" Hadjimanolis looks into the role of small and medium size enterprises (SMEs) in innovation. Using theoretical lenses of the resource/capabilities-based view and the systems theory, this chapter critically assesses and integrates the various literature streams and proposes an innovation management framework.

This part closes with the last chapter looking into innovation management in public and private sector. In "Public and private sector innovation management", Katsigiannis looks at the specific characteristics and differences between these two critical innovation contexts.

DOI: 10.4324/9780429346033-14

11

'HOUSTON, WE HAVE A PROBLEM

Ambiguity in perceiving 'open innovation' by academia, business, and policy-makers'

Ekaterina Albats and Daria Podmetina

Introduction

Since its initial inception by Professor Chesbrough in 2003 the 'open innovation' (OI) concept has received remarkable popularity. It is seen in the constantly growing number of academic publications on the topic, in OI becoming an inherent element of the leading companies' strategies (Huston & Sakkab, 2006) and growing forums for scientific, business, and policy-making advancement led by 'The World Open Innovation Conference'. However, as any 'trendy' and yet emerging notion, 'open innovation' is still going through conceptualization and operationalization, faces criticism, ambiguity, and duality (Dahlander et al., 2021; Groen & Linton, 2010; Trott & Hartmann, 2009). Furthermore, as 'open innovation' is a term coined by a university professor for executives, it is called to speak to both worlds – academic and business. Moreover, open innovation has become a field for policy-making (Bogers et al., 2018) and thus, policy-makers are part of the OI discourse too. Does the OI concept cope well with such a difficult 'multilingual' job? – this chapter is to find out.

The original, 'academic' definition of OI reads as '*a paradigm that assumes that firms can and should use external ideas as well as internal ideas, and internal and external paths to market, as the firms look to advance their technology*' (Chesbrough, 2003a, p. xxiv). This notion of external ideas used internally later evolved into an academic term of 'outside-in'/'inbound' OI. The opposite phenomenon, internal ideas used externally, has evolved conceptually into 'inside-out'/'outbound' OI (Chesbrough and Crowther, 2006; Gassmann and Enkel, 2004). Accordingly, the growing scientific community has identified more than a dozen of 'open innovation activities' each classified as either 'inbound' or 'outbound' in logic (Chesbrough & Brunswicker, 2014; Teplov et al., 2019). Chesbrough and Bogers defining OI in the later work (2014, p. 27) highlight its link with companies'

DOI: 10.4324/9780429346033-15

business model: '*a distributed innovation process based on purposively managed knowledge flows across organizational boundaries, using pecuniary and non-pecuniary mechanisms in line with each organization's business model*'. This embeddedness of OI into the nature of organizations and inter-organizational relations make it particularly critical to understand but simultaneously more difficult to disentangle from more well-known organizational practices.

Business community, in turn, inspired by the OI 'paradigm' took it in use and it went somewhat viral leaving a lot of room for interpretation and, thus, dispute.[1] Furthermore, relying on more than 20 years of experience and in line with research findings NineSigma '*Open innovation basics*' highlight the prevailing role of inbound OI over outbound in the business world (NineSigma, 2019). Whether practicing (or not) certain activities limits managers' perception of OI, our prior research results (Teplov et al., 2019) suggest that predominantly only 'inbound' OI activities (yet not all of them) are seen as 'open innovation' by practitioners, with only 'free revealing' being an exception for 'outbound' ones.

This chapter is written to not only stress the issue of ambiguity in perception toward OI by business and research communities or contribute the 'dispute' message, but also point out which practices show a mismatch and whether practitioners and policy-makers could enhance an academic definition of OI with their experiences. We follow the theoretical roots of OI (Vanhaverbeke & Cloodt, 2014), as well as a critique perceiving OI concept as 'an old wine in new bottles' (Trott & Hartmann, 2009) and explore the perceptions of various organizational groups.

What is this thing called 'open innovation'? Academia, business, and policy-making perspectives

Given our exploratory goal of analyzing and comparing the perceptions of OI existing in academia, business, and policy-making communities, we first review the perspectives within each group, which also show some diversity.

Academic perspective toward OI and OI in science

The academic perspective toward open innovation has been shaping for decades before Henry Chesbrough introduced its first formal definition (2003a) and has its roots in multiple theories of organization. The resource-based view (Barney, 1991; Barney et al., 2001) and knowledge-based view (Felin & Hesterly, 2007) pointed out the value and scarcity of organizational resources, which itself demands searching for alternative, external resources and knowledge. OI also has its roots linked to the transaction-cost theory, where inter-organizational transactions are essential (Vanhaverbeke & Cloodt, 2014; Williamson, 1981). In the transaction-cost theory, organizations tend to minimize the transaction costs, may be inclined to opportunistic behavior and thus, fear of similar attitude from the partners. A relational view (Dyer & Singh, 1998), in turn, focuses on 'maximizing the transactional value' through picking partners with greater resource complementarity and optimal governance. OI paradigm, which embraces complementarity, reciprocity, and trust-building (Abu El-Ella et al., 2016; Pullen et al., 2012; Simeth & Raffo, 2013), thus follows a *transaction value theory* approach (Vanhaverbeke & Cloodt, 2014).

In terms of the literature streams, OI paradigm is also rooted into several management science fields (Bogers et al., 2019; Dahlander et al., 2021; Vanhaverbeke & Cloodt, 2014). Those include strategy and business model literature (Chesbrough, 2007), as if OI takes place it is tightly integrated with both. More recently, the OI philosophy has been actively engaged with the literature on ecosystems (Ferreira & Teixeira, 2019) and platform-based business models (Dahlander et al., 2021; Nambisan et al., 2018). These developments led to distinguishing between different levels in analyzing OI. Bogers et al. (2017) overview the levels where OI is seen, those include: intra-organizational (individual, team, project, functional area, business unit); organizational (organization, strategy, business model); extra-organizational (external stakeholders, communities); inter-organizational (alliances, network, ecosystem); industry, regional, innovation systems (industry, inter-industry, region, nation, citizens, public policy, and society). Still, what specific organizational practices are perceived as OI?

The variety of OI practices discussed in academic research come from the existing innovation surveys, such as Community Innovation Survey (Ebersberger et al., 2012; Grimpe & Sofka, 2009; Spithoven et al., 2013) and practices elaborated by researchers (Clausen et al., 2013; Hung & Chou, 2013; Remneland Wikhamn & Wikhamn, 2013; Theyel, 2013). The OI practices were first aggregated into inbound, outbound, and coupled groups (Chesbrough & Crowther, 2006; Dahlander & Gann, 2010; Gassmann & Enkel, 2004), and later classified into inbound-outbound-pecuniary-non-pecuniary matrix by Chesbrough and Brunswicker (2013). The list of these practices was used for our survey and can be seen in Appendix 11.1. Burhcharth et al. (2014) also developed a literature-based list of OI practices: inbound – using external sources to search for new trends or technology; purchasing external R&D, licenses, patents, knowhow; involving lead users; and outbound – participating in others' innovation projects, selling patents, licenses, knowhow; freely revealing innovation. Chesbrough and Brunswicker revised the list of OI practices in 2018 by introducing categories, which somewhat aggregate the previously defined practices into: multi-actor/ collaborative (communities and professional networks, firm-sponsored OI communities, informal networking); multi-actor/ transactional (OI intermediaries, innovation contests and tournaments); bilateral / collaborative (bilateral partnerships); and bilateral / transactional (bilateral contracts). The globalization and digitalization of recent decades posed significant, "game-changing" challenges to organizations of all types worldwide, thus, we feel that it is time to revise our comprehension of OI practices in order to understand the meaning of OI process and specifically link those to the practical implementation across organizational boundaries of academia, business and policy-making communities.

Speaking of going beyond conceptualizing OI in solely corporate context, Beck et al. (2020, p. 4) define OI for the context of science (academia):

> a process of purposively enabling, initiating, and managing inbound, outbound, and coupled knowledge flows and (inter/ transdisciplinary) collaboration across organisational and disciplinary boundaries and along all stages of the scientific research process, from the formulation of research questions and the obtainment of funding or development of methods (i.e. conceptualisation) to data collection, data processing, and data analyses (exploration and/or testing) and the dissemination of results through writing, translation into innovation, or other forms of codifying scientific insight (i.e. documentation).

As we can see, although the context differs from corporate, the principles of multi-directional knowledge flows across the entire cycle of the research process remain. The OI practices in science context according to Beck et al. (2020) could be grouped by the stakeholders involved, for example, solely academics collaborating in cross-disciplinary projects (Gibbons et al., 1994) or involved in and open publishing (Maxwell et al., 2019); general public involved in citizen science or crowd science (Franzoni & Sauermann, 2014). Industry actors may also be co-creators in the scientific research with universities spinning out the research, running contract research, consulting, and staff mobility with companies (Perkmann et al., 2013; Perkmann & Walsh, 2007) as well as establishing strategic partnerships with firms (Albats et al., 2020).

Business perspective toward OI

Instead of sourcing business perspective on OI from the literature, we turn to the actual companies' voices – their websites and the websites of their partners – to grasp the variety of perceptions existing in the business community.

In our prior work on OI conceptualization, we found that in business mindset, inbound OI practices dominate (Teplov et al., 2019). While browsing through corporate definitions in the internet, we see the same tendency remaining. For example, one of the FMCG giants, Unilever, on its 'open innovation' webpage is rather encouraging externals to meet Unilever challenges: "...*If you have a new design or technology that could help us grow our business and solve the challenges we've set, we'd like to work with you through Open Innovation...*"[2] The legendary "Connect + Develop" program of another FMCG giant, P&G (Huston & Sakkab, 2006) keeps embracing collaboration:

> Our external partnership program, Connect + Develop, is based on the belief that collaboration accelerates innovation... Our global team searches for trailblazers outside the company. Then, we create and nurture

partnerships with these inventors, patent holders and other innovators – ultimately leading to new solutions in every area of business, from supply chains to products and technologies to in-store and e-commerce experiences.

P&G' Signal program, in turn, introduced in 2012 promotes outbound OI: "*Since 2012, we have produced Signal P&G, a remarkable 'inside out' conference that welcomes the world's most innovative business leaders into the company's headquarters in Cincinnati…*"[3]

Working on this chapter during the global COVID-19 pandemic, we could not neglect the view of Big Pharma. One of the vaccine-developing pioneers, AstraZeneca, when communicating their OI strategy, stresses the importance of sharing knowledge and resources across stakeholder groups for solving global challenges:

> AstraZeneca has spent decades creating unique enabling tools and technologies of interest to the scientific community of investigators… At the same time, academic, research foundation and biotech investigators have been developing insights, tools, technologies, platforms, resources and facilities that complement those of AstraZeneca… By bringing all of this together through partnering, we can test hypotheses that may otherwise not be possible. Sharing ideas and enabling scientific innovation to cross boundaries between academia, industry, government and non-profit organisations will help us translate innovative ideas into scientific breakthroughs and potential new medicines more quickly and effectively.[4]

LEGO in their FORMA program continuously engages adults and their non-traditional partners through crowdfunding website Indiegogo to create something different from what they usually do.[5] IBM among others puts stakes on open source.[6] OI intermediaries (as InnoCentive, Qmarkets), as well as traditional businesses (as General Electric) continue to develop digital platforms and software for matchmaking, connecting, and supporting OI partners. All these diverse examples refer to OI, but focus on different OI practices and aspects, while mostly staying at organizational, extra-organizational or inter-organizational levels (Bogers et al., 2017). The following policy-making perspective would help us climb higher in levels.

Policy-making perspective toward OI

OI paradigm has also received a wide recognition on a policy-making level. Governments of countries and regions apply OI principles to policy-making initiatives. Policy-makers, as expected, are inclined to take an overarching perspective toward OI, oversee all the OI actors and support them in a targeted way. Governmental bodies support open collective actions with funding (Gläser & Laudel, 2016), establishing policy labs where various stakeholder groups run scientific foresight activities – for example, IdeaLab in Denmark, Sitra in Finland, and the EU Policy Lab of the European Commission (Beck et al., 2020). Furthermore, state supports OI via developing regulations for the best social impact (Bogers et al., 2018; Robaczewska et al., 2019). One of the examples on regulations related to OI are the ongoing policy-making efforts in regulating platform-based business and user data usage – as the more open and accessible the user data are, the more businesses leverage that user data, the more privacy issues arise especially in non-regulated settings (Cusumano et al., 2019; Dahlander et al., 2021).[7]

Among the examples of OI definitions in the policy-making space, the EU-based initiative "Open Innovation 2.0" says:

> Open Innovation 2.0 is a new paradigm based on a Quadruple Helix Model where government, industry, academia and civil participants work together to co-create the future and drive structural changes far beyond the scope of what any one organization or person could do alone. This model encompasses also user-oriented innovation models to take full advantage of ideas' cross-fertilisation leading to experimentation and prototyping in real world setting.[8]

This definition clearly implies coupled OI practices. We observe the perception of OI varies not only across the groups as business, academia, and government, but also within the groups. The US Government Accountability Office for example, shares mostly organizational-level and rather inbound view of OI on their website: "*Open innovation uses activities and technologies to harness the ideas, expertise, and resources of those outside an organization to address an issue or achieve specific goals*".[9] Notably, these above mentioned definitions do not contradict each other, they rather emphasize different "faces" of OI. Such conceptual ambiguity is a very natural step in theoretical development and conceptualization of such a developing OI phenomenon (Teplov et al., 2019). Those might still create confusions and misinterpretations both between the groups of academia, business, government, and within each of those. Our study is to help the views' alignment process take its steps forward.

Research approach

Given an exploratory goal of our research, this study applies predominantly qualitative research strategy, with some of the data being quantified. In the analysis we used quantitative and qualitative data collected as a part of the OI-Net project[10] with a large-scale survey on OI practices, capabilities, and industrial needs for OI skills and abilities conducted in 2014–2015.

In total, 525 (N=525) responses from 38 countries were collected. Most of the samples are large companies with 250 employees and more (44.17%), while micro companies with less than ten employees are least represented.

The major quantitative variables taken for our analysis are (1) 1–7 Likert scale intensity of adopting each of the specific OI practices – 13 OI practices as per Chesbrough and Brunswicker (2013); and (2) "OI status", which implies six stages of generally OI adoption (Appendix 11.1). To avoid pitfalls associated with self-reported data and minimize risk of common method bias we adjusted the design of the questionnaire in such manner that respondents could not associate the question related to OI practices adoption and question on OI status. Of qualitative variables, the respondents were asked "*How do you define open innovation? Please provide your own definition (optional)*", although in the cover letter the respondents were provided with the definition of OI by Chesbrough (2003b, p. 43). Among multiple control variables there are respondent' position and experience at the company, their company' country, company size, and others. All applied variables are allocated into Appendix 11.1.

Driven by our exploratory goals we started the analysis from looking at the definitions of OI provided by our respondents. All together 188 respondents (out of 525) replied to the OI definition question, after removing seven responses containing irrelevant text, we analyzed 181 definitions. First, two researchers independently analyzed the OI definitions and then compared their analyses. We compared the definitions with the established definition of OI provided by Chesbrough and Bogers (2014) and identified the following categories coded qualitatively and quantitatively: inbound / outbound directions of OI definition; pecuniary / non-pecuniary aspects; OI practices associated with the definitions; additional practices proposed; aspects different from the traditional definition; keywords; level of relevance and novelty; level of analysis spotted in the definition. In terms of the OI definition relevance and novelty, we assessed the definitions by comparing those to the widely accepted definition by Chesbrough and Bogers (2014, p. 27), and identified whether the respondent' definition shared the logic with this classical, 'book' definition, adds any novelty or goes to a completely different direction in its logic. Furthermore, we checked if the definitions shared by the respondents explicitly refer to any specific OI practice (Appendix 11.1 based on Chesbrough & Brunswicker, 2013). In addition to qualitative analysis, the data was quantified and analyzed in SPSS.

As the definitions were provided by individual respondents, we treat each of those as individual perspective, not as their organization perspective. Accordingly, we also analyzed the positions of the respondents and coded them into eight categories (Table 11.1). The majority of our respondents are top managers, managers in different fields, and leaders of R&D/innovation management departments working in companies for more than ten years. Now, let's move toward analyzing their perceptions of OI.

TABLE 11.1 Respondent positions and length of work in a company

		Less than 1 year	1–3 years	3–5 years	5–10 years	Longer than 10 years	Total
R&D and innovation management	Count	3	9	4	5	4	25
	%	12,0%	36,0%	16,0%	20,0%	16,0%	100,0%
Top management	Count	6	14	8	13	26	67
	%	9,0%	20,9%	11,9%	19,4%	38,8%	100,0%
Quality manager	Count	0	0	3	1	1	5
	%	0,0%	0,0%	60,0%	20,0%	20,0%	100,0%
Project manager	Count	1	2	1	0	3	7
	%	14,3%	28,6%	14,3%	0,0%	42,9%	100,0%
Management	Count	2	3	4	8	16	33
	%	6,1%	9,1%	12,1%	24,2%	48,5%	100,0%
Other	Count	3	3	7	5	5	23
	%	13,0%	13,0%	30,4%	21,7%	21,7%	100,0%
HR	Count	0	2	1	2	2	7
	%	0,0%	28,6%	14,3%	28,6%	28,6%	100,0%
University professor/lecturer	Count	1	1	1	1	5	9
	%	11,1%	11,1%	11,1%	11,1%	55,6%	100,0%
Total	Count	16	34	29	35	62	176
	%	9,1%	19,3%	16,5%	19,9%	35,2%	100,0%

Research results

Practitioners defining open innovation versus theory-based practices

Aiming at understanding how the relevance and novelty of OI definition provided by our respondents (Variable 14 in Appendix 11.1) is explained by the factual adoption of OI in the company, we compared the definitions' relevance with OI adoption intensity (Var 9, Appendix 11.1) and OI Status (Var2, Appendix 11.1). The majority (117/181) of respondents tend to define open innovation very closely to the classical Chesbrough (2003a, 2006)'s definition (see Table 11.2). These respondents represent mostly companies with higher than average OI adoption intensity positioned on early to medium stage of OI adoption. Thirty respondents gave a definition of OI, which is far from Chesbrough (2003a, 2006)' definition. They reported lower than average adoption intensity but many of them identified OI status of company as 4 – "We are in the process of refining OI activities to help establish best practices in OI". This may indicate that these respondents interpret OI concept far differently than Chesbrough's school of thought and perceive their company' OI strategy in their own specific way. Furthermore, four respondents defined OI as activities as the ones focused exclusively on internal openness, however, the OI adoption level reported is above average. Six respondents provided definitions that follow Chesbrough's logic but add novel ideas and practices into it. However half of them stated that "we are not adopting and not planning to adopt open innovation". Very interesting category identified by us are the respondents who gave a rather traditional definition but add some novelty (24). Twenty-five percent of them do not adopt OI and don't plan, but the rest reported some of OI adoption. Let's first look at a few illustrative examples of the definitions that are 'close-to-the-book' and the ones which sound far from Chesbrough's logic.

Two examples of 'close-to-the-book' definitions follow. The first one reads like:

> Open innovation means to me the use of others and to share our innovative knowledge. As a supplier of machines and systems we use innovative components in the end product. We share those products with our customers. We make use of students and universities to find out together about new technologies, solutions and ideas. Sharing innovations is done via students and universities and by delivering solutions to the end user of equipment.
>
> *(Coordinator of Technical training/HR, Industrials, The Netherlands; OI status*
> *3: Early stages of implementing OI activities)*

The second example says: "*Not all good ideas are developed within the own company, and not all ideas should necessarily be further developed within the own firm's boundaries*" (Position: n/a, Latvia, Materials, OI status 3: Early stages of implementing OI activities). Those clearly reflect the boundary crossing nature and inbound and

TABLE 11.2 Comparison of OI definitions novelty and real OI adoption in the company (OIA average intensity and OI status)

Definition classification	N	OIA intensity, mean	1	2	3	4	5	6	Total
not correct definition	30	2,4885	20%	16,7% (5)	20% (6)	**33,3%** **(10)**	10% (3)	0%	100,0%
internal OI focus	4	3,2548	0%	25% (1)	25% (1)	25% (1)	25% (1)	0%	100,0%
some novelty	24	2,9213	**25%** **(6)**	12,5% (3)	**29,2%** **(7)**	16,7% (4)	16,7% (4)	0%	100,0%
novel approach	6	2,0662	**50%** **(3)**	0%	16,7% (1)	16,7% (1)	16,7% (1)	0%	100,0%
traditional OI	117	3,0935	11,3% (13)	**19,1%** **(22)**	**35,7%** **(41)**	20,9% **(24)**	12,2% (14)	0,9% (1)	100,0%
Total	181	2,9399	28	31	56	40	23	1	179

outbound dimensions of OI identified by the literature (Chesbrough & Bogers, 2014; Gassmann & Enkel, 2004).

Among the respondents, who see OI as a predominantly internal practice, a good illustrative example of a definition would be: '*Open innovation – an excellent approach for encouraging employees to create new products and services*' (Top manager, strategic development, Slovenia, Industrials, OI status 5: Experienced adopters of OI). Here, the logic of sourcing ideas is present, but there is no emphasis on crossing organizational boundaries. Of the definitions, that go far from Chesbrough's tradition, Table 11.3 provides a few examples. As we can see, those come from managers of different levels and functional areas, countries, companies of different sizes having various levels of OI adoption as per the respondents themselves assessing it.

If we go deeper in the comparison of OI definitions (Var14, Appendix 11.1) and real adoption of OI practices in companies (Var1, Appendix 11.1), we see that not all OI practices find their reflection in the definitions shared by the respondents in our sample (only practices 1–4, 7, 9, 11–13, see Table 11.4 and Appendix 11.1 for respective practices). Respondents providing the definitions that are different from the book report that their companies adopt OI practices rather intensively, especially '*Scanning for external ideas*' and '*Collaborative innovation with external partners*'. Respondents, who see open innovation as predominantly internal practice report most of the 'book-based' OI practices adopted intensively (especially practices 1–4, 11, 12, see Appendix 11.1). Among the respondents, whose definition is close to the book or follows its logic and offers novelty, practices are overall adopted at a high level, with '*Scanning for external ideas*', '*Collaborative innovation with external partners*' and '*Free Revealing (e.g. Ideas, IP) to external parties*' adopted at above average intensity.

TABLE 11.3 "Problematic" definitions different from Chesbrough's tradition of OI

OI Definition	Position	OI Status 1-6	Country	Company size*
To be constantly looking for improvements and coming forward with tangible ideas to improve processes and procedures.	Top manager	5	Malta	Large
Open innovation is the tool to make real progress and in the near future every company would go through it to make success.	Top manager	2	Malta	Medium
Products to help our everyday work activities	Manager	4	Macedonia	Small
Open innovation is creative approach to processes.	HR	3	Latvia	Large
Innovations that help the general public, business environment, public and third sector.	Top manager	1	Slovakia	Micro
The ability to overcome internal and external barriers in the company in the management of innovation processes.	Other (consultant)	2	Czech Republic	Large
I have experience and I have a problem with the concept of "open innovation". Innovations and improvements understood as intellectual effort and investment to achieve the competitiveness of the product portfolio and the implementation still somewhat "closed" to the outside world".	Top manager	1	Slovenia	Medium
Open innovation is the best way to deliver most up-to-date and "fresh" services to their customers without spending too much funds on it.	Manager	4	Latvia	Large
Create by out of the box thinking a solution that is large in simplicity	R&D and innovation management (head)	4	The Netherlands	Medium
Putting money into laziness	Product manager	1	Spain	Large

Note: By headcount, Large: >250; Medium-sized: 50–249; Small: 10–49; Micro: 1–9.

TABLE 11.4 Comparison of OI definitions' novelty and factual adoption of OI

Definition novelty coded		1	2	3	4	7	9	11	12	13
not correct definition	Mean	3,21	1,47	3,52	3,93	3,23	1,96	1,42	2,71	1,34
	N	29	30	29	29	30	28	24	28	29
internal OI focus	Mean	4,75	4,33	5,00	5,00	3,25	1,75	2,33	4,50	1,67
	N	4	3	3	4	4	4	3	4	3
some novelty	Mean	4,29	1,91	4,50	4,83	4,04	2,00	1,23	3,29	1,60
	N	24	23	24	24	24	23	22	24	20
novel approach	Mean	3,83	,40	4,50	3,67	2,67	,17	,00	2,50	1,00
	N	6	5	6	6	6	6	5	6	6
traditional OI	Mean	4,02	1,90	4,70	4,78	3,38	2,04	1,88	3,36	1,64
	N	116	112	116	116	114	108	97	111	104
Total	Mean	3,93	1,83	4,48	4,62	3,42	1,95	1,66	3,24	1,56
	N	179	173	178	179	178	169	151	173	162

Definitions and respondents' positions

To enhance our understanding of the OI definitions offered by our respondents (Var14, Appendix 11.1) we turn to our unit of analysis – individual employees at surveyed organizations, as whatever they share is their individual perception. Referring to the general approach to sampling and respondents (see methodology part), we coded the position of the respondents (Var18, Appendix 11.1). We found that most of our respondents are top managers, managers, R&D, and innovation managers (Table 11.5). Majority of R&D and Innovation managers (22/25) gave definitions which are very close to Chesbrough's tradition or proposed some novelty. Top managers (47/69) and other managers also stick to the traditional definition. Some novelty was mostly proposed by R&D and innovation managers as well as top managers, and radical innovative approach is rather rare and is mostly seen among managers and top managers (Table 11.5).

Definitions and specific OI practices

Qualitative analysis of OI definitions revealed that a number of those refer to specific OI practice(s), which we coded (Var10, Appendix 11.1) according to the list of OI practices in the quantitative survey (Var1, Appendix 11.1). We also specified if "none" of the practices were specifically mentioned in the definition (in 38 definitions we were unable to identify any OI practice) as well as if the definition is rather "generic" referring not to a specific practice but to rather general logic of a 'book' OI definition (15/181) – see Table 11.6. An example of only a single OI practice taken into consideration: *"The involvement of consumers in product development process, allowing for more efficient understanding of their needs, taking that into account (immediate feedback). Using a user can directly take advantage of their knowledge and creativity in connection with the products"* (Head of business development, Industrials, Hungary, OI status 2: We are not currently adopting open innovation, but plan to implement OI in the nearest future). The 'generic' examples, which rather refer to an attitudinal aspect of OI include: *"Openness to external technologies and techniques and the level of their respect"* (Junior developer, Energy, Croatia, OI status 3: Early stages of implementing OI activities) and *"Open innovation is a creative lifestyle aimed at creating the material and spiritual values to future generations"* (Project Manager, Consulting, Latvia, OI status 3: Early stages of implementing OI activities).

The OI practices most commonly referred in the OI definitions are: "Collaborative innovation with external partners (i.e. suppliers, universities, competitors)" (56/181), "Scouting for external ideas" (38/181), and "Free Revealing (e.g. Ideas, IP) to external parties" (12/181). Although we did spot some of the OI practices within the 'incorrect' definitions, these practices are either dominating the definition shared by a respondent or changing the overall definition logic. See, for example, this definition, which positions open innovation as a predominantly 'free-revealing' practice: *"Open innovation must be all innovations, which*

TABLE 11.5 Comparison of OI definitions novelty and respondents' positions

	R&D and innovation management	Top management	Quality manager	Project manager	Management	Other	HR	University professor /lecturer	Total
Not correct definition	10,0% (3)	**43,3% (13)**	0,0%	0,0%	23,3% (7)	10,0% (3)	6,7% (2)	6,7% (2)	100,0% (30)
Internal OI focus	0,0%	25,0% (1)	25,0% (1)	0,0%	0,0%	25,0% (1)	25,0% (1)	0,0%	100,0% (4)
Some novelty	**20,8% (5)**	**25,0% (6)**	8,3% (2)	8,3% (2)	12,5% (3)	12,5% (3)	4,2% (1)	8,3% (3)	100,0% (24)
Novel approach	0,0%	**33,3% (2)**	0,0%	16,7% (1)	**33,3% (2)**	16,7% (1)	0,0%	0,0%	100,0% (6)
Traditional OI	14,5% (17)	**40,2% (47)**	1,7% (2)	3,4% (4)	18,8% (22)	14,5% (17)	2,6% (3)	4,3% (5)	100,0% (117)
Total	25	69	5	7	34	25	7	9	181

TABLE 11.6 Comparison of OI definitions novelty and OI practice found in definition

	1	2	3	4	7	9	11	12	13	14	15	Total
Not correct definition	0,0%	0,0%	13,3% (4)	3,3% (1)	0,0%	3,3% (1)	0,0%	0,0%	0,0%	**80,0%** **(24)**	0,0%	100,0% (30)
Internal OI focus	0,0%	0,0%	0,0%	0,0%	0,0%	0,0%	0,0%	0,0%	0,0%	**75,0 %** **(3)**	25,0% (1)	100,0% (4)
Some novelty	8,3% (2)	0,0%	16,7% (4)	**29,2%** **(7)**	0,0%	8,3% (2)	0,0%	8,3% (2)	0,0%	16,7% (4)	12,5% (3)	100,0% (24)
Novel approach	0,0%	0,0%	16,7% (1)	0,0%	16,7% (1)	16,7% (1)	0,0%	0,0%	0,0%	**33,3%** **(2)**	16,7% (1)	100,0% (6)
Traditional OI	4,3% (5)	0,9% (1)	**24,8%** **(29)**	**41,0%** **(48)**	2,6% (3)	6,8% (8)	1,7% (2)	3,4% (4)	1,7% (2)	4,3% (5)	8,5% (10)	100,0% (117)
Total Count	7	1	**38**	**56**	4	12	2	6	2	**38**	15	181
% within Definition novelty coded	3,9%	0,6%	**21,0%**	**30,9%**	2,2%	6,6%	1,1%	3,3%	1,1%	**21,0%**	8,3%	100,0%

TABLE 11.7 Open innovation definition novelty vs. dummy novel practices

	N	New OI practice offered		Inbound/outbound/coupled (1-inbound, 2-outbound, 3-coupled, 4=other)				Pecuniary-1; Non-pecuniary-2; (non)-pecuniary/both-3; Not-relevant/Other-4				
		Yes	No	Inbound	Outbound	Coupled	Other	Pecuniary	Non-Pecuniary	Both	Other	Total
Not correct definition	30	23,3% (7)	**76,7% (23)**	10,0% (3)	0,0%	0,0%	**90,0% (27)**	3,3% (1)	23,3% (7)	30,0% (9)	**43,3% (13)**	100,0%
Internal OI focus	4	50,0% (2)	50,0% (2)	25,0% (1)	0,0%	0,0%	**75,0% (3)**	25,0% (1)	25,0% (1)	**50,0% (2)**	0,0%	100,0%
Some novelty	24	**66,7% (16)**	33,3% (8)	**45,8% (11)**	8,3% (2)	**41,7% (10)**	4,2% (1)	0,0%	37,5% (9)	**62,5% (15)**	0,0%	100,0%
Novel approach	6	33,3% (2)	**66,7% (4)**	16,7% (1)	**33,3% (2)**	16,7% (1)	33,3% (2)	16,7% (1)	33,3% (2)	**50,0% (3)**	0,0%	100,0%
Traditional OI	117	31,6% (37)	**68,4% (80)**	**65,8% (77)**	6,0% (7)	28,2% (33)	0,0%	5,1% (6)	29,9% (35)	**65,0% (76)**	0,0%	100,0%
Total	181	35,4% (64)	64,6% (117)	**51,4%** 93	6,1% 11	24,3% 44	18,2% 33	5,0% 9	29,8% 54	**58,0%** 105	7,2% 13	100,0%

are intended for the public good and helpful man and the environment" (Top manager, Slovenia, OI status – 2: We are not currently adopting open innovation, but plan to implement OI in the nearest future). Definitions with "some novelty" are mostly based on "Collaborative innovation with external partners" as OI practice (see Table 11.7).

Going across levels and novel definitions proposed

Already at the stage of initial coding, we noted that the respondents perceive OI differently also in terms of the analytical level (Table 11.8). Relying on Bogers et al. (2017), we coded the shared definitions as the ones referring to a single or few levels of the following: Intra-organizational (Individual Group/Team, Project, Functional area, Business unit); Organizational (Firm, Other (non-firm), Organization, Strategy, Business model); Extra-organizational (External stakeholders, Individual, Community, Organization); Inter-organizational (Alliances, Network, Ecosystem); Industry, regional, innovation systems (Industry development, Inter-industry differences, Local region, Nation, Supra-national institution, Citizens, Public policy and Society) (Var17, Appendix 11.1). Most of the definitions in our sample refer to either extra-organizational level of external stakeholders or to the inter-organizational level of collaborative projects (see Table 11.8). Let's look at a few examples of how we distinguished between different levels in the definitions.

We saw the intra-organizational level focus in the definitions where open innovation is perceived as an attitude, a mindset, or an intra-organizational aspect is highlighted. For example: *"Open innovation – a mind set for new creations open to all possibilities and risks"* or *"Internal independent department innovating together with needed external partners by following customer needs to find out which innovations would be in need"*. The first definition mentions a mindset, which could be an individual or an intra-organizational, while the second example mentions an intra-organizational department. Obviously, both examples also refer to the other levels: the first one refers to organizational, strategy level mentioning the openness to externals, while the second one clearly refers to extra-organizational level and mentions specific external partners. So, these definitions were coded accordingly as having multiple levels referred. The highest, policy level, just like intra-organizational level was referred by only a minority of our respondents, but one of the prominent examples of a public policy level reads as:

> Many government programmes such as the one my organization is administrating ("ForskEL") can partly be considered to be open innovation. Basically, it invites new ideas and concepts on renewable energy to be screened by a board of experts. If accepted, the concept or idea will be sponsored by the programme but applying to conditions on sharing knowledge obtained. If multiple actors manage to promote a joint concept this is an advantage as the programme encourages joint efforts among participating companies.

TABLE 11.8 OI definition novelty and levels of analysis

	N	Intra-organizational		Organizational		Extra-organizational		Inter-organizational		Ecosystem	
		No	Yes	No	Yes	No	Yes	No	Yes	No	Yes
Not correct definition	30	93,3% (28)	6,7% (2)	56,7% (17)	43,3% (13)	93,3% (28)	6,7% (2)	100,0% (30)	0,0%	96,7% (29)	3,3% (1)
Internal OI focus	4	100,0% (4)	0,0%	50,0% (2)	50,0% (2)	50,0% (2)	50,0% (2)	100,0% (4)	0,0%	100,0% (4)	0,0%
Some novelty	24	91,7% (22)	8,3% (2)	66,7% (16)	33,3% (8)	45,8% (11)	54,2% (13)	75,0% (18)	25,0% (6)	91,7% (22)	8,3% (2)
Novel approach	6	100,0% (6)	0,0%	50,0% (3)	50,0% (3)	66,7% (4)	33,3% (2)	83,3% (5)	16,7% (1)	100,0% (6)	0,0%
Traditional OI	117	99,1% (116)	0,9% (1)	73,5% (86)	26,5% (31)	35,0% (41)	65,0% (76)	76,9% (90)	23,1% (27)	96,6% (113)	3,4% (4)
Total	181	176 97,2%	5 2,8%	124 68,5%	57 31,5%	86 47,5%	95 52,5%	147 81,2%	34 18,8%	174 96,1%	7 3,9%

TABLE 11.9 "New additions" to defining open innovation

OI definition	Inbound/ outbound	(Non-) pecuniary	What's new	Position	OI status	Country	Company size★
Freely available and useable information of an innovation	Coupled	Non-pecuniary	Innov. for everyone	Top Mngt.	3	Hungary	Medium
What we know, the world must know.	Outbound	(Non-) pecuniary	Innov. for everyone	Manager	1	Portugal	Large
OI represents innovation for all. OI are innovation that have been widely disseminated.	Coupled	Non-pecuniary	Innov. for everyone	Quality manager	4	Bosnia and Herzegovina	Large
Innovations that help the general public, business environment, public and third sector.	Other	(Non-) pecuniary	Innov. for everyone	Top Mngt.	1	Slovakia	Micro
Open Innovation – cooperation with companies with goal to produce products which can make cheaper, better products, with low production costs, energy hybrid savings systems for energy savings environment friendly and other benefits for better life on the earth.	Inbound	Non-pecuniary	Sustainab. aspects	Top Mngt.	3	Macedonia	Micro
Getting the most out of open-source projects and tools, implementing every stage of innovation	Coupled	Non-pecuniary	Open source	Manager	3	Greece	Small
The best example is the case of open-source software and possibly hardware 3D printing or loose patents [of] Tesla	Coupled	(Non-) pecuniary	Open source, Loose patents	Manager	1	Czech Republic	Large

Description							
Open innovation represents the creation of a sort of collaboration platform (virtual) that will enable the smooth flow of internal ideas and information that will lead to new ideas and innovation, and that will contribute to the placement of these innovations in the external environment.	Coupled	(Non)-pecuniary	OI Platform	Top Mngt.	N/A	Croatia	Small
It is an environment that allows the free exchange of ideas and that values the most beneficial and inventive solutions but does not penalize failures.	Coupled	Non-pecuniary	OI as environment / Failure tolerance	Top Mngt.	4	Switzerland	Large
The process by which the company not only takes into account the knowledge of the organization but also collaborates or provides external information, seeking collaboration, synergy with outsiders, professionals who can contribute their knowledge, mentoring or expert mentoring…	Coupled	Both	Mentoring	Top Mngt.	3	Spain	Micro
Putting money into laziness	Other	(Non-)pecuniary	Being lazy	Manager	1	Spain	Large

Note: By headcount, Large: >250; Medium-sized: 50–249; Small: 10–49; Micro: 1–9

This Danish program aims to go beyond an inter-organizational level and supports both administratively and financially as an umbrella program.

We close our analysis with a few examples of the novel definitions or particularly, novel OI practices proposed. One group of these "new additions" (Table 11.9) are the definitions, which refer to open innovation as innovation available for everyone (for free), innovation for the public good and society. Several definitions refer to sustainability aspects in a similar attitude of 'innovation for everyone'. Notably, this 'innovation for everyone' and mostly non-pecuniary tone is heard predominantly from the top management group in our sample with the OI status varying from low to high.

Another mention of specific practices close to 'innovation for everyone' is 'open source' and 'loose patents', but as we all know, those are strategic practices, which are done with not just altruistic motives (Dahlander et al., 2021; Wang & Peng, 2020). One more idea of OI practice shared by our respondents is perceiving OI as a certain environment, being not material, but spiritual space for ideas and knowledge exchange, which may take a form of a virtual platform. This is an example, which indeed is not very easy to touch, codify, and maybe add to the list of 'standard' OI practices, but as we already passed the platform revolution age (Parker et al., 2016) and the power of network effects is widely acknowledged (Evans & Gawer, 2016), this stream of practices deserves a separate mention. Expert mentoring is also standing out as a practice that helps to spark internal innovation as well as achieve synergy in innovating with others. Finally, as a fly in the ointment, there is a mention of OI perceived as 'putting money into laziness', where if we interpret our respondent correctly, engaging others for resources reflects laziness. If we speculate further, such an approach may lead to the 'not-invented-here' syndrome (Burcharth et al., 2014), when getting an external help is perceived as inappropriate or 'lazy' approach.

Practical applications

Following the most recent theoretical insights (Bhattacharyya & Thakre, 2021; Dahlander et al., 2021; Valdez-Juárez & Castillo-Vergara, 2021) and empirical findings we identified several dimensions where tensions in perceiving OI are spotted. The major dimensions of tensions include transdisciplinarity of the OI phenomenon, perspectives varying in levels, novel OI practices getting saturation in business context but not yet in theory, and synergy between these dimensions.

Open innovation goes beyond borders again: toward transdisciplinarity – OI is everywhere!

Since its introduction in 2003 OI concept has been mostly business-oriented and heavily relied on various literature streams. Being tightly related to established theories as relational view, OI has been heavily criticized for being "old wine in new bottles" (Trott & Hartmann, 2009). At the same time, globalization, climate change, and digitalization intensified in the past decades have generally enhanced the embeddedness and interconnectedness of such phenomena (and literature on those) as corporate social responsibility, sustainability, circular economy, green energy, platform-based economies, open innovation, big data, and ecosystems (Dahlander et al., 2021). This overlapping of trends somehow smudges the borders between concepts, ensure the mutual saturation, and increase the transdisciplinarity of a wide spectrum of organizational practices. We found that open innovation is not an exception, and it is rather a mix of "old and new wines", the "taste" or perception of which heavily depends not only on the environmental factors but also on who exactly is trying the "wine".

Knowledge transformation and theory development – Big data eats OI for breakfast!

Nowadays, with the emergence and power of big data and platform-based businesses, both new opportunities and challenges emerge (Del Vecchio et al., 2018; Nambisan et al., 2018). Managing big data is less linear than classical inbound and outbound OI practices. *"The data economy pushes us to consider competitive dimensions of open innovation where data may not be freely available and where the interests of multiple players must be considered simultaneously"* (Dahlander et al., 2021, p. 4). Furthermore, social and legal responsibilities of multiple big data players demand an agile balance in open value creation and capture (Saebi & Foss, 2015; Sjödin et al., 2020). Thus, it becomes more and more problematic to perceive OI in isolation and solely through the lens of pecuniary logic.

From organizational through ecosystem toward policy-making – OI is embedding!

Following the big data spread, in their recent paper Dahlander et al. (2021, p. 4) stated that

> …open innovation researchers should consider the wider picture. Research has often focused on the use of open innovation from one target firm's perspective. But as data is growing in importance and the practice of open innovation becomes ubiquitous, inherent trade-offs are revealed and need to be addressed. These concerns clearly connect open innovation to the growing field of ecosystems.

Thus, and in line with some of our respondents' opinions, OI could not and should not be perceived solely from a single organization viewpoint, as every organization is not just a stand-alone player, which could opportunistically and irresponsibly rely on others (e.g. trade user data in absence of regulations for that), but is a player in an ecosystem and in society, now more than ever, where the actors are increasingly interdependent and are watched more and more for their sustainable practices, social contribution, or harm (Bhattacharyya & Thakre, 2021; Radziwon & Bogers, 2019; Vasudeva et al., 2020). Data trading and platform-based businesses are no more irregulated fields (Cusumano et al., 2019; Yun et al., 2020), environmental innovations at organizations tend to heavily depend on both – the behavior of their ecosystem actors as well as governmental measures to support changes for sustainable future.

Emergence of novel OI practices: something old, something new, something borrowed, and something blue

The understanding and practical implementation of OI by management community went beyond traditional Chesbrough definition (2003a, 2006) and novel OI practices emerged while OI has been penetrating multiple organizational types and levels. For example, citizen science, where public is directly involved in scientific research (Sauermann et al., 2020), is called to democratize science, make it more open as well as help to achieve sustainable development goals. Indeed, the literature on social innovation suggests us that the best innovators are citizens who "spot needs which aren't being adequately met by the market or the state" (Mulgan, 2006, p. 150). Patent "open-source" strategy is becoming more and more visible beyond computer-based businesses with Tesla that offered a "good faith" patent pledge being a prominent example (Dahlander et al., 2021; Wang & Peng, 2020). Tesla case, however, also demonstrates how revealing of internal technology to potential partners could have indirect effects and be an instrument for fighting the competitive sector, traditional automotive one for Tesla (Dahlander et al., 2021). The general corporate interest in open-source platforms (GitHub, Red Hat, Linux) indirectly shows the hidden power of an open source practice, while triggers a question of 'how open the commons will remain?' (Dahlander et al., 2021). Generally, the increased usage of platforms and software for managing and exchanging knowledge deserves consideration as a separate OI practice.

Synergy of OI

Similarly to Weber and Rohracher (2012) we argue that a multi-level research approach is needed to study OI and boost transformational changes. A recent event demanding such changes and collaboration, is the global COVID-19 pandemic. A single theoretical stream is not enough to comprehend so complex phenomenon and the role of OI in it (Bhattacharyya & Thakre, 2021). Even a 'system'-type of approach is apparently not enough to grasp the essence of complex transformational processes in relations of businesses, academia, policy-making institutions, and society (Weber & Rohracher, 2012). Accordingly, a further revision of OI definition would call for a more comprehensive and inclusive approach. That first implies an inclusion of all the relevant levels at which OI could be analyzed (Bogers et al., 2017). Second, such a future definition would admit and highlight the interconnectedness of OI with day-to-day organizational operations and inter-organizational relations. More of theorization efforts are needed for OI: as fashion and strategy it works, but practices and recommendations are blurry, perceptions are ambiguous, instruments are taken from other theories (relational view, strategy, etc.) and own measurement instruments are underdeveloped.

We want to conclude with the following chain of thoughts shared with us recently in a conversation by a technology transfer expert:

> Open innovation is now often very misunderstood. Most people using the term "open innovation" have not actually read the books about open inno-vation and are therefore not familiar [with] the different concepts thereof. They wouldn't know that there [is] a quite different number of flavors, ... and that open innovation, first of all, doesn't mean that results are owned by everybody. Reasons that open innovation is not [enough] widespread... include that universities are not really trained to engage with open inno-vation projects and concepts yet, but companies aren't either. ... Yeah, there are a few companies who have opened themselves to an open inno-vation concept very successfully, but a lot of the companies, and also really technical companies are unable (or unwilling?) to change themselves and implement open innovation concepts and practices yet.
>
> *(technology transfer expert, head of the university technology transfer office in Germany)*

As we can see, a dedicated training of multiple organizational and professional groups could become one of the practical steps toward improving understand-ing of OI between the groups and if not unify their perceptions (which is not an ultimate goal) allow them to speak and understand the OI languages of each other.

Conclusions

Aim of our chapter is not to provide any strong claims on 'right' or 'wrong' perceptions of open innovation. It is rather about the need to perceive open innovation as a natural phenomenon, like sunshine. It can be shining bright and reaching every corner – as open innovation penetrates organizational strat-egy, inter-organizational ecosystems, regions, and policy-making. The sun can be hidden behind the clouds but still providing the daylight – as specific open innovation practices being on hold in a certain organization, but still existing elsewhere and reaching out. It can also hit with sunburns – as when too much openness could become harmful in terms of intellectual property leakages or data-related issues. Or, periods of polar day and night could be observed – as when the economic, business and social environment becomes more or less favorable to openness. Just like the sun, open innovation is an alive phenomenon, and we learn new things about it day by day.

In terms of our contribution and future research, this chapter is among a few works, which try to perceive open innovation critically, but still comprehensively and take into account the viewpoints of the diverse communities as business, academia, and policy-makers. Future research should probably work toward developing an overarching OI definition which would speak to different communities, so everyone could still explain in their own words what is open innovation but reach a deeper consensus than exists now. Furthermore, based on our findings, future research could develop and validate a revised list of open innovation practices for multiple organizational groups.

Acknowledgement

The data behind this chapter were collected by the European Academic Network for Open Innovation (OI-Net project), which received funding from the European Union Lifelong Learning Programme under the Grant Agreement Number 2013–3830 (for more information please visit www. oi-net.eu).

Note: By headcount, Large: >250; Medium-sized: 50–249; Small: 10–49; Micro: 1–9.

Notes

1 As for June 2021 the page on 'Open innovation' in 'Wikipedia' states: 'The neutrality of this article is disputed. (May 2013)' (Wikipedia, 2020): https://en.wikipedia.org/wiki/Open_innovation#cite_note-schuttemarais2010–11
2 See www.unilever.com/brands/innovation/open-innovation/
3 See www.us.pg.com/innovation/
4 See www.openinnovation.astrazeneca.com/
5 See www.lego.com/en-us/service/help/products/themes-sets/lego-forma/about-lego-forma-408100000016059
6 See www.ibm.com/opensource/innovation/
7 Examples of those policy-making efforts are GDPR policy in the EU, a package of acts in the US, as well as the efforts of non-profits like MyData.org. See www.mydata.org/about/
8 See www.ec.europa.eu/digital-single-market/en/open-innovation-20
9 See www.gao.gov/open-innovation
10 The data behind this chapter were collected by the European Academic Network for Open Innovation (OI-Net project), which received funding from the European Union Lifelong Learning Programme under the Grant Agreement Number 2013-3830 (for more information, please visit www.oi-net.eu).

References

Abu El-Ella, N., Bessant, J., & Pinkwart, A. (2016). Revisiting the honorable merchant: The reshaped role of trust in open innovation. *Thunderbird International Business Review*, *58*(3). https://doi.org/10.1002/tie.21774

Albats, E., Bogers, M., & Podmetina, D. (2020). Companies' human capital for university partnerships: A micro-foundational perspective. *Technological Forecasting and Social Change*, *157*, 120085. https://doi.org/10.1016/j.techfore.2020.120085

Barney, J. (1991). Firm resources and sustained competitive advantage. *Journal of Management*, *17*(1), 99–120. https://doi.org/10.1177/014920639101700108

Barney, J., Wright, M., & Ketchen, D. J. (2001). The resource-based view of the firm: Ten years after 1991. *Journal of Management*, *27*, 625–641.

Beck, S., Bergenholtz, C., Bogers, M., Brasseur, T. M., Conradsen, M. L., Di Marco, D., Distel, A. P., Dobusch, L., Dörler, D., Effert, A., Fecher, B., Filiou, D., Frederiksen, L., Gillier, T., Grimpe, C., Gruber, M., Haeussler, C., Heigl, F., Hoisl, K., … Xu, S. M. (2020). The Open Innovation in Science research field: A collaborative conceptualisation approach. *Industry and Innovation*, *29*21–50. https://doi.org/10.1080/13662716.2020.1792274

Bhattacharyya, S. S., & Thakre, S. (2021). Coronavirus pandemic and economic lockdown; study of strategic initiatives and tactical responses of firms. *International Journal of Organizational Analysis*. https://doi.org/10.1108/IJOA-05-2020-2198

Bogers, M., Chesbrough, H., Heaton, S., & Teece, D. J. (2019). Strategic management of open innovation: A dynamic capabilities perspective. *California Management Review*, *62*(1), 77–94. https://doi.org/10.1177/0008125619885150

Bogers, M., Chesbrough, H., & Moedas, C. (2018). Open innovation: Research, practices, and policies. *California Management Review*, *60*(2), 5–16. https://doi.org/10.1177/0008125617745086

Bogers, M., Zobel, A.-K., Afuah, A., Almirall, E., Brunswicker, S., Dahlander, L., L., Gawer, A., Gruber, M., Haefliger, S., Hagedoorn, J., Hilgers, D., Laursen, K., Magnusson, M. G., Majchrzak, A., McCarthy, I. P., Moeslein, K. M., Nambisan, S., Piller, F. T., … Ter Wal, A. L. J. (2017). The open innovation research landscape: Established perspectives and emerging themes across different levels of analysis. *Industry and Innovation*, *24*(1), 8–40. https://doi.org/10.1080/13662716.2016.1240068

Burcharth, A. L. D. A., Knudsen, M. P., & Søndergaard, H. A. (2014). Neither invented nor shared here: The impact and management of attitudes for the adoption of open innovation practices. *Technovation*, *34*(3), 149–161. https://doi.org/10.1016/j.technovation.2013.11.007

Chesbrough, H. (2003a). *Open Innovation the New Imperative for Creating and Profiting from Technology Xerox PARC the Achievements and Limits of Closed Innovation*. Harvard Business School Press, 1–10. https://doi.org/10.1111/j.1467-8691.2008.00502.x

Chesbrough, H. W. (2003b). *Open Innovation: The New Imperative for Creating and Profiting from Technology*. Harvard Business School Press. http://ictlogy.net/bibliography/reports/projects.php?idp=2546

Chesbrough, H. (2006). *Open Innovation: The New Imperative for Creating and Profiting from Technology*. Harvard Business School Press. https://books.google.fi/books?id=OeLIH89YiMcC

Chesbrough, H. W. (2007). Why companies should have Open Business Models? *MIT Sloan Management Review*, *48*(2), 22–28. https://doi.org/10.1111/j.1540-5885.2008.00309_1.x

Chesbrough, H., & Bogers, M. (2014). Explicating open innovation: Clarifying an emerging paradigm for understanding innovation keywords. In *New Frontiers in Open Innovation*. Oxford University Press, 1–37. https://doi.org/10.1093/acprof

Chesbrough, H., & Brunswicker, S. (2013). Managing open Innovation in Large firms. In Executive Survey on Open Innovation 2013, Fraunhofer Verlag.

Chesbrough, H., & Brunswicker, S. (2014). A fad or a phenomenon? The adoption of open innovation practices in large firms. *Research Technology Management*, *57*(2), 16–25. https://doi.org/10.5437/08956308X5702196

Chesbrough, H., & Crowther, A. K. (2006). Beyond high tech: Early adopters of open innovation in other industries. *R&D Management Management*, *36*(3), 229–236. https://doi.org/10.1111/j.1467-9310.2006.00428.x

Clausen, T. H., Korneliussen, T., & Madsen, E. L. (2013). Modes of innovation, resources and their influence on product innovation: Empirical evidence from R&D active firms in Norway. *Technovation, 33*(6–7), 225–233. https://doi.org/10.1016/j.technovation.2013.02.002

Cusumano, M. A., Gawer, A., & Yoffie, D. B. (2019). *The Business of Platforms: Strategy in the Age of Digital Competition, Innovation, and Power.* HarperCollins.

Dahlander, L., & Gann, D. M. (2010). How open is innovation? *Research Policy, 39*(6), 699–709. https://doi.org/10.1016/j.respol.2010.01.013

Dahlander, L., Gann, D. M., & Wallin, M. W. (2021). How open is innovation? A retrospective and ideas forward. *Research Policy, 50*(4), 104218. https://doi.org/10.1016/j.respol.2021.104218

Del Vecchio, P., Di Minin, A., Petruzzelli, A. M., Panniello, U., & Pirri, S. (2018). Big data for open innovation in SMEs and large corporations: Trends, opportunities, and challenges. *Creativity and Innovation Management, 27*(1), 6–22. https://doi.org/10.1111/caim.12224

Dyer, J. H., & Singh, H. (1998). The relational view : Cooperative strategy and sources of interorganizational competitive advantage. *Academy of Management Review, 23*(4), 660–679.

Ebersberger, B., Bloch, C., Herstad, S. J., & Van De Velde, E. L. S. (2012). Open innovation practices and their effect on innovation performance. *International Journal of Innovation and Technology Management, 9*(6). https://doi.org/10.1142/S021987701250040X

Evans, P. C., & Gawer, A. (2016). The rise of the platform enterprise a global survey. In *The Emerging Platform Economy Series.* Surrey: University of Surrey, 2016.

Felin, T., & Hesterly, W. S. (2007). The knowledge-based view, nested heterogeneity, and new value creation: Philosophical considerations on the locus of knowledge. *The Academy of Management Review, 32*(1), 195–218.

Ferreira, J. J., & Teixeira, A. A. C. (2019). Open innovation and knowledge for fostering business ecosystems. *Journal of Innovation and Knowledge, 4*(4), 253–255. https://doi.org/10.1016/j.jik.2018.10.002

Franzoni, C., & Sauermann, H. (2014). Crowd science: The organization of scientific research in open collaborative projects. *Research Policy, 43*(1), 1–20. https://doi.org/10.1016/j.respol.2013.07.005

Gassmann, O., & Enkel, E. (2004). Towards a theory of open innovation: Three core process archetypes. *R&D Management Conference,* 1–18. https://doi.org/10.1.1.149.4843

Gibbons, M., Limoges, C., Nowotny, H., Schwartzmann, S., Scrott, P., & Trow, M. (1994). *The New Production of Knowledge: The Dynamics of Science and Research in Contemporary Societies.* Sage.

Gläser, J., & Laudel, G. (2016). Governing science: How science policy shapes research content. *European Journal of Sociology, 15*(1), 117–168. https://doi.org/10.1017/s0003975616000047

Grimpe, C., & Sofka, W. (2009). Search patterns and absorptive capacity: Low- and high-technology sectors in European countries. *Research Policy, 38*(3), 495–506. https://doi.org/10.1016/j.respol.2008.10.006

Groen, A. J., & Linton, J. D. (2010). Is open innovation a field of study or a communication barrier to theory development? *Technovation, 30*(11), 554.

Hung, K. P., & Chou, C. (2013). The impact of open innovation on firm performance: The moderating effects of internal R&D and environmental turbulence. *Technovation, 33*(10–11), 368–380. https://doi.org/10.1016/j.technovation.2013.06.006

Huston, L., & Sakkab, N. (2006). Connect and develop inside procter & gamble's new model for innovation. *Harvard Business Review, 84*(3), 58–66.

Maxwell, J. W., Hanson, E., Desai, L., Tiampo, C., O'Donnell, K., Ketheeswaran, A., Sun, M., Walter, E., & Michelle, E. (2019). Mind the gap: A landscape analysis of open source publishing tools and platforms. *Mind the Gap: A Landscape Analysis of Open Source Publishing Tools and Platforms.* https://doi.org/10.21428/6bc8b38c.2e2f6c3f

Mulgan, G. (2006). The process of social innovation. *Innovations: Technology, Governance, Globalization, 1*(2), 145–162. https://doi.org/10.1162/itgg.2006.1.2.145

Nambisan, S., Siegel, D., & Kenney, M. (2018). On open innovation, platforms, and entrepreneurship. *Strategic Entrepreneurship Journal, 12*(3). https://doi.org/10.1002/sej.1300

NineSigma. (2019). *Open Innovation Basics.* Open Innovation Basics. https://www.ninesigma.com/open-innovation-basics/

Parker, G. G., Van Alstyne, M. W., & Choudary, S. P. (2016). *Platform Revolution: How Networked Markets Are Transforming the Economy and How to Make Them Work for You.* W. W. Norton & Company.

Perkmann, M., Tartari, V., McKelvey, M., Autio, E., Broström, A., D'Este, P., Fini, R., Geuna, A., Grimaldi, R., Hughes, A., Krabel, S., Kitson, M., Llerena, P., Lissoni, F., Salter, A., & Sobrero, M. (2013). Academic engagement and commercialisation: A review of the literature on university-industry relations. *Research Policy, 42*(2), 423–442. https://doi.org/10.1016/j.respol.2012.09.007

Perkmann, M., & Walsh, K. (2007). University-industry relationships and open innovation: Towards a research agenda. *International Journal of Management Reviews, 9*(4), 259–280. https://doi.org/10.1111/j.1468-2370.2007.00225.x

Pullen, A. J. J., De Weerd-Nederhof, P. C., Groen, A. J., & Fisscher, O. A. M. (2012). Open innovation in practice: Goal complementarity and closed NPD networks to explain differences in innovation performance for SMEs in the medical devices sector. *Journal of Product Innovation Management, 29*(6), 917–934. https://doi.org/10.1111/j.1540-5885.2012.00973.x

Radziwon, A., & Bogers, M. (2019). Open innovation in SMEs: Exploring inter-organisational relationships in an ecosystem. *Technological Forecasting and Social Change, 146*(May 2018), 573–587. https://doi.org/10.1016/j.techfore.2018.04.021

Remneland Wikhamn, B., & Wikhamn, W. (2013). Structuring of the open innovation field. *Journal of Technology Management and Innovation, 8*(3), 173–185. https://doi.org/10.4067/s0718-27242013000400016

Robaczewska, J., Vanhaverbeke, W., & Lorenz, A. (2019). Applying open innovation strategies in the context of a regional innovation ecosystem: The case of Janssen Pharmaceuticals. *Global Transitions, 1*, 120–131. https://doi.org/10.1016/j.glt.2019.05.001

Saebi, T., & Foss, N. J. (2015). Business models for open innovation: Matching heterogeneous open innovation strategies with business model dimensions. *European Management Journal, 33*(3), 201–213. https://doi.org/10.1016/j.emj.2014.11.002

Sauermann, H., Vohland, K., Antoniou, V., Balázs, B., Göbel, C., Karatzas, K., Mooney, P., Perelló, J., Ponti, M., Samson, R., & Winter, S. (2020). Citizen science and sustainability transitions. *Research Policy, 49*(5), 103978. https://doi.org/10.1016/j.respol.2020.103978

Simeth, M., & Raffo, J. D. (2013). What makes companies pursue an Open Science strategy? *Research Policy, 42*(9), 1531–1543. https://doi.org/10.1016/j.respol.2013.05.007

Sjödin, D., Parida, V., Jovanovic, M., & Visnjic, I. (2020). Value creation and value capture alignment in business model innovation: A process view on outcome-based business models. *Journal of Product Innovation Management, 37*(2), 158–183. https://doi.org/10.1111/jpim.12516

Spithoven, A., Vanhaverbeke, W., & Roijakkers, N. (2013). Open innovation practices in SMEs and large enterprises. *Small Business Economics, 41*(3), 537–562. https://doi. org/10.1007/s11187-012-9453-9

Teplov, R., Albats, E., & Podmetina, D. (2019). What does open innovation mean? Business versus academic perceptions. *International Journal of Innovation Management, 23*(1). https://doi.org/10.1142/S1363919619500026

Theyel, N. (2013). Extending open innovation throughout the value chain by small and medium-sized manufacturers. *International Small Business Journal, 31*(3), 256–274. https://doi.org/10.1177/0266242612458517

Trott, P., & Hartmann, D. (2009). Why "open innovation" is old wine in new bottles. *International Journal of Innovation Management, 13*(4), 715–736. http://www.worldscinet. com/abstract?id=pii:S1363919609002509

Valdez-Juárez, L. E., & Castillo-Vergara, M. (2021). Technological capabilities, open innovation, and eco-innovation: Dynamic capabilities to increase corporate performance of smes. *Journal of Open Innovation: Technology, Market, and Complexity, 7*(1), 1–19. https://doi.org/10.3390/joitmc7010008

Vanhaverbeke, W., & Cloodt, M. (2014). Theories of the Firm and Open Innovation. In Henry William Chesbrough, W. Vanhaverbeke, & J. West (Eds.), *New Frontiers in Open Innovation*. Oxford University Press, 256–278.

Vasudeva, G., Leiponen, A., & Jones, S. (2020). Dear enemy: The dynamics of conflict and cooperation in open innovation ecosystems. *Strategic Management Review, 1*(2), 355–379. https://doi.org/10.1561/111.00000008

Wang, J., & Peng, X. (2020). A study of patent open source strategies based on open innovation: The case of Tesla. *Open Journal of Social Sciences, 8*(7), 386–394. https:// doi.org/10.4236/jss.2020.87031

Weber, K. M., & Rohracher, H. (2012). Legitimizing research, technology and innovation policies for transformative change: Combining insights from innovation systems and multi-level perspective in a comprehensive "failures" framework. *Research Policy, 41*(6), 1037–1047. https://doi.org/10.1016/j.respol.2011.10.015

Wikipedia. (2020). *Open Innovation*. Open Innovation. https://en.wikipedia.org/wiki/ Open_innovation#cite_note-schuttemarais2010-11

Williamson, O. E. (1981). The economics of organization: The transaction cost approach. *American Journal of Sociology, 87*(3), 548–577.

Yun, J. H. J., Zhao, X., Wu, J., Yi, J. C., Park, K. B., & Jung, W. Y. (2020). Modelo de negócios, inovação aberta e sustentabilidade na indústria de compartilhamento de automóveis – comparando três economias. *Sustainability (Switzerland), 12*(6), 27. https://www.mdpi.com/journal/sustainability

APPENDIX 11.1

Operationalization of variables
  Survey variables

N	Variable	Code	Source and measurement
1	*Open innovation Activities* – Measurement of actual level of open innovation adoption		Do you adopt the following activities in your company?
	1. Customer and consumer co-creation in R&D projects	OIA1	*Based on Chesbrough and Brunswicker, 2013 and*
	2. Crowdsourcing	OIA2	*2014 and interpreted by*
	3. Scanning for external ideas	OIA3	*authors*
	4. Collaborative innovation with external partners	OIA4	Intensity of adoption: 8 – point scale, where
	5. Subcontracting R&D	OIA5	0 – No, we don't (adopt), 1 – Very
	6. Idea & start-up competitions	OIA6	seldom, 4 – regularly;
	7. Using external networks	OIA7	7 – Very intensively
	8 Participation in standardisation / influencing industry standards	OIA8	
	9. Free Revealing (e.g. Ideas, IP) to external parties	OIA9	
	10. IP in-licensing	OIA10	
	11. IP out-licensing	OIA11	
	12. External technology acquisition	OIA12	
	13. Selling unutilised / unused technologies	OIA13	

(*Continued*)

N	Variable	Code	Source and measurement
2	Self-perception of open innovation adoption – Companies were asked to evaluate themselves as adopters or non-adopters of open innovation		Please evaluate your current open innovation status. Choose one option.
	1 – We are not adopting and not planning to adopt open innovation	OI status	Self-elaborated nominal:
	2 – We are not currently adopting open innovation, but plan to implement OI in the nearest future		
	3 – We are in the early stages of implementing OI activities		
	4 – We are in the process of refining OI activities and shaping programmes to help establish best practices in OI		
	5 – We are experienced adopters of OI (processes, procedures, and best practices are in place)		
	6 – We had OI practices, but decided to discontinue them		
3	Size of the firm[a]	Size	Nominal, four categories: Large, >250, Medium-sized 50–249, Small 10–49, Micro 1–9
4	Industry[b] Industry. Please select the Industry. Tick the one which provides the main source of revenue.	Industry	Nominal: 28 categories
5.	Work Experience How long have you worked for the company?	Experience	1 = Less than 1 year 2 = 1–3 years 3 = 3–5 years 4 = 5–10 years 5 = Longer than 10 years
	Qualitative questions		
6.	How do you define open innovation? Please provide your own definition (optional)		Qualitative
7.	What is your position in the company?		Qualitative
	Coded variables		
8	High-tech industry 1 = High-tech 0 = Mid and low-tech		High-techn industry classification, based on Kile and Phillips 2009
9	Intensity of OI adoption, average	OIA intensity	Cumulative variables as MEAN of 13 OIA variables

[a]Based on the European Union classification: http://ec.europa.eu/growth/smes/business-friendly-environment/sme-definition/index_en.htm
[b]Global Industry Classification System (GI)

Qualitative data quantified

N	Variable	Code	Source and measurement
	Based on the analysis of qualitative data in answers of the question "How do you define open innovation? Please provide your own definition (optional)" we defined following categories		
10	*OI practices associated with definitions (generic, none or according to the list of practices)*		Do you adopt the following activities in your company?
	1. Customer and consumer co-creation in R&D projects	OIA1	*Based on Chesbrough and Brunswicker (2013,*
	2. Crowdsourcing	OIA2	*2014) and interpreted by*
	3. Scanning for external ideas/ Scouting for external ideas	OIA3	*authors (see previous table). Dummy variable 0 – no,*
	4. Collaborative innovation with external partners	OIA4	*1 yes*
	5. Subcontracting R&D	OIA5	
	6. Idea & start-up competitions	OIA6	
	7. Using external networks	OIA7	
	8 Participation in standardisation / influencing industry standards	OIA8	
	9. Free Revealing (e.g. Ideas, IP) to external parties	OIA9	
	10. IP in-licensing	OIA10	
	11. IP out-licensing	OIA11	
	12. External technology acquisition	OIA12	
	13. Selling unutilised / unused technologies	OIA13	
	12. External technology acquisition	OIA12	
	13. Selling unutilised / unused technologies	OIA13	
	14. None	OIA14	
	15. Generic practices associated with OI definition	OIA15	
11	*New practices proposed*	New OIA Coded	Qualitative and coded as dummy 1 – yes, 0 – no
12	*Aspects different from traditional definitions;*		Qualitative
13	*Keywords*		Qualitative
14	*Relevance and novelty of OI definition*	DefNovCoded	Coded: 1 – not correct definition 2 – internal OI focus 3 – some novelty 4 – novel approach 5 – traditional OI definition

(Continued)

N	Variable	Code	Source and measurement
15	*Inbound / outbound directions of OI definition*	InOuCoCoded	(Chesbrough and Crowther, 2006; Gassmann and Enkel, 2004) Coded 1 – inbound, 2 – outbound, 3 – coupled, 4 – other
16	*Pecuniary / non-pecuniary aspects of OI definition*	PeNonCoded	(Dahlander & Gann, 2010) Coded: 1 – pecuniary; 2 – non-pecuniary; 3 – both; 4 – other
17	*Level of analysis spotted in OI definition*	OIDefLevel	(Bogers et al., 2017) Coded *1 – intra-organizational; 2 – organizational; 3 – extra-organizational; 4 – inter – organizational; 5 – Ecosystem and policy level*
18	*What is your position in the company? 1 – R&D and Innovation Management (Head); 2 – Top Management; 3 – Quality Manager; 4 – Project manager; 5 – Management; 6 – Other; 7 – HR; 8 – University professor / lecturer*	PositionCoded	Coded based on qualitative analysis (categories, themes) and grouped

12

INNOVATION MANAGEMENT IN SMALL AND MEDIUM SIZE ENTERPRISES (SMES)

New perspectives and directions

Athanasios Hadjimanolis

Introduction

Innovation is a key success factor in the current globalized competitive environment for all firms, large and small (Adams et al., 2006). Most attention in innovation research is focused on the activities of large firms. Innovation in small and medium size enterprises (SMEs) is, however, important due to their large numbers and their share in radical and disruptive innovations. SMEs usually form the large, or even the dominant, majority of firms in most countries and their prosperity is critically important for creation of wealth, employment, and economic growth (Usman et al., 2018). Innovation is a significant contributor to the survival and performance of SMEs, especially in a knowledge-based economy (Mazzarol and Reboud, 2011). The management of innovation in such firms presents, however, several challenges due to their peculiarities and it is relatively less well researched than that in large firms (Pierre and Fernandez, 2018). There is then a relative research gap in this area.

Innovation management has become even more demanding and complicated than in the past due to some recent societal and environmental trends like increasing concerns about the sustainability of the physical environment, and the effects of digitalization and artificial intelligence on innovation design and diffusion (Horn and Brem, 2013). New forms of innovation have appeared like open innovation and disruptive innovation and new ways of managing dependency on environmental factors like innovation ecosystems (Adner, 2017; Chesbrough, 2003).

The recent COVID-19 crisis with the lockdowns and other restrictive measures, had a negative impact on SMEs (much more than that on large firms). The lower purchasing power of consumers, the reduced demand, and the paralysis of the tourist sector have reduced the liquidity of SMEs and increased the financial barriers to their innovation (Roper and Turner, 2020). The latter is

DOI: 10.4324/9780429346033-16

however necessary in order to move to new business models like use of digital technologies for electronic purchasing and digital marketing (Ibarra et al., 2020).

While there are several approaches to innovation management a very useful framework of analysis is that of the resource/capabilities based view (Barney, 1991; Teece et al., 1997). A systems perspective provides a complementary approach that can be usefully applied to interorganizational cooperation (Teece, 2018). The construct of innovation capacity (or sometimes called innovation capability) will be examined in this chapter as a key antecedent factor of successful innovation management and performance of SMEs (Adams et al., 2006).

The present chapter will consider the following research questions:

1. How recent trends and developments in technology, economy, society, and the physical environment have affected innovation in SMEs?
2. Why do recent innovation forms demand new ways of managing innovation in SMEs?
3. Which are the main challenges of building and maintaining innovation capacity and managing innovation within the current environment in SMEs?
4. What is the impact of innovation capacity on the performance of firms?

The chapter will critically examine the existing literature, especially that of the last few years, and recent changes in the practice of innovation management in SMEs and propose new avenues for further research as well as some practical recommendations for owners/managers of SMEs. It covers the broad spectrum of innovation activities, but does not elaborate on the differences between innovation types (product, process, or organizational).

The second section presents the theoretical frames and foundations, while the third section analyzes the concept of innovation capacity and its components and characteristics. The fourth section considers the current trends in environmental changes and their implications for innovation management. The fifth section outlines the gaps in the literature and opportunities for studies, while the sixth section the research approach. The seventh section considers innovation management in SMEs in the new socio-economic environment, while the eighth section summarizes the conclusions and offers some recommendations for SME owners/ managers and state authorities.

Theoretical frames

Resource-based view and dynamic capabilities

The resource-based view (RBV) has been a dominant theoretical framework in management for the last 30 years. It states that the performance of firms does not only depend on external factors, as previous theories on the competitive environment have stressed, but to a large extent on internal factors which explain the heterogeneity of firms and their performance differences in the same competitive environment (Barney, 1991; Helfat and Peteraf, 2003). These internal factors are assets or resources that are rare, unique, and not easily imitated by competitors. After the initial focus on assets, capabilities were also considered. They are either ordinary capabilities, which refer to routines and practices that are relatively stable, or dynamic ones that change over time (Teece et al., 1997). From the RBV there is then a move to the CBV (capabilities based view). CBV is considered as an extension of RBV (Barreto, 2010). The dynamic aspect of capabilities addresses the static view, one of the weaknesses of the RBV, and enhances the resource based view considering time effects (Breznik and Hisrich, 2014).

There are many definitions of dynamic capabilities. One of the early and widely cited ones is that by the pioneers of the concept. Teece et al. (1997, p. 516) define dynamic capability "as the firm's ability to integrate, build, and reconfigure internal and external competences to address rapidly changing environments". Dynamic capabilities enable the organization to achieve new and innovative forms of competitive advantage. They could also lead to the creation of new resources (Helfat and Peteraf, 2003; Schilke, 2014).

Innovation capabilities overlap to some extent with dynamic ones. They can be considered as part of the broader concept of dynamic capabilities (Breznik and Hisrich, 2014). Other types of capabilities, directly or indirectly related to innovation, but of wider scope include dynamic relational capabilities, adaptive, and absorptive capabilities. In another view innovation capabilities form the core of dynamic capabilities. Therefore the nature, development, and impact of the dynamic capabilities have to be examined in order to prepare the ground for the deeper study of innovation capabilities (Stroenen et al., 2017). Felin et al. (2012) have proposed three components or micro-foundations underlying capabilities, that is individuals, social processes, and structure of the firm.

While RBV is a widely studied and cited approach it has received considerable criticism. Several problematic issues have been highlighted. It is considered to be static in nature, tautological, with an unworkable definition of resources and therefore weak in exposing causal mechanisms (Kraaijenbrink et al., 2010). While the capabilities-based view addresses some of the issues of criticism, for example, the static nature, it has also been criticized. The construct "dynamic capabilities" is characterized as an underspecified one with lack of empirical support (Shilke et al., 2018).

Apart from the criticisms of the theory as such there are also empirical problems, for example, difficulties of measuring dynamic capabilities. Some authors refer to the black box of dynamic capabilities (Pavlou and El Sawy, 2011). A useful practical approach in order to identify the capabilities of a particular firm is to use the three criteria of sensing opportunities and threats, seizing value from opportunities, and transforming intangible and tangible assets in a continuous renewal (Stroenen et al., 2017; Teece, 2019). Firms should formulate their strategy in such a way as to use their dynamic capabilities in order to take advantage of opportunities and respond effectively to threats. Whether SMEs actually do it is a matter for empirical investigation.

The systems view

Although the resource and capabilities-based view is adequate for the study of the strategy of firm and to some extent its ability to compete in its task or industry environment, a more holistic approach is needed for a multi-level analysis of strategy that would go beyond the firm and its industry and take into account regional, national, and supranational factors. The systemic view is such a holistic approach. It complements, therefore, the capabilities view.

Teece has referred to the nested nature of systems, where the firm as a system is nested and interconnected with wider systems such as the innovation ecosystem, which could be further nested within the national innovation system (Teece, 2018). The systems theory is a useful approach, but the complexity and diversity of studying innovation systems is not to be overlooked. A key issue is the determination of the boundaries of the system, its main components and their interrelationships. The components include actors (for example, firms and universities) and institutions. The operationalization of innovation system boundaries is not well documented in the literature (Autio and Thomas, 2014).

The innovation ecosystem is a recently introduced term to describe the sectoral, technological, regional, or national actors and institutions and their set of relationships (Adner, 2012; Walrave et al., 2018). Firms can be considered as open to the environment systems possessing and exchanging resources and capabilities. They cooperate with other firms (suppliers, buyers or intermediaries), universities, and the government, which are within the same ecosystem. The cooperative relationships serve for obtaining complementary resources and knowledge exchange.

Most articles in the literature focus on the benefits of innovation ecosystems for firms, communities and countries, but their risks should not be underestimated. There are three fundamental types of risk: initiative risks (referring to the uncertainties of managing a project), interdependence risks arising from uncertainties in coordinating with complementary innovators, and integration risks created by the adoption process across the value chain (Adner, 2006).

While the innovation ecosystem is a fashionable new term in the literature there has been considerable critique of the concept. Some authors consider it as a loose metaphor applying the natural ecological systems in innovation (Oh et al., 2016). The main strength of this construct is the emphasis on the analogy of the symbiotic relationships of species in a natural ecosystem with the synergistic interrelationships of firms in a particular setting (Autio and Thomas, 2014). Apart from the theoretical limitations there are also difficulties in measurement and heterogeneity of innovation ecosystems (Brown and Mason, 2017). There is also considerable debate on ecosystem design and the roles of the government, hub firms, or other agents as designers and orchestrators of an ecosystem (Jacobides et al., 2018).

Innovation capacity

Innovation capacity is a concept that is difficult to define and delineate from other similar concepts (Borgesson and Elmquist, 2011; Forsman, 2011). It can be defined as a firm's ability to combine, integrate, and improve resources and capabilities in order to exploit opportunities for development of new products, processes, or business models (Boly et al., 2014; Forsman, 2011; Pierre and Fernandes, 2018).

The term "innovation capability" is frequently used interchangeably with "innovation capacity" as a collective term for particular capabilities. The term capacity, for the overall ability to innovate, is preferred in this chapter in order to reserve the "capability" for specific capabilities, considered as dimensions of innovation capacity. This approach is supported by the fact that the term "capacity" is also used for other complementary abilities like, for example, absorption capacity (Zawislaw et al., 2018). Firms have different innovation capabilities like design, development, and commercial exploitation of innovation, which together form innovation capacity (Saunila and Ukko, 2014). Iddris (2016), considers knowledge management, organizational learning, culture, leadership, and collaboration as major innovation capacity dimensions. Another categorization could be into exploration and exploitation capabilities (Brix, 2019). Exploration refers to the development of radical innovations, while exploitation to appropriating the benefits of existing innovation or developing incremental innovation.

Innovation capacity is an inherently unobservable entity. As a latent construct presents challenges in establishing its validity and boundaries (Grant and Verona, 2015). It is difficult to measure and there are no universally accepted measurement scales. For example, in some studies innovation capabilities are based on estimates of managers about the level of their possession or the intention of the companies to develop those capabilities (Iddris, 2016). There is a further difficulty of measuring innovative activities and defining innovation capacity in SMEs since their innovation activities are informal.

Various internal and external factors affect innovation capacity and there are important feedback effects. These factors can be classified as facilitators, barriers, and motivators (Kim et al., 2018). They are summarized in Table 12.1. Examples of facilitators include top management leadership and external networking, while barriers form the costs and risks of collaboration and lack of resources. Motivators include opportunity exploitation and customer and supplier pressure (Kim et al., 2018). Innovation capacity has a significant impact, synergistically with other capacities or capabilities, on innovation practices and eventually performance. There are various ways of classifying such additional capabilities as mentioned in the literature. They can be classified as technological, operational, and transactional capabilities (Zawislaw et al., 2018). Other sources refer to absorptive capacity, managerial capabilities, and stakeholder engagement capability (Saunila and Ukko, 2014).

TABLE 12.1 Facilitators, barriers, and motivators of innovation capacity

Facilitators	Barriers	Motivators
Leadership	Costs of collaboration	Opportunity exploitation
External networking	Risks of collaboration	Competitive pressure
Innovation culture	Inadequate resources	Supplier/customer pressure
Flexible structure	Lack of time	Managerial ambition

The development and maintenance of innovation capabilities is a time-consuming and costly exercise. Careful consideration should be given to the different types of costs in their development, including opportunity costs (Arndt and Gould, 2010). Innovation capabilities can then be seen as following a maturity model of evolution over time with development, maturation, and decline stages (Corsi and Neau, 2015; Helfat and Peteraf, 2003; Narcizo et al., 2018). Some authors have proposed a hierarchical capability framework, which includes ordinary, first-order dynamic, and second-order dynamic capabilities (Breznik and Hisrich, 2014; Watson et al., 2018; Winter, 2003). The hierarchical model can be adapted to the innovation capabilities and can be combined with the maturity or life cycle model (Helfat and Peteraf, 2003).

Innovation capacity is desirable since it is assumed to lead to a higher performance of the firms. The relationship of innovation capacity with performance indicators of the firm has been evaluated in empirical research. While in many studies the relationship was positive, there are some other studies reporting no relationship or even a negative one (Kafetzopoulos and Psomas, 2015; Kim et al., 2018). There is also a problem of selection of appropriate performance indicators (profitability, sales growth, market share, etc.). Another issue is that innovation capacity that is available, but not adequately used by the firm, will not lead to better performance results.

Many studies combine the theoretical framework of resources and capabilities, and the innovation capacity concept in order to investigate innovation management approaches in SMEs. Due to space considerations only two examples of studies are mentioned. Kim et al. (2018) report in their empirical investigation the positive effect of innovation capabilities on firm performance and the role of facilitators (like commercial capabilities) and barriers like organizational rigidity. Forsman (2011) has examined the degree of innovation capacity and the types of innovation patterns in both manufacturing and service small enterprises with fewer than 50 employees. The systems view is rather rarely used as a framework for empirical studies (for example, O'Connors, 2008) (but for large firms). The latter paper uses a framework of seven system elements, like organizational structure and exploration processes, in order to investigate dynamic capabilities for the management of major innovation.

New trends and their implications for innovation capacity development

There are several recent developments and trends that have changed the competitive environment of firms, increased uncertainty, and aggravated the difficulties and complexities of innovation management (Horn and Brem, 2013). Due to the limited available space only some of them are briefly considered. They are illustrated in Table 12.2 with a short description of their nature.

I. Globalization and the recent commercial wars, for example, between the USA and China, have increased the environmental dynamism and require fast adaptation. Global competition accelerates innovation, leading to shorter product life cycles through global innovation networks (Horn and Brem, 2013).

II. Digitalization and artificial intelligence are not just technological trends that open new possibilities, but have revolutionized business by introducing new forms of competition and facilitating the development and implementation of new products and services and new business models (Nambisan et al., 2017). They imply that firms have to develop the capability for digital innovation and increase customer participation and co-creation of what is called synergistic innovation.

III. Sustainability of the natural environment is a much debated societal requirement that is increasingly affecting managerial decisions. Sustainable innovations are then what firms should aim for (Watson et al., 2018).

IV. New forms of innovation include open innovation and disruptive innovation. Open innovation has been a relatively recent approach to innovation that is widely discussed in the literature (Bigliardi and Galati, 2016). The basic idea behind it is simple. Firms, even large ones, benefit from collaboration with others in innovation development or by offering their inventions, etc. to outside entities for commercial exploitation (Chesbrough, 2003). Open innovation is particularly important for SMEs which frequently lack the resources and capabilities and cannot follow a closed model of innovation to develop in house their innovations from start to end (Vanhaverbeke and Frattini, 2018).

TABLE 12.2 Developments and trends affecting innovation management

Number	Development/trend	Description
I.	Globalization and trade wars	Commercial
II.	Digitalization and artificial intelligence	Technological
III.	Sustainability of natural environment	Ecological
IV.	New forms of innovation (Open innovation, Disruptive innovation)	Innovation form

Disruptive innovation is a particular type of innovation, usually radical, that upsets markets and creates problems for the dominant incumbent firms (Christensen, 1997). Specific innovation capabilities are needed for disruptive innovation since the acceptance of a revolutionary value proposition by societal stakeholders, despite the strong resistance of established sociotechnical systems, sets particular challenges for the firm (Christensen et al., 2018; Walrave et al., 2018).

Gaps in the literature and opportunities for further studies

The above review has identified the main gaps in the literature. The present section summarizes and evaluates these gaps and deficiencies with appropriate references.

Open innovation practices in the small and medium-sized enterprises (SMEs) context is under-researched, while the corresponding practices in large firms have received considerable attention in the literature (Kim et al., 2018; Usman et al., 2018). Similarly the impact of the open innovation paradigm on innovation efficiency is an issue requiring further investigation (Kim et al., 2018).

The extant empirical research on innovation capabilities and their utilization in the innovation management of SMEs is rather scarce (Stroenen et al., 2017). The proposed models of innovation capacity do not consider SME specificities, while the latter have an important impact on innovation development and implementation (Pierre and Fernandez, 2018). How innovation capabilities can be developed in practice in SMEs is a controversial issue. Extensive empirical research is needed, especially of the longitudinal type as Borgesson and Elmquist (2011) have already done for large firms. The impact of complementary capacities (absorptive capacity, managerial capacity) and their synergistic effect to that of innovation capacity has been neglected (Kim et al., 2018). The relationship between innovation capacity and firm performance (financial, etc.) is under-researched (Kafetzopoulos and Psomas, 2015; Kim et al., 2018; Narcizo et al., 2018).

Many studies focus on innovation determinants, while the process view of innovation over a period of time in SMEs is rather neglected (Oliveira et al., 2019). Methods, strategies, and systematized processes of implementation in the innovation management of SMEs are still little discussed (Oliveira et al., 2019). The pervasive effect of digital technologies on innovation and the undermining of the assumptions of established innovation theories, for example, regarding the boundaries of innovation processes and outcomes and the connectivity of innovation agents has not been fully explored in the literature (Nambisan et al., 2017).

There are some frameworks for innovation capabilities in SMEs and their antecedents and impact (Kim et al., 2018; Pierre and Fernandez, 2018). There are also frameworks on open innovation determinants in SMEs (Oliveira et al.,

2019). There is, however, no holistic framework for the management of innovation in SMEs, which takes into account the antecedents and hierarchy of innovation capabilities, the synergistic effects of complementary capabilities and the impact of innovation barriers. The present study is aiming to fill this gap as explained below.

The above specific gaps illustrate the limitations of the current literature. Although there are many review articles on open innovation, innovation capacity, and individual technological trends there is still a need for an integrative review that applies all of them to the strategic management of innovation in SMEs with a practical approach and develops a suitable framework for that purpose.

Research approach

The main purpose of the research approach was to evaluate the theory and empirical evidence in the area of innovation management and get a "state-of-the-art" snapshot of the particular domain. Specific answers were sought to the research questions as stated in the introduction. The approach then is a combination of a review and a conceptual synthesis and integration of the specific area defined as "innovation management in SMEs" that will generate new insights for managerial application and further research.

A systematic and critical assessment of the literature was used with a specific search strategy as described below. The emphasis was not, however, on the examination of all the vast literature related to the topic with its several research streams and the classification of this literature. It was rather the identification of specific themes in the literature and the comparison of different approaches and their critical appraisal and synthesis. The literature review does not then include descriptive aspects like the summarization and classification of articles under thematic categories, statistics about journals, etc.

The search was kept deliberately broad because the purpose was not to summarize a particular area, for example, innovation capabilities for radical or incremental product innovation, process innovation or open innovation as such, but a holistic innovation management approach taking into account all the above sub-topics. The research approach with an integrative viewpoint attempted to identify core constructs (like innovation capacity and its dimensions and measures and open innovation) and their patterns of relationships and assess the disagreements and inconsistencies that appear in the extant literature. The result is a conceptual framework for effective innovation management in SMEs in the current demanding environment and its managerial implications.

The search was broad-based using a number of databases like Google Scholar, EBSCOHost, Proquest ABI/Inform, and Scopus with combinations of keywords and Boolean operators such as "innovation management" and "innovation capabilities" or "open innovation" as search terms. Pre-specified inclusion and exclusion criteria were used. For example articles concerning SMEs were used, not multinationals or large firms.

After the initial selection of articles an evaluation stage led to the most important ones for the purposes of this chapter. Systematic literature reviews and influential articles with significant contribution (as judged by their citations) published in high-quality journals (like *Strategic Management Journal* and *Research Policy*) were given high priority in the analysis. Articles after the year 2000 were mostly used with emphasis to the most recent ones after the year 2010.

Innovation management in SMEs

SME characteristics

The peculiarities of SMEs are first briefly reviewed. These characteristics are directly related to the challenges of innovation management in such firms as explained below. Some of them support, while others hinder innovation (Ibarra et al., 2020). SMEs have therefore both strengths and weaknesses in comparison to larger firms (Pierre and Fernandez, 2018). The main strengths and weaknesses are summarized in Table 12.3. SMEs are defined here as firms with fewer than 250 employees following the simple criterion of employment according to the definition of the European Union (EUC, 2016).

Strengths include fast decision-making and flexibility in adaptation to environmental changes, lack of rigid hierarchies, and a personal interest and dedication of owners/managers (O/M) in the survival and success of the firm. The performance of the firm is usually closely related to the personal and family welfare of the owners (Terziovski, 2010).

Weaknesses include insufficient resources including human ones, lack of time since managers are overburdened with duties and responsibilities, and frequently lack of knowledge, brand power, and managerial skills and capabilities (Kim et al., 2018). Their position in business networks and lobbying capacity toward the government and its rules and regulations are usually weak. The main strengths and weaknesses are illustrated in Table 12.3.

TABLE 12.3 Main strengths and weaknesses of SMEs in relation to innovation

Strengths	*Weaknesses*
Fast decision making	Insufficient resources
Flexibility toward market demands	Lack of time
Flat structure	Lack of knowledge and skills
Personal interest and motivation of O/M	Weak position in business networks and innovation ecosystems
High adaptability of operations	Limited innovation portfolio (increasing failure risk)

Key issues in SME innovation management

The current state of innovation management in SMEs could be described as rather informal and unsystematic. Few of them use formal mechanisms and procedures. Innovation processes in such firms are typically ad hoc and not well organized (Mazzarol and Reboud, 2011). An innovation team is formed, led by the owner/manager, whenever there is a need for developing or adopting an innovation that will exploit a particular opportunity.

There are some key questions regarding SME approaches to innovation as illustrated in Table 12.4. The first question is whether SMEs simply adopt learning strategies of large firms and if this is the case the feasibility and desirability of such an adoption.

The second question is whether there is or should be a single approach to innovation management with applicability into different industries (for example, manufacturing versus services), different technological intensity levels and both start-up and established SMEs.

The third question is how managers develop and use their innovation capabilities in order to obtain competitive advantage (Eisenhardt and Martin, 2000).

Regarding the first question, SMEs cannot, even if they wanted to, adopt the learning strategies of larger firms due to lack of the groups of specialized people that larger firms have, and the resources for such an endeavor (Adams et al., 2006). They have to use alternative sources of knowledge like use of informal contacts with suppliers, customers or universities. Due to lack of resources they have to collaborate with other firms sharing costs and risks with them. In this network of collaborators SMEs have many opportunities for learning and knowledge transfer including vicarious learning from the failures or successes of others.

Concerning the second question, the diversity and heterogeneity of SMEs precludes a single approach to innovation management. While it is expected that firms in high technology sectors should have a high innovation capacity in order to survive in a fast changing technological environment, firms in relatively low technology sectors should also develop some key innovation capabilities in order to differentiate themselves from competitors and obtain competitive advantage. Start-up firms have different approaches than established firms. In view of the

TABLE 12.4 Key questions regarding innovation management in SMEs

Number	Key question
1.	Same learning approach to large firms?
2.	Single universal approach to Innovation Management for all types of SMEs?
3.	How managers develop and use innovation capabilities?

above a contextual approach has gradually evolved for innovation management (Ortt and van der Duin, 2008).

The third question is actually about the actions and influence of the top manager. The key role of the owner/manager (O/M) in all activities of an SME is widely recognized in the literature (Hadjimanolis, 2000; Pierre and Fernandez, 2018). Kevill et al. (2017) emphasize the perceived self-efficacy of the owner/manager as a key component of the micro-foundations of dynamic capabilities in micro-enterprises. The O/M is the main orchestrator of innovative capabilities (Breznik and Hisrich, 2014).

We can illustrate the innovation capacity building as a process with several stages. Figure 12.1 shows a simplified framework of this process and at the same time an approach to innovation management. Many aspects like feedback effects and other nonlinear interactions between the stages are omitted in order to keep the framework simple and easy to present.

The framework could also be seen as taking a systems view of the firm as embedded in a larger ecosystem of innovation. Actors within the system of the firm, such as managers and employees are implicitly involved, but interdependent elements like strategy, resources, capabilities, and performance metrics are explicitly treated. Similarly O'Connor (2008) takes a systems view of innovation, but at the project level in large firms.

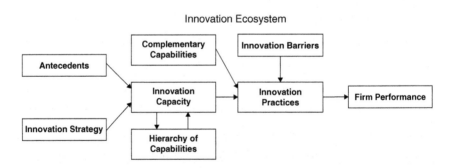

Notes to Figure 1:
1. Antecedents: Leadership, innovation culture, structure, resources
2. Complementary capabilities: Absorptive capacity, managerial capabilities
3. Hierarchy of capabilities: ordinary, 1st-order, 2nd order capabilities
4. Innovation barriers: Internal, external
5. Innovation practices: Forms (open or disruptive), type (new product, etc.)

FIGURE 12.1 Framework of innovation management in SMEs.

Source: Compiled by the author from various literature sources (Breznik and Hisrich, 2014; Kim et al., 2018; Pierre and Fernandez, 2018; Watson et al., 2018; Zawislaw et al., 2018).

Overall framework of innovation management in SMEs

It all starts with the strategy of the firm. The strategy determines the overall objectives and actions taking into account the existing capabilities and the necessary new ones for these actions. It should be noted, however, that in SMEs strategy is sometimes informal and not fully formulated as intended strategy, but it develops as emergent strategy (Vanhaverbeke et al., 2017). Innovation strategy should match with the overall firm strategy. Since SMEs are frequently embedded in innovation eco-systems, as explained above, their innovation strategies should "fit" to their innovation ecosystem, in the sense that they should take into account their position and relationships in that system (Adner, 2006; Shipilov and Gawer, 2020). Therefore they should develop an explicit ecosystem strategy with an integrated value proposition to the final customer that is formed together with the other partners (Adner, 2012, 2017).

A practical example from the literature will illustrate issues of strategy. It refers to a study that explored how SMEs perceive, organize, and manage open innovation in the particular context of a regional innovation ecosystem (Radziwon and Bogers, 2019). Their results highlight the consideration of the firm's collaboration choices and the level of undertaken risk according to their resources and capabilities and selection of the right and credible partners. Then preparation for capturing knowledge and learning within the ecosystem.

Managers have to determine their relationship management capabilities that are required to manage ecosystem-level interdependencies with other firms and institutions (Agarwal and Selen, 2009). One of the first stages of capability building involves diagnosis or identification of capability gaps that have then to be closed through the development of appropriate capabilities (Teece, 2019). The diagnosis should include the assessment of their own capabilities relative to those of competitors.

The antecedents of innovation capacity, facilitators like top leadership and external networking and barriers like organizational rigidity and lack of resources play a key role in the process (Kim et al., 2018). Top leaders are the initiators and supporters of the process and the key links in external network formation, while they have to find ways to overcome the barriers in order to go ahead with the building process. The process includes the use and development of the employees' knowledge, skills and decision making in building innovation capacity (Brix, 2019).

The hierarchical model of innovation capability building, that is the attainment of higher levels of capabilities from lower level ones, as mentioned above, is a way of both understanding better the process of developing innovation capabilities, and guiding this process in practice (Breznik and Hisrich, 2014). The first level could start from existing ordinary capabilities, for example, operational capabilities or even ad hoc solutions given to the firm's problems. The next level is first-order dynamic capabilities for adjusting to environmental changes and then second-order ones, that is, capabilities to transform the existing first-order ones (Watson et al., 2018; Winter, 2003). It is an incremental building process. The second-order innovation capabilities include the change of existing mindsets and unlearning of current routines so that new learning is possible, while they establish learning mechanisms (learning to learn) for the firm.

Although the particular set of capabilities that will make the overall innovation capacity may differ according to the particular circumstances of each SME, there are some widely applicable capabilities. They include the search for new ideas, and acquisition of knowledge both internally and externally according to the open innovation mindset. Project management and product design and development are further examples of rather universal innovation capabilities. The set of innovation capabilities that managers should aim to develop should be limited to the few critical ones for the particular firm, because of the cost and time resources for their development and the associated risk.

The main challenges of building innovation capacities relate to cultural and structural issues. The literature recommends a flat and flexible structure and an open culture with a focus on participation of employees, encouragement of initiative, and tolerance for mistakes (Brix, 2019). An innovation culture is such an open culture. It is characterized by commitment of managers, as shown by specific measures and actions, encouragement of the creativity of employees through recognition and rewards, and provision of opportunities for personal growth (Popa et al., 2017). Some other features include informal social relations, knowledge sharing, and close collaboration across functional areas. A firm would need an efficient innovation culture fitting with its innovation strategy in order to support open innovation initiatives (Terziovski, 2010).

While the roles of the internal structure and culture in innovation success are recognized in the literature, the importance of overcoming cultural conflict for cooperation in a network of actors in an innovation ecosystem for an integrated value proposition by the ecosystem is frequently neglected (Walrave et al., 2018).

Complementary capabilities like absorption capacity and managerial capabilities have been discussed in previous sections. They can play a crucial role in innovation processes. Innovation barriers are internal factors like costs and fear of imitation by competitors and external ones like problems in obtaining finance or market and institutional failures. They potentially discourage firms in attempting innovation.

Innovation practices refer to processes with their formal systems, routines, and procedures that are used in innovation development (Brunswicker and Vanhaverbeke, 2015). They are embedded in a particular form or paradigm like open or disruptive innovation. The innovation output (or type) is a product, process, business model or a new organizational design.

An example from the literature will illustrate some successful innovation practices. Pullen et al. (2012) have examined open innovation practices in the demanding and highly regulated high tech sector of medical devices. Their findings show that goal complementarity, resource and capability complementarity, trust, and network position strength characterize the more successful firms versus the less successful ones.

Recognizing and measuring the outcomes of the innovation efforts and therefore the successful management of innovation in SMEs is a key and ambiguous issue for both researchers and practicing managers. There are several indicators of successful innovation management like reduced time-to-market in product innovation and the extent of customer and employee involvement in innovation relative to competitors (Grant and Verona, 2015). There is no agreement on the exact set of indicators, and the proper balance of input, process and output measures of innovation performance, to be used in specific cases or adequate empirical research to support such a set. Finally the impact of innovation on the overall performance of the firm, both short and especially long term, is an issue for continuous evaluation.

Conclusions and recommendations

Recent trends and developments have a significant impact on innovation management in both large and small firms and there is a need for new approaches in order to take advantage of the new opportunities offered by these trends and avoid the considerable threats especially for small firms. Although the trends have been presented as separate for convenience of discussion, there are significant interactions between them. Open innovation, for example, has been stimulated by digital collaboration technologies and globalization. The need for sustainable development has implications on innovation within global collaboration networks.

The above review suggests that barriers to building and maintenance of innovation capacity have to be identified and imaginative ways of overcoming them must be found. Such barriers are internal ones like the cost of intellectual property protection or external originating from institutional and environmental factors.

The proposed framework acknowledges that the firm is embedded in an innovation ecosystem, while it mainly focuses on forces inside the firm. It considers the firm as a system with interacting components, relationships, and attributes (O'Connor, 2008). The complex interactions of the firm with other actors of the ecosystem are not explicitly treated in order to keep the model simple, easy to comprehend, and actionable. The framework does not claim to be a model, but rather an outline of the main factors involved. A model would specify the exact relationships between constructs in a more formal way. It also does not claim complete originality, since elements of it are already included in models of the literature for some of the constructs involved, for example, innovation capacities (Kim et al., 2018; Pierre and Fernandez, 2018). It integrates them, however, into a parsimonious framework following the familiar sequence of strategy formulation, implementation, and performance (control) phases.

The framework emphasizes the key role of strategy that dictates the types of capabilities needed (Fainshmidt et al., 2019). It shows the antecedents of innovation capacity and the hierarchy of capabilities that lead to this capacity. It takes into account the complementary capabilities needed and shows how innovation capacity affects innovation practices like new product development or process innovation. Such practices are also affected by barriers, some of them related to innovation capacity, but many others independent of it. The framework also illustrates the impact of innovation practices on the overall firm performance. This is a complicated issue that needs further research in the context of SMEs. Overall performance is a critical aspect in practice because what matters to SMEs is their survival, profitability, and growth.

Regarding the contribution of the chapter to the study of innovation and areas for future study the following comments summarize the issues. The above framework is a first attempt for an integrated perspective of innovation management in SMEs. It suggests the need for future research on the individual constructs of the framework and their interactions, especially from a process view and a dynamic perspective.

Furthermore, future studies should focus on particular categories of firms, since the specific requirements of innovation management are expected to differ by category and the framework should be adapted accordingly. The industry type, its structure and maturity (or life-cycle stage), but also the level of competition and technological intensiveness affect innovation and its management (Waldner et al., 2015). For example a study of high tech versus low tech firms is proposed. Also investigation of innovation management practices through categorization of firms by industrial sector, country, and size of firms (distinguishing between micro-firms with less than 10 employees, small ones with less than 50, and medium size firms between 50 and 250). Management of innovation presents special challenges in "start-ups" worthy of relevant studies.

Future research could focus more narrowly on innovation capacity and complementary capacities. Different firms in various circumstances need different sets of capacities. Innovation in the services sector, an increasingly important type of innovation since services form a significant part of modern economies, requires special capabilities like process management and relationship management capabilities to handle customer interface and interaction with business partners (Agarwal and Selen, 2009). The configurational approach and the strategy fit offer a way of approaching the problem of the required set of capacities. The configuration approach, which is currently under-researched, classifies firms into a limited number of groups according to certain criteria (for example, size, age, sector, technology, innovation type, and level of environmental uncertainty)

(Fainshmidt et al., 2019). The usefulness of this approach to managers is that it can serve as a guide for the necessary set of innovation capabilities suitable for the group closer to their conditions and the formulation of a strategy matching these conditions.

Managerial implications and practical applications of the present chapter are briefly stated as follows. Managers should start first with the context, both internal and external of the firm, and then consider the practices to follow. They can analyze the antecedents to innovation capacity, their complementary capacities, and innovation barriers in order to identify their strengths and weaknesses and decide which innovation capabilities to develop. They can build innovation capabilities starting from the initial resource base of the firm and its ordinary capabilities and gradually developing them. Psychological and sociocultural factors should not be neglected since they are frequently major barriers for the building and maintenance of dynamic innovation capabilities (Arndt and Gould, 2010). The various innovation capabilities should then be integrated into an overall innovation capacity that will improve the chances of innovation success (Pierre and Fernandez, 2018). As a practical example, an SME in the digital health services, which are much in demand during pandemics or other health crises, can use the proposed framework as a guide. It will help the firm to build and develop the required interactive system of digital innovation capabilities and create the appropriate network relations.

Most authors advise SMEs to adopt an open innovation (OI) approach in order to overcome their inherent weaknesses regarding insufficient resources and limited market power (Usman et al., 2018). It makes sense, however, to start with the relatively easy and less costly activities of OI like the inbound activities (for example, external knowledge acquisition through collaboration) (Brunswicker and Vanhaverbeke, 2015). The more sophisticated outbound open innovation activities, for example, intellectual property licensing to other firms, can be added at a later stage (Horn and Brem, 2013). SMEs should find ways to overcome internal barriers to open innovation like financial, organizational, and strategic factors (Bigliardi and Galati, 2016). Some of the external barriers, like low market power or brand recognition, can be overcome by engaging their stakeholders in the OI process through customer integration, user involvement, and participation in external research networks (Marullo et al., 2018).

Establishing long term relationships with external partners in the context of open innovation is a slow and resource demanding process (Bigliardi and Galati, 2016; van de Vrande et al., 2009). Therefore managers should give due attention to the selection and evaluation of few such partners among the most promising ones following a focused search strategy (Marullo et al., 2018). Criteria of selection could include partner reputation, financial position, and trust. After the selection of partners, the long-term management of the key dependencies on other firms in order to develop and then to commercialize innovation is particularly challenging. The idea is to maximize the benefits (for example, learning from them), while minimizing the substantial risks (for example, knowledge leakage to competitors) (Watson et al., 2018).

Managers can take advantage of new forms of innovation tools such as crowd-sourcing for ideas and crowd-financing for obtaining seed capital. A digital innovation strategy covering learning, knowledge management, collaboration, commercialization, and various other aspects should then be developed (Nambisan et al., 2017). Advances in digital technology facilitate such actions and allow SMEs to keep costs at relatively low levels. Vicarious learning, that is learning from the experiences of other firms that have pioneered broadly similar radical or even incremental innovations, is a relatively low-cost practice (Walrave et al., 2018).

Governments in recent years have realized the potential of innovation for economic growth and are, at least verbally, supporting it. In order to go beyond the rhetoric a long-term political vision is needed and a well-developed innovation policy with specific incentives and measures. It should be a holistic innovation policy integrating all public actions with a potential influence on innovation processes (Edquist, 2019). The innovation policy should aim at supporting existing, and promoting the building of new, innovation ecosystems. While the traditional approach was to support the formation of key firms in promising sectors selected by the government, the new trend is to rely more on market forces by building a suitable institutional framework and providing incentives for innovators in all economic sectors.

The particular needs of SMEs, which are more vulnerable than large firms, should be specifically addressed in such policies. The shock of COVID-19 pandemic cannot be easily overcome by SMEs without Government support through specific policies and action plans (Roper and Turner, 2020). For example, firms may need support in adopting and making full use of newer digital technologies and R&D subsidies in order to develop innovations needed in the new economic and societal environment.

References

Adams, R., Bessant, J. and Phelps, R. (2006). Innovation management measurement: A review. *International Journal of Management Reviews*, 8(1), 21–47. https://doi.org/10.1111/j.1468-2370.2006.00119.x

Adner, R. (2006). Match your innovation strategy to your innovation ecosystem. *Harvard Business Review*, 84(4), 98–107.

Adner, R. (2012). *The Wide Lens: A New Strategy for Innovation*. London, UK: Penguin Books.

Adner, R. (2017). Ecosystem as structure: An actionable construct for strategy. *Journal of Management*, 43(1), 39–58. doi: 10.1177/0149206316678451

Agarwal, R. and Selen, W. (2009). Dynamic capability building in service value networks for achieving service innovation. *Decision Sciences*, 40(3), 431–475. doi: 10.1111/j.1540-5915.2009.00236.x

Arndt, F. and Gould, R.B. (2010). Revisiting dynamic capabilities through the lens of complexity theory. In *Conference Paper 24th ANZAM (Australian New Zealand Academy of Management)*. Adelaide, Australia, 8–10 September 2010.

Autio, E. and Thomas, L.D.W. (2014). Innovation ecosystems: Implications for innovation management. In: Dogson, M., Gann, D., and Philips, N. (Eds.), *Oxford Handbook of Innovation Management*. Oxford: Oxford University Press, pp. 204–228.

Barney, J. (1991). Firm resources and sustained competitive advantage. *Journal of Management*, 17(1), 99–120.

Barreto, I. (2010). Dynamic capabilities: A review of past research and an agenda for the future. *Journal of Management*, 36, 256–280. https://doi.org/10.1177%2F014920630 9350776

Bigliardi, B. and Galati, F. (2016). Which factors hinder the adoption of open innovation in SMEs? *Technology Analysis & Strategic Management*, 28(8), 869–885. doi: 10.1080/09537325.2016.1180353.

Boly, V., Morel, L., Assielou, N.G. and Camargo, M. (2014). Evaluating innovative processes in French firms: Methodological proposition for firm innovation capacity evaluation. *Research Policy*, 43(3), 608–622. doi.org/10.1016/j.respol.2013. 09.005

Börjesson, S. and Elmquist, M. (2011). Developing innovation capabilities: A longitudinal study of a project at Volvo cars. *Creativity and Innovation Management*, 20(3), 171–184. https://doi.org/10.1111/j.1467-8691.2011.00605.x

Breznik, L. and Hisrich, R.D. (2014). Dynamic capabilities vs. innovation capability: Are they related? *Journal of Small Business and Enterprise Development*, 21(3), 368–384. http://dx.doi.org/10.1108/JSBED-02-2014-0018.

Brix, J. (2019). Innovation capacity building: An approach to maintaining balance between exploration and exploitation in organizational learning. *Learning Organization*, 26(1), 12–26. doi: 10.1108/TLO-08-2018-0143.

Brown, R. and Mason, C. (2017). Looking inside the spiky bits: A critical review and conceptualisation of entrepreneurial ecosystems. *Small Business Economics*, 49(1), 11–30. doi: 10.1007/s11187-017-9865-7

Brunswicker, S. and Vanhaverbeke, W. (2015). Open innovation in small and medium-sized enterprises (SMEs): External knowledge sourcing strategies and internal organizational facilitators. *Journal of Small Business Management*, 53, 1241–1263. https://doi.org/10.1111/jsbm.12120.

Chesbrough, H.W. (2003). *Open Innovation: The New Imperative for Creating and Profiting from Technology*. Boston, MA: Harvard Business Press.

Christensen, C.M. (1997). *The Innovator's Dilemma: When New Technologies Cause Great Firms to Fail*. Boston, MA: Harvard Business School Press.

Christensen, C.M., McDonald, R., Altman, E.J. and Palmer, J.E. (2018). Disruptive innovation: An intellectual history and directions for future research. Special Issue on Managing in the Age of Disruptions. *Journal of Management Studies*, 55(7), 1043–1078. https://doi.org/10.1111/joms.12349.

Corsi, P. and Neau, E. (2015). *Innovation Capability Maturity Model*. London and New York: John Wiley & Sons, ISTE.

Edquist, C. (2019). Towards a holistic innovation policy: Can the Swedish National Innovation Council (NIC) be a role model? *Research Policy*, 48(4), 869–879. https://doi.org/10.1016/j.respol.2018.10.008.

Eisenhardt, K.M. and Martin, J.A. (2000). Dynamic capabilities: What are they? *Strategic Management Journal*, 21(10–11), 1105–1121. https://doi.org/10.1002/1097-0266(200010/11)21:10/11%3C1105::AID-SMJ133%3E3.0.CO;2-E.

European Commission. (2016). User guide to SME definition Ref. Ares (2016)956541 24/02/2016. https://ec.europa.eu/regional_policy/sources/conferences/state-aid/sme/smedefinitionguide_en.pdf accessed on 14/01/2020.

Fainshmidt, S., Wenger, L., Pezeshkan, A. and Mallonc, M. (2019). When do dynamic capabilities lead to competitive advantage? The importance of strategic fit. *Journal of Management Studies*, 56(4), 758–787. https://doi.org/10.1111/joms.12415.

Felin, T., Foss, N., Heimeriks, K. and Madsen, T. (2012). Microfoundations of routines and capabilities: Individuals, processes, and structure. *Journal of Management Studies*, 49, 1351–1374. https://doi.org/10.1111/j.1467-6486.2012.01052.x.

Forsman, H. (2011). Innovation capacity and innovation development in small enterprises. A comparison between the manufacturing and service sectors. *Research Policy*, 40(5), 739–750. https://doi.org/10.1016/j.respol.2011.02.003.

Grant, R. and Verona, G. (2015). What's holding back empirical research into organizational capabilities? Remedies for common problems. *Strategic Organization*, 13(1), 61–74. https://doi.org/10.1177%2F1476127014565988.

Hadjimanolis. (2000). An investigation of innovation antecedents in small firms in the context of a small developing country. *R&D Management*, 30(3), 235–245. https://doi.org/10.1111/1467-9310.00174.

Helfat, C.E. and Peteraf, M.A. (2003). The dynamic resource-based view: Capability lifecycles. *Strategic Management Journal*, 24, 997–1010. https://doi.org/10.1002/smj.332

Horn, C. and Brem, A. (2013). Strategic directions on innovation management – A conceptual framework. *Management Research Review*, 36(10), 939–954. http://dx.doi.org/10.1108/MRR-06-2012-0142

Ibarra, D., Bigdeli, A.Z., Igartua, J.I. and Ganzarain, J. (2020). Business model innovation in established SMEs: A configurational approach. *Journal of Open Innovation: Technology, Market, and Complexity*, 6(3), 76. https://doi.org/10.3390/joitmc6030076.

Iddris, F. (2016). Innovation capability: A systematic review and research agenda. *Interdisciplinary Journal of Information, Knowledge, and Management*, 11, 235–260. http://dx.doi.org/10.28945/3571.

Jacobides, M.G., Cennamo, C. and Gawer, A. (2018). Towards a theory of ecosystems. *Strategic Management Journal*, 39(8), 2255–2276. https://doi.org/10.1002/smj.2904.

Kafetzopoulos, D. and Psomas, E. (2015). The impact of innovation capability on the performance of manufacturing companies: The Greek case. *Journal of Manufacturing Technology Management*, 26(1), 104–130. http://dx.doi.org/10.1108/JMTM-12-2012-0117

Kevill, A., Trehan, K. and Easterby-Smith, M. (2017). Perceiving 'capability' within dynamic capabilities: The role of owner-manager self-efficacy. *International Small Business Journal*, 35(8), 883–902. https://doi.org/10.1172F/0266242616688523.

Kim, M.-K., Park, J.-H. and Paik, J.-H. (2018). Factors influencing innovation capability of small and medium-sized enterprises in Korean manufacturing sector: Facilitators, barriers and moderators. *International Journal Technology Management*, 76(¾), 214–235. https://doi.org/10.1504/IJTM.2018.091286

Kraaijenbrink, J., Spender, J.C. and Groen, A.J. (2010). The resource-based view: A review and assessment of its critiques. *Journal of Management*, 36(1), 349–372. https://doi.org/10.1177%2F0149206309350775.

Marullo, C., Di Minin, A., De Marco, C.E. and Piccaluga, A. (2018). The "hidden costs" of open innovation in SMEs: From theory to practice. World Scientific Book Chapters. In: Vanhaverbeke, W., Frattini, F., Roijakkers, N., and Usman, M. (Eds.), *Researching Open Innovation in SMEs*. Singapore: World Scientific Publishing Co. Pvt. Ltd., chapter 2, pp. 37–68.

Mazzarol, T. and Reboud, S. (2011). *Strategic Innovation in Small Firms: An International Analysis of Innovation and Strategic Decision Making in Small to Medium Sized Enterprises.* Cheltenham, UK and Northampton, MA: Edward Elgar Publishing.

Nambisan, S., Lyytinen, K., Majchrzak, A. and Song, M. (2017). Digital innovation management: Reinventing innovation management research in a digital world. *MIS Q*, 41(1), 223–238. http://dx.doi.org/10.25300/MISQ/2017/41:1.03.

Narcizo, R.B., Canen, A.G. and Tammela, I. (2018). A framework for Innovation Capability performance assessment in Brazilian low-tech small business, article presented in 14th International Conference on Industrial Logistics, Beer-Sheva, Israel, 14–16th May, 2018.

O'Connor, G. (2008). Major innovation as a dynamic capability: A systems approach. *Journal of Product Innovation Management*, 25(4), 313–330. doi: 10.1111/j.1540–5885. 2008.00304.x

Oh, D.-S., Phillips, F., Park, S. and Lee, E. (2016). Innovation ecosystems: A critical examination. *Technovation*, 54, 1–6. https://doi.org/10.1016/j.technovation.2016.02.004.

Oliveira, L.S.de, Soares Echeveste, M.E. and Nogueira Cortimiglia, M. (2019). Framework proposal for open innovation implementation in SMEs of regional innovation systems. *Journal of Technology Management and Innovation*, 14(2), 14–20. https://doi.org/10.4067/S0718-27242019000200014.

Ortt, J.R. and van der Duin, P.A. (2008). The evolution of innovation management towards contextual innovation. *European Journal of Innovation Management*, 11(4), 522–538. http://dx.doi.org/10.1108/14601060810911147.

Pavlou, P.A. and El Sawy, O.A. (2011). Understanding the elusive black box of dynamic capabilities. *Decision Sciences*, 42(1), 239–273. https://doi.org/10.1111/j.1540-5915.2010.00287.x.

Pierre, A. and Fernandez, A.S. (2018). Going deeper into SMEs' innovation capacity, an empirical exploration of innovation capacity factors. *Journal of Innovation Economics Management*, 1(25), 139–181. doi: 10.3917/jie.pr1.0019.

Popa, S., Soto-Acosta, P. and Martínez-Conesa, I. (2017). Antecedents, moderators, and outcomes of innovation climate and open innovation: An empirical study in SMEs. *Technological Forecasting and Social Change*, 118, 134–142. http://dx.doi.org/10.1016/j. techfore.2017.02.014.

Pullen, A.J., Weerd-Nederhof, P.C., Groen, A.J. and Fisscher, O.A. (2012). Open innovation in practice: Goal complementarity and closed NPD networks to explain differences in innovation performance for SMEs in the medical devices sector. *Journal of Product Innovation Management*, 29(6), 917–934. doi: 10.1111/j.1540-5885.2012.00973.x

Radziwon, A. and Bogers, M. (2019). Open innovation in SMEs: Exploring inter-organizational relationships in an ecosystem. *Technological Forecasting & Social Change*, 146, 573–587. doi.org/10.1016/j.techfore.2018.04.021

Roper, S. and Turner, J. (2020). R&D and innovation after COVID-19: What can we expect? A review of prior research and data trends after the great financial crisis. *International Small Business Journal*, 38(6), 504–514. doi: 10.1177/02662426 20947946.

Saunila, M. and Ukko, J. (2014). Intangible aspects of innovation capability in SMEs: Impacts of size and industry. *Journal of Engineering and Technology Management*, 33, 32–46 http://dx.doi.org/10.1016/j.jengtecman.2014.02.002.

Schilke, O. (2014). On the contingent value of dynamic capabilities for competitive advantage: The nonlinear moderating effect of environmental dynamism. *Strategic Management Journal*, 35, 179–203. https://doi.org/10.1002/smj.2099.

Schilke, O., Hu, S. and Helfat, C. (2018). Quo vadis, dynamic capabilities? A content-analytic review of the current state of knowledge and recommendations for future research. *Academy of Management Annals*, 12(1), 390–439. http://dx.doi.org/10.5465/annals.2016.0014.

Shipilov, A. and Gawer, A. (2020). Integrating research on inter-organizational networks and ecosystems. *Academy of Management Annals*, 14(1), 92–121. https://doi.org/10.5465/annals.2018.0121.

Strønen, F., Hoholm, T., Kværner, K. and Støme, L.N. (2017). Dynamic capabilities and innovation capabilities: The case of the 'Innovation Clinic'. *Journal of Entrepreneurship*, 13(1), 89–116. doi: 10.7341/20171314.

Teece, D.J. (2018). Dynamic capabilities as (workable) management systems theory. *Journal of Management & Organization*, 24(3), 359–368. https://doi.org/10.1017/jmo.2017.75

Teece, D.J. (2019). A capability theory of the firm: An economics and (strategic) management perspective. *New Zealand Economic Papers*, 53(1), 1–43. https://doi.org/10.1080/00779954.2017.1371208.

Teece, D.J., Pisano, G. and Shuen, A. (1997). Dynamic capabilities and strategic management. *Strategic Management Journal*, 18(7), 509–533. Doi.org/10.1002/(SICI)1097-0266(199708)18:7%3C509::AID-SMJ882%3E3.0.CO;2-Z.

Terziovski, M. (2010). Innovation practice and its performance implications in small and medium enterprises (SMEs) in the manufacturing sector: A resource based view. *Strategic Management Journal*, 31(8), 892–902. https://doi.org/10.1002/smj.841

Usman, M., Roijakkers, N., Vanhaverbeke, W. and Frattini, F. (2018). A systematic review of the literature on open innovation in SMEs. In Vanhaverbeke, W., Frattini, F., Roijakkers, N., and Usman, M. (Eds.), *Researching Open Innovation in SMEs*. Ch. 1, pp. 3–35.

Van de Vrande, V., Jong, J.P.J., Vanhaverbeke, W. and Rochemont, M. (2009). Open innovation in SMEs: Trends, motives and management challenges. *Technovation*, 29, 423–437. http://dx.doi.org/10.1016/j.technovation.2008.10.001.

Vanhaverbeke, W. and Frattini, F. (2018). A systematic review of the literature on open innovation in SMEs. *Journal of Engineering and Technology Management*, 31, 43–57. http://dx.doi.org/10.1142/9789813230972_0001.

Vanhaverbeke, W., Roijakkers, N., Lorenz, A. and Chesbrough, H. (2017). The importance of connecting open innovation to strategy. In: Pfeffermann, N., and Gould, J. (Eds.), *Strategy and Communication for Innovation: Integrative Perspectives on Innovation in the Digital Economy*. Cham, Switzerland: Springer International Publishing AG, Ch. 1, pp. 3–16.

Waldner, F., Poetz, M.K., Grimpe, C. and Eurich, M. (2015). Antecedents and consequences of business model innovation: The role of industry structure. In Baden-Fuller, C., and Mangematin, V. (Eds.), *Business Models and Modelling*. Volume 33, *Advances in Strategic Management*. Chapter 12. Emerald Press. http://dx.doi.org/10.1108/s0742-332220150000033013.

Walrave, B., Talmar, M., Podoynitsyna, K.S., Romme, A.G.L. and Verbong, G.P.J. (2018). A multi-level perspective on innovation ecosystems for path-breaking innovation. *Technological Forecasting and Social Change*, 136, 103–113. http://dx.doi.org/10.1016/j.techfore.2017.04.011.

Watson, R., Wilson, H.N., Smart, P. and Macdonald, E.K. (2018). Harnessing difference: A capability-based framework for stakeholder engagement in environmental innovation. *Journal of Product Innovation Management*, 35(2), 254–279. https://doi.org/10.1111/jpim.12394.

Winter, S.G. (2003). Understanding dynamic capabilities. *Strategic Management Journal*, 24, 991–995. https://doi.org/10.1002/smj.318.

Zawislak, P.A., Fracasso, EM. and Tello-Gamarra, J. (2018). Technological intensity and innovation capability in industrial firms. *Innovation & Management Review*, 15(2), 189–207. https://doi.org/10.1108/INMR-04-2018-012.

13

LEADING PUBLIC SECTOR INNOVATION MANAGEMENT

Tony Katsigiannis

Introduction

Innovation is an area of great importance to the private and public sectors. It involves embracing digital, reinventing products and services, and transforming the customer experience. For the private sector, innovation is primarily about sustainable competition and the creation of wealth. In the public sector, innovation has been harnessed to meet unmet needs and achieve efficiencies in service delivery, attempting to do this through similar mechanisms to those in the private sector.

Innovation is the process of making changes, and it can be radical or incremental. The term innovation is often associated with products,[1] but can also occur in a service, process, organization or method.

A considerable amount of innovation research has been conducted since the 1960s, which this chapter draws upon. However, it does not purport to be a systematic overview of innovation. The public sector constitutes the general government sector – largely funded by taxes, fines and regulatory fees – and the public trading enterprise sector, comprising entities largely funded by the sales proceeds of their services.

This chapter examines how the private sector innovates, and compares and contrasts it to the way the public sector innovates, drawing on relevant research. It examines how the public sector can become more innovative by leveraging off learnings in the private sector, and provides frameworks for successful innovation. The chapter is divided into three sections: why innovate? What is innovation? Practical considerations and next steps.

Although there is no one agreed definition of innovation, innovation may be defined broadly as the creation and exploitation of new ideas (Kanter, 1988) or the implementation of new ideas which create some form of value (Kastelle, 2015).

DOI: 10.4324/9780429346033-17

Joseph Schumpeter defined innovation as a process of creative destruction in which new combinations of existing resources are achieved. A related concept is that of the 'entrepreneur', someone with the will and ability to covert a new idea into a successful innovation.

The Nobel Prize-winning economist Edmund Phelps says that the dynamism of an economy is directly related to its willingness and capacity to innovate (Phelps, 2013). This dynamism can be distinguished from Schumpeter's entrepreneurialism or alertness to opportunities.

Although the public sector traditionally has tended to discourage innovation (Borins, 2006), the sector is generally "far more dynamic and innovative than many people think" (Cankar and Petkovsek, 2013, p. 1602). Examples include labour market policies, preventive healthcare, emissions reduction, new digitalized services and organizational reform.

Anecdotally, it would appear that the private sector is more innovative than the public sector. However, in 2016 researchers from Denmark's National Center for Public Sector Innovation found that only 44% of Danish companies were innovative, compared with 80% of public workplaces.[2] The researchers found also that budget limitations was the single most important barrier to public sector innovation, accounting for 36% of cases, while 72% of public sector innovations were inspired by or direct copies of other people's/workplace's solutions (i.e., reuse). While these figures should be treated with some caution, as they are specific to Denmark, they show the importance of further empirical research in this area.

Why innovate?

The systematic practice of innovation is the means by which entrepreneurs create new wealth or endow existing resources with the potential for creating new wealth (Drucker, 2002). The main goal of business is to develop new and innovative products that generate economic growth which, in turn, improves people's lives (Ahlstrom, 2010). This concurs with the ideas of Schumpeter who argued that the development of new combinations of elements by entrepreneurs is the major factor behind long-term economic growth.

The main drivers of innovation in the private sector are increased market share and improvements to performance and efficiency. However, it is generally acknowledged that the magnitude of the challenges facing society – such as climate change, crime, aging societies, unsustainable public finances and global crises – will require innovative solutions (Bekkers et al., 2011). As well, there is a growing demand for more public services at the same time as citizens' expectations of the quality of those services are increasing.

Innovation is the key to sustainable competitive advantage and a major driving force for the economic growth of nations, as it creates new ways of doing things or new products and processes that contribute to wealth (Neely and Hii, 1998). The central process of innovation derives from design, not science (Kline and Rosenberg, 1986).

Innovation did not really take off until the emergence of the world's first modern economies (i.e., modern capitalism) in the 19th century. Phelps (2013) says the main source of innovation in Britain and America from the 1820s to the 1960s was a dynamic form of grassroots innovation[3] – and not scientific advance. Examples from this period include new railways, steel, textiles and other technologies. Furthermore, there was no significant public subsidy for research and development before 1940 (Ridley, 2020).

Initially, innovation was simply the mechanism for creating new goods and services. But in time, it was found that innovating firms could achieve larger market share and higher growth rates and profits (Geroski and Machin, 1992) so it became imperative to continue the process of innovation. Research from the UK indicates that innovative activities enhance business performance because they lead to the firm being more competitive in terms of profits, market share and the penetration of new markets, and they transform a firm's internal capabilities[4] (Neely and Hii, 1998).

How does the public sector compare

Some commentators believe there is a strong history of public sector innovation, notwithstanding the

> widely held assumption that the public sector is inherently less innovative than the private sector. Imputed reasons include a lack of competition and incentives; a culture of risk aversion and bureaucratic conservatism; a workforce which is unresponsive to, and unwilling to change.
>
> *(Mulgan and Albury, 2003, pp. 5–6)*

In Australia, public sector innovations have included the polymer banknote, bionic ear, vaccine for cervical cancer, WiFi, no-fault divorce and anti-discrimination legislation.

In 2003, a UK Cabinet Office discussion paper argued that innovation should be seen as a core activity in the public sector, with the aim of increasing the responsiveness of services to local and individual needs and keeping up with public needs and expectations (Mulgan and Albury, 2003). The private sector's ability to harness technology to improve service provision (e.g. 24/7 banking, retailing and media services), has had the effect of raising people's expectations of Government services. So, too, has the move away from a 'one size fits all' approach to the provision of services and towards a more customized or customer-centric approach.

As the public sector became a large employer and provider of services,[5] it became important to innovate as a means of achieving better services and cost efficiencies. Now that the biggest sectors of the economy are health, education and care, all sectors where government is a major player, public sector innovation has become critical. These sectors need continuous revitalization and innovation if a sustainable competitive economy is to be achieved.

Nevertheless, the barriers to innovation in the public sector are significant, and the introduction of innovations has often failed (Wipulanusat et al., 2016). A recent example of innovation failure in Australia is Robodebt, the automatic debt recovery scheme operated by Centrelink.[6] The way the scheme operated was found to be unlawful by the courts, and the Australian Government was ordered to pay $1.8 billion to 381,000 affected individuals.

What is innovation

The reality

This section explores the definitions and drivers of innovation, and explores how innovation happens.

While there is no single agreed definition of innovation, there are similarities in the way researchers define innovation in the private and public sectors, as can be seen from the following:

While there is no single agreed definition of innovation, the OECD's Oslo Manual defines a business innovation as a "new or improved product or business process (or combination thereof) that differs significantly from the firm's previous products or business processes and that has been introduced on the market or brought into use by the firm" (2018, p. 20). For the first time, the Oslo Manual provides a common framework for measuring innovation across the economy, including in government.

The major point of difference is that private sector innovation is driven by profit maximization, while public sector innovation focusses on maximizing social welfare creation through public investments (Bloch, 2010). A common feature is that both sectors share consumer demand as a driver of service innovation (Arundel at al., 2018).

Rather than define what innovation means, a better approach according to Eggers and Singh (2009), is to define what innovation means in the context of your organization: "Organizations such as Tesco have clearly defined what they mean by innovation. An idea has to meet three criteria to be considered innovative: better for customers, simpler for staff, and less expensive for Tesco" (Eggers and Singh, 2009, p. 131).

The drivers of innovation differ between the two sectors. In the private sector, innovation is seen as the way to achieve increased revenue, profits and shareholder value. The public sector, by comparison, is not subject to competitive pressure to innovate, but is required to achieve efficiencies and effectiveness, and reduce the cost of services.

Typically, innovation in government happens as a response to a crisis, or because an individual champions a particular innovation. In other words, innovation is the result of an unusual occurrence. Innovation in government often falls down during the execution stage (Eggers and Singh, 2009). Furthermore, public sector innovation is problem driven (Windrum, 2008). For example, finding a solution to bottlenecks.

By comparison, many innovations in the private sector are the result of new combinations of existing knowledge, new uses and creativity in product design (Neely and Hii, 1998). While this applies to the public sector as well, a considerable amount of public sector innovation occurs through the process of copying. Researchers from Denmark's National Center for Public Sector Innovation have found that almost three out of four solutions in public sector innovation reused (or adapted) other people's solutions; brand new innovations accounted for only 18% of cases.

In the private sector, entrepreneurs draw on innovation to build new businesses. An entrepreneur is an individual who discovers, recognizes, or creates opportunities and then exploits those opportunities by managing resources and bearing risks (Dodgson and Gann, 2018). The term is also used in the public sector, though does not have the same connotations.[7] More often, the public sector will refer to intrapreneurs who are essentially employees who use their entrepreneurial skills to create and develop new projects or services.

Innovative organizations "undertake experiments, put in place a process for evaluating the results, and, depending on those results, expand, modify, or scrap the innovation" (Borins, 2006, p. 32). Furthermore, successful managers do not innovate through a process of rational planning, but by trial and error (Behn, 1988). Contrast this with the public sector, which requires top down planning, rigid timelines and budgets and which is "highly risk-averse, attempting to avoid errors by avoiding innovation" (Borins, 2006, p. 32).

Mulgan and Albury (2003) propose that some organizations which are consistently innovative (e.g. Unilever and Shell) do not focus on innovation at all. Rather, they focus on outcomes, culture, rewards and methods for ensuring that innovation is pervasive.

The challenges of innovating are great, and most innovations fail (Bowers and Khorakian, 2014; Dodgson and Gann, 2018). But failure is often the inability to see where old knowledge fits into new situations, rather than the result of ignorance/lack of knowledge (Thompson et al., 2000).

Theories and dimensions of innovation

Researchers like to formulate theories to help guide their work. While there is no single theory of innovation, Dodgson and Gann (2018) suggest two useful theories:

- Evolutionary economics puts its faith in entrepreneurs and research groups working together to produce endless varieties of ideas, firms and technologies.
- Dynamic capabilities theory is about "the ways firms search for, select, configure, deploy and learn about innovations" (Dodgson and Gann, 2018, p. 214). Its focus is on skills, processes and structures.

In the context of this chapter, both theories are applicable to the private and public sectors.

Further, Neely and Hii (1998) identify three dimensions of innovation in the private sector:

- Product innovation: a new or improved product, equipment or service.
- Process innovation: a new or improved production or distribution process, or a new method of social service.[8]
- Organizational innovation: changes in management, work organization, and the working conditions and skills of the workforce.

Based on a systematic literature review covering the period 1990–2014, De Vries et al. (2014) have classified four dimensions of innovation in the public sector, two of which mirror those of Neely and Hii (product / process / organizational innovation) and two which are different (governance / conceptual innovation):

- Product or service innovation – the creation of new public services or products. An example is a new passport.
- Process Innovation:
  - Administrative process innovation – creation of new organizational forms, new management techniques and new working methods (such as the one-stop shop).
  - Technological process innovation – creation or use of new technologies to provide services (such as the digital assessment of taxes).
- Governance innovation – new ways of engaging citizens. An example is giving citizens more autonomy when choosing which hospital to go to.
- Conceptual innovation – a new way of looking at problems, challenging current assumptions, or both. An example is looking at someone's ability to work, not his/her disability.

A possible taxonomy of public sector innovation of six categories[9] is suggested by Windrum (2008):

1. Service innovation – a new or improved service. An example is the National Broadband Network which provides high-speed internet access to the public.
2. Service delivery innovation – a new or altered way (or ways) of providing a service. An example is the Australian Government Business website, which provides businesses with information on government services and access to online registration for those services.
3. Administrative or organizational innovation – a new process. An example is the Child Support Scheme, which provides an administrative approach to assessment of child support through a formula, rather than using courts to determine payments.

4. Conceptual innovation – a new way of looking at problems, challenging current assumptions, or both. An example is the National Respite for Carers Program, which provides support for carers.
5. Policy innovation – a change to policy thinking or behavioural intentions. An example is the Higher Education Contribution Scheme (HECS), which improves access to higher education for all students.
6. Systemic innovation – new ways of interacting with other organizations or sources of knowledge. An example is the establishment of Centrelink, which provides government services to the public.
   Another two categories are suggested by Hartley (2005):
7. Governance innovation – new forms of citizen engagement and democratic institutions. For example, area forums and devolved government.
8. Rhetorical innovation – new language and new concepts. For example, the concept of congestion charging for London, or a carbon tax.

All these innovation categories are applicable in the private sector.

The enormity of the problems faced by institutions often exceeds their capacity to tackle them. These complex or "wicked" problems have led both firms and governments to use a systems approach[10] and design thinking[11] to find solutions.

Systemic innovation is more than an additional performance dimension: "It requires systemic change in most aspects of management, training, planning, decision making and the deeper levels of culture, routines and accountability" (Green et al., 2013, p. 45).

Systemic innovation is more than an additional performance dimension. It is a "set of interconnected innovations, where each is dependent on the other, with innovation both in the parts of the system and in the ways that they interact" (Davies et al., 2012, p. 3.)

Systemic innovation requires putting desired outcomes ahead of institutional interests and controls, and designing functions and organizations around users instead of around government (OECD, 2017).

A systems perspective enables a holistic approach to problems that cross organizational boundaries and government levels, and allows new practices to be implemented alongside core processes (OECD, 2017). In the Netherlands, transforming the child protection system required changes to a multiplicity of services and the legal framework.

A systems perspective may, in turn, lead to a partnering approach or an open innovation[12] approach.

Partnering among government agencies, and between government, private industry, universities and non-profits helps individual agencies to: overcome bureaucratic and financial constraints; meet demands for more personalized services; open new channels for service delivery; share ideas and experiences; and mitigate the risks of initiating new programmes. Open innovation, by comparison, involves an open approach to sourcing ideas, problem identification, and innovations that are worth replicating or learning from.

A related concept is that of 'milieux of innovation' (Bekkers and Tummers, 2018). This approach stresses the importance of organizations sharing vital resources (like ideas, knowledge, funds and people) across organizational boundaries.

Types of innovation

From a private sector perspective, innovations can be classified into two types: radical or incremental (Neely and Hii, 1998).

For the public sector, Mulgan and Albury (2003) propose three types of innovations, two of which are similar to the above:

- Radical – new services (e.g. Diagnostic Centres) or new ways of organizing or delivering a service (e.g. online tax returns).
- Incremental – small scale improvements to services or processes (e.g. using ICT to handle school finances).
- Systemic or transformative – new technologies (e.g. printing, electrification, mass production) or changes in mindsets or new policies (e.g. Welfare to Work).

The public sector is usually incremental in its approach to innovation (Green et al., 2013). Many of the examples of radical innovation are driven by Ministers. In the UK, these included the creation of the National Health System in the 1940s, and the privatization of utilities in the 1980s.

A further distinction is between 'top-down' and 'bottom-up' innovation.[13] Half of all innovations in the public sector are not initiated at the top of the organization (Mulgan and Albury, 2003).

In the private sector, it is possible to distinguish between sustaining and disruptive innovations (Christensen et al., 2015):

- Sustaining innovations are product improvements. The improvements are usually incremental advances, but occasionally major breakthroughs. Sustaining innovation targets demanding, high-end customers.
- Disruptive innovation describes a process where a challenger moves into a market from one of two footholds:
  - Low-end footholds

As incumbents are focussed on improving their product and service offerings to their most profitable and demanding customers, they leave the door open to disrupters who will target the incumbents' low-end customers with less expensive and more accessible/convenient products, and then relentlessly move upmarket, eventually displacing the incumbents.

  - New-market footholds

Disrupters create a market where none existed, by turning non-consumers into consumers.

An example of disruptive innovation was Netflix's challenge to Blockbuster video in the late 1990s. Blockbuster dominated the US video rental market through a vast network of physical stores. Netflix introduced DVDs into the market, which they distributed via the postal service. DVDs were lighter and cheaper than their video cassette counterpart.

Government innovation is rarely disruptive, it is typically sustaining (Green et al., 2013). An example of a disruptive innovation in the public sector is replacing prisons with electronic monitoring. Some sustaining innovations are incremental, others are dramatic. However, sustaining innovations have a major shortcoming: they tend to result in price inflation. In the context of the public sector, this means the most common type of innovation drives costs up, not down (Green et al., 2013).

As previously mentioned, many innovations in the private sector are the result of new combinations of existing knowledge, new uses and creativity in design. This has application in the public sector.

Two concepts which are difficult to replicate in the public sector are Schumpeter's heroic, risk taking entrepreneur and the idea (also from Schumpeter) that innovation unleashes creative destruction. Public sector innovation is rarely disruptive, let alone destructive, and it is the rare politician who would propose a risky transformative policy.

However, also attributable to Schumpeter are "formal, organized innovative efforts in large companies" (Dodgson and Gann, 2018, p. 22). This is an eminently viable approach for large public sector organizations to adopt. In fact, a committee of the Australian Government has articulated a set of guiding principles for innovation in the public sector which includes integrating innovation into an agency's strategy and planning (AMAC, 2010).

It is notable that a considerable amount of innovation in the private and public sectors is technology-driven. However, this approach requires the ability to imagine new possibilities, and then to design and implement the necessary changes.

Based upon research conducted in a telecommunications service provider and its partnering organizations, Agarwal and Selen (2009) highlight that innovation in services is different to process or product innovation, or even performance and productivity improvements. The research provides several findings. Firstly, organizational forms of innovation and collaboration are powerful tools for achieving service innovation. Second, the true value creation comes from the customer engagement and co-creation of value. Third, through collaboration and learning by the stakeholders, higher-order dynamic capabilities[14] evolve over time.

By comparison, collaboration, co-creation and learning have also been identified as factors influencing the innovation process in the public sector (Arundel et al., 2018).

Characteristics of innovation

Kanter (1988) outlines four distinctive characteristics of innovation:

1. The innovation process is uncertain
   The process is characterized by unpredictability, delays and cost overruns. Time from invention to financial success is 7–15 years.
2. The innovation process is fragile and knowledge-intensive
   The innovation process relies on a combination of knowledge, creativity and interactive learning. New knowledge is often uncodified and can easily be lost.
3. The innovation process is political
   Potential innovations can pose a threat to vested interests. Innovations compete internally with alternative courses of action.
4. The innovation process is imperialistic (crosses boundaries)
   The innovation is rarely contained within one unit. Many of the best ideas are interdisciplinary or interfunctional. The innovation will influence the behaviour of other units, or require their co-operation.

To summarize Kanter:

> [Innovation] is most likely to flourish where conditions allow flexibility, quick action and intensive care, coalition formation and connectedness. It is most likely to grow in organizations that have integrative structures and cultures emphasizing diversity, multiple structural linkages both inside and outside the organization, intersecting territories, collective pride and faith in people's talents, collaboration and teamwork.
>
> *(Kanter, 1988, p. 95)*

These characteristics are found also in the public sector.

By way of contrast, Drucker (2002) says that most innovations come about due to a conscious, purposeful search for innovation opportunities. They rarely happen by accident. Drucker has a simple formula for innovators to take action, what he calls the systematic practice of innovation (Drucker, 2002):

- Go out and look, ask, and listen.
- Analyse all the opportunity sources – and work out what the innovation has to be to satisfy the opportunity.
- Study potential users – their expectations, values and needs.
- An innovation has to be simple, focussed and do one thing only.
- An effective innovation starts small, but aims at leadership from the beginning.
- Innovation requires not only knowledge, but hard, focussed, purposeful work.

He outlines seven sources of opportunities for innovation, of which four exist within any company or industry, and three are external to the company or industry. They are:

Internal

- Unexpected occurrences: Unexpected successes and failures in business can be productive sources of innovation opportunities. For example, Novocaine, the first synthesized non-addictive narcotic, had been developed for use in major surgical procedures like amputation, but failed to find a market. It was instead taken up by dentists.
- Incongruities: Innovation opportunities may arise out of incongruities, such as a seeming mismatch between a company's expectations and results, or a discrepancy between an industry's assumptions and its realities. An example of the former was the growing market for steel manufacturing in developed countries between 1950 and 1970, which was accompanied by falling profit margins; the response was mini-mills.
- Process needs: Identifying the weak spots in processes, and the ways they can be improved, can be a source of opportunity for innovation. An example is the Linotype which made it possible to produce newspapers quickly and in large volume, by creating one line of type at a time rather than relying on individual letter typesetting.
- Industry and market changes: Industry and market structures can change, sometimes quickly, and such changes can create opportunities for innovation. An example is the deregulation of Australia's rigid and highly centralized labour market arrangements in the 1980s. The response was enterprise agreements and individual contracts.

External

- Demographic changes: The demographic changes in age, education, income and geographic location affect the direction that a business takes, and can provide opportunities for innovation if properly managed. An example is the Japanese investment in robotics in the 1980s, which was designed to take advantage of the decline in blue-collar workers in manufacturing.
- Changes in perception: The way people view products, brands or industries can change, thereby creating opportunities for businesses to develop new products and services that align with the new perspective of the customer. An example: the consolidation of the beer industry since the early 2000s was accompanied by a drop in beer consumption. This seems to have caused, or exacerbated, a change in perception among drinkers of craft beer that saw the rise of micro-breweries.
- New knowledge: Knowledge-based innovations are those which draw on scientific, technical or social knowledge. Innovations of this kind have a long

lead time, and are usually market dependent. An example is De Havilland, while an early innovator in the commercial jet-aircraft industry, failed to maintain its lead due to a lack of adequate analysis of market needs.

The innovator will determine which of the opportunity sources are most relevant within the context of the changing industry or market.

There is no reason why Drucker's systematic practice of innovation cannot also be applied in the public sector.

Research conducted by Borins (2001) into the public sector in the US, Canada and the countries of the Commonwealth concludes that the following characteristics of public sector innovation look like private sector innovation:

* The most frequent characteristic, observed in 60% of cases, encompassed one of three 'holistic' approaches: the innovation depended on inter-organization co-operation, it delivered multiple services to individuals, or it took a systems approach to a problem.
* The three next most frequent responses, observed in 35% of cases involved the following: process re-engineering; the application of information technology; the development of alternative service delivery mechanisms such as contracting to the private sector or partnerships with the voluntary sector.
* The fifth most frequent characteristic, observed in 25% of cases, relates to the empowerment of citizens or staff.

The total is more than 100% as some respondents sometimes gave multiple answers.

Another interesting finding from Borins' research is that a great deal of public sector innovation originates at the front line: approximately 50% of the innovations originate from front-line workers or middle managers. This compares with 25% of innovations originating from agency heads, 20% from politicians, 15% from interest groups, and 10% from individuals outside government. Again, the total is more than 100% as some respondents sometimes gave multiple answers (Borins, 2001).

Factors or dimensions influencing the capacity of organizations to innovate (i.e. innovative capacity)

The concept of innovative capacity refers to the potential of an organization, region or nation to generate innovative outputs. Some of the critical factors influencing the capacity of firms to innovate are summarized below (Kanter, 1988):

* Culture
  * Align innovation with the firm's strategy or direction.
  * Contact with those who have new angles on problems.
  * Diversity of views.

- Multiple sources of information.
- Flat organizational structure.
- Celebrate achievements.[15]
- Make people feel valued and secure.
- Collaborate.
- Maintain open communication.
- Facilitate the free flow of ideas and alternative points of view.
- Keep project teams small and give them sufficient operating autonomy.
- Internal (or managerial) processes
  - Be aware of customers' changing needs.
  - Shake reality into new patterns ('kaleidoscopic thinking').
  - Face outwards as well as inwards.
  - Facilitate an integrative structure: looser boundaries, cross-cutting[16] access, flexible assignments.
  - Have more angles on the problem, more ways to pull in resources.
  - Use multi-disciplinary project teams.
  - Avoid narrow job definitions.
  - Focus on results to be achieved, not rules or procedures to be followed.
  - Measure success or allocate rewards for results rather than adherence to plan.
  - Have slack resources available.[17]
  - Establish special innovation funds.
  - Promote interactive learning.
  - Adopt a flexible approach to deal with unforeseen problems.
  - Assemble a working team to create a prototype or model of the innovation.
  - Review progress against milestones.
- External Environment
  - Be close to customers (users).
  - Manage the boundary.[18]
  - Form networks.
  - Seek creativity at the boundary of disciplines.
  - Facilitate cross-disciplinary exchanges.

Similar conclusions have been reached by other researchers. For example, the Confederation of British Industry and Department of Trade and Industry (1993)[19] identified the following critical factors influencing the capacity of firms to innovate:

- Culture
  - A clear mission and purpose.
  - Well thought out and clearly articulated strategy, which includes innovation.
  - A philosophy of continuous improvement and customer satisfaction.
  - Team based working.

- Empowered employees.
- A commitment to innovation from the top.
- Encouragement of risk-taking and change.
- Flat organizational structure.
- Regular communication with customers, suppliers, investors and employees.
- An open environment.
- Constant feedback from stakeholders.
- Internal (or managerial) processes
  - Capture ideas through employee suggestion schemes.
  - Reward successful ideas.
  - View failure as part of the learning process.
  - Seek ideas from customers and suppliers.
  - Encourage contacts between R&D, design, production, sales and marketing, and customers.
  - Use a screening process to identify key projects.
  - Use multi-functional teams and project champions.
  - Review progress against milestones.
  - Set clear targets.
  - Continuous training and development of staff.
- External environment
  - Strong customer satisfaction.
  - Benchmark performance against competitors.
  - Strong supplier relationships.
  - Active collaboration with academia and other companies
  - Regular dialogue with investors.
  - Partner with the government.

How does the public sector compare

Green et al. (2013) argue that public sector organizations are at the commencement stage of the challenges posed by innovation, and do not have a capacity for innovation. Specifically, most public sector organizations lack the following:

- An explicit innovation strategy and innovation-related goals.
- Resources allocated for innovation.
- User engagement.
- Innovation competency development.
- Innovation leaders and champions.
- A diversity of skill sets and perceptions.
- Empowered staff.
- Processes for encouraging new ideas, developing ideas and experimenting.
- Staff competencies in designing and implementing change.
- The capacity to capture and re-use lessons learnt.

As well, public sector organizations have several features which make them resistant to innovation: a restrictive approach to collaboration with the private sector: few incentives for change; a tradition of secrecy; an intolerance of risk taking and mistakes; top down communication and decision making; and entrenched hierarchies.

In their literature review covering the period from 1980 to 2017, Moussa et al. (2018) have highlighted the following shortcomings of the public sector in respect of innovation:

- Effective ideas are frequently blocked or forgotten.
- Public services are ineffective at learning from better models.
- Lack of investment models for innovation in organizations.
- Lack of resources.
- Inadequate reward and incentive systems.
- Lack of mature risk management strategies.
- Lack of methods for experimentation.

So what needs to be done?

Based on research from both the private and public sectors, Borins (2006) provides a number of suggestions:

- Get support from the top.
- Reward innovative individuals.
- Provide resources, including funds.
- Ensure diversity of backgrounds and ways of thinking.
- Seek out information from the outside, for example, by benchmarking, making site visits, and participating in professional networks.
- Draw ideas from people at all levels.
- Experiment and evaluate.
- Windrum (2008) cites five important factors which determine how innovation occurs in a public sector organization, and whether innovation is successful:
- The nature of the incentive structures and support mechanisms to promote creativity and disseminate innovation.
- The presence of individuals who want to challenge the status quo (i.e., entrepreneurs).[20]
- The mix of top-down (politicians) and bottom-up (public sector managers and service personnel) innovation.
- The impact of the New Public Management. This refers to public sector reforms such as the use of performance targets for customer satisfaction, efficiency and expenditure. These reforms favour innovations that support the decentralization, privatization and contracting out of services, and promotes competition between public providers and private firms/not-for-profit organizations.

- The implications of consumerism (i.e., the implications of looking through the lens of informed and empowered consumers of services).

Based upon surveys of government initiatives and interviews with public sector innovators, Sahni et al. (2013) suggests the following "framework" of five conditions which are conducive to innovation in public organizations:

- Create opportunities for experimentation.[21]
- Sunset outdated technology and business models.
- Introduce feedback loops[22] for product or service improvements.
- Provide incentives[23] for employees to make improvements.
- Work around budget constraints.

It has been argued by Demircioglu and Audretsch (2017) that the second condition – "sunset outdated technology and business models" – should be replaced with "responding to low performers", as both concepts refer to similar actions, i.e., the elimination/improvement of poor job practices and performances and the elimination/improvement of poor performers.

The use of feedback loops, as proposed by Sahini et al. (2013), is fundamental to the operation of Citizens Connect, a community hotline in Boston which operates by way of a mobile app. Citizens Connect not only allows people to report problems (such as potholes or graffiti) but provides feedback showing whether the city responded to the problem and fixed it.

According to De Vries et al. (2014) the factors influencing innovation capacity in the public sector include: a learning culture; political mandates; availability of organizational slack; isomorphism or looking alike;[24] innovative leaders; creative entrepreneurs; empowered employees; job-related knowledge and skills; and individual autonomy.

Many of these elements can be created within, or imported from outside, the relevant agency by enlightened leaders.

A recent trend is that citizens are demanding more user-centric services, and services designed and often delivered in collaboration with citizens and community sector partners (Wipulanusat et al., 2016).

A literature review by Moussa et al. (2018) covering the period from 1980 to 2017 found:

- There is some evidence that participative and empowering styles of leadership are positively related to innovation.
- A high level of managerial autonomy can develop a more innovation-oriented culture.
- Support for creativity contributes to an innovative climate.
- Innovators often succeed in less dominant structures and systems.

By drawing on published surveys of innovation in the public sector, Arundel et al. (2018) have identified the key factors that influence the innovation process in the public sector:

- Be open to experimentation.
- Have tools to encourage creativity and learning.
- Offer incentives and rewards to encourage new ideas.
- Provide training in innovation.
- Collaborate.
- Implement strategies for managing risk and failure.
- Adopt design thinking and co-creation.[25]
- Set objectives for innovation; monitor and measure the outcomes.

Finally, McGuiness and Slaughter (2019) argue that the way public problems are solved – in other words, the policy-making[26] process – is arduous, time consuming and made for another era. This has the effect of encouraging activists, non-government organizations and social entrepreneurs to bypass the policy making process and experiment with direct-service solutions that address public needs. The factors influencing this work are as follows:

- Put people at the centre of policies and engage them in real time about their needs (human-centred or user-centred design).
- Experiment – start small and scout for local solutions.
- Use data to assess problems, monitor progress, and make improvements.
- Design to scale.

Examples of this approach include:

- In the US, the community-based "Built for Zero" created a list of homeless people in the community as the first step towards servicing their needs. Stakeholders use this list to co-ordinate the work of many agencies and not-for-profits.
- In Germany, the "Stiftung Neue Verantwortung", a not-for-profit organization specializing in public policy relating to technology's effect on society, tests different policy options with affected stakeholders.

Models and frameworks

Models of innovation help explain how individuals and organizations innovate. Rothwell (1994) provides five models on how the innovation process works in the private sector:

1. Technology-push model (1950s to mid-1960s): new products are developed through R&D, and involve a linear and sequential process of design of new products, manufacturing and sales. This model is simplistic and lacks customer feedback.

2. Market pull model (late 1960s to early 1970s): market/customer needs drive the innovation process, with an emphasis on marketing as a strategy.
3. Coupling model (mid 1970s to early 1980s): this model couples technological innovation with market needs (i.e., technology push and market pull). The process is sequential, but feedback is non-linear.
4. Integrated model (mid 1980s to 1990s): takes a parallel approach in respect of development, manufacture, marketing, communication, suppliers and customers. It involves a high level of functional integration and parallel activities across functions. This model is complex, non-sequential and requires feedback.
5. Systems integration and networking model: enables integration of the various functions within a firm, while connecting the firm to the outside world (i.e., external networks).

It is the last model – systems integration and networking – that has raised considerable interest in the public sector, and was covered in the section above of this chapter.

Other models from the private sector include:

- Business model innovation: occurs by making changes to an organization's value proposition to customers and to its underlying operating model.
- Brokerage models: innovation occurs by recombining past knowledge, practices and people in new ways.

Both approaches involve a process of reframing. In the case of business model innovation, a new firm may challenge long-held core beliefs about how to create value in an industry (De Jong and Van Dijk, 2015). For example, Uber's ride-hailing service disrupted the taxicab licence franchise model.

It is possible to use the business model approach to innovation to create an improved public service. For example, the NSW Government franchised the operation of Sydney Ferries to the private sector, with a requirement that the operator improve the customer experience.

The brokerage model involves brokers dis-assembling and re-assembling (or disentangling and recombining) past experiences, in order to understand and respond to new situations (Hargadon, 2014). For example, in response to Nike's new Air athletic shoe technology, Reebok produced the Reebok Pump shoe incorporating elements from medical and diagnostic equipment.

An important innovation framework is Kanter's four innovation tasks (Kanter, 1988). These four tasks sometimes occur in sequence, sometimes overlap:

1. Idea generation
   Innovators initiate a process of departing from the organization's established routines or systems. An awareness of changing user needs is beneficial in activating solutions.

2. Coalition building
   The innovator engages in political activity in order to build support for the innovation and create the conditions necessary for it to thrive. This may require access to data, technical knowledge, political intelligence, expertise, funds, materials, space, time, endorsement, backing, approval and legitimacy.
3. Idea realization and innovation production
   This involves assembling a team[27] to create a prototype or model that can be touched or experienced. Kanter suggests the team should have "procedural autonomy coupled with multiple milestones that must be reached in order for the project to continue" (Kanter, 1988, p. 119).
4. Transfer or diffusion
   The final stage is the transfer or diffusion[28] of the innovation to those who will exploit or embed it in ongoing organizational practice. Effective transfer may require an alignment with strategy or a strategic decision to allocate resources, which, in turn, requires a top management link to the innovation project. Agents of diffusion can include product managers and transition teams.

This framework mirrors similar frameworks in use in the public sector. For example:

- The four-cycle innovation framework is a simple approach to understanding how innovation may be fostered in the public sector (Mulgan and Albury, 2003):
  1. Generating possibilities: Identify new needs and alternative possibilities.
  2. Incubating and prototyping: Test and develop promising ideas while managing the risks of innovation.
  3. Replicating and scaling up: Use formal evaluations, qualitative assessments, assessments of organizational capacity, and political viability to select a small proportion of ideas and pilots to replicate.
  4. Analysing and learning: Evaluate what works and what doesn't in order to promote continuous learning and improvement.
- This is similar to the four-phase innovation cycle (Eggers and Singh, 2009):
  5. Idea generation and discovery.
  6. Idea selection.
  7. Idea implementation (or idea conversion).
  8. Idea diffusion.

There are similarities between the above two examples and also differences. However, taken together, they are very similar to Kanter's four innovation tasks, the private sector framework presented above. Kanter's framework has the added benefit of "coalition building" as a task, a clear omission from the above two frameworks. Coalition building is very important, and involves political activity to build support for the innovation and create the conditions necessary for it to thrive.

The Australian National Audit Office (ANAO, 2009) proposes a four phase innovation process model for managing innovation in the public sector: develop options and solutions; implement; check and evaluate; adjust and disseminate.

The Australian Management Advisory Committee (AMAC, 2010) has adapted the Eggers and Singh model, and added a fifth step in the process, calling it sustaining ideas, as shown in Figure 13.1. This recognizes that, in the absence of profit as a dominant driver of innovation, the public sector may require specific assistance and effort to embed innovation activity.

Borins (2006) proposes the five building blocks of innovation:

1. Adopt a systems approach[29] (i.e., a systems approach assumes everything is inter-related and interdependent).
2. Use information technology.
3. Process improvement.
4. Involve the private or voluntary sectors.
5. Empower communities, citizens or staff.

There are also the five strategies of innovation (Eggers and Singh, 2009):
1. Cultivate: Engage employees at all levels to generate ideas.
   How: Tap into the tacit knowledge of employees. Use prediction markets and collaboration tools. Build safe havens to permit low risk experimentation.
2. Replicate: Borrow and adapt an existing innovation to a new context.
   How: Discover and track innovations and best practice. Build relationships, networks and communities of practice.

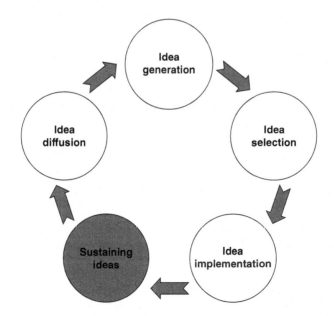

FIGURE 13.1 Five-step innovation process adopted from the Eggers and Singh model.

3. Partner: Partner with government agencies and with government, private industry, universities and non-for-profits.

   How: Work with public or private partners. Obtain resources and new skills from partners.

4. Network: Establish informal global networks to discover, develop and implement ideas in and out of organizational boundaries.

   How: Co-create solutions with suppliers. Engage citizens in developing innovations.

5. Open source: Collaborate with people from diverse disciplines to create free solutions.

   How: Develop an infrastructure that supports the open source model and build a community of developers (collaborators). Promote flexibility and open knowledge sharing.

Practical considerations and next steps

This chapter has considered the similarities and differences between private and public sector innovation. Innovation in the private sector is driven by competitive pressure; one could say innovation defines success. The public sector, on the other hand, has no competitive pressure to innovate, and innovation is often undertaken on an ad hoc basis, for example, in response to a new policy or demand for a new or improved service (Arundel et al., 2018).

Many of the success factors for private sector innovation are capable of being replicated in the public sector in part or full. Factors such as: openness to ideas; the presence of champions for innovation; teamwork; engagement of stakeholders; organizational learning; and recognition and support.

Of course, simply taking tools from the private sector, and transplanting them into the public sector is problematic, due to differences in the objectives, culture, structure and processes of the two sectors.

As well, most organizations are better at executing than at adapting to the future, and few do both well (Beinhocker, 2006). Adaptation requires a new approach, one that overcomes the barriers imposed by rigid mental models, hierarchies and fixed ways of doing things (path dependence). Innovation offers the new approach.

However, Green et al. (2013) argue that – unlike in the private sector where there is an array of competencies that support innovation – most public sector organizations do not have the capacity to innovate. They have not developed the management and staff competencies in designing and implementing change. In fact, the culture, management style, incentive structures and other features of the public sector make it hostile to innovation.

At the same time, the impetus for innovation in the public sector remains great. Wicked problems remain intractable. The community is demanding better, cheaper and more user-centric services; but also services designed and delivered in collaboration with citizens and community sector partners (Bowden, 2005).

What is required is a shift in how the public sector creates solutions. The following approach is proposed by Bason (2010):

- Move from random innovation to a conscious and systematic approach.
- Build innovation capacity.
- Create new approaches where solutions are designed with people, not for them (i.e., co-creation, co-design).
- Shift the focus away from administering public organizations and towards leading innovation across the public sector.

Fortunately new forms of creativity and participation (crowd sourcing, user-driver innovation etc.) are available; and we live in an increasingly experimental society where learning by doing and improvisation methods is becoming the new norm (Crossan & Sorrenti, 1997).

Political and public sector leaders can play a critical role in encouraging innovation. This ranges from allocating funds for projects through to driving the change in strategies, resource allocation, decision making and incentive structures required to facilitate innovation approaches at the organizational or sector level. Other important leadership activities include: promoting creativity and independent thinking; opening spaces for experiment and learning; creating a culture that embraces calculated risk-taking; celebrating the role of innovation champions and intrapreneurs; managing the tensions between competing objectives; accepting there will sometimes be failures; and managing the consequences of failure.

Innovation practitioners can take action to encourage innovation in the public sector by drawing on the practical considerations across nine dimensions (Values, Strategy, Resources, Create processes, Structures, Funding, Incentives and rewards, Learning, and Stakeholder, customers and citizens) adapted from Serrat (2018) and Green et al. (2013).

Values
- Be open to new ideas and new ways of doing things.
- Support experimentation and calculated risk taking.
- Give permission to employees to question and challenge.

Strategy
- Develop an innovation strategy.
- Support experimentation.
- Understand customer and citizen needs and views and integrate them into organizational plans.

Resources
- Identify priorities for innovation.
- Set up dedicated teams and networks responsible for innovation.
- Engage people who think creatively and see new patterns.

- Provide safe spaces for dissenting opinions and outsider perspectives.
- Push and pull to create pressure for innovation.
- Tap new technology.
- Manage knowledge flows to facilitate creative thought.
- Identify what is working, promising or emerging.
- Implement management and human resource strategies to support the transition to greater innovativeness – through engaging, developing, motivating and rewarding staff.
- Collaborate to create and spread innovations.

Create processes
- Conduct an internal audit to identify the barriers to innovation, opportunities for innovation and capacity development needs.
- Develop explicit processes for capturing and assessing ideas for innovation, both from internal and external sources.
- Develop processes for identifying and understanding problems and opportunities, assessing alternative ideas and testing prototypes.
- Use approaches that support re-framing of problems.
- Embrace insights from frontline staff, suppliers, outsiders and end users.
- In-source ideas from idea scouts, network partners, open networks, knowledge-brokers and prediction markets.
- Improve knowledge brokering of ideas from generation to selection, implementation and diffusion.
- Make innovation a job prerequisite and define jobs around it.
- Provide time to think.
- Open up the space for ideas and draw these from people at all levels.
- Develop approaches for trying things out, including incubators, laboratories, pathfinders, pilots and skunk works.
- Conduct innovation experiments, initially at a relatively low level of risk.
- Tinker with prototypes and pilots.
- Evaluate experiments.
- Collaborate with outsiders to help solve problems.
- Seek information from the outside, for example, by benchmarking, making site visits, and participating in professional networks.
- Shape inducements for adoption, scaling and diffusion by teams and networks.
- Strike an appropriate balance between risk and opportunity.
- Stimulate and support innovation by suppliers of products and services.
- Develop a framework for assessing progress with innovation performance and strengthening innovation capability.

Structures
- Reduce organizational hierarchies
- Give business units more autonomy.

Funding
- Divert a small proportion of the budget for generating, selecting, implementing and diffusing innovation, including training.
- Fund for outcomes achieved, not rules adhered to.
- Draw on private, venture or philanthropic investment to help trial new approaches.
- Link funding to carefully defined outcomes.
- Invest in incubating new ideas and in scaling the best ones.

Incentives and rewards
- Provide incentives to develop innovations.
- Recognise and reward staff for good ideas or systems design.

Learning
- Support continuous improvement and learning.
- Dynamic capability building through collaboration.
- Acquire change management skills.
- Build systems for capturing and sharing learning.

Stakeholder, customers and citizens
- Build and actively manage relationships with external stakeholders in order to: obtain feedback on performance; identify problems or opportunities for innovation; obtain ideas for innovation; and partner with stakeholders in developing or implementing innovations.
- Collaborate with citizens and community sector partners in planning designing, producing, delivering and evaluating services.
- Create feedback loops.

Some suggested further areas of research include the following: case studies of the failure of innovations to fulfil expectations of higher efficiency and better service; hard data on the value of service innovations to citizens; the impact of innovation at the individual, organizational and societal levels; the cross-national impact of innovations; linkages between structural organizational characteristics and organizational antecedents such as leadership; and why certain types of innovations succeed in one context but fail in another.

Notes

1 A product is sometimes defined as a good or service, and some products can have characteristics of both goods and services.
2 Lykkebo, O.B., Præstbro, M. (2019), *Eight myths about public sector innovation – debunked.* The Centre has confirmed there has been very little change in the statistics since the article appeared.
3 'Grassroots innovation' means that the conception, development and spread of new methods or goods stemmed from the ground up. The dynamism of this form of

innovation derived from a new set of *values* – creativity, exploration and personal growth.

4 Neely and Hii, p 5: … "the effect of innovation is to transform a firm's inner capabilities, making it more adaptive, better able to learn, to exploit new ideas".

5 In Australia total government expenditure as a proportion of GDP in 2018 was 38.6% (OECD).

6 Centrelink provides government services to the Australian public.

7 There is a view that public servants can develop an 'entrepreneurial mindset' and exhibit entrepreneurial behaviours. See Iliashenko (2020)

8 Product and process innovations are not mutually exclusive; one may lead to the other.

9 Windrum says the first three categories have been examined in studies of private sector innovation. The other three have been added by Windrum as a result of research he presents.

10 Complex problems are frequently referred to as "wicked" because it is difficult to assess the true nature of the problems and how to manage them. Some governments have started to view complex or "wicked" problems as *complex systems* whose solution requires a *systemic approach*, working across organizational boundaries and government levels, with multiple actors and interventions, in a holistic manner (OECD, 2017).

11 Design thinking uses the designer's creativity and tools to match people's needs with what is technologically feasible.

12 An open innovation approach is one that promotes collaboration with people and organizations external to the organization.

13 This refers to the source of the innovation, whether it is high up in the organizational hierarchy or lower down.

14 Dynamic capabilities can be defined as routines within an organization. Higher-order dynamic capabilities relate to customer engagement, collaborative agility, entrepreneurial alertness and collaborative innovation.

15 Kanter calls this a "culture of pride".

16 "Cross cutting" means cutting across formal lines and levels in the organization.

17 These resources may include people who float freely without a "home" or who lack defined tasks.

18 Sentries control the transactions that occur at the boundaries, deciding how much can come in; guards control how much goes out of the group.

19 This is based on a study of companies carried out by the Confederation of British Industry (CBI) and Department of Trade and Industry (DTI) (1993). The assessment of the companies was based on structured interviews. Chief executives and senior managers of 76 UK companies across different sectors, sizes and types of company were interviewed. Manufacturing to services ratio was 3:1.

20 It needs to be remembered that public sector organizations are risk averse and the word 'entrepreneurs' does not have the same significance as in the private sector. However, in this context, entrepreneurs may include politicians who wish to challenge the status quo.

21 Experiments should be validated with data.

22 The feedback loops operate between citizens and public servants.

23 Incentives include increased revenue, reduced costs, prestige, etc.

24 This covers copying, conformity and mimicking.

25 Co-creation is the contribution of time and effort to the creation of public services by service users and citizens.

26 A policy is a service or course of action operating within a legislative framework which responds to a perceived need or societal problem or ministerial pledge.

27 These teams sometimes operate in special settings called 'skunkworks' where they can create new things without distractions.

28 The innovation is diffused throughout the organization and to affected stakeholders.

29 Karen Manley (2002) – "The *systems* perspective recognises that innovation is a collective undertaking where innovating organizations interact with others in particular institutional settings" (p. 96). The focus is on knowledge, relationships and learning, in the context of collaborations with external parties.

References

Agarwal, R. and Selen, W. (2009), Dynamic capability building in service value networks for achieving service innovation. *Decision Sciences, 40*(3), 421–475.

Ahlstrom, D. (2010), Innovation and growth: How business contributes to society. *Academy of Management Perspectives, 24*(3), 11–24.

AMAC (Australian Management Advisory Committee). (2010), *Empowering Change: Fostering Innovation in the Australian Public Service*. Canberra: Australian Government.

ANAO (Australian National Audit Office). (2009), *Innovation in the Public Sector: Enabling Better Performance, Driving New Directions. Better Practice Guide*. Canberra: Australian National Audit Office.

Arundel, A., Bloch, C. and Ferguson, B. (2018), Advancing innovation in the public sector: Aligning innovation measurement with policy goals. *Research Policy, 48*, 789–798.

Bason, C. (2010), *Leading Public Sector Innovation: Co-Creating for a Better Society*. The Policy Press, UK.

Behn, R. D. (1988), Managing by groping along. *Journal of Policy Analysis and Management, 7*(4), 643–663.

Beinhocker, E. (2006), The adaptable organization. *McKinsey Quarterly No 2*.

Bekkers, V., Edelenbos, J. and Steijn, B. (2011), *Innovation in the Public Sector*. Palgrave Macmillan, New York.

Bekkers, V. and Tummers, L. (2018), Innovation in the public sector: Towards an open and collaborative approach. *International Review of Administrative Sciences, 84*(2), 209–213.

Bloch, C. (2010), Towards a conceptual framework for measuring public sector innovation. Nordic project. *Measuring Innovation in the Public Sector in the Nordic Countries: Toward a Common Statistical Approach ("Copenhagen Manual")*.

Borins, S. (2001), Encouraging innovation in the public sector. *Journal of Intellectual Capital, 2*(3), 310–319. MCB University Press.

Borins, S. (2006), *The Challenge of Innovating in Government* (second edition). Arlington, VA: IBM Centre for the Business of Government.

Bowden, A. (2005), Knowledge for free? Distributed innovation as a source of learning. *Public Policy and Administration, 20*(3), 56–58.

Bowers, J. and Khorakian, A. (2014), Integrating risk management in the innovation project. *European Journal of Innovation Management, 17*(1), 25–40.

Cankar, S. S. and Petkovsek, V. (2013), Private and Public Sector Innovation and the Importance of Cross-Sector Collaboration. *Journal of Applied Business Research, 29*(6), 1597–1605.

Christensen, C. M., Raynor, M. and McDonald, R. (2015), What is disruptive Innovation? *Harvard Business Review, 93*(12), 44–53.

Confederation of British Industry and Department of Trade and Industry. (1993), *Innovation: The Best Practise*. CBI/DTI.

Crossan, M. and Sorrenti, M. (1997), Making sense of improvisation. *Advanced Strategic Management, 14*, 155–180.

Davies, A., Mulgan G., Norman, W., Pulford, L., Patrick, R. and Simon, J. (2012), *Systemic Innovation*. Social Innovation Europe.

De Jong, M. and Van Dijk, M. (2015), Disrupting beliefs: A new approach to business model innovation. *McKinsey Quarterly July.*

De Vries, H. A., Bekkers, V. J. J. M. and Tummers, L. G. (2014), Innovations in the public sector: A systematic review and future research agenda. *Ottawa: IRSPM Conference. Public Administration, 2016.*

Demircioglu, M. A. and Audretsch, D. B. (2017), Conditions for innovation in public sector organizations. *Research Policy,* 46(9), 1681–1691.

Dodgson, M. and Gann, D. (2018), *Innovation: A Very Short Introduction.* Oxford University Press, Oxford.

Drucker, P. F. (2002), The discipline of innovation. *Harvard Business Review, August 2002,* Harvard Business School Publishing Corporation.

Eggers, W. D. and Singh, S. K. (2009), *The Public Innovator's Playbook: Nurturing Bold Ideas in Government.* Deloitte and the Ash Institute for Democratic Governance and Innovation.

Geroski, P. A. and Machin, S. (1992), Do innovating firms outperform non-innovators? *Business Strategy Review,* 3(2), 79–90.

Green, R., Roos, G., Agarwal, R. and Scott-Kemmis, D. (2013), *Australian Public Sector Innovation: Actively Shaping the Future Through Co-Creation.* Institute of Public Administration Australia.

Hargadon, A. (2014), *Brokerage and Innovation.* The Oxford Handbook of Innovation Management, Oxford University Press.

Hartley, J. (2005), Innovation in governance and public services: Past and present. *Public Money & Management,* 25(1), 27–34.

Iliashenko, I. (2020). The entrepreneurial mindset adjustment as a tool to foster innovations in public sector organizations. *Economia Aziendale Online,* 11(2), 145–164.

Kanter, R. M. (1988), When a thousand flowers bloom: Structural, collective, and social conditions for innovation in organizations. *Research in Organizational Behavior,* 10, 169–211.

Kastelle, T. (2015), How does innovation work in the public sector? *Australian Journal of Public Administration,* 74(1), 68–71.

Kline, S. and Rosenberg, N. (1986), An overview of innovation. In: *The Positive Sum Strategy: Harnessing Technology for Economic Growth.* National Academies Press, Washington, DC.

Lykkebo, O. B. and Præstbro, M. (2019), *Eight Myths about Public Sector Innovation— Debunked.* Opinion piece written by Ole Bech Lykkebo and Majken Præstbro from Denmark's National Centre for Public Sector Innovation for *apolitical.*

Manley, K. (2002), The systems approach to innovation studies. *Australasian Journal of Information Systems,* 9(2), 94–102.

McGuiness, T. and Slaughter, A.-M. (2019), The new practice of public problem solving. *Stanford Social Innovation Review, Spring 2019.*

Moussa, M., McMurray, A. and Muenjohn, N. (2018), Innovation in public sector organizations. *Journal of Cogent Business & Management,* 5(1) 1475047.

Mulgan, G. and Albury, D. (2003), *Innovation in the Public Sector.* UK Government, London.

Neely, A. and Hii, J. (1998), *Innovation and Business Performance: A Literature Review.* The Judge Institute of Management Studies, Cambridge University, 1998. Report Commissioned by the Government Office for the Eastern Region (GO-ER).

OECD. (2017), *Systems Approaches to Public Sector Challenges: Working with Change.* OECD Publishing, Paris.

Phelps, E. (2013), *Mass Flourishing – How Grassroots Innovation Created Jobs, Challenge and Change.* Princeton University Press. (Edmund Phelps was the 2006 Nobel Laureate in Economics.)

Ridley, M. (2020), *How Innovation Works.* 4th Estate, London.

Rothwell, R. (1994), Industrial innovation: Success, strategy, trends. In: Dodgson, M. and Rothwell, R. (eds.), *The Handbook of Industrial Innovation.* Edward Elgar Publishing, Hants.

Sahni, N. R., Wessel, M. and Christensen C. M. (2013), Unleashing breakthrough innovation in government. *Stanford Social Innovation Review, Summer 2013.*

Serrat, O. (2018), *Knowledge Solutions: Tools, Methods, and Approaches to Drive Organizational Performance.* Asian Development Bank and Springer Open.

Thompson, L., Gentner, D. and Loewenstein, J. (2000), Avoiding missed opportunities in managerial life: Analogical training more powerful than case-based training. *Organizational Behaviour and Human Decision Processes, 82,* 60–75.

Windrum, P. (2008), Innovation and entrepreneurship in public services. In: Windrum, P. and Koch, P. (eds.), *Innovation in Public Sector Services: Entrepreneurship, Creativity and Management.* Edward Elgar Publishing Limited, Cheltenham, 3–20.

Wipulanusat, W., Panuwatwanich, K. and Stewart R. A. (2016), Innovation in the Australian public service: A qualitative analysis. 40th Annual Conference of the Australia New Zealand Regional Science Association International, 5-7 December 2016, Melbourne, Australia, Australia New Zealand Regional Science Association International.

PART 5

New standards for managing innovation effectively

The final part for the Handbook encompasses Future Agendas in innovation management. This part is all about accepting a dynamic environment where innovation needs to occur in volatile, uncertain, complex and ambiguous conditions, and from the real people at the coalface.

This part begins with looking at effectuation in innovation management. In "Effectuation: A decision logic for innovation in dynamic environments", Killen explores into effectuation, a decision logic first observed in entrepreneurship, to present a 'new way of thinking' to support innovation management. By using effectuation, organisations may benefit by developing awareness among managers and using their abilities to apply it effectively.

Yang in "Benefiting from innovation – Playing the appropriability cards" shows how innovation can benefit in different ways. Using appropriability literature, Yang presents a framework addressing the three paths (exclusion of others, leveraging the appropriability premises, and abandoning of protection) and suggests how it can help innovators adjust their appropriability portfolios and align the appropriability premises with the ways in which they are utilised.

In "Frugal innovation: A structured literature review of antecedents, enablers, implications and directions for future research" Jaiswal et al., looks at frugal innovation literature to understand the concept and identify the knowledge gaps in the current literature for future research directions in frugal innovation. Their literature review concludes by presenting a conceptual framework for frugal innovation.

In "Dynamic capabilities and innovation" Ahmadi and Arndt provide an overview of the relationships between the four areas of dynamic capabilities and seek to provide some ideas for future research.

DOI: 10.4324/9780429346033-18

As the last chapter of the Handbook, we look at innovation in volatile, uncertain, complex and ambiguous (VUCA) environment. Patterson et al. in "Innovation in a volatile, uncertain, complex and ambiguous world with dynamic capabilities" uses a case-based approach to understand the innovation under volatile, uncertain, complex and ambiguous (VUCA) conditions. The study explores how organisations can use innovation management as a dynamic capability to help them create sustained value during times of disruption.

14

EFFECTUATION

A decision logic for innovation in dynamic environments

Catherine Killen

Introduction

Managing innovation in the face of relentless change is further complicated by the diversity of types of change and the increasing pace of change. Traditional innovation management approaches are not designed for such highly dynamic environments and can inhibit innovation in such contexts. A succession of new approaches has been introduced to support innovation that is faster, more responsive, and adaptable. Agile project management, design thinking, and lean startup methods are some of these contemporary approaches for managing innovation. While new ways of thinking are important for supporting these increasingly agile and responsive ways of working (Cicmil, Williams, Thomas, & Hodgson, 2006; Conforto, Salum, Amaral, Da Silva, & De Almeida, 2014), research is only just starting to identify types of thinking that will best support innovation (Sauer & Reich, 2009; Svejvig & Andersen, 2015). The 'rational' or 'causative' mindset that underpins traditional innovation approaches may not be relevant during times of rapid change.

This chapter overviews the latest research on a relatively new concept, 'effectuation', highlighting its potential as an alternate mindset to better support innovation management in dynamic and uncertain times. Effectuation is a decision logic identified by Saras Sarasvathy in studies of entrepreneurship (2001, 2008). Effectuation is positioned as a contrasting type of decision logic from 'causation', the rational type of thinking that underpins many innovation processes and decision frameworks. A primary differentiating principle of effectuation is the focus on using available resources to generate innovation ideas, rather than developing ideas and setting goals and only later considering resourcing to meet those goals. Other effectuation principles promote considering the level of loss that is 'affordable' when pursuing risky projects, emphasising partnerships and networks over competitive analyses, and encouraging the proactive identification of contingency

DOI: 10.4324/9780429346033-19

options to enable adaptability to changing circumstances (Sarasvathy, 2001). In contrast, causation logic advocates thorough up-front planning to avoid failure and meet pre-defined goals.

A growing stream of literature on effectuation highlights its relevance in a range of disciplines. While effectuation has been studied most often in entrepreneurship and could be seen to be a quality of entrepreneurs, increasing evidence indicates that effectual logic plays a role in innovation management environments, including project management and new product and service development (see, for example, Berends, Jelinek, Reymen, & Stultiëns, 2014; Brettel, Mauer, Engelen, & Küpper, 2012; Nguyen, Killen, Kock, & Gemuenden, 2018; Read, Song, & Smit, 2009; Wiltbank, Read, Dew, & Sarasvathy, 2009; Wiltbank & Sarasvathy, 2010).

Managing innovation involves a degree of risk and uncertainty; the ability to create value from something new is never assured. However, there are differing degrees and types of innovation, and each requires innovation management approaches tailored to the context. Many organisational innovation efforts are devoted to relatively low-risk incremental innovations that employ tried-and-tested methods and offer a good chance of modest success. These incremental innovations are often successfully managed through 'phase-gate' processes that guide an innovation project through multiple phases from idea to launch and ensure that criteria are satisfied along the way.

However, to establish innovation leadership and obtain long-term competitive advantages, organisations need to develop innovations that involve high levels of change. These radical or breakthrough innovations entail higher levels of risk and uncertainty than incremental innovation. The traditional approaches that provide benefits for incremental innovation in fairly stable innovation environments can actually hinder the development of radical innovations in more dynamic environments by slowing the innovation process and applying outdated criteria that block relevant and promising new ideas. The resulting 'incrementalism' prevents organisations from making the larger innovative leaps that are required for sustainable success.

Contemporary innovation approaches aim to address the downsides from traditional, causation-based innovation management methods; however, these approaches require organisations to think differently. Promoting awareness of alternative ways of thinking, such as effectuation, may assist organisations meet the challenge of innovation in dynamic and uncertain times; in fact, studies are starting to emerge that demonstrate how effectuation has played a role in organisational responses to the COVID-19 pandemic.

This chapter outlines the impact of Sarasvathy's (2001) identification of 'effectuation' as an alternate decision logic on contemporary innovation management. An overview of the origins and definitions of effectuation is followed by a summary of the research relating effectuation to innovation management. Emphasis is placed on the findings about the role of effectuation in several prominent innovation management themes, including strategy and dynamic capabilities, ambidexterity, and agile methodologies. Implications for practice include promoting awareness of effectuation as an alternate decision logic, identifying contexts where effectuation logic may support innovation, and providing guidance on applying effectual thinking in contemporary innovation practices. The chapter concludes with recommendations for future research to strengthen the understanding and provide further insights on whether and how effectuation can enhance innovation outcomes.

What is effectuation?

The origins of effectuation lie in the field of entrepreneurship. Effectuation is best described as a 'decision logic' – defined by a set of principles that were first observed in entrepreneurial decision-making (Sarasvathy, 2001). Sarasvathy refers to effectuation as a "comprehensive alternate frame" (2008, p. 23) that is "the inverse of causation" (2008, p. 16). Causation is the decision logic underpinned by rational assumptions about cause and effect. Causation is characterised by goal-setting and up-front planning before identifying and deploying resources; many traditional innovation approaches designed to reduce risk and gain predictability are built upon the logic of causation. In contrast, approaches using effectuation logic "take a set of means as given and focus on selecting between possible effects that can be created with that set of means" (Sarasvathy, 2001, p. 245). An approach guided by effectuation draws inspiration from the resources currently available and accepts that risk is a part of creating something new. Instead of trying to eliminate risk, effectuation asks what level of risk is 'affordable' – recognising the potential loss up-front when deciding to pursue new endeavours.

Metaphors assist with understanding the difference between causation and effectuation. Sarasvathy uses a simple example of the process of cooking. Starting with a menu and recipes and then shopping for ingredients and obtaining any necessary equipment or skills are a causation-based approach. In contrast, when applying effectuation logic, the menu and recipes evolve from looking in the kitchen and seeing what ingredients are available and considering existing skills and equipment (Sarasvathy, 2001). This example demonstrates one of the five principles of effectuation, the 'available means' principle, also referred to as 'bird-in-hand' (drawing up on the proverb *a bird in the hand is worth two in the bush* that emphasises the value of currently held resources).

Effectuation and causation have different benefits. While causation provides structured approaches to achieve identified goals, effectuation promotes creative ways of thinking and working that are more closely influenced by current resources and constraints. Multiple studies document evidence of a mixed use of the two logics (see, for example, Berends et al., 2014; Lingelbach, Sriram, Mersha, & Saffu, 2015; Nguyen et al., 2018; Reymen et al., 2015). Effectuation approaches are regarded as more effective than causation when the future is unpredictable (Sarasvathy, 2001) or for exploratory phases of the innovation process (Reymen et al., 2015). For these reasons, effectuation is attracting growing interest in disciplines such as innovation management that deal with a high level of uncertainty and exploration.

Sarasvathy's seminal paper on effectuation (2001) documented findings from a study that compared the ways that decisions were made by entrepreneurs and bankers. Sarasvathy observed entrepreneurs using rational, causation-based logic, along with an alternate way of viewing the world that she labelled 'effectuation'. Effectuation involves decision-making "starting with means and creating new effects" (Sarasvathy, 2008, p. 74).

Debates and proposed refinements abound in the literature, but the original principles presented by Sarasvathy still anchor the field. Characteristics of the decision-maker – "who are they, what do they know, whom do they know" (Sarasvathy, 2001, p. 249) – and the available resources form the starting point for the effectuation principles Sarasvathy proposed in 2001. Effectuation contrasts

TABLE 14.1 Effectuation principles compared with causation approaches

Effectuation	*Causation*
Available means principle (also referred to as the bird-in-hand principle) - using the resources that are currently available as a starting point. Including the answers to: Who am I? What do I know? Whom do I know?	Goal-driven - setting goals and targets, and then identifying and securing the resources needed
Affordable loss principle - accepting a level of risk, and determining up front the level of 'loss' that is possible, proceeding if this level is acceptable, "determination of how much one is willing to lose and leveraging limited means in creative ways" (Sarasvathy, 2008, p. 81)	Expected returns - focusing on commercial analysis and the expected returns - up-front planning and analysis focused on achieving returns on investment
Adaptability principle (also called the lemonade principle, or referred to as exploitation of contingencies) - responding to change, flexibility - viewing unexpected events as opportunities (when life gives you lemons, make lemonade)	Planning and control - attempting to predict the future, using up-front planning and monitoring that aims to control the situation and to avoid being surprised by unexpected change
Partnership principle (also called the crazy quilt principle) - using networks and partnerships that commit to the endeavour and influence its direction - involving strategic alliances, pre-commitments to partnerships	Competitive analysis - undertaking detailed competitive analysis using casual models such as Porter's principles of competition and strategic advantage (Porter, 1980)
Control of an unpredictable future (also called the pilot-in-the-plane principle) - based on non-predictive control related to the above four principles, acknowledging the role of human agency in responding to opportunity, and developing networks and teams.	Prediction of an uncertain future - planning based on projections of future conditions - focusing on technological developments and other trends as drivers of opportunity

Derived from Sarasvathy (2001, 2008).

with causation by promoting "(1) affordable loss, rather than expected returns; (2) strategic alliances, rather than competitive analyses; (3) exploitation of contingencies, rather than pre-existing knowledge; and (4) the control of an unpredictable future, rather than prediction of an uncertain one" (Sarasvathy, 2001, p. 259). Table 14.1 compiles the principles introduced by Sarasvathy (2001, 2008) and compares these with the corresponding causation approaches.

Twenty years of effectuation research: extending beyond entrepreneurship

It has been 20 years since the effectuation concept was first introduced in the field of entrepreneurship. Interest and further research on the theme grew slowly at first, with escalating interest in recent years. Rapid growth in fields beyond entrepreneurship position effectuation as a "general theory of decision-making in uncertain situations" (Sarasvathy, 2008, p. 227). However, the word 'theory' with respect to effectuation has been strongly contested, most prominently by Arend, Sarooghi, and Burkemper (2015), who argue that the elements of Experience, Explain, and Establish required for theory building have not been satisfied. In response, some authors suggest that effectuation should be evaluated as a process theory using different criteria (Gupta, Chiles, & McMullen, 2016) and others contribute guidance for effectuation research to progress and support the evolution of the effectuation concept as a potential theory (Read, Sarasvathy, Dew, & Wiltbank, 2016; Reuber, Fischer, & Coviello, 2016).

Recent additions to the debate confirm that there is still no consensus on whether effectuation can be considered a theory and suggest that further studies are needed that focus on the theoretical aspects of effectuation (Dias, Lizuka, & Boas, 2019). The increasing number of publications in recent years is helping to build the understanding of effectuation and its theoretical application, providing evidence to support claims that effectuation is transitioning to the mature stage of theoretical development (Matalamäki, 2017). However, claims that effectuation represents a theory of entrepreneurship have been contested, as effectuation represents only one aspect of the entrepreneurship process (Kitching & Rouse, 2020).

The scholars in this debate agree that effectuation is still a relatively new concept, and that further studies are needed to strengthen the understanding and efficacy of effectuation as a valuable lens for research. Effectuation has been given many different labels – for example, it has been called a theory, a framework, a set of behaviours, and a type of logic. To avoid the controversy about whether effectuation can be considered a theory, this chapter uses the common description of effectuation as a decision-making logic.

As effectuation matures as a lens for research, the focus of the research is moving well beyond entrepreneurship. Innovation and new product development now represent the strongest areas for effectuation research (Matalamäki, 2017). Effectuation research has also moved from focussing on the individual entrepreneur and small startups to testing its applicability in larger organisational settings; most of the research related to effectuation is now situated in established organisations.

One sign of the maturation of a field of research is the emergence of review papers summarising the developments in the field. Read et al. (2009) conducted an early review of effectuation, noting the growing interest in the discipline, and encouraging further research in this area. Perry, Chandler and Markova's (2012) review observed a steady increase in publications, with 29 articles where effectuation was the primary focus. Most of the papers were conceptual at that stage, with only 13 empirical studies – and the context for research was still largely within entrepreneurship. Recent reviews that analysed 64 (Grégoire & Cherchem, 2020) and 81 empirical studies (McKelvie, Chandler, DeTienne, & Johansson, 2020) reveal that effectuation research is influencing fields outside entrepreneurship. This finding is emphasised in the special issue of the journal *Small Business Economics* on "Effectual exchange: from entrepreneurship to the disciplines and beyond" which identifies a research agenda to continue to "move effectuation from entrepreneurship to the disciplines and beyond into new futures" (Alsos, Clausen, Mauer, Read, & Sarasvathy, 2020, p. 605).

Effectuation has influenced research in a wide variety of disciplines to date, many of which align with future-oriented and contemporary innovation management themes. A growing stream of publications reveal how effectuation perspectives contribute to research on aspects such as foresight (Djuricic & Bootz, 2019), leadership (Miles & Morrison, 2020), disaster response (Nelson & Lima, 2020), the evolution of art (Olive-Tomas & Harmeling, 2020), strategy (Guo, 2019; Hauser, Eggers, & Güldenberg, 2020; Zahra, Sapienza, & Davidsson, 2006), business model innovation (Futterer, Schmidt, & Heidenreich, 2018), social innovation (Corner & Ho, 2010), sustainability (Keskin, Wever, & Brezet, 2020; Sarasvathy & Ramesh, 2019), operations (Golicic & Sebastiao, 2011), design thinking (Abrell, 2016; Mansoori & Lackéus, 2020), lean startup methods (Ghezzi, 2019; Mansoori & Lackéus, 2020; Roach, Ryman, & Makani, 2016), and project management and agile project management approaches (Hansen & Svejvig, 2018; Xu & Koivumäki, 2019).

In addition to embracing multiple disciplines, research on effectuation now spans the globe – Africa (see for example Lingelbach et al., 2015), the Middle East (Jisr & Maamari, 2017), Russia (Laine & Galkina, 2017), Brazil (Nelson & Lima, 2020), New Zealand (Corner & Ho, 2010), Australia (Miles & Morrison, 2020), Spain (Ortega, García, & Santos, 2017), the Netherlands (Keskin et al., 2020; Reymen et al., 2015), and other European nations, as well as the UK, the USA, and Canada.

Most recently, publications have identified effectuation in practice in response to the COVID-19 pandemic. Especially in times of great change and turmoil, effectual logic is proposed to be more appropriate than using causation logic since detailed plans quickly become obsolete (Giones et al., 2020). Effectuation logic has underpinned the ability to respond to previous crises, such as the 2012

Earthquakes in Italy (Kuckertz et al., 2020). Early research on the COVID-19 pandemic demonstrates effectuation in practice for business model innovation (Harms, Alfert, Cheng, & Kraus, 2021), in supporting entrepreneurship by educators as they respond to the rapid change (Langston, 2020), and in the use of 'frugal' innovation approaches (Corsini, Dammicco, & Moultrie, 2021). Effectual thinking and the development of dynamic capabilities supported small business entrepreneurs cope with the COVID-19 (Rashid & Ratten, 2021). The ability to respond quickly was highlighted in a study on the ways that businesses adjusted to the turmoil of COVID-19 pandemic; while incumbents found it more difficult than startups to respond quickly, the study suggests that adopting effectuation logic will assist incumbents to improve response time (Ebersberger & Kuckertz, 2021).

The increasing volume and quality of research suggests that effectuation is a "healthy and growing theoretical perspective that represents a major shift" in the ways that innovation and entrepreneurship are understood (McKelvie et al., 2020, p. 659). Suggestions for future development of the field include understanding and clarifying the scope and assumptions underpinning each research study – and ensuring that methods and measurements suit the context.

Effectuation research – questions and methods

The methods used to conduct research on effectuation are overviewed here to provide context for the findings on effectuation and implications for innovation management that are presented in the following sections. The growing number of empirical studies on effectuation draw upon a wide range of research methodologies, including quantitative, qualitative and mixed method studies. Methods include case studies, surveys, interviews, 'think aloud' protocols, process analyses, simulations and experiments. Each study has unique aims, often exploring these types of questions:

- Is effectuation used – and if so, is effectuation used more often in certain types of environments or conditions at conditions (antecedents and contexts for effectuation)?
- What are the outcomes from the use of effectuation?

Qualitative studies are most useful for exploring new areas and gaining insights into questions about 'how' and 'why'. The original work by Sarasvathy (2001) used a 'think aloud' protocol to provide insights into the decision-making thought processes and logic used as the participants considered scenarios about business opportunities. Other methods include case studies, document analysis, content analysis and alternate templates. The alternate template approach (Fisher, 2012; Ortega et al., 2017) applies multiple theoretical perspectives to interpret what is known about a situation. In such cases, "the different interpretations are less like true 'tests' of theory and more like alternate complementary readings that focus on different variables and levels of analysis and reveal different types of dynamics" (Langley, 1999, p. 699).

Quantitative studies on effectuation often employ surveys to capture perceptions and determine statistical relationships between concepts, such as the relationship between the use of effectuation principles and innovation outcomes. Effectuation is a relatively new concept, and the modes of questioning on surveys are still maturing. Survey items are generally statements that are rated on a five-point Likert scale ranging from "Strongly agree" to "Strongly disagree". Alternatively, respondents may be asked to provide a rating along a scale anchored by two endpoints – for example between 'desired goals have been the starting point for this project' (to represent causation) and 'available resources and capabilities have been the starting point for this project' (to represent the 'available means' principle of effectuation). Using these approaches, survey items measure the degree to which effectuation or causation behaviours were used and other input on innovation processes and outcomes. Each aspect is measured by multiple related items (usually 3–4 items for each factor). Table 14.2 provides examples of selected survey items.

Research on effectuation is in the early stages, and a wide variety of methods are being used to learn more about whether and how effectuation is used in practice. Other methods for research on effectuation include experimentation and simulations (Welter & Kim, 2018) and process trajectory analysis (Berends et al., 2014). The wide variety of research methods support broad exploration of the concept; however, each method requires further use and refinement to improve the rigor and reliability of effectuation research. There are ongoing debates "on the more detailed aspects of the use of effectuation and how we, as scholars, can, and should, examine it empirically" (McKelvie et al., 2020, p. 690).

TABLE 14.2 Example survey items on the use of effectuation logic

Items on use of effectuation-based logic:

We evaluated the set of resources and means we had at our disposal and thought about different options (related to 'available means')

We were careful not to commit more resources than we could afford to lose (related to 'affordable loss')

We allowed the business to evolve as opportunities emerged (related to 'flexibility'/'adaptability')

Items on the use of causation-based logic:

We designed and planned business strategies

We organized and implemented control processes to make sure we met objectives

We researched and selected target markets and did meaningful competitive analysis

Items measured in a five-point Likert scale.
Selected from Table 2 in Chandler, DeTienne, McKelvie, and Mumford (2011, p. 382).

What do we know about effectuation in innovation practice?

This chapter highlights the effectuation research that is related to innovation management (beyond entrepreneurship). Studies of effectuation in the field of entrepreneurship have consistently shown that effectuation provides entrepreneurs with a new lens to broaden opportunity identification. Effectuation principles are found to reflect entrepreneurial thinking on risk (or affordable loss) and provide new insights into the processes of entrepreneurship (Grégoire & Cherchem, 2020; McKelvie et al., 2020). Entrepreneurship studies have also explored the new venture creation processes, including setting up business models and business model innovation (Futterer et al., 2018; Xu & Koivumäki, 2019). Studies in entrepreneurship have developed scales for measuring the aspects of effectuation and causation (Chandler et al., 2011; Roach et al., 2016), and have repeatedly demonstrated that effectuation is used alongside causation – in different proportions depending on context (Hauser et al., 2020).

Innovation management is a wide field and, although it is quite distinct from entrepreneurship, the two fields are strongly associated with one another. Using the broad definition of innovation as 'creating value from something new', entrepreneurship with its focus on the creation of new value-producing ventures represents a specific aspect of innovation. The escalating interest in effectuation in the field of innovation management emphasises its role in processes for developing new products and services from the initial idea through to launch. Effectuation concepts influence research on approaches to new product and service development, including design thinking, agile project management and concepts such as the 'lean startup' that bridge innovation management and entrepreneurship. Effectuation is also aligned with the movement to 'rethink' the project management discipline, moving away from the 'hard' rational or positivist perspectives to embrace subjective 'soft' perspectives (Svejvig & Andersen, 2015). As part of this move, effectuation is of interest in project management (Blauth, Mauer, & Brettel, 2014; Brettel et al., 2012; Huff, 2016; Midler & Silberzahn, 2008) and the strategic decision processes that constitute project portfolio management (Nguyen et al., 2018).

The role of effectuation principles in innovation management

To determine whether and how effectuation is used, research studies generally look for behaviours across some or all of the effectuation principles, and some also measure causation behaviours. This section briefly overviews findings on the use of each principle and the impact.

Available means: Although some studies have identified distinct 'available means' behaviours (Brettel et al., 2012), measuring such behaviours has been difficult in some settings (Nguyen et al., 2018). About half of the survey-based studies did not measure or did not find evidence of distinct behaviours related to available means (see, for example, Chandler et al., 2011; Guo, 2019). However, two studies focussed strongly on available means, producing findings that highlight the importance of tacit knowledge (what I know) and its positive influence on innovative outcomes (Jisr & Maamari, 2017), and the resulting strategic advantages (Svensrud & Åsvoll, 2012).

Affordable loss: Research has consistently confirmed the existence of 'affordable loss' as a distinct aspect of an effectuation mindset (Brettel et al., 2012; Chandler et al., 2011; Guo, 2019). Affordable loss behaviours had a positive impact on projects with high levels of innovativeness, while causation behaviours focussing on expected returns were more effective for projects with low levels of innovativeness (Brettel et al., 2012). The affordable loss concept has been linked to the 'innovation funnel' concept, where multiple ideas are initially considered, with the intention of culling most ideas at early stages once the best ideas can be determined (Svensrud & Åsvoll, 2012). The 'affordable loss' can be considered the investment in ideas that will be culled to make way for the selected idea(s).

Adaptability – exploiting contingencies through flexibility and experimentation: Behaviours related to these themes are strongly represented in the research; however, the emphasis differs among studies. Some studies have focussed on flexibility and experimentation (Cai, Guo, Fei, & Liu, 2017; Chandler et al., 2011; Guo, 2019), while others have looked at a contingency orientation (Szambelan, Jiang, & Mauer, 2020) or iteration (Berends et al., 2014; Nguyen et al., 2018). Adaptability has been proposed to enhance an organisation's exploration capabilities (Svensrud & Åsvoll, 2012), and to reduce perceptions of market-based innovation barriers (Szambelan et al., 2020).

Partnerships: Effectuation research has extensively explored the partnerships theme. Some studies have focussed on the use of pre-commitments from customers, and the degree to which partners commit resources to the shared endeavour. Such pre-commitments were associated with improved performance in new ventures (Cai et al., 2017; Guo, 2019), and were shown to solidify the supply chain (Golicic & Sebastiao, 2011). Partnerships that become strategic alliances can become important dynamic capabilities, providing advantages through additional opportunities to adjust the resource base in response to change in the environment (Svensrud & Åsvoll, 2012).

Control an unpredictable future: Most of the effectuation studies consider this principle as an underlying condition or perspective, such as the entrepreneurial control orientation mindset (Szambelan et al., 2020) that is reflected in the other principles. This mindset underpins the ability to create opportunities with respect to uncertainties in the future (Svensrud & Åsvoll, 2012). Acknowledging the unexpected in highly innovative environments is associated with increased innovation output and efficiency (Brettel et al., 2012), and (along with available means and the use of partnerships), supports increased levels of creativity in new product development under high uncertainty (Blauth et al., 2014).

Primary themes and findings on effectuation and innovation

Effectuation research aligns with some of the major innovation management themes. This section overviews findings related to strategy and context.

Strategy, dynamic capabilities, and emergence

Strategic concepts about competition, differentiation, organisational capabilities, and the development of competitive advantage underpin much of the innovation management research. From a strategic perspective, questions about what underpins organisational success generally take an external or internal perspective (Barney, 1991). The external perspective focusses on how organisations compete by differentiating their offerings and analyse the environment in order to succeed in a competitive environment (Porter, 1980). In contrast, the internal perspective takes a 'resource-based view' and focusses on the resources and capabilities within the organisation, and how those resources enable superior performance (Barney, 2001). Effectuation research from a strategic perspective is aligned with the internal 'resource-based view' and the associated 'dynamic capabilities' perspective. Dynamic capabilities are specific organisational capabilities that enable organisations to effectively respond to changes in the environment (Eisenhardt & Martin, 2000; Teece, Pisano, & Shuen, 1997). Dynamic capabilities are not valuable by themselves – the benefits are achieved through the ability afforded by the dynamic capability to update, extend or otherwise modify other resources and capabilities to meet changing requirements.

The dynamic capability concept is an emerging theme in contemporary innovation management. Effectuation has been proposed to act as a dynamic capability in large organisations, prompting a call for further research at the strategy level in that context (Svensrud & Åsvoll, 2012). Effectuation is also proposed to support the higher use of experimentation in growing organisations as resource constraints ease, and in this way to lead to competitive advantage through dynamic capability (Zahra et al., 2006). Tacit knowledge is linked to the effectuation principle of available means (what I know), and proposed to lead to dynamic capabilities, with gut feeling proposed to be a valuable type of tacit knowledge (Svensrud & Åsvoll, 2012). The role of effectuation in venture creation is also thought to contribute advantages as a dynamic capability (Corner & Wu, 2012); however, very little research has explored these concepts. One study found that the degree of innovativeness in a project was associated with increased use of effectuation in strategic PPM decision-making, and suggested that effectuation enhances the ability of project portfolio management to act as a dynamic capability (Nguyen et al., 2018).

The strong level of interest in dynamic capabilities reflects the increasing levels of uncertainty and change in innovation management environments, and the importance of strategy. However, further research is required to better understand whether and how effectuation can act as a dynamic capability or enhance other dynamic capabilities.

Effectuation has also been linked to emergent strategy. Strategic management concepts have evolved to recognise that strategy is not a one-way (top-down) process, and that emergent strategies have an important role to play in informing future strategic directions (Mintzberg & Waters, 1985). Deliberate strategy is planned – and implemented as planned. In contrast, emergent strategy is not initially planned, but instead represents strategic actions that 'emerge' in the course of doing business. These emergent strategies are increasingly recognised as important indicators of changes in circumstance, opportunity, and response. The counterintuitive concept of 'planned emergence' suggests that organisations can improve their ability to recognise and even to promote and build on emergent strategies, and that effectuation may have a role to play (Kopmann, Kock, Killen, & Gemuenden, 2017). Chandler et al. (2011) align the concept of causation logic with deliberate strategy implementation – such as through business planning processes, and effectuation logic with emergent strategy processes – for example, where experiments are used to identify alternatives to be considered in the context of potential affordable loss.

Ambidexterity and effectuation

Effectuation contributes to organisational ambidexterity, the ability to successfully pursue both exploitative innovation and explorative innovation (O'Reilly & Tushman, 2004). Exploitative innovation uses existing resources and methods to create incremental innovation that involves low levels of change and risk. Explorative innovation is a higher risk endeavour that offers the potential for high reward through the development of radical or breakthrough innovations. Effectuation, as a decision logic for uncertain contexts, is associated with explorative innovation, while causation is aligned primarily with exploitative innovation. The mindful and strategic combination of the two decision logics (Agogué, Lundqvist, & Middleton, 2015) builds understanding, and the repeatedly observed combination of effectuation and causation is considered a form of organisational ambidexterity (Brettel et al., 2012; Midler & Silberzahn, 2008; Yu, Tao, Tao, Xia, & Li, 2018). Such ambidextrous use of both causation and effectuation provides advantages, as deficiencies in one approach are filled by strengths in the other approach (Yu et al., 2018). The complementary combination of clear goals with opportunities to improvise and explore supports strategic decisions for both the short and long term, providing a balanced information base that avoids extremes (Villani, Linder, & Grimaldi, 2018).

Another perspective on effectuation, causation, and ambidexterity builds on the regularly reported shift in the emphasis on effectuation to causation over time (Evers & Andersson, 2020). Sequential ambidexterity is a recognised form of ambidexterity where, instead of simultaneous exploration and exploration, an organisation does both in succession (O'Reilly & Tushman, 2013). This temporal separation is observed when effectuation is used to provide advantages in early explorative stages of innovation, while causation is considered more appropriate for the later development and commercialisation stages (exploitation) (Evers & Andersson, 2020).

Contextual influences on effectuation use

Research findings repeatedly emphasise that the innovation management approach should be tailored to suit the context. Studies of effectuation reinforce the role of context in guiding whether and how effectuation is used alongside causation, and how the balance changes according to the context and over time.

Managing under uncertainty is at the core of effectuation logic. While uncertainty is inherent in innovative endeavours, the level of uncertainty is heightened for radical or breakthrough innovation. In contrast, incremental innovation often follows 'tried and tested' methods and entails a low level of uncertainty. Therefore, effectuation is seen as especially important for the sought-after radical innovations or when uncertainty is high (Fisher, 2012; Hauser et al., 2020; Reymen et al., 2015). Growth speed is also associated with the choice and balance of decision logics. Effectuation is found to be more appropriate in high-growth contexts, whereas lower growth is associated with causation (Futterer et al., 2018). In a simulation-based study, effectuation was shown to perform better under risky and uncertain contexts (Welter & Kim, 2018). While some researchers suggest that effectuation-based approaches are more effective for smaller organisations (Berends et al., 2014), others propose that the decision context is more important than the size of the organisation (Hauser et al., 2020).

The relationship between the degree of innovation and effectuation goes both ways. Highly innovative projects or environments are more likely to use effectuation-based decision processes and, when effectuation is used, the innovative outcomes are enhanced (Ortega et al., 2017). One study found that exploratory learning was the link between effectuation use and improved performance; when effectuation was used, exploratory learning was enhanced, which, in turn, led to better performance of new ventures (Cai et al., 2017).

Time-based shifts in effectuation use are often tied to the stage of the innovation process. Higher levels of effectuation are generally effective for decision-making related to the iteration and experimentation associated with early-stage product and process development, while causation is more effective during later stages of development (Berends et al., 2014; Ortega et al., 2017; Reymen et al., 2015; Svensrud & Åsvoll, 2012). In emerging economies, changes in resource constraints were the main triggers for a shift between the use of effectuation and causation; more effectuation was used when resources were constrained, whether early or late in the process. (Lingelbach et al., 2015). Aligned with the concept of ambidexterity, the ability to switch between the two decision logics to suit the evolving context provides strategic advantages (Hauser et al., 2020).

Effectuation and innovation management methods

Interest in effectuation is particularly strong in innovation management, new product and service development, and project management research. These three overlapping areas share a range of management approaches that were traditionally underpinned by causative concepts, along with a series of contemporary innovation management practices that prompt new ways of thinking. In these disciplines, effectuation is repeatedly identified as a suitable approach for uncertain and risky endeavours – and there is a push to explore alternative decision-making approaches because "deeply rooted beliefs in causal logic are an impediment in intrinsically unpredictable environments" (Huff, 2016, p. 8). The following sections outline some of the findings on effectuation related to methods used in innovation management, new product and service development, and project management.

Phased and gated processes (also called stage-gate™ processes) are prevalent in guiding projects from idea to completion in innovation management, new product and service development, and project management disciplines. Such processes employ a rational sequence of phases (idea generation, business planning, development, testing, etc.) with gating criteria used to control the progression to the next phase. Phased and gated processes are associated with better innovation outcomes (Cooper, Edgett, & Kleinschmidt, 1999; Killen, Hunt, & Kleinschmidt, 2008), but they are less beneficial when there are high levels of uncertainty, such as in radical innovations (Loch, 2000). Duening, Shepherd, and Czaplewski (2012) recognise the value of the commonly used phased and gated processes, but propose that the incorporation of effectuation logic could improve effectiveness. Their model demonstrates how effectuation could be incorporated through actions such as promoting consideration of available resources during the screening/scoping phases, or by seeking partnerships to extend resources flexibly in later phases.

Lean startup and design thinking methods (Blank, 2013; Brown, 2008) guide entrepreneurs and innovators through customer-focussed, iterative methods for managing innovation. Evidence of the use of effectuation practices was revealed in a large-scale survey-based study on lean startups (Yang, Sun, & Zhao, 2019). Mansoori and Lackéus (2020) analysed effectuation as an 'entrepreneurial method' rather than a decision logic, and found that methods associated with effectuation (such as evaluating means and estimating affordable loss) were closely aligned to the Lean startup and design thinking methods. Design thinking has been shown to support entrepreneurial thinking and action (Abrell, 2016), and a range of studies have emphasised links between effectuation and the ways that lean startup and design thinking create value in an iterative, knowledge-, and learning-focussed, connected environment (Ghezzi, 2019; Mansoori & Lackéus, 2020; Roach et al., 2016; Xu & Koivumäki, 2019).

Agile project management and effectuation

Traditionally project management approaches have taken a causative perspective; up-front planning has been emphasised to clearly define the desired outcomes and the ways the project will unfold in a top-down fashion, referred to as a 'waterfall' approach. In situations of change and uncertainty, traditional 'waterfall' project management approaches make it difficult to adjust goals and plans, resulting in outcomes that can be expensive and irrelevant. In response, agile project management methods enable organisations to respond quickly and efficiently. Agile project management promotes incremental planning, where the goal will be determined iteratively in a process that continually assesses customer needs and available resources. It has proven difficult to shift organisational ways of working to embrace agile methodologies; these agile methodologies need a cultural shift or a 'new way of thinking' for effective transition from traditional methods (Conforto et al., 2014).

An effectuation mindset is proposed to offer a 'new way of thinking' to support the 'new ways of working' required to implement agile project management methods. Research in this area is only just beginning. The close association of agile project management, lean startups, and effectuation is explored in conceptual papers (Frederiksen & Brem, 2017; Mansoori & Lackéus, 2020), revealing high alignment between the concepts, but lacking empirical evidence to demonstrate whether and how effectuation is used in agile project management practice. In a mixed method study involving 227 digital startups, Ghezzi (2019) built on the empirical findings that link agile project management with lean principles to propose a model combining effectuation, bricolage and opportunity-creation approaches for lean and agile environments; however, the relationships have not been explored through targeted research. In a similar vein, a conceptual paper proposes a model for effectuation principles in a digital context to support emerging IT technology development using 'frugal' innovation approaches (Khanal, 2018), and suggest how the spread of agile and lean approaches make this type of digital effectuation particularly important. Similarly, effectuation is linked to frugal innovation practices that support digital fabricators' ability to respond to the challenges of COVID-19 (Corsini et al., 2021),

In a slightly different area, an empirical study extends agile software development concepts to business model development, employing a case study on digital business models that showed how effectuation principles can provide benefits and align with the agile approach (Xu & Koivumäki, 2019). Another study on business model innovation demonstrated how effectuation and causation work together to enable organisations to adapt and respond to COVID-19; organisations employed 'hybrid' decision logics where the balance of effectual and causal logics was aligned with the organisation's strategic approach (Harms et al., 2021).

Finally, alignment between effectuation and agile project portfolio management practices is suggested, with similar mechanisms that support strategy emergence (Kaufmann, Kock, & Gemünden, 2020). Current organisations adopt 'agile at scale' to become more adaptable but must make a transition from a hierarchical mindset to one that is more flexible (Rigby, Sutherland, & Noble, 2018). However, agile practices have not worked well at the project portfolio level and a radical new way of thinking may be required (Sweetman & Conboy, 2018). Adopting an effectuation mindset (alongside causation) may assist organisation's transition to agile methods.

Effectuation and multi-project perspectives – lineage management and project portfolio management

In addition to its role in agile project portfolio management, effectuation principles support other multi-project perspectives on innovation management and contribute to strategic dynamic capabilities. Project lineage management concepts are shown to be aligned with and supported by effectuation principles (Midler & Silberzahn, 2008). Project lineage concepts take a longitudinal project portfolio perspective and recognise the connectedness between projects as components of longer-term strategic innovation trajectories (Kock & Gemünden, 2019). In innovative contexts, research at the project portfolio management level also suggests benefits from the use of effectuation logic, along with causation (Nguyen et al., 2018). Project portfolio management is an important dynamic capability associated with improving innovation outcomes (Killen & Hunt, 2010), and further studies are recommended to better understand the role of effectuation in these multi-project management capabilities. Multi-project perspectives and the use of effectuation are associated with the sought-after ability for organisations to recognise emerging strategies and improve agility and responsiveness to succeed in dynamic times (Kaufmann et al., 2020).

Conclusion

The challenge of innovation management is intensified as organisations cope with uncertainty, change and increasing competition. In such environments, organisational strategies must be responsive and adaptive; organisations need innovation capabilities that can shift and change to meet evolving needs. To meet these challenges, new innovation management approaches encourage iterative, open and dynamic ways of working. The emerging interest and research on effectuation provide insights on how 'new ways of thinking' can support these 'new ways of working' for managing innovation under uncertainty.

Sarasvathy's (2001) identification of effectuation as an alternate decision logic has implications for innovation management beyond entrepreneurship. From initial observations in startups and entrepreneurial environments, effectuation is now shown to support new ways of working in established organisations. This chapter has overviewed a range of research studies that show how innovation managers use effectuation logic in combination with causation logic, highlighting situations where effectuation logic is particularly useful.

Effectuation logic provides advantages in uncertain, fast changing environments, with increasing interest in the application of effectuation for innovation management, new product and service development, and project management. The emerging research on effectuation provides examples of how effectuation is applied in a variety of environments, and evidence on how it can provide performance advantages. Effectuation logic is used in combination with causation logic to support innovation management approaches such as design thinking, lean startup, and agile project management. Decisions in the early stages of innovation processes benefit from a stronger emphasis on effectuation logic, whereas a balance of the decision logics that is weighted towards causation is better aligned for decisions later in the innovation process.

Importantly, effectuation may have relevance for organisational strategy and competitiveness beyond its influence on innovation management methods. The use of effectuation logic is also associated with organisational ambidexterity, strategy emergence, and the development of dynamic capabilities. Overturning traditional thinking about the need for high-level long-term strategic planning, effectuation logic promotes a more adaptable approach. Effectuation logic recognises the value of tacit knowledge and 'gut feelings' ('what I know'), which are often ignored or downplayed in traditional strategic planning approaches (Svensrud & Åsvoll, 2012).

Organisations that are able to harness an effectuation mindset for innovation management stand to possess a dynamic capability that enables them to succeed in times of change and uncertainty. The ability to apply effectuation logic in combination with causation logic, and to shift the balance between the two logics when appropriate, will enhance organisational ambidexterity and improve competitiveness. The emerging research on effectuation repeatedly highlights the benefits of effectuation in highly innovative contexts and suggests that effectuation can enhance an organisation's flexibility, adaptability, and creativity in an increasingly uncertain and dynamic environment.

Implications for innovation management

The concept of effectuation and the emerging body of research provide new insights that may assist management to incorporate contemporary innovation management approaches into their organisations. The alternate logic represented by effectuation principles can help promote the 'new ways of thinking' needed to support the implementation of 'new ways of working' to meet contemporary innovation management challenges.

Organisations may benefit from programmes that help managers recognise and apply effectuation logic in conjunction with causation logic to support open, iterative and creative innovation management and the development of organisational dynamic capability. Such programmes may assist organisations gain the best advantages from innovation practices, especially in uncertain and dynamic environments.

Managers also will benefit from learning how to evaluate the context and determine when effectuation may be more beneficial than causation in supporting decision-making. As effectuation is almost always used in combination with causation, decision-makers that can shift the balance between the two logics in response to the environment and context will improve their ability to manage innovation effectively.

Organisations implementing culture-change programmes could use the example of effectuation as an alternate decision logic to raise awareness of how different ways of thinking support different behaviours and decisions. Similarly, effectuation principles could be promoted to support the introduction of new ways of working, such as design thinking or agile project management approaches. Effectuation principles can be used to demonstrate the types of 'new ways of thinking' that support these approaches; for example, the emphasis on iteration experimentation in these innovation management approaches is supported by effectuation principles of affordable loss, adaptability and concepts about control of an unpredictable future.

Research findings on the positive influence of effectuation on innovation outcomes also have implications for education to prepare students for management, especially innovation management. Awareness of the benefits of integrating effectuation into entrepreneurial studies has been increasing since Sarasvathy (2001) posed a question about whether, and what, MBA students need to learn about effectuation. Others have also highlighted the role of education in developing awareness of both causative and effectual decision-making to prepare students to operate across both sides when managing innovation. Students need to develop the ability to plan but also to adapt; skills to pursue competitive strategies when appropriate, while also embracing collaborative partnerships; and the ability to consider projected returns while also valuing and accepting some risks inherent in innovation (Fisher, 2012; Reymen et al., 2015). There is strong support for innovation management education that raises awareness of the existence and influence of the underlying decision logic on organisational performance. Innovation management educators should consider including modules that explain the principles of effectuation and causation decision logics and demonstrate how and when such decision-making logics are best applied. This includes highlighting how to apply a combination of both decision-making logics, and how to evaluate the context and shift the balance between the logics for effective innovation management.

Future research on effectuation and innovation management

Effectuation research, while growing strongly, is still at an early stage. Many avenues for future research relate to contemporary innovation management. Research on the use of effectuation decision logic in specific innovation management contexts will add further insights to build on findings from existing studies. Such research should explore whether and how effectuation logic is applied in a range of environments, and identify the impact on outcomes. Such research could focus on specific types or stages of innovation, targeted innovation approaches, or focus on certain industries or types of organisations. This section outlines a few avenues for such future research.

Agile project management is making a strong impact across a wide range of industry sectors and sizes of organisations. Adaptation to change is highlighted in recent research on the potential for effectuation logic as an aid for innovation management. Studies on 'agile' methodologies have emphasised the need for a cultural shift in order to effectively transition from traditional methods (Conforto et al., 2014), and recent research (Hansen, Rode, Sommer, & Svejvig, 2019) has highlighted that effectuation may play a role in the evolution of strategic approaches for long term innovation management.

Future research should aim to better understand the role of effectuation in agile project management, and identify whether, where and how effectuation principles can best support agile practices and the related 'new ways of thinking'. Research is currently being planned to build upon the early studies on the role of effectuation for agile project management. Early findings suggest that, although the label 'effectuation' is not known in industry, the effectuation principles may align with agile project management goals and 'ways of working'.

Longitudinal research is also suggested to explore the use and benefits of effectuation during different stages of the innovation process, with the aim of identifying the stages and environments where effectuation is most helpful. There could be additional benefits from conducting such research in large organisations to explore whether effectuation enables these large organisations to be "more experimental in their opportunity practice to assure a higher number of successes" (Svensrud & Åsvoll, 2012, p. 84) by exploring multiple projects quickly and cheaply before moving to larger project investments.

Finally, future research could explore the role of effectuation as an agent for organisational agility and the development of dynamic capabilities. Further studies are recommended to explore the role of effectuation in strategic decision-making. Such studies could build on earlier findings on the use of effectuation in project portfolio management and the ways that project portfolio management can provide advantages as a dynamic capability (Killen & Hunt, 2010; Nguyen et al., 2018). Future research is also suggested to explore the role of effectuation in fostering emergent strategy recognition and the ability to respond to emergence (Kopmann et al., 2017).

References

Abrell, T. (2016). Design thinking and corporate entrepreneurship: An integration and avenues for future research. In W. Brenner & F. Uebernickel (Eds.), *Design thinking for innovation: Research and practice* (pp. 25–39). Cham: Springer International Publishing.

Agogué, M., Lundqvist, M., & Middleton, K. W. (2015). Mindful deviation through combining causation and effectuation: A design theory-based study of technology entrepreneurship. *Creativity & Innovation Management, 24*(4), 629–644. doi:10.1111/caim.12134

Alsos, G. A., Clausen, T. H., Mauer, R., Read, S., & Sarasvathy, S. D. (2020). Effectual exchange: From entrepreneurship to the disciplines and beyond. *Small Business Economics, 54*(3), 605–619. doi:10.1007/s11187-019-00146-9

Arend, R. J., Sarooghi, H., & Burkemper, A. (2015). Effectuation as ineffectual? Applying the 3E theory-assessment framework to a proposed new theory of entrepreneurship. *Academy of Management Review, 40*(4), 630–651. doi:10.5465/amr.2014.0455

Barney, J. B. (1991). Firm resources and sustained competitive advantage. *Journal of Management, 17*(1), 99–120.

Barney, J. B. (2001). Is the resource-based 'view' a useful perspective for strategic management research? Yes. *Academy of Management Review, 26*(1), 41–56.

Berends, H., Jelinek, M., Reymen, I., & Stultiëns, R. (2014). Product innovation processes in small firms: Combining entrepreneurial effectuation and managerial causation. *Journal of Product Innovation Management, 31*(3), 616–635.

Blank, S. (2013). Why the lean startup changes everything. *Harvard Business Review, 91*(5), 63–72.

Blauth, M., Mauer, R., & Brettel, M. (2014). Fostering creativity in new product development through entrepreneurial decision making. *Creativity & Innovation Management, 23*(4), 495–509.

Brettel, M., Mauer, R., Engelen, A., & Küpper, D. (2012). Corporate effectuation: Entrepreneurial action and its impact on R&D project performance. *Journal of Business Venturing, 27*(2), 167–184.

Brown, T. (2008). Design thinking. *Harvard Business Review, 86*(6), 84.

Cai, L., Guo, R., Fei, Y., & Liu, Z. (2017). Effectuation, exploratory learning and new venture performance: Evidence from China. *Journal of Small Business Management, 55*(3), 388–403. doi:10.1111/jsbm.12247

Chandler, G. N., DeTienne, D. R., McKelvie, A., & Mumford, T. V. (2011). Causation and effectuation processes: A validation study. *Journal of Business Venturing, 26*(3), 375–390. https://doi.org/10.1016/j.jbusvent.2009.10.006

Cicmil, S., Williams, T., Thomas, J., & Hodgson, D. (2006). Rethinking Project Management: Researching the actuality of projects. *International Journal of Project Management, 24*(8), 675–686.

Conforto, E. C., Salum, F., Amaral, D. C., Da Silva, S. L., & De Almeida, L. F. M. (2014). Can agile project management be adopted by industries other than software development? *Project Management Journal, 45*(3), 21–34.

Cooper, R. G., Edgett, S. J., & Kleinschmidt, E. J. (1999). New product portfolio management: Practices and performance. *Journal of Product Innovation Management, 16*(4), 333–351. doi:10.1111/1540-5885.1640333

Corner, P. D., & Ho, M. (2010). How opportunities develop in social entrepreneurship. *Entrepreneurship Theory and Practice, 34*(4), 635–659. doi:10.1111/j.1540-6520.2010.00382.x

Corner, P. D., & Wu, S. (2012). Dynamic capability emergence in the venture creation process. *International Small Business Journal, 30*(2), 138–160. doi:10.1177/0266242611431092

Corsini, L., Dammicco, V., & Moultrie, J. (2021). Frugal innovation in a crisis: The digital fabrication maker response to COVID-19. *R&D Management, 51*(2), 195–210. https://doi.org/10.1111/radm.12446

Dias, S. E. F., Lizuka, E. S., & Boas, E. P. V. (2019). Effectuation theoretical debate: Systematic review and research agenda. *Innovation & Management Review, 17*(1), 41–57. doi:10.1108/INMR-12-2018-0094

Djuricic, K., & Bootz, J. -P. (2019). Effectuation and foresight – An exploratory study of the implicit links between the two concepts. *Technological Forecasting and Social Change, 140*, 115–128. https://doi.org/10.1016/j.techfore.2018.04.010

Duening, T., Shepherd, M., & Czaplewski, A. (2012). How entrepreneurs think: Why effectuation and effectual logic may be the key to successful enterprise entrepreneurship. *International Journal of Innovation Science.*

Ebersberger, B., & Kuckertz, A. (2021). Hop to it! The impact of organization type on innovation response time to the COVID-19 crisis. *Journal of Business Research, 124*, 126–135. https://doi.org/10.1016/j.jbusres.2020.11.051

Eisenhardt, K. M., & Martin, J. A. (2000). Dynamic capabilities: What are they? *Strategic Management Journal, 21*(10/11), 1105–1121.

Evers, N., & Andersson, S. (2020). Predictive and effectual decision-making in high-tech international new ventures – A matter of sequential ambidexterity. *International Business Review, forthcoming*, 101655. https://doi.org/10.1016/j.ibusrev.2019.101655

Fisher, G. (2012). Effectuation, causation, and bricolage: A behavioral comparison of emerging theories in entrepreneurship research. *Entrepreneurship Theory and Practice, 36*(5), 1019–1051. doi:10.1111/j.1540–6520.2012.00537.x

Frederiksen, D. L., & Brem, A. (2017). How do entrepreneurs think they create value? A scientific reflection of Eric Ries' Lean Startup approach. *International Entrepreneurship and Management Journal, 13*(1), 169–189. http://dx.doi.org/10.1007/s11365-016-0411-x

Futterer, F., Schmidt, J., & Heidenreich, S. (2018). Effectuation or causation as the key to corporate venture success? Investigating effects of entrepreneurial behaviors on business model innovation and venture performance. *Long Range Planning, 51*(1), 64–81. https://doi.org/10.1016/j.lrp.2017.06.008

Ghezzi, A. (2019). Digital startups and the adoption and implementation of lean startup approaches: Effectuation, bricolage and opportunity creation in practice. *Technological Forecasting and Social Change, 146*, 945–960. https://doi.org/10.1016/j.techfore.2018.09.017

Giones, F., Brem, A., Pollack, J. M., Michaelis, T. L., Klyver, K., & Brinckmann, J. (2020). Revising entrepreneurial action in response to exogenous shocks: Considering the COVID-19 pandemic. *Journal of Business Venturing Insights, 14*, e00186. https://doi.org/10.1016/j.jbvi.2020.e00186

Golicic, S. L., & Sebastiao, H. J. (2011). Supply chain strategy in nascent markets: The role of supply chain development in the commercialization process. *Journal of Business Logistics, 32*(3), 254–273. doi:10.1111/j.2158-1592.2011.01021.x

Grégoire, D. A., & Cherchem, N. (2020). A structured literature review and suggestions for future effectuation research. *Small Business Economics, 54*(3), 621–639. doi:10.1007/s11187-019-00158-5

Guo, R. (2019). Effectuation, opportunity shaping and innovation strategy in high-tech new ventures. *Management Decision, 57*(1), 115. http://dx.doi.org/10.1108/MD-08-2017-0799

Gupta, V. K., Chiles, T. H., & McMullen, J. S. (2016). A process perspective on evaluating and conducting effectual entrepreneurship research. *Academy of Management Review, 41*(3), 540–544. doi:10.5465/amr.2015.0433

Hansen, L. K., Rode, A., Sommer, A., & Svejvig, P. (2019). *Toward a project portfolio management evaluation framework.* Paper presented at the EURAM Lisbon.

Hansen, L. K., & Svejvig, P. (2018). *Agile project portfolio management, new solutions and new challenges: preliminary findings from a case study of an agile organization.* Paper presented at the IRIS41/SCIS9 Conference 2018.

Harms, R., Alfert, C., Cheng, C. -F., & Kraus, S. (2021). Effectuation and causation configurations for business model innovation: Addressing COVID-19 in the gastronomy industry. *International Journal of Hospitality Management, 95*, 102896. https://doi.org/10.1016/j.ijhm.2021.102896

Hauser, A., Eggers, F., & Güldenberg, S. (2020). Strategic decision-making in SMEs: Effectuation, causation, and the absence of strategy. *Small Business Economics, 54*(3), 775–790. doi:10.1007/s11187-019-00152-x

Huff, A. S. (2016). Project innovation: Evidence-informed, open, effectual, and subjective. *Project Management Journal, 47*(2), 8–25. doi:10.1002/pmj.21576

Jisr, R. E., & Maamari, B. E. (2017). Effectuation: Exploring a third dimension to tacit knowledge. *Knowledge & Process Management, 24*(1), 72–78. doi:10.1002/kpm.1536

Kaufmann, C., Kock, A., & Gemünden, H. G. (2020). Emerging strategy recognition in agile portfolios. *International Journal of Project Management.* https://doi.org/10.1016/j.ijproman.2020.01.002

Keskin, D., Wever, R., & Brezet, H. (2020). Product innovation processes in sustainability-oriented ventures: A study of effectuation and causation. *Journal of Cleaner Production, 263*, 121210. https://doi.org/10.1016/j.jclepro.2020.121210

Khanal, P. B. (2018). *IT enabled frugal innovation.* Paper presented at the Proceedings of the 2018 ACM SIGMIS Conference on Computers and People Research.

Killen, C. P., & Hunt, R. A. (2010). Dynamic capability through project portfolio management in service and manufacturing industries. *International Journal of Managing Projects in Business, 3*(1), 157–169.

Killen, C. P., Hunt, R. A., & Kleinschmidt, E. J. (2008). Project portfolio management for product innovation. *International Journal of Quality and Reliability Management, 25*(1), 24–38.

Kitching, J., & Rouse, J. (2020). Contesting effectuation theory: Why it does not explain new venture creation. *International Small Business Journal*, forthcoming. doi:10.1177/0266242620904638

Kock, A., & Gemünden, H. G. (2019). Project lineage management and project portfolio success. *Project Management Journal, 50*(5), 587–601. doi:10.1177/8756972819870357

Kopmann, J., Kock, A., Killen, C. P., & Gemuenden, H. G. (2017). The role of project portfolio management in fostering both deliberate and emergent strategy. *International Journal of Project Management, 35*, 557–570.

Kuckertz, A., Brändle, L., Gaudig, A., Hinderer, S., Morales Reyes, C. A., Prochotta, A., … Berger, E. S. C. (2020). Startups in times of crisis – A rapid response to the COVID-19 pandemic. *Journal of Business Venturing Insights, 13*, e00169–e00169. doi:10.1016/j.jbvi.2020.e00169

Laine, I., & Galkina, T. (2017). The interplay of effectuation and causation in decision making: Russian SMEs under institutional uncertainty. *International Entrepreneurship and Management Journal, 13*(3), 905–941. doi:10.1007/s11365-016-0423-6

Langley, A. (1999). Strategies for theorizing from process data. *The Academy of Management Review, 24*(4), 691–710.

Langston, C. (2020). Entrepreneurial educators: Vital enablers to support the education sector to reimagine and respond to the challenges of COVID-19. *Entrepreneurship Education, 3*(3), 311–338. doi:10.1007/s41959-020-00034-4

Lingelbach, D., Sriram, V., Mersha, T., & Saffu, K. (2015). The innovation process in emerging economies: An effectuation perspective. *The International Journal of Entrepreneurship and Innovation, 16*(1), 5–17. doi:10.5367/ijei.2015.0172

Loch, C. (2000). Tailoring product development to strategy: Case of a European technology manufacturer. *European Management Journal, 18*(3), 246–258.

Mansoori, Y., & Lackéus, M. (2020). Comparing effectuation to discovery-driven planning, prescriptive entrepreneurship, business planning, lean startup, and design thinking. *Small Business Economics, 54*(3), 791–818. http://dx.doi.org/10.1007/s11187-019-00153-w

Matalamäki, M. J. (2017). Effectuation, an emerging theory of entrepreneurship – Towards a mature stage of the development. *Journal of Small Business and Enterprise Development, 24*(4), 928–949. http://dx.doi.org/10.1108/JSBED-02-2017-0030

McKelvie, A., Chandler, G. N., DeTienne, D. R., & Johansson, A. (2020). The measurement of effectuation: Highlighting research tensions and opportunities for the future. *Small Business Economics, 54*(3), 689–720. doi:10.1007/s11187-019-00149-6

Midler, C., & Silberzahn, P. (2008). Managing robust development process for high-tech startups through multi-project learning: The case of two European start-ups. *International Journal of Project Management, 26*(5), 479–486. http://dx.doi.org/10.1016/j.ijproman.2008.05.003

Miles, M. P., & Morrison, M. (2020). An effectual leadership perspective for developing rural entrepreneurial ecosystems. *Small Business Economics, 54*(4), 933–949. doi:10.1007/s11187-018-0128-z

Mintzberg, H., & Waters, J. A. (1985). Of strategies, deliberate and emergent. *Strategic Management Journal, 6*(3), 257–272.

Nelson, R., & Lima, E. (2020). Effectuations, social bricolage and causation in the response to a natural disaster. *Small Business Economics, 54*(3), 721–750. doi:10.1007/s11187-019-00150-z

Nguyen, N. M., Killen, C. P., Kock, A., & Gemuenden, H. G. (2018). The use of effectuation in projects: The influence of business case control, portfolio monitoring intensity and project innovativeness. *International Journal of Project Management, 38*(8), 1054–1067.

O'Reilly, C. A., & Tushman, M. L. (2004). The ambidextrous organization. *Harvard Business Review, 82*(4), 74–81.

O'Reilly, C. A., & Tushman, M. L. (2013). Organizational ambidexterity: Past, present, and future. *Academy of Management Perspectives, 27*(4), 324–338. doi:10.5465/amp.2013.0025

Olive-Tomas, A., & Harmeling, S. S. (2020). The rise of art movements: An effectual process model of Picasso's and Braque's give-and-take during the creation of Cubism (1908–1914). *Small Business Economics, 54*(3), 819–842. doi:10.1007/s11187-019-00154-9

Ortega, A. M., García, M. T., & Santos, M. V. (2017). Effectuation-causation: What happens in new product development? *Management Decision, 55*(8), 1717–1735. http://dx.doi.org/10.1108/MD-03-2016-0160

Perry, J. T., Chandler, G. N., & Markova, G. (2012). Entrepreneurial effectuation: A review and suggestions for future research. *Entrepreneurship Theory and Practice, 36*(4), 837–861. doi:10.1111/j.1540-6520.2010.00435.x

Porter, M. E. (1980). *Competitive strategy: Techniques for analyzing industries and competitors.* New York and London: Free Press; Collier Macmillan.

Rashid, S., & Ratten, V. (2021). Entrepreneurial ecosystems during COVID-19: The survival of small businesses using dynamic capabilities. *World Journal of Entrepreneurship, Management and Sustainable Development, ahead-of-print* (ahead-of-print). doi:10.1108/WJEMSD-09-2020-0110

Read, S., Sarasvathy, S. D., Dew, N., & Wiltbank, R. (2016). Response to Arend, Sarooghi, and Burkemper (2015): Cocreating effectual entrepreneurship research. *Academy of Management Review, 41*(3), 528–536. doi:10.5465/amr.2015.0180

Read, S., Song, M., & Smit, W. (2009). A meta-analytic review of effectuation and venture performance. *Journal of Business Venturing, 24*(6), 573–587.

Reuber, A. R., Fischer, E., & Coviello, N. (2016). Deepening the dialogue: New directions for the evolution of effectuation theory. *Academy of Management Review, 41*(3), 536–540. doi:10.5465/amr.2015.0217

Reymen, I. M. M. J., Andries, P., Berends, H., Mauer, R., Stephan, U., & van Burg, E. (2015). Understanding dynamics of strategic decision making in venture creation: A process study of effectuation and causation. *Strategic Entrepreneurship Journal, 9*(4), 351–379. doi:10.1002/sej.1201

Rigby, D. K., Sutherland, J., & Noble, A. (2018). Agile at scale. *Harvard Business Review, 96*(3), 88–96.

Roach, D., Ryman, J., & Makani, J. (2016). Effectuation, innovation and performance in SMEs: An empirical study. *European Journal of Innovation Management, 9*(2), 214–238. https://doi.org/10.1108/EJIM-12-2014-0119

Sarasvathy, S. D. (2001). Causation and effectuation: Toward a theoretical shift from economic inevitability to entrepreneurial contingency. *Academy of Management Review, 26*(2), 243–263. doi:10.5465/amr.2001.4378020

Sarasvathy, S. D. (2008). *Effectuation: Elements of entrepreneurial expertise.* Cheltenham: Edward Elgar Publishing Limited.

Sarasvathy, S. D., & Ramesh, A. (2019). An effectual model of collective action for addressing sustainability challenges. *Academy of Management Perspectives, 33*(4), 405–424. doi:10.5465/amp.2017.0090

Sauer, C., & Reich, B. Z. (2009). Rethinking IT project management: Evidence of a new mindset and its implications. *International Journal of Project Management, 27*(2), 182–193.

Svejvig, P., & Andersen, P. (2015). Rethinking project management: A structured literature review with a critical look at the brave new world. *International Journal of Project Management, 33*(2), 278–290. https://doi.org/10.1016/j.ijproman.2014.06.004

Svensrud, E., & Åsvoll, H. (2012). Innovation in large corporations: A development of the rudimentary theory of effectuation. *Academy of Strategic Management Journal, 11*(1), 59–89.

Sweetman, R., & Conboy, K. (2018). Portfolios of agile projects: A complex adaptive systems' agent perspective. *Project Management Journal, 49*(6), 18–38. doi:10.1177/8756972818802712.

Szambelan, S., Jiang, Y., & Mauer, R. (2020). Breaking through innovation barriers: Linking effectuation orientation to innovation performance. *European Management Journal, 38*(3), 425–434. https://doi.org/10.1016/j.emj.2019.11.001

Teece, D. J., Pisano, G., & Shuen, A. (1997). Dynamic capabilities and strategic management. *Strategic Management Journal (1986–1998), 18*(7), 509–533.

Villani, E., Linder, C., & Grimaldi, R. (2018). Effectuation and causation in science-based new venture creation: A configurational approach. *Journal of Business Research, 83*, 173–185. https://doi.org/10.1016/j.jbusres.2017.10.041

Welter, C., & Kim, S. (2018). Effectuation under risk and uncertainty: A simulation model. *Journal of Business Venturing, 33*(1), 100–116. https://doi.org/10.1016/j.jbusvent.2017.11.005

Wiltbank, R., Read, S., Dew, N., & Sarasvathy, S. D. (2009). Prediction and control under uncertainty: Outcomes in angel investing. *Journal of Business Venturing, 24*(2), 116–133.

Wiltbank, R., & Sarasvathy, S. D. (2010). *What effectuation is not: Further development of an alternative to rational choice.* Paper presented at the Academy of Management Conference, Batten Institute at the Darden Graduate School of Business, Virginia, EUA.

Xu, Y., & Koivumäki, T. (2019). Digital business model effectuation: An agile approach. *Computers in Human Behavior, 95*, 307–314. https://doi.org/10.1016/j.chb.2018.10.021

Yang, X., Sun, S. L., & Zhao, X. (2019). Search and execution: Examining the entrepreneurial cognitions behind the lean startup model. *Small Business Economics, 52*(3), 667–679.

Yu, X., Tao, Y., Tao, X., Xia, F., & Li, Y. (2018). Managing uncertainty in emerging economies: The interaction effects between causation and effectuation on firm performance. *Technological Forecasting and Social Change, 135*, 121–131. https://doi.org/10.1016/j.techfore.2017.11.017

Zahra, S. A., Sapienza, H. J., & Davidsson, P. (2006). Entrepreneurship and dynamic capabilities: A review, model and research agenda. *Journal of Management Studies, 43*(4), 917–955.

15

BENEFITING FROM INNOVATION – PLAYING THE APPROPRIABILITY CARDS

Jialei Yang and Pia Hurmelinna-Laukkanen

Introduction

Innovation management does not stop to the point where a new idea has emerged and gained its form. It does not stop when the innovation has been successfully offered to customers either. This is, however, the point where innovation appropriability starts to turn into appropriation – if the premises have been well managed, and if subsequent innovation management is equipped and ready to deal with hurdles related to value capture. This chapter addresses these issues.

Most innovators pursue strongly to benefit from their investments in innovation and find incentives to engage in complex and uncertain development work in the underlying potential for capturing some value in the process. This benefit does not have to be monetary, even if in many instances it comes down to making profits – at least at some point. In these situations – for capturing value – having some control over the innovation is needed, which, in turn, necessitates careful management. As most innovation is profoundly intellectual and intangible, it may be misappropriated by competitors and customers without any compensation to the innovator.

In the contemporary world, appropriability of innovation – the potential of an innovator to benefit from their innovation – realizes in complex ways. Innovation appropriability can be built, like suggested in many studies, on formal mechanisms such as patents and/or other intellectual property rights (IPRs), or on informal and strategic mechanisms such as (partial or full) secrecy and/or careful human resource management (Cohen et al., 2000; Hannah et al., 2019; Hurmelinna-Laukkanen & Puumalainen, 2007; Levin et al., 1987b; Liebeskind, 1996, 1997; Olander et al., 2014, 2016; Teece, 1986). However, this building of appropriability needs to be aligned with the innovation and value creation processes quite early on. Succeeding in this, in turn, is dependent on contextual

DOI: 10.4324/9780429346033-20

features. For example, while some control is generally needed, different industries and countries have different effective appropriability premises, and aspects such as networkedness of firms are relevant; an overly protective approach may make important collaborators shy away, in which case it makes sense to open up and selectively reveal ideas (Alexy et al., 2018). That is, when building appropriability, understanding the contingencies and logics of value creation and matching managerial approach accordingly is needed.

Appropriation as the realizing of appropriability potential is not straightforward either. It does not follow automatically from good appropriability premises or conditions. The actual appropriation requires an understanding of the market and the dynamics within it. Having control is only the starting point, and how this control (or lack thereof) is exercised is a completely different thing. The varying appropriability mechanisms can be put in use for quite different purposes from ensuring that the innovator becomes the sole beneficiary of monopolistic profits, to making sure that other actors do not block free and wide dissemination of the innovation and its free use (Appleyard & Chesbrough, 2017; Jacobides et al., 2006; Teece, 1986). Importantly, the mechanisms can also be utilized to support the generation of new innovation based on the initial innovation (Ahuja et al., 2013; Alnuaimi & George, 2016), and thereby receiving future benefits.

The challenge is, that the practices in between appropriability and appropriation are not all that clear or visible in the current theorizing or managerial writings. Existing literature tends to address the combinations of appropriability premises (the combinations of mechanisms and/or complementary assets) and the uses of individual mechanisms, such as patent strategies, separately. Current theories and frameworks lack the explaining of, for example, the emerging appropriation failures of firms that have a strong appropriability regime and sufficient complementary assets (such as IBM Watson Health) (Yang et al., 2020). This chapter intends to narrow this gap with insights and a framework that elaborates the strategic and managerial premises of connecting appropriability and appropriation. We propose the concept of interactive appropriability – context-specific, dynamic aligning of appropriability premises (constituted with appropriability mechanisms and complementary assets) and interacting with other agents by relying on exclusion of others, leveraging the appropriability premises, and abandoning of protection, to benefit from innovation and appropriate value.

The rest of this chapter is structured as follows. The next section traces the theoretical origins of relevant research streams and advances profiting-from-innovation framework with value capture theory, thereby introducing the bases of our suggested framework with the emphasis on the three paths of turning appropriability into appropriation. We then explicate the realizing of the possibilities to capture value by building on conceptual consideration and illustrative examples. We conclude with the theoretical and practical contributions of this study and suggestions for future research.

Value capture theory: refining the original Profiting from innovation (PFI) framework with a cooperative game theory

David Teece's "Profiting from innovation" (PFI) framework (Teece, 1986, revisited in 2006 and 2018b; see also Gambardella et al., 2021) is highly influential in the innovation and strategic management fields. Many ideas presented in the PFI framework, such as building appropriability premises with appropriability mechanisms (e.g., intellectual property rights) and complementary assets (e.g., distribution channels), are still relevant today and in the central discussion of innovation management scholars and practitioners (Table 15.1 presents typical appropriability mechanisms and complementary assets). With decades of scholars' efforts, the question "how to benefit from innovation" has been explored across varying innovations (Battisti & Stoneman, 2010; e.g., Ritala & Hurmelinna-Laukkanen, 2009), analysis levels (e.g., Alexander, 2012), and contexts (such as industry context, country context, and more recently, digitalization context) (e.g., Faria & Sofka, 2008; Miric et al., 2019; Seo et al., 2017; Tech et al., 2019). Among these studies, open innovation, a distributed innovation model introduced by Henry Chesbrough (2003), goes beyond the firm boundaries and opens a new research avenue in terms of purposively managing knowledge flows to benefit from innovation (Chesbrough & Bogers, 2014).

Value capture theory has been recently outlined by Gans and Ryall (2017). Like the PFI framework, it addresses value appropriation and explains the

TABLE 15.1 Typical appropriability mechanisms and complementary assets

Appropriability mechanisms

Formal appropriability mechanisms
Patent
Copyright
Registered design — Intellectual property rights (IPRs)
Trademark

Informal appropriability mechanisms
Secrecy (a part of IPR when considered as trade secrets defined in legislation)
Lead time/speed to market
Tacitness/complexity (of design)

Complementary assets

Reputation (sometimes narrowed to brand)
Distribution channels
Complementary technologies/products/goods
Marketing/sales
Service
Expertise/additional know-how

heterogeneity of a firm's performance. However, in this theorizing, the object of value capturing does not necessarily have to be innovation – it can also be products that have been existing for long, for example. More importantly, the unit of analysis in the value capture theory is agent, and the focus of the theory shifts toward engaging agents in productive activities (Gans & Ryall, 2017). Being placed in the contexts of value networks composed of agents, heterogeneity of a firm's performance is explained with a cooperative game theory. For a firm, appropriating value is like a "bargaining game" between players.

In innovation appropriability literature (see James et al., 2013; Sun & Zhai, 2018 for reviews), the phrase "to appropriate value" is used interchangeably with "to capture value". However, these two research streams – PFI and value capture theory, have been hardly contrasted and aligned. Yet, value capture theory's modeling of the cooperative game stage could be valuable for the PFI framework in terms of assessing how to capture value with collaboration and competition, as this kind of modeling makes it possible to analytically study the interactions in multi-player settings and the value allocated to individual players (Ross, 2018). On the other hand, the PFI framework could help value capture theory to narrow the chasm existing in the identification of issues for empirical development (Chatain & Mindruta, 2017; Gans & Ryall, 2017), as factors determining value capture from innovation have been long discussed in PFI studies. As a result, value capture theory could be expanded from the predominantly conceptual and theoretical works to empirical domains.

In this section, the origins (as well as underlying assumptions) of PFI and value capture theory are presented and compared first. After converging the different streams of research, we discuss how the realizing of the possibilities to capture value could be reconsidered by looking at the paths from appropriability potential to realized appropriation. Finally, we present a framework that emphasizes the process to realize appropriability (i.e., appropriation process) as the outcome of integrating the two perspectives.

Value-based strategy versus knowledge-based view

The possibility to draw together concepts from the PFI framework and value capture theory lies in the resource-based view of the firm in the field of strategic management. Figure 15.1 illustrates the links between the PFI framework (and open innovation) and value capture theory by tracing their theoretical origins.

Both PFI and value capture theory assume that resources are scarce (i.e., in finite supply) and that mobility barriers of resources exist, which accounts for profit differentials between firms (Gans & Ryall, 2017). Particularly, for the PFI framework, knowledge is the most important resource of the firm for creating and maintaining competitive advantage (Grant, 2015). Hence, preventing others from copying and exploiting the innovation by protecting knowledge

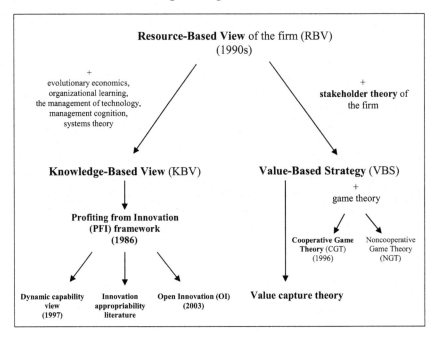

FIGURE 15.1 Developments of PFI and value capture theory, and their links (commonly used abbreviations in the brackets) (Teece, 1986; see Chesbrough, 2003; Gans & Ryall, 2017; Grant, 2015).

(and innovation) with different appropriability mechanisms has dominated appropriability discussions. However, changes in the innovation and business environments have produced quite different and parallel views. Especially open innovation literature challenges the assumption that exclusivity is desirable (Huizingh, 2011), and argues the importance of allowing knowledge to flow across firm boundaries (in the way of inside-out and outside-in open innovation). It has raised coopetition discussions upon knowledge protection and sharing, as well as aspects of knowledge acquisition and integration that are closely related to the absorptive capabilities of a firm (Bacon et al., 2020; Estrada et al., 2016; Ritala & Hurmelinna-Laukkanen, 2013).

As already briefly noted above, value capture theory analyzes the tension between collaboration and competition with game theory, placed in the context of a network of players. Game theory has two distinct areas: noncooperative game theory (NGT) and cooperative game theory (CGT). While NGT focuses on individual strategies and is action-oriented, CGT focuses on coalitions and agent added value, and it is payoff-oriented (Gans & Ryall, 2017; Ross, 2018). Placed in a commercial setting, NGT's and CGT's modeling of a firm's value capture addresses the aspect of how much profit or utility a firm obtains from a transaction

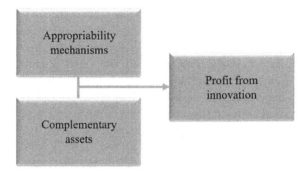

FIGURE 15.2   The original profit from innovation (PFI) framework.

(e.g., a sale, collaboration, or investment) (Ross, 2018). CGT stage and NGT stage can be linked with a "biform game" model, where NGT is the first stage, followed by CGT (Brandenburger & Stuart, 2007); or an inverse biform game, where NGT stage is placed after a CGT stage (see Nagarajan & Sošić, 2008 for a review). Taking CGT and NGT together models coopetition (Ross, 2018).

In terms of using value capture theory to refine the PFI model at the abstract and general levels, CGT modeling of value capture seems particularly suitable. CGT can be used to understand interactions in relatively limited settings such as an acquisition or a strategic alliance, or those among a larger number of agents, such as in ecosystems, collaborative communities, and platforms (Gans & Ryall, 2017: 24; Ross, 2018). The core idea of CGT is that while a firm engages in the game and forms coalitions with other players to co-create value (or so-called "bake the cake"), it also competes to capture value from resulting collective payoffs (or so-called "divide the cake") (see Ritala & Hurmelinna-Laukkanen, 2019). The aggregate value arises from the firm's engagement (or so-called "bigger cake"), and agents can benefit from cooperation, where binding agreements determine their roles and positions (Gans & Ryall, 2017: 24; Ross, 2018).

Value capture theory's consideration of cooperation and bargaining for value appropriation is valuable for the PFI framework. PFI argues that a firm with strong appropriability premises ('the cards with which they play') will lead to profits from innovation (see Figure 15.2). However, the concrete value capture activities ('playing the cards') are missing in this discussion. This is where the value capture theory could provide the needed insight. These aspects are discussed in the following.

Appropriation processes and outcomes

Traditional views suggest that appropriation can build on the *exclusivity of the innovation and the related knowledge assets*: innovation is treated as proprietary, and the innovator takes actions to prevent others from using the innovation and related knowledge (e.g., Ceccagnoli, 2009; Harabi, 1995; Teece, 1998).

This view is changed when insights of value capture theory are brought into the discussion. Value capture theory indicates that it is possible to capture a larger share of value by engaging in coalitions constituted by agents with binding agreements. It leads to reconsidering the path from appropriability to appropriation: profiting from innovation does not necessitate exclusivity. Appropriation can also build on *leveraging the innovation and the related appropriability mechanisms*, that is, on using them in different ways according to emerging opportunities and threats. For example, Petricevic and Teece (2019, p. 1504) note that in the international markets,

> the driver of individual MNEs' actions should not be the conventional 'profiting from innovation' target, but rather the insight that a rising tide will lift many boats, with IPR protection recognized as the global economic system's premier public good that logically deserves exceptional and impassioned collective action.

Leveraging does not emphasize the individual, preventive use of innovation, or the proprietary nature of innovation; it rather treats appropriability mechanisms and complementary assets as bargaining chips, means of signaling capabilities, or vehicles for transactions and (intended, wanted) knowledge sharing (see Gans & Stern, 2003; Pisano, 2006). Analysis of this process can be conducted at the level of individual transactions (e.g., transaction of IP), or more broadly, at the coalition level (e.g., Apple's iOS system where agents are in a coalition to build compatible technologies).

A further insight is that *appropriability premises, especially the mechanisms, can also be purposively abandoned,* meaning that exclusive rights are not applied for or executed, and knowledge is disclosed. It is frequently the case for corporates, who do research and development and patent their inventions, that they find some patents redundant. In a cooperative environment, this kind of approach might turn out particularly challenging; on top of taking resources for no reason, it might affect the performance of firms negatively due to impeding innovation adoption and/or cooperation. Deliberate abandonment of some appropriability mechanisms may enable attracting external contribution and accessing external capabilities (Appleyard & Chesbrough, 2017; Henkel et al., 2013; Jacobides et al., 2006). Exclusive rights may remain as owned (although not executed for exclusion purposes) by the innovator, which means that others cannot limit the free and wide use of the innovation and the related knowledge. This may notably enhance the firm's value capture. However, this requires combining the traditional PFI views with insights on cooperation, coopetition, and competition, as well as open innovation.

By converging the different streams of research, we propose a refined PFI framework, where the processes for realizing value capturing, from appropriability to appropriation, are emphasized (Figure 15.3). We argue that strong appropriability premises do not automatically lead to success, but that playing

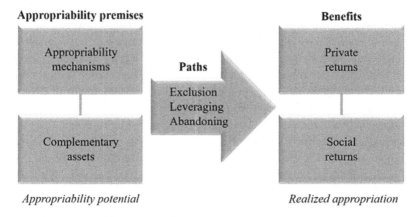

FIGURE 15.3 Benefit from innovation framework.

the "appropriability cards" in the right way with consideration of contextual factors and other agents in the game is important. In addition, as many collaborative communities include non-profit actors (Ross, 2018), this framework separates social returns from private returns, which are more relevant to non-profit-oriented actors such as universities. In the following, we propose how *interactive appropriability* may work.

Realizing the potential for value appropriation – leaning on interactive appropriability

The model in Figure 15.3 illustrates how benefit from innovation can accrue from the following three central paths. With this general model in mind, we consider how firms can realize value appropriation in practice. The following discussion shows, in particular, how appropriability is interactive; it is dependent on the context in which it exists and the dynamics within.

Exclusion

As noted, extant appropriability research largely focuses on exclusivity where the use of appropriability mechanisms (see Table 15.1), especially intellectual property rights viewed from the proprietary perspective, dominates the discussion. Although these appropriability mechanisms cannot perfectly block others (e.g., it is always possible to "invent around" a patent or an idea protected with secrecy can be developed by someone else independently), these appropriability mechanisms can at least slow down excessive competition. Besides defensive motives, offensive motives to use appropriability premise emerge. These include bargaining, standard setting, and even retaliation (Granstrand, 1999; Holgersson, 2013). Sophisticated use of appropriability mechanisms can generate new revenues for a firm, such as penalty income. However, the conditions under which these outcomes are pursued, are relevant.

Size of firms affecting the exclusive approach

Empirical studies have observed that small firms find patents less valuable as a tool to secure exclusivity and thus they rely more on secrecy and other means of appropriability when they pursue proprietary benefits (e.g., Arundel, 2001). Small firms usually have fewer patents per R&D investment than large firms (Minniti, 2011), but they can still be safe from imitation if they rely on tacit knowledge, for example. Adopting such an approach is understandable, as the value of formal appropriability mechanisms depends on ability of a firm to pose a credible threat of litigation (Gans & Stern, 2003; Laursen & Salter, 2014; Sherry & Teece, 2004). IPRs are not self-enforcing and they come often at great expense. With IPRs, there are usually filing, issuance, and maintenance fees in addition to ongoing costs for identifying misappropriation and costs for negotiation or litigation to defend rights (James et al., 2013; Teece, 2018a).

Industry contexts

Next to firm-level conditions, industries have their specific trajectories regarding the reliance on appropriability mechanisms. Certain industries have been empirically observed to be particularly prone to show reliance on patent protection to secure exclusivity, including, for example, pharmaceuticals and biotechnology industries, drugs, and medical equipment industries (Al-Laham et al., 2010; Cohen et al., 2000, 2005; Hall et al., 2003). Such an approach is understandable, as pharmaceutical products may require huge efforts to discover, but are relatively easy to manufacture; and they are typically covered with clear standards for assessing and claiming patent infringement (Ivus et al., 2017; Levin et al., 1987a). Industry context also explains why firms choose not to patent. For example, biotechnology start-up executives are concerned about technology disclosure (Graham & Sichelman, 2016). In many cases, the usefulness of the different appropriability premises depends on whether the industry can be considered discrete or complex, and on how fast the development cycles are. Patents, for instance, may be too slow a means, and they eventually will expire.

Appropriability conditions of countries

Other aspects that may define the feasibility of exclusive uses emerge from the wider, international environment. Different countries have different legal systems and enforcement levels of legal protection. As most IPRs are country-specific and the exclusive rights are limited to issuing countries, firms having international business usually must cover multiple countries at one time, with operated and targeted countries included. However, the lawsuit results of infringement (and the exclusivity and appropriation results) can vary across countries (Santangelo et al., 2016). In countries with weak intellectual property regimes, firms struggle to execute their rights, and even if they win disputes, they may have a hard time retrieving any compensation. Furthermore, a problem might emerge, if a government decides to support local firms by putting up limitations to foreign firms – despite their IPRs (see Pao-Tsung, 2013). Therefore, companies operating across multiple countries or located in countries with weaker IPR and legal systems may find formal appropriability mechanisms to be of limited efficiency for exclusive purposes.

Nature of technologies – emerging technologies and exclusive approach

Emerging technologies and advancements illustrate the applicability of exclusive paths to appropriation. In particular, they demonstrate how appropriability is interactive in terms of connecting in various ways to the innovation and the environment in which it emerges. In recent years, Artificial Intelligence (AI) has come to the focus of the public again and attracted interest from scholars and practitioners. AI's achievements (e.g., AlphaGo's beating human chess players with a surprising move; Google AI's more precise prediction of gender through eyes than humans) excite investors and portray a promising future (Qi, 2018). However, firms with AI-related technologies find it difficult to generate significant profits from it, and the traditional way of building appropriability premises for exclusion seems to slow down the development and commercialization of AI, where numerous experiments are needed for finding the best use cases of it (Yang et al., 2020). Taking the exclusivity strategy, where innovation is treated as property, means that outsiders have limited access to the innovation and make contributions. Therefore, the tasks to explore and experiment with different use cases, as well as continuously develop the algorithms, are conducted by their own staff. For firms that attempt to apply AI in slowly digitalized industries (such as healthcare, where data are not centralized and structured), it is a challenge: they need to do all the tasks mainly by themselves, including data governance and technology development in a context that they do not necessarily know well. When the technologies are treated as property, trust concerns also arise. For example, when AI is applied to give diagnosis suggestions (used as a clinical decision support system), physicians want to know how AI produces certain conclusions. Based on the transparency of conclusion making, physicians may or may not approve AI's suggestions, which influences their future acceptance and adoption of AI. Furthermore, applying exclusivity also implies communication costs, not only for developing the technology but also for making outsiders understand the technology during commercialization. Different approaches may be then needed.

Leveraging as the focal approach

As suggested above, leveraging refers to utilizing appropriability mechanisms and complementary assets that do not emphasize exclusion, but rather controlled transfer and wider utilization of innovation and the related knowledge. It includes practices such as licensing (and property transactions), inter-organizational collaboration (e.g., team-up, alliances, and ecosystems), bargaining/negotiations, and orchestration/coordination. The focus is on allowing others to access the innovation in purposeful ways. To continue the discussion on the nature of technology as a relevant aspect, and looking at AI as an example of emerging technologies, the Watson OpenScale of IBM can be an example of leveraging for appropriating value. It is an open platform allowing IBM Watson – a cognitive computing technology that integrated different facets of artificial intelligence (Chen et al., 2016) – to be used across clouds. It enables clients to use and build AI at their choice (IBM, 2018). Nevertheless, leveraging can emerge in different forms, and is conditioned by the features of the innovation environments.

Licensing (and property transaction)

Licensing has been regarded as an important means to profit from innovation. A license is "a contract by which an IPR holder firm (licensor) transfers the right to exploit its innovation to another firm (licensee) under certain conditions and for a certain period of time" (Avagyan et al., 2014). In this regard, IPRs can be used as bargaining chips for cross-licensing agreements (Fischer & Henkel, 2013). Such agreements facilitate accessing such assets and resources that would otherwise be difficult to obtain and would likely be in the proprietary use of some other parties. Licensing IPRs out generates revenues, which can be significant. For example, license fees collected by IBM exceed $1 billion a year (Bhatia & Carey, 2007). This kind of approach is particularly useful when the innovator does not have resources to manufacture or disseminate the innovation widely, or if the innovation involves such creations that are not in the core activity of the innovator. An innovator can also appropriate economic returns from innovation by selling its intellectual rights and assets (Chesbrough, 2003, 2006). Selling unused IP and assets will not influence much the competitive advantage or bargaining power of firms such as Ericsson and IBM who have numerous patents, but help free their cash (Holgersson et al., 2018; Stasik & Cohen, 2020).

Inter-organizational collaboration

An innovator conducts inter-organizational collaboration for, for example, when building industry standards or dominant designs (Ahuja et al., 2008), jointly solving problems and exploiting technological opportunities (Milesi et al., 2013), and/or "borrowing" resources (e.g., expertise and assets) from others to fill its resource gap (Dattée et al., 2018). Its collaboration partners can be both private and public actors (such as universities and research institutes), even competitors (i.e., coopetition). In these activities, the benefit does not necessarily originate from the current innovation as such, but from combining it and the related knowledge with that of others for additional value, or for the generation of completely new innovation. Indeed, appropriability discussions have expanded from focal firm level to network level, thereby getting closer to the approach of value capture theory. Viewed from the network perspective, inter-organizational collaborations are dynamic, with actors entering and exiting the relationships and re-encounters happening (Hurmelinna, 2018). In the multi-innovation context, innovation ecosystem gathers private and public organizations to combine complementary resources and achieve joint innovative goals, and firms can appropriate value from the joint innovation activities (Di Minin & Faems, 2013; Leten et al., 2013; Ritala & Hurmelinna-Laukkanen, 2019). Digital ecosystems have emerged recently as a result of the development of interactive digital technology, Cloud, Internet of Things, Internet of services, etc. (Pagani, 2013). They have provided a new basis for innovators and innovation, and firms increasingly offer platforms that enable ecosystems and make it easier for outsiders to engage in the development and commercialization of technology (Boudreau, 2010; Teece, 2018a). However, control and protective elements remain relevant. Cooperation failures happen, and this needs to be considered. Cooperative game theory provides some tools for increasing readiness: a firm's engagement should be considered in light of the configurations of the networks constituted by agents with different portfolios (Lichtenthaler, 2015; Ross, 2018). This idea is valuable for today's collaborative communities, where innovations are produced across disciplinary and industry boundaries. It is especially valuable for them when, for example, deciding the group size for collaboration and/or accessing the role of suppliers, buyers, or complementors who have heterogeneous complementary resources (see Ross, 2018).

Bargaining/negotiation and orchestration/coordination

Generally speaking, those with strong appropriability premises have a better bargaining position, which is also one of the reasons why innovators obtain the appropriability mechanisms (Appleyard & Chesbrough, 2017; Holgersson et al., 2018). The more diversified, effective portfolio one has, the more the bargaining position can be strengthened (Bessen & Maskin, 2009; Bos et al., 2015). The improved transferability of knowledge assets incentivizes firms to use formal appropriability mechanisms such as IPRs and contracts over informal ones. Tacitness or secrecy, might, in fact, pose challenges in this regard. However, also in bargaining situations, control has a role to play. In networks, there might be a "hub" organization that takes an orchestrator role in negotiating agreements (Bogers et al., 2011). Less central actors in the network may find it difficult to exploit information and orchestrate resources for their advantage, and they have weaker bargaining power for capturing value from collective payoffs (Dahlander & Wallin, 2006). If these actors were able to communicate that they have relevant innovation (covered with formal mechanisms) and tacit knowledge that is valuable for the other actors, the more likely they will be able to affect their positioning.

Abandoning appropriability mechanisms for value capturing

In contemporary business environments, practical examples indicate that sometimes any control is deliberately put to the background. In most cases, this is due to the interactive nature of appropriability. The IBM example expands to this path too. IBM has been contributing to open-source communities (and utilized the abandoning approach of appropriability mechanisms), receiving social returns as well as monetary returns as AI gets more widely adopted. That is, building on the ideas in value capture theory, the appropriability mechanisms (e.g., IPRs) and complementary assets held by IBM are not used for exclusion, nor leveraged, but rather forfeited to allow for wider use and experimentation.

Promoting free access

Practices of abandoning appropriability mechanisms include open license, defensive patents, and the so-called 'copyleft' (e.g., Belenzon & Schankerman, 2015; Schultz & Urban, 2012). Through open license (sometimes called "free license"), the innovator intends to cooperatively work with other parties and instead of maintaining a monopoly (Bessen & Maskin, 2009; Grindley & Teece, 1997). Open Invention Network (OIN)'s defensive patent pool is a good example for clarifying the concept of defensive patent. OIN, backed by six companies – IBM, NEC, Novell, Philips, Red Hat, and Sony, established a patent pool, but not to generate revenues by asserting those patents, but rather to defend against attacks of Linux, which is an open-source operating system, and its related technologies (Nicholson, 2012). 'Copyleft', for its part, describes a reverse copyright scheme, where openness is preserved, for example, with the license called the General Public License (GPL), and individual appropriation is prevented by requiring subsequent developers to share the improved software following the original open terms (Giordani et al., 2018). Returns to innovation are mainly social returns. For firms that turn proprietary software into open source software (OSS), "non-copyleft" is suggested, as it allows converting future versions back into proprietary, exclusive ones; or they can use an OSS and a proprietary license in parallel (Henkel, 2006).

Waiving exclusive rights

Besides using the appropriability mechanisms to ensure free use of the innovation, exclusive rights can also be waived: there is a waiver paradigm where firms pledge that they will not assert exclusive rights when infringement occurs. For example, IBM, Novell, and Nokia have done this when promoting OSS (Alexy et al., 2013). Another example is found in the patent waiving pledge made by the CEO of Tesla Motors in 2014 with a blog, with the statement that "Tesla will not initiate patent lawsuits against anyone who, in good faith, wants to use our technology" (Musk, 2014). Traditionally, Tesla Motors has had strictly protected its intellectual property, so not surprisingly, this waiving pledge for all patents attracted great interest from the public (Rimmer, 2014). In 2018, Tesla Motors also started to release some Linux source codes for the Tesla Model S and X cars. From the appropriability perspective, these Tesla's activities of abandoning and forfeiting their rights generate significant social returns to Tesla with regard to the spilled knowledge to other firms, and the environmental contributions based on facilitating the use of electric vehicles, for example. However, Tesla also does have monetary benefits available, as the spreading of e-cars has all the potential to increase interest in and demand for Tesla's charging stations. Disclosing innovation related knowledge without applying any protection also signifies abandoning approach.

Conclusions

This chapter responds to a focal question in the field of innovation management: how to benefit from innovation. We add to existing knowledge by turning attention to *interactive appropriability*: we remind that appropriation does not emerge automatically from (a portfolio of) appropriability mechanisms and complementary assets, but that these connect to varying uses and to the relevant contexts in dynamic ways. We identify three specific paths where this aspect emerges: in a nutshell, *exclusion* is about protecting innovation and excluding others from accessing the innovation to prevent unwanted imitation, *leveraging* focuses on knowledge transfer and bargaining power with appropriability premises, and *abandoning* deliberately gives up control to gain social returns and future-oriented private returns.

It is worth noticing that our framework does not mean that a firm can only choose one of three approaches to realize appropriation. It does not mean either that the strategic choice of approach should be one-off: it is possible, at least to an extent, to switch between paths, even the firm is already following one alternative. The objects of value capture can also be different parts or different versions of an innovation, which allows for multiple approaches to co-exist. We highlight the importance of managing the processes strategically, utilizing exclusion, leveraging, and abandoning in an intentional manner.

Theoretical contributions and practical implications

Appropriating returns from innovation is an important motivation for firms to engage in innovation activities, including open innovation endeavors. This chapter contributes to the current innovation study by explicating how to "play the appropriability cards" to realize appropriation.

Our study started from the distinctive, theoretical discussions of Profiting from innovation (PFI) framework and value capture theory. We suggest, that by combining insights from these two views, it is possible to understand how innovation appropriability as potential can be turned into realized value capturing. While the building blocks of appropriability and appropriation come from the PFI, value capture theory brings in the context where varying agents interact. In particular, the cooperative game theory as a part of value capture theory analyzing the tension between collaboration and competition in networked context allows seeing how different approaches to competition and collaboration, and matching the use of appropriability mechanisms and complementary assets to these approaches, promote appropriating value from innovation in different ways. In particular, this framing has the potential to explain better the appropriability and appropriation of emerging technological innovations. Our attempt to align value capture theory with the PFI framework further gives a start to translating the mathematical language of value capture theory into a view that is applicable in strategy research and practice. Value capture theory unpacks the "bargaining ability" box, showing how appropriability mechanisms and complementary assets can be treated as bargaining chips. It allows analyzing and understanding the interactions in inter-organizational collaborations with the consideration of the added value of agents, which range from small (like an individual transaction) to large (like collaborative communities and ecosystems) (Ross, 2018). Additionally, we push the framing to cover social, and not just private return, which may be relevant when considering value capturing in relation to the grand societal and environmental challenges.

This chapter's proposed framework has significant implications for practice. It reminds and helps firms to reconsider and revise their appropriation strategies continuously. Nowadays, actors are increasingly networked, and open for collaboration and knowledge sharing. For example, the ongoing pandemic has prompted more discussion on collaboration and sharing of proprietary technologies and other solutions as an essential aspect in responding to global challenges (Chesbrough, 2020). It could be expected that the value of leveraging and abandoning paths could be emerging more in the future. Expanding the appropriability view from traditional exclusion toward leveraging and abandoning to turn appropriability potential to realized appropriation updates the managerial understanding of innovation appropriability and the related value capturing. Especially, the leveraging concept, enriched with cooperative game theory, offers firms ideas on how to strengthen bargaining power in the inter-organizational collaborations with the help of appropriability mechanisms and complementary assets. In such settings, building collaborative communities benefits from assessment of complementary resources owned by different agents, and from being knowledgeable of the firm's own control over the innovation and related knowledge – overemphasis of openness is not advisable either. In governing collaborative communities, cooperative game theory (CGT) may shed light on opportunistic behavior when developing shared norms (Kolbjørnsrud, 2014; Ross, 2018), and instruct managers on the appropriate levels of exclusivity and leverage.

Future research

The paths connecting appropriability and appropriation as well as interactive appropriability with consideration of other agents and context-specificity open avenues for future innovation studies falling under resource-based view, especially value-based strategy, and knowledge-based view, to understand how to capture value from innovation in competition and networks. Correspondingly, value capture theory is in its infancy in terms of being applied to guide strategy practices.

Details of the three approaches proposed here, that is, exclusion, leveraging, and abandoning, await examination. Empirical research on the selection of the paths and deciding when to switch paths is needed. It will be valuable not only to examine successes, but also failures of firms, who make choices on different paths. Emerging contexts warrant attention: we need studies on the emergence and building of inter-organizational collaboration platforms (e.g., IBM OpenScale), which introduce different types of dynamics of value capture. Modeling digital transactions is a relevant topic for future research. Limited research focusses on the bargaining rules and configurations of agents with different complementary resources (Piller & West, 2014; Ross, 2018). What are the optimal configurations? How to select collaborative communities with regard to a firm's own bargaining power and appropriability level? How do bargaining failures influence innovation activities and appropriation outcomes? How does value appropriation change with a firm's bargaining power?

Finally, we acknowledge that besides private returns, it is also valuable to study the social returns from innovation. For example, researchers can trace the process starting from a firm's purposive abandoning of its appropriability premises, looking at what social returns come up, and ending with an examination of how these social returns eventually influence the private profiting. Contemporary global challenges, such as the COVID-19 pandemic, gather collective and collaborative efforts to achieve technological progress and advancements (Bertello et al., 2021; Chesbrough, 2020). As a response, many firms (such as AbbVie) announced waving exclusive rights to speed up the discovering of the treatments. We hope that this study provides a starting point for work that increases understanding of the premises of abandoning path and the related returns.

Acknowledgments

We are in debt to many colleagues and co-researchers who have listened to our ideas and helped us develop them further with their questions and comments. Likewise, we thank practitioners for sharing their insight during our research activities. Funding of this research is gratefully received from Finnish Cultural Foundation, Marcus Wallenberg Foundation, Foundation for Economic Education, Tauno Tönning Foundation, Scholarship Fund of the University of Oulu, University of Oulu Graduate School, Savings Banks Research Foundation, Martti Ahtisaari International Doctoral Scholarship, HPY Research Foundation, and University of Oulu Academics.

References

Ahuja, G., Lampert, C. M., & Novelli, E. (2013). The second face of appropriability: Generative appropriability and its determinants. *Academy of Management Review, 38*(2), 248–269. doi: 10.5465/amr.2010.0290

Ahuja, G., Lampert, C. M., & Tandon, V. (2008). Chapter 1: Moving beyond Schumpeter: Management research on the determinants of technological innovation. *Academy of Management Annals, 2*(1), 1–98. Retrieved from http://10.0.4.56/19416520802211446

Al-Laham, A., Amburgey, T. L., & Baden-Fuller, C. (2010). Who is my partner and how do we dance? Technological collaboration and patenting speed in US biotechnology. *British Journal of Management, 21*(3), 789–807. Retrieved from http://10.0.4.87/j.1467-8551.2010.00689.x

Alexander, E. A. (2012). The effects of legal, normative, and cultural-cognitive institutions on innovation in technology alliances. *Management International Review, 52*(6), 791–815. doi: http://dx.doi.org/10.1007/s11575-011-0123-y

Alexy, O., George, G., & Salter, A. J. (2013). Cui Bono? The selective revealing of knowledge and its implications for innovative activity. *Academy of Management Review, 38*(2), 270–291. doi: 10.5465/amr.2011.0193

Alexy, O., West, J., Klapper, H., & Reitzig, M. (2018). Surrendering control to gain advantage: Reconciling openness and the resource-based view of the firm. *Strategic Management Journal, 39*(6), 1704–1727. doi: 10.1002/smj.2706

Alnuaimi, T., & George, G. (2016). Appropriability and the retrieval of knowledge after spillovers. *Strategic Management Journal, 37*(7), 1263–1279. doi: 10.1002/smj.2383

Appleyard, M. M., & Chesbrough, H. W. (2017). The dynamics of open strategy: From adoption to reversion. *Long Range Planning, 50*(3), 310–321. doi: 10.1016/J.LRP.2016.07.004

Arundel, A. (2001). The relative effectiveness of patents and secrecy for appropriation. *Research Policy, 30*(4), 611–624. doi: 10.1016/S0048-7333(00)00100-1

Avagyan, V., Esteban-Bravo, M., & Vidal-Sanz, J. M. (2014). Licensing radical product innovations to speed up the diffusion. *European Journal of Operational Research, 239*(2), 542–555. doi: 10.1016/j.ejor.2014.05.031

Bacon, E., Williams, M. D., & Davies, G. (2020). Coopetition in innovation ecosystems: A comparative analysis of knowledge transfer configurations. *Journal of Business Research, 115*, 307–316. doi: 10.1016/j.jbusres.2019.11.005

Battisti, G., & Stoneman, P. (2010). How innovative are UK firms? Evidence from the fourth UK community innovation survey on synergies between technological and organizational innovations. *British Journal of Management, 21*(1), 187–206. doi: 10.1111/j.1467-8551.2009.00629.x

Belenzon, S., & Schankerman, M. (2015). Motivation and sorting of human capital in open innovation. *Strategic Management Journal, 36*(6), 795–820. doi: 10.1002/smj.2284

Bertello, A., Bogers, M. L., & De Bernardi, P. (2021). Open innovation in the face of the COVID-19 grand challenge: Insights from the Pan-European hackathon 'EUvsVirus'. *R&D Management*. doi: 10.1111/radm.12456

Bessen, J., & Maskin, E. (2009). Sequential innovation, patents, and imitation. *RAND Journal of Economics, 40*(4), 611–635. doi: 10.1111/j.1756-2171.2009.00081.x

Bhatia, V., & Carey, G. I. B. (2007). Patenting for profits. *MIT Sloan Management Review, 48*(4), 15–16.

Bogers, M., Bekkers, R., & Granstrand, O. (2011). Intellectual property and licensing strategies in open collaborative innovation. In *Open innovation in firms and public administrations: Technologies for value creation* (pp. 37–58). University of Southern Denmark, Denmark: IGI Global. doi: 10.4018/978-1-61350-341-6.ch003

Bos, B., Broekhuizen, T. L. J., & de Faria, P. (2015). A dynamic view on secrecy management. *Journal of Business Research, 68*(12), 2619–2627. doi: 10.1016/j.jbusres.2015.04.009

Boudreau, K. (2010). Open platform strategies and innovation: Granting access vs. devolving control. *Management Science, 56*(10), 1849–1872. doi: 10.1287/mnsc.1100.1215

Brandenburger, A., & Stuart, H. (2007). Biform games. *Management Science, 53*(4), 537–549. doi: 10.1287/mnsc.1060.0591

Ceccagnoli, M. (2009). Appropriability, preemption, and firm performance. *Strategic Management Journal, 30*(1), 81–98. doi: 10.1002/smj.723

Chatain, O., & Mindruta, D. (2017). Estimating value creation from revealed preferences: Application to value-based strategies. *Strategic Management Journal, 38*(10), 1964–1985. doi: 10.1002/smj.2633

Chen, Y., Argentinis, E., & Weber, G. (2016, April 1). IBM Watson: How cognitive computing can be applied to big data challenges in life sciences research. *Clinical Therapeutics, 38*(4), 688–701. doi: 10.1016/j.clinthera.2015.12.001

Chesbrough, H. W. (2003). *Open innovation: The new imperative for creating and profiting from technology.* Boston, MA: Harvard Business School Press.

Chesbrough, H. W. (2006). *Open business models: How to thrive in the new innovation landscape.* Boston, MA: Harvard Business School Press (1st ed.).

Chesbrough, H. (2020). To recover faster from Covid-19, open up: Managerial implications from an open innovation perspective. *Industrial Marketing Management, 88,* 410–413. doi: 10.1016/j.indmarman.2020.04.010

Chesbrough, H., & Bogers, M. (2014). Explicating open innovation: Clarifying an emerging paradigm for understanding innovation keywords. In H. Chesrbough, W. Vanhaverbeke, & J. West (Eds.), *New frontiers in open innovation* (pp. 3–28). Oxford: Oxford University Press.

Cohen, J. E., Rajz, G., Lylyk, P., Ben-Hur, T., Gomori, J. M., & Umansky, F. (2005). Protected stent-assisted angioplasty in radiation-induced carotid artery stenosis. *Neurological Research, 27*(Suppl. 1), S69–S72. doi: 10.1179/016164105X25333

Cohen, W. M., Nelson, R. R., & Walsh, J. P. (2000). *Protecting their intellectual assets: Appropriability conditions and why U.S. manufacturing firms patent (or not)* (Working Paper 7552). National Bureau of Economic Research Inc.

Dahlander, L., & Wallin, M. W. (2006). A man on the inside: Unlocking communities as complementary assets. *Research Policy, 35*(8 SPEC. ISS.), 1243–1259. doi: 10.1016/j.respol.2006.09.011

Dattée, B., Alexy, O., & Autio, E. (2018). Maneuvering in poor visibility: How firms play the ecosystem game when uncertainty is high. *Academy of Management Journal, 61*(2), 466–498.

Di Minin, A., & Faems, D. (2013). Building appropriation advantage: An introduction to the special issue on intellectual property management. *California Management Review, 55*(4), 7–14. doi: 10.1525/cmr.2013.55.4.7

Estrada, I., Faems, D., & de Faria, P. (2016). Coopetition and product innovation performance: The role of internal knowledge sharing mechanisms and formal knowledge protection mechanisms. *Industrial Marketing Management, 53,* 56–65. doi: 10.1016/j.indmarman.2015.11.013

Faria, P., & Sofka, W. (2008). Appropriability mechanisms of multinational firms – A cross country comparison. In *2008 IEEE International Engineering Management Conference* (pp. 1–5). doi: 10.1109/IEMCE.2008.4617978

Fischer, T., & Henkel, J. (2013). Complements and substitutes in profiting from innovation – A choice experimental approach. *Research Policy, 42*(2), 326–339. doi: 10.1016/j.respol.2012.06.004

Gambardella, A., Heaton, S., Novelli, E., & Teece, D. J. (2021). Profiting from enabling technologies? *Strategy Science, 6*(1), 75–90. doi: 10.1287/stsc.2020.0119

Gans, J., & Ryall, M. D. (2017). Value capture theory: A strategic management review. *Strategic Management Journal, 38*(1), 17–41. doi: 10.1002/smj.2592

Gans, J. S., & Stern, S. (2003). The product market and the market for "ideas": Commercialization strategies for technology entrepreneurs. *Research Policy, 32*(2 SPEC.), 333–350. doi: 10.1016/S0048-7333(02)00103-8

Giordani, P. E., Rullani, F., & Zirulia, L. (2018). Endogenous growth of open collaborative innovation communities: A supply-side perspective. *Industrial and Corporate Change, 27*(4), 745–762. doi: 10.1093/icc/dty004

Graham, S. J. H., & Sichelman, T. S. (2016). Intellectual property and technology start-ups: What entrepreneurs tell us. In *Advances in the study of entrepreneurship, innovation, and economic growth* (Vol. 26, pp. 163–199). UK: Emerald Group Publishing Ltd. doi: 10.1108/S1048-473620160000026006

Granstrand, O. (1999). *The economics and management of intellectual property.* MA: Edward Elgar Publishing.

Grant, R. M. (2015). Knowledge-based view. In *Wiley encyclopedia of management* (pp. 1–2). Chichester, UK: John Wiley & Sons, Ltd. doi: 10.1002/9781118785317.weom120172

Grindley, P. C., & Teece, D. J. (1997). Managing intellectual capital: Licensing and cross-licensing in semiconductors and electronics. *California Management Review, 39*(2), 8–41.

Hall, M., Oppenheim, C., & Sheen, M. (2003). Barriers to the use of patent information in SMEs. In R. A. Blackburn (Ed.), *Intellectual property and innovation management in small firms* (pp. 144–160). London, New York: Routledge.

Hannah, D., Parent, M., Pitt, L., & Berthon, P. (2019). Secrets and knowledge management strategy: The role of secrecy appropriation mechanisms in realizing value from firm innovations. *Journal of Knowledge Management, 23*(2), 297–312. doi: http://dx.doi.org/10.1108/JKM-09-2017-0389

Harabi, N. (1995). Appropriability of technical innovations an empirical analysis. *Research Policy, 24*(6), 981–992. doi: 10.1016/0048-7333(94)00812-4

Henkel, J. (2006). Selective revealing in open innovation processes: The case of embedded Linux. *Research Policy, 35*(7), 953–969. doi: 10.1016/j.respol.2006.04.010

Henkel, J., Baldwin, C. Y., & Shih, W. (2013). IP modularity: Profiting from innovation by aligning product architecture with intellectual property. *California Management Review, 55*(4), 65–82. doi: 10.1525/cmr.2013.55.4.65

Holgersson, M. (2013). Patent management in entrepreneurial SMEs: A literature review and an empirical study of innovation appropriation, patent propensity, and motives. *R and D Management, 43*(1), 21–36. doi: 10.1111/j.1467-9310.2012.00700.x

Holgersson, M., Granstrand, O., & Bogers, M. (2018). The evolution of intellectual property strategy in innovation ecosystems: Uncovering complementary and substitute appropriability regimes. *Long Range Planning, 51*(2), 303–319. doi: 10.1016/j.lrp.2017.08.007

Huizingh, E. K. R. E. (2011). Open innovation: State of the art and future perspectives. *Technovation, 31*(1), 2–9. doi: 10.1016/j.technovation.2010.10.002

Hurmelinna, P. (2018). Exiting and entering relationships: A framework for re-encounters in business networks. *Industrial Marketing Management, 70,* 113–127. doi: 10.1016/j.indmarman.2017.07.010

Hurmelinna-Laukkanen, P., & Puumalainen, K. (2007). Formation of the appropriability regime: Strategic and practical considerations. *Innovation : Management, Policy & Practice, 9*(1), 2–13.

IBM. (2018, October 15). *IBM introduces ai openscale to spur artificial intelligence adoption and transparency.* US: IBM Corporation.

Ivus, O., Park, W. G., & Saggi, K. (2017). Patent protection and the composition of multinational activity: Evidence from US multinational firms. *Journal of International Business Studies, 48*(7), 808–836. doi: 10.1057/s41267-017-0100-1

Jacobides, M. G., Knudsen, T., & Augier, M. (2006). Benefiting from innovation: Value creation, value appropriation and the role of industry architectures. *Research Policy, 35*(8 SPEC. ISS.), 1200–1221. doi: 10.1016/j.respol.2006.09.005

James, S. D., Leiblein, M. J., & Lu, S. (2013). How firms capture value from their innovations. *Journal of Management, 39*(5), 1123–1155. doi: 10.1177/0149206313488211

Kolbjørnsrud, V. (2014). *On governance in collaborative communities* [BI Norwegian Business School]. Retrieved from https://core.ac.uk/download/pdf/52094914.pdf

Laursen, K., & Salter, A. J. (2014). The paradox of openness: Appropriability, external search and collaboration. *Research Policy, 43*(5), 867–878. doi: 10.1016/j.respol.2013.10.004

Leten, B., Vanhaverbeke, W., Roijakkers, N., Clerix, A., & Van Helleputte, J. (2013). IP models to orchestrate innovation ecosystems: IMEC, a public research institute in nano-electronics. *California Management Review, 55*(4), 51–64. doi: 10.1525/cmr.2013.55.4.51

Levin, R. C., Klevorick, A. K., Nelson, R. R., & Winter, S. G. (1987a). Appropriating the returns from industrial research and development; Comments and discussion. *Brookings Papers on Economic Activity, 3*, 783. doi: 10.2307/2534454

Levin, R. C., Klevorick, A. K., Nelson, R. R., Winter, S. G., Gilbert, R., & Griliches, Z. (1987b). Appropriating the returns from industrial research and development. *Brookings Papers on Economic Activity, 1987*(3), 783. doi: 10.2307/2534454

Lichtenthaler, U. (2015). A note on outbound open innovation and firm performance. *R and D Management, 45*(5), 606–608. doi: 10.1111/radm.12138

Liebeskind, J. P. (1996). Knowledge, strategy, and the theory of the firm. *Strategic Management Journal, 17*(Suppl. Winter), 93–107. doi: 10.1002/smj.4250171109

Liebeskind, J. P. (1997). Keeping organizational secrets: Protective institutional mechanisms and their costs. *Industrial and Corporate Change, 6*(3), 623–663. doi: 10.1093/icc/6.3.623

Milesi, D., Petelski, N., & Verre, V. (2013). Innovation and appropriation mechanisms: Evidence from Argentine microdata. *Technovation, 33*(2–3), 78–87. doi: 10.1016/j.technovation.2012.12.001

Minniti, A. (2011). Knowledge appropriability, firm size, and growth. *Journal of Macroeconomics, 33*(3), 438–454. doi: 10.1016/j.jmacro.2011.02.004

Miric, M., Boudreau, K. J., & Jeppesen, L. B. (2019). Protecting their digital assets: The use of formal & informal appropriability strategies by App developers. *Research Policy, 48*(8), 103738. doi: 10.1016/j.respol.2019.01.012

Musk, E. (2014). *All our patent are belong to you.* Retrieved from https://www.tesla.com/blog/all-our-patent-are-belong-you

Nagarajan, M., & Sošić, G. (2008). Game-theoretic analysis of cooperation among supply chain agents: Review and extensions. *European Journal of Operational Research, 187*(3), 719–745. doi: 10.1016/j.ejor.2006.05.045

Nicholson, D. (2012). Open invention network: A defensive patent pool for open source projects and businesses. *Technology Innovation Management Review, 2*(1), 12–17. doi: 10.22215/timreview/511

Olander, H., Vanhala, M., & Hurmelinna-Laukkanen, P. (2014). Reasons for choosing mechanisms to protect knowledge and innovations. *Management Decision, 52*(2), 207–229. doi: 10.1108/MD-11-2012-0791

Olander, H., Vanhala, M., Hurmelinna-Laukkanen, P., & Blomqvist, K. (2016). Preserving prerequisites for innovation: Employee-related knowledge protection and organizational trust. *Baltic Journal of Management, 11*(4), 493–515. doi: 10.1108/BJM-03-2015-0080

Pagani, M. (2013). Digital business strategy and value creation: Framing the dynamic cycle of control points. *MIS Quarterly, 37*(2), 617–632.

Pao-Tsung, K. (2013). *Institutional change and foreign market entry behaviour of the firm: A longitudinal study of three Swedish firms in China.* Sweden: Uppsala University.

Petricevic, O., & Teece, D. J. (2019). The structural reshaping of globalization: Implications for strategic sectors, profiting from innovation, and the multinational enterprise. *Journal of International Business Studies, 50*(9), 1487–1512. doi: 10.1057/s41267-019-00269-x

Piller, F., & West, J. (2014). Firms, users, and innovation. In H. Chesrbough, W. Vanhaverbeke, & J. West (Eds.), *New frontiers in open innovation* (pp. 29–49). Oxford: Oxford University Press. doi: 10.1093/acprof:oso/9780199682461.003.0002

Pisano, G. (2006). Profiting from innovation and the intellectual property revolution. *Research Policy, 35*(8 SPEC. ISS.), 1122–1130. doi: 10.1016/j.respol.2006.09.008

Qi, S. R. (2018). *Google's AI can see through your eyes what doctors can't.* Retrieved from https://medium.com/health-ai/googles-ai-can-see-through-your-eyes-what-doctors-can-t-c1031c0b3df4

Rimmer, M. (2014). *Tesla motors: Intellectual property, open innovation, and the carbon crisis* (Issue August). Retrieved from http://ir.teslamotors.com/secfiling.cfm?filingID=1193125-13-96241&CIK=1318605

Ritala, P., & Hurmelinna-Laukkanen, P. (2009). What's in it for me? Creating and appropriating value in innovation-related coopetition. *Technovation, 29*(12), 819–828. doi: 10.1016/j.technovation.2009.07.002

Ritala, P., & Hurmelinna-Laukkanen, P. (2013). Incremental and radical innovation in coopetition-the role of absorptive capacity and appropriability. *Journal of Product Innovation Management, 30*(1), 154–169. doi: 10.1111/j.1540-5885.2012.00956.x

Ritala, P., & Hurmelinna-Laukkanen, P. (2019). Dynamics of coopetitive value creation and appropriation. Chapter 5. In A.-S. Fernandez, P. Chiambaretto, F. Le Roy, & W. Czakon (Eds.), UK: *Routledge companion to coopetition strategy* (80–89). Routledge.

Ross, D. G. (2018). Using cooperative game theory to contribute to strategy research. *Strategic Management Journal, 39*(11), 2859–2876. doi: 10.1002/smj.2936

Santangelo, G. D., Meyer, K. E., & Jindra, B. (2016). MNE subsidiaries' outsourcing and insourcing of R&D: The role of local institutions. *Global Strategy Journal, 6*(4), 247–268. Retrieved from http://10.0.3.234/gsj.1137

Schultz, J., & Urban, J. (2012). Protecting open innovation: The defensive patent license as a new approach to patent threats, transaction costs, and tactical disarmament. *Harvard Journal of Law & Technology, 26.* Retrieved from https://scholarship.law.berkeley.edu/facpubs/2149

Seo, H., Chung, Y., & Yoon, H. D. (2017). R&D cooperation and unintended innovation performance: Role of appropriability regimes and sectoral characteristics. *Technovation, 66–67,* 28–42. doi: 10.1016/j.technovation.2017.03.002

Sherry, E. F., & Teece, D. J. (2004). Royalties, evolving patent rights, and the value of innovation. *Research Policy, 33*(2), 179–191. doi: 10.1016/S0048-7333(03)00088-X

Stasik, E., & Cohen, D. L. (2020). Royalty rates and licensing strategies for essential patents on 5g telecommunication standards: What to expect. *Les Nouvelles*

– *Journal of the Licensing Executives Society, 3.* Retrieved from https://papers.ssrn.com/abstract=3658472

Sun, Y., & Zhai, Y. (2018). Mapping the knowledge domain and the theme evolution of appropriability research between 1986 and 2016: A scientometric review. *Scientometrics, 116*(1), 203–230. doi: 10.1007/s11192-018-2748-0

Tech, R. P., Kahlert, J., & Schmeiss, J. (2019). Blockchain-enabled open business models: New means to shared value capturing? In *Co-creation* (pp. 63–76). Chambrigde: Springer.

Teece, D. J. (1986). Profiting from technological innovation: Implications for integration, collaboration, licensing and public policy. *Research Policy, 15*(6), 285–305. doi: 10.1016/0048-7333(86)90027-2

Teece, D. J. (1998). Capturing value from knowledge assets: The new economy, markets for know-how, and intagible assets. *California Management Review, 40*(3), 55–79. doi: 10.2307/41165943

Teece, D. J. (2006). Reflections on "profiting from innovation." *Research Policy, 35*(8 SPEC. ISS.), 1131–1146. doi: 10.1016/j.respol.2006.09.009

Teece, D. J. (2018a). Profiting from innovation in the digital economy: Enabling technologies, standards, and licensing models in the wireless world. *Research Policy, 47*(8), 1367–1387. doi: 10.1016/j.respol.2017.01.015

Teece, D. J. (2018b). Reply to Nelson, Helfat and Raubitschek. *Research Policy, 47*(8), 1400–1402. doi: 10.1016/j.respol.2018.03.016

Yang, J., Chesbrough, H., & Hurmelinna-Laukkanen, P. (2020). *The rise, fall, and resurrection of IBM Watson Health.* Berkeley, CA: University of California. Retrieved from http://jultika.oulu.fi/Record/nbnfi-fe2020050424858

16

FRUGAL INNOVATION

A structured literature review of antecedents, enablers, implications and directions for future research

Jayshree Jaiswal, Amit Anand Tiwari, Samrat Gupta and Renu Agarwal

Introduction

In the current times of growing economic instability and environmental turbulence during COVID-19, innovation as a dynamic capability plays a crucial role for businesses to capitalize on market opportunities (Lei et al., 2019) and to gain competitive edge so as to meet customer needs (Hossain, 2020). Earlier, innovation was mainstream for developed countries to achieve market performance, competitive advantage and productivity. It involved setting up of national policies, formal research with businesses and educational institutions, clusters, precincts and raising funds for research and development (Oslo Manual, 2018). However, it was largely criticized as in this process demand side factors were largely ignored and concentration was only on the supply side factors (Kaplinsky, 2011). Presently, in developed countries, the economic growth is stagnated while in developing countries there is a huge potential to serve large customer base and opportunity for massive economic growth (OECD, 2015). This has led to the rise in scholarly interest in the field of management and innovation in developing countries (Hossain, 2021).

A fact well known is that developing countries are strapped for resources. In such a constrained environment, businesses are pushed to adapt to the changing needs which forces them to rethink their strategy executed via creating new innovative products and services (Baker & Nelson, 2005) in emerging and developed markets. These innovative services and products not only create value at a firm level but also support economic development at a national level (Lei et al., 2019). Thus, shortage of resources has rather shaped the ability to innovate. Additionally, becoming lean and cutting down of use of the resources to a bare minimum has led to the emergence of the concept of innovation called "frugal innovation (FI)". Frugal, derived from the Latin word, frugalis means 'sparing or

DOI: 10.4324/9780429346033-21

economical as regards money or food'. FI can be distinguished from conventional innovation on the basis of its drivers (especially resource and cost constraint), the bottom-up processes (from emerging or developing market to developed market) and core values delivered to the customers such as ease of operation, cost-effectiveness, resource efficiency (more can be done with less without compromising the quality) (Basu et al., 2013). Frugal often linked with concepts like "asceticism, self-restriction or free-chosen poverty" (Bouckaert et al., 2008, p. 3), as such presents a phenomenal opportunity for the world's wealthiest businesses to bring prosperity to the resource poor economies (Prahlad and Hart, 2002). It also has religious (e.g. Buddhism or Christianity) and philosophical (e.g. Epicurean ethics or Stoa) roots (Albert, 2019, p. 2).

FIs are mainly developed keeping in mind the needs of the respective home countries and not necessarily for worldwide consumption or distribution. Even though these countries often lack core capabilities in terms of raw material, labour, capital, policy support, infrastructure and, skilled manpower at the grassroots level, FIs have emerged as a new entrepreneurial phenomenon and a potential model delivering value to the customers (Radjou et al., 2012). The FI model is underpinned by simplifying the eco-system, lowering costs and optimizing resource usage (Zeschky et al., 2014). The rise in the number of innovations in the last decade from emerging markets like India has shifted the traditional view that innovations are developed only in the West and transferred to the rest (Hossain, 2021). FI is thus a paradigm shift in the innovation and management literature. The use of IT systems and services coupled with frugal innovation practices is another nascent phenomenon (Ahuja and Chan, 2016). Frugal IT Innovation Capability (FITIC), a higher-order capability at a strategic level, is defined as "*the capability of a firm to redesign its processes, products, and services, to minimize resource usage and increase affordability and sustainability by combining business innovation, information technology/systems innovation, and social innovation*". It facilitates the provision frugal IT innovation capabilities along with opportunities for strategic differentiation and competitive advantage to the firms (Ahuja and Chan, 2016).

Most developed countries have not yet recognized the importance of embracing FI and continue the use of conventional products and services that have ultimately led to the contribution to environmental degradation, resource scarcity and other issues (Rosca et al., 2018; Winkler et al., 2020). Recently, in developed markets owing to their commitment to Sustainable Development Goals (SDGs), FI is being considered as the future of innovation management for cleaner production and sustainable development that meets the needs of next generation (Khan, 2016; Rosca et al., 2017). As per the WCED (1987) report, '*sustainable development is a development that meets the needs of the present without compromising the ability of future generations to meet their own needs*' (WCED, 1987, p. 8). To meet the needs of future generation it is crucial that resources are used aptly, thus there is an increased focus on the concept of circular economy, which is now gaining traction in developed economies. Circular economy involves "*reduction of material input in production, different reuse and reproduction opportunities, intelligent, resource management (including energy resources) and changes in consumer behaviour and business models"* (Levänen and Lindemann, 2016, p. 2). Also, there is a gradual shift of the outputs of FI from developing markets to developed markets (Nesta, 2016; Tiwari et al., 2016). This is often referred to as a phenomenon of reverse innovation *"where an innovation is adopted first in poor (emerging) economies before 'trickling up' to rich countries"* (Govindarajan and Ramamurti, 2013, p. 191). FI has thus emerged as a central innovation topic in the context of scarcity and sustainability in the developed markets.

The existing research has certainly enriched our understanding of FI from various aspects, such as conceptualization (e.g. Weyrauch and Herstatt, 2017), development (e.g. Niroumand et al., 2021) and diffusion (e.g. Hossain et al., 2016). As FI research continues to expand its legitimacy, it is apparent that researchers from various other disciplines apart from innovation management will take interest in conducting research at the intersection of FI and their respective multidisciplinary fields. For example, recent studies have advocated the cross-pollination of research in FI with social entrepreneurship (Bhatti, 2014; Mishra, 2021), marketing (Costa et al., 2021), sustainable development (Hossain, 2021), information and communication technology (Peša, 2018), healthcare (Mishra and Sharma, 2021), energy (Numminen and Lund, 2017), supply chain (Dubey et al., 2021) and economics (Meagher, 2018). The fragmentation of FI research into numerous literature streams and theoretical approaches makes it difficult to obtain a holistic picture of the collective current evidence base, and there is an urgent need to provide an overview of FI research that would help scholars position their scholarly efforts within a broader realm of FI phenomena.

Given the influx of the scholarly articles in this field, a systematic review of FI is timely and warranted. Accordingly, we aim to develop a structured review of the FI literature published in scholarly journals to synthesize the literature and put forward important research agendas. Through a detailed review of FI with a specific focus on its antecedents, enablers, emerging areas of application, and the impact FI has on sustainable development, we aim to propose a conceptual framework in this chapter.

There are several FI review papers that already exist that do enhance our understanding of FI but they focus in the context of developing and emerging markets with closest relation at the Bottom of the Pyramid concept (e.g. Hossain, 2018). The term "Bottom of Pyramid (BoP)" was coined by Prahalad and Stuart in 2002 in their article "The fortune at the bottom of the pyramid" are the 4 billion people, who live on less than US$2 a day (Prahalad and Stuart, 2002). We believe that our understanding can further be advanced by taking a different approach through linking FI in close connection with 'reverse innovation', 'sustainability', 'circular economy' and how these concepts are crucial in scaling up the FI from developing markets to developed economies. The chapter thus particularly aims to focus on the flow of innovation from developing to developed market context. In the present work, we also reviewed FI's antecedents, enablers, sector-wise applications and impact on sustainable development, thereby proposing a conceptual framework for FI.

Against this backdrop, this study presents a literature review in the field of FI and aims to answer the following questions, namely:

i)   what is the current state of research in the field of FI?
ii) what are the antecedents of FI?
iii) what are the key enablers of FI?
iv) what are the different applications of FI across different industries and domains?
v)   what are the implications of FI on sustainable development, circular economy, digital effectuation and scaling up the FI from emerging markets to developed markets?
vi) what are the future research directions in FI?

Answering these specific research questions will help us identify the research gaps that remain to be addressed with our major and unique contribution being connecting the hitherto missing link of FI with sustainable development for scaling it up from emerging markets to developed markets. We also provide explicit research directions for future.

This article is structured as follows: it starts by explaining the background related to FI thus positioning it against previous FI-related literature review studies and classifying theories related to FI. Then, the methodological choices in the identification and selection of suitable studies for the review are explained. Subsequently, findings are presented that help construct a comprehensive view of antecedents, enablers and sector-wise case applications of FI. Then implications of FI are discussed. The next section proposes and discusses a number of important future research avenues and a conceptual framework for future research on FI. Finally, we conclude this study.

Background

The origin of the concept of FI in the management and innovation literature is not clear (Hossain, 2018). However, the concept of FI gained prominent attention after one of the pioneering studies on FI defined FI as *"good-enough, affordable products that meet the needs of resource-constrained consumers"* (Zeschky et al., 2011, p. 23). In 2010, it was introduced by The Economist in press and emerged as *"frugal engineering"* concept coined in 2006 by Carlos Ghosn, the Chairman and CEO of the Renault-Nissan Alliance (Hossain et al., 2016).

Besides frugal engineering, constraint-based innovation, Gandhian innovation, jugaad innovation, reverse innovation, catalytic innovation, grassroots innovation and indigenous innovation are other concepts linked with FI (Brem and Wolfram, 2014). The other FI concepts consider low cost, good-enough, the base of the pyramid, inclusive, grassroots, disruptive, jugaad and reverse innovation notions in connection with developing nations (Rosca et al., 2017). Concepts like reverse innovation, blowback innovation and trickle-up innovation are often used for scaling up the innovation from developing to the developed markets (Hossain, 2016). Linking the FI concept with sustainable development is yet to be sufficiently documented in the literature.

History of the evolution of the concept of frugal innovation

Beyond the discussion above, FI as an emerging paradigm is been explored through distinct lens. Different definitions of the concept exist. In the current work, we have used the classification suggested by Pisoni et al. (2018) to understand the evolution of its conception through four phases which are described in Table 16.1.

First phase of evolution (2012–2013)

This phase provides a product-oriented view of FI that highlights the key features of product or services, namely, reduced cost, limited use of resources, ease-of-use, advanced technology, compact design, etc. (Rao, 2013; Tiwari and Herstatt, 2012). Hossain (2021) argued that this was vague as it is simply focussing on efficiency. Bound and Thornton (2012) pointed that frugal products and services not only offer low cost but also are superior in comparison to its alternate and can be made available at a large scale. Agarwal and Brem (2012) emphasized localization and identification of core values for FI. Basu et al. (2013) find FI as an innovation process design with a customer-centric approach. Bhatti et al. (2013) further proposed that FI requires a business model approach rather than a new technology or product or service, comprising of the key building blocks of value proposition, target customer, value chain and revenue model (Boons and Lüdeke-Freund, 2013).

TABLE 16.1 Phases of evolution of frugal innovation

Phase of evolution	Focus area	References
First phase (2012–2013)	Product-oriented	Tiwari and Herstatt (2012), Rao (2013)
Second phase (2014–2015)	Product-market-process-oriented	Zeschky et al. (2014), Soni and Krishnan (2014), Brem and Wolfram (2014), Agnihotri (2015), Prabhu and Jain (2015)
Third phase (2016–2017)	Holistic view in developing and developed markets	Weyrauch and Herstatt (2017), Tiwari et al. (2017), Rossetto et al. (2017), Agarwal et al. (2016), Hossain et al. (2016)
Current phase (2018–present)	Advanced FI, Sustainable Development, Scaling up, Digital Effectuation	Rao (2018), Pansera (2018), Hossain (2018), Hossain (2021)

Second phase of evolution (2014–2015)

In the second phase, the definition moved beyond product centric view and incorporated market and process view. Zeschky et al. (2014) argued that technical novelty and market novelty are key features for the success of the frugal offering. Soni and Krishnan (2014) emphasized on the role of resource constrained environment for the development of FI. They proposed FI as a process with three stages, namely input, process and output. First, at the input level, for example, a housewife with limited budget using her resources prudently to buy basic necessities for her family is exhibiting a frugal mindset. FI at this stage can be done through providing proper training, teaching best practices and using behavioural change approaches. Second, FI at the process stage can be done through following lean manufacturing and process reengineering. Lastly at the output level FIs can be done by adapting to new business models and new market offerings at the grassroots level, domestic firms and Multinational Corporation (MNC) subsidiaries. Brem and Wolfram (2014) proposed that FI is characterized by sustainability, low to medium sophistication, and emerging market orientation to distinguish it from other innovation. Cunha et al. (2014) used three key terms – "scarcity", "bricolage" and "improvisation" and considered FI as a product innovation where the target customers are scarce and distinguish it from bricolage which means to do with whatever is at hand (Lévi-Strauss, 1967) and from improvisation when time is scarce. Agnihotri (2015) highlighted the frugal mindset of the innovators in meeting the need of producing low-cost products and services. As per the process-oriented definitions, "frugal innovation is the means and ends to do more with less for more people" (Prabhu and Jain, 2015, p. 857). This was later refined to *doing better with less* (Radjou and Prabhu, 2015, p. 54) which accounts for promising quality and a win-win situation for both the society and business as well as results in sustainable outcomes.

Third phase of evolution (2016–2017)

The third phase of evolution (2016–2017) took a holistic view and identified three criteria namely "substantial cost reduction, concentration on core functionalities, and optimized performance level" in both emerging and developed market context (Agarwal et al., 2016; Hossain et al., 2016; Weyrauch and Herstatt, 2017). Hossain et al. (2016, p. 133) defined

> Frugal innovation as a resource scarce solution (i.e., product, service, process, or business model) that is designed and implemented despite financial, technological, material or other resource constraints, whereby the final outcome is significantly cheaper than competitive offerings (if available) and is good enough to meet the basic needs of customers who would otherwise remain un(der)served.

Weyrauch and Herstatt (2017) proposed the need to explore how FIs can develop and what challenges we face when pursuing FIs. Tiwari et al. (2017) proposed to gain insights into how small and medium firms with limited capabilities can do research and development to create innovation. Rossetto et al. (2017) used the three dimensions namely, frugal functionality (i.e. ability of the firm to focus on core values); frugal cost (i.e. ability of the firm to sustainably reduce the cost while maintaining quality) and frugal ecosystem (i.e. ability of firm to maintain relationship and promote sustainability).

Current phase of evolution (2018–present)

This phase demonstrates the role and importance of technology. Rao (2018) focussed on the role of advanced technology in driving the low-cost innovation which he termed "Advanced Frugal Innovation". According to this study, the three main features of advance FIs are low cost, advanced engineering and product design, and involvement of workers through the use of advanced technology. Pansera (2018) effectively linked the triple bottom line approach across social, environmental and economic underpinned by technological innovations will lead to sustainable development resulting in FI. Ahuja and Chan (2016) emphasized on the role IT systems and services coupled with frugal innovation practices to add to the firms' capabilities. Table 16.1 summarizes these phases and key focus during each period.

A summary of FI reviews to-date

There are number of review papers that attempt to understand the concept of FI as shown in Table 16.2. For example, Hossain (2016) analysed more than 60 research papers on FI and offered country-wise, journal-wise and sector-wise description of FIs. They also reviewed eminent cases of FI in different industries to understand the evolution of FI. Agarwal et al. (2016) systematically reviewed more than a hundred research works focussing on the term "constraint-based innovations" and provided quantitative analyses of the articles. Hossain (2018) defined FI as a phenomenon and used the three stages of input, process and output to propose a framework. According to the findings of this study, "leadership, institutional gaps, new financial model, flexible local sales force, awareness and training" are the critical success factors, and "weak infrastructure, weak policy and law, cannibalization, dual business model and slow diffusion" are barriers. Von Janda et al. (2020) discussed frugality as a formative construct with two additional dimensions of sustainability and cost of consumption. Thus, numerous definitions and conceptions of FI as a product, service, technology, phenomenon and business model have led to divergent views (Hossain, 2021), however they lack a coherent understanding of the boundaries of FI.

Theories related to frugal innovation

Since FI is a young field, different theories have been used to understand diverse aspects of the concept. A concrete theory to explain FI is still at an early stage of evolution. Examples of significant theories used in explaining FI phenomenon are transaction theory, international product life cycle theory, agency theory, network theory, institutional theory, disruptive innovation theory, diffusion theory, and resource dependency theory (Table 16.3). Further, more and more empirical studies are evaluating and testing existing and new theories supporting FI. Most of the existing theories used to explain FI provide a limited explanation of the phenomenon (Ahuja and Chan, 2014). Therefore, extending theories into the FI context is essential to comprehend the phenomenon (Hossain, 2018). George et al. (2012, p. 5) proposed to use the theoretical lenses:

> 1) resource assembly, deployment, and development; 2) social and organizational networks; 3) governance and agency; 4) transaction cost and organizational economics; 5) competition and strategy; 6) stakeholder engagement and property rights; and 7) adoption of innovation' to understand the phenomenon of FIs.

The vision of FI is to cater to the needs of developing markets by offering customer value at the lowest price as compared to conventional ones. Some FIs have found their foothold in the developed markets too. Due to the salient features that FI possess, the existing innovation paradigms cannot be used to fully explain the FI concept. Scholars suggest that a separate theoretical framework is needed because of the contextual differences across countries, the way FI diffuses is different, and different FIs need separate business models as well as distribution channels (Hossain, 2018).

TABLE 16.2 Existing review papers on frugal innovation

Authors	Title, Journal and publication year	Description
Nivedita Agarwal, Michael Grottke, Shefali Mishra, Alexander Brem	A Systematic Literature Review of Constraint-Based Innovations: State of the Art and Future Perspectives *IEEE Transactions on Engineering Management*, 2016	The study systematically reviewed more than 100 research works focussing on the term "constraint-based innovations" and provided quantitative analyses of the articles. The findings suggest increasing applications of these innovations to emerging as well as developed markets

(Continued)

Authors	Title, Journal and publication year	Description
Mokter Hossain	Frugal innovation: A review and research agenda. *Journal of Cleaner Production*, 2018	The study analysed the various definitions and overlapping concepts of FI by reviewing 101 relevant articles, he. The study proposed that theory driven studies are needed and emphasized on the role of FI on sustainability.
Eugenia Rosca, Jack Reedy, Julia C. Bendul	Does Frugal Innovation Enable Sustainable Development? A Systematic Literature Review. *The European Journal of Development Research*, 2018	The study sheds light on the drivers to link FI with sustainable development especially in relation to different types of private sector actors by systematically reviewing the existing literature.
Ronny Reinhardt, Sebastian Gurtner, Abbie Griffin	Towards an adaptive framework of low-end innovation capability – A systematic review and multiple case study analysis. *Long Range Planning*, 2018	The study developed a framework to understand what constitutes a low-end innovation capability by systematically reviewing articles and case studies. The study found the specific internal capabilities and external capabilities required to meet the needs of low-end market.
Sergejvon von Janda, Sabine Kuestera, MonikaC. Schuhmacherb, G. Shainesh	What frugal products are and why they matter: A cross-national multi-method study. *Journal of Cleaner Production*, 2020	The study found frugality as a multi-dimensional construct with two addition dimensions namely low cost and environmental sustainability.
Janet Molina-Maturano, Stijn Speelman, Hans De Steur	Constraint-based innovations in agriculture and sustainable development: A scoping review. *Journal of Cleaner Production*, 2020	The study found 'inclusive' and 'smallholder' innovation as key concepts used in an agricultural context; and the innovation networks, direction of the innovation and scale are key attributes by analysing 30 cases in the agriculture sector.
Marjan Niroumand, Arash Shahin, Amirreza Naghsh, Hamid Reza Peikari	Frugal innovation enablers, critical success factors and barriers: A systematic review. *Creativity and Innovation Management*, 2021	The study developed a model for the critical success factors (CSF), enablers and barriers to FI by reviewing 372 documentaries of five databases and conducting semi-structured interviews with experts.

TABLE 16.3 Theories related to frugal innovation

Theories	Linkage to frugal innovation	References
Transaction theory	Knowledge transfer	Fischer et al. (2020), Prabhu (2017)
International product life cycle theory	Mature products launching in the emerging markets	Rosca et al. (2018)
Agency theory	Agencies involved in FI are different	Leliveld and Knorringa (2018), Ploeg et al. (2021)
Network theory	Network elements	Leliveld and Knorringa (2017)
Institutional theory	New types of institutions	Zeschky et al. (2014)
Disruptive innovation theory	Value for money, convenience and affordability of products	Soni and Krishnan (2014), Slavova (2014)
Diffusion theory	Cost of product lower down with innovation diffusion	Hossain et al. (2016), Hang et al. (2015)
Resource dependency theory	Resource scarcity	George et al. (2012), Hessels and Teriesen (2010)

Review methodology

We conducted a structured literature review to address the research objectives highlighted in this study. A structured literature review aims to survey scientific literature related to a particular field in a reproducible and unbiased way, enabling the study and evaluation of all existing work that meet the set criteria. The criteria for excluding or including studies are agreed upon and explicitly stated before searching for relevant literature. We use the guidelines proposed by Kitchenham and Charters (2007).

Structured literature review methodology

As the initial step in this structured literature review, we formulate a set of principal research questions along with clear articulation of the exclusion and inclusion criteria. These research questions encompass the motivation behind this review and exclusion and inclusion criteria help in focussing the scope of the research. In the second step, we plan and design an appropriate search strategy for querying relevant databases. Once results have been consolidated, the exclusion and inclusion criteria are applied so as to filter and narrow down the final set of papers to review. We start this iterative process by looking at the title and keywords, followed by the perusal of the abstract, and finally going through the full paper to decide whether to exclude or include the paper. In the following subsections, we explain how we applied the aforementioned methodology in this study.

Strategy for searching relevant papers

In this study, we used the keyword "frugal innovation" for searching relevant papers. Figure 16.1 shows the number of hits generated when the search string "frugal innovation" was applied to each database. At this stage, not all exclusion and inclusion criteria have been applied. A total of 1,351 hits were generated which consists of some duplicates as some papers were indexed in multiple databases. These 1,351 hits consisted of papers on different aspects of FI such as its drivers, enablers, impact on sustainability, applications and case studies in various domains.

Exclusion and inclusion criteria

The following exclusion and inclusion criteria were used to filter the results of search:

1. Only papers related to FI, low-cost innovation, jugaad innovation, reverse innovation, and resource constrained innovation are included.
2. The timeline used for selection process is from January 2001 to August 2021. We selected 2001 as the starting point because that was the time when the research and application of FI took off with a primary focus on Bottom-of-pyramid (BoP). Since the beginning of last decade this area has started gaining considerable momentum from prominent scholars in the innovation and management literature.
3. Only papers published in English language, i.e. research work available to the wider research audience is included. Research papers published in any other language than English (American and British spelling) are excluded.

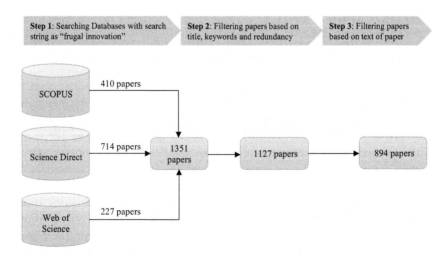

FIGURE 16.1 Paper selection and review process.

Study selection process

The database searches were conducted in September 2021, and subsequently the reviewing and filtering process took place. The iterative process of literature selection was followed, where the search results were screened based on the structured literature review method detailed in the relevant sections. With the exclusion and inclusion criteria at hand, filtering of the database results was done based on the keywords and title resulting in a total of 1,127 papers. The last filtering iteration was based on a cursory glance at the full papers, resulting in a set of 894 papers. This final set of papers were reviewed in full so as to answer the research objectives pertaining to this study.

Findings

Based on the structured literature review of the selected papers we analyse and the relevant papers to synthesis and describe the antecedents of FI, enablers of FI, sector wise application, and impact of FI on sustainability in this section.

Antecedents of frugal innovation

Since the research in the area of FI is in nascent stage, most of the literature has focussed on the conceptualization and theory development as detailed in Costa et al. (2021). There is less literature that sheds light on the antecedents of FI. However, in the last few years, researchers have focussed on studying the few antecedents of FI namely scarcity of resources, BoP economics, income inequality, social inequality, climate change and globalization (Table 16.4).

It is also evident from the extant literature that the researchers so far have placed more inclination on the developing or emerging markets for understanding the FI concept, its antecedents and diffusion. A systematic review by Pisoni et al. (2018) highlighted that studies in this field have focussed only on few countries with the UK as the largest contributor followed by India, the USA and Germany. He argued that the UK and India are the largest contributors due to the intense commercial and cultural ties between the authors from both these countries. Recently, studies from the countries, namely, Denmark, Belgium, Ireland, Uruguay, Jamaica, Mexico, Portugal, Philippines, Russia, Slovakia, Singapore, Netherlands and South Korea started making contribution in this area. The study pointed out India ranks first among the countries under investigation (35%), followed by the UK (17%), the USA (10%) and a number of countries with emerging economies, such as Brazil, China and Kenya (between 7% and 8%). There are calls to understand the development and diffusion of FI in developed countries because of demographic, environmental, social and economic changes which is an under-researched area (Agarwal et al., 2016; Hossain, 2020; Kroll and Gabriel, 2020). Recently, few studies explored the process of the diffusion of FI in the developing markets (e.g. Costa et al., 2021; Zhang 2018).

TABLE 16.4 Antecedents of frugal innovation

Antecedents of frugal innovation	References
Scarcity of resources	Zeschky et al. (2011), Bhatti (2012), Rao (2013), Bhatti and Ventresca (2013), Cunha et al. (2014), Sarkar and Pansera (2017), Corsini et al. (2021), Pleog et al. (2021)
BoP economics	Bhatti (2012), Bhatti et al. (2013), Prahalad (2012), Chataway et al. (2014), Soni and Krishnan (2014), Brem and Wolfram (2014), Agarwal and Brem (2017), Laliveld and Knorringa (2018), Sarkar (2021)
Income inequality	Bhatti (2012), Chataway et al. (2014), Tiwari et al. (2017), Laliveld and Knorringa (2018), Roscaet al. (2018)
Social inequality	Bhatti (2012), Bhatti et al. (2013), Basu et al. (2013), Brem and Wolfram (2014), Soni and Krishnan (2014), Hossain (2016), Khan (2016), Knorringa et al. (2016), Tiwari et al. (2016), Sarkar and Pansera (2017), Rosca et al. (2017), Tiwari et al. (2017), Laliveld and Knorringa (2018), Corsini et al. (2021), Sarkar (2021)
Climate change	Bhatti et al. (2013), Rosca et al. (2017), Albert (2019), Winkler et al. (2020), Hossain et al. (2016)
Globalization	Jha and Krishnan (2013), Altmann and Engberg (2016), Hossain (2016), Le Bas (2016), Tiwari et al. (2017), Krohn and Herstatt (2019), Gerybadze and Klein (2020)

Enablers of frugal innovation

The ability of an organization to convert an idea into something that has economic value is based on its enablers. When understanding the enablers of FI, it is crucial to identify and match the external opportunity with the internal environment. There are few studies in the extant literature that focus on understanding the enablers of FI. Niroumand et al. (2021) noted that no existing studies have exclusively addressed the enablers and barriers to FI. They conducted a systematic review of literature on enablers and barriers to FI and found that *"not paying attention to the enablers and critical success factors (CSFs) and their mismanagement can turn them into barriers to FI"*, and in contrast, *"proper attention and management of barriers to FI can turn them into enablers for FI"*. Through this structured review, we identified the following (see Table 16.5) as enablers of FI.

Applications of frugal innovation in key industries and domains

We have explored FI across key industries and domains (see Figure 16.2). We discuss some key industry and domain examples which include agriculture, transportation, healthcare, energy and finance, including a brief description of some specific examples from the water, education, sharing economy, eco-innovation, supply chain sectors. Agriculture is the recent promising sector where FI is

TABLE 16.5 Enablers of frugal innovation

Enablers of frugal innovation	References
Organizational support to employees	Ramdorai and Herstatt (2015), Bocken and Short (2016), Farooq (2017), Gupta and Thomke (2018), Srivastava (2018)
Frugal mindset	Soni and Krishnan (2014), Rosca et al. (2017), Tiwari et al. (2017), Agarwal et al. (2016), Igwe et al. (2020)
Government and policy support	Radjou et al. (2012), Prabhu and Jain (2015), Hossain (2018), Thun (2018), Krishnan and Prashantham (2019), Lim et al. (2021), Sarkar (2021)
Infrastructural support	Ahuja and Chan (2014), Sood and Szyf (2011), Sun et al. (2016), Bianchi et al. (2017), Tiwari et al. (2017)
Marketing	Tiwari and Herstatt (2012), Gault (2018)

picking up at greater pace (Molina-Maturano et al., 2020). In the agricultural sector, agricultural machinery and water for irrigation are the focus areas whereas alternate and innovative farming systems, agricultural biomass gasifiers are the emerging areas (Molina-Maturano et al., 2020). FI in this sector are the collaborative initiatives of small farmers, local developers, civil societies and researchers to promote sustainable agriculture. They aim to bring out some novel, cost-effective and efficient solution for the existing agricultural practices. For example, CPlantae is a social enterprise in Mexico maintains innovative natural wastewater systems by integrating biotechnological solutions that use aquatic plants, microorganisms, and worms (Molina-Maturano et al., 2020). A study by Duker et al. (2020) highlighted that individual-geared solar-powered irrigation system developed from aquifers in ephemeral rivers has immense utility in bringing water to the dry areas of southern Africa. Scarcity of farmlands, lack of resources and capacities, infrastructure support are the driving forces for FI in agriculture.

In the transportation sector, emergency transport and eco-friendly transport are the growing areas. For example, Dial 1298 in India helps in the transportation of rural patients at an affordable rate or free of charge using a cross-subsidy model (Mandal, 2014). E-Ranger motor ambulance that works 24/7 is providing service for maternity emergency and also to ill and injured. Besides, considering the global warming issues, development of frugal electric vehicles is also gearing up. For example, Chinese firms adopted FI strategy to develop low-speed electric vehicles to meet the needs of resource constrained customers (Lu et al., 2020). In India, e-Rickshaw and e-Bikes are examples of disruptive FI that is leveraging constraints as opportunity to better address the environmental issues (Koch, 2021). Thus, it is evident that investment in research and development miniaturization and localness are the key factors for the success of FIs in the transportation sector.

In the healthcare sector, FI facilitates access to affordable and quality solutions in a resource-scarce environment. General practice and neonatology are the focus areas whereas ophthalmic and orthopaedics are emerging areas in this sector. For example, an ECG test at around US$1 (Angot and Plé, 2015) and Hepatitis B vaccine at ten cents per jab are effective solutions for BoPs. Narayana Hridulaya hospital and Kerala's Palliative Care work for the well-being of severely ill people by application of principles of lean manufacturing and mass production. In the neonatal care, Lullaby baby warmer by General Electric have been effectively used to serve the base of pyramid customers. Seimens developed an affordable heart rate monitor to measure the heart rate of foetuses in the womb in India (Hossain, 2017). mOm and Embrace founded in the UK and the USA respectively are low-cost infant incubator built to reduce the infant mortality rate. In the orthopaedics area, Jaipur foot is a simple, affordable, easy to produce and highly performing artificial limb suitable for the uneven terrain (Bhatti, 2012). In the ophthalmic area, Aravind Eye Care Hospital in India provides cataract surgeries at a marginal cost with cross-subsidy (Hossain, 2016). The aforementioned cases highlight that the focus on core values, simplification, reduction of unnecessary features of products and services, using local resources, respecting the needs of local people are critical factors for the successful creation and diffusion of FI in healthcare sector.

In the energy sector, renewable forms of energy like Solar and Wind have gained prominent attention. SELCO (solar power) and Husk Power (power from waste rice husk) in India have successfully catered to the local needs and now eying to scale up to developed markets (Bhatti and Ventresca, 2013; Prabhu and Jain, 2015). Nuru Energy based in Canada provides devices like USB, lights that can be recharged through the solar panels. Grameen Shakti based in Bangladesh provides renewable energy to the underprivileged people using an innovative monthly instalment financial model. The solar cooker of Tibet New Energy Research and Demonstration Centre is also a well-known household device promoted by the Government of China. MyShelter Foundation's A Liter of Light provides sun lighting for the underprivileged in Metro Manila, the Philippines (Kuo, 2017). It is important to design and develop keeping in mind the social and environmental issues, reusing old and recycling materials as an input, collaborations with others, local research and development, world class design and local manufacturing, developing infrastructure with the support of local people and government to scale up are key factors for the success of FIs in the energy sector.

In the finance sector, the concept of microfinance or the Grameen bank has revolutionized the banking sector in the developing as well as the developed nations. Vortex's frugal ATM solutions, that run on solar power and are based on biometric systems, are now available for rural Indian consumers (Hossain et al., 2016). The Rickshaw Bank of the Center for Rural Development is empowering rickshaw pullers for providing frugal finance in rural areas in India (Sahay and Walsham, 2014). M-Pesa in Kenya and EKO in India, the mobile phone-based money transfer service, allow a user to make financial transactions with the help of mobile phones. Zoona a similar service is an icon of successful FI in Tanzania. The various cases discussed above suggest that the use of information and communication technology, biometric design, restructuring business model, use of local manpower are key for the success of FIs in finance sector.

The other sectors where FI is gaining attention are water, education, sharing economy, eco-innovation and supply chain. For example, FI grounded water purifiers and water conservation devices make pure water access and conservation affordable to people. Water purifiers such as Tata Swatch, Lifestraw and Solvatten have made pure water reachability to a large population at the low cost (Hossain, 2016). Airbnb, a sharing economy platform, is also a service innovation example that used frugal approach to achieve success (Winkler et al., 2020). Agooday's bamboo toothbrush is a social enterprise in Taiwan that offer eco-friendly plastic free toothbrush. Among consumer goods, washing-cum-exercise machine is a prominent innovation. This washing machine does not require electricity to wash and dry cloths. Another innovative product, Chotuwash, is a nano washing machine at low cost. The famous lunch box delivery system called 'dabbawallas' in Mumbai, India is an apt case of frugal supply chain system. A summary of FI across industries and domains is provided in Figure 16.2. The grassroots level innovation is described as "neglected, but potentially important site of innovative activity" (Seyfang and Smith, 2007, p. 584). At the grassroots level, the focus is on creating novel solutions that meet the needs of local people and solve their problems with local knowledge (Jain and Verloop, 2012; Pansera and Sarkar, 2016; Smith et al., 2014). In this context, two classic FI examples standout: i) Mitticool fridge, invented by Mansukhbhai Prajapati from Gujarat State, made of clay can be used to freeze necessary perishables. The local region where the inventor lived is deprived of electricity and he invented the refrigerator that works on the principle of cooling through evaporation. The success stories of this product helped it to be adopted in many developed countries like Germany and France. Besides refrigerator, there are many other innovative clay products developed by Mitticool such as water bottles, crockery, pressure cookers, and tableware. ii) The other well-known case is Jayashree Industries, owned by Arunachalam Muruganantham, which invented a machine that produces low-cost sanitary napkins. Another example of how FIs can promote sustainable development is the milking machine developed by Ksheera Enterprises owned by Raghava Gowda. The key feature of this machine is that it can work without electricity too. This product marked in presence not only in Indian market but also in developed countries like New Zealand, Sweden, Mexico, etc.

A challenge for FI at grassroots level is they lack support from formal institutions and often fail to scale at a larger level. To combat this in India, the grassroots level FI are supported by the National Innovation Foundation and SRISTI (Gupta, 2006). Policymakers should effectively design the policies to help the grass-level innovators for the development of FI (Hossain, 2021).

At the domestic level, small and medium firms are adapting new business models and reconfiguring their processes to target the bottom of pyramid market.

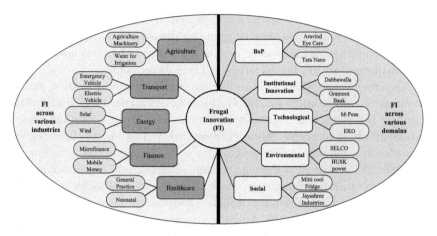

FIGURE 16.2 Representation of frugal innovation across various industries and domains.

FI at the domestic levels in India include affordable and quality healthcare services provided by Aravind Eye Care Hospital, and Narayana Hrudayalaya, solar lamps developed by SELCO and cheap and sustainable power produced from husk by Husk Power Systems. These firms not only provide economically viable solutions but also address the social needs of the BoP markets (Jayashankar and Goedegebuure, 2012; Prasad and Suri, 2011).

Lastly the FI by the multinationals companies aims to meet the goals of serving the untapped emerging and developing market of India and China. Considering the fact that multinational companies are equipped with immense resources and competencies that can be utilized effectively to cater to the needs of low-income countries (Prabhu and Jain, 2015). As part of their long-term strategy, they are shifting from large-scale funding and elaborate processes to an approach that is more frugal, affordable and inclusive (Prahalad and Mashelkar, 2010). Recently many emerging MNCs like Tata, Godrej, Vodafone and Lenovo are successfully targeting low-income countries, which have demonstrated that FIs require investment and scaling up. Mahindra and Mahindra's small tractors, Tata's Swach low-priced water purifier, Ace and Nano affordable cars and Godrej's ChotuKool refrigerator are currently competing in the local markets (Levänen et al., 2016) for market expansion and achievement of SDGs.

Implications of the study

This study demonstrates that FI discipline has emerged over the last decade as a novel, new or disruptive solution. Some researchers argue that FI is a mindset (George et al., 2012; Prahalad and Mashelkar, 2010; Soni and Krishnan, 2014), while for some it is a process (Radjou et al., 2012) and for others it is an outcome (Prahalad and Mashelkar, 2010). As evident, FI has operated mainly at three levels, namely, domestic-enterprises, grassroots, and MNC subsidiaries. New forms of collaborations, business models, alliances and networks are needed for each type.

First, the theoretical understanding of FI is still at the embryonic stage of research (as discussed in Section 2.3). Rigorous attempts at exploratory studies, empirical research and hypothesis testing are needed to gain firm theoretical perspectives. Since FI is characterized by low cost, resource scarcity, local resources, ease of use, minimum product features and core functionalities, they are different from the conventional and mainstream innovations. Substantial changes in the mindset, business culture, skill-sets and business environment can drive the success of FI.

Secondly, there is a need for collaboration with the government, local authorities, regulatory bodies and pressure groups to scale up the innovation at a broader level. Focussing on FI that originated to cater the needs of BoP could offer interesting and valuable insights for extending it to developed markets. Besides the knowledge about how sustainable development and innovation can be integrated to capture value for all the stakeholders is useful for sustainable solutions. Moreover, considering the triple bottom line, the environmental issues are also addressed by making the use of more sustainable and local resources and following the principles of conservation.

Lastly, FI provides useful ways to overcome social problems by better serving underprivileged people with novel and disruptive business models that are characterized by a frugal mind and assured quality. It also has the potential to successfully address economic concerns by creating jobs at the local level and enhancing the quality of life.

Frugal innovation and its implications on sustainability

There is a growing criticism that MNCs are embracing sustainability features. Bouckaert et al. (2008) in their book *Frugality: Rebalancing Material and Spiritual Values in Economic Life* argued that frugality is the necessary condition for sustainable development to meet the needs of future generation. FI is an effective business model to promote sustainable development that can effectively address economic, social and environmental concerns (Albert, 2019). Tiwari et al. (2016) suggested a strong association between both these concepts. Brem and Ivens (2013) pointed out that there are not many evidences to establish or understand the link of frugality with sustainability. Levänen et al. (2016) emphasized the need to focus on empirical evidences to establish this association with the three dimensions of environmental, sustainability, social and economic. The positive association between FI and environmental sustainability is characterized by no-frills design, resource constraints, reduced complexity, robustness, and simplicity (Albert, 2019). The positive association between FI and social sustainability is characterized by indirect and direct effects of access to this innovation type and the affordability. Lastly, the positive association between FI and economic sustainability is characterized by economic development, increased profitability of the firms, enhanced completion and employment opportunities.

There are few studies that present a negative association between FI and sustainable development due to rebound effect (e.g. Rosca et al., 2017; Sharma and Iyer, 2012; Wohlfart et al., 2016). The rebound effect occurs when more people are able to buy affordable products and increased consumption causes environment degradation. The authors also argued that increased demand for affordable frugal products and services could lead to the disposal of obsolete and goods (planned obsolescence) that, in turn, could deteriorate the environment. Also, highly affordable products may lead to the cannibalization of existing products.

Frugal innovation and its implications on circular economy

Most big and small firms are operating on linear value chains where the products are disposed in an unsustainable way piling up landfills, thus causing environmental issues (Merli et al., 2018). Business leaders must adapt to new sustainable methods, for example, cradle to cradle design which works on the 3 R principles, namely, reduce, reuse and recycle (Levänen and Lindemann, 2016). They proposed that FI at a micro level can leverage the impact of FI on circular economy. For example, Tarkett is sports surface and flooring solutions provider that uses materials like pine resin, walnut shells, linseed oil, cork and jute as well as pre- and post-consumer recycled plastic material. This allows use of waste materials, thereby reducing the waste into the landfills.

Frugal innovation and its implications on IT-enabled digital effectuation

The exploration of link between FI and digital effectuation has been attempted in a few studies but has largely remained an under explored area of research. The theoretical lens of FI and effectuation has been used to understand the digital entrepreneurial practices by exploring the case of a movie named *Lucia* (Khanal et al., 2021). According to the theory of effectuation entrepreneurs following effectual logic are flexible towards their goals in order to deal with uncertainty (Sarasvathy, 2001). They are approximate, adaptive and iterative that helps them to overcome their environmental constraints. They also work with knowledge corridors and create alliance with partners to share risks. Since movie making is a risky business (Gupta et al., 2016), Lucia made use of digital technologies to overcome the shortcomings such as resource-scarcity and institutional voids. It not only helped gain financial benefits but also stimulate localness, social, and cultural betterment (Khanal et al., 2021). Another case of a mobile banking solution to help the local people in getting the access to banking service provides insights on how IT affordances can support frugal effectuation (Khanal et al., 2017). The developer of this mobile banking solution used the online sources such as Wikipedia and YouTube, to advance his understanding while relying upon his own savings, personal assets and partnership with local group to create the venture. While being very flexible, adaptive and receptive, he made a good use of digital information system which led to a successful creation of his entrepreneurial venture so as to meet the demands of resource constrained consumers. One of the prior studies also seeks to understand the role of ICT in capturing and creation of value for non-commodity products at the BoP and found that ICT-enabled awareness creation positively impacts value-added, but this effect decreases with an increase in product complexity (Parthiban et al., 2021). Another study explores the case of digital transformation of a public service namely *'certification of authenticity of a signature'* in Greece to explore the role of frugal approach in achieving low-cost digital transformation. This study concludes that *'e-services can meet the basic relevant needs of citizens, but cannot meet some more complex ones that may appear'* thus highlighting the importance of trust in frugal digital transformation and suggesting the implications of trust in frugal innovation (Loukadounou et al., 2020). Therefore, IT affordances have several implications on frugal entrepreneurs and digital effectuation.

Scaling-up the frugal innovation

Emerging economies are considered as an ideal hub and a lead market for the conception and development of FI (Kaur, 2016). For example, India is referred to as an "ideal laboratory" for conducting experiments related to the FIs (Tiwari and Herstatt, 2012; Shivdas and Chandrasekhar, 2016). The Government of India has also set up FI for inclusive growth as one of the agendas (Arora, 2011; Nair et al., 2015; Prabhu and Jain, 2015). As there are three types of innovators namely grassroots, domestic and multinational (Soni and Krishnan, 2014), the scaling up of FI from the local level to the domestic level and from the emerging markets to the developed markets is the key challenge faced by emerging FIs. Most FIs are developed with the aim of solving a local need effectively at a low cost and not with the intention of scaling up. Since the values held by the participants at a global level differs from the local values, scaling up requires a unique approach keeping the target market in mind. The economic, social, political, environment and technological factors drive the process. A study by Rosca et al. (2017) figured out that reverse innovation for health-related products and services such as Tomography Scanner and VScan opens up new market segments in developed markets mainly because of the mobility of devices as they are optimized in terms of weight, size, and robustness and also affordable for smaller institutions. Price sensitivity among customers is different in different markets. There is an association of poor product image with low price so firms need to strategically avoid this while positioning their offerings.

Discussion

Based on the structured literature review and the subsequent analysis and synthesis of the literature conducted in Section 4, we present a future research agenda and a conceptual framework for future research on FI (see Figure 16.3). We propose numerous research opportunities that can be explored further. While our suggestions are not an exhaustive list, yet the future research can aim to address the following research questions as identified from this structured literature review and fill the different knowledge gaps that exist in extant literature.

RQ1. Is resource scarcity the only driver in the development of frugal innovation or is it a thoughtful business strategy that is used to capture large untapped BoP markets?

BoP is the future unexploited and, unlimited market segment. The loci and foci of the innovations have changed recently and now FI are mainly developed to address the urgent local needs of low-income markets under resource scarcity. It is in the interest of global and local companies to target the BoP market due to the immense growth potential and business opportunities. FI capable of meeting the needs of people at an ultra-low cost without quality compromise has the potential of diffusing rapidly. Therefore, we propose that future research should gain a better understanding on how FI can be used as a thoughtful business strategy to capture the large untapped BoP markets. There is a need to develop insights on the changes required in the operating business model, the role of the firm size and where it is headquartered, and the changes required in distribution channel to target the BoP market at a broader level. Besides, marketing and awareness programmes need to be properly designed to fill the information accessibility gap. For instance, Siemens in the healthcare environment initially

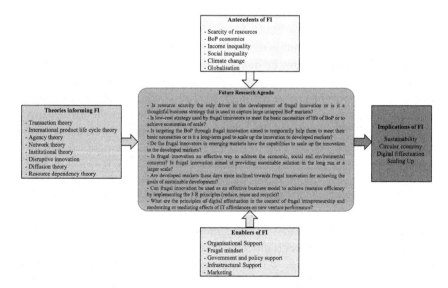

FIGURE 16.3 Conceptual framework for future research on FI.

faced difficulty in changing the traditional mindset. BoP can be effectively targeted by building upon the local competencies through the local resources and capabilities.

RQ2. Is low-cost strategy used by frugal innovators to meet the basic necessities of life of BoP or to achieve economies of scale?

As discussed in RQ1, FIs are developed at an ultra-low cost to meet the necessities of BoP market. Since BoP markets are large in size, it is possible to achieve economies of scale. For instance, Bharti and M-Pesa are only successful because of achieving a large scale. FI can thus address the objective of achieving resource efficiency (i.e. maximizing output and minimizing input). Therefore, we propose that firms are more likely to adopt FI as it can help increase profit in two ways: first by reducing cost due to reduced inputs and second by increasing sales. However, more sales also imply inviting more competitors in the market, which, in turn, will drive firms to create more value for the customers. Therefore, better insights on the raw material sourcing, handling supply chains, designing and product packaging and better customer's engagement needs to be understood.

RQ3. Is targeting the BoP through frugal innovation aimed to temporarily help them to meet their basic necessities or is it a long-term goal to scale up the innovation to developed markets?

As discussed in RQ2, firms initially targeting the BoPs to meet their basic needs can achieve economies of scale and generate business growth. However, FI is often compared to reverse innovation. Reverse innovation refers to innovations that first target the emerging markets and migrates to the developed or wealthier markets. In the developed market, there are concerns over the declining real incomes, lesser government spending, resource scarcity and environmental degradation. People in the developed markets are also becoming more resource conscious committed to positive social and environmental impact. For example, Western MNCs such as TATA Consultancy Services (TCS) and General Electric (GE) are turning FI into reverse innovation by bringing them to developed markets. GE handheld electrocardiogram (ECG) and Ultrasound Machine are successful in the Western market especially the USA. However, such cases are few mainly due to differences in socio-economic contexts and the geographic regions.

RQ4. Do the frugal innovators in emerging markets have the capabilities to scale up the innovation to the developed markets?

As discussed in RQ3, the scaling up of FI from emerging market to the developed markets is limited owing to geographic and socio-economic challenges. Therefore, better insights into the understanding the capabilities of FI for global diffusion is needed. There is a need to explore dimensions like functional and technological competencies of the offering, business model, supply chain and logistics channels, marketing channel and target customer segment to proper position the offering. Vortex Gramateller with high-end materials and state-of-the-art technologies could make a global diffusion due to its well-fitted strategy along with a substantial product offering while Tata Nano and Godrej's

ChotuKool failed to scale up to the developed markets due to product quality issues, huge investment requirement and geographical differences. This study informs policy making on the ways to influence and scale up frugal innovation at local as well as global level.

RQ5. Is frugal innovation an effective way to address the social, economic, and environmental concerns? Is frugal innovation aimed at providing sustainable solution in the long run at a larger scale?

There may be a need to transform to a frugal business model (that use less resources and only sustainable resources, focus only on core functionalities and localization) to allow the global economy to function in a sustainable way. This requires efforts from multiple actors ranging from large or small firms to policy makers to consumers. The development of frugal products and services and its diffusion is crucial for addressing the need of sustainable development. However, there is little empirical evidence linking FI and sustainability. More research is required to understand the ties between FI and sustainable development through the triple bottom line approach (social, economic and environmental). In the long run, it is argued that more people will be able to buy such products, so there would be market pressure on firms to match the demand-supply with valuable offering on other hand as well as dealing with finding out innovative ways to continue delivering value to the customers in a resource-constrained environment. A major threat that could negate the link between the FI and sustainability is the rebound effect and planned obsolescence. Future research must carefully analyse this and the policy level interventions required to shape up a sustainable frugal innovation ecosystem.

RQ6. Are developed markets these days more inclined towards frugal innovation for achieving the goals of sustainable development?

Western developed markets could relate to FI through their sustained change in consumer behaviour. There are growing aspirations towards simple living among them and they are more conscious of their consumption. Most of the developed countries have agreed to work towards energy and climate targets set by the Paris Agreement. Thus, the consumers in the developed markets have a drive towards embracing a lifestyle that works towards sustainable development. There is a need to better understand how the market and consumer characteristics of emerging and developed markets differ to better position their offerings.

RQ7. Can frugal innovation be used as an effective business model to achieve resource efficiency by implementing the 3 R principles (reduce, reuse and recycle)?

FI is important for the development of circular economy for overcoming the problem of resource scarcity. In the developed markets, there is a shift from linear economy to a bio-based circular economy to attain SDGs. New emerging business models encompassing principles of 3 Rs, namely, reduce, reuse and recycle are essential for the sustainable growth. The emergence and growth of sharing economy, collaborative consumption in the developed and developing markets will require multiple actors to play their role in the process. For example, TATA

Swach that make use of rice husk, Bamboo Bike, Solar Bulb made up from waste plastic, Oorja Stove that can be borrowed and shared are emerging paradigms that are creating value. Future research should focus on generating more insights in these areas. Government intervention in terms of market mechanism, regulation, policy support and incentives are required to foster collaboration and competition.

RQ8. What are the principles of digital effectuation in the frugal intrapreneurship context and mediating or moderating effects of IT affordances on performance of new ventures?

Challenges such as institutional voids and resource constraints can leverage the use of digital technologies to create affordable offerings. Therefore, understanding how international and national economies are influenced by digital effectuation in frugal context is required. More research is needed to ascertain how digital platforms, digital partnerships and alliances can help the effectuators in sharing risk and reducing uncertainty. The negative influence of IT affordances on effectuation also needs to be explored. Future research should also investigate how effectuators use their knowledge corridors to deepen the breadth of their knowledge while extending both explicit and tacit knowledge.

Conclusion

The dramatic increase in number of publications on FI since 2011 and level of interest indicates the dynamic evolution of research on FI as a viable research paradigm. However, despite a decade of research in this stream, it can be deciphered that the boundary or scope of FI is not clearly established and current theoretical narratives of FI are disjointed for capturing its essence. The prominence of case-based studies on FI acting in isolation calls for empirical research in this domain so as to guide theory building and bring conceptual synergy. A clear theoretical understanding of the concept of FI will help scholars, practitioners and policy makers in preparing better for a strategic implementation. The connection between sustainability and FI has not been examined rigorously yet. An integration of FI and sustainability transition literature would be most beneficial for driving research and development in this field. FIs at the grassroots level are mostly confined to local areas. They need policy support and finance to scale up to other geographies. Scholars have not yet focussed on understanding the role of FI in sectors like housing and education.

This study is not devoid of limitations. First, we have considered only the articles from the databases of Web of Science, Scopus and Science Direct. Further, addition of databases like ACM digital library, IEEE Xplore and EBSCO could provide a larger database for more robust interpretation. Besides, the nature of the analysis and synthesis of the literature in the present work is subjective and interpretive and the literature can be interpreted and organized in different ways by the scholars who take an alternate approach. We believe that this study will impart rigor and guide future research in the field of FI.

References

Agarwal, N., & Brem, A. (2017). The frugal innovation case of solar-powered automated teller machines (Atms) of vortex engineering in India. *Journal of Entrepreneurship and Innovation in Emerging Economies, 3*(2), 115–126.

Agarwal, N., Grottke, M., Mishra, S., & Brem, A. (2016). A systematic literature review of constraint-based innovations: State of the art and future perspectives. *IEEE Transactions on Engineering Management, 64*(1), 3–15.

Agnihotri, A. (2015). Low-cost innovation in emerging markets. *Journal of Strategic Marketing, 23*(5), 399–411.

Ahuja, S., & Chan, Y. (2014). The enabling role of IT in frugal innovation. UK: ICIS.

Ahuja, S., & Chan, Y. E. (2016). Digital innovation: A frugal ecosystem perspective. UK: ICIS.

Albert, M. (2019). Sustainable frugal innovation-The connection between frugal innovation and sustainability. *Journal of Cleaner Production, 237,* 117747.

Altmann, P., & Engberg, R. (2016). Frugal innovation and knowledge transferability: Innovation for emerging markets using home-based R&D Western firms aiming to develop products for emerging markets may face knowledge transfer barriers that favor a home-based approach to frugal innovation. *Research-Technology Management, 59*(1), 48–55.

Angot, J., & Plé, L. (2015). Serving poor people in rich countries: The bottom-of-the-pyramid business model solution. *Journal of Business Strategy, 36*(2), 3–15.

Arora, P. (2011). Innovation in Indian firms: Evidence from the pilot national innovation survey. *ASCI Journal of Management, 41*(1), 75–90.

Baker, T., & Nelson, R. E. (2005). Creating something from nothing: Resource construction through entrepreneurial bricolage. *Administrative Science Quarterly, 50*(3), 329–366.

Basu, R. R., Banerjee, P. M., & Sweeny, E. G. (2013). Frugal innovation. *Journal of Management for Global Sustainability, 1*(2), 63–82.

Bhatti, Y. A. (2012). *What is frugal, what is innovation? Towards a theory of frugal innovation.* February 1, 2012.

Bhatti, Y. (2014). Frugal innovation: Social entrepreneurs' perceptions of innovation under institutional voids, resource scarcity and affordability constraints (Doctoral dissertation, Oxford University, UK).

Bhatti, Y., Khilji, S. E., &Basu, R. (2013). Frugal innovation. In *Globalization, change and learning in South Asia* (pp. 123–145). Chandos Publishing.

Bhatti, Y. A., &Ventresca, M. (2013). How can 'frugal innovation'beconceptualized? *Available at SSRN 2203552.*

Bianchi, M., Di Benedetto, A., Franzò, S., & Frattini, F. (2017). Selecting early adopters to foster the diffusion of innovations in industrial markets: Evidence from a multiple case study. *European Journal of Innovation Management, 20*(4), 620–644.

Bocken, N. M., & Short, S. W. (2016). Towards a sufficiency-driven business model: Experiences and opportunities. *Environmental Innovation and Societal Transitions, 18,* 41–61.

Boons, F., & Lüdeke-Freund, F. (2013). Business models for sustainable innovation: State-of-the-art and steps towards a research agenda. *Journal of Cleaner Production, 45,* 9–19.

Bouckaert, L., Opdebeeck, H., & Zsolnai, L. (Eds.). (2008). *Frugality: Rebalancing material and spiritual values in economic life* (Vol. 4). Peter Lang.

Bound, K., & Thornton, I. W. (2012). Our frugal future: Lessons from India's innovation system. London: NESTA.

Brem, A., & Ivens, B. (2013). Do frugal and reverse innovation foster sustainability? Introduction of a conceptual framework. *Journal of Technology Management for Growing Economies, 4*(2), 31–50.

Brem, A., & Wolfram, P. (2014). Research and development from the bottom up-introduction of terminologies for new product development in emerging markets. *Journal of Innovation and Entrepreneurship, 3*(1), 1–22.

Chataway, J., Hanlin, R., & Kaplinsky, R. (2014). Inclusive innovation: An architecture for policy development. *Innovation and Development, 4*(1), 33–54.

Corsini, L., Dammicco, V., & Moultrie, J. (2021). Frugal innovation in a crisis: The digital fabrication maker response to COVID-19. *R&D Management, 51*(2), 195–210.

Costa, L., Teixeira, A., & Brochado, A. (2021). Determinants of consumers' frugal innovation acceptance in a developed country. *Young Consumers, 22*(2), 185–201.

Cunha, M. P. E., Rego, A., Oliveira, P., Rosado, P., & Habib, N. (2014). Product innovation in resource-poor environments: Three research streams. *Journal of Product Innovation Management, 31*(2), 202–210.

Dubey, R., Bryde, D. J., Foropon, C., Tiwari, M., & Gunasekaran, A. (2021). How frugal innovation shape global sustainable supply chains during the pandemic crisis: Lessons from the COVID-19. *Supply Chain Management: An International Journal, 27*(2), 295–311.

Duker, A., Cambaza, C., Saveca, P., Ponguane, S., Mawoyo, T. A., Hulshof, M., & van der Zaag, P. (2020). Using nature-based water storage for smallholder irrigated agriculture in African drylands: Lessons from frugal innovation pilots in Mozambique and Zimbabwe. Environmental Science & Policy, 107, 1–6.

Farooq, R. (2017). A conceptual model of frugal innovation: Is environmental munificence a missing link? *Science, 9*(4), 320–334.

Fischer, B., Guerrero, M., Guimón, J., & Schaeffer, P. R. (2020). Knowledge transfer for frugal innovation: Where do entrepreneurial universities stand? *Journal of Knowledge Management, 25*(2), 360–379.

Gault, F. (2018). Defining and measuring innovation in all sectors of the economy. *Research Policy, 47*(3), 617–622.

George, G., McGahan, A. M., & Prabhu, J. (2012). Innovation for inclusive growth: Towards a theoretical framework and a research agenda. *Journal of Management Studies, 49*(4), 661–683.

Gerybadze, A., & Klein, M. (2020). Frugal innovation strategies and global competition in wind power. *International Journal of Technology Management, 83*(1–3), 114–133.

Govindarajan, V., & Ramamurti, R. (2013). Delivering world-class health care, affordably. *Harvard Business Review, 91*(11), 117–122.

Gupta, A. K. (2006). From sink to source: The Honey Bee Network documents indigenous knowledge and innovations in India. *Innovations: Technology, Governance, Globalization, 1*(3), 49–66.

Gupta, S., Kumar, S., & Kumar, P. (2016). Evaluating the predictive power of an ensemble model for economic success of Indian movies. *Journal of Prediction Markets, 10*(1), 30–51.

Gupta, B., & Thomke, S. (2018). An exploratory study of product development in emerging economies: Evidence from medical device testing in India. *R&D Management, 48*(4), 485–501.

Hossain, M. (2016). *Frugal innovation: A systematic literature review.* Available at SSRN 2768254.

Hossain, M. (2017). Mapping the frugal innovation phenomenon. *Technology in Society, 51*, 199–208.

Hossain, M. (2018). Frugal innovation: A review and research agenda. *Journal of Cleaner Production, 182*, 926–936.

Hossain, M. (2020). Frugal innovation: Conception, development, diffusion, and outcome. *Journal of Cleaner Production, 262*, 121456.

Hossain, M. (2021). Frugal innovation and sustainable business models. *Technology in Society, 64*, 101508.

Hossain, M., Simula, H., & Halme, M. (2016). Can frugal go global? Diffusion patterns of frugal innovations. *Technology in Society, 46*, 132–139.

Igwe, P. A., Odunukan, K., Rahman, M., Rugara, D. G., & Ochinanwata, C. (2020). How entrepreneurship ecosystem influences the development of frugal innovation and informal entrepreneurship. *Thunderbird International Business Review, 62*(5), 475–488.

Jain, A., & Verloop, J. (2012). Repositioning grassroots innovation in India's S&T policy: From divider to provider. *Current Science, 103*(3), 282–285.

Jayashankar, P., & Goedegebuure, R. V. (2012). The impact of marketing strategies on the double bottom line of MFIs: A cross-country study. *IUP Journal of Marketing Management, 11*(1), 7–41.

Jha, S. K., & Krishnan, R. T. (2013). Local innovation: The key to globalisation. *IIMB Management Review, 25*(4), 249–256.

Kaplinsky, R. (2011). Schumacher meets Schumpeter: Appropriate technology below the radar. *Research Policy, 40*(2), 193–203.

Kaur, R. (2016). The innovative Indian: Common man and the politics of jugaad culture. *Contemporary South Asia, 24*(3), 313–327.

Khan, R. (2016). How frugal innovation promotes social sustainability. *Sustainability, 8*(10), 1034.

Khanal, P. B., Aubert, B. A., Bernard, J. G., Narasimhamurthy, R., & Dé, R. (2021). Frugal innovation and digital effectuation for development: The case of Lucia. *Information Technology for Development, 28*(1), 1–30.

Khanal, P. B., Bernard, J. G., & Aubert, B. A. (2017, June). IT enabled frugal effectuation. In *Proceedings of the 2017 ACM SIGMIS conference on computers and people research* (pp. 71–78).

Kitchenham, B., & Charters, S. (2007). Guidelines for performing systematic literature reviews in software engineering. Technical Report EBSE 2007-001, Keele University and Durham University Joint Report.

Knorringa, P., Peša, I., Leliveld, A., & Van Beers, C. (2016). Frugal innovation and development: Aides or adversaries? *The European Journal of Development Research, 28*(2), 143–153.

Koch, A. H. (2021). Implementing Frugal Innovation: Leveraging Constraints as Opportunities for Electric Rickshaws in India. In Frugal Innovation and Its Implementation (pp. 219–232). New York: Springer, Cham.

Krishnan, R. T., & Prashantham, S. (2019). Innovation in and from India: The who, where, what, and when. *Global Strategy Journal, 9*(3), 357–377.

Krohn, M., & Herstatt, C. (2019). Vision for frugal innovation: The power of mindsets for transformation. In *Frugal Innovation* (pp. 164–176). Routledge.

Kroll, H., & Gabriel, M. (2020). Frugal innovation in, by and for Europe. *International Journal of Technology Management, 83*(1–3), 34–54.

Kumar, N., & Puranam, P. (2012). Frugal engineering: An emerging innovation paradigm. *Ivey Business Journal, 76*(2), 14–16.

Kuo, A. (2017). Harnessing frugal innovation to foster clean technologies. *Clean Technologies and Environmental Policy, 19*(4), 1109–1120.

Le Bas, C. (2016). Frugal innovation, sustainable innovation, reverse innovation: Why do they look alike? Why are they different? *Journal of Innovation Economics Management*, (3), 9–26.

Lei, H., Ha, A. T. L., & Le, P. B. (2019). How ethical leadership cultivates radical and incremental innovation: The mediating role of tacit and explicit knowledge sharing. *Journal of Business & Industrial Marketing, 35*(5), 849–862.

Leliveld, A., & Knorringa, P. (2018). Frugal innovation and development research. *The European Journal of Development Research, 30*(1), 1–16.

Levänen, J., Hossain, M., Lyytinen, T., Hyvärinen, A., Numminen, S., & Halme, M. (2016). Implications of frugal innovations on sustainable development: Evaluating water and energy innovations. *Sustainability*, *8*(1), 4.

Levänen, J., & Lindemann, S. (2016, June). Frugal innovations in circular economy: Exploring possibilities and challenges in emerging markets. In *The international society for ecological economics 2016 conference, transforming the economy: Sustaining food, water, energy and justice*. Washington DC, USA.

Lévi-Strauss, C. (1967), *The savage mind*. Chicago, IL: University of Chicago Press.

Lim, C., Lee, J. H., Sonthikorn, P., &Vongbunyong, S. (2021). Frugal innovation and leapfrogging innovation approach to the Industry 4.0 challenge for a developing country. *Asian Journal of Technology Innovation*, *29*(1), 87–108.

Loukadounou, S., Koutsona, V., & Loukis, E. (2020, November). Analyzing a frugal digital transformation of a widely used simple public service in Greece. In *European, mediterranean, and middle eastern conference on information systems* (pp. 223–237). Cham: Springer.

Lu, C., Chang, F., Rong, K., Shi, Y., & Yu, X. (2020). Deprecated in policy, abundant in market? The frugal innovation of Chinese low-speed EV industry. *International Journal of Production Economics*, *225*, 107583.

Mandal, S. (2014). Frugal innovations for global health—Perspectives for students. *IEEE Pulse*, *5*(1), 11–13.

Meagher, K. (2018). Cannibalizing the informal economy: Frugal innovation and economic inclusion in Africa. *The European Journal of Development Research*, *30*(1), 17–33.

Merli, R., Preziosi, M., & Acampora, A. (2018). How do scholars approach the circular economy? A systematic literature review. *Journal of Cleaner Production*, *178*, 703–722.

Mishra, O. (2021). Principles of frugal innovation and its application by social entrepreneurs in times of adversity: An inductive single-case approach. *Journal of Entrepreneurship in Emerging Economies*, *13*(4), 547–574.

Mishra, V., & Sharma, M. G. (2021). Telemedicine as frugal intervention to health care: A case of diabetes management. *International Journal of Healthcare Management*, *1*, 1–6.

Molina-Maturano, J., Bucher, J., & Speelman, S. (2020). Understanding and evaluating the sustainability of frugal water innovations in México: An exploratory case study. *Journal of Cleaner Production*, *274*, 122692.

Nair, A., Guldiken, O., Fainshmidt, S., & Pezeshkan, A. (2015). Innovation in India: A review of past research and future directions. *Asia Pacific Journal of Management*, *32*(4), 925–958.

Nesta. (2016) *Cheaper, better, more relevant. Is frugal innovation an opportunity for Europe?* Available from: https://www.isi.fraunhofer.de/content/dam/isi/dokumente/ccp/2016/FrugalInnovationSummary_ISI_Nesta_mit-ISI.pdf

Niroumand, M., Shahin, A., Naghsh, A., & Peikari, H. R. (2021). Frugal innovation enablers, critical success factors and barriers: A systematic review. *Creativity and Innovation Management*, *30*(2), 348–367.

Numminen, S., & Lund, P. D. (2017). Frugal energy innovations for developing countries–a framework. *Global Challenges*, *1*(1), 9–19.

OECD. (2015). *Innovation policies for inclusive development: Scaling up inclusive innovations*. Paris: OECD.

Oslo Manual. (2018). *Guidelines for collecting, reporting and using data on innovation. The measurement of scientific, technological and innovation activities*. Luxembourg: OECD Publishing.

Pai, D. C., Tseng, C. Y., &Liou, C. H. (2012). Collaborative innovation in emerging economies: Case of India and China. *Innovation*, *14*(3), 467–476.

Pansera, M. (2018). Frugal or fair? The unfulfilled promises of frugal innovation. *Technology Innovation Management Review*, *8*(4), 6–13.

Pansera, M., & Sarkar, S. (2016). Crafting sustainable development solutions: Frugal innovations of grassroots entrepreneurs. *Sustainability*, *8*(1), 51.

Parthiban, R., Qureshi, I., Bandyopadhyay, S., & Jaikumar, S. (2021). Digitally mediated value creation for non-commodity base of the pyramid producers. *International Journal of Information Management, 56*, 102256.

Peša, I. (2018). The developmental potential of frugal innovation among mobile money agents in Kitwe, Zambia. *The European Journal of Development Research, 30*(1), 49–65.

Pisoni, A., Michelini, L., & Martignoni, G. (2018). Frugal approach to innovation: State of the art and future perspectives. *Journal of Cleaner Production, 171*, 107–126.

Ploeg, M., Knoben, J., Vermeulen, P., & van Beers, C. (2021). Rare gems or mundane practice? Resource constraints as drivers of frugal innovation. *Innovation, 23*(1), 93–126.

Prabhu, J. (2017). Frugal innovation: Doing more with less for more. *Philosophical Transactions of the Royal Society A: Mathematical, Physical and Engineering Sciences, 375*(2095), 20160372.

Prabhu, J., & Jain, S. (2015). Innovation and entrepreneurship in India: Understanding jugaad. *Asia Pacific Journal of Management, 32*(4), 843–868.

Prahalad, C. K. (2012). Bottom of the pyramid as a source of breakthrough innovations. *Journal of Product Innovation Management, 29*(1), 6–12.

Prahalad, C. K., & Hart, S. L. (2002). *The fortune at the bottom of the pyramid.* Strategy+ Business, 26.

Prahalad Coimbatore, K., & Stuart, H. (2002). The fortune at the bottom of the pyramid. Strategy+ Business, 26, 1–14.

Prahalad, C. K., & Mashelkar, R. A. (2010). Innovation's holy grail. *Harvard Business Review, 88*(7–8), 132–141.

Prasad, U. C., & Suri, R. K. (2011). Modeling of continuity and change forces in private higher technical education using total interpretive structural modeling (TISM). *Global Journal of Flexible Systems Management, 12*(3–4), 31–39.

Radjou, N., & Prabhu, J. (2012). Mobilizing for growth in emerging markets. *MIT Sloan Management Review, 53*(3), 81.

Radjou, N., & Prabhu, J. (2015). *Frugal innovation: How to do more with less.* The Economist.

Radjou, N., Prabhu, J., & Ahuja, S. (2012). *Jugaad innovation: Think frugal, be flexible, generate breakthrough growth.* John Wiley & Sons.

Ramdorai, A., & Herstatt, C. (2015). Frugal innovation in healthcare. *India Studies in Business and Economics, 127.*

Rao, B. C. (2013). How disruptive is frugal? *Technology in Society, 35*(1), 65–73.

Rao, B. C. (2018). Science is indispensable to frugal innovations. *Technology Innovation Management Review, 8*(4), 49–56.

Rosca, E., Arnold, M., & Bendul, J. C. (2017). Business models for sustainable innovation – An empirical analysis of frugal products and services. *Journal of Cleaner Production, 162*, S133–S145.

Rosca, E., Reedy, J., & Bendul, J. C. (2018). Does frugal innovation enable sustainable development? A systematic literature review. *The European Journal of Development Research, 30*(1), 136–157.

Rossetto, D. E., Borini, F. M., Bernardes, R. C., & Frankwick, G. L. (2017). A new scale for measuring Frugal Innovation: The first stage of development of a measurement tool. In *VI SINGEP–International Symposium on Project Management, Innovation, and Sustainability* (Vol. 6).

Sahay, S., & Walsham, G. (2014). Building a better world: Frugal hospital information systems in an Indian state. India: CIS 2014 Proceedings. 1. https://aisel.aisnet.org/icis2014/proceedings/ConferenceTheme/1.

Sarasvathy, S. D. (2001). Causation and effectuation: Toward a theoretical shift from economic inevitability to entrepreneurial contingency. *Academy of Management Review, 26*(2), 243–263.

Sarkar, S. (2021). Breaking the chain: Governmental frugal innovation in Kerala to combat the COVID-19 pandemic. *Government Information Quarterly, 38*(1), 101549.

Sarkar, S., & Pansera, M. (2017). Sustainability-driven innovation at the bottom: Insights from grassroots ecopreneurs. *Technological Forecasting and Social Change, 114*, 327–338.

Seyfang, G., & Smith, A. (2007). Grassroots innovations for sustainable development: Towards a new research and policy agenda. *Environmental Politics, 16*(4), 584–603.

Sharma, A., & Iyer, G. R. (2012). Resource-constrained product development: Implications for green marketing and green supply chains. *Industrial Marketing Management, 41*(4), 599–608.

Shivdas, A., & Chandrasekhar, J. (2016). Sustainability through frugal innovations: An application of Indian spiritual wisdom. *Prabandhan: Indian Journal of Management, 9*(5), 7–23.

Smith, A., Fressoli, M., & Thomas, H. (2014). Grassroots innovation movements: Challenges and contributions. *Journal of Cleaner Production, 63*, 114–124.

Soni, P., & Krishnan, R. T. (2014). Frugal innovation: Aligning theory, practice, and public policy. *Journal of Indian Business Research, 6*(1), 29–47.

Sood, A., & Szyf, Y. A. (2011). Productivity and technology for Asia's growth. *Global Journal of Emerging Market Economies, 3*(3), 313–334.

Srivastava, M. (2018). New product strategy/innovation: Challenges and opportunities in emerging market. In *Strategic marketing issues in emerging markets* (pp. 99–105). Singapore: Springer.

Sun, Y., Cao, H., Tan, B., & Shang, R. A. (2016). Developing frugal IS innovations: Applied insights from weqia. com. *International Journal of Information Management, 36*(6), 1260–1264.

Thun, E. (2018). Innovation at the middle of the pyramid: State policy, market segmentation, and the Chinese automotive sector. *Technovation, 70*, 7–19.

Tiwari, R., Fischer, L., & Kalogerakis, K. (2017). *Frugal innovation in Germany: A qualitative analysis of potential socio-economic impacts* (No. 96). Working paper.

Tiwari, R., & Herstatt, C. (2012). Assessing India's lead market potential for cost-effective innovations. *Journal of Indian Business Research, 4*(2), 97–115.

Tiwari, R., Kalogerakis, K., & Herstatt, C. (2016, July). Frugal innovations in the mirror of scholarly discourse: Tracing theoretical basis and antecedents. In *R&D management conference*, Cambridge, UK.

Von Janda, S., Kuester, S., Schuhmacher, M. C., & Shainesh, G. (2020). What frugal products are and why they matter: A cross-national multi-method study. Journal of Cleaner Production, 246, 118977.

WCED, Special Working Session. (1987). World commission on environment and development. Our common future, 17(1), 1–91.

Weyrauch, T., & Herstatt, C. (2017). What is frugal innovation? Three defining criteria. *Journal of Frugal Innovation, 2*(1), 1–17.

Winkler, T., Ulz, A., Knöbl, W., & Lercher, H. (2020). Frugal innovation in developed markets–Adaption of a criteria-based evaluation model. *Journal of Innovation & Knowledge, 5*(4), 251–259.

Wohlfart, L., Bünger, M., Lang-Koetz, C., & Wagner, F. (2016). Corporate and grassroot frugal innovation: A comparison of top-down and bottom-up strategies. *Technology Innovation Management Review, 6*(4), 5–17.

Zeschky, M., Widenmayer, B., & Gassmann, O. (2011). Frugal innovation in emerging markets. *Research-Technology Management, 54*(4), 38–45.

Zeschky, M. B., Winterhalter, S., & Gassmann, O. (2014). From cost to frugal and reverse innovation: Mapping the field and implications for global competitiveness. *Research-Technology Management, 57*(4), 20–27.

Zhang, X. (2018). Frugal innovation and the digital divide: Developing an extended model of the diffusion of innovations. *International Journal of Innovation Studies, 2*(2), 53–64.

17

DYNAMIC CAPABILITIES AND INNOVATION

Ali Ahmadi and Felix Arndt

Introduction

Innovation has been a central driver of the economy in the 21st century. For firms, innovation is related to constant change, survival, growth, and competitive advantage. Firms that are able to address and co-create changing environments, those that possess dynamic capabilities, will excel in such environments. We propose the innovation roundabout to offer guidance for navigating this literature in a practical manner. Our innovation roundabout has four pillars of innovations that have been pertinent for advancing our understanding of innovation in the last decade: innovation capabilities, product/process innovation, business model innovation and open innovation.

While managers are fully aware of the necessity and gravity of fostering innovation to create new capabilities in the face of change and competitive market situation, the body of knowledge they have access to through scholarly articles is scattered (Di Stefano et al., 2010). The ambiguity and volatility of the environment can create a bottleneck situation for executive managers and innovative officers in firms, rushing them into short-sighted decisions that may drive managers into the safe haven of traditional methods of budgeting and risk-management that are doomed to fail in the face of a turbulent environment (Schoemaker et al., 2018). Dynamic capabilities offer a comprehensive framework under which strategic renewal and innovation takes place, our innovation roundabout presents guidelines how to utilize this framework in organizations.

On the other hand, technological progress over time enables new business models to emerge, thus disrupting the market equilibrium and increasing the need for change by all players (Teece, 2018). Thus, the emergence of the internet and the flood of new business models in different forms and shapes increases the speed of environmental change for digital business managers from whom faster

DOI: 10.4324/9780429346033-22

and more effective innovation capabilities are expected (Teece, 2018). Similarly, digitalization has offered new opportunities to organize and partner; both central drivers of a modern organization.

In this chapter, we intend to provide a holistic overview of dynamic capabilities and innovation. We start with a historical perspective of dynamic capabilities and related constructs such as combinative capabilities to lay a foundation for our proposed innovation roundabout. Then, we discuss each of the four components of the roundabout and conclude with ideas for future research.

A Brief History of Dynamic Capabilities

The contribution of dynamic capabilities to the literature of innovation has been invaluable. Dynamic capabilities have been a major contributor to better understand dynamic processes such as the resource creation processes, and the renewal of resources to moving environments (Bowman & Ambrosini, 2003; Teece et al., 1997).

Thinking about dynamic processes is not entirely new. Joseph Schumpeter suggested that the disruption of the economic equilibrium is one of the critical roles of entrepreneurs, which then results in disruptive and sudden changes in the environment (Schumpeter, 1934). Other entrepreneurship scholars, such as Israel Kirzner, believed that the entrepreneur find opportunities in markets that are in disequilibrium and exploits these opportunities in an innovative way. Both of these approaches single out the innovative behavior of entrepreneurs and managers that change the state of the market (Teece, 2009).

These ideas also found space in newer perspectives such as the evolutionary theory of the firm (Nelson & Winter, 1982) and the resource-based view (Barney, 1991), inspired by the works of Penrose (1959). The resource-based view (RBV) suggests that firms should focus on their set of valuable and rare resources and their fit to market competition (Barney, 1991). The RBV considers valuable, rare, inimitable, and non-substitutable assets with the capacity to create sustainable competitive advantage. Innovation in this setting refers to the innovation capacity of firms to access and deploy resources.

Aiming at developing a more dynamic perspective, Kogut and Zander (1992) advanced our understanding of combinative capabilities. Their view on knowledge-creation in firms suggests that it is through recombining the current capabilities that new skills and tacit assets are created. The cumulative knowledge of an organization and the adjustable clusters and patterns of this knowledge shape opportunities for a firm to grow in uncertain market. Combinative capabilities present a way to face changing markets dynamically. Combinative capabilities have been a starting point for empirical inquiries regarding dynamic capabilities (Arndt et al., 2018).

In an attempt to overcome the static nature of prior approaches, Teece et al. (1997) introduced the concept of dynamic capabilities as *"the firm's ability to integrate, build and reconfigure internal and external competencies to address rapidly changing environments.*" The nature of dynamic capabilities implies that changes happen from within and outside of firms and lead to novel firm responses. Teece argues that dynamic capabilities could not only help firms to adapt to changing business environments, but they can also drive changes by innovation and collaboration with others. He defines three dimensions of dynamic capabilities that hitherto became very influential: sensing (and shaping) capabilities as a set of systems and capacities to "*learn and to sense, filter, shape, and calibrate opportunities,*" seizing capabilities as "*enterprise structures, procedures, designs and incentives for seizing opportunities,*" and reconfiguring capabilities as "*continuous alignment and realignment of specific tangible and intangible assets.*" In general, their framework intended to explain how firms can find profitable, invest, and implement opportunities. Helfat and Peteraf (2015) highlight the role of the manager by introducing the "*managerial cognitive capabilities*" as a concept that urges capabilities to consider both physical and mental activities. They emphasize the importance of cognitive capabilities for sensing, seizing, and transforming. They argue that dynamic managerial capabilities are a source of heterogeneity between firms (Arndt & Bach, 2015; Arndt & Pierce, 2018).

Aiming at making dynamic capabilities more empirically tangible, Eisenhardt and Martin (2000) proposed a reconceptualization of dynamic capabilities. They focused on best practices, noting that the nature of dynamic capabilities in high-velocity markets changes from complex, deeply embedded processes to simple and fragile rules. Possibly, one of the main contributions of the work of Eisenhardt and Martin (2000) was the observation that dynamic capabilities could be found as specific practices such as new product development, alliancing, and decision-making that turn current assets into value-creating strategies. Arguably, a core contribution of dynamic capabilities is that they locate a source of adaptation within the firm and not like Schumpeter in the market. They identify a lack of imitation and replicability as two mechanisms that work in favor of the entrepreneurial manager (Langlois, 1992; Teece & Pisano, 2003). We explore the elements that entrepreneurial managers have at hand to make their firms dynamically capable in the next section with the innovation roundabout.

Dynamic Capabilities and the Innovation Roundabout

This chapter provides an overview of four kinds of innovation that centrally contribute to a firm's dynamic capabilities. For this very purpose, we developed the innovation roundabout that helps us structuring the discussion in four parts (see Figure 17.1).

We intend to offer a holistic view of how the four pillars of the innovation roundabout shows the dynamic capabilities of a firm. The roundabout of dynamic capabilities and innovation could be seen as a tool that offers managers options that they could follow to face market challenges. Thus, the innovation roundabout helps demystify a plethora of concepts to facilitate informed managerial decisions.

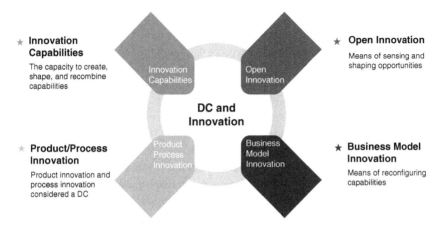

★ **Innovation Capabilities**

The capacity to create, shape, and recombine capabilities

★ **Open Innovation**

Means of sensing and shaping opportunities

★ **Product/Process Innovation**

Product innovation and process innovation considered a DC

★ **Business Model Innovation**

Means of reconfiguring capabilities

FIGURE 17.1 Roundabout of dynamic capabilities and innovation.

Innovation Capabilities and Dynamic Capabilities

The concept of dynamic capabilities is generally about the capabilities that reconfigure and refresh the resource base thus bringing innovation to the organization (Ambrosini & Bowman, 2009; Arndt, 2011). Only through innovation and constant renewal can organizations make continuous changes and keep up with market demands (Chakravarthy & Doz, 1992).

Breznik and Hisrich (2014) compare dynamic capabilities and innovation capabilities. The comparison reveals a meaningful overlap. First, innovation capabilities have deep roots in learning processes. Learning processes are the birthplace for dynamic capabilities and their capacity to create and shape new capabilities from scratch or by recombining previous capabilities. Second, continuous exploration and search for opportunities from internal and external sources (open innovation) are also crucial to creating innovation capabilities. And finally, since innovation is often idiosyncratic to the firm, innovation capabilities are regularly firm-specific and heterogeneous. While replication across firms is common to create best practices, these best practices are still idiosyncratic to the firm by their nature (see Figure 17.2).

One key source of this heterogeneity is the firm's management. Both concepts dynamic capabilities and innovation capabilities are about a firm's ability to work with change whether; reactive or proactive change. In Figure 17.2, these five commonalities are illustrated.

Zooming into the micro-foundations of innovation and dynamic capabilities is helpful to better understand the formation and transformation of firm capabilities (Arndt, 2011; Wei & Lau, 2010). According to Felin et al. (2012), dynamic capabilities are higher-order capabilities that affect processes, activities, and behaviors, resulting in innovation behavior in employees. As mentioned earlier, three useful analytical dimensions of dynamic capabilities have been introduced to shape the understanding of the three dimensions of dynamic capabilities sensing, seizing, and reconfiguring capabilities. Figure 17.3 six perspectives to view the relationship between dynamic capabilities and innovation capabilities.

Alves et al. (2017) looks at the role of performance and technology to describe innovation capabilities and dynamic capabilities. They suggest that a firm is "a technological set of products and processes that operates under a specific business model to transact with and profit from the market" (Alves et al., 2017). Alves et al. (2017) stated that an organization's innovation capabilities are a function of the companies' business and technological drivers (*"development, operations, management, and transaction capabilities"*).

Lawson and Samson (2001) brings attention to innovation capabilities as an integration capability, effective in managing and shaping other capabilities. Their idea was that innovation capability should be considered a higher-order capability that results in high innovation performance, and in order to be able to gain economic rent by innovation, firms need to make use of such capabilities. Lawson and Samson (2001) have shown that the dynamic nature of innovation capabilities is imprinted in their impact on quick sensing, seizing, and reconfiguring of knowledge and resources of firms.

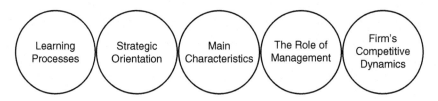

FIGURE 17.2 Commonalities between dynamic capabilities and innovation capabilities.

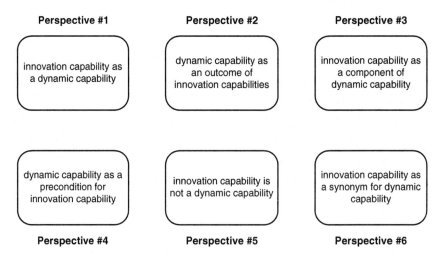

FIGURE 17.3 The six perspectives to view the relationship between dynamic capabilities and innovation capabilities (Breznik & Hisrich, 2014).

Other studies have added further to this stream of literature. For example, Wang et al. (2015) take a behavioral perspective of organizational innovation. Strønen et al. (2017) argue that according to Helfat et al. (2007) and (Teece et al., 1997), typical innovation activities can only be considered a dynamic capability if they add to the change adaptability of the company in the changing environments, so if certain innovation capabilities conduct these functions they can be considered a dynamic capability. They have derived a series of "dynamic innovation capabilities" in a case-study at an innovation clinic. Fallon-Byrne and Harney (2017) draw from human resource management and the innovation management literature to clarify the ambiguous roots that create the micro-foundations of dynamic capabilities for innovation. Their work provides insights about processes that promote certain behaviors that relate dynamic capabilities to innovation, more interestingly, in employees' individual-level perception of innovation strategies. Their work looked at the two concepts of "employee perspective" and "employee motivation" from a behavioral view of the firm (Fallon-Byrne & Harney, 2017).

Overall, the literature strongly suggests a stronger focus on longitudinal and comparative research studies and analysis to better disentangle how innovation capabilities and dynamic capabilities lead to sustainable competitive advantage (Arndt, 2019).

Product and Process Innovation and Dynamic Capabilities

The second pillar to search for the commonalities between innovation and dynamic capabilities, is the area of product and process innovation. This pillar of the innovation roundabout has been extensively developed for the significant and profound impact it has on firm performance. In this part, we discuss the dynamic capabilities views on new product development and process improvements.

In order to bring novel products to market, firms need to cope with change and make it into a continuous process (Eisenhardt & Tabrizi, 1995). Firms often integrate disseminated knowledge to inform their product development processes (Grant, 1996; Henderson & Cockburn, 1994; Kogut & Zander, 1996). A set of empirical research has explored and tried to formulate strategies that activate the capacity of rapid and continuous product innovation, many of which pointed out resources as the most crucial factor to fathom continuous innovation (Verona, 1999). Dynamic capabilities make use of market players, assets, firm structure, and culture to generate continuous product innovation, so a firmwide effort to develop dynamic capabilities is crucial to bring concurrent and continuous knowledge creation, absorption, and integration (Verona & Ravasi, 2003). To maintain continuous product innovation in the face of change, firms should develop a structure that fosters creativity in the whole organization and does not merely focus on one aspect (Arndt & Jucevicius, 2013; Liu et al., 2018). For instance, the literature on dynamic capabilities emphasizes the importance of continuous organizational learning for product innovations (Leonard-Barton, 1992; Verona & Ravasi, 2003).

Dynamic capabilities make use of human and tangible assets, along with the structure, systems, and culture of an organization as the founding basis of product innovation (Verona & Ravasi, 2003). Dixon et al. (2014) noted that long-term adaptability is the necessary attribute that makes new product development and R&D work as a dynamic capability.

Innovation in products is about the final end-products/services offered by an organization and innovation in the process discusses insights about the means by which organizations come up with such products/services (Piening & Salge, 2015). Moreover, as Damanpour and Gopalakrishnan (2001) noted, process innovations and product innovations walk hand in hand, and they are "*mutually supportive*," meaning that maintaining both of them at the same time can benefit firm performance. Furthermore, Zollo and Winter (2002) posit that process innovation in firms alters the organization's usual approaches, and the capacity to make such innovations can be considered a dynamic capability.

The dynamic capabilities literature emphasizes activities that empower the generation, integration, acquisition, and dissemination of knowledge that reconfigures firm processes (Eisenhardt & Martin, 2000; Pavlou & El Sawy, 2011). In order to foster process innovation, Teece (2007) suggests examples for such activities as sensing customer needs and market developments, and Pisano (1994) notes domestic R&D and prototyping.

Internal and external knowledge acquisition/generation activities are essential in the innovation process as well. Extending the knowledge of organizations by committing to these activities helps the organization to become alert of process innovations and to internalize them (Cohen & Levinthal, 1990; Zahra & George, 2002). Internal R&D makes it possible for organizations to better understand process technologies, thus gain a higher ability to improve processes (Hatch & Mowery, 1998; Pisano, 1994). The Schumpeterian notion of innovation as a "*new combination of existing knowledge*" (Schumpeter, 1934), is consistent with the previously stated works, that broad organizational knowledge creates capacity for more combination of previously untapped knowledge bases (Kogut & Zander, 1992). On the other hand, outsourcing knowledge to other players by using alliances, licensing, and agreements can also renew the organization's knowledge base (Cassiman & Veugelers, 2006).

A great example of the intersection between product innovation and dynamic capabilities is the study by (Verona & Ravasi, 2003) about a health/engineering company with notable performance in continuous innovation, called Oticon A/S. They find that dynamic capabilities are essential for product innovation. Oticon A/S invested a large amount of funds in a research center in their specific area of expertise, and also followed a project-based structure that allowed the three previously mentioned knowledge components to disperse throughout the firm, leading to sustainable product innovation. Oticon research center benefited from the "structural, managerial, and cultural" freedom that are often associated with the presence of dynamic capabilities (Verona & Ravasi, 2003).

Business Model Innovation and Dynamic Capabilities

In the past two decades, the most vigorous disrupting force of the business environment was a surge of innovative ventures in technology-based startup' business models. Digital platforms, the sharing economy, and social media are popular keywords inside the realm of business model innovation. In this part, we look at business model innovation from the lens of dynamic capabilities to provide insights about their common roots and interrelations.

Teece (2018) defined business model in this way: "*A business model describes an architecture for how a firm creates and delivers value to customers and the mechanisms employed to capture a share of that value.*" He then moved on to describe three main components of the business model through which the companies can make changes or innovate: the cost model, the revenue model, and the value proposition.

Capabilities are either available in the market or have to be crafted inside the company, and it is in the combination of these that fruitful business models are chosen, thus praised as innovation. Schoemaker et al. (2018) noted that organizations with a better hold of dynamic capabilities have a higher ability to create, integrate, and reconfigure their resources and business models.

Teece (2018) suggests that there is a close link between business model innovation and dynamic capabilities within a firm. Organizations should be able to reconfigure their previous and novel assets to obtain business model-related capabilities and skills (Teece, 2018). Čirjevskis (2019) defined three sets of dynamic capabilities to "*reinvent and transform a business model to achieve competitive advantage.*" The first set is "*sensing and shaping*," which selects new activities and customer segments, shapes the market and assets needed. The second set, "*Identifying and seizing*," supports companies in obtaining key assets, capabilities, and network expansion. The third set, "*transforming and reconfiguring*," transforms customer retention for more efficient value capturing. Making use of these three sets of dynamic capabilities, organizations can renew their cost structure, revenue streams, and value proposition, thus sustaining a new competitive advantage. Amit and Zott (2012) proposed an interesting new way of looking at the subject, they stated that business model innovation can be obtained by adding new activities ("*content*"), linking activities in different ways ("*structure*"), and changing teams that do the activities ("*governance*").

Although small to medium enterprises (SMEs) possess unique dynamic capabilities, letting them compete and innovate, academic research on the relations between dynamic capabilities and business model innovation has focused on incumbent companies. SMEs have attracted less attention, possibly due the nature of dynamic capabilities that have been conceptualized to primarily exist in larger organizations (Hülsbeck et al., 2017; Sapienza et al., 2006). Large incumbent organizations use dynamic capabilities to develop new ventures, penetrate new markets, gain novel skills, make use of assets and push strategic change, while, on the other hand, SMEs with low access to resources to reconfigure their assets face a barrier to value creation (Bowman & Ambrosini, 2003; Zollo & Winter,

2002). Still, SMEs' degree of specialization often gives them the ability to adapt to high-velocity contexts. With their compact size, they benefit from flat hierarchies, easy-to-use tacit knowledge, informal high-efficiency communication, and an entrepreneurial mindset (Fiegenbaum & Karnani, 1991; Liu & Cui, 2012).

The issue of business model innovation in digital businesses is rather more complicated and challenging (Arndt et al., 2021c; Correani et al., 2020; Nambisan, 2017). Easterby-Smith and Prieto (2008) suggest three distinct dynamic capabilities that are more relevant in digital business model innovation. *"Knowledge Exploitation Capabilities," "Risk Management Capabilities,"* and *"Marketing Capabilities."* These capabilities find and internalize assets, help them manage the threats and uncertainties, and provide them with new market insights and brand repositioning respectively (Helfat & Winter, 2011; Teece, 2017, 2018). According to Soluk and Kammerlander (2021), digital business model innovation is more complicated, more distributed, and much more complex than conventional business model innovations; thus, the three sets of dynamic capabilities we introduced in this section become arguably even more relevant. Platforms like Uber or the Apple App Store are well-known examples of such platforms for which content, governance and structure appear much more complex than in many traditional business models.

Open Innovation and Dynamic Capabilities

Open innovation has become increasingly common with the emergence of the internet and unlocked the possibility of segregating work tasks into fragments that could be readily divided for a geographically dispersed work force with temporary project-based employment. In organizations, the concept became a helpful tool for engaging external stakeholders, such as customers or partners, in processes and routines that have changed the business landscape dramatically. In this part, we discuss open innovation as a special case of dynamic capabilities.

Open innovation is defined as *"the use of purposive inflows and outflows of knowledge to accelerate internal innovation, and expand the markets for external use of innovation respectively"* (Chesbrough et al., 2008). Organizations need to engage internal and external stakeholders. Often invention and creativity are sourced by various parts of an organization and its partners. Open innovation has become crucial for the innovativeness of firms (Kump et al., 2016).

Bogers et al. (2019) emphasize that since sensing capabilities are about identifying valuable external resources and sources of knowledge outside of the firm, it is crucial to obtain many ideas as a starting point for better outcomes. This is what outside-in open innovations are about and the reason that open innovation relies on *"sensing, sense-making, and filtering externally developed technologies."* In terms of sensing, open innovation includes a wide range of techniques including crowdsourcing. Since many of the outside-in technologies and ideas are not fully compatible with previous systems and procedures, major adaptation and integration capacity is required to use them in the market. That is why implementing a fruitful open innovation requires seizing capabilities (Bogers et al., 2019). Teece et al. (2016) suggest open innovation processes as one of the ways of seizing opportunities by which the firm can preserve its agility.

Bogers et al. (2019) categorized open innovation based on the mode of technology development and intellectual property strategies. When the company does not focus on keeping its intellectual properties secured, whether it uses domestic R&D or outsources to external players, it will engage in open sourcing or open patent systems. On the other side of the spectrum, if the trademarks and rights are to be kept to the company's ownership, it has to create an open ecosystem or be involved in open innovation through acquisition (see Figure 17.4).

The case of Kraft Foods Australia is an excellent example of following mass customer choice. Kraft held a public competition to choose the name for Vegemite-based cheese snack that the company was introducing. "iSnack 2.0" was not popular with customers and the company eventually had to drop it. In another itinerary, the popular vote chose "Vegemite Cheesybite" for the same snack. This name was more successful (Bogers et al., 2019).

Organization culture is an important element for innovativeness and accepting new ways of innovation. Adopting knowledge from the outside traditionally meets "not-invented-here" attitudes that can have devastating effects on the adoption of innovations. As such, firms benefit from a change-friendly culture to be better able to reconfigure their processes and routines, leaving them inevitably in need for transformation capabilities (Bogers et al., 2019; Chesbrough & Crowther, 2006). For example, Mention et al. (2019) propose the use of social media as an effective enabler of open innovation practices by creating an open and collaborative culture. Their framework shows that firms can use the nature of social media to access distributed knowledge sources, promote their innovation capabilities, and foster a culture of openness and collaboration.

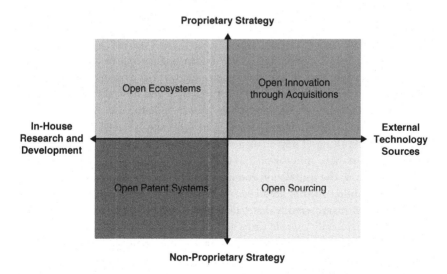

FIGURE 17.4 Categories of open innovation (Bogers et al., 2019).

Future Research and Conclusion

The Innovation Roundabout is a practical toolkit that offers easy orientation for managers on how to prepare their firms for changing environments. It offers avenues that many firms have to consider to stay relevant in the 21st century. Building innovation capability has become a complex undertaking as it includes internal and external processes and does not only look at products and new technologies, but also the business models that enable their market success.

While the innovation roundabout offers much help to find orientation to make a firm more innovative and dynamically capable, we'd like to refer to some recent work that offers further avenues for practice and research alike.

The macropolitical environment post-corona brings significant challenges for firms. First, we expect to see a re-organization of global value chains with deep implications for dynamic capabilities (Arndt et al., 2021a). Deglobalization is a trend that for many industries may take place well beyond the China-US tensions, but also to secure bottlenecks in critical industry for national subsistence all over the world. In this new world order, political actors play an important role for developing an entrepreneurial management as one of the cornerstones of dynamic capabilities (Dai et al., 2020).

Second, firms face new challenges regarding the degree of digitalization and the organization of the workspace. Firms that follow the innovation roundabout and those that have dynamic capabilities in place may understand how to reorganize their offers and business models, find new ways of partnering and adopt their structures flexibly to the new rapidly changing environment.

Third, new forms of work also include a highly diverse and inclusive environment. Increasingly, entrepreneurs and employees have ambicultural backgrounds that challenge narrow cultural conceptions and offer new opportunities for latent and undiscovered customer needs (Arndt & Ashkanasy, 2015). Those firms that embrace such changes are likely to fully reap the fruits of the innovation roundabout.

In this chapter, we presented a range of ideas managers can use to work with the innovation roundabout and affect their practice. For example, being dynamically capable means being aware of best practices and how they can be implemented in the focal firm. These practices may include the use of social media to keep employees at the innovation frontier, includes the use of lean start-up methods, or the rethinking of how managers can change the cognition of innovation, use emotions to drive innovation and change inert cultures.

In conclusion, the innovation roundabout offers a versatile tool for managers and scholars alike to think about strategic renewal. The pandemic has accelerated a range of macro-trends that had begun to shape life in organizations and for which dynamically capable firms actively use these capabilities to renew and reshape their innovation capabilities, products and processes, business models, and ways of partnering.

References

Alves, A. C., Barbieux, D., Reichert, F. M., Tello-Gamarra, J., & Zawislak, P. A. (2017). Innovation and dynamic capabilities of the firm: Defining an assessment model. *RAE Revista de Administracao de Empresas, 57*(3), 232–244. https://doi.org/10.1590/S0034-759020170304

Ambrosini, V., & Bowman, C. (2009). What are dynamic capabilities and are they a useful construct in strategic management? *International Journal of Management Reviews, 11*(1), 29–49. https://doi.org/10.1111/j.1468-2370.2008.00251.x

Amit, R., & Zott, C. (2012). Creating value through business model innovation. *MIT Sloan Management Review, 53*, 41–49. https://doi.org/https://www.researchgate.net/publication/279555624_Creating_Value_Through_Business_Model_Innovation

Arndt, F. (2011). Assessing dynamic capabilities: Mintzberg's schools of thought. *South African Journal of Business Management, 42*(1), 1–8.

Arndt, F. (2019). Dynamic capabilities: A retrospective, state-of-the-art, and future research agenda. *Journal of Management & Organization, 2019*(1), 1–4.

Arndt, F., & Ashkanasy, N. (2015). Integrating ambiculturalism and fusion theory: A world with open doors. *Academy of Management Review, 40*(1), 144–147.

Arndt, F., & Bach, N. (2015). Evolutionary and Ecological conceptualization of dynamic capabilities: Identifying elements of the Teece and Eisenhardt schools. *Journal of Management & Organization, 21*(5), 701–704.

Arndt, F., Fourné, S. P., & MacInerney-May, K. (2018). The merits of playing it by the book: Routine versus deliberate learning and the development of dynamic capabilities. *Industrial and Corporate Change, 27*(4), 723–743.

Arndt, F., Galvin, P., Jansen, R., & JM, G. (2021a). Special Issue Journal of Management and Organization Dynamic Capabilities: New Ideas, Microfoundations, and Criticism. *Feedback, 1*(1st).

Arndt, F., & Jucevicius, G. (2013). Antecedents and outcomes of dynamic capabilities: The effect of structure. *Social Sciences, 81*(3), 35–12.

Arndt, F., Katic, M., Mistry, A., & Nafei, S. (2021b). From selection to deployment. In *The Routledge Companion to Global Value Chains: Reinterpreting and Reimagining Megatrends in the World Economy* (p. 23). Oxfordshire: Routledge.

Arndt, F., Ng, N., & Huang, T. (2021c). Do-It-Yourself laboratories, communities of practice, and open innovation in a digitalised environment. *Technology Analysis & Strategic Management, 33*(10), 1186–1197. doi: 10.1080/09537325.2021.1931674

Arndt, F., & Pierce, L. (2018). The behavioral and evolutionary roots of dynamic capabilities. *Industrial and Corporate Change, 27*(2), 413–424.

Barney, J. B. (1991). Firm resources and sustained competitive advantage. *Journal of Management, 17*(1), 99–120. https://doi.org/10.1177/014920639101700108

Bogers, M., Chesbrough, H., Heaton, S., & Teece, D. J. (2019). Strategic management of open innovation: A dynamic capabilities perspective. *California Management Review, 62*(1), 77–94. https://doi.org/10.1177/0008125619885150

Bowman, C., & Ambrosini, V. (2003). How the resource-based and the dynamic capability views of the firm inform corporate-level strategy. *British Journal of Management, 14*(4), 289–303. John Wiley & Sons, Ltd. https://doi.org/10.1111/j.1467-8551.2003.00380.x

Breznik, L., & Hisrich, R. D. (2014). Dynamic capabilities vs. innovation capability: Are they related? *Journal of Small Business and Enterprise Development, 21*(3), 368–384. https://doi.org/10.1108/JSBED-02-2014-0018

Cassiman, B., & Veugelers, R. (2006). In search of complementarity in innovation strategy: Internal R & D and external knowledge acquisition. *Management Science, 52*(1), 68–82. https://doi.org/10.1287/mnsc.1050.0470

Chakravarthy, B. S., & Doz, Y. (1992). Strategy process research: Focusing on corporate self-renewal. *Strategic Management Journal, 13*(1 S), 5–14. https://doi.org/10.1002/smj.4250131003

Chesbrough, H., & Crowther, A. K. (2006). Beyond high tech: Early adopters of open innovation in other industries. *R and D Management, 36*(3), 229–236. https://doi.org/10.1111/j.1467-9310.2006.00428.x

Chesbrough, H., Vanhaverbeke, W., & West, J. (2008). *Open Innovation: Researching a New Paradigm.* https://www.researchgate.net/publication/232957368_Open_Innovation_Researching_A_New_Paradigm

Čirjevskis, A. (2019). What dynamic managerial capabilities are needed for greater strategic alliance performance? *Journal of Open Innovation: Technology, Market, and Complexity, 5*(2), 1–11. https://ideas.repec.org/a/gam/joitmc/v5y2019i2p36-d242473.html

Cohen, W. M., & Levinthal, D. A. (1990). Absorptive capacity: A new perspective on learning and innovation. *Administrative Science Quarterly, 35*(1), 128–152. https://doi.org/10.2307/2393553

Correani, A., De Massis, A., Frattini, F., Petruzzelli, A. M., & Natalicchio, A. (2020). Implementing a digital strategy: Learning from the experience of three digital transformation projects. *California Management Review, 62*(4), 37–56. https://doi.org/10.1177/0008125620934864

Dai, W., Arndt, F., & Liao, M. (2020). Hear it straight from the horse's mouth: Recognizing policy-induced opportunities. *Entrepreneurship & Regional Development, 32*(5–6), 408–428.

Damanpour, F., & Gopalakrishnan, S. (2001). The dynamics of the adoption of product and process innovations in organizations. *Journal of Management Studies, 38*(1), 45–65. https://doi.org/10.1111/1467-6486.00227

Di Stefano, G., Peteraf, M., & Verona, G. (2010). Dynamic capabilities deconstructed : A bibliographic investigation into the origins, development, and future directions of the research domain. *Industrial and Corporate Change, 19*(4), 1187–1204. https://doi.org/10.1093/ICC/DTQ027

Dixon, S., Meyer, K., & Day, M. (2014). Building dynamic capabilities of adaptation and innovation: A study of micro-foundations in a transition economy. *Long Range Planning, 47*(4), 186–205. https://doi.org/10.1016/j.lrp.2013.08.011

Easterby-Smith, M., & Prieto, I. M. (2008). Dynamic capabilities and knowledge management: An integrative role for learning? *British Journal of Management, 19*(3), 235–249. John Wiley & Sons, Ltd. https://doi.org/10.1111/j.1467-8551.2007.00543.x

Eisenhardt, K. M., & Martin, J. A. (2000). Dynamic capabilities: What are they? *Strategic Management Journal, 21*(10–11), 1105–1121. https://doi.org/10.1002/1097-0266(200010/11)21:10/11<1105::AID-SMJ133>3.0.CO;2-E

Eisenhardt, K. M., & Tabrizi, N. B. (1995). Accelerating adaptive processes: Product innovation in the global computer industry. *Administrative Science Quarterly, 40*(1), 84–110. https://doi.org/10.2307/2393701

Fallon-Byrne, L., & Harney, B. (2017). Microfoundations of dynamic capabilities for innovation: A review and research agenda. *Irish Journal of Management, 36*, 21–31. https://doi.org/10.1515/ijm-2017-0004

Felin, T., Foss, N. J., Heimeriks, K., & Madsen, T. L. (2012). Microfoundations of routines and capabilities: Individuals, processes, and structure. *SSRN Electronic Journal.* https://doi.org/10.2139/ssrn.1988881

Fiegenbaum, A., & Karnani, A. (1991). Output flexibility—A competitive advantage for small firms. *Strategic Management Journal, 12*(2), 101–114. https://doi.org/10.1002/smj.4250120203

Grant, R. M. (1996). Prospering in dynamically-competitive environments: Organizational capability as knowledge integration. *Organization Science, 7*(4), 375–387. https://doi.org/10.1287/orsc.7.4.375

Hatch, N. W., & Mowery, D. C. (1998). Process innovation and learning by doing in semiconductor manufacturing. *Management Science, 44*(11 Part 1), 1461–1477. https://doi.org/10.1287/mnsc.44.11.1461

Helfat, C. E., Finkelstein, S., Mitchell, W., Peteraf, M. A., Singh, H., Teece, D. J., & Winter, S. G. (2007). *Dynamic Capabilities Understanding Strategic Change in Organizations.* Blackwell Publishing Ltd.

Helfat, C. E., & Peteraf, M. A. (2015). Managerial cognitive capabilities and the microfoundations of dynamic capabilities. *Strategic Management Journal, 36*(6), 831–850. https://doi.org/10.1002/smj.2247

Helfat, C. E., & Winter, S. G. (2011). Untangling dynamic and operational capabilities: Strategy for the (N)ever-changing world. *Strategic Management Journal, 32*(11), 1243–1250. https://doi.org/10.1002/smj.955

Henderson, R., & Cockburn, I. (1994). Measuring competence? Exploring firm effects in pharmaceutical research. *Strategic Management Journal, 15*(1 S), 63–84. https://doi.org/10.1002/smj.4250150906

Hülsbeck, M., Gärtner, C., Duschek, S., Ortmann, G., Schüßler, E., & Müller-Seitz, G. (2017). Emergence of responsiveness across organizations, networks, and clusters from a dynamic capability perspective. *Journal of Competence-Based Strategic Management, 9*, 7–32.

Kogut, B., & Zander, U. (1992). Knowledge of the firm, combinative capabilities, and the replication of technology. *Organization Science, 3*(3), 383–397. http://www.jstor.org/stable/2635279

Kogut, B., & Zander, U. (1996). What firms do? Coordination, identity, and learning. *Organization Science, 7*(5), 502–518. https://doi.org/10.1287/orsc.7.5.502

Kump, B., Engelmann, A., Kessler, A., & Schweiger, C. (2016). Towards a dynamic capabilities scale: Measuring sensing, seizing, and transforming capacities. *Academy of Management Proceedings, 2016*(1), 13839. https://doi.org/10.5465/ambpp.2016.13839abstract

Langlois, R. N. (1992). Transaction-cost economics in real time. *Industrial and Corporate Change, 1*(1), 99–127. https://doi.org/10.1093/ICC/1.1.99

Lawson, B., & Samson, D. (2001). Developing innovation capability in organisations: A dynamic capabilities approach. *International Journal of Innovation Management, 5*(3), 377–400. https://doi.org/10.1142/s1363919601000427

Leonard-Barton, D. (1992). Core capabilities and core rigidities: A paradox in managing new product development. *Strategic Management Journal, 13*(1 S), 111–125. https://doi.org/10.1002/smj.4250131009

Liu, Z. G., & Cui, J. (2012). Improve technological innovation capability of enterprises through tacit knowledge sharing. *Procedia Engineering, 29*, 2072–2076. https://doi.org/10.1016/j.proeng.2012.01.264

Liu, Y., Lv, D., Ying, Y., Arndt, F., & Wei, J. (2018). Improvisation for innovation: The contingent role of resource and structural factors in explaining innovation capability. *Technovation, 74*, 32–41.

Mention, A. L., Barlatier, P. J., & Josserand, E. (2019). Using social media to leverage and develop dynamic capabilities for innovation. *Technological Forecasting and Social Change, 144*, 242–250. https://doi.org/10.1016/j.techfore.2019.03.003

Nambisan, S. (2017). Digital entrepreneurship: Toward a digital technology perspective of entrepreneurship. *Entrepreneurship Theory and Practice, 41*(6), 1029–1055. https://doi.org/10.1111/etap.12254

Nelson, R. R., & Winter, S. G. (1982). *An Evolutionary Theory of Economic Change* (6th ed.). Belknap Press of Harvard University Press. https://books.google.com/books?id=n1xvngEACAAJ&dq=An evolutionary theory of economic change&lr&source=gbs_book_other_versions

Pavlou, P. A., & El Sawy, O. A. (2011). Understanding the elusive black box of dynamic capabilities. *Decision Sciences, 42*(1), 239–273. https://doi.org/10.1111/j.1540-5915.2010.00287.x

Penrose, E. T. (1959). The Theory of the Growth of the Firm. New York: John Wiley.

Piening, E. P., & Salge, T. O. (2015). Understanding the antecedents, contingencies, and performance implications of process innovation: A dynamic capabilities perspective. *Journal of Product Innovation Management, 32*(1), 80–97. Blackwell Publishing Ltd. https://doi.org/10.1111/jpim.12225

Pisano, G. P. (1994). Knowledge, integration, and the locus of learning: An empirical analysis of process development. *Strategic Management Journal, 15*(1 S), 85–100. https://doi.org/10.1002/smj.4250150907

Sapienza, H. J., Autio, E., George, G., & Zahra, S. A. (2006). A capabilities perspective on the effects of early internationalization on firm survival and growth. *The Academy of Management Review, 31*(4), 914–933. https://doi.org/10.2307/20159258

Schoemaker, P. J. H., Heaton, S., & Teece, D. (2018). Innovation, dynamic capabilities, and leadership. *California Management Review, 61*(1), 15–42. https://doi.org/10.1177/0008125618790246

Schumpeter, J. A. (1934). *The Theory of Economic Development an Inquiry into Profits, Capital, Credit, Interest, and the Business Cycle.* Harvard Economic Studies.

Soluk, J., & Kammerlander, N. (2021). Digital transformation in family-owned Mittelstand firms: A dynamic capabilities perspective. *European Journal of Information Systems*, 1–36. https://doi.org/10.1080/0960085X.2020.1857666

Strønen, F., Hoholm, T., & Nathalie, L. (2017). Dynamic capabilities and innovation capabilities: The case of the 'innovation clinic.' *Journal of Entrepreneurship, Management and Innovation, 13*(1), 89–116. https://doi.org/http://dx.doi.org/10.7341/20171314

Teece, D. J. (2007). Explicating dynamic capabilities: The nature and microfoundations of (sustainable) enterprise performance. *Strategic Management Journal, 28*(13), 1319–1350. https://doi.org/10.1002/smj.640

Teece, D. (2009). *Dynamic Capabilities and Strategic Management: Organizing for Innovation and Growth.* Oxford University Press.

Teece, D. J. (2017). Towards a capability theory of (innovating) firms: Implications for management and policy. *Cambridge Journal of Economics, 41*(3), 693–720. https://doi.org/10.1093/cje/bew063

Teece, D. J. (2018). Business models and dynamic capabilities. *Long Range Planning, 51*(1), 40–49. https://doi.org/10.1016/j.lrp.2017.06.007

Teece, D., Peteraf, M., & Leih, S. (2016). Dynamic capabilities and organizational agility: Risk, uncertainty, and strategy in the innovation economy. *California Management Review, 58*(4), 13–35. https://doi.org/10.1525/cmr.2016.58.4.13

Teece, D. J., & Pisano, I. (2003). *The Dynamic Capabilities of Firms* (pp. 193–212). https://doi.org/10.1007/978-3-540-24748-7_10

Teece, D. J., Pisano, G., & Shuen, A. (1997). Dynamic capabilities and strategic management. *Strategic Management Journal, 18*(7), 509–533. https://doi.org/10.1002/(SICI)1097-0266(199708)18:7<509::AID-SMJ882>3.0.CO;2-Z

Verona, G. (1999). A resource-based view of product development. *Academy of Management Review, 24*(1), 132–142. https://doi.org/10.5465/AMR.1999.1580445

Verona, G., & Ravasi, D. (2003). Unbundling dynamic capabilities: An exploratory study of continuous product innovation. *Industrial and Corporate Change, 12*(3), 577–606. https://doi.org/10.1093/icc/12.3.577

Wang, C. L., Senaratne, C., & Rafiq, M. (2015). Success traps, dynamic capabilities and firm performance. *British Journal of Management, 26*(1), 26–44. https://doi.org/10.1111/1467-8551.12066

Wei, L. Q., & Lau, C. M. (2010). High performance work systems and performance: The role of adaptive capability. *Human Relations, 63*(10), 1487–1511. https://doi.org/10.1177/0018726709359720

Zahra, S. A., & George, G. (2002). Absorptive capacity: A review, reconceptualization, and extension. *The Academy of Management Review, 27*(2), 185–203. https://doi.org/10.2307/4134351

Zollo, M., & Winter, S. G. (2002). Deliberate learning and the evolution of dynamic capabilities. *Organization Science, 13*(3), 339–351. https://doi.org/10.1287/orsc.13.3.339.2780

18

INNOVATION MANAGEMENT AS A DYNAMIC CAPABILITY FOR A VOLATILE, UNCERTAIN, COMPLEX AND AMBIGUOUS WORLD

Eric Patterson, Sancheeta Pugalia and Renu Agarwal

Introduction

For organisational leaders, innovation is a top priority (Guo et al., 2017). Innovation helps operational improvements (Calantone et al., 2002) and firm performance (Mone et al., 1998). Across entire economies, innovation accounts for up to 50% of economic growth (OECD, 2015). In recognition of its importance, organisations are actively coordinating resources to innovate (Hargadon, 2014) and installing specific administrative structures and organisational processes to successfully manage innovation (Dougherty & Hardy, 1996).

Our modern understanding of innovation management is aligned to theories of evolutionary economics, which urges organisations to innovate in order to remain relevant and competitive (Nelson, 2009). These highly structured approaches to innovation management have been largely recognised across the globe (Tidd, 2001). However, what seemed like an acceptable approach pre-COVID in 2019 was turned on its head during the pandemic in 2020 and the global economic, political and social problems brought about by the COVID pandemic were extremely disruptive. As markets went into lockdown and global supply chains shut down, nations, institutions and individuals struggled to navigate and survive those turbulent times. These unique experiences surfaced shortcomings in how organisations should manage innovations during periods of disruption and that no longer can we assume stable operating conditions and certainty with respect to the external environment. The new norm is that businesses need to operate increasingly in a VUCA environment.

According to the Dynamic Capability View firms need to adjust their organisational resources with environmental needs (Teece, 2017), however many organisations were not able to do this during the crisis. This pointed to a wider gap in our ability to embed innovation management as a dynamic

DOI: 10.4324/9780429346033-23

capability to respond to customer demands and external pressures (Slater et al., 2014) under VUCA conditions (Miller et al., 2018). Consequently, our traditional approach to innovation management built highly structured coordination of organisational resources and structures in support of innovation (Dodgson et al., 2013) was challenged, and despite these challenges some organisations were able to ride this wave of VUCA conditions and excel in their performance. How could they do it, that many others could not contemplate achieving? These successful companies included leaders in supply chain logistics, service delivery and government sectors in particular. It is for this reason that we want to look at why and how these successful firms survived and succeeded. To explore this proposition and enhance our understanding further we look at the specific ways these firms were able to manage innovation under VUCA conditions.

Through the 2020 pandemic, notable success stories surfaced across industry sectors and government. We look to such companies that excelled, as an inspiration to how to navigate that unprecedented point in history. Importantly, we can look at the qualities, features and, ultimately, capabilities that allowed these businesses to thrive during notable VUCA conditions. These success stories contrasted with the global disruption and provide an opportunity for us to consider what enabled fortunes and amplified fallout. They let us understand how organisations are able to navigate innovation under VUCA conditions (Johansen & Euchner, 2013) and manage innovation as a dynamic capability (Teece, 2017). This paper will take the learnings from these organisations to understand what key innovation management practices can be adopted by companies to effectively operate in VUCA conditions.

To explore the lessons around VUCA innovation management this paper is structured as follows. The second section provides a literature review of innovation management capabilities, VUCA innovation and dynamic capabilities. Following that in the third section we discuss the innovation accounts for up to 50% of economic growth (OECD, 2015). Findings of the five case study analysis provide a coherent assessment of commonalities between those able to innovate during VUCA conditions. Delivery of a framework to embed VUCA innovation as a dynamic capability is presented. Lastly, the fourth section presents conclusions from this research across government, organisations and individuals, added with research limitations and future research opportunities.

Literature Review

This section provides an overview of the extant literature. First, it presents the new paradigm of firm operations and their management characterised by VUCA conditions. Second, we consider the role of Dynamic Capabilities in Innovation Management. Finally, we present a visionary perspective, highlight specific challenges that will be addressed by this research and lastly discuss the role of DC in a VUCA environment.

Firm Operating Environment and Recognition of External Conditions

In *The world is Flat*, Thomas Friedman sees the rapid flattening of the world due to its reach, but also the speed and breadth with which profound changes are happening. This has indeed led to creation of a new environment that refers to a much more chaotic, turbulent, riskier and quickly changing business world that is increasingly volatile, uncertain, complex and adaptable (VUCA) (Bennis & Nanus, 1985). An example of a new form of global disruption is the recent COVID-19 disruptions which see businesses operating under the new VUCA environment, which is taxing organisations as they see their capabilities deplete and become obsolete in this unpredictable global landscape. Bennett and Lemoine (2014) provide a framework to capture these specific conditions relating to VUCA. This includes:

- Complexity: The situation has many interconnected parts and variables. Some information is available or can be predicted, but the volume or nature of it can be overwhelming to process.
- Volatility: The challenge is unexpected or unstable and may be of unknown duration, but it's not necessarily hard to understand; knowledge about it is often available.
- Ambiguity: Causal relationships are completely unclear. No precedents exist; you face "unknown unknowns".
- Uncertainty: Despite a lack of other information, the event's basic cause and effect are known. Change is possible but not a given.

These conditions present a challenging situation for businesses. More importantly, businesses are increasingly subject to such conditions and need a dynamic approach to strategy and planning to circumvent such circumstances. Consequently, George (2017) coined the concept VUCA 2.0, which referred to having vision, understanding, courage and adaptability as a dynamic leadership response to innovate, grow and be more productive under VUCA conditions.

The management of innovations requires understanding of both internal and external factors simultaneously. The systems view of innovation emphasises the significance of the external environment that firms are subject to by conceptualising different innovation activities of firms embedded in political, social, organisational and economic systems (Lundvall, 2008). These external factors can influence a firm's ability to innovate, its innovation activities, capabilities and outcomes. Further, these external factors are also seen as an object of a business strategy, public policy or concerted social action by different interest groups. In an endeavour to measure, collect and interpret innovation data on business innovation, the OSLO manual (2018) recognises that understanding the context in which businesses operate is essential.

Given this, it is beyond a firm's management ability to control the factors that influence the external environment. When subjected to such external factors, business managers need to consider the challenges and opportunities they face as a consequence of making strategic choices. According to the OSLO manual (2018) external factors are bundled into five main categories, namely the spatial and locational factors, markets, knowledge flows and networks, public policy and society and the natural environment. Underpinning these are a range of structural and economic external factors which influence business innovation, namely, the activities of customers, competitors and suppliers; the labour market; legal, regulatory, competitive and economic conditions; and the supply of technological and other types of knowledge of value to innovation. A tension exists because there is between responding to the external environment and focussing on a firms' internal environment. Central to this challenge is that internal factors are under the control of firm management and take a predominant focus. Items in this domain include the firm's business model, production and innovation capabilities, as well as financial and human resources, which firms manage through their varied management capabilities, resources and processes.

To date, in an attempt to innovate, the traditional approaches to strategy and decision making assume a relatively static and predictable business operating environment (Dodgson et al., 2013). However, at present we are living in an era of uncertainty, instability and volatility prescribed by VUCA, and more importantly, the business landscape has far greater complexity and is riskier. The recognition of different forces of globalisation, technological disruptions and the unprecedented need for greater transparency is paramount. Further, there has been limited recognition of external dynamics in tandem with firms' internal content in real time. If firms align too closely to traditional ways of operating, their success will be hampered (Schoemaker et al., 2018). Firms indeed have been devoid of these joint forces – internal and external – and the need for building such capabilities that can steer strategy, decision making through dynamic capability building as well as policy making (Teece, 2020).

The overall gap in the VUCA literature is that it is a new field of study, needs future operational details, and is not adopted nor integrated into organisations' current strategic management processes.

The Role of Dynamic Capabilities in Innovation Management

Most businesses under the VUCA environment grapple with industry dynamics to formulate a strategic response. Schoemaker et al. (2018) highlight that traditional ways of operating are already hampered and that businesses should leverage their product or process innovations concurrently with business model innovation through leverage of strategic leadership, dynamic capabilities and business model innovation.

The OSLO manual (2018, p. 35) describes business capabilities to include the "knowledge, competencies and resources that a firm accumulates over time and draws upon in pursuit of its objectives". The manual clearly articulates that skills and abilities of a firm's workforce are a critical part of innovation-relevant capabilities. Given this, firms mostly possess the more well understood "ordinary management capability which are amenable to transfer and testing in an experimental setting" (Teece, 2020). However, Teece criticises work on management practices to date by Bloom and others (Bloom & Van Reenen, 2007; Bloom, Sadun and Van Reenen, 2010; Bloom & Van Reenen, 2010; Bloom, Genakos, Sadun and Van Reenen, 2012; Bloom, Eifert, Mahajan, McKenzie and Roberts, 2013; Bloom, Lemos, Sadun, Scur and Van Reenen, 2014; Bloom, Sadun and Van Reenen, 2014; Bloom, Lemos, Sadun, Scur and Van Reenen, 2016; Bloom, Sadun and Van Reenen, 2017). He say that we were "merely the tip of the iceberg in terms of the ways that management matters" (Teece, 2017, p.711). Teece (1997, p. 516) introduced the term dynamic capabilities as those to integrate, build, and reconfigure internal and external competences to address rapidly changing environments. Clearly, there is a need for inculcating higher order capabilities that are strategic in nature in order to maintain a competitive advantage. More importantly, 'dynamic capabilities' are integral to selecting, developing, and coordinating ordinary capabilities (Teece, 1990).

Another aspect equally and strategically important is the unprecedented rate at which new technologies are emerging and their use in business model innovation is shaping future businesses and causing disruptions (Singh et al., 2021). Kapoor and Teece (2021) see technology as a "multifaceted construct that encompasses production know-how, problem solving, and functionality" (p. 1) and for innovation to happen, the three features – emerging, enabling, and embedding nature of technology – are a distinct source of technology's value creation and its value capture. These new technologies in different forms present significant opportunities for firms, industries and technologies over time. Therefore, situating technology in this context can have a significant impact on its value creation, especially when new business models emanate, which can facilitate technological progress to help spur economic growth.

For example, Agarwal et al. (2021) discuss the LPG gas in India enabled business model innovation through emerging, enabling and embedding nature of the technology, and the ecosystem within which the technology trajectories was commercialised over 70 years in the Indian public sector. Therefore, situating the technology in its commercialisation context can have significant impact on the fundamentals of strategy, as well as value creation, capture and appropriation, and indeed this enables new business model innovations. Understanding of this intertwining dynamic across these strategic angles is pivotal as firms and policy makers can then contribute to technological and economic progress and generate superior performance.

While multiple definitions of capabilities exist, it is clear that organisations would benefit from a holistic approach and some practical advice on how to deploy these in complex and fast changing environments to capitalise on technological opportunities and drive value creation.

Vision and Need for Managing Innovation Capabilities

Business capabilities include the knowledge, competencies and resources that a firm accumulates over time and draws upon in pursuit of its objectives. The skills and abilities of a firm's workforce are a particularly critical part of innovation-relevant capabilities. Innovation capabilities are of critical importance because they evidence the effect of innovation management on firm performance and why some firms engage in and are successful in innovation activities and others are not.

Defined within the OSLO manual (2018, p. 304) are the four types ofinnovation-related capabilities that are relevant and crucial for businesses to have such that they can have a sustainable impact on the innovation performance of all firms:

- the **resources** controlled by a firm
- the general **management capabilities** of a firm
- the **skills** of the workforce and how a firm manages its human resources
- the ability to design, develop and adopt **technologica**l tools and data resources, with the latter providing an increasingly important source of information for innovation.

Resources: The resources available to a firm have a strong influence on its ability to pursue its objectives by engaging in different types of activities, including innovation-related activities. Relevant resources for the firm include its own workforce, physical and intangible assets (comprising knowledge-based capital), accumulated experience in conducting business activities and available financial resources. Resources that influence the innovation activities include firm size, business assets consisting of tangible fixed assets, intangible fixed assets, goodwill and current assets (e.g. cash, accounts receivable, inventories); firm age, internal financial sources, firm's ownership status.

Management capabilities: These can influence a firm's ability to undertake innovation activities, introduce innovations and generate innovation outcomes. Two key capabilities areas affecting innovation performance include the firm's business strategy and the organisational managerial capabilities. A business strategy includes the formulation of goals and the identification of policies to reach these goals. Organisational and managerial capabilities include all of a firm's internal abilities, capacities, and competences that can be used to mobilise, command and exploit resources in order to meet the firm's strategic goals.

A further concept of relevance to innovation is a firm's "dynamic managerial capabilities" which refers to the ability of managers to organise an effective response to internal and external challenges (Helfat & Martin, 2015). Dynamic managerial capabilities include three main dimensions, namely, (i) Managerial cognition: knowledge structures that influence managers' biases and heuristics when, for example, anticipating market changes or understanding the implications of different choices; (ii) Managerial social capital: goodwill derived from relationships that managers have with others and can use to obtain resources and information and (iii) Managerial human capital: learned skills and knowledge that individuals develop through their prior experience, training and education.

Skills: To bring innovation in any company, the workforce plays a crucial role. People are the most important resource for innovation as they are the source of creativity and new ideas (Høyrup, 2012). The design, development and implementation of innovations require a variety of skills and the cooperation of different individuals. Human resource management practices can influence the ability of a firm to profit from the creative potential and skills of its workforce. Many of these practices can benefit both innovation and other goals.

Technology: The novelty or improved characteristics of an innovation are often due to the use of new or modified technology. At the same time, the accumulated innovation activities of one or more actors can advance knowledge within specific technological domains, creating new markets and opportunities for innovation. The ability of a firm to take advantage of these opportunities will depend on its technological capabilities within relevant domains. Three types of technological capabilities are of particular interest to potential users of innovation data: technical expertise, design capabilities, and capabilities for the use of digital technologies and data analytics.

The Importance of External Factors and Firms' Responsiveness

The system's view of innovation stresses the importance of the external environment by conceptualising the innovation activities of firms as embedded in political, social, organisational and economic systems (Granstrand et al., 1997; Lundvall, 2008). These external factors can influence a firm's incentives to innovate and its innovation activities, capabilities and outcomes. External factors can also be the object of a business strategy, public policy or concerted social action by public interest groups. External factors include customers, competitors and suppliers; labour markets, legal, regulatory, competitive and economic conditions, and the supply of technological and other types of knowledge of value to innovation.

Spatial and locational factors define the firm's jurisdictional location and its proximity to product and labour markets. Markets are leading contextual factors that are also shaped by the firm's own decisions.

Public policy can influence business activities in direct and indirect ways. The regulatory and enforcement framework influences how firms can appropriate the outcomes of their innovation efforts and the multiple relationships and transactions that firms engage in. Governments can also use public policy interventions to firms, including support for innovation.

Society and the natural environment can directly and indirectly affect business activities. Societal aspects can influence the public acceptance of innovations as well as firm policies on corporate social responsibility. Larger societal changes can drive system wide innovations, such as in support of the environment, large public infrastructure investment or focus on public services.

The above are all factors in the external environment that require appropriate consideration in managing innovation through VUCA conditions.

The Role of Dynamics Capabilities in a VUCA Environment

Business leaders are able to use innovation management as a dynamic capability in the face of environmental conditions. However, this is still an emerging and fragmented area of the literature without clear views to systematise and consistently manage innovation in VUCA environments (Teece, 2020). There have been key lessons taken on how to manage VUCA (Miller et al., 2018), these include four main aspects, namely, (i) do not turn away from the VUCA environment but make it work for you by understanding it and creating context-dependent management innovations; (ii) understand the customer and customer satisfaction needs and engineer all functions and processes into management innovations to deliver on these needs, (iii) approach entrepreneurial opportunity identification, pivoting and strategic vision in combination to build agility and lastly, (iv) integrate functions and processes within the company to create dynamic capabilities.

Maier et al. (2016) proposes the concept of 'approaches to futures' which sees specific interventions targeted at VUCA conditions. This includes agility in response to volatility, information and knowledge in response to uncertainty, restructure in response to complexity and experimentation in response to ambiguity. Lahiri et al. (2008) identify a set of mindsets required to respond to VUCA, including: global, virtual, collaborative and innovation. While all useful, these perspectives appear as an optional pursuit at the fringe of core business activities. They do not embed the approaches into core operations. Given the wide scale and profound VUCA conditions created by the COVID pandemic, this is a global situation that lets us explore what allowed leaders in industry to navigate VUCA and effectively innovate.

Research Approach

For this study a pragmatism research philosophy is most appropriate as it helps construct a real-life experience of innovation management in VUCA conditions presented during the global COVID-19 pandemic (Saunders et al., 2011). Using an explorative design (Creswell, 2013) approach we look at why innovation manifested as it did in selected examples (Lee et al., 1999) during the VUCA duration.

This research uses qualitative analysis to examine the relationships and deeper organisational experiences surrounding VUCA innovation in key organisations during COVID-19. Qualitative research is appropriate for studying the complex phenomenon of VUCA innovation (Cavana et al., 2001) and to generalise the learnings from specific cases.

Candidates are selected for this case based on those who have reported strong performance during COVID-19 in the form of revenue preservation and respective increase in revenue, increased market share, notable new product service development and/or positive customer feedback and public awareness and publicity. By exploring these firms we identify themes to help understand the reasoning for the results that addresses our research questions. This questioning will examine the environmental, institutional and interpersonal factors (Denzin & Lincoln, 2011) affecting the innovation successes. It is important that these cases explore the following aspects namely, (i) why organisations were able or unable to successfully innovate; (ii) what capabilities they demonstrate to enable this success; and (iii) how other organisations can replicate these behaviours and outcomes.

Part of the research process examines the outcome to be used to build theories (Cooper et al., 2006) into how to better design, deliver and manage innovation through VUCA environments. We further create a framework to compare innovation management before and after the global pandemic. To explore this we consider the relationship between the dynamic capabilities literature (Teece, 2020) and conditions brought about by VUCA (Maier et al., 2016).

In this research the following five cases of notable responses to VUCA were considered:

1. Telemedicine: Observing the ability to shift health services onto virtual phone-based delivery
2. Virtual classes and workshops: Movement of education and workplace settings to digital delivery
3. Intelligent Office franchisees: Creation of pop-up offices and mobile businesses
4. Australian National Government Emergency Cabinet: Formation of a virtual and dynamic national government bringing together state and national leaders
5. COVID Disaster Payments National, Australia: examination of how the responsible government agency was able to create a new cross government payment system in response to economic disruption caused by COVID.

Findings

Analysis of the five case studies is presented below covering the experience of the organisation through the pandemic. Each case includes a set of takeaways and observed innovation capabilities required to operate under VUCA condition framework.

Telemedicine

As the global context increasingly becomes unsteady, unpredictable, complicated and unclear, the capacity to learn and respond rapidly is becoming extremely important. Hence, given the VUCA environment raised due to COVID -19, it is important to adapt and respond quickly (Laksono & Darmawan, 2021). As Laksono and Darmawan (2021) identified, the healthcare sector has faced huge disruption due to COVID-19 including problems pertaining to digitalisation of the healthcare system. However, it's rapid adaptation to the new environment through innovation, which earlier felt difficult to achieve, is the solution towards addressing upcoming challenges.

One such innovation in the healthcare industry was telemedicine. Though telehealth is not a new concept, it has entered into a key clinical practice. Patients and clinicians have been required to participate in live video consultations that have been quite successful. Healthcare providers have turned to telehealth to bridge distances in times of physical separation (Philips, 2021). A national medical director named Michael Okun from Parkinson's Foundation shared *"We accomplished in 10 days what we have been trying to do for 10 years – fighting and advocating and trying to get telemedicine up and going"*. Data from the US Centers for Disease Control and Prevention shows an incredible increase in telehealth services, i.e. from 43% in 2019 to 95% in 2020 (Marquez, 2021). People may use LiveMD's new app to follow COVID in their region, self-diagnose using an AI-based integrated tool, submit their coronavirus status for tracking, and interact with local government and medical organisations for assistance and guidance (LiveMD Inc, 2020).

Takeaway: Given the rapid change required by the healthcare industry during COVID-19, through its remarkable agility and accelerated innovation it was able to sense, seize and reform clinical practices. In effect, the pandemic has inspired unparalleled agility and inventiveness in its health processes and systems affecting patient delivery. Moreover, the resilience shown from different stakeholders, including patients, doctors and service providers to adapt to the changing and disruptive environment is crucial. Sometimes, it takes a cataclysmic event to force change and modernisation and such was the COVID-19. Thus, leaning into **agility and resilience** has been effective and profitable during such VUCA conditions.

Innovation Capabilities Required:

- Operations – delivery of standards activities must flexible to be offered virtually
- Business Model – Firms need integrated and connected business models (Guo et al., 2017)

Virtual Classes and Workshops

COVID-19, like so many other elements of daily life, has had a significant influence on students, educators and educational institutions across the world (Adnan & Anwar, 2020). Due to the lockdown, education institutions as well as multiple affiliated organisations as providers of education services were shut down. For example, the communication software provider of Zoom was essential for keeping the organisation running efficiently in disruptive times. They are crucial to the process of communication and collaboration. Most universities employed video conferencing capabilities to conduct virtual lectures and workshops for their clients/students during the COVID-19 pandemic. Numerous colleges and universities largely concentrated on the transition of academic material available via digital platforms, rather than explicitly via online teaching and delivery pedagogies, as the unanticipated shift to online learning became a measure of organisational agility (Wu, 2020).

Another familiar instance was the Gyms and fitness studios, as one of the most popular instances of service delivery. These firms have shifted their products to cater to a stuck-at-home clientele, from online yoga sessions to virtual training camps. Another example is Microsoft who is planning to combine it's new as well as existing learning materials from LinkedIn and GitHub units, as well as from inside the rest of the company. They are planning to make them available to those who are interested in upskilling and/or retraining for new careers for either free or at low cost.

Takeaway: Companies have restructured their core product to cater to a wider customer market by offering its services virtually. The **responsiveness to adapt to new environments through collaboration** such as joining different video conferencing platforms such as Microsoft teams, zoom or Webex (from Cisco) helped to adapt to the VUCA environment. Multiple experimentation and use of technical knowledge specifically contributed towards the transition of virtual learning systems. Thus, the key response strategies to adopt for this industry are **collaboration, experimentation** and **knowledge sharing**.

Innovation Capabilities Required:

- Operations – operating environments needs to by dynamically adjusted under constantly changing conditions, which can be planned or unplanned
- Technologies – technology need to be deployed quickly and flexibly to rapidly changing operating environments (Kapoor & Teece, 2021).

Virtual Business Solutions

The COVID-19 crisis has transformed the way we operate for the new normal. For instance, more employees than ever before are working from home. The way modern companies do business is changing, which can be seen from the Intelligent Office franchisees across North America. One example of such changes can be seen in the rise of the popup offices (Farris, 2020).

Pop-up offices can be used by small and medium-sized teams for renting office space based on their needs. These offices do not have long-term leases, thus making it attractive to business owners who are unsure of the requirement of huge office space.

As Intelligent Office's President, Brian Farris, explains,

> Businesses of all sizes have realized that paying fixed rent is no longer necessary and the sublease market proves it. Smart business owners also realize

that culture suffers without human connection and have opted for Pop-Up Offices where the entire team can rent space on-demand to connect and socialize.

Virtual office spaces are also a great solution for businesses that want their employees to get back to work safely (Beauregard, 2020).

Takeaway: When considering spaces required by the team to do the work, there are a number of options available. Whether you need a meeting room rental for a single day, a private office on a monthly basis or something else entirely, virtual office providers like Intelligen**t Office have the options you need. Thus, collaboration with multiple virtual business solutions and government as well as entrepreneurial capabilities** such as instead of renting a big corporate office using a hybrid model or sharing office space can lead to building and adapting a VUCA instigated environment.

Innovation Capabilities Required:

- Supply chain – business must be able to have leaders that are flexible to proactively resign their operating and delivery model to meet changing internal and external conditions (Ivanov & Dolgui, 2020)
- Asset Base – the asset base of organisation must be reconfigured across both sites, products/services and people to adjust to the specific needs of the time.

Australian National Government Emergency Cabinet

The global nature of the pandemic highlighted the need for governments to lead the response and, out of necessity, innovate (Heinonen & Strandvik, 2021). Beyond the obvious support in the quest for the cure, the institutional response of governments across the globe was at an unprecedented scale (Sampat & Shadlen, 2021).

Within Australia, with the government's significant interventions to stop the spread of the virus, it is estimated that this reduced cases by over 60% (Varghese & Xu, 2020). Underpinning this response was the Australian Government's nationally coordinated response that included border enforcement, health policy and economic management.

This response to COVID, the organisational and operational response, was unprecedented. One element of this included the rapid formation and frequent meeting of a combined national and state government crisis cabinet (Bromfield & McConnell, 2021). There were many 'first ever' events for this forum including meetings on a near weekly basis and providing public press briefings at a high frequency. In addition, this group fully virtualised parliament and allowed online parliamentary voting for the first time in Australian history.

Takeaway: This sequence of events was a credit to the government and its leaders, and shows a rapid and profound policy and institutional change in the Australian government landscape. It shows increased **agility to redefine public**

services and shift away from processes and procedures over 100+ years in the making. Underpinning this was rapid political leadership as an enabler of business model innovation (Agarwal et al., 2021).

Other factors include an openness to develop new and strong **stakeholder relationships** (Van der Wal, 2020) and, importantly, political mastering and collaborative networks. A third factor in these changes was a clear **openness in data** (Temiz & Broo, 2020) in the form of exchange of information across political boundaries and parties, as well as from politicians to the public.

Innovation Capabilities Required:

- Business Model – the business model for delivering services needs to be open for new ways of operating in a much more open organisational context in order to respond to cross institutional challenges
- Leadership – the frameworks for leadership decisions must need to be flexible to occur outside of traditional organisational and geographic boundaries, with leaders operating faster than the changing operating environment (Schoemaker et al., 2018).

Disaster Payments to Businesses across Multiple Australian States

With the mass closure of Australian business and enforcement of stay at home requirements, the COVID pandemic saw a sharp reduction in business activities. In response the government installed widespread rapid fiscal support that was the largest in Australia history during peacetime and equivalent to 7% of GDP (Chen & Langwasser, 2021a).

To deliver these payments the national government was able to rapidly put in place the payment infrastructure to support over $120 billion of payments (Chen & Langwasser, 2021b). These announcements, development and delivery of COVID payments represented a new ecosystem of business and individual payments. This included new capabilities supporting policy determination, process delivery and technology support to operate at this scale and speed across the Australian Government. Under the leadership of Services Australia, the Central government was able to set up new digital payments for Victoria, ACT and NSW governments within a matter of weeks.

Takeaway: The clear allocation of people and flexible technology assets. This shows the **ability to restructure, and agility and capacity to experiment**. This includes **leadership and collaboration** across government bodies including policy and delivery commonwealth agencies, and state/territory government. In addition, a partner ecosystem involving the Reserve Bank of Australia and technology service providers was rapidly and effectively mobilised. Another thing evident was the ability to **build innovation capacity**, keeping active investments and also capacity to change (Mazzucato & Kattel, 2020). This shows a dual ability to build assets to deliver innovation alongside the organisation ability to respond to change

Innovation Capabilities Required:

- Growth and Operations – Building organisations assets needs to be done with open sharing with potential partners to identify opportunities and quickly scale to meet adjacent customer needs (Bennett & Lemoine, 2014)
- Technologies – there needs to be a dynamic and decoupled approach for designing, delivering and scaling technology capabilities in fast paces organisations (Kapoor & Teece, 2021).

Overall Learnings

Clearly, the above five cases highlight the key dynamic capability characteristics which provided business their competitive advantage and differentiated these cases through the pandemic across these specific aspects of a business operations, namely business planning, operations and supply chain, growth, asset base and technologies, and lastly leadership and business models. We have captured the capabilities to manage innovation before, during and after COVID in Table 18.1.

TABLE 18.1 Capabilities to manage innovation before, during and after COVID

Capability	Pre-COVID 2019 characteristics	During pandemic	Post pandemic
Business Planning, operations and supply chain	• Linear and structured business planning (Dodgson et al., 2013)	• Rapid and reactionary (Case study 1) • Virtualisation of the office (Case study 2)	• Agile and iterative business planning (Temiz & Broo, 2020) • Design Capabilities (OECD, 2018) • Virtualisation of supply / value chain (Ivanov and Dolgui, 2020)
Growth, Asset Base and Technologies	• Standard and repeatable yearly planning cycle based on return on investment (Tidd, 2001) • Clear resistance to digital adoption (Talwar et al., 2020)	• Restructure (Case Study 3 and 4)	• Strategic triangulation of strategy, leadership and dynamic capabilities (Schoemaker et al., 2018) • Dynamic approach to adopting new technology utilising rent and decoupled / scalable services (Kapoor & Teece, 2021)
Leadership and Business Model	• Hierarchical (Keum and See, 2017) • Innovation is a one way process (Kahn, 2018)	• Disrupted and Distributed (Case study 1 and 5)	• Integrated and connected (Guo et al., 2017) • Open sharing of information (Bennett & Lemoine, 2014)

Based on the case studies and key changes during each period, we take away a set of common interventions that characterise successful response to VUCA conditions that allow organisations to innovate through disruption.

Innovation Management Interventions include:

- **Forced agility and experimentation as a standard operating process**: business processes can adjust to sudden externally driven change. This may include restructure (short and long terms) and business model adjustments
- **Information and knowledge exchange systems and processes**: Organisations can openly communicate across its employees, with partners and external stakeholders. This includes the infrastructure to produce and disseminate material. There also needs to be the means to collaborate and communicate
- **Leadership and Focus**: Organisations need its decision makers ready to decide on VUCA related decisions with commitment. In terms of resources, leaders need to structurally commit to keep slack resources to respond to VUCA conditions and drive new capabilities (resources, business models, processes and technologies). This leadership applies in the public and private sector equally.

This list of interventions and capabilities should act as a takeaway from individuals and organisations to be ready for and responding to VUCA conditions.

Conclusion

With the COVID-19 outbreak, almost every aspect of one's life was affected across professional (where companies had to reinvent their business model or make changes to their supply to reach to their consumers) as well as personal (shifting to the virtual environment) contexts. A survey conducted by Mckinsey in 2020 shows that executives and managers are looking at this pandemic more as an opportunity to innovate and grow (Mckinsey Global Institute, 2020). Less than a third of these same executives are optimistic in their ability to deal with the changes they anticipate (Am et al., 2020). The key obstacle for them is delivering new growth possibilities.

COVID-19 has aided executives in recognising the risks of business inertia. "In this new era – or the future forward – innovation will be a cornerstone of organizational resiliency", explains Jeff Wong, Global Chief Innovation Officer at EY, "one that will drive a company's ability to shift rapidly in response to unexpected events and evolving customer needs" (Wong, 2020) This pandemic is a perfect example of the VUCA world, where businesses had to rethink to be in the market. This new environment impacted every business – both small and large – and across individuals through to government (Gibbons, 2021). Out of this research and observing leadership in respective fields, there are key capabilities organisations need to hold to respond to the specific VUCA condition. These forced agility and experimentation as a standard operating process, information and knowledge exchange systems and processes, and leadership and focus. As we are now operating in a period of continuous change and disruption, organisations need to actively be able to deploy the capabilities to manage innovation in VUCA conditions.

This research contributes positively to the innovation management literature by breaking away from an often linear approach to innovation management that was proven inadequate for the global pandemic scenario. We have learnt from leaders of businesses and propose a framework to succeed in managing innovation in the face of environmental, digital and global disruption. This research presents a way forward to embed innovation management as a dynamic capability for individuals, businesses and nations to navigate turbulent times.

As the research is focussed on only a small subset of cases, this sample size can be increased to a broader set of organisations to test the robustness of the framework and relative impact of the different interventions and capabilities recommendations. Further to this research, it will be important to understand how economies and organisations bounce back from the pandemic and continue to respond to residual challenges. It will be important to see how any positive changes stick together, and whether organisations can get back to a true sense of normality. In learning from the pandemic, it will be important to see how organisations keep capacity to innovate and embed sustainable innovation management capabilities (Mazzucato & Kattel, 2020) in the future.

References

Adnan, M., & Anwar, K. (2020). Online learning amid the COVID-19 pandemic: Students' perspectives. *Online Submission*, 2(1), 45–51.

Agarwal, R., Mittal, N., Patterson, E., & Giorcelli, M. (2021). Evolution of the Indian LPG industry: Exploring conditions for public sector business model innovation. *Research Policy*, 50(4), 104196.

Am, J. B., Furstenthal, L., Jorge, F., & Roth, E. (2020). Innovation in a crisis: Why it is more critical than ever. McKinsey, Retrieved June, 17.

Beauregard, B. (2020). How to (safely) get your employees back to work. Accessed on 9th September 2021 from https://www.intelligentoffice.com/blog/how-to-safely-get-your-employees-back-to-work

Bennett, N., & Lemoine, J. (2014). What VUCA really means for you. *Harvard Business Review*, 92(1/2), 27.

Bennis, W., & Nanus, B. (1985). The strategies for taking charge. Leaders, New York: Harper. Row, 41.

Bloom, N., Eifert, B., Mahajan, A., McKenzie, D., & Roberts, J. (2013). Does management matter? Evidence from India. *The Quarterly Journal of Economics*, 128(1), 1–51.

Bloom, N., Genakos, C., Sadun, R., & Van Reenen, J. (2012). Management practices across firms and countries. *Academy of Management Perspectives*, 26(1), 12–33.

Bloom, N., Lemos, R., Sadun, R., Scur, D., & Van Reenen, J. (2014). JEEA-FBBVA Lecture 2013: The new empirical economics of management. *Journal of the European Economic Association*, 12(4), 835–876.

Bloom, N., Lemos, R., Sadun, R., Scur, D., & Van Reenen, J. (2016). International data on measuring management practices. *American Economic Review*, 106(5), 152–56.

Bloom, N., Sadun, R., & Van Reenen, J. (2010). Does product market competition lead firms to decentralize? *American Economic Review*, 100(2), 434–438.

Bloom, N., Sadun, R., & Van Reenen, J. (2014). Does management matter in healthcare. Boston, MA: Center for Economic Performance and Harvard Business School.

Bloom, N., Sadun, R., & Van Reenen, J. (2017). Why do we undervalue competent management. *Harvard Business Review*, 95(5), 120–127.

Bloom, N., & Van Reenen, J. (2007). Measuring and explaining management practices across firms and countries. *The Quarterly Journal of Economics*, 122(4), 1351–1408.

Bloom, N., & Van Reenen, J. (2010). Why do management practices differ across firms and countries? *Journal of Economic Perspectives*, 24(1), 203–224.

Bromfield, N., & McConnell, A. (2021). Two routes to precarious success: Australia, New Zealand, COVID-19 and the politics of crisis governance. *International Review of Administrative Sciences*, 87(3), 518–535.

Calantone, R. J., Cavusgil, S. T., & Zhao, Y. (2002). Learning orientation, firm innovation capability, and firm performance. *Industrial Marketing Management*, 31(6), 515–524.

Cavana, R. Y., Delahaye, B. L., & Sekaran, U. (2001). Applied business research: Qualitative and quantitative method. Australia: John Wiley & Sons.

Chen, J., & Langwasser, K. (2021a). COVID-19 Stimulus Payments and the Reserve Bank's Transactional Banking Services| Bulletin–June Quarter 2021. *Bulletin*.

Chen, J., & Langwasser, K. (2021b). COVID-19 Stimulus Payments and the Reserve Bank's Transactional Banking Services. 1. COVID-19 Stimulus Payments and the Reserve Bank's Transactional Banking Services 2. How Far Do Australians Need to Travel to Access Cash? 3. An Initial Assessment of the Reserve Bank's Bond Purchase Program 4. Monetary Policy, Liquidity, and the Central Bank Balance Sheet, 1.

Cooper, D. R., Schindler, P. S., & Sun, J. (2006). Business research methods. New York: McGraw-Hill Irwin.

Creswell, J. W. (2013). Research design: Qualitative, quantitative, and mixed methods approaches. Sage Publications.

Denzin, N. K., & Lincoln, Y. S. (2011). The Sage handbook of qualitative research. Sage.

Dodgson, M., Gann, D. M., & Phillips, N. (2013). The Oxford handbook of innovation management. Oxford: OUP.

Dougherty, D., & Hardy, C. (1996). Sustained product innovation in large, mature organizations: Overcoming innovation-to-organization problems. *Academy of Management Journal*, 39(5), 1120–1153.

Farris, B. (2020). The rise of the pop-up office. Accessed on 9th September 2021 from https://www.intelligentoffice.com/blog/the-rise-of-the-popup-office

George, B. (2017). VUCA 2.0: A strategy for steady leadership in an unsteady world. Forbes. Retrievable from forbes. com/sites/hbsworkingknowledge/2017/02/17/vuca-2-0-a-strategv-for-steadv-leadership-in-anunsteadv-world, 199701.

Gibbons, S. (2021). How Covid-19 is shaping the future of innovation. Forbes, January 2021.

Granstrand, O., Patel, P., & Pavitt, K. (1997). Multi-technology corporations: Why they have "distributed" rather than "distinctive core" competencies. *California Management Review*, 39(4), 8–25.

Guo, W., Katila, R., Maggitti, P. G., & Tesluk, P. E. (2017). Innovation at the Top: Proactive CEO, Top Executive Attention Focus, and Product Innovation. Paper presented at the Academy of Management Proceedings.

Hargadon, A. (2014). Brokerage and innovation The Oxford Handbook of Innovation Management (pp. 163–180). Oxford University Press.

Heinonen, K., & Strandvik, T. (2021). Reframing service innovation: COVID-19 as a catalyst for imposed service innovation. *Journal of Service Management*, 32(1), 101–112.

Helfat, C. E., & Martin, J. A. (2015). Dynamic managerial capabilities: Review and assessment of managerial impact on strategic change. *Journal of Management*, 41(5), 1281–1312.

Høyrup, S. (2012). Employee-driven innovation: A new phenomenon, concept and mode of innovation. In Employee-driven innovation (pp. 3–33). London: Palgrave Macmillan.

Ivanov, D., & Dolgui, A. (2020). A digital supply chain twin for managing the disruption risks and resilience in the era of Industry 4.0. *Production Planning & Control*, 32(9), 1–14.

Johansen, B., & Euchner, J. (2013). Navigating the VUCA world. *I*, 56(1), 10–15.

Kahn, K. B. (2018). Understanding innovation. *Business Horizons*, 61(3), 453–460.

Kapoor, R., & Teece, D. J. (2021). Three faces of technology's value creation: Emerging, enabling, embedding. *Strategy Science*, 6(1), 1–4.

Keum, D. D., & See, K. E. (2017). The influence of hierarchy on idea generation and selection in the innovation process. *Organization Science*, 28(4), 653–669.

Lahiri, S., PerezNordtvedt, L., & Renn, R. W. (2008). Business horizons, will the new competitive landscape cause your firm's decline? It depends on your mindset. *Business Horizons*, 51(4), 311–320.

Laksono, S., & Darmawan, E. S. (2021). The new leadership paradigm in digital health and its relations to hospital services. *Jurnal Ilmu Kesehatan Masyarakat*, 12(2), 89–103.

Lee, T. W., Mitchell, T. R., & Sablynski, C. J. 1999. Qualitative research in organizational and vocational psychology: 1979–1999. *Journal of Vocational Behavior*, 55, 161–187.

LiveMD Inc, (2020). LiveMD Global Telehealth Platform launches artificial intelligence tracking and triaging tools to help combat COVID-19 (CoronaVirus) pandemic. Accessed on 9th September 2021 from https://www.globenewswire.com/news-release/2020/03/25/2006187/0/en/LiveMD-Global-Telehealth-Platform-launches-artificial-intelligence-tracking-and-triaging-tools-to-help-combat-COVID-19-CoronaVirus-Pandemic.html

Lundvall, B. Å. (2008). Innovation system research: Where it came from and where it might go. Georgia Institute of Technology.

Maier, H. R., Guillaume, J. H., van Delden, H., Riddell, G. A., Haasnoot, M., & Kwakkel, J. H. (2016). An uncertain future, deep uncertainty, scenarios, robustness and adaptation: How do they fit together? *Environmental Modelling & Software*, 81, 154–164.

Marquez, J. R. (2021). How the telehealth trend is revolutionizing medical care as we know it. Accessed on 9th September 2021 from https://www.jnj.com/innovation/how-telehealth-is-revolutionizing-medical-care

Mazzucato, M., & Kattel, R. (2020). COVID-19 and public-sector capacity. *Oxford Review of Economic Policy*, 36(Supplement_1), S256–S269.

McKinsey Global Institute. (2020). What 800 executives envision for the postpandemic workforce. Accessed on 9th September 2021 from https://www.mckinsey.com/featured-insights/future-of-work/what-800-executives-envision-for-the-postpandemic-workforce; https://www.mckinsey.com/business-functions/risk-and-resilience/our-insights/covid-19-implications-for-business

Millar, C. C., Groth, O., & Mahon, J. F. (2018). Management innovation in a VUCA world: Challenges and recommendations. *California Management Review*, 61(1), 5–14.

Mone, M. A., McKinley, W., & Barker, V. L. (1998). Organizational decline and innovation: A contingency framework. *Academy of Management Review*, 23(1), 115–132.

Nelson, R. R. (2009). An evolutionary theory of economic change. Harvard University Press.

OECD. (2015). OECD innovation strategy: An agenda for policy action. Paris.

OECD. (2018). Oslo manual: Guidelines for collecting, reporting and using data on innovation. Paris: OECD.

Philips. (2021). 10 innovative examples of telehealth in action. Accessed on 9th September 2021 from https://www.philips.com/a-w/about/news/archive/features/2021/20210401-10-innovative-examples-of-telehealth-in-action.html

Sampat, B. N., & Shadlen, K. C. (2021). The COVID-19 innovation system: Article describes innovations that emerged during the COVID-19 pandemic. *Health Affairs*, 40(3), 400–409.

Saunders, J., Wong, V., & Saunders, C. (2011). The research evaluation and globalization of business research. *British Journal of Management*, 22(3), 401–419.

Schoemaker, P. J., Heaton, S., & Teece, D. (2018). Innovation, dynamic capabilities, and leadership. *California Management Review*, 61(1), 15–42.

Singh, A., Triulzi, G., & Magee, C. L. (2021). Technological improvement rate predictions for all technologies: Use of patent data and an extended domain description. *Research Policy*, 50(9), 104294.

Slater, S. F., Mohr, J. J., & Sengupta, S. (2014). Radical product innovation capability: Literature review, synthesis, and illustrative research propositions. *Journal of Product Innovation Management*, 31, 552–566.

Talwar, S., Talwar, M., Kaur, P., & Dhir, A. (2020). Consumers' resistance to digital innovations: A systematic review and framework development. *Australasian Marketing Journal (AMJ)*, 28(4), 286–299.

Teece, D. J. (1997). Economies of scope and the scope of the enterprise. *Resources, Firms and Strategies*, 103–116.

Teece, D. J. (2017). Towards a capability theory of (innovating) firms: Implications for management and policy. *Cambridge Journal of Economics*, 41, 693–720.

Teece, D. J. (2020). Hand in glove: Open innovation and the dynamic capabilities framework. *Strategic Management Review*, 1(2), 233–253.

Teece, D.J., Pisano, G., & Shuen, A. (1990). Firm capabilities, resources, and the concept of strategy. (Working Paper 90–8). Berkeley, CA: Center for Research on Management, University of California

Temiz, S., & Broo, D. G. (2020). Open innovation initiatives to tackle Covid-19 crises: Imposter open innovation and openness in data. *IEEE Engineering Management Review*, 48(4), 46–54.

Tidd, J. (2001). Innovation management in context: Environment, organization and performance. *International Journal of Management Reviews*, 3, 169–183.

Van der Wal, Z. (2020). Being a public manager in times of crisis: The art of managing stakeholders, political masters, and collaborative networks. *Public Administration Review*, 80(5), 759–764.

Varghese, C., & Xu, W. (2020). Quantifying what could have been–the impact of the Australian and New Zealand governments' response to COVID-19. *Infection, Disease & Health*, 25(4), 242–244.

Wong, J. (2020). The path forward: Building a bolder, better post-COVID-19 pandemic world. Accessed on 9th September 2021 from https://www.linkedin.com/pulse/path-forward-building-bolder-better-post-covid-19-pandemic-jeff-wong/

Wu, Z. (2020). How a top Chinese university is responding to coronavirus. Accessed on 9th September 2021 from World Economic Forum: https://www.weforum.org/agenda/2020/03/coronavirus-china-the-challenges-of-online-learning-for-universities/

INDEX

Note: **Bold** page numbers refer to tables, *italic* page numbers refer to figures and page numbers followed by "n" denote end notes.

Printed in the United States
by Baker & Taylor Publisher Services